SPEAKERS
SOURCEBOOK
II

Also by Eleanor Doan ...

A Child's Treasury of Verse

SPEAKERS
SOURCEBOOK
II

ELEANOR DOAN

Ministry Resources Library

Zondervan Publishing House • Grand Rapids, MI

Speaker's Sourcebook II

Ministry Resources Library is an imprint of Zondervan Publishing House,
1415 Lake Drive S.E.,
Grand Rapids, Michigan, 49506.

Copyright © 1968 by Zondervan Publishing House

Library of Congress Cataloging-in-Publication Data

Doan, Eleanor Lloyd, 1914–
    Speakers sourcebook II / Eleanor Doan.
        p.   cm.
    Includes index.
    ISBN 0-310-24201-0
    1. Quotations, English. I. Title. II. Title: Speakers sourcebook 2.
PN6081.D56   1989   89-12547
082—dc20   CIP

ISBN 0-310-24201-0

Printed in the United States of America

    90 91 92 93 94 95 / AK / 10 9 8 7

Dedicated to

My Father, who unknowingly started me on this series
of books, and

My Mother, whose help with the first book inspired
continuance with this volume

and with grateful appreciation to

Jackie McGregor for invaluable assistance in classifying and checking materials,

Helena Wiebe for her faithful help in typing, recheck-
ing contents, and finalizing copy,

and to many others whose names I do not know, but
whose contributions are invaluable.

ACKNOWLEDGMENTS

Grateful acknowledgment is made to the following who have granted permission to include copyrighted selections in this book:

ABINGDON PRESS for the quotation on p. 187 from Costen J. Harrell, *Walking With God*. Copyright renewal 1956. Reprinted by permission.

Herm Albright for the quotation on p. 252 which appeared in *Family Weekly*.

ALLIANCE WITNESS for poems and quotations by A. B. Simpson.

AMERICAN SUNDAY-SCHOOL UNION for two stories on pp. 230 and 335 from *Sunday School World*.

ASSOCIATION PRESS for the poem on p. 241, "Take Time to Live" by Thomas Curtis Clark; for the paragraph headings on p. 152 from Harry Emerson Fosdick, *The Meaning of Faith*, Chapter I.

Frances Benson for the anecdote on p. 123 from *Family Weekly*.

GEOFFREY BLES LTD., London, England, for four quotations from C. S. Lewis, *Mere Christianity*.

William M. Bower for two poems on pp. 44 and 166 by Helen Frazee-Bower, "The Book" and "The Land of the Free" which appeared in *The King's Business*.

THE BRETHREN PRESS for the poem on p. 115, "Seed" by Myra Brooks Welch, from her book *The Touch of the Master's Hand*, copyright © 1957.

CHRISTIAN HERALD for the quotations on pp. 291 and 305 by J. C. Penney, and other anecdotes.

CHRISTIAN LIFE PUBLICATIONS for the selections from *Christian Life* Magazine, copyright by Christian Life Publications, Inc., Gunderson Drive and Schmale Road, Wheaton, Illinois 60187.

CHURCH MANAGEMENT for the poem on p. 95, "Birth of a Committee" by Leslie Conrad, Jr.; the poem on p. 260 "First Missionaries" by Donna Dickey Guyer; the paragraphs on p. 380 by Dr. William H. Leach. Copyright Church Management, Inc., reprinted by permission.

DAVID C. COOK PUBLISHING COMPANY for the item on p. 43 from *The Leader*; the story on p. 267 from *The Christian Mother*.

THE CURTIS PUBLISHING COMPANY for quotations from the *Saturday Evening Post*, one each from Franklin P. Jones (Copyright October 11, 1952 by The Curtis Publishing Company); Raymond Duncan (Copyright February 25, 1956 by The Curtis Publishing Company); G. Norman Collie (Copyright November 22, 1958 by The Curtis Publishing Company); Chon Day (Copyright February 13, 1960 by The Curtis Publishing Company).

DECISION Magazine for quotations by Billy Graham, Roy W. Gustafson, Sherwood E. Wirt, and the Christmas greeting from the *Decision* staff, "A Square, Honest Look" by Sherwood E. Wirt on pp. 84-85.

DEFENDER Magazine for "A Christmas Compliment" on p. 85, and the poem "Preachers Can Talk" on p. 297.

T. S. DENISON & COMPANY, INC. for the poem on p. 319, "School Days" by Nick Kenny, from *Poems to Inspire* by Nick Kenny, published by T. S. Denison & Co., Inc., Minneapolis, Minn.

DOUBLEDAY & COMPANY, INC. for two quotations from Billy Graham, *The Secret of Happiness*.

LIFE Magazine for the quotation on p. 144 by Billy Graham from the article "Billy Graham Makes Plea for an End to Intolerance," October 1, 1956.

LOG OF THE GOOD SHIP GRACE for poems, illustrations, anecdotes, etc. by various authors; for poems, sayings, illustrations by Nat Olson.

LOIZEAUX BROTHERS, INC. for four lines by Frances R. Havergal on p. 244 from the poem "Seldom Can a Heart . . ." from the November 25th meditation in *Opened Treasures* by Frances Ridley Havergal, published by Loizeaux Brothers, and reprinted by permission.

LUTHERAN STANDARD for the poem on p. 189, "Grandma" by Ann Johnson. Copyright Augsburg Publishing House, *The Lutheran Standard*, February 16, 1963.

THE MACMILLAN COMPANY for the selection on pp. 196-197 from J. B. Phillips, *Your God Is Too Small*, first published in the United States by The Macmillan Company, 1953; for four quotations on pp. 39, 97, 102, 104 from C. S. Lewis, *Mere Christianity*, copyright 1952 by The Macmillan Company, New York.

Virgil Markham for poems by Edwin Markham: two stanzas on p. 59 entitled "Why Build?" and four lines on p. 323.

METHODIST PUBLISHING HOUSE for selections from *Together* Magazine, copyright 1959, 1960, 1961 by Lovick Pierce Publisher; copyright 1963 by The Methodist Publishing House, Nashville, Tennessee.

Phyllis C. Michael for the poems "On Graduating," p. 134, and "A Girl Is A Girl," pp. 172-173, copyright 1963 by Phyllis C. Michael in *Poems for Mothers*, Zondervan Publishing House.

Wanda Milner for her poem on p. 75, "Fingers," which appeared in December 1963 *Decision* Magazine.

MOODY MONTHLY for the selection on p. 254 by Anne Nunemaker, reprinted by permission.

MOODY PRESS for seven poems by Martha Snell Nicholson: p. 40, "My Advocate," copyright 1938; p. 262, "The Voice of One Who Wept," copyright 1943; p. 362, "Treasures," copyright 1946; p. 325, "Remembered Sin," copyright 1952 in *Her Best For the Master;* p. 200, "From a Loved One in Heaven," and p. 366, "Trusting," copyright 1945 in *In Heaven's Garden;* p. 131, "Easter," copyright 1950 in *Her Heart Held High.*

NATIONAL CONFERENCE OF CHRISTIANS AND JEWS, INC. for the poem on p. 67 by Jo Tenjford, "Some Children Are."

NATIONAL EDUCATION ASSOCIATION JOURNAL for stories and quotations and the poem on p. 345 by Beth Blue. Copyright *NEA Journal.*

Tom and Marie Olson for poems and illustrations from *Now.*

Theo Oxenham for three poems by John Oxenham: p. 108, "Credo" from *Bees in Amber;* p. 153, "Lord, Give Me Faith," and p. 110, "The Cross of Calvary," copyright by Theo Oxenham.

PENTECOSTAL EVANGEL for the anecdotes on pp. 164, 194.

RAND MCNALLY & COMPANY for the poems of Ella Wheeler Wilcox, copyright by the W. B. Conkey Company.

Lucy Lolli Rankin for the poem "One Weigh" which appeared in *Family Weekly.*

READER'S DIGEST for five anecdotes by the following: Mrs. Roy Carter, p. 130; Mrs. Frank Watson, p. 189; Louise Paw, pp. 249-250; Ethel M. Anderson, p. 281; Lula M. Olds, p. 329.

REFORMED CHURCH IN AMERICA for the item by William R. Buitendorp, "You Are Not Cheap," from the *Church Herald.*

HENRY REGNERY COMPANY for Edgar A. Guest's poems: p. 42, "Believe in Yourself"; p. 101, "The Signal Lights"; p. 231, "It's the Laymen"; p. 326, four lines from "He Did It"; copyright Henry Regnery Company, Reilly & Lee Company, Chicago.

FLEMING H. REVELL CO. for the quotation on p. 151 from Vance Havner, *Peace in the Valley.*

May Richstone for her poem "Might Have Been" on p. 307.

THE RODEHEAVER COMPANY for the two poems on pp. 267 and 334 by Strickland Gillilan from *Gillilan, Finnigan and Company* published by The Rodeheaver Co.: "Stewardship," and four lines from "The Reading Mother."

THE SALVATION ARMY for materials from *The War Cry*.

Margaret E. Sangster for her poem on p. 86, "The Christmas List."

CHARLES SCRIBNER'S SONS for the following by Henry van Dyke: pp. 26-27, "America For Me" from *The Poems of Henry van Dyke*, copyright 1911, Charles Scribner's Sons, renewal copyright 1939, Tertius van Dyke; pp. 79-80, "The Psalm of the Good Teacher" from *Songs Out of Doors*, copyright 1922 by Charles Scribner's Sons, renewal copyright 1950 by Tertius van Dyke; pp. 45-46, an excerpt from *Companionable Books*, copyright 1922 by Charles Scribner's Sons, renewal copyright 1950 by Tertius van Dyke; p. 355, six lines entitled "Time Is" from "Katrina's Sun Dial" from *Music and Other Poems*, 1904; and four lines from "Three Best Things" p. 229, stanza 4 of "The Gospel of Labor" from *The Toiling of Felix*.

SCRIPTURE PRESS PUBLICATIONS for the poem on p. 73, "My Choice" by Bill McChesney, copyright 1965, Scripture Press Publications, Inc., Wheaton, Illinois, reprinted by permission from *Power for Living*; p. 60, the poem "Too Busy?" and other anecdotes and sayings from *The Christian Parent*.

THE SOCIETY FOR PROMOTING CHRISTIAN KNOWLEDGE, London. England, for the poem by Amy Carmichael on p. 371.

STANDARD PUBLISHING for the quotation on p. 340 from James DeForest Murch, *Christian Education and the Local Church*, copyright 1943; revised edition copyright 1958.

THE SUNDAY SCHOOL BOARD OF THE SOUTHERN BAPTIST CONVENTION for the six selections on pp. 66, 144, 168, 189, 295 from *Home Life*, copyright by the Sunday School Board of the Southern Baptist Convention, Nashville, Tenn., and used by permission.

THE SUNDAY SCHOOL TIMES for the poem on pp. 174, 192-193 and 315 by Barbara C. Ryberg, and other stories and paragraphs. Copyright by The Sunday School Times.

THE SUNSHINE PRESS for "Marking Time" by Luther Markin, p. 53; "Business Trends," p. 59; "Life's Melody by Ruth Smeltzer, p. 236; the poem by Paul P. Wentz, p. 248; selection by Doris LaGasse, p. 321; and other materials, reprinted from *Sunshine Magazine*.

THIS DAY for the poem on p. 221, "Instruction" by Beth Applegate. Copyright 1957 by *This Day* Magazine.

THE UNITED PRESBYTERIAN CHURCH IN THE UNITED STATES OF AMERICA for Mary Seth's article on p. 243; the poem "First Bible" on pp. 48-49, from the *United Presbyterian*.

WORLD VISION for excerpts from Paul Rees's editorial, "Heal as You Travel," copyright *World Vision* Magazine.

ZONDERVAN PUBLISHING HOUSE for excerpts from Martin P. Simon, *Points for Parents;* the excerpt on p. 230 from *Religious Digest;* the quotation on p. 233 by C. B. Eavey; the poem on p. 350 by Clifford Lewis from *212 Victory Poems;* quotations by Richard C. Halverson from *Perspective*.

Diligent effort has been made to locate the original source of all copyrighted materials in this book and to secure permission for their inclusion. If such acknowledgments have been inadvertently omitted, the compiler and publisher would appreciate receiving full information so that proper credit may be given in future editions.

PLEASE SHARE ANOTHER SOURCEBOOK . . .

which I have enjoyed preparing for you to use when you need an illustration, aphorism, ancedote, poem, quotation or attention-getter.

This book began several years ago when I came across two note-books containing materials which I had wanted to use but could not find while preparing the *Speaker's Sourcebook* manuscript. I began adding to these cherished scrapbooks and often had occasion to share their content with others. A high school neighbor boy needed illus-trations for an essay, a collegian requested quotations to support a report, a minister wanted some sentence-sermons for the church bulletin, a toastmaster needed stories, a school teacher asked for maxims, a service club friend wanted attention-getters for a meeting, a Sunday school teacher needed a paraphrase, a writer asked for anecdotes about children. . . . And, because others, many others, found the collection helpful, this new Sourcebook was prepared.

Since this book originated from scrapbooks compiled for personal use, it contains materials selected primarily for their practical help-fulness and not necessarily for their literary quality. Many selections are from great books, others from outstanding incidents and persons in history, some from personal experiences and the experiences of friends. Still others are from the delightful world of children. And a number are from sources and authors unknown to me although every possible effort was made to acknowledge the publications and/or author. Regrettably numerous selections bear the credit line, "Author Unknown," "Source Unknown," "Anonymous," etc.

The more than 5000 selections in this book are arranged under more than 600 alphabetized subjects. This broad classification and the carefully detailed index are dependable guides in finding prac-tical helpfulness and personal enjoyment as you share the pages of my second sourcebook.

ELEANOR DOAN

Glendale, California

A

Abide

Abiding And Confiding

I have learned the wondrous secret
　Of abiding in the Lord;
I have found the strength and sweet-
　ness
　Of confiding in His word.
I have tasted life's pure fountain;
　I am drinking of His blood;
I have lost myself in Jesus,
　I am sinking into God.

I am crucified with Jesus,
　And He lives and dwells with me;
I have ceased from all my struggling;
　'Tis no longer I but He.
All my will is yielded to Him,
　And His Spirit reigns within,
And His precious blood each moment
　Keeps me cleansed and free from sin.

For my words I take His wisdom,
　For my works, His Spirit's power;
For my ways, His ceaseless Presence
　Guards and guides me every hour.
Of my heart, He is the portion,
　Of my joy, the boundless spring;
Saviour, Sanctifier, Healer,
　Glorious Lord and Coming King!

A. B. SIMPSON

———o———

The Blessed Secret
(Philippians 4:11)

I have learned the blessed secret
　Of the soul that's satisfied,
Since the Saviour dwells within me
　And in Him I now abide.
I have learned the joy of trusting
　In the sureness of His Word,
Knowing that each promise spoken
　Will be honored by my Lord.

In the silence I have heard Him:
　(O, the music of His voice!)
"Peace I give thee, be not troubled,
　Let thy heart and soul rejoice."
Yes, I've found my Lord sufficient,
　For He meets my ev'ry need,
Satisfies my soul's deep longings,
　Guards and guides each thought and
　deed.

Peace that passeth understanding
　Is His gift of grace so free.
And the power of His presence
　Is His promise unto me.
Blessed peace, divine contentment
　From the heart of God above!
All the shadows turn to sunshine,
　Walking with the Lord of love.

AUTHOR UNKNOWN

Ability

Ability means responsibility.

———o———

There is great ability in knowing how
to conceal one's ability.

FRANÇOIS, DUC DE LA ROCHEFOUCAULD,
Maxim 245

———o———

Every one excels in something in
which another fails.

PUBLILIUS SYRUS, Maxim 17

———o———

They can because they think they
can.

VIRGIL, Aeneid

———o———

There is something that is much more
scarce, something rarer than ability.
It is the ability to recognize ability.

ROBERT HALF

———o———

Ability is a poor man's wealth.

M. WREN

———o———

Most of us live too near the surface
of our abilities, dreading to call upon
our deeper resources. It is as if a strong
man were to do his work with only one
finger.

JOHN CHARLES WYNN

———o———

We are sometimes born into wealth,
but not ability. Ability must be acquired by an earnest effort; it is not
inherited.

PAUL P. PARKER

———o———

As we advance in life, we learn the
limits of our abilities.

JAMES ANTHONY FROUDE

Heal As You Travel

Dr. Paul Rees talks about life for the Christian as a "healing journey." "The Samaritan concerned himself with just one thing: saving the life of a mortal brother. Compassion . . . oil and wine . . . his own beast . . . two pence — he gave it all."

The healing journey, Dr. Rees explains, is made according to ability and not according to expediency.

Expediency says: "I must look after my own safety."

Ability says: "At all cost I must rescue this dying man."

Expediency asks: "How little can I get by with?"

Ability asks: "How much can I do?"

Expediency mumbles: "I must save up for a rainy day."

Ability cries: "I must give now, for this may be my last day."

Yes, for the Samaritan life was a healing journey. He took the wounded of the way and made them whole.

The Great Physician is looking for more "Samaritans" who will walk the way of the wounded with Him.

PAUL REES in World Vision Magazine

———o———

A man seldom knows what he can do until he tries to undo what he did.

Leader, Bridgeport, Ill.

———o———

Most men underestimate their ability but overestimate their performance.

———o———

You can do anything you ought to do.

Voice for Health

———o———

Ability is of little value without dependability.

———o———

It is not enough to know how to load the Gospel gun; you have to be able to shoot it.

AN UNKNOWN CHRISTIAN

Absence, Absentminded

Distance sometimes endears friendship, and absence sweeteneth it.

JAMES HOWELL, Familiar Letters

Our hours in love have wings; in absence crutches.

COLLEY CIBBER, Xerxes

———o———

Four-year-old Danny and his family went camping for their vacation. Since they weren't near a church, the family had Sunday school together at their campsite. During prayer time Danny prayed, "Dear God, please help my Sunday school teacher to be able to get along without me this morning!"

MRS. IRIS ELDRIDGE, Teach

———o———

A Pastor Explains His Absence

Dear Members:

I feel that a word of explanation is due concerning my absence from the pulpit last Sunday morning. I had not anticipated it causing such an uproar among the members, but I feel that when you hear of the circumstances you'll understand.

I had fully intended to be present as usual, but Saturday afternoon a whole carload of my wife's folks from Arkansas pulled into the driveway. We hadn't seen them in almost a year and since they had their children with them, we packed a hurried picnic supper and headed for the lake. It was after dark when we got back and aside from the fact that I hadn't been able to finish my sermon preparation; my wife's relatives had decided that they would spend the night with us and leave right after lunch Sunday to drive on to the mountains.

I tried to phone the chairman of our deacons, but as most of you know he is out of town a great deal and I was unable to contact him. However, I did leave a message with his wife and she promised to let him know as soon as he got home. Naturally, I felt that this was all that was necessary and that everything would work out fine.

I stayed home Sunday morning visiting with the folks, and it wasn't until Sunday afternoon, when the committee from the deacons came to visit me, that I found out that you hadn't been able to line up a supply preacher. I had just taken for granted that the chairman's wife would tell her husband when he came in Saturday night and that he would work something out. And besides this, how was I to know that this was the Sunday our organist had planned to be out of town, and that our choir director would be called away to announce a Sunday baseball game.

I regret that you had to dismiss the services. It just never occurred to me that the more than 500 people present had come expecting to hear me preach. And, I was deeply sorry to hear from the deacons' committee that there were four people present who had come to make a profession of faith but had to leave disappointed. I'll try not to let this happen again, but I can't promise anything, at least until vacation is over. So, as my favorite barber tells me when I get my hair cut, "I'll see you next Sunday, unless company drops in."

Almost sincerely,
Your Pastor

P.S. — Absurd? Unthinkable? Yes, but the same Person who expects the pastor to be present is depending just as much on every Sunday school teacher and officer to be present too — Jesus Christ. He's the one whom we fail.

Original Source Unknown,
printed in *Biblical Recorder*

———o———

If absence really made the heart grow fonder, a lot of people would miss church more than any place in the world.

———o———

I am not absentminded. It is the presence of mind that makes me unaware of everything else.

GILBERT KEITH CHESTERTON

Accidents, Accidental

Some people get to the top just by being stuck in the back of the elevator.

———o———

Accidents will occur in the best regulated families.

CHARLES DICKENS, *David Copperfield*

At first laying down, as a fact fundamental,
That nothing with God can be accidental.

HENRY W. LONGFELLOW

———o———

A man became sleepy. He rammed his motorcycle into a parked trailer truck, and he was killed. Two trailer trucks stopped at the scene. Two motorcycles smashed into the rear truck, killing both the motorcyclists. Another truck, unable to stop in time, hit the wreckage and hurled two bodies over an embankment. A fourth motorcyle plunged into that truck. Rider and another critically injured. Six automobiles piled up in opposite lane. Traffic stalled for hours. All because of one man!

Newspaper item

Accomplish, Achieve

I found Rome brick, I left it marble.

AUGUSTUS CAESAR

———o———

Almost never killed a fly.

German Saying

———o———

Take the obvious, add a cupful of brains, a generous pinch of imagination, a bucketful of courage and daring, stir well and bring it to a boil.

BERNARD BARUCH

———o———

If you would go to the top, first go to the bottom.

THOMAS A. EDISON

———o———

It is impossible for a man who attempts many things to do them all well.

Xenophon

———o———

Others have done so much with so little, while we have done so little with so much.

BOB PIERCE

———o———

All men are born equal, but what they are equal to later on is what counts.

I "can't" is a quitter;
I "don't know" is too lazy;
I "wish I could" is a wisher;
I "might" is waking up;
I "will try" is on his feet;
I "can" is on his way;
I "will" is at work;
I "did" is now boss.

AUTHOR UNKNOWN

———o———

The shortest way to do anything is to do only one thing at a time.

MARTIN LUTHER

———o———

Nothing is impossible to the man who doesn't have to do it himself.

———o———

It isn't what you wish to do, it's what you will do for God that transforms your life.

HENRIETTA C. MEARS

———o———

I long to accomplish a great and noble task, but it is my chief duty to accomplish tasks as though they were great and noble. The world is moved along, not only by the mighty shoves of its heroes, but also by the aggregate of the tiny pushes of each honest worker.

HELEN KELLER

———o———

The fellow who's on his toes doesn't usually have any trouble keeping other people from stepping on them.

———o———

People forget how fast you did a job . . . but they remember how well you did it.

HOWARD W. NEWTON

———o———

Not by self-seeking, but by self-sacrifice, not by dodging difficulties, but by overcoming them; not by giving supreme attention to outer things, but to inner worth — do men achieve.

CLIFF COLE

———o———

We have achieved plenty but lost quality.

The life of achievement is a life of hard work.

Councillor

———o———

It isn't how much you know, but what you get done that the world rewards and remembers.

DONALD LAIRD

Account, Accountable

God's Plan

If we don't like the sermon we can
    turn the dial
And tune in another station;
If we don't like the church we can
    stay away
For this is a broad creation.

But stop and think as you go your way:
    We'll each have to answer to God
    some day;
There'll be no dial that we can turn,
    There'll be no way of escape;
We'll face our God, and to Him
    A full confession make.

AUTHOR UNKNOWN

———o———

God Keeps Account

Of every self-denial true,
Of every thing we say or do,
Of every good intention, too,
    God keeps account.

Of each cup of cold water given,
Of each encouragement toward heaven,
To one, despairing, tempest driven,
    God keeps account.

Of every prayer to heaven we send,
Of every helping hand we lend,
Of every brother's wrong we mend,
    God keeps account.

May every word and deed and thought
Be prompted by the love of God,
And prove that I have only sought
    A good account.

O. F. HINZ

———o———

Bankrupt

One midnight, deep in starlight still,
I dreamed that I received this bill:
"(. . . . . in account with Life):

Five thousand breathless dawns all
new;
Five thousand flowers fresh in dew;
Five thousand sunsets wrapped in gold;
One million snow-flakes served ice-
cold;
Five quiet friends; one baby's love;
One white-mad sea with clouds above;
One hundred music-haunted dreams
Of moon-drenched roads and hurrying
streams;
Of prophesying winds, and trees;
Of silent stars and browsing bees;
One still night in a fragrant wood;
One heart that loved and understood."
I wondered when I waked at day,
How — how in God's name — I could
pay!

> CORTLAND W. SAYRES,
> *Golden Book of Faith*

Accuse

The breath of accusation kills an innocent name,
And leaves for lame acquittal the poor
life,
Which is a mask without it.

> PERCY BYSSHE SHELLEY, *The Cenci*

———o———

When you point your finger accus-
ingly at someone else, you've three
fingers pointing at yourself.

Acts, Actions, Active
(See also Do, Doing)

Everywhere in life, the true question
is not what we gain, but what we do.

> THOMAS CARLYLE

———o———

It is not necessary for all men to be
great in action. The greatest and sub-
limest power is often simple patience.

> HORACE BUSHNELL

———o———

I have never heard anything about
the resolutions of the apostles, but a
great deal about their acts.

> HORACE MANN

———o———

Actions, not words, are the true characteristic mark of the attachment of
friends.

> GEORGE WASHINGTON

Distinction between virtuous and
vicious actions has been engraven by
the Lord in the heart of every man.

> JOHN CALVIN

———o———

Do unto others as though you were
the others.

———o———

The need of the hour is not so much
to discuss the genuineness of the Bread,
as to break it and pass it out to the
hungry multitude.

———o———

Have you ever noticed that there
are two kinds of people who always
seem to be in bad luck; those who did
it but never thought, and those who
thought but never did it?

———o———

It is better to wear out than to rust
out.

> BISHOP RICHARD CUMBERLAND

———o———

If I rest, I rust.

> MARTIN LUTHER

———o———

The great end of life is not knowledge but action.

> THOMAS H. HUXLEY,
> *Technical Education*

———o———

Every man feels instinctively that all
the beautiful sentiments in the world
weigh less than a single lovely action.

> JAMES RUSSELL LOWELL

———o———

It is not always your actions that
count, but your reactions.

———o———

It is possible to be so active in the
service of Christ as to forget to love
him.

> PETER TAYLER FORSYTH

———o———

To be active for God is one thing
. . . but to be *effective* in that work is
quite another thing.

———o———

The story is told of a supersalesman
who sold an incredibly efficient filing

system to a certain business concern. A few months later he dropped by the office of the company to check up on its operation.

"How is the system working?" he inquired eagerly.

"Beyond our wildest dreams," the manager replied.

"And how's business?" the salesman asked.

The manager smiled, "We had to give up our business in order to run the filing system!"

———o———

You can't plow a field by turning it over in your mind.

———o———

When You Do An Act

You can never tell when you do an act
Just what the result will be;
But with every deed you are sowing a
seed,
Though its harvest you may not see.

Each kindly act is an acorn dropped
In God's productive soil;
Though you may not know, yet the
tree shall grow
And shelter the brows that toil.

AUTHOR UNKNOWN

Adapt

One learns to itch where one can scratch.

ERNEST BRAMAH

———o———

You might as well fall flat on your face as to lean over too far backward.

———o———

He who does not stretch himself according to the coverlet, finds his feet uncovered.

JOHANN WOLFGANG VON GOETHE

———o———

The wise man does no wrong in changing his habits with the times.

DIONYSIUS CATO

———o———

You must cut your coat according to your cloth.

Old Proverb

Admire

In reality, we do not admire a man so much for his success as we do for the qualities he has that makes success possible.

———o———

We always love those who admire us, and we do not always love those whom we admire.

FRANÇOIS, DUC DE LA ROCHEFOUCAULD,
Maxim 294

———o———

The greatest admiration gives rise, not to words, but to silence.

MUSONIUS

———o———

Admiration is our polite recognition of another man's resemblance to ourselves.

AMBROSE BIERCE

Adolescence
(See also Age)

Adolescence is a time of rapid changes. Between the ages of 12 and 17, for example, a parent ages as much as 20 years.

Changing Times, The Kiplinger Magazine

———o———

Adolescence is that period when a boy refuses to believe that some day he will be as ignorant as his parents.

———o———

Adolescent: One who is well informed about anything he doesn't have to study.

———o———

The world is full of people suffering from delayed or ingrown adolescence.

STORM JAMESON

Adopted

Ode To An Adopted Child

Not flesh of my flesh,
Nor bone of my bone;
But still, miraculously, my own!

Never forget, for a single minute:
You didn't grow under my heart
But in it!

FLEUR CONKLING HEYLINGER

Advantage

Shed no tears over your lack of early advantages. No really great man ever had any advantages that he himself did not create.

ELBERT HUBBARD

Next to knowing when to seize an opportunity, the most important thing in life is to know when to forego an advantage.

BENJAMIN DISRAELI

Adversary, Adversities

When the adversary strikes, watch God's answer. It may seem long in coming, but let us always remember that God will have the last word.

Adversities act as if they were the victors, but inwardly they are the vanquished.

RUSSELL H. VOIGHT

Adversity brings out talents which in prosperous circumstances would have lain dormant.

Be modest in good fortune, prudent in misfortune.

PERIANDER

Prosperity is a great teacher; adversity is a greater.

WILLIAM HAZLITT

Gold is tried by fire, brave men by affliction.

SENECA

Prosperity proves the fortunate, adversity the great.

PLINY THE YOUNGER

He who has not tasted bitter does not know what sweet is.

From the German

Storms make oaks take deeper root.

Kites rise highest against the wind – not with it.

SIR WINSTON CHURCHILL

It is in the furnace of affliction that our Savior watches for Christlikeness to be brought out in us. He is pictured as a purifier and refiner of silver, and we are told that he counts the process complete only when he can see his likeness in the molten metal.

NORMAN B. HARRISON

My business as a preacher is to afflict the comfortable and comfort the afflicted.

RALPH W. SOCKMAN

Advertising

The Sunday school teacher had carefully prepared his lesson. He was lecturing the youngsters on keeping their minds as clean as their bodies. Then, to emphasize his point, he held up a bar of soap.

"Oh, oh," murmured one lad. "Here comes the commercial."

Presbyterian Life

Advertising is the mouthpiece of business.

JAMES R. ADAMS

When business is good, it pays to advertise;
When business is bad you've got to advertise.

The first time six-year-old Lisa attended Sunday School she brought home a Sunday School paper.

"What is that?" her mother asked, reaching for the paper.

"Oh," said Lisa, "It's a give-away sheet full of ads about heaven!"

Advice

A woman's advice is not worth much, but he who doesn't heed it is a fool.

PEDRO CALDERON DE LA BARCA

A famous pediatrician was asked by

a mother what the best time was to put her children to bed.

"While you still have the strength," was the answer.

———o———

We wonder why it is that well-meant advice and constructive criticism, like a hat someone else has put on your head, never feels just right.

———o———

There is no situation in human life or experience for which advice from God cannot be found in the Bible — whether it be personal, social, national or international.

G. CAMPBELL MORGAN

———o———

We give advice by the bucket, but take it by the grain.

WILLIAM R. ALGER

———o———

Be quiet enough to hear it,
    The plan of God.
Be brave enough to speak it,
    The message of God.
Be honest enough to live it,
    The life of God.

———o———

One little hint may be worth a ton of advice.

———o———

Many receive advice, few profit by it.

PUBLILIUS SYRUS, *Maxim 149*

———o———

To stimulate her young pupils, a first-grade teacher arranged to take her class on an "educational tour" of a farmyard. But one small boy saw right through her scheme. "Don't look, don't look!" he warned his buddy. "If we look we'll have to tell about it tomorrow."

AL RHOADES, Newburgh, N.Y.,
Newburgh-Beacon News

———o———

Advice is like castor oil, easy enough to give but dreadful uneasy to take.

"JOSH BILLINGS"
(HENRY WHEELER SHAW)

———o———

When Billy Sunday was converted and joined the church, a Christian man put his arm on the young man's shoulder and said, "William, there are three simple rules I can give to you, and if you will hold to them you will never write 'backslider' after your name.

"Take fifteen minutes each day to listen to God talking to you; take fifteen minutes each day to talk to God; take fifteen minutes each day to talk to others about God."

The young convert was deeply impressed and determined to make these rules of his life. From that day onward throughout his life he made it a rule to spend the first moments of his day alone with God and God's Word. Before he read a letter, looked at a paper or even read a telegram, he went first to the Bible, that the first impression of the day might be what he got directly from God.

———o———

Advice is what you take for a cold.

THOMAS J. O'BRIEN

———o———

To a young man learning to perform on the flying trapeze a veteran circus performer once said, "Throw your heart over the bars and your body will follow."

———o———

To find fault is easy; to do better may be difficult.

———o———

Doctor: "The thing for you to do is to stop thinking about yourself; try burying yourself in your work."

Patient: "Mercy, and me a concrete mixer!"

———o———

Walk softly, speak tenderly, pray fervently, do not run up stairs, do not run down God's people.

T. J. BACH

Advocate

My Advocate

I sinned. And straightway, posthaste, Satan flew
Before the presence of the most High God,

And made a railing accusation there.
He said, "This soul, this thing of clay
   and sod,
Has sinned. 'Tis true that he has named
   Thy Name,
But I demand his death, for Thou hast
   said,
'The soul that sinneth, it shall die.'
   Shall not
Thy sentence be fulfilled? Is justice
   dead?
Send now this wretched sinner to his
   doom.
What other thing can righteous ruler
   do?"
And thus he did accuse me day and
   night,
And every word he spoke, oh God, was
   true!

Then quickly One rose up from God's
   right hand
Before whose glory angels veiled their
   eyes,
He spoke, "Each jot and tittle of the law
Must be fulfilled; the guilty sinner dies!
But wait — suppose his guilt were all
   transferred to Me, and that I paid his
   penalty!
Behold My hands, My side, My feet!
   One day
I was made sin for him, and died that
   he
Might be presented faultless, at thy
   throne!"
And Satan fled away. Full well he knew
That he could not prevail against such
   love,
For every word my dear Lord spoke
   was true!
               MARTHA SNELL NICHOLSON

Age

If you want to be a dear old lady at
seventy you have to begin early, say
about seventeen.
                     MAUDE ROYDEN

———o———

To avoid old age keep taking on new
thoughts and throwing off old habits.

———o———

Middle age is the time of life when
your idea of getting ahead is to stay
even.

The most dangerous age for women is
poundage.

———o———

When a man has a birthday he takes
the day off, but when a woman has a
birthday, she takes a year off.

———o———

Going On

Growing old, but not retiring
   For the battle still is on;
Going on without relenting,
   Till the final victory's won.
Ever on, nor think of resting,
   For the battle rages still,
And my Saviour still is with me
   And I seek to do His will.

Years roll by, the body weakens;
   But the spirit still is young;
Breath of God — it never ages,
   Is eternal, ever strong.
Rather, year by year it strengthens,
   Gaining o'er the things of sense.
By Thy Spirit, lead my spirit,

Saviour, till Thou call me hence.
Things of earth decrease in value,
   Brighter shines the light above;
Less the power of human hatred,
   Sweeter far the Saviour's love.
Let me tell it to the needy,
   Far and wide Thy worth proclaim;
That my closing years may praise Thee
   Glorify Thy blessed name.

Let me labor in Thy harvest
   More than ever in the past,
Reaping in what Thou hast planted,
   Till I dwell with Thee at last;
That before Thy throne eternal
   I may have some fruit to bring,
Not my work — the fruit of Calvary,
   All are Thine, my Lord and King.
                 AUTHOR UNKNOWN

———o———

To keep young, associate much with
young people. To get old in a hurry,
try keeping up with them.

———o———

You are as young as your faith,
   As old as your doubt,
As young as your self-confidence,
   As old as your fear,

As young as your hope,
As old as your despair.

CINDY

The Ages Of Man

Baby	Working
Bottle	Saving
Rocking crib	Bride and groom
Walking	Children
Talking	Cottage
Tidy bib	Money boom
Pencil	Christmas
Paper	Easter
Grammar school	Mountain lakes
Reading	Meetings
Writing	Hobbies
Golden Rule	Leaves and rakes
Growing	Prestige
Learning	Wall Street
In a daze	Pain in head
Rockin'	Doctors
Rollin'	Ulcers
Hi Fi craze	Rest in bed
College	False teeth
Buddies	Fatty
Actions rude	Lots of dough
Liquor	Fifty
Army	Sixty
Language crude	Had to go

GEORGE LOUKIDES in *Suburbia Today*

———o———

Some folks go to seed long before spring planting time.

———o———

No man is really old until his mother stops worrying about him.

WILLIAM RYAN

———o———

Why is it that a person your own age always looks older than you do?

———o———

When a woman filling out an application blank came to the square marked "Age," she didn't hesitate. She simply wrote: "Atomic."

Adolescence is when you think you'll live forever. Middle age is when you wonder how you've lasted so long.

———o———

To be seventy years young is sometimes far more cheerful and hopeful than to be forty years old.

OLIVER WENDELL HOLMES

———o———

Middle age is when you start for home about the same time you used to start for somewhere else.

Review, Conrad, Iowa

———o———

For Friends Of The Aged

BLESSED are they who understand
My faltering step and palsied hand.
BLESSED are they who know that my
ears today
Must strain to catch the things they
say.
BLESSED are they who seem to know
That my eyes are dim and my wits
are slow.
BLESSED are they who looked away
When coffee was spilled at table to-
day.
BLESSED are they who never say:
"You've told that story twice today."
BLESSED are they who know the ways
To bring back memories of yester-
days.
BLESSED are they who make it known
That I'm loved, respected and not
alone.
BLESSED are they who know I'm at a
loss
To find the strength to carry the
Cross.
BLESSED are they who ease the days
Of my journey home in loving ways.

ESTHER M. WALKER,
The Glass "Chatterbox"

———o———

Middle age is the time when you can do everything you could in your youth, but not until tomorrow.

CHICK WELCH

———o———

Look them over and you will find that people don't stop playing because they get old, but they get old because they stop playing.

———o———

You're an old-timer if you can remember when a housewife's meals were carefully thought out instead of thawed out.

ANNA HERBERT

———o———

Age makes you take twice as long to rest and half as long to get tired.

———o———

Old age and the wear of time teach many things.

———o———

A Prayer For Older Folk

Lord, Thou knowest that I am growing older.

Keep me from becoming talkative and possessed with the idea that I must express myself on every subject.

Release me from the craving to straighten out everyone's affairs.

Keep my mind free from the recital of endless details. Give me wings to get to the point.

Seal my lips when I am inclined to tell of my aches and pains. They are increasing with the years and my love to speak of them grows sweeter as time goes by.

Teach me the glorious lesson that occasionally I may be wrong.

Make me thoughtful but not nosey; helpful but not bossy.

With my vast store of wisdom and experience it does seem a pity not to use it all, but Thou, knowest, Lord, that I want a few friends left at the end. Amen!

AUTHOR UNKNOWN

———o———

Life Begins At Forty?

I completed my preparations,
  But, alas, I found with chagrin,
I had worked so hard getting ready
  That I was too tired to begin.

———o———

At age twenty we don't care what the world thinks of us; at age fifty we find out it wasn't thinking of us at all.

When a man ceases to grow, no matter what the years, then and there he begins to be old.

———o———

Talking about growing old, a man isn't old until everything seems wrong. It may happen at seventy or twenty.

CLIFF COLE

———o———

Isn't it silly to fuss about getting old? When we stop growing older, we're dead.

———o———

About the only thing that comes to us without effort is old age.

———o———

Several elderly church members were being asked to what they attributed their longevity. "And why do you think God has permitted you to reach the age of 92?" one wealthy old lady was asked.

Without hesitation she responded: "To test the patience of my relatives."

MARY LYNN SHELTON, *Reader's Digest*

———o———

We do not count a man's years, until he has nothing else to count.

RALPH WALDO EMERSON

———o———

Adult to small boy: "How old is your father?"

Small boy: "He's in the middle ages."

———o———

Middle age is the time when a man is always thinking that in a week or two he will feel as good as ever.

DONALD ROBERT PERRY MARQUIS

———o———

Age, A Quality Of Mind

Age is a quality of mind;
If you have left your dreams behind,
If hope is cold,
If you no longer look ahead,
If your ambition's fires are dead,
Then you are old.

But if from life you take the best,
And if in life you keep the zest,
If love you hold,
No matter how the years go by,
No matter how the birthdays fly,
You are not old.

AUTHOR UNKNOWN

Agree

The quickest way to take the starch out of a man who is always blaming himself is to agree with him.

"JOSH BILLINGS" (HENRY WHEELER SHAW)

———o———

Be pretty if you can;
Be witty if you must;
But be agreeable if it kills you.

———o———

The Home With The Two Bears

It was observed by friends that old Brother and Sister Brown were getting on more agreeably together than they had formerly done. Asked for an explanation, Brother Brown replied: "Well, about a year ago we decided to keep two bears in the house all the time. One of these bears is 'bear ye one another's burdens,' and the other is 'Forbear one another in love.' And since we took these two bears in we have found the going easier."

———o———

When you say that you agree to a thing in principle you mean that you have not the slightest intention of carrying it out.

OTTO VON BISMARCK

———o———

When everyone agrees, there is very little thinking.

———o———

Fools bite one another, but wise men agree.

———o———

When two men in business always agree, one of them is unnecessary.

WILLIAM WRIGLEY, JR.

———o———

You can't expect people to see eye to eye with you if you look down on them.

Aim

Slight not what's near through aiming at what's far.

EURIPIDES, Rhesus

Next in importance to having good aim is to recognize when to pull the trigger.

ELMER G. LETERMAN

———o———

Everything worth-while has a high wall around it; but by looking to God He will give you the key to open the gate and go through.

———o———

An aim in life is the only fortune worth finding.

ROBERT LOUIS STEVENSON

———o———

The Christian's aim should be less at goods and more at goodness.

———o———

When man understands that the aim of life is not material profit but life itself, he ceases to fix his attention exclusively on the external world. He considers more attentively his own existence and the existence of those around him. He realizes that he depends on others and that others depend on him.

ALEXIS CARREL

Alcohol

The liquor dealers advertise
    In many magazines,
We see their "ads" on street cars, too,
    And on the movie screens.
Pictures of happy, laughing girls
    And wholesome, healthy lads;
But where's their finished product?
    It's never in their ads.

———o———

Balanced judgment will certify that intoxicating liquor leaves an unbalanced budget, unbalanced men and women, an unbalanced home and an unbalanced social order.

CLIFF COLE

———o———

Our Silly Ways

We license a saloon to teach vice and then tax people for schools to teach virtue!
We license a man to make drunken pau-

pers and then tax sober men to take care of them!

We license a man to sell that which will make a man drunk, and then punish the man for being drunk!

SOURCE UNKNOWN

———o———

A physician once said of alcoholic beverages:

It gives you a red nose,
a black eye,
a white liver,
a dark brown breath,
a blue outlook.

But who wants that color scheme in life?

———o———

Abstinence is as easy to me as temperance would be difficult.

SAMUEL JOHNSON

———o———

Some of the domestic evils of drunkenness are houses without windows, gardens without fences, fields without tillage, barns without roofs, children without clothing, principles, morals or manners.

BENJAMIN FRANKLIN

———o———

The steady drinker soon becomes the unsteady drinker.

———o———

Liquor talks mighty loud when it gets loose from the bottle.

———o———

The man who drinks a little, drinks too much.

Alone

Never Alone

"*I will never leave thee, nor forsake thee*" (Hebrews 13:5).

I'm never alone in the morning
As I rise at the break of day,
For Jesus who watched through the darkness
Says, "Lo, I am with you alway."

I'm never alone at my table,
Though loved ones no longer I see;
For dearer than all who have vanished,
Is Jesus who breaks bread with me.

I'm never alone through the daylight,
Though nothing but trials I see;
Though the furnace be seven times heated,
The "form of the fourth" walks with me.

I'm never alone at the twilight
When darkness around me doth creep;
And spectres press hard round my pillow,
He watches and cares while I sleep.

I'm walking and talking with Jesus,
Each day as I journey along;
I'm never alone, Hallelujah!
The joy of the Lord is my song.

AUTHOR UNKNOWN

———o———

I was never less alone than when by myself.

EDWARD GIBBON

———o———

Who lives unto himself, he lives to none.

FRANCIS QUARLES

———o———

There's a path that leads through a woodland — a path that I love to trod,
To get away from this wild world's rush and be alone with God.

From a Very Old Scrapbook

Alphabet

Bible Alphabet

A—Ask and it shall be given you.
B—Be still, and know that I am God.
C—Commit thy works unto the Lord.
D—Do good, O Lord, unto those that do good.
E—Enter into his gates with thanksgiving.
F—For by grace are ye saved through faith.
G—Give, and it shall be given unto you.

H—Honor and majesty are before him.
I — In his hands are the deep places of the earth.
J—Judge not, that ye be not judged.
K—Keep thy heart with all diligence.
L—Let all the people praise thee, O God.
M—My help cometh from the Lord.
N—Nevertheless, I tell ye the truth.
O—O worship the Lord in the beauty of holiness.
P—Praise ye the Lord.
Q—Quench not the Spirit.
R—Rest in the Lord, and wait patiently for him.
S—Sing unto the Lord a new song.
T—Take my yoke upon you.
U—Unto thee lift I up mine eyes.
V—Vanity, vanity, all is vanity.
W—Where there is no vision, the people perish.
X—(X-ray).
Y—Ye are my witnesses, saith the Lord.
Z—Zion heard and was glad.

VERNA B. WADDELL

Ambition

Your ambition, not your worded prayer, is your real creed.

ELLA WHEELER WILCOX

———o———

Ambition can move mountains — providing the tools are there to do the job.

———o———

Some people are like blisters, they do not show up until the work is done.

———o———

Many a man with an ambition to find fame and fortune failed because he didn't find himself first.

———o———

A little boy came home from Sunday School and said to his grandmother "We have been singing 'Jesus wants me for a sunbeam.'"

"How lovely," replied Grandmother.

Looking rather put out, the little chap said: "But Granny, I want to be an engine driver."

Life Story

The evolution of a man's ambitions:
To be a circus clown.
To be like dad.
To be a fireman.
To do something noble.
To get wealthy.
To make ends meet.
To get the old-age pension.

Sunshine Magazine

———o———

The tallest trees are most in the power of the winds, and ambitious men of the blasts of fortune.

WILLIAM PENN

———o———

A man will remain a rag-picker as long as he has only the vision of a rag-picker.

O. S. MARDEN

———o———

Every man is capable of being something better than he is.

ROY L. SMITH

———o———

The desire of power in excess caused the angels to fall; the desire of knowledge in excess caused man to fall; but in charity there is no excess, neither can angel or man come in danger by it.

FRANCIS BACON, *Essay: Of Goodness*

———o———

Well it is known that ambition can creep as well as soar.

EDMUND BURKE

———o———

Let proud Ambition pause
And sicken at the vanity that prompts
His little deeds.

DAVID MALLETT, *The Excursion, Cante ii*

———o———

There is a loftier ambition than merely to stand high in the world. It is to stoop down and lift mankind a little higher.

HENRY VAN DYKE

America

"America For Me"

'Tis fine to see the Old World, and travel up and down

Among the famous places and cities of
renown,
To admire the crumbly castles and
statues of the Kings, —
But now I think I've had enough of
antiquated things.

So it's home again, and home again,
America for me!
My heart is turning home again, and
there I long to be,
In the land of youth and freedom be-
yond the ocean bars,
Where the air is full of sunlight and the
flag is full of stars.

Oh, London is a man's town, there's
power in the air;
And Paris is a woman's town, with
flowers in her hair;
And it's sweet to dream in Venice, and
it's great to study Rome;
But when it comes to living there is no
place like home.

I like the German fir-woods, in green
battalions drilled;
I like the gardens of Versailles with
flashing fountains filled;
But, oh, to take your hand, my dear,
and ramble for a day
In the friendly western woodland where
Nature has her way!

I know that Europe's wonderful, yet
something seems to lack:
The Past is too much with her, and
people looking back.
But the glory of the Present is to make
the Future free, —
We love our land for what she is and
what she is to be.

Oh, it's home again, and home again,
America for me!
I want a ship that's westward bound
to plough the rolling sea,
To the blessed Land of Room Enough
beyond the ocean bars,
Where the air is full of sunlight and the
flag is full of stars.

HENRY VAN DYKE

———o———

It's a great country, but you can't live
in it for nothing.

WILL ROGERS

The World In Miniature

Imagine that we could compress the
world's population of more than three
and a quarter billion into one town of
1,000 persons in the exact proportions in
which the world population is actually
divided. In such a town of 1,000 there
would be only 60 Americans! And these
60 Americans would receive half the income of the entire town. Only about
330 of the remaining 940 townsfolk
would be classed as Christians. At least
80 townspeople would be practicing
Communists and 370 others under Communist domination.

The 60 Americans would have an
average life expectancy of 70 years;
the other 940 less than 40 years. The
60 Americans would have 15 times as
many possessions per person as all of
their neighbors. The Americans would
produce 16 percent of the town's food
supply and, although they'd eat 72 percent above the maximum food require-
ments, they would either eat most of
what they grew, or store it for their
own further use, at enormous cost.
(With most of the 940 non-Americans
hungry, the food supply disparity might
understandably lead to some ill-feel-
ing.)

There would be 53 telephones in this
one-town world . . . Americans would
have 28 of them. The Americans would
enjoy a disproportionate share of electric power, coal, fuel, steel, and general
equipment.

The lowest income group among the
Americans would be better off by far
than the average of the other towns-
men. The 60 Americans and about 200
others representing Western Europe
and a few classes in South America,
South Africa, Australia, and Japan
would be relatively well off, by comparison.

Half of the inhabitants of our one-
town world would be ignorant of Jesus
Christ, but more than half would have
heard, and would continue to hear of
Karl Marx, Lenin, Stalin, and Khrush-
chev.

Out of his average income of $3,000
per year, the gift of each American per-

son for all purposes other than private and personal gifts would average less than $60 per year. This might raise a question as to how seriously he regards the Christian faith or the meaning of Christmas with its emphasis on peace and good will among men.

HENRY SMITH LEIPER

Of This I Am Proud

That I am an American
  And have the right to vote as
  And for whom I please

That I have the right to choose
  My friends
  And live where I please

That I have the right to worship
  At the church and religion of my
    choice
  When and where I please

That I have the right
  And may always live worthy of
  And do honor to this country
  Of which I am proud

STERLING SNYDER

Let independence be our boast,
Ever mindful what it cost;
Ever grateful for the prize,
Let its altar reach the skies!
JOSEPH HOPKINSON, *Hail, Columbia*

I shall know but one country. The ends I aim at shall be my country's, my God's and Truth's. I was born an American; I will live an American; I shall die an American.

DANIEL WEBSTER

Give me your tired, your poor,
Your huddled masses yearning to breathe free,
The wretched refuse of your teeming shore,
Send these, the homeless, tempest-tossed to me:
I lift my lamp beside the golden door.
EMMA LAZARUS —
Inscription on the Statue of Liberty

Ancestors

Little Tommy: "What kind of things are ancestors?"
Papa: "Well, I'm one and so is Grandpa."
Little Tommy: "Then why is it people go around bragging about them?"

It is indeed a desirable thing to be well descended, but the glory belongs to our ancestors.

PLUTARCH

They that on glorious ancestors enlarge, Produce their debt, instead of their discharge.

EDWARD YOUNG, *Love of Fame*

He who serves well his country has no need of ancestors.

VOLTAIRE

People will not look forward to posterity who never looked backward to their ancestors.

EDMUND BURKE

If there be no nobility of descent, all the more indispensable is it that there should be nobility of ascent — a character in them that bear rule so fine and high and pure that as men come within the circle of its influence they involuntarily pay homage to that which is the one pre-eminent distinction, the royalty of virtue.

HENRY CODMAN POTTER

The kind of ancestors we have had is not as important as the kind of descendants our ancestors have.

A man who has ancestors is like a representative of the past.
EDWARD GEORGE BULWER-LYTTON

Many a family tree needs trimming.
FRANK MCKINNEY HUBBARD

Angels

Five-year-old Betty had been told that the noise of a thunderstorm was only the angels making their beds. One morning, after a storm in which there had been considerable thunder and lightning, the little girl said:

"You know, Mommy, I didn't mind the noise when the angels made their beds last night, but I certainly didn't like it when they couldn't make up their minds whether to turn the lights off or not."

——o——

It's easy to be an angel when nobody ruffles your feathers.

Anger, Angry

It is he who is in the wrong who first gets angry.

WILLIAM PENN

——o——

Anger improves nothing except the arch of a cat's back.

COLEMAN COX

——o——

Consider how few things are worthy of anger, and thou wilt wonder that any fool should be wroth.

ROBERT DODSLEY

——o——

Getting mad will never get you anything else!

——o——

When tempted to anger, read —

The Humility Verse — Job 18:4
The Punishment Verse — Matthew 5:22
Cruel Wrath — Proverbs 27:4
A Soft Answer — Proverbs 15:1

——o——

He who can suppress a moment's anger may prevent a day of sorrow.

TRYON EDWARDS

——o——

When angry, count ten before you speak; if very angry, count a hundred.

THOMAS JEFFERSON

——o——

Form the habit of closing your mouth firmly when angry.

——o——

If you are patient in one moment of anger, you will escape a hundred days of sorrow.

Chinese Proverb

——o——

Be strong enough to control your anger instead of letting it control you.

——o——

Be not angry that you cannot make others as you wish them to be, since you cannot make yourself as you wish to be.

THOMAS À KEMPIS

——o——

Whatever is begun in anger ends in shame.

——o——

He that strives not to stem his anger's tide,
Does a wild horse without a bridle ride.

COLLEY CIBBER, Love's Last Shift

Animals

I have found . . . that those who love
a deer, a dog, a bird and flowers . . .
are usually thoughtful of the larger
needs that may be ours . . .
. . . Who for God's creatures small will
plan . . . will seldom wrong his fellow man.

AUTHOR UNKNOWN

——o——

You can't buy loyalty, they say.
I bought it though, the other day.
You can't buy friendship tried and true.
Well, just the same, I bought that, too.

I made my bid, and on the spot
Bought love and faith and a whole job lot
Of happiness; so all in all
The total price was pretty small.

I bought a simple, trusting heart
That gave devotion from the start.
If you think these things are not for sale,
Buy a brown-eyed pup with a wagging tail!

AUTHOR UNKNOWN

——o——

Animals are such agreeable friends — they ask no questions, they pass no criticisms.

GEORGE ELIOT (MARY ANN EVANS)

When the donkey saw the Zebra
He began to switch his tail;
"Well, I never," was the comment,
"Saw a mule that's been in jail."
Southwest Collegian

---o---

School Essay On The Cow

The cow is an animal. At the back it has a tail. On it hangs a brush. With this it sends the flies away so that they do not fall into the milk. The head is for the purpose of growing horns and so the mouth can be somewhere. The horns are to butt with, and the mouth is to moo with. Under the cow hangs the milk. It is arranged for milking. When people milk, the milk comes. How the cow does it, I don't know. The cow has a fine sense of smell. One can smell it far away; this is the reason for fresh air in the country. The cow does not eat much, but eats it twice, so that it gets enough. When it is hungry, it moos, but when it says nothing, it is because it is all full up with grass.

SIR ERNEST GOWERS, *Plain Words*
Observer

---o---

The first-grade children in a Raleigh, N.C., school were having a wonderful time playing with a stray cat. After a while one little lad asked the teacher if it was a boy cat or a girl cat. Not wishing to get into that particular subject, she said that she didn't believe she could tell. "I know how we can find out," said the boy.

"All right," said the teacher, resigning herself to the inevitable. "How can we find out?"

"We can vote," said the child.

SAM RAGAN, Raleigh, N.C.,
News and Observer

---o---

The Tale Of A Dog

There was a dachshund, once, so long
He hadn't any notion
How long it took to notify
His tail of his emotion;
And so it happened, while his eyes
Were filled with woe and sadness,
His little tail went wagging on
Because of previous gladness.

AUTHOR UNKNOWN

Why a dog has so many friends: his tail wags instead of his tongue.

---o---

During World War II a mother and her little girl were sent from a city to the country home of parents. One day the little girl came in and said, "Mummy, I saw four little pigs blowing up the mother pig!"

---o---

There was a young man from a city
Who saw what he thought was a kitty.
He gave it a pat, said nice little cat —
And they buried his clothes out of pity.

---o---

It's nice for children to have pets until the pets start having children.

The Wildrooter

---o---

Dachshund

A dog-and-a-half long
And a half-a-dog high;
All the family can pet him
While he's passing by.

VIRGIE EVANS ROGERS

Announcement

A Clean Announcement

DUZ you just DREFT along with the TIDE of unconcern? VEL now is the time to CHEER up. If you want real JOY the TREND is for ALL the family to BREEZE right into our Sunday School. Hear our SOS. Don't let us have to DIAL you this week to have you WHISK yourself to Sunday School next Sunday. Come on and let's ALL pull together like a 20 MULE TEAM.

Temple Evangelist

---o---

A young wife, wishing to announce the birth of her first child to a friend in a distant city, sent this telegram:
"Isaiah 9:6."

Her friend, not familiar with the Scriptures, said to her husband:

"Margaret evidently has a boy who weighs nine pounds and six ounces, but why on earth did they name him Isaiah?"

Answer

Gracious Care

God answered prayer!
Not in the way I sought:
Not in the way that I had thought He
ought!
But in His own good way and I could
see
He answered in the fashion best for me.
And I was glad that I had such a share
In His parental love and gracious care,
That thus He answered prayer.

God answered prayer!
But not in my brief hour:
I looked to see the fruit ere yet the
flower
Had shed its gales of sweetness o'er my
path!
But I have learned that slowest blos-
soms yield
The choicest fruit; and so I leave them
there
Upon the boughs, assured that they
will bear
In time my answered prayer!

God answered prayer!
So sweetly that I stand
Amid the blessing of His wondrous
Hand,
And marvel at the miracle I see,
The fashion that His love has wrought
for me.
Pray on for the impossible and dare,
Upon thy banner this brave motto bear,
"My Father answers prayer."

The Good Shepherd

———o———

Usually reluctant to participate in
class discussions, Alfred was wildly
waving his hand in response to the
question, "What causes tides?" I was
happy to call on him.

"Dead people!" he said with some
smugness. "It says so right in the ge-
ography book: 'Tides are caused by
heavenly bodies.'"

MARTHA VOGEN in *Grade Teacher*

———o———

The trouble with some people who
always "have all the answers" is that
so few of them are the right ones.

A child can ask a thousand questions
that the wisest man cannot answer.

JACOB ABBOTT

———o———

God's Answer

One day I prayed that God would lay
a soul upon my heart;
And in my prayer I promised Him that
I would do my part.
I'd call on strangers, write some cards,
and use the telephone;
Then trust Him — in His wisdom — to
lead me to that one.

Just then my doorbell rang so hard it
shook me from my prayer.
Before me stood a ten-year-old, his
head and feet were bare.
His small, dark face was far from clean,
his speech was bold and rough.
His brother said, "He's awful mean";
his manner said, "I'm tough."

But as I stood there at the door, the
Saviour whispered low,
"Here is that soul I charge to you. Oh,
do not let him go!"
That's why I baked these cookies; I've
put them out to cool
For my small friend — no longer tough
— he's in our Sunday school.

AUTHOR UNKNOWN

———o———

It is a good answer which knows
when to stop.

Italian Proverb

———o———

There cannot be a precise answer to
a vague question.

WENDELL JOHNSON

———o———

It is not every question that deserves
an answer.

PUBLILIUS SYRUS, *Maxim 581*

———o———

If you desire a wise answer, you must
ask a reasonable question.

JOHANN WOLFGANG VON GOETHE

———o———

A Sunday school teacher was telling
a Junior boy the story of Zacchaeus.
When he came to the part where Jesus
looked up into the tree and saw Zac-

chaeus, he asked, "What did Jesus say to the little man?" Without hesitation the lad answered, "Don't climb trees!"

MOLLIE MCCALL

Anticipation

As watchmen look for the morning, so do we look for Thee, O Christ. Come with the dawning of the day, and make Thyself known to us in the breaking of the bread; for Thou art our God for ever and ever.

Clare College Rite

———o———

Not many sounds in life, and I include all urban and all rural sounds, exceed in interest a knock at the door.

CHARLES LAMB, *Essays of Elia. Valentine's Day*

———o———

Many count their chickens before they are hatched.

MIGUEL DE CERVANTES, *Don Quixote*

———o———

Let's fear no storm, before we feel a shower.

MICHAEL DRAYTON, *The Baron's Wars*

———o———

The misfortunes hardest to bear are those which never came.

JAMES RUSSELL LOWELL

———o———

Nothing is so good as it seems beforehand.

GEORGE ELIOT (MARY ANN EVANS), *Silas Marner*

Anxiety

What does your anxiety do? It does not empty tomorrow, brother, of its sorrow; but ah! it empties today of its strength. It does not make you escape the evil; it makes you unfit to cope with it if it comes.

IAN MCLAREN

———o———

There is such a thing as taking ourselves and the world too seriously, or at any rate too anxiously. Half of the secular unrest and dismal, profane sadness of modern society comes from the vain idea that every man is bound to be a critic of life, and to let no day pass without finding some fault with the general order of things, or projecting some plan for its general improvement. And the other half comes from the greedy notion that a man's life does consist, after all, in the abundance of things that he possesseth, and that it is somehow or other more respectable and pious to be always at work trying to make a larger living, than it is to lie on your back in the green pastures and beside the still waters, and thank God that you are alive.

HENRY VAN DYKE

———o———

Oh, how great peace and quietness would he possess who should cut off all vain anxiety and place all his confidence in God.

THOMAS À KEMPIS

———o———

Nothing in the affairs of men is worthy of great anxiety.

PLATO

———o———

Anxiety reveals a lack of faith.

———o———

Anxiety is the poison of human life; the parent of many sins and of more miseries.

HUGH BLAIR

———o———

You cannot carry easily and well today's duties if you pile anxiety concerning the morrow on top of them.

Apology

A preacher's small son had to apologize for forgetting his aunt's birthday. He wrote, "I am sorry I forgot your birthday. I have no excuse, and it would serve me right if you forgot mine, which is next Friday."

———o———

From a son, now twice the age of which he speaks, came to his parents this one-line note: "If I was ever sixteen, pardon me!"

Apologies only account for that which they do not alter.

BENJAMIN DISRAELI

Appearance

You can't judge a horse by the harness.

Old Proverb

————o————

All is not false which seems at first a lie.

ROBERT SOUTHEY

————o————

Appearances to the mind are of four kinds. Things either are what they appear to be; or they neither are, nor appear to be; or they are, and do not appear to be; or they are not, and yet appear to be. Rightly to aim in all these cases is the wise man's task.

EPICTETUS

————o————

Half the work that is done in this world is to make things appear what they are not.

ELIAS ROST BEADLE

————o————

Appearances do not make the man, but it will pay any man to make the best appearance possible.

ROY L. SMITH

————o————

The dress does not make the monk.

FRANÇOIS RABELAIS

Application
(See also Action)

If a girl sits and reads the recipes in the cook-book, and does nothing more about it, she will never get a dinner ready. Reading the Bible can be done in the same easy way — with the same lack of results.

The Brethren Evangelist

————o————

Few men are lacking in capacity, but they fail because they are lacking in application.

CALVIN COOLIDGE

————o————

When a minister in a new parish preached the same sermon three Sundays in a row there was quite a bit of fuss and talk.

At last, one of the deacons called the young minister aside and said, "Pastor, you have used the sermon three times in a row. When are you going to preach a new one?"

The young pastor answered, "I will preach a new sermon when the people of my church start practicing the message of this one."

The Log of the Good Ship Grace

————o————

Application is the price to be paid for mental acquisition. To have the harvest we must sow the seed.

————o————

Application in youth enriches old age.

CHARLES SIMMONS

Appreciation
Appreciation

Let me be very patient with the old
And gladly listen to their tales thrice-
told;
My hurrying feet I would more gently
stay,
And fit my steps to theirs, along the
way.

Perhaps the fertile future holds for me
Bright days the lonely old shall never
see;
And so I fain would share their joy,
their pain,
Because they shall not pass this way
again.

Then let me not forget to give my smile,
And let me not forget that all the while
The old are giving too, of wisdom rare,
Rich gifts to me, though I be unaware.

RUBY M. SLOAN
in *South Carolina Methodist Advocate*

————o————

The only place you can be sure to find appreciation is in the dictionary.

————o————

Don't be stingy with words of appreciation when they are justly due.

He who seeks only for applause from without has all his happiness in another's keeping.

OLIVER GOLDSMITH

———o———

Applause is the spur of noble minds, the end and aim of weak ones.

CHARLES CALEB COLTON

———o———

Prayer For Appreciation

Oh teach me, Lord, to treasure much
The simple things of life — the touch
Of wind and snow, of rain and sun;
And when the hours of work are done,
The quietness of rest, the fair
And healing sustenance of prayer.
And, Lord of living, help me keep
A shining, singing gladness deep
Within for blessings yet to be
Through all eternity.

AUTHOR UNKNOWN

Architects

All are architects of fate,
    Working in these walls of Time;
Some with massive deeds and great,
    Some with ornaments of rhyme.

HENRY WADSWORTH LONGFELLOW

———o———

Every man is the architect of his own fortune.

SALLUST

———o———

Every man's fortune is moulded by his character.

CORNELIUS NEPOS

———o———

If you seek a monument, look about you.

*Inscription on Sir Christopher Wren's Tomb,
in St. Paul's Cathedral, London*

———o———

We must not only be architects of our fate; we must also be builders.

———o———

Let us not say, Every man is the architect of his own fortune; but let us say, Every man is the architect of his own character.

GEORGE DANA BOARDMAN

Argue, Argument

A man who has only an argument is no match for a Christian who has an experience.

———o———

No matter what side of an argument you get on, you will always find some people with you that you wish were on the other side.

JASCHA HEIFETZ

———o———

Many a person can recall ruefully having gone out of his way to get an argument, only to lose it.

Glendale News-Press, Glendale, Calif.

———o———

The best way I know of to win an argument is to start by being in the right.

LORD HAILSHAM

———o———

One way to avoid arguments is to be a good listener.

———o———

Note found in a Wauwatosa, Wisconsin, household written by a nine-year-old girl after an argument: "Good-bye family. You all hate me. I love you all very much. God bless you.
"P.S. In case of fire, I'm in the attic."

———o———

The only people who listen to both sides of an argument are the neighbors.

———o———

When all is said and done makes a a dandy time to quit arguing.

Changing Times, The Kiplinger Magazine

———o———

You can't prove anything in an argument, except that you're just as bullheaded as the other fellow.

———o———

I never make the mistake of arguing with people for whose opinions I have no respect.

EDWARD GIBBON

———o———

Don't win the argument and lose the sale.

ROY L. SMITH

Argument is the worst sort of conversation.

JONATHAN SWIFT

———o———

In a heated argument we are apt to lose sight of the truth.

PUBLILIUS SYRUS

———o———

There is no good in arguing with the inevitable. The only argument available with an east wind is to put on your overcoat.

JAMES RUSSELL LOWELL

———o———

A long dispute means that both parties are wrong.

VOLTAIRE

———o———

Behind every argument is someone's ignorance.

LOUIS DEMBITZ BRANDEIS

Aspiration

What we truly and earnestly aspire to be, that in a sense we are.

———o———

The one who aspires highly is the one who achieves highly.

———o———

What shall I do to be forever known, And make the age to come my own?

ABRAHAM COWLEY

———o———

Our aspirations are our possibilities,

ROBERT BROWNING

———o———

There is not a heart but has its moments of longing, yearning for something better, nobler, holier than it knows now.

HENRY WARD BEECHER

Assets

If you count all your assets, you always show a profit.

ROBERT QUILLEN

———o———

Enthusiasm is the greatest asset in the world. It beats money and power and influence.

HENRY CHESTER

Good will is the one and only asset that competition cannot undersell or destroy.

MARSHALL FIELD

———o———

The greatest asset of a man, a business or a nation is faith.

THOMAS J. WATSON

Assurance

This I Know

I do not know the depths of love
  It took to die on Calvary;
I do not know the shame and grief
  He suffered there to set me free.
Nor can I tell how bitter was
  His cup in dark Gethsemane,
The pain He bore — heartbroken, poor;
  But this I know: He died for me!

I know not why that for my sins
  His precious blood so freely flows,
Nor fathom why the Lord of All
  Did not such cruel death oppose.
I cannot understand the power
  Which triumphed over death and
    foes.
They sealed His tomb 'midst dark'ning
    gloom;
  But this I know: for me He rose!

I do not know why oftentimes
  The skies are dark and overcast;
Nor why, in grave temptations, all
  My problems seem so hard, so vast.
I cannot tell what things may come —
  Sore heartaches, all my hopes to blast
The shades of night obscure the light;
  But this I know: He'll hold me fast.

GRACE V. WATKINS

———o———

Rock And Roll

I'm on the roll up there
and on the rock down here.

———o———

Robert Louis Stevenson tells the story of a ship at sea in time of storm. The passengers were in great distress. After a while one of them, against orders, went up on deck and made his way to the pilot.

The seaman was at his post of duty at the wheel and when he saw the man was greatly frightened he gave him a reassuring smile. Then the passanger turned and went back to the other passengers and said, "I have seen the pilot and he smiled, 'All is well.'"

When our small boat of life is storm-tossed and our hearts are fearful, we may push through the storm to our Pilot who is standing at the wheel, and when we see His face we shall know that all is well.

Atheist

I can see how it might be possible for a man to look down upon the earth and be an atheist, but I cannot conceive how a man could look up into the heavens and say there is no God.

ABRAHAM LINCOLN

———o———

He who does not believe that God is above all is either a fool or has no experience of life.

CAECILIUS STATIUS, *Fragments No. 15*

———o———

It takes no brains to be an atheist.

DWIGHT DAVID EISENHOWER

———o———

An atheist has a reason, but no hope for his reason. A hypocrite has a hope, but no reason for his hope. A Christian has a reason for his hope and hope for his reason.

The United Brethren Magazine

———o———

An atheist is a man without any invisible means of support.

JOHN BUCHAN, LORD TWEEDSMUIR

———o———

An atheist cannot find God for the same reason a thief cannot find a policeman.

———o———

The atheist's most embarrassing moment is when he feels profoundly thankful for something but can't think of anybody to thank for it.

MARY ANN VINCENT

———o———

An atheist spent a few days with Fenelon, a saintly Christian. He was moved to say: "If I stay here much longer, I shall become a Christian in spite of myself." Fenelon had used no word of controversy or of pleading. It was only the quiet, convincing argument of a holy life — a consistent walk and conversation.

———o———

"There is no God," the wicked saith,
   "And truly it's a blessing,
For what He might have done with us
   It's better only guessing."

Some others also, to themselves
   Who scarce so much as doubt it,
Think there is none, when they are well
   And do not think about it.

And almost every one when age,
   Disease, or sorrows strike him,
Inclines to think there is a God,
   Or something very like Him.

ARTHUR HUGH CLOUGH, *Dipsychus*

———o———

The science to which I pinned my faith is bankrupt.... Its counsels which should have established the millennium led directly to the suicide of Europe. I believed them once.... In their name I helped to destroy the faith of millions of worshippers in the temples of a thousand creeds. And now they look at me and witness the great tragedy of an atheist who has lost *his* faith.

GEORGE BERNARD SHAW,
Too True To Be Good

Attention

If a pupil is not giving attention, he's absent.

———o———

The easiest way for a man to get his wife's attention is by looking comfortable.

———o———

Attention is the stuff that memory is made of, and memory is accumulated genius.

JAMES RUSSELL LOWELL

———o———

When you can do the common things of life in an uncommon way you will command the attention of the world.

GEORGE WASHINGTON CARVER

What makes men great is their ability to decide what is important, and then focus their attention on it.

Attitude

The posture of Christianity toward the religions of the world is not one of condemnation. It is rather one of illumination and the offering of the Good News.

GARY W. DEMAREST

———o———

One's attitude toward life is determined largely by one's altitude.

———o———

The best attitude to have toward one's daily work is a keep-at-it-tude.

———o———

One ship drives east and another west,
  With the self-same winds that blow;
'Tis the set of the sails and not the gales
  That determines where they go.
Like the winds of the sea are the ways
    of fate,
  As we voyage along through life;
'Tis the set of a soul that decides the
    goal —
  And not the calm or the strife.

REBECCA R. WILLIAMS

Authority

The best time for a man to assert his authority and let his wife know who's boss is the first time he gets up the courage.

———o———

Greatness does not depend on the size of your command, but on the way you exercise it.

MARSHALL FERDINAND FOCH

———o———

Nothing pleases a little man more than an opportunity to crack a big whip.

———o———

The one in authority has responsibility.

———o———

Nothing so soon overthrows a weak character as a bit of authority.

Authors

Choose an author as you choose a friend.

WENTWORTH DILLON, EARL OF ROSCOMMON,
Essay on Translated Verse

———o———

A small number of men and women think for the million; through them the million speak and act.

JEAN-JACQUES ROUSSEAU

———o———

I think the author who speaks about his own books is almost as bad as a mother who talks about her own children.

BENJAMIN DISRAELI

———o———

The greatest part of a writer's time is spent in reading, in order to write; a man will turn over half a library to make one book.

SAMUEL JOHNSON

———o———

A man may write at any time if he will set himself doggedly to it.

SAMUEL JOHNSON

Automation

Automation is man's effort to make work so easy that woman can do it all.

In a Nutshell

———o———

We are turning out machines that act like men, and men that act like machines.

ERICH FROMM

———o———

A tool is but the extension of a man's hand and a machine is but a complex tool; and he that invents a machine augments the power of man and the well-being of mankind.

HENRY WARD BEECHER

Automobile

Nothing keeps the family together as much as owning just one car.

———o———

"This car is the opportunity of a lifetime," remarked the enterprising salesman.

"Yes," replied the prospective buyer, "I can hear it knocking."

———o———

The trouble is that the car of tomorrow is being driven on the highway of yesterday by the driver of today.

———o———

Car sickness: The feeling you get each month when the payment's due.

———o———

Safety slogan: Look out for school children — especially if they are driving cars.

———o———

The worst kind of car trouble is when the engine won't start and the payments won't stop.

Autumn

God painted all the autumn leaves
And put to sleep the flowers,
And told the birds to find a place
To spend their winter hours.

CHARLES BOWMAN

———o———

Coming Of Autumn

Autumn came this morning
Scarlet slippers on her feet,
Her eyes were blue as asters,
Her breath was honey sweet.

Like a brook's soft whispering
She crooned a lullaby,
And all the flowers nodded
As she passed by.

She walked along the roadside,
And where her footsteps fell
Swamp maple and young sassafras
Felt her magic spell.

Low dogwood and the sweet-gum,
Pin oak and tulip, too,
Stood clad in gold and scarlet
When she passed through.

She ran across the marshes
Free as the sea-blown air,
And turned to gold the sedges
To warn the heron there.

They heeded not her warning,
But stood with me to stare
At all the wealth of beauty
Around us, everywhere.

M. K. S.

———o———

It takes two kinds of people to make the world — poets to write about the glories of autumn and the rest of us to rake them.

MARJORIE JOHNSON in NEA Journal

———o———

Autumn is when an unwatched boy, raking, leaves.

———o———

November

November is an outdoor month
Of crisp and sparkling weather,
A time for playing outdoor games,
For doing chores together.
November is a harvest month
Of richly laden tables,
A time for roaring winter fires
And barnyard turkey fables.
November is a solemn month,
A time reserved for prayer
Of thankfulness for blessings past
And for God's loving care.

CHRISTINE GRAHAME

Average

The average man never gets mad, because he never thinks the things being said about the average man mean him.

Press, London, Ohio

———o———

It is so much easier to live down to the average than to rise above it.

B

Baby

What Is A Baby?

What is a baby?
A baby is a lot of things:
A baby is a soft little hand, curling warmly around your finger. . . .
A baby is a lively little pair of legs, kicking happily in the air after a bath. . . .
A baby is a puckered and trembling lower lip, trying hard, — oh so hard — to tell you something. . . .
A baby is a cry in the night, calling you swiftly out of sleep and to its crib. . . .
A baby is an eloquent pair of eyes — one time dancing with glee and sparkle as they watch a bouncing toy, another time staring at you with sober and steady reflection, until you wonder what goes on within that little head. . . .
And above all a baby is a priceless gift from God. Those little hands must learn to move in His service . . . those little feet must grow up to walk in His ways . . . those little eyes must learn to focus on His Word.

EWA Family Counselor

———o———

As a young mother was bathing her baby, a neighbor's little girl was holding a doll minus an arm.
"How long have you had your baby?" asked the little visitor.
"Three months," replied the mother.
And the little girl said: "But you've kept her nice."

Bachelor

She: "And how is your bachelor friend?"
He: "When I saw him last he was mending very slowly."
She: "Indeed. I didn't know he'd been ill."
He: "He hasn't been. He was darning his socks."

A bachelor is a person who has to fix only one breakfast.

———o———

A bachelor is a fellow who can take a nap on top of a bedspread.

Spectator, Somerset, Mass.

———o———

A bachelor should learn to sew on his own buttons and darn his socks — he may marry some day.

Bargain

It's a bad bargain where nobody gains.

English Proverb

———o———

It is extraordinary to what an expense of time and money people will go in order to get something for nothing.

ROBERT LYND

———o———

Two small children were engaged in selling pink lemonade, side by side. Tom's glasses were the same size as Mike's but his lemonade was marked "2 glasses for 5c" while Mike's were marked "5c each." Of course Tom was doing a bigger business.
Feeling sorry for Mike, a neighbor stopped to buy a glass of lemonade from him. "Your lemonade looks just the same as Tom's and your glasses are the same size," he said. "How is it that your price is higher than Tom's?"
"Well, you see," Mike explained, "the cat fell into Tom's bucket just before our sale began so he's having a bargain sale!"

Beauty

Beautiful young people are accidents of nature, but beautiful old people are works of art.

———o———

Beauty is the mark God sets on virtue.

RALPH WALDO EMERSON

Everything has its beauty, but not everyone sees it.

CONFUCIUS

———o———

There is no beautifier of complexion, or form, or behavior, like the wish to scatter joy and not pain around us.

RALPH WALDO EMERSON, *Conduct of Life*

———o———

"What do you think of mul as a beautifier?"
"It hasn't done much for pigs."

———o———

A man should hear a little music, read a little poetry, and see a fine picture every day of his life, in order that worldly cares may not obliterate the sense of the beautiful which God has implanted in the human soul.

JOHANN WOLFGANG VON GOETHE

———o———

Beauty without grace is a hook without a bait.

NINON DE LENCLOS

———o———

Beauty is but a flower,
Which wrinkles will devour.

THOMAS NASH

———o———

A beautiful mother, a more beautiful daughter.

HORACE

———o———

That is the best part of beauty, which a picture cannot express.

FRANCIS BACON, *Of Beauty*

Begin, Beginning

Be active
Be vital
Be responsible
Begin

———o———

A good start makes for a good ending only if you don't start something you can't finish.

———o———

A mosquito doesn't wait for an opening, he makes one.

Life is full of endings, but every ending is a new beginning.

———o———

You will never reach second base if you keep one foot on first base.

VERNON LAW

———o———

The beginning is the most important part of the work.

PLATO, *The Republic*

———o———

Tender twigs are bent with ease,
Aged trees do break with bending.

ROBERT SOUTHWELL, *Loss in Delay*

Behavior

Behavior is a mirror in which everyone shows his true image.

JOHANN WOLFGANG VON GOETHE

———o———

To really know a man, observe his behavior with a woman, a flat tire and a child.

———o———

Always behave like a duck. Remain calm and unruffled on the surface, but keep paddling like fury underneath.

———o———

If one fights for good behavior, God makes one a present of the good feelings.

JULIANA H. EWING

———o———

The Art Of Getting Along

Sooner or later, a man, if he is wise, discovers that life is a mixture of good days and bad, victory and defeat, give and take.

He learns that it doesn't pay to let things get his goat; that he must let some things go over his head like water off a duck's back.

He learns that carrying a chip on his shoulder is the quickest way to get into a fight.

He learns that buck-passing acts as a boomerang.

He learns that carrying tales and gossip about others is the surest way to become unpopular.

He learns that giving others a mental lift by showing appreciation and praise is the best way to lift his own spirits.

He learns that the world will not end when he fails or makes an error; that there is always another day and another chance.

He learns that all men have burnt toast for breakfast now and then, and that he shouldn't let their grumbling get him down.

He learns that people are not any more difficult to get along with in one place than another, and that "Getting along" depends about 98% on his own behavior.

"As much as lieth in you, live peaceably with all men." Romans 12:18.

WILFRED A. PETERSON

———o———

The sum of behavior is to retain a man's own dignity, without intruding upon the liberty of others.

FRANCIS BACON

———o———

The Sunday school teacher had finished her talk on behavior.

"Now, Billy," she questioned, "tell me what we must do before we can expect forgiveness of sin."

There was a moment's thought, then Billy replied, "We gotta sin."

———o———

Perfection consists not in doing extraordinary things, but in doing ordinary things extraordinarily well.

ANGÉLIQUE ARNAULD

———o———

Your moral behavior is governed by your inner grace.

Believe

If you believe in God, in the principles on which our nation was founded, in a personal code of ethics, then exemplify them for us.

Spoken by a Youth

———o———

Teacher to parent about child: Don't believe everything he tells you about me and I won't believe everything he tells me about you.

———o———

I did not use to believe the story of Daniel in the lions' den until I had to take some of these awful marches [through the leopard forests of Nigeria]. Then I knew it was true, and that it was written for my comfort.

MARY SLESSOR

———o———

I Believe God

I believe God —
Though angry breakers
Cast their spray
Upon the shore,
I know that through the storm
He'll keep me safe
Forevermore.

I believe God —
Though neither sun
Nor stars appear
For many days,
I trust Him in the darkest,
Wildest hours.
He knows my ways.

I believe God —
Though this frail ship
Be swept along
By tempest force,
I am assured at last
Of Harbor Home.
He charts my course.

PAUL T. HOLLIDAY

———o———

Why is it that some people so often will more readily believe a lie than the truth?

———o———

Believe God's Word

It is strange we trust each other
And only doubt our Lord.
We take the word of mortals
And yet distrust His Word.
But oh, what light and glory
Would shine o'er all our days,
If we always would remember
God means just what He says.

A. B. SIMPSON

———o———

The world says, "show me and I'll

believe." Christ says, "Believe Me and I'll show you."

———o———

To those who believe no explanation is necessary; to those who do not believe no explanation will satisfy.

FRANZ WERFEL

———o———

One who does not believe in God does not believe in self.

ROGER BABSON

———o———

Philanthropic unbelievers and unphilanthropic believers are equally monstrosities.

———o———

A London missionary, who had before him three hundred ragged children, placed a coin under a book on the table and said, "Whosoever believeth, let him come and take it." He waited; they were all "whosoevers," but only one was "whosoever believeth;" a little ragged chap who came up, lifted the Bible, and took the coin, saying, "Thank you, Sir."

"What is your name?" asked the missionary.

"Cecil Smithers."

"I did not say Cecil Smithers could have the coin.

"No, Sir," said the half-frightened boy, "but you did say 'whosoever,' and that means me."

The missionary's "whosoever" meant anyone, and the boy believed it; and God's "whosoever" means anyone. Have you believed this?

"Whosoever believeth in Him (that is, in Christ, Who died and rose again) shall receive the remission (the pardon) of sins."

The Little Lutheran

———o———

One person with a belief is equal to a force of ninety-nine who have only interests.

JOHN STUART MILL

———o———

People will believe anything if you whisper it.

Believe In Yourself

Believe in yourself! Believe you were made
To do any task without calling for aid.
Believe, without growing too scornfully proud,
That you, as the greatest and least are endowed.
A mind to do thinking, two hands and two eyes
Are all the equipment God gives to the wise.

Believe in yourself! You're divinely designed
And perfectly made for the work of mankind.
This truth you must cling to through danger and pain;
The heights man has reached you can also attain.
Believe to the very last hour, for it's true,
That whatever you will you've been gifted to do.

The wisdom of ages is yours if you'll read
But you've got to believe in yourself to succeed.

EDGAR A. GUEST

———o———

Upon the wreckage of thy yesterday
Design thy structure of tomorrow, lay
Strong corner-stones of purpose, and prepare
Great blocks of wisdom cut from past despair.
Shape mighty pillars of resolve, to set
Deep in the tear-wet mortar of regret.
Believe in God — in thine own self believe,
All thou hast hoped for thou shalt yet achieve.

ELLA WHEELER WILCOX

———o———

If I believed [the Gospel], I would crawl across England on broken glass on my hands and knees to tell men it was true!

CHARLES PEACE, *On The Scaffold*

———o———

A belief that does not express itself in action soon ceases to be even a belief.

I believe in God as I believe in my friends, because I feel the breath of his affection, feel his invisible and intangible hand drawing me, leading me, grasping me.

MIGUEL DE UNAMUNO, *Prosa Diversa*

———o———

He does not believe that does not live according to his belief.

THOMAS FULLER

Best

God's Best

God has His best things for the few
   That dare to stand the test;
God has His second choice for those
   Who will not have His best.

It is not always open ill
   That risks the Promised Rest;
The better, often, is the foe
   That keeps us from the best.

Some seek the highest choice,
   But, when by trials pressed
They shrink, they yield, they shun the
    cross
And so they lose the best.

Give me, O Lord, Thy highest choice;
   Let others take the rest.
Their good things have no charm for
   me,
   I want Thy very best.

I want, in this short life of mine,
   As much as can be pressed
Of service true for God and man:
   Make me to be Thy best.

A. B. SIMPSON

———o———

Do the very best you can today and tomorrow you can do better.

MARTIN VANBEE

———o———

God does not seek better methods, or better means, but He seeks for better men.

———o———

It is a sin to take the good when the best can be had.

———o———

The search for the best is a constant challenge to high adventure.

When we do the best that we can, we never know what miracle is wrought in our life, or in the life of another.

HELEN KELLER

Betray

Thomas Cranmer, Archbishop of Canterbury in the sixteenth century, was cast into prison because of his faith. His imprisoners thrust a written document into his hands and said: "Sign that!" When Cranmer read it, he exclaimed: "Nay, 'tis a downright denial of my Christ! I will not sign." "Sign it or die," they threatened, and they badgered and tortured him until in a weak moment he took the pen and wrote his name. When he finished, the horror of his betrayal leapt upon his soul, and he stared at his right hand that had signed his name. For days and nights he was tormented with remorse. Jesus had said: "If thy hand offend thee, cut it off," and he gladly would have taken a knife and severed his traitor hand. When, in spite of his recantation, they led him out to die, he walked to the martyr pyre and thrust his right arm first into the flames. "This unworthy hand," he said, "this which hath sinned, having signed the writing, must be the first to suffer," and he held it there until it was blackened and consumed. Then he plunged into the fire himself.

The Leader

Bible

The Bible! There It Stands!

Where childhood needs a standard
   Or youth a beacon light,
Where sorrow sighs for comfort
   Or weakness longs for might,
Bring forth the Holy Bible,
   The Bible! There it stands!
Resolving all life's problems
   And meeting its demands.

Though sophistry conceal it,
   The Bible! There it stands!
Though Pharisees profane it,
   Its influence expands;

It fills the world with fragrance
   Whose sweetness never cloys,
It lifts our eyes to heaven,
   It heightens human joys.

Despised and torn in pieces,
   By infidels decried —
The thunderbolts of hatred
   The haughty cynic's pride —
All these have railed against it
   In this and other lands,
Yet dynasties have fallen,
   And still the Bible stands!

To paradise a highway,
   The Bible! There it stands!
Its promises unfailing,
   Nor grievous its commands;
It points man to the Saviour,
   The lover of his soul;
Salvation is its watchword,
   Eternity its goal!

JAMES M. GRAY

———o———

God's Book does not yield up its
secrets to those who will not be taught
of the Spirit.

JAMES I. PACKER

———o———

The Bible is a great and powerful
tree. Each word is a mighty branch.
Each of these branches have I well
shaken. And the shaking of them has
never disappointed me.

MARTIN LUTHER

———o———

Sampling the Word of God only occasionally will never give you a real
taste for it.

Give me a Bible and a candle and
shut me up in a dungeon and I will
tell you what the world is doing.

CECIL DICHARD

———o———

Apply yourself to the whole text,
and apply the whole text to yourself.

J. A. BENGEL

———o———

A Navy chaplain had just completed
a lengthy tour of sea duty and was
happily headed for home when he was
ordered back to sea. Disturbed, he
wired the office of the chief of chap-
lains: "How long, O Lord? Isaiah 6:
11."

His chief's reply came fast: "It would
be for a time, two times, and half a
time. — Daniel 12:7."

SHIRLEY LINDE in Together

———o———

Men do not reject the Bible because
it contradicts itself but because it contradicts them.

———o———

The Book

The books men write are but a fra-
   grance blown
   From transient blossoms crushed by
     human hands;
But high above them, splendid and
   alone,
   Staunch as a tree, there is a Book
     that stands
Unmoved by storms, unchallenged by
   decay:
   The winds of criticism would pro-
     fane
Its sacred pages, but the Truth, the
   Way,
   The Life are in it — and they beat in
     vain.

Oh, traveler from this to yonder world,
   Pause in the shade of God's magni-
     ficent,
Eternal World — that tree whose roots
   are curled
   About our human need. When
     strength is spent,
Stretch out beneath some great, far-
   reaching limb
   Of promise and find rest and peace
     in HIM.

HELEN FRAZEE-BOWER

———o———

It is of the greatest importance then
that we should feed our minds with
facts; with reliable information; with
the results of human experience; and
above all with the teachings of the
Word of God. It is matter for the utmost admiration to notice how full the
Bible is of biography and history: so
that there is hardly a single crisis in
our lives that may not be matched
from those wondrous pages. There is

no book like the Bible for casting a light on the dark landings of human life.

F. B. MEYER

————o————

The Holy Scriptures are full of divine gifts and virtues . . . In a word, the Holy Scripture is the Highest and Best of Books, abounding in comfort under all afflictions and trials. It teaches us to see, to feel, to grasp and to comprehend faith, hope and charity. . . . And when evil oppresses us, it teaches how these virtues throw light upon the darkness and how, after this poor, miserable existence of ours on earth, there is another and an eternal life.

MARTIN LUTHER

Secret Study

Pre-eminent, supreme among the helps to secret prayer I place, of course, the secret study of the holy written Word of God.

Read it on your knees, at least on the knees of your spirit. Read it to reassure, to feed, to regulate, to kindle, to give to your secret prayer at once body and soul.

Read it that you may hold faster your certainty of being heard.

Read it that you may know with blessed definiteness whom you have believed, and what you have in Him, and how He is able to keep your deposit safe.

Read it in the attitude of mind in which the apostles read it, in which the Lord read it. Read it, not seldom, to turn it at once into prayer.

H. C. G. MOULE

————o————

Does It Matter What I Say?

What if I say —
 "The Bible is God's Holy Word,
 Complete, inspired, without a flaw" —
But let its pages stay
 Unread from day to day,
And fail to learn therefrom God's law;
What if I go not there to seek
 The truth of which I glibly speak,
 For guidance on this earthly way —
Does it matter what I say?

What if I say —
 "That Jesus Christ is Lord divine — "
Yet fellow-pilgrims can behold
Naught of the Master's love in me,
No grace of kindly sympathy?
If I am of the Shepherd's fold,
Then shall I know the Shepherd's voice
And gladly make His way my choice.
 We are saved by faith, yet faith is one
 With life, like daylight and the sun.
 Unless they flower in our deeds,
 Dead, empty husks are all the creeds.
To call Christ Lord, but strive not to obey —
Belies the homage that with words I pay.

MAUD FRAZER JACKSON

————o————

Heed the exhortation of one who, with all the passion of his heart, urges you to lay hold on the Bible until the Bible lays hold on you.

WILL H. HOUGHTON

————o————

Other books were given for our information; the Bible was given for our transformation.

————o————

God's Word

Where is comfort for your sorrow,
 Wounded heart that peace would know?
Where is help to aid and strengthen,
 Weary pilgrim here below?
Where is wisdom that will guide you,
 Puzzled youth with questioning plea?
Where is cleansing for transgression,
 Sinner longing to be free?
All is answered, all provided
 In God's Word to you and me.

DELLA ADAMS LEITNER

————o————

The Bible

Born in the East and clothed in Oriental form and imagery, the Bible walks the ways of all the world with familiar feet and enters land after land to find its own everywhere. It comes to the palace to tell the monarch that he is a servant of the Most High, and into the cottage to assure the peasant that he can be a son of God. Children listen to its stories with wonder and delight, and wise men ponder them as parables of life.

It has a word of peace for the time of peril, a word of comfort for the time of calamity, a word of light for the hour of darkness. Its oracles are repeated in the assembly of the people, and its counsels whispered in the ear of the lonely. The wicked and the proud tremble at its warnings, but to the wounded and penitent it has a mother's voice.

No man is poor or desolate who has this treasure for his own. When the landscape darkens and the trembling pilgrim comes to the valley named of the shadow, he is not afraid to enter; he takes the rod and staff of Scripture in his hand, he says to his friend and comrade, "Goodbye, we shall meet again"; and comforted by that support, he goes toward the lonely pass as one who walks through darkness into light.

HENRY VAN DYKE

———o———

A preacher entered a Sunday school class while the lesson was in progress and asked this question, "Who broke down the walls of Jericho?" A boy answered, "Not me, sir." The preacher turned to the teacher and asked, "Is this the usual behavior in this class?" The teacher answered, "This boy is honest and I believe him. I really don't think he did it."

Leaving the room, the preacher sought out an elder and explained what had happened. The elder said, "I have known both the teacher and the boy for years, and neither of them would do such a thing."

By this time the preacher was heartsick and reported it to the Department of Christian Education. They said, "We see no point in being disturbed. Let's pay the bill for the damage to the walls and charge it to upkeep."

Modern Maturity

It is illegal to read the Bible in the public schools of Illinois, but a law requires the STATE to provide a Bible for every convict! Don't worry, young people, if you can't read the Bible in school, you'll be able to when you get to prison!

Baptist Beacon

———o———

I have spent seventy years of my life studying that Book to satisfy my heart; it is the Word of God. I bank my life on the statement that I believe this Book to be the solid rock of Holy Scripture.

WILLIAM EWART GLADSTONE

———o———

A scholarly Chinese was employed to translate the New Testament into the Chinese language. After a while, he exclaimed, "What a marvelous Book this is!"

"Why do you think so?" asked the missionary.

"Because it tells me so exactly about myself. It knows all that is in me. The One who made this Book must be the One who made me!"

As we read God's Word, it searches our innermost being. It reveals to us the sinfulness of the human heart — "deceitful above all things, and desperately wicked." It prescribes the sure remedy for our spiritual sickness: "The blood of Jesus Christ his Son cleanseth us from all sin." (I John 1:7).

———o———

Comments By Great Men About The Bible

Abraham Lincoln — I am profitably engaged in reading the Bible. Take all of this Book upon reason that you can and the balance by faith, and you will live and die a better man.

George Washington — Above all, the pure and benign light of Revelation has had a meliorating influence on mankind, and increased the blessings of society.

Thomas Jefferson — I always have said, and always will say, that the studious perusal of the sacred Volume will make better citizens, better fathers, and better husbands.

John Quincy Adams — The first and almost the only Book deserving of universal attention is the Bible. I speak as a man of the world . . . and I say to you, "Search the Scriptures."

Zachary Taylor — It was for the love of the truths of this great and good Book that our fathers abandoned their native shore for the wilderness.

Daniel Webster — The Bible is a book of faith, and a book of doctrine, and a book of morals, and a book of religion, of special revelation from God; but it is also a book which teaches man his own individual responsibility, his own dignity, and his equality with his fellow-man.

William H. Seward, Secretary of State in Lincoln's cabinet — I know not how long a republican form of government can flourish among a great people who have not the Bible.

Herbert Hoover — There is no other book so various as the Bible, nor one so full of concentrated wisdom. Whether it be of law, business, morals or that vision which leads the imagination in the creation of constructive enterprises for the happiness of mankind, he who seeks for guidance . . . may look inside its covers and find illumination.

William Ewart Gladstone — I have known ninety-five great men of the world in my time and of these eighty-seven were followers of the Bible.

———o———

Where To Look In The BIBLE

When God seems far away, read Psalm 139.

When sorrowful, read John 14; Psalm 46.

When men fail you, read Psalm 27.

When you have sinned, read Psalm 51; I John 1.

When you worry, read Matthew 6:19-34; Psalm 43.

When in sickness, read Psalm 41.

When in danger, read Psalm 91.

When you have the blues, read Psalm 34.

When you are discouraged, read Isaiah 40.

When you are lonely or fearful, read Psalm 23.

When you forget your blessings, read Psalm 103.

When you want courage, read Joshua 1:1-9.

When the world seems bigger than God, read Psalm 90.

When you want rest and peace, read Matthew 11:25-30.

When you want assurance, read Romans 8.

When looking for joy, read Colossians 3.

When you leave home to travel, read Psalm 121.

When you grow bitter or critical, read I Corinthians 13.

When you think of investments, read Mark 10:17-31.

Some rules of conduct? Read Romans 12.

Why not follow Psalm 119:11?

———o———

Search The Scriptures

When Jesus walked the shore of Galilee,
Not all Capernaum turned out to see;
When He worked miracles within that town,
Some even turned their casement shutters down!

And Nazareth? He did no wonders there!
To thrust Him from its cliff they'd even dare;
But there were some who followed Him, and learned
His way of life, and truth — of hearts which burned.

A wistful feeling lies with men today,
Who wish that they could meet Him on their way
Down country lanes, or on some city street,
Or resting by a rock in desert heat.

And He is there — if one has faith to see;
And He abides in men like you and me —

His living temples – passing to and
fro
Along the very way He bid them go.
In Nazareth, men spurned God's holy
writ,
And people still are few who study it;
Your footsteps – do they press the
world's Broadway?
Then read, lest when you meet, it's
Judgment Day.

MILDRED ALLEN JEFFERY

———o———

Bobby Richardson, Yankee baseball
star, says this about the Bible: "Put a
man in a baseball suit, give him a
glove and a hat – but all that doesn't
make him a star. Nor will all the practice in the world get some people into
the major leagues. Something more is
needed.

"It's also true if you put a man in
church and give him a hymn book or
a Bible, it doesn't make him a Christian. Not singing all the hymns in the
world will do that – or even reading
the Bible from cover to cover.

"That's why something more is needed when you read the Bible. We call
it the Spirit. Read the Bible and let
its message live in you, for 'not the
readers of the law are just before God,
but the doers shall be justified.' "

———o———

"I have never in my whole life met
a man who really knew the Bible, and
rejected it. The difficulty has always
been an *unwillingness* to give it an
honest trial. Our Lord Himself says,
'Ye will not come unto me, that you
may have life.' "

HOWARD A. KELLY

———o———

A man who loves his wife will love
her letters and her photographs because they speak to him of her. So if
we love the Lord Jesus we shall love
the Bible because it speaks to us of
him.

JOHN R. W. STOTT

———o———

If you accept the Bible with reservations, the devil has a reservation for
you.

RALPH BREWER

The English Bible is the first of our
national treasures.

GEORGE V, KING OF ENGLAND

———o———

The Bible is a revelation of God's
thoughts for the happiness of His children.

———o———

If a man's Bible is coming apart, it
is an indication that he himself is fairly
well put together.

JAMES E. JENNINGS

———o———

I consider an intimate knowledge of
the Bible an indispensable qualification
of a well-educated man.

ROBERT ANDREWS MILLIKAN

———o———

The Bible is criticized most by those
who read it the least.

———o———

The Bible contains the vitamins of
soul health.

PALMER

———o———

A Christian woman wrote upon the
fly-page of her Bible the following
words: "Lay any burden upon me, only sustain me; send me anywhere,
only go with me; sever any tie but that
which binds me to thy service and to
thy heart."

———o———

If our children have the background
of a godly, happy home and this un-
shakeable faith that the Bible is indeed
the Word of God, they will have a
foundation that the forces of hell cannot shake.

MRS. BILLY GRAHAM

———o———

The Bible is broad as life, having,
indeed, the same Author.

SCHMAUK

The Bible and Children

First Bible

A little boy's first Bible
Is the greatest thrill he's known;
There's a sweet, unique excitement
In a Bible all his own!

And yet my heart is smitten
As this touching sight I see —
Has his reverence for that Bible
Depended much on me?
As I see him with his Bible,
I bow my head and pray —
May he always love that Bible
The way he does today.
Then I hear a voice within me
Speak in solemn words and true;
How he cherishes that Bible
Will depend a lot on you!
I love my Bible better
Since I've seen the beaming joy
This wonderful possession
Has afforded to my boy.
May I seek to give mine daily
A devotion he can see,
For the love he bears his Bible
Will depend a lot on me.

AUTHOR UNKNOWN

---o---

"Mother, I found an old dusty thing
High on the shelf — just look!"
"Why, that's a Bible, Tommy dear;
Be careful — that's God's book!"
"God's book!" the child exclaimed;
"Then, mother, before we lose it,
We'd better send it back to God,
For, you know, we never use it."

Christian Life

---o---

Dusty Bibles

When the pastor called he found little Mary crying, and inquired as to the cause of her tears.

"Mamma got my apron all dirty," she sobbed.

"And how did that happen?" he asked.

"When she saw you coming she used it to wipe the dust off the Bible."

---o---

The preacher was visiting the home, and asked if he might read a chapter from the Bible. The man of the house said to his little son, "Bobby, go and get the Bible — you know, the big Book we read so much."

In a little while Bobby came in carrying the mail-order catalog!

Big

God is looking for men who are big enough to be small enough to be used of Him in a big way.

Christian Digest

---o---

Only a truly big person can graciously accept a favor he doesn't deserve and may never be able to repay.

---o---

What a superb thing it would be if we were all big enough in mind to see no slights, accept no insults, cherish no jealousies and admit into our heart no hatred!

ELBERT HUBBARD

Birth (New)

We really begin to live only when we are born twice.

---o---

Second Birth

I never loved the pleasant earth
  So much as since my second birth!
The shy forget-me-not's soft blue
  Seems bits of Heaven shining
    through!
The golden buttercup's bright face
  Proclaims the glory of *His* face.
The red of maples in the fall,
  His precious Blood that washes all.
My sin forever far away,
  As white as hawthorn buds in May —
The saints' new shining linen dress —
  The robe of His own righteousness.
I touch the pansy's purple face —
  His kingly majesty I trace.
Green pasture breathes refreshment,
    rest,
  And sweet communion on His breast;
While bird song from the orchard trees
  Suggests celestial harmonies.
I see in river, hill and glen
  New charms since I've been born
    again!

LOIS REYNOLDS CARPENTER

Blessings

Whatever seeming calamity happens to you, if you thank God and praise him for it you turn it into a blessing.

WILLIAM LAW

———o———

God gives our blessings, but we have to take them.

———o———

Reflect upon your present blessings, of which every man has many; not on your past misfortunes, of which all men have some.

CHARLES DICKENS

———o———

Our Business

We are not store-rooms, but channels;
We are not cisterns, but springs;
Passing our benefits onward,
Fitting our blessings with wings;

Letting the water flow outward
To spread o'er the desert forlorn.
Sharing our bread with our brothers,
Our comfort with those who mourn.

AUTHOR UNKNOWN

———o———

Countless Blessings

For the quiet of the forest
And the grandeur of the hills,
For the glory of the sunsets
And the music of the rills,
For the flowers that bloom so sweetly
Along the woodland ways —
For these, and countless blessings,
Dear Lord, we render praise!

A. M. S. ROSSITER

———o———

The blessings we evoke for another descend upon ourselves.

EDMUND GIBSON

———o———

No Christian can be an "avenue" of blessing if he's not willing to cross the "street" to church.

NAT OLSON

———o———

With Blessings Everywhere
(Ezekiel 16:49)

Not only, Lord, in time of trial
Would I hold fast to Thee,
Not only when false friends revile,
Seek help on bended knee;
But also when victorious,
When pain has found release,
When all my way is glorious,
When I am filled with peace
Would I rejoice in Thee, my Friend,
For all the good that Thou dost send.
Not only then, when troubles breed
Would I seek Thee in prayer,
But also in the greater need
With blessings everywhere.
For in Thy holy Word, we know
Men seek Thee to be fed,
And then forget the thanks they owe
When they are filled with bread.
Thou callest this iniquity;
From it, O God, deliver me.

MILDRED ALLEN JEFFERY

Blind

My Personal Testimony

I cannot see that of which others tell:
The beauties of this earth on which we dwell;
The jeweled perfection of the starry sky;
Great sights that please and tantalize the eye.

But there are precious jewels which are not seen:
Things everlasting, wholesome, pure, and clean.
Such gems are found within God's Holy Book,
Wherein a man, though blind, may freely look.

And I have looked within that Book, and found
A source of perfect peace, a footing sound.
I've found, portrayed therein, a gracious Friend,
Whose tender loving care will never end.

So now I see His hand upon my life,
Directing all my way, through peace or strife;
And though my way is dark, I'm not alone;
With Christ I am content, while walking home.

ALVY E. FORD

Boast

Boasters by nature are from truth aloof.

GEOFFREY CHAUCER

———o———

There's less chance of your friends not letting you down if you don't build yourself up so high.

———o———

You can't push yourself ahead by patting yourself on the back.

———o———

The saying is true, "The empty vessel makes the greatest sound."

WILLIAM SHAKESPEARE, *King Henry V*

———o———

We rise in glory, as we sink in pride; Where boasting ends, there dignity begins.

EDWARD YOUNG

———o———

Boasting is the refuge of those more able to talk than to do.

———o———

Deeds done and work accomplished need not be bolstered by words.

———o———

For every person who brags about being bright, there are a dozen ready to polish him off.

———o———

The trouble with singing your own praises is that you seldom get the right pitch.

ARNOLD GLASGOW

———o———

The trouble with blowing one's own horn is that it seldom leaves any wind for climbing.

———o———

Some folks would rather blow their own horn than listen to a military band.

Whenever you boast too much, you pray too little.
Whenever you pray too little, you act too soon.

Body

If there are a thousand miles of blood vessels in my body, if there are 1,500,000 sweat glands on its surface, if my lungs are composed of 700,000,-000 cells, if my heart-beats for a single day were "concentrated into one huge throb of vital power, it would be sufficient to throw a ton of iron 120 feet into the air" then, since it has already beat 3,000,000,000 times since I was born, and has lifted what would equal the weight of 600,000 tons, if my nervous system is controlled by a brain that has 3,000,000,000,000 nerve cells of which 9,200,000,000 are in the cortex or covering of the brain alone, and if in my veins there are 3,000,000 white corpuscles and 180,000,000,000,000 red ones — then it is *some job* for (it just to evolve) . . . I grant! It sounds to me more like the work of God!

The Psalmist wrote: "*I will praise Thee: for I am fearfully and wonderfully made.*" (Psalm 139:14).

W. B. RILEY

———o———

Our body is a wonderful engine of marvelous energy. Overfed, underfed, over-burdened, neglected, abused, weakened, shamefully talked about, yet it goes on generating from year to year the most divine thing in the universe — Life.

DR. CROFT

———o———

Definition Of Anatomy
(*by a very small boy*)

"Your head is kind of round and hard, and your brains are in it. Your hair is on it. Your face is the front of your head where you eat and make faces. Your neck is what keeps your head out of your collar. It is hard to keep clean . . . Your stummick is something that if you don't eat enough it hurts, and spinach don't help none. Your spine is a long bone in your back that keeps you from folding up. Your back is always behind you no matter how quick you turn around. Your arms you have to have to pitch with and so you can reach the butter. Your fingers stick out of your hand so you can throw a curve and add up rithmetic. Your legs is what if you have not got two of you can't get to first base. Your feet are what you run on; your toes are what always get stubbed. And that's all there is to you except what's inside and I never saw it."

———o———

God gave us two ears and one mouth to use in that proportion.

Bold

What you can do, or dream you can — begin it. Boldness has genius, power, and magic in it.

JOHANN WOLFGANG VON GOETHE

———o———

A minister without boldness is like a smooth file, a knife without an edge, a sentinel that is afraid to let off his gun. Men will be bold in sin, and ministers must be bold to reprove.

WILLIAM GURNALL

———o———

Be bold in what you stand for, but careful what you fall for.

———o———

Boldness is unembarrassed freedom of speech.

———o———

We make way for the man who boldly pushes past us.

———o———

He who never ventures will never cross the sea.

Books

A house without books is like a room without windows.

HORACE MANN

———o———

There is no reason to make either books or education easy, any more than

tennis or football is easy. . . . Books require a certain amount of hard work and practice and, like sports, they can be both a challenge and a delight.

GILBERT W. CHAPMAN

———o———

Books are the quietest and most constant of friends; they are the most accessible and wisest of counsellors, and the most patient of teachers.

CHARLES WILLIAM ELIOT

———o———

A book is a book only when it is in the hands of a reader. The rest of the time it is an artifact.

WILLIAM SLOANE

———o———

Get books and read and study them carefully.

ABRAHAM LINCOLN

———o———

When we are collecting books, we are collecting happiness.

VINCENT STARRETT

———o———

The books that help you most are those that make you think the most.

THEODORE PARKER

———o———

Even in life the best friendships are based not so much on propinquity and contact as on the touching of minds and spirits, and this is almost completely obtainable in a book.

MARY WRIGHT PLUMMER

———o———

Read not to contradict and confute; nor to believe and take for granted; nor to find talk and discourse; but to weigh and consider. Some books are to be tasted, others to be swallowed, and some few to be chewed and digested: that is, some books are to be read only in parts, others to be read, but not curiously; and some few to be read wholly, and with diligence and attention.

FRANCIS BACON, *Of Studies*

———o———

There are three schoolmasters for everybody that will employ them — the senses, intelligent companions, and books.

HENRY WARD BEECHER

———o———

Someone has said that the three most important books are the Bible, the Cook Book, and the Check Book.

———o———

A book is a success when people who haven't read it pretend they have.

———o———

The true University of these days is a Collection of Books.

THOMAS CARLYLE,
Heroes and Hero Worship

———o———

But words are things, and a small
    drop of ink,
Falling like dew upon a thought, pro-
    duces
That which makes thousands, perhaps
    millions, think.

LORD BYRON, *Don Juan*

———o———

It is a man's duty to have books. A library is not a luxury, but one of the necessaries of life.

HENRY WARD BEECHER

———o———

One man browsing in a bookstore is worth 100 men gathering in the market place.

———o———

Books are lighthouses erected in the great sea of time.

EDWIN PERCY WHIPPLE

———o———

A taste for books is the pleasure and glory of my life. I would not exchange it for the riches of the Indies.

EDWARD GIBBON

———o———

Except a living man there is nothing more wonderful than a book! A message to us from the dead — from human souls whom we never saw, who lived perhaps thousands of miles away; and yet these, on those little sheets of paper, speak to us, teach us, comfort us, open their hearts to us as brothers.

CHARLES KINGSLEY

A home without books and ideas can be almost as bad for a child as a broken home, an alcoholic home, or a criminal home, because it leaves a vacuum into which rush corrupting values.

MAX LERNER

———o———

The voice of books can be heard for years!

Sunshine Magazine

———o———

Marking Time

A book is more than printer's ink.
It is a friend who helps me think;
In a short time I can obtain
What took him many years to gain.

LUTHER MARKIN in *Sunshine Magazine*

———o———

Books are sepulchres of thought.

HENRY WADSWORTH LONGFELLOW

———o———

Books, the children of the brain.

JONATHAN SWIFT, *Tale of a Tub*

———o———

Wear the old coat and buy the new book.

AUSTIN PHELPS

———o———

Dreams, books are each a world;
    And books, we know,
Are a substantial world,
    Both pure and good;
Round these, with tendril strong
    As flesh and blood,
Our pastime and our happiness
    Will grow.

WILLIAM WORDSWORTH, *Personal Talk*

———o———

Since the invention of printing about 18,000,000 different titles of books have been published, and about one-third of these have appeared since 1960.

Bore, Boredom

Bore: a person who talks when you wish him to listen.

AMBROSE BIERCE

Some people can stay longer in an hour than others can in a week.

———o———

The secret of being a bore is to tell everything.

VOLTAIRE

———o———

We may forgive those who bore us, we cannot forgive those whom we bore.

FRANÇOIS, DUC DE LA ROCHEFOUCAULD

———o———

A man of learning is never bored.

JEAN PAUL RICHTER

———o———

Work is the best escape from boredom.

ELEANOR L. DOAN

———o———

America is said to have the highest per capita boredom of any spot on earth. We know because we have the greatest variety and number of artificial amusements of any country. People have become so empty that they can't even entertain themselves. They have to pay other people to amuse them, to make them happy and comfortable for a few minutes, to try to lose that awful, frightening, hollow feeling of being lost and alone.

BILLY GRAHAM

Borrow

Don't worry if you borrow, only if you lend.

Russian Proverb

———o———

The borrower runs in his own debt.

RALPH WALDO EMERSON

———o———

Neither a borrower nor a lender be;
For a loan oft loses both itself and friend,
And borrowing dulls the edge of husbandry.

WILLIAM SHAKESPEARE, *Hamlet*

Boys

Definition Of A Junior Boy

After a male baby has grown out of long clothes and triangles, and has acquired pants, freckles, and so much dirt that relatives don't dare to kiss it between meals, it becomes a boy. A boy is nature's answer to that false belief that there is no such thing as perpetual motion. A boy can swim like a fish, run like a deer, climb like a squirrel, balk like a mule, bellow like a bull, eat like a pig, or act like a fool. He is called a tornado because he comes in at the most unexpected times, hits most unexpected places, and leaves everything a wreck behind him. He is a piece of skin stretched over an appetite. A noise with smudges. He is a growing animal of superlative promise to be fed, watered, and kept warm; a joy forever, a periodic nuisance, the problem of our times, the hope of a nation.

Every boy born is evidence that God is not discouraged with man. Were it not for boys, newspapers would go unread and a thousand TV shows would go bankrupt. Boys are useful in running errands. A boy can easily do the family errands with the help of five or six adults. The zest with which a boy does an errand is equaled only by the speed of a turtle on a hot day in July.

The boy is a natural spectator. He watches parades, fires, ballgames, automobiles, boats, and airplanes with equal fervor, but will not watch the clock. The man who invents a clock that will stand on its head and sing a song when it strikes will win the undying gratitude of millions of families whose boys are forever coming to lunch about suppertime. Boys faithfully imitate their dads in spite of all efforts to teach them good manners. A boy, if not washed too often and if kept in a cool, quiet place after each accident, will survive broken bones, hornets, swimming holes, fights, and nine helpings of pie.

AUTHOR UNKNOWN

———o———

A boy becomes a man when he wears out the seat of his pants instead of the soles of his shoes.

———o———

Small boys are washable, though most of them shrink from it.

Times, Fort Mill, S.C.

Diamonds In The Rough

A diamond in the rough
  Is a diamond sure enough,
For, before it ever sparkled,
  It was made of diamond stuff.
Of course someone must find it
  Or it never will be found.
And then, someone must grind it
  Or it never will be ground.

But when it's found, and when it's
    ground
  And when it's burnished bright,
That diamond's everlastingly
  Flashing out its radiant light.
O! Christian, please, who'er you be,
  Don't say you've done enough,
That worst boy in the class may be
  A Diamond in the Rough.
AUTHOR UNKNOWN

---o---

A Little Boy In Church

He ruffles through his hymn book,
He fumbles with his tie,
He laces up his oxfords,
He overworks a sigh;
He goes through all his pockets,
Engrossed in deep research;
There's no one quite so busy
As a little boy in church.
THELMA IRELAND

---o---

A boy is a bank where you can
deposit your most precious treasures
— the hard won wisdom, the dreams
of a better world. A boy can guard
and protect these, and perhaps invest
them wisely and with a profit — a profit larger than you ever dreamed. A
boy will inherit your world. All the
work will be judged by him. Tomorrow he will take your seat in Congress,
own your company, run your town.
The future is his and through him the
future is yours. Perhaps he deserves
a little more attention now.
SOURCE UNKNOWN

---o---

For Any Mother Of A Small Boy

Was it for this I rendered sterile
Bottles, blankets, and apparel,
Scrubbed and boiled and disinfected,
Let no one touch unless inspected,
That now, quite innocent of soap,
My erstwhile pride, my one-time hope,
In spite of all the books assert
Should thrive on good old-fashioned
    dirt?
ELIZABETH-ELLEN LONG

---o---

Seven Year Old

STEM the force behind a tide!
Have you tried?

Direct the hurricane's wild path,
Appease its wrath;

Reduce the forest's red-tongued flames
With words and names;

Then you have curbed with order's
    rules
Beyond the power of sages, fools,

What's in a boy!

Electric, alien, proud creation!
But you'll have silenced the ovation
Nature raised to Joy!
IDA ELAINE JAMES
in *The Christian Parent*

---o---

A little girl was once asked to write
an essay on boys. She wrote: Boys are
noisy, pesty, and dirty. They hate soap
and never wash themselves. They have
bugs and worms in their pockets. I
don't want to play with them. But
girls are nice. They are quiet and play
together in a ladylike way. My daddy
must have been a little girl when he
was a little boy because he is so nice.
Church School Teacher

---o---

Among the papers of the late Dr.
Harper of the University of Chicago
was found a memorandum which read
like this:

"If I were a boy again, I would
strive to find out from good books how
good men lived.

"If I were a boy again I would more
and more cultivate the company of
those whose graces of person and mind
would help me on in my work. I
would always seek good company.

"If I were a boy again, I would
study the life and character of our

Savior persistently, that I might become more and more like Him.

"If I were a boy again, I would study the Bible even more than I did. The Bible is a necessity to every boy."

War Cry

Brain

You must nourish the brain as well as the body. The man who despises music as a luxury and non-essential is doing the Nation an injury.

THOMAS ALVA EDISON

———o———

I use not only all the brains I have, but all I can borrow.

WOODROW WILSON

———o———

As we sit and watch the train go by, along with a hundred other autoists, it occurs to us that the human brain is somewhat like a freight car, guaranteed to have a certain capacity, but too often running empty.

———o———

The Brain

The top-floor apartment in the Human Block, known as the Cranium, and kept by the Sarah Sisters — Sarah Brum and Sarah Belum, assisted by Medulla Oblongata. All three are nervous, but are always confined to their cells. The Brain is done in gray and white and furnished with light and heat, hot or cold water, (if desired), with regular connections to the outside world by way of the Spinal Circuit. Usually occupied by the Intellect Bros. — Thoughts and Ideas — as an Intelligence Office.

———o———

The brain is as strong as its weakest think.

———o———

Our brains, like our bodies, don't come with a set of directions attached.

KEYES

———o———

A brain is known by its fruit.

H. G. WELLS

Brave, Bravery

Bravery is the capacity to perform properly even when scared half to death.

OMAR BRADLEY

———o———

The brave man seeks not honor of man but does always the best he can.

———o———

The brave man is not one who feels no fear, but one who conquers his fear and boldly does his duty.

Brevity

A short saying often carries much wisdom.

SOPHOCLES

———o———

'Tis better to be brief, than tedious.

WILLIAM SHAKESPEARE

———o———

Brevity is the best recommendation of speech, whether in a senator or an orator.

MARCUS TULLIUS CICERO

———o———

Whatever you teach, be brief, that your readers' minds may readily comprehend and faithfully retain your words. Everything superfluous slips from the full heart.

HORACE

———o———

Have something to say; say it, and stop when you've done.

TRYON EDWARDS

———o———

Brevity is very good when we are, or are not, understood.

SAMUEL BUTLER

———o———

Brevity is not a virtue; it is a result. In a word, if you would be brief, first be long. To make a telephone conversation short, think it over and anticipate as far as possible what needs to be said. To make . . . an annual report pointed, let it first be written in fullness, or at least outlined in some . . . detail. Only then will it be possible to make it brief.

CHARLES W. FERGUSON in *THINK*

Bride

Dear Bride

Love in your heart . . . a ring on your
    finger;
Flowers in your hand . . . a groom to
    share life with;
The prospect of a future family of your
    own.
What more could a woman ask for?
You stand there, hands slightly trem-
    bling
Yet with confidence in your heart —
Confident that yours will be the "per-
    fect marriage."
And it can be just that!
O, there will be those well-meaning
    friends
Who will tell you otherwise.
But don't you listen to them in their
    unhappiness.
    If you will keep the love you feel to-
    day;
If you will guard the confidence you
    sense today,
Yours can be "a bit of heaven on earth."
Go walking daily with your lover
Through the pages of God's Word, es-
    pecially I Corinthians 13
For there you will find the secret of
    "abiding love" that never fails!

NAT OLSON
in The Log of the Good Ship Grace

———o———

Two Brides

A faithful bride, in garments spotless,
    fair,
    Is waiting, watching, for her coming
    lord.
She knows that he will quickly meet
    her there
    Because she has the promise of his
    word.

The Bride of Christ, in garments spot-
    less, fair,
    Is waiting, watching, for her coming
    Lord.
She knows that she will meet Him in
    the air
    Because she has the promise of His
    Word.

EMMA BELLE YOURDON in Today

A wise bride is one who loses her
temper — permanently.

HAL CHADWICK

Build

Building For The Future

The angels from their thrones on high
    Look down on us with wondering
    eye,
That where we are but passing guests
    We build such strong and solid nests;
And where we hope to dwell for aye
    We scarce take heed a stone to lay.

The Sunday School Times

———o———

Why Build?

We are all blind until we see
That in the human plan
Nothing is worth the making, if
It does not make the man.

Why build those cities glorious
If man unbuilded goes?
In vain, we build the work, unless
The builder also grows.

EDWIN MARKHAM, Man-Making

———o———

The loftier the building the deeper
must the foundation be laid.

THOMAS À KEMPIS

No matter what your lot, build something on it.

———o———

You cannot erect a sound super-
structure on a foundation of thinking
based upon error.

———o———

I watched them tearing a building
down,
A gang of men in a busy town.
With a ho-heave-ho and a lusty yell,
They swung a beam, and the sidewall
fell.
I asked the foreman: "Are these men
skilled?
"And the men you'd hire if you had to
build?"
He gave a laugh and said: "No, in-
deed
"Just common labor is all I need.

"With them I can wreck in a day or
two,
"What builders have taken years to do."
So I thought to myself as I went my
way,
Which of these roles have I tried to
play?
Am I a builder who works with care,
Measuring life by the rule and square?
Am I shaping my deeds to a well made
plan,
Patiently doing the best I can?
Or am I a wrecker, who walks the
town,
Content with the labor of tearing
down?

AUTHOR UNKNOWN

Burden

The greatest burden we have to carry
in life is self. The most difficult thing
we have to manage is self.

HANNAH WHITALL SMITH

———o———

Pray not for lighter burdens but for
stronger backs.

THEODORE ROOSEVELT

———o———

None knows the weight of another's
burthen.

GEORGE HERBERT, *Jacula Prudentum*

———o———

Burdens become light when cheerfully borne.

OVID

———o———

A biologist tells how he watched an
ant carrying a piece of straw which
seemed almost too heavy for it to drag.
The ant came to a crack in the ground
which was too big for it to cross. It
stood still for a time, as though perplexed by the situation, then put the
straw across the crack and walked over
on the straw.

If only we were as wise as that ant!
We speak much about the burdens
we must bear. But have we ever
thought of converting our burdens into
bridges, of having our burdens bear *us*
up instead of us bearing *them* up?

The Log of the Good Ship Grace

Not the load but the overload kills.

Spanish Proverb

———o———

The story is told of a poor man who
plodded along toward home in an Irish
town carrying a huge bag of potatoes.
A horse and wagon carrying a stranger
came along, and the stranger stopped
the wagon and invited the man on foot
to climb inside. This the poor man
did, but when he sat down in the
wagon he held the bag of potatoes in
his arms. And when it was suggested
that he should set it down, he said very
warmly: "Sure, I don't like to trouble
you too much. You're giving me a ride.
I'll carry the potatoes!"

Sometimes we think we are doing
the Lord a favor when we carry the
burden. But the work is His, and the
burden is His, and He asks us only to
be faithful.

ISAAC PAGE

———o———

Our Burden Bearer

The little sharp vexations
    And the briars that catch and fret,
Why not take all to the Helper
    Who has never failed us yet?

Tell Him about the heartache,
    And tell Him the longings, too;
Tell Him the baffled purpose
    When we scarce know what to do.

Then, leaving all our weakness
    With One divinely strong,
Forget that we bore the burden,
    And carry away the song.

PHILLIPS BROOKS

———o———

Everyone thinks his own burden
heavy.

French Proverb

Business

A Busy Business Man's Prayer

Take my wife and let her be
Consecrated, Lord, to Thee.
Take her moments and her days;
Leave me mine for my own ways.

Take my weekly offering
That so grudgingly I bring

Yet report as 10 per cent
So that more will be exempt.

Take my voice and let me pray
Sundays — maybe twice that day;
Otherwise, O Lord, my mother
Handles prayers for me and others.

Take my children, show them how
Respect is due me here and now;
Make them do just what I say,
Not to follow in my way.

Finally, Lord, at end of life
Make me faithful as my wife,
That together we may be
Ever, only, all for Thee!

FRANCES R. LONGINO

———o———

Sign in store window: "This is a non-profit organization — please help us change."

———o———

Business Trends

"My business is looking up," said the astronomer.

"Mine is all write," declared the author.

"Mine is growing," boasted the farmer.

"Mine is picking up," chuckled the cheerful rag picker.

"Mine is just sew, sew," ventured the tailor.

"Mine is looking better," smiled the optician.

"Mine is pretty light," snapped the electric light man.

Sunshine Magazine

———o———

To be a success in business: Be daring, be first, be different.

MARCHANT

———o———

Business makes a man, as well as tries him.

———o———

No business is a success which must ruin men to make money.

ROY L. SMITH

———o———

Success or failure in business is caused more by mental attitude even than by mental capacities.

WALTER DILL SCOTT

The men who made fortunes in business always precede, never follow, the crowd.

———o———

Some people regard private enterprise as a predatory tiger to be shot. Others look on it as a cow they can milk. Not enough people see it as a healthy horse pulling a sturdy wagon.

SIR WINSTON CHURCHILL

Busy

Too Busy

"I sometimes think we are in danger of being too busy to be really useful," said an old lady, thoughtfully. "We hear so much about making every minute count, that there is no place left for small wayside kindnesses. We visit the sick neighbor, and relieve the poor neighbor, but for the common, everyday neighbor, who has not fallen by the way, we haven't a minute to spare. But everybody who needs a cup of cold water isn't calling the fact out to the world. There are a great many little pauses by the way which are no waste time."

SELECTED

———o———

If You Were Busy

If you were busy being kind,
Before you knew it you would find
You'd soon forget to think 'twas true
That someone was unkind to you.

If you were busy being glad,
And cheering people who are sad,
Although your heart might ache a bit,
You'd soon forget to notice it.

If you were busy being good,
And doing just the best you could,
You'd not have time to blame some man
Who's doing just the best he can.

If you were busy being true
To what you know you ought to do,
You'd be so busy you'd forget
The blunders of the folks you've met.

If you were busy being right,
You'd find yourself too busy, quite,
To criticize your neighbor long
Because he's busy being wrong.

REBECCA FORESMAN

Too Busy?

You are too busy this morning
In the maelstrom of family care,
The husband must rush to the office,
So there isn't a moment for prayer?

The children are sent to the school-
room,
And the grind of the day then begins
With no Word from God to remember,
Nor the echo of strengthening hymns?

What wonder the burdens seem heavy
And the hours seem irksomely long!
What wonder that rash words are spo-
ken
And life seems discordant and wrong!

Oh, pause for a little each morning
And again at the close of the day,
To talk to the Master, who loves you.
Remember, He taught us to pray!
                    AUTHOR UNKNOWN

———o———

If you're too busy to read God's Word,
If you're too busy to pray,
If you're too busy to hear His voice,
You're too busy today.

———o———

I Was Too Busy

The Lord Christ wanted a tongue one
day
To speak a message of cheer
To a heart that was weary and worn
and sad,
And weighed with a mighty fear.
He asked me for mine, but 'twas busy
quite
With my own affairs from morn till
night.

The Lord Christ wanted a hand one
day
To do a loving deed;
He wanted two feet, on an errand for
Him
To run with gladsome speed.
But I had need of my own that day;
To his gentle beseeching I answered,
"Nay!"

So all that day I used my tongue,
My hands, and my feet as I chose;
I said some hasty, bitter words
That hurt one heart, God knows.
I busied my hands with worthless play,
And my wilful feet went a crooked way.

And the dear Lord Christ, was His
work undone
For lack of a willing heart?
Only through men does He speak to
men?
Dumb must He be apart?
I do not know, but I wish today
I had let the Lord Christ have His way.
                    Christian Endeavor World

C

Call

The Call of Calls

I am the everlasting Christ.
I stand and call from the heights,
    in the places of the paths,
        at the coming in at the doors,
And my voice is to the sons of men.

Hear, for I will speak of excellent
        things,
    and my mouth shall say truth:
The life which I am
    is better than rubies
        and fine gold
            and choice silver;
Earth has nothing to compare with it.

Counsel is mine, and sound wisdom;
I am understanding, I am strength.
I lead in the wheelruts of righteousness,
In the paths of justice;
For it is by me that rulers declare
    what is just.
The kind of honor and substance that
        I give
    is the kind that endures.

To seek me early is to find me,
    for I love those who love me,
And my delight is with the sons of
        men,
    to endow them
        with the treasuries of their hearts.

It has always been this way;
I was with the Father from the be-
    ginning;
Before the hills were did I set forth
    to teach men to hate the evil way,
    to live in me and for me
        and to rejoice in the dowry of
        earth.

Hear instruction, then, and be wise:
Watch for me, wait for me, listen for
    me;
Discern the riffling of the water,
    the waving of the treetops,
        the moving of the Spirit,
Lest you fall in love with death
    and lose out on eternity.

The man who finds me finds life,
    the only real life there is,
        in the favor of the Lord.
                Adapted from Proverbs 8:2-35

———o———

There is a terrible fact that if I
hadn't heard the call of Christ, I might
have been a physician in Harley Street
being driven about in my Rolls-Royce.
                SIR WILFRED GRENFELL,
                a missionary to Labrador

Camp

Summer camps are places where little boys and girls go for mother's vacation.

———o———

Counselor to new boy at camp: "We
want you to be happy, so enjoy yourself here. If there's something you want
we haven't got, I'll show you how to
get along without it."

———o———

Thank You, God

Thank you, God, for all these things —
    For the moon, the stars and the sun;
Thank you for the beautiful sky
    When the day has just begun.

Thank you, God, for mountains high,
    Thank you for the trees;
Thank you for all creatures that live;
    For the mighty, crashing seas.

Thank you for my friends so dear,
    Thank you for my family;

Thank you for the whole wide world,
    And especially, God, for me.

Thank you for Jesus Christ
    And all that He has done,
That we may go to heaven
    And live with Thee as one.
        *This poem was written by a ten-year-old
        girl at Forest Home Christian Conference
        Center, Calif.*

Can't

The man who says, "It can't be done,"
is liable to be interrupted by someone
doing it.

———o———

It can't be done, it never has been
done; therefore I will do it.

———o———

When someone says something can't
be done, it only means *he* can't do it.

———o———

"I can't do it" never yet accomplished anything; "I will try" has performed wonders.
                GEORGE P. BURNHAM

Care

If a care is too small to be turned
into a prayer, it is too small to be made
into a burden.

———o———

Careful For Nothing

Casting all your care upon Him; for He careth
for you. (I Peter 5:7)

Cease your thinking, troubled Chris-
    tian;
    What avail your anxious cares;
God is ever thinking for you,
    Jesus every burden bears.
Casting all your care upon Him,
    Sink into His blessed will;
While He folds you to His bosom,
    Sweetly whispering, "Peace be still."

Jesus knows the way He leads me,
    I have but to hold His hand;
Nothing from His thought is hidden,
    Why need I to understand?

Let me, like the loved disciple,
  Hide my head upon His breast;
Till upon His faithful bosom,
  All my cares are hushed to rest.
                              A. B. SIMPSON

———o———

Millions dying there have never heard.
Millions living here have never cared.

———o———

Out In The Fields

The little cares that fretted me,
  I lost them yesterday
Among the fields above the sea,
  Among the winds at play;
Among the lowing of the herds,
  The rustling of the trees,
Among the singing of the birds,
  The humming of the bees.

The foolish fears of what may happen,
  I cast them all away
Among the clover-scented grass,
  Among the new-mown hay;
Among the hushing of the corn
  Where drowsy poppies nod,
Where ill thoughts die and good are
    born,
  Out in the fields with God.
                              ANONYMOUS

———o———

"It Matters To Him About You"

Casting all your care upon Him; for He careth
for you. (I Peter 5:7)

Be not troubled with thought of the
    morrow —
Of duties you surely must do —
On the Lord cast thy burden of sor-
    row —
"It matters to Him about you!"

Be not weary in fighting with Satan —
But, buckle His armour so true —
He will make all your troubles to
    straighten —
"It matters to Him about you!"

Be patient, until His appearing —
'Tis dawn, almost, now, on your
    view —
The mists of this dark age are clear-
    ing —
"He is planning in love about you!"
                              AUTHOR UNKNOWN

Challenge
These Slogans are Timely

Have voice . . . . will invite
Have phone . . . . will call
Have pen . . . . . will write
Have interest . . . will come
Have car . . . . . will bring
Have concern . . . will pray
Have ability . . . . will use
Have conviction . . will share
Have hope . . . . will rejoice
Have money . . . . will tithe

———o———

Before Napoleon Bonaparte invaded
Russia, he told the Russian ambassador
that he would destroy that empire. The
ambassador's reply was, "Man proposes,
but God disposes." "Tell your master,"
thundered the arrogant and self-con-
fident Corsican, "that I am he that
proposes, and I am he that disposes."
It was a challenge to the living God
to show who was the ruler of this
world, and God accepted the challenge.
He moved not from His august throne.
But He sent one of His most humble
messengers, the crystal snowflake, from
Heaven to punish the audacious boast-
er. Napoleon flung his army into Mos-
cow, but in his retreat he left on the
frozen plains the bulk of his vast army,
and the official returns of the Russian
authorities reported 213,516 French
corpses and 95,816 dead horses.
                              A. T. PIERSON

———o———

Never challenge another to do
wrong, lest he sin at thy bidding.

———o———

Flaming Torch

That flaming torch — it fell,
It fell among the trees,
Cut down by cruel hands.
It fell, and falling cast
Long shadows on the ground,
Shadows of men in chains,
Shadows of prison walls.

It fell, and yet it burns —
Not smoldering, not flickering,
But sending up long fingers
To the sky,

Fingers that point,
Fingers that plead,
Fingers that beckon me
To quit this life of deadly ease
And lift that torch on high.

O God,
And shall my heart
Be cold —
When men go out to die
For Thee?

E.L.S., *Source Unknown*

Chance

Chance is a nickname for Providence.

SEBASTIEN R. N. CHAMFORT,
Maxims and Thoughts

———o———

The successful man is one who had the chance and took it.

ROGER BABSON

———o———

Every day gives you another chance.

———o———

Chances rule men and not men chances.

HERODOTUS

Change

When one life is changed, the world is changed.

THOMAS L. JOHNS

———o———

Blessed is the man who has discovered that there is nothing permanent in life but change.

A. P. GOUTHEY

———o———

A wise man changes his mind, a fool never.

Spanish Proverb

———o———

Changing one thing for the better does more good than proving a dozen things are wrong.

———o———

Lincoln used to tell the story of a man who heated a piece of iron in the forge, not knowing just what he was going to make out of it. At first he thought he would make a horseshoe; then he changed his mind and thought he would make something else out of it. After he had hammered on this design for a little while, he changed his mind and started on something else. By this time, he had so hammered the iron that it was not good for much of anything; and, holding it up with his tongs, and looking at it in dusgust, the blacksmith thrust it hissing into a tub of water. "Well, at least I can make a fizzle out of it!" he exclaimed.

CLARENCE E. MACARTNEY

———o———

The past cannot be altered; the future can.

Character

You can't carve rotten wood.

Chinese Proverb

———o———

Character is a victory, not a gift.

Try Square

———o———

A wise observer of human nature once said that a sure test of a person's character was for him to list honestly what things are luxuries to him and what are necessities. Try it. The result will show what kind of a person you are. Under the heading "necessities," some people will put down such items as an expensive car, a house in a "nice" neighborhood, fashionable clothes, membership in exclusive clubs. These will soon crowd out things needed for the life of the soul. Other people will put down as necessities integrity and independence of spirit, no matter what they cost in social approval. They will put down the religious quality and influence of the home, and the sharing of one's goods in the work of the Kingdom of God. What are the "necessities" of life to you?

———o———

You cannot dream yourself into a character; you must hammer and forge yourself into one.

JAMES ANTHONY FROUDE

———o———

The grand aim of man's creation is the development of a grand character — and grand character is, by its very nature, the product of probationary discipline.

AUSTIN PHELPS

Reputation is what you have on arrival. Character is what you have on departure.

————o————

A river becomes crooked by following the line of least resistance! So does a man!

————o————

Character is like the foundation to a house . . . it is below the surface.

————o————

Youth and beauty fade; character endures forever.

————o————

A noble character is the sum of many ordinary days well used.

————o————

Persons with any weight of character carry, like planets, their atmosphere along with them in their orbits.

THOMAS HARDY

————o————

Character is Destiny.

HERACLITUS

————o————

Character cannot be made except by a steady, long continued process.

PHILLIPS BROOKS

————o————

The measure of a man's real character is what he would do if he knew he would never be found out.

THOMAS BABINGTON MACAULAY

————o————

How a man plays the game, shows something of his character. How he loses, shows all of it.

————o————

Character is a by-product; it is produced in the great manufacture of daily duty.

WOODROW WILSON

————o————

Reputation is what men think we are; character is what God knows we are.

LEVIER

————o————

If I take care of my character, my reputation will take care of itself.

DWIGHT L. MOODY

In times like these it is our task to build into America's children what psychologists call 'internalized systems.' This capacity for self-discipline is called character: the building of character is a life-long process; it is built at the mother's knee — and sometimes over the mother's knee.

REV. FRED GREVE
in The Log of the Good Ship Grace

————o————

Every man has three characters: that which he exhibits, that which he has, and that which he thinks he has.

A. KARR

————o————

A man shows what he is by what he does with what he has.

————o————

Character is not a gift but an achievement.

H. A. PARK

Charity

It is not charity to any man to give him what he needs. Offer him an opportunity to earn what he needs and you are his benefactor.

————o————

People who have no charity for the faults of others are generally stoneblind to their own!

————o————

What Is Charity?

It's silence when your words would hurt;
It's patience when your neighbor's curt;
It's deafness when the scandal flows;
It's thoughtfulness for another's woes;
It's promptness when stern duty calls;
It's courage when misfortune falls.

World Christian Digest

————o————

Real charity doesn't care if it's tax-deductible or not.

DAN BENNETT

————o————

Charity is a virtue of the heart, and not of the hands.

JOSEPH ADDISON, The Guardian

Feel for others — in your pocket.

CHARLES HADDON SPURGEON

Charm

"Charm" — which means the power to effect work without employing brute force — is indispensable to women.

Charm is a woman's strength just as strength is a man's charm.

HAVELOCK ELLIS

Prescription For Charm

For *lips* — truth, kind, words, and a smile.

For *eyes* — friendliness and sympathetic understanding.

For *ears* — courteous attention and wholesome listening.

For *hands* — honest work and thoughtful deeds.

For *figure* — helpful and right living.

For *voice* — prayer, praise, and the lilt of joy.

For *heart* — love for God, for life, and for others.

AUTHOR UNKNOWN

Cheerful

A cheerful heart makes its own blue sky.

Brightening up the life of someone else will put a fresh shine on your own.

Give a cheerful, kind and courteous answer to the meanest grouch (if there is such a person) and you are mighty sure to have a kind answer in return.

Well, you're richer tonight than you were this morning, if a little child has smiled at you, or a stray dog has licked your hand, or if you have managed to be cheerful even though harassed and troubled.

Cheerfulness keeps up a kind of daylight in the mind, and fills it with a steady and perpetual serenity.

JOSEPH ADDISON, *The Spectator*

Cheerfulness means a contented spirit; a pure heart, a kind and loving disposition; it means humility and charity, a generous appreciation of others, and a modest opinion of self.

WILLIAM MAKEPEACE THACKERAY

Cheerful people, the doctors say, resist disease better than the glum ones. In other words, the surly bird catches the germ.

Merely to share another's burden is noble. To do it cheerfully is sublime.

Cheerfulness and content are great beautifiers, and are famous preservers of youthful looks.

CHARLES DICKENS

Children

Let Me Guide A Little Child!

Dear Lord, I do not ask
That Thou should'st give me some high
    work of Thine,
Some noble calling, or some wondrous
    task.
Give me a little hand to hold in mine;
Give me a little child to point the way
Over the strange, sweet path that leads
    to Thee;
Give me a little voice to teach to pray;
Give me two shining eyes Thy face to
    see.
The only crown I ask, dear Lord to
    wear
Is this: that I may teach a little child.
I do not ask that I may ever stand
Among the wise, the worthy, or the
    great;
I only ask that softly, hand in hand,
A child and I may enter at the gate.

AUTHOR UNKNOWN

The most important in child training is love.

REX

We are apt to forget that children watch examples better than they listen to preaching.

ROY L. SMITH

Children are what we make them.
French Proverb

———o———

The Heart Of A Child

The heart of a child is a tremulous
thing;
Lovely and frail as a butterfly's wing.

Kissed by the beam of a summer sun,
Or crushed by the word of a careless
one.

A look or a smile will cause it to sing,
For the heart of a child is a tremulous
thing.

MILLICENT M. SLABY

———o———

Be careful of your life lest a child
stumble over you.

———o———

Children are contagious to character
and conduct.

———o———

I love little children, and it is not a
slight thing when they, who are fresh
from God, love us.

CHARLES DICKENS

———o———

A torn jacket is soon mended, but
hard words bruise the heart of a child.

HENRY WADSWORTH LONGFELLOW

———o———

Mothers who raise
A child by the book,
Can, if sufficiently vexed,
Hasten results
By applying the book
As well as the text.

Evangelical Beacon

———o———

The thing most apt to drive a parent
wild,
Is a child behaving like a child.

———o———

Children: Today's investment, tomorrow's dividend.

———o———

The Child's Appeal

I am the Child.
All the world waits for my coming.
All the earth watches with interest to
see what
I shall become.
Civilization hangs in the balance,
For what I am, the world of tomorrow
will be.

I am the Child.
I have come into your world, about
which
I know nothing.
Why I came I know not;
How I came I know not.
I am curious; I am interested.

I am the Child.
You hold in your hand my destiny.
You determine, largely, whether I shall
succeed or fail.
Give me, I pray you, those things that
make
for happiness.
Train me, I beg you, that I may be a
blessing
to the world.

MAMIE GENE COLE

———o———

Trail Of Woe

There's a well-trodden path from nursery to sink
From eternal nocturnally fetching his
drink.

PAT CUNNINGHAM in *Home Life*

———o———

Personalized Music

In spite of all the toys I buy
Equipped with "built-in" tunes
My child prefers to improvise
With my best *pans* and *spoons!*

CATHERINE CLARK

———o———

Four

It's such a sweet and helpful age;
Too bad it's just a passing stage.

ALICE CHANDLER DUCH in *Home Life*

———o———

There's no faith like that of children.
They know that God is quiet and calm
and wonderful — big and interested in
them, and kind. Their requests of God
usually are reasonable and honest,

modest. They seldom ask for more than they deserve. They know of no reason why the world, in fact, shouldn't be mostly good.

Leader, Stuttgart, Ark.

———o———

Children are God's apostles sent forth, day by day, to preach of love, and hope and peace.

JAMES RUSSELL LOWELL

———o———

Those that allow and countenance their children in any evil way and do not use their authority to restrain and punish them, do in effect honor them more than God being more tender of their reputation than of His glory, and more desirous to humor them than to honor Him.

MATTHEW HENRY

———o———

Children begin by loving their parents; as they grow older they judge them; sometimes they forgive them.

OSCAR WILDE, *The Picture of Dorian Gray*

———o———

Some Children Are . . .

Some children are brown
  like newly baked bread,
some children are yellow
  and some are red,
some children are white
  and some almost blue.
Their colors are different —
  the children like you!

Some children eat porridge
  and some eat figs,
some children like ice-cream
  and some roasted pigs!
Some eat raw fishes
  and some Irish stew —
Their likings are different —
  the children like you!

Some children say "yes"
  and some say "oui,"
some say "ja"
  and some say "si,"
some children say "peep,"
  and some say "booh —"
Their words may be different
  the children like you!

Some children wear sweaters
  and some rebozos,
some children wear furs
  and some kimonos,
some children go naked
  and wear only their queue.
Their clothes may be different —
  the children like you!

Some children have houses
  of stone in the streets,
some live in igloos,
  and some live on fleets.
Some live in old strawhuts
  and some in new —
Their homes may be different —
  the children like you!

Oh, if they could dance
  and if they could play
altogether together
  a wonderful day!
Some could come sailing
  and some could just hike!
So much would be different —
  the children alike!

JO TENJFORD

———o———

Children now love luxury, have bad manners, contempt for authority, show disrespect for their elders, and love chatter in place of exercise. Children are now tyrants, not the servants of their households. They no longer rise when elders enter the room. They contradict their parents, chatter before company, gobble up their dainties at table, cross their legs and tyrannize over their teachers.

SOCRATES

———o———

First talk to God about your children — Then talk to your children about God.

———o———

Rearing children is like drafting a blueprint; you have to know where to draw the line.

———o———

Our earnest suggestion to the person who feels that she has been hurrying through life a bit too fast and has, in the process, grown a bit indifferent to life: Take the hand of a three-year-old

and walk with him two or three blocks.
The child can do to a person what any
amount of philosophizing cannot.
News-Herald, Morning Sun, Iowa

———o———

Father our children keep!
  We know not what is coming on the
      earth;
Beneath the shadow of Thy heavenly
      wing
  O keep them, keep them, Thou who
      gav'st them birth.

Father, draw nearer us!
  Draw firmer round us Thy protecting
      arm;
Oh, clasp our children closer to Thy
      side,
  Uninjured in the day of earth's alarm.

Oh, keep them undefiled!
  Unspotted from a tempting world of
      sin;
That, clothed in white, through the
      bright city gates,
  They may, with us, in triumph enter
      in.
                                    HORATIUS BONAR

———o———

The Child Was Shy

The child was shy.
One moist hand
Clung tightly to her mother.
Quite close she stood,
Her head pressed hard
Against her dress.
But between two fingers
A troubled eye
Peered into a strange, new world,
The Nursery Room.
For a long time she stood —
Afraid.

And then she saw
A small, familiar thing —
A crooked house
Built out of blocks.
Slowly she made her way
Across the room,
Forgetful of its strangeness.
And as her hand
Caught up a block,
She smiled back at her mother.
"You can go," she said,
"I think I'll build a house."
                                    AUTHOR UNKNOWN

The Faith Of A Child

As I tucked my little boy into bed and
      waited
for the prayers he always said,
He closed his eyes, and with his hands
      held
  tight, said "Jesus, I'm tired, so I'll
      just say good night."
And the smile on his face showed a
      faith so
  grand that I knew in my heart God
      would understand.

As I left him all snuggled with peace
      and content,
  I thought to myself if I was this con-
      fident,
And this child-like faith was at my
      command,
  so I'd put my hand in the nail-scarred
      hand
And leave it there all nestled tight so
      God
  would guide me day and night.
I'd have no fear of the future then for
      my
  broken dreams I know He'd mend,
And if life at times seemed hard to
      take I'd
  know my God had made no mistake.
I'd just hold tighter to His arm and
      He would
  quiet the raging storm.

Some folk would say such a faith is
      "blind"
  and think they had it well defined.
But I've never seen any brighter eyes
      than
  those of a child who completely
      relies
On the mighty grace of God above and
      there
  abides within His love.
                                    VELMA WOODS
                      in *Log of the Good Ship Grace*

———o———

Children's Beatitudes

Blessed is the child who has someone who believes in him, to whom he
can carry his problems unafraid.

Blessed is the child who is allowed
to pursue his curiosity into every worthwhile field of information.

Blessed is the child who has some-one who understands that childhood's griefs are real and call for understanding and sympathy.

Blessed is the child who has about him those who realize his need of Christ as Saviour and will lead him patiently and prayerfully to the place of acceptance.

Blessed is the child whose love of the true, the beautiful, and the good has been nourished through the years.

Blessed is the child whose imagination has been turned into channels of creative effort.

Blessed is the child whose efforts to achieve have found encouragement and kindly commendation.

Blessed is the child who has learned freedom from selfishness through responsibility and cooperation with others.

AUTHOR UNKNOWN

Sayings And Stories Of Children

PRESCHOOL AGES

Three-year-old Nancy was going down the stairs, holding a cup and saucer.

"Be careful you don't fall down the steps, dear!" her mother called out to her.

"Oh, that's all right, Mother. I won't fall," Nancy replied blithely. "I'm holding real tight to the cup."

ALICE CHRISTIE in *The Instructor*

Three children were debating whether they dared take candy mints to church to eat during the service.

"Mother wouldn't let us," Terry warned.

"Then put them in my pocket," the smallest volunteered. "She thinks I'm too little to know better."

REX CAMPBELL in *Together*

My small daughter had spent some time with her grandmother and broke something for which she had been reprimanded.

A few days later, she was listening to a discussion a friend and I were having about weapons, and afterward my daughter asked me what the word meant. I answered that it usually referred to an object that did damage.

She thought about this for a moment, then asked in a little voice, "Mother, am I a weapon?"

MRS. W. H. DE MOURE in *Coronet*

Little Mary was visiting her grandmother in the country. Walking in the garden, Mary chanced to see a peacock, a bird that she had never seen before.

After gazing in silent admiration, she ran into the house and cried out: "Oh, Granny, come and see! One of your chickens is in bloom!"

Christian Herald

When my baby brother was three or four years old, he had to be watched quite closely as he liked to play with kitchen knives.

One day, however, he did manage to sneak a sharp, pointed paring knife out of the house. He carried it carefully across the fields to where my uncle worked at quite a distance from home. Handing it to him he said, "Please put this in your pocket so the kids don't get it."

MRS. R. J. G. in *The Christian Parent*

Grandmother brought home some lovely color books and crayons to her little four-year-old granddaughter, Vickie. She did not want the little girl to mark the book carelessly, so she patiently tried to show her how to color within the confines of the book. Vickie did her best, but Grandmother wanted her to do better. Vickie tried, but finally to her Grandmother's numerous suggestions replied, "Grandma, this is the first time you have ever hounded me!"

The father took his young son (five years old) to a nursery school to be enrolled, and the teacher brought out a long form and started asking questions.

"Does the boy have any older brothers?" she asked.

"No."

"Any younger brothers?"

"No."

"Younger sisters?" "No."

"Older sisters?" "No."

Young Johnny, who had been looking more and more unhappy during this dialogue, finally burst out wistfully, "But I've got friends."

───o───

A pre-schooler with considerable TV-watching experience wasn't stumped for a remedy when her mother lost her voice in a recent siege of laryngitis. "You got no sound, Mama," diagnosed the tot. "Maybe you need a new tube."

Christian Herald

───o───

Johnny was very grown-up for his four-and-one-half years. One day I was inspecting our gardens after returning from a vacation and this little fellow from next door joined me. "Look at those nice gourds, Johnny," I said. Johnny disagreed, "They're not gourds, they're squash." "No, Johnny," said I, "those are gourds." "Well," said the little gardener, "they're gourds in your yard, but they're squash in my yard.!"

ELEANOR L. DOAN

───o───

KINDERGARTEN AGES

The beginners' Sunday school teacher used gold stars at the top of pupils' papers to reward excellent work.

One boy who received a large zero on his took the paper home and explained to his mother: "Teacher ran out of stars, so she gave me a moon!"

FLORENCE NAGLE in *Together*

───o───

Tommy and his little brother Jack had taken their sled out to have some fun while the snow lasted. After a little while mother looked out of the window to see how they were getting on. "I hope you are letting Jack have his share, Tommy," she said. "Oh, yes, Mother," was the reply. "I have it down hill and he has it up."

A little girl at Christmas had ten cents given her — ten bright, new pennies. "This," she said, laying aside one, "is for Jesus."

"But," said her mother, "you have already given one to Jesus."

"Yes," said the child, "but that belonged to Him; this is a present."

Selected

───o───

Young Susan, an avid television fan, was told to come to the dinner table to say grace. Bowing her head, but with her mind still on the program, she said in a clear small voice: "Thank Thee, God, for the food we are about to receive and speed it up so I can get back to Woody Woodpecker."

Watchman Examiner

───o───

The family was preparing to go to the mission field, and each person had to receive several shots. Finally little Janie asked her mother, "Mommie, do you have to get a shot to go to heaven?"

MRS. EARL CARTER in *Teach*

───o───

PRIMARY AGES

One of my seven-year-old twins came to me one day and said, "Daddy, when we sin we get smaller, don't we?" "No," I replied. "Why do you say that?" "Well," she exclaimed, "the Bible says, 'All have sinned and come short!'"

R. J., Norwalk, Calif.

───o───

"It's Sunday, Bobby. Don't play in the street. Go out and play in the back yard," his mother instructed.

"But, Mother, it's Sunday there, too," Bobby replied.

───o───

"Mommy, Mommy," called Richard half crying.

"What is it, dear?" Mother asked.

"I was just trying to whistle like Daddy," explained Richard, "and my teeth stepped on my tongue."

───o───

The Sunday school teacher asked the class to act out the Bible story they had just heard of Joseph's brothers selling him to an Egyptian merchant. This delighted the children, particularly one little boy who took the part of the merchant. Carefully he began to count out the money. "One . . . two . . . three . . . four . . . five . . . six . . . seven . . . Oh, this is so much work," the lad complained. "I'll just write out a check!"

MRS. BILL SMITH, Chattanooga, Tenn.

It was Promotion Sunday in our church. Wondering how much my primary class understood about this concept, I asked, "Who can tell me what special day this is?"

Without hesitation one bright-eyed youngster said, "I know! It's COM-MOTION SUNDAY!"

MRS. F. W. ROSEBURG in *Teach*

A third-grader's definition:

"A contraction is made by putting two words together to make one word. You leave out some of the letters, but you put in a catastrophe."

BETTY KOWALLIK in *NEA Journal*

When classes were dismissed for the day at Goodman Point School, a first-grader walked up to teacher, Mrs. Marie Story, tugged on her skirt, and said: "Mrs. Story, could you please tell me what I learned in school today? My daddy always wants to know."

Cortez, Colo. (AP)

Our seven-year-old daughter looks forward each evening to reading time when we all gather in the living room while Daddy reads. It was following family devotions after studying a series on the Gospel of John, that she asked Christ to be her Saviour.

While discussing the Bible story about Pilate's attempt to release Jesus, our 3½-year-old daughter said, "But they wanted the bunnies instead." Our first thought was that she had not been listening as we read the story, but her further comment that "they wanted the rabbits" revealed her interpretation of the name Barabbas.

MRS. JOHN R. COLOMBO
in *The Christian Parent*

A small boy in church with his mother heard the preacher talk on *What Is a Christian?* Every time he asked the question, the minister banged his fist on the pulpit.

"Mama, do you know?" the boy whispered to his mother.

"Yes, dear, now be quiet," she replied.

Finally, when the minister demanded once more, "What is a Christian?" and banged especially hard, the boy yelled, "Mama, tell 'im!"

GLENDA GOSS in *Together*

Immediately after opening exercises, Robin waved an urgent hand for attention. I called on her, and she asked, "What is a widget?"

In response to my obvious mystification, she explained: "You know, in the pledge we say, 'I pledge allegiance for widget stands . . .'"

BONNIE K. PEZZOPANE in *Grade Teacher*

JUNIOR AGES

Doctors had conferred with the parents of a ten-year-old boy suffering with an incurable disease. They agreed to explain the true situation to him. After this was done, the boy faced the doctors and asked, "How shall we break the news to my parents?"

The solar system was the subject and the teacher had permitted each pupil in her fourth grade to select his own topic about which to study and report to the rest of the class. Jim took "Pluto," Henry "Mars," but Walter selected "Earth," and his reason seemed most logical. Explained Walter, "It's the only planet I have visited."

Sunday School Teacher: "In what order do the Gospels come?"

Student: "One after the other."

A San Jose teacher suggested that her sixth graders stage a United Nations session. One of the first youngsters to volunteer to represent a nation was a boy who wanted to be Russia. When the session got underway, the "Russian" delegate promptly got up and walked out of the room.

FRANK FREEMAN
in San Jose, Calif., *Mercury*

———o———

The Sunday school teacher was telling the class about the Christian's armor. After speaking of the breastplate of righteousness and a shield of faith, she said, "And Paul also says we should carry a weapon, which he says is the Word of God. Do you remember what he called the Word of God?"

There was no answer so she added, "It's something very sharp, something that cuts."

Then one little fellow answered vigorously, "I know. I know. It's the axe of the Apostles!"

Baptist & Reflector

———o———

"If you had been living when Noah was building the ark, what would you have said about him if you had watched him?" the first grade Sunday School teacher asked her class. "Martha, do you want to tell us?"

"I would have said, 'Noah is a silly, foolish man!'" the little girl replied.

"Now," said the teacher, "pretend that I am Noah and tell me what you would say to me."

"No," objected Martha. "I don't know what I would say to you."

"But you just said it," the teacher reminded her.

"Yes, I know," Martha replied. "But I didn't say it to his face!"

———o———

Recently, our young son was listening to a broadcast of the Milwaukee Braves ball game which opened with the singing of the national anthem.

During the singing, he stood up very solemnly and, as the anthem came to a close, he sang, "And the homers of the Braves."

MRS. M. OTTERBEIN in *Coronet*

Asked if she could spell banana, a little girl said, "I know how to spell banana but I never know when to stop."

QUOTED BY CHARLES POORE
in *New York Times*

Choice

It's not a question of good or bad — but a choice of good or best.

———o———

The rich young ruler, in his famous interview with Christ,

Asked the *right* question,
Asked the *right* Person,
Received the *right* answer,
But made the *wrong* choice.

BILLY GRAHAM

———o———

It is not in life's chances but in its choices that happiness comes to the heart of the individual.

———o———

This Thing I Choose

Some folk enjoy talking about trouble,
and insults, and burdens, and pain;
They talk about losses and crosses,
but seldom of sunshine and gain.
Their troubles they list without number,
but blessings, if ever, are told;
No wonder they bog down in spirit,
and grow sad before they grow old.

Sure I could join them in sadness,
for sorrow has oft come to me;
I could tell all my blights and my blunders,
and heartache that folks cannot see.
But would this make our world any brighter?
Wouldn't I lend to its sorrow and care?
Why then scatter gloom in this dark world,
When God has sunbeams to spare?

No, I won't join the ranks of complainers,
for God's been too good to me;
I refuse to find fault with His leadings;
I refuse to weep on bitterly.

I want to be grateful and humble,
 and ever His sweet praises sing;
I want to enjoy every moment the
    victory
 that Christ came to bring!
                                    NAT OLSON
          in The Log of the Good Ship Grace

———o———

Three choices every young person
needs to make right: master, mission,
and mate.

———o———

Evangelist Billy Graham told an interesting story about a man who had
trouble with his eyes. In fact, he was
rapidly becoming blind.
The doctor advised that he have an
operation. So this was done. The man's
eyesight became normal, but his memory seemed affected. So the doctor
operated once more. The man's memory improved, but his eyesight failed.
Finally the perplexed doctor asked
his patient, "What do you choose —
your memory or your eyesight?"
After a moment of deep thought, the
man replied, "I choose my eyesight
because I would rather spend my life
looking ahead than remembering the
things that are past."

———o———

Make worthy choices but avoid taking foolish chances.

———o———

Where there is no choice, we do well
to make no difficulty.
                          GEORGE MACDONALD

———o———

If you are willing to choose the seeming darkness of faith instead of the
illumination of reason, wonderful light
will break out upon you from the
Word of God.
                        ADONIRAM J. GORDON

———o———

My Choice

*Written during his training days by Bill Mc-
Chesney, who became a missionary martyr in
the Congo, November 25, 1964*

I want my breakfast served at "eight,"
With ham and eggs upon the plate;

A well-broiled steak I'll eat at "one,"
And dine again when day is done.

I want an ultra modern home,
And in each room a telephone;
Soft carpets, too, upon the floors,
And pretty drapes to grace the doors.

A cozy place of lovely things,
Like easy chairs with innersprings,
And then I'll get a small TV —
Of course, "I'm careful what I see."

I want my wardrobe, too, to be
Of neatest, finest quality,
With latest style in suit and vest.
Why shouldn't Christians have the
   best?

But then the Master I can hear,
In no uncertain voice, so clear,
"I bid you come and follow Me,
The lowly Man of Galilee.

"Birds of the air have made their nest,
And foxes in their holes find rest;
But I can offer you no bed;
No place have I to lay My head."

In shame I hung my head and cried.
How could I spurn the Crucified?
Could I forget the way He went,
The sleepless nights in prayer He
   spent?

For forty days without a bite,
Alone He fasted day and night;
Despised, rejected — on He went,
And did not stop till veil He rent.

A Man of sorrows and of grief,
No earthly friend to bring relief —
"Smitten of God," the prophet said —
Mocked, beaten, bruised, His blood ran
   red.

If He be God and died for me,
No sacrifice too great can be
For me, a mortal man, to make;
I'll do it all for Jesus' sake.

Yes, I will tread the path He trod,
No other way will please my God;
So, henceforth, this my choice shall be,
My choice for all eternity.
              BILL MCCHESNEY, Power For Living

Christ

Christ is not valued at all — unless He is valued above all.

ST. AUGUSTINE

———o———

All that I had, He took; all that He has, He has given me in Jesus Christ!

SUBODH SAHU, "Evangelism and The Church" in *Commission, Conflict, Commitment*

———o———

Christ with me sleeping,
Christ with me waking,
Christ with me watching
Every day and night
Each day and night.

God with me protecting,
The Lord with me directing,
The Spirit with me strengthening
Forever and forevermore,
Ever and evermore. Amen.

Translated from the Gaelic

———o———

What the sunshine is to the flower, the Lord Jesus Christ is to my soul.

ALFRED, LORD TENNYSON

———o———

Christ never says He is a high delicacy, a rare luxury, a feast which the rich alone can afford. He says that He is Bread, He is Water, He is Light, He is the Door, He is the Shepherd. These words, so simple, stretch their meaning around the whole circle of human life.

Selected

———o———

The world doesn't want Christ, but it needs Him.

DR. EARLE STEVENS

———o———

John 14:6

I am the Way, the Truth, and the Life.
Without the Way, there is no going,
Without the Truth there is no knowing,
Without the Life there is no living.

———o———

My Saviour

There is no time too busy for His leisure,
There is no task too hard for Him to share.
There is no soul too lowly for His notice,
There is no need to trifling for His care.
There is no place too humble for His presence,
There is no pain His bosom cannot feel.
There is no sorrow that He cannot comfort,
There is no sickness that He cannot heal.

From *The Banner* — Bethany Presbyterian Church, Fort Lauderdale, Florida

———o———

Our Wonderful Lord

Whatever Christ touched was transformed by His love
The manger, the cross and the tomb.
The Light of the World turned sin's night into day,
And death has been shorn of its gloom.

The multitudes fed of the bread from His hand;
The lame leaped for joy at His word;
The blind saw His beauty, and shouted His praise;
The leper was healed by the Lord.

One wonderful day His great love touched my heart,
And then by His mercy and grace
The darkness all fled as His love-light shone in,
Transformed by His tender embrace.

Then let us speak forth the glad tidings anew,
And words of salvation proclaim;
For still He is mighty to save and to keep
Through faith in His marvelous Name.

ALBERT SIMPSON REITZ

———o———

Excellency Of Christ

He is a path, if any be misled;
He is a robe, if any naked be;
If any chance to hunger, he is bread;
If any be a bondman, he is free;
If any be but weak, how strong is he!
To dead men life is he, to sick men, health;

To blind men, sight, and to the
needy, wealth;
A pleasure without loss, a treasure
without stealth.
                        GILES FLETCHER

————o————

Christ has outlived the empire which
crucified Him nineteen centuries ago.
He will outlast the dictators who defy
Him now.
                    RALPH W. SOCKMAN

————o————

If Jesus Christ is a man —
And only a man — I say,
That of all mankind I will cleave to
Him,
And to Him will I cleave alway.

If Jesus Christ is God —
And the only God — I swear,
I will follow Him through heaven and
hell,
The earth, the sea and the air!
            RICHARD WATSON GILDER,
                    The Song of a Heathen

————o————

Jesus Christ is a FRIEND of sinners;
but a COMPANION only of the godly.

————o————

We know what God is like because
we know the character of Jesus Christ.
                        GEORGE HODGES

————o————

Jesus was not a man of remarkable
spiritual powers with big and ambitious
ideas. He was a man under orders.
His unique vocation was to establish
the Kingdom of God.
                        W. R. FORRESTER

————o————

There is a reward for the obedient
disciple, there are power and authority
for the faithful disciple, there is glory
of achievement for the zealous disciple;
but there is the whisper of his love, the
joy of his presence, and the shining
of his face, for those who love Jesus
for himself alone.
                    SUSAN B. STRACHAN

Christ's Birth
(See also Christmas)

Fingers
Newborn petal-pink fingers destined to
Tangle Mary's hair.

Clasp a magi's thumb,
Handle saw and plane,
Explore the Law and the Prophets,

Beckon to fishermen,
Cleanse and heal,
Wash a sinner's feet,
Dangle from a gibbet,
Break bread at Emmaus!
                        WANDA MILNER

————o————

Sadhu Sundar Singh used to illustrate
the incarnation mystery in this way.
A simple countryman was being shown
a red glass bottle full of milk. They
asked him what was in the bottle.
"Wine? Brandy? Whiskey?" he replied, questioningly. He could not believe it was filled with milk till he saw
the milk poured out from it. The red-
ness of the bottle hid the color of the
milk.
So, he said, it was and is with our
Lord's humanity. Man saw Him tired,
hungry, suffering, weeping, and thought
He was only man. "He was made in
the likeness of men," yet He ever is
"God over all, blessed for ever."

————o————

The whole question of the virgin
birth of Jesus need not afflict the average man. If Jesus is unique, unlike
any other person, it is not illogical to
believe that his birth was unique.
                    WILLIAM LYON PHELPS

————o————

If Christ Had Not Been Born. . .

Suppose that Christ had not been born
That far away Judean morn.
Suppose that God, Whose mighty hand
Created worlds, had never planned
A way for man to be redeemed.
Suppose the wise men only dreamed
That guiding star whose light still glows
Down through the centuries. Suppose
Christ never walked here in men's
sight,
Our blessed Way, and Truth, and
Light.

Suppose He counted all the cost,
And never cared that we were lost,
And never died for you and me,
Nor shed His blood on Calvary

Upon a shameful cross. Suppose
That having died, He never rose,
And there was none with power to save
Our souls from death beyond the grave!
Oh, far away Judean morn —
Suppose that Christ had not been born!

But praise His name, the Christ was
born
That far away Judean morn —
Beloved of our Father God, Whose
mighty hand
Created worlds; and while they stand,
Redemption's door is open still
Through Him proclaimed on Judah's
hill!
The guiding star leads to Him now
And we may in the presence bow
Of Him who walked here in men's
sight
Our blessed Way, and Truth, and
Light.

He never stopped to count the cost,
Oh, how He loved His sheep — the
lost!
Christ gave His life for you and me
And shed His blood on Calvary,
Upon a shameful cross. But none
Could overcome God's only Son! —
Assurance of His power to save
Our souls from death beyond the grave.
O far away Judean morn —
We praise Him in the manger born!
MARTHA SNELL and MARY R. KEFFER

---o---

Lamb Of God

We think it strange the Son of God
Should in a manger lie;
His room, a stable floored with sod,
And animals close by.

We think it strange; we sigh and
mourn.
A stable seems so odd.
But where else should a lamb be born?
Behold the Lamb of God!
BESS A. OLSON

Christ's Death

As A Lamb

As a Lamb to the slaughter my Saviour
was led,
With the thorns in His heart, and the
thorns on His head.

By His stripes I am healed, by His
death I now live,
And He died that my sins He might
fully forgive.

In the Garden of Sorrows He suffered
for me,
In the cold judgment hall He was sentenced for me,
In the midst of the mob He was nailed
to the tree
And in love He was willing to die there,
for me.

In this wonderful Saviour no fault
could be found,
But through envy they led Him to
Calvary's mound
"O forgive them" He cried, ere in an-
guish He died,
And He loved to the end, my dear
Lord crucified.

Oh, how can I repay Thee, my Saviour
divine.
All I am and I have shall forever be
Thine.
I will give Thee my life, I will give
Thee my love,
And forever I'll praise Thee in man-
sions above.
ALBERT SIMPSON REITZ

---o---

The biggest fact about Joseph's tomb
is that it wasn't a tomb at all, it was
a room for a transient. Jesus just
stopped there a night or two on his
way back to glory.
HERBERT BOOTH SMITH

Christ's Return

The King Is Coming . . .

The skies are growing darker,
With the passing of the years,
And life becomes more restless,
And on every hand are fears:
Men know not what is coming,
Yet feel something lies ahead,
Which fills them with foreboding
And a solemn sense of dread.

But Christians we are waiting
For the breaking of the day:
We are certain Christ is coming —
He may now be on the way.

Deeper still will grow earth's dark-
ness —
Still more awesome grow its night,
But for Christ our eyes are looking,
Quick may come the Rapture bright.
Doorstep Evangel

———o———

Looking

There are two ways of looking at the
Lord's coming: a looking *for* it and a
looking *at* it. It is possible to look at it
with keen intellect and profound interest, and yet have it mean nothing to
us personally. It is also possible to
know but little of the theology of the
subject, and yet have a deep and holy
longing for our Lord to appear. May
this theme be not only our study but
also our personal hope; for "unto them
that look for him shall he appear a
second time without sin unto salvation."
A. B. SIMPSON

———o———

What Would He Say?

If He should come today
And find my hands so full
Of future plans, however fair,
In which my Saviour had no share,
What would He say?

If He should come today
And find I had not told
One soul about my heavenly Friend
Whose blessings all my way attend,
What would He say?

If He should come today,
Would I be glad, quite glad?
Remembering He had died for all,
And none through me had heard His
call,
What would He say?
AUTHOR UNKNOWN

———o———

Are You Ready?

The Scriptures give constant testimony to the fact that our Lord Jesus
Christ will come again. If you take
your Bible and read through from the
beginning you will be amazed at the
reiterated truth of the Second Advent.
If we were to take out of the Bible

every reference to the second coming
of the Lord we would have a terribly
mutilated Book! This is no "pet theory"
accepted by a few "cranks"; it is a
major doctrine of the Word of God. It
has been said by scholars that the
second coming of Christ is mentioned
no less than 1,200 times in the Old
Testament and 300 times in the New
Testament. If we read our Bible and
believe our Bible we cannot do other
than be certain that our Saviour is coming again. The fact of His return is
clearly and emphatically stated, in
prediction, type, parable and promise.
REV. FRANCIS W. DIXON

———o———

He Is Coming Again

I stood one day on a busy street
And watched the restless throng.
And heard the tramp of countless feet,
As they hurriedly marched along.
All bent on pleasure; no thought of
care,
The rich, the poor all were there;
Making the most of the time at hand,
But starving their souls in a bounte-
ous land.
And I thought of the Master, as He
wept to see
The thoughtless crowd at Galilee.
I thought of the awful price He paid
When all of our sins on Him were
laid.
How He bore the cross — endured the
pain:
We know He's coming back again.
What a wondrous morning that will be
When all of His glory we shall see.
We'll reign with Him a thousand years;
No more heartaches, no more tears,
No more sorrow, grief or pain
When Jesus comes to earth again.
W. A. BARNES

———o———

A Wonderful Day

Glorious day when we stand in His
presence,
All of our heartaches and sorrows are
past,
No more burdens too heavy to carry —
We shall see Jesus at last!

Wonderful day when we shall be like
Him,
  Features were marred by sin here
    below,
Now they are radiant, beautiful, glori-
    ous!
  Cleansed by His blood, made whiter
    than snow.

Marvelous day, all suffering ended,
  Glorious bodies now, like to His own;
We will be kings and priests in God's
    kingdom,
  With glory and honor around the
    white throne.

Radiant day — the day of His crown-
    ing —
  The thought of this day is immea-
    surably sweet;
Then we will stand transformed in His
    likeness,
  Casting our trophies and crowns at
    His feet.

Victorious day — the day of the Rap-
    ture,
  The Lamb who was slain is now be-
    come King!
The Bride of the Lamb in garments all
    glorious
  Is singing sweet songs the Bride only
    can sing.

Triumphant day — great day of His
    power!
  All the kingdoms of earth will crum-
    ble and fall;
The saints of all ages in garments of
    splendor
  Are crowning Him King to rule over
    all!

A. H. DIXON

Christian

As burning candles give light until
they be consumed, so likewise godly
Christians must be occupied in doing
good so long as they shall live.

CAWDRAY

A Christian's Relationships:

Get right with God;
Get together with other Christians;
Get going for others.

SAMUEL M. SHOEMAKER

It doesn't take much of a man to be
a Christian . . . it takes all of him.

DAWSON TROTMAN

If every Christian in your church
were the kind of Christian that you
are, what kind of a church would your
church be?

A visitor asked an old bedridden
woman who said she was trying to be
a Christian: "Are you trying to be Mrs.
Whyte?"
"No, I am Mrs. Whyte."
"How long have you been Mrs.
Whyte?"
"Ever since this ring was put on my
finger."
"That is how it is with me. I do not
try to be a Christian. I have been one
ever since I put out my empty hand
and received Christ as my Saviour."

The Prairie Overcomer

What is a Christian put into the
world for, except to do the impossible
in the strength of the Lord?

GENERAL S. C. ARMSTRONG

It has been said that a Christian is
one who believes what Christ believes,
hates what Christ hates, and loves what
Christ loves.

Christians are like the first half of a
round trip ticket — not good if de-
tached.

ROBERT E. SPEER

Some Christians are like porcupines.
They have many fine points but it's
hard to get next to them.

VANCE HAVNER

Many Christians are like the man
who bought a book on reducing exercises and lies down to read it.

A Christian should be a striking likeness of Jesus Christ. You have read
lives of Christ, beautifully written; but
the best life of Christ is His living

biography, written out in the words and action of His people.

CHARLES HADDON SPURGEON

———o———

Three Pictures

A believer may see three pictures of himself in God's Word — what he was, what he is, and what he shall be. As to his former condition, he reads in Ephesians 2:12: "That at that time ye were without Christ, being aliens from the commonwealth of Israel, and strangers from the covenants of promise, having no hope, and without God in the world." As to his present position, he reads in I John 3:2: "Beloved, now are we the sons of God." As to his future glory, he reads in the same verse: "It doth not yet appear what we shall be: but we know that . . . we shall be like Him."

F. J. HORSEFIELD

———o———

The true Christian is marked by his selflessness.

RODGER GOODMAN

———o———

Only a great Christian can be a great Biblical scholar.

KENNETH SCOTT LATOURETTE

———o———

A Christian is someone to whom God entrusts all his fellow men.

DWIGHT L. MOODY

———o———

If a man cannot be a Christian in the place where he is, he cannot be a Christian anywhere.

HENRY WARD BEECHER

———o———

This cold world needs warm-hearted Christians.

———o———

Some Christians crawl into a spiritual bomb shelter and sing, "Safe am I."

———o———

When a Christian is in the wrong place, his right place is empty.

T. J. BACH

A true and faithful Christian does not make holy living a mere incidental thing. It is his great concern. As the business of the soldier is to fight, so the business of the Christian is to be like Christ.

JONATHAN EDWARDS

———o———

These Christians love each other even before they are acquainted!

CELUS, Roman anti-Christian philosopher, 3rd Century A.D.

———o———

Christians and camels receive their burdens kneeling.

AMBROSE BIERCE

———o———

Christians are in the world to do the things that unbelievers say cannot be done!

———o———

One can be a Confucianist without knowing Confucius. One can be a Mohammedan without knowing Mohammed. One can be a Buddhist without knowing Buddha. But one cannot be a Christian without knowing Christ.

CARL ARMERDING

———o———

Without Christ I was like a fish out of water. With Christ I am in the ocean of love.

SADHU SUNDAR SINGH

Christian Education

The Psalm Of The Good Teacher

The Lord is my teacher,
I shall not lose the way.
He leadeth me in the lowly path of learning,
He prepareth a lesson for me every day;
He bringeth me to the clear fountains of instruction,
Little by little he showeth me the beauty of truth.

The world is a great book that he hath written,
He turneth the leaves for me slowly;
They are all inscribed with images and letters,

He poureth light on the pictures and the words.

He taketh me by the hand to the hill-top of vision,
And my soul is glad when I perceive his meaning;
In the valley also he walketh beside me,
In the dark places he whispereth to my heart.

Even though my lesson be hard it is not hopeless,
For the Lord is patient with his slow scholar;
He will wait awhile for my weakness,
And help me to read the truth through tears.

HENRY VAN DYKE

Pod Of Christian Peas

The goal and aim of every Sunday School board can be summed up in this group of Christian P's.
CHRISTIAN Planning.
CHRISTIAN Praying.
CHRISTIAN Playing.
CHRISTIAN Purpose.

In *P.A.S.S.*

To help the individual develop into an ever better Christian in all of life's relationships is an aim of Christian education.

Christian Living

Do not strive to make yourself holy by working, but by believing, by living out of yourselves, entirely on the strength of Christ; the believer's life is a life hid with Christ in God.

The Weaver

My life is but a weaving
  Between my Lord and me,
I cannot choose the colors
  He worketh steadily.

Ofttimes He weaveth sorrow,
  And I in foolish pride
Forget He sees the upper
  And I, the underside.

Not till the loom is silent
  And the shuttles cease to fly
Shall God unroll the canvas
  And explain the reason why.

The dark threads are as needful
  In the Weaver's skillful hand
As the threads of gold and silver
  In the pattern He has planned.

AUTHOR UNKNOWN

The Christian life is like an airplane; when you stop, you drop.

The argument for the risen Christ is the living Christian.

WINIFRED KIRKLAND

Christian love is a road sign to the lost.

HAROLD G. SARLES

The Way of the Cross is not a free-way: the toll is heavy.

RALPH BREWER

Christian ABC's

Act instead of Argue
Build instead of Brag
Climb instead of Criticize
Dig instead of Deprecate
Encourage instead of Envy
Fight instead of Faint
Give instead of Grumble
Help instead of Harm
Invite instead of Ignore
Join instead of Jeer
Kneel instead of Kick
Love instead of Lampoon
Move instead of Mould
Nurture instead of Neglect
Obey instead of Obstruct
Pray instead of Pout
Quicken instead of Quit
Rescue instead of Ridicule
Shout instead of Shrink
Try instead of Tremble
Undergird instead of Undermine
Vindicate instead of Vilify
Witness instead of Wilt

Exterminate instead of Excuse
Yield instead of Yell
Zip instead of Zigzag.

ALVY E. FORD

———o———

One advantage of traveling the straight and narrow is that no one is trying to pass you.

Clarion-Ledger, Jackson, Mississippi

———o———

The straight and narrow way seems to have no detours nor places to park, and the folk who travel it are supposed to keep going right on to its end.

———o———

I grew up in the generation of the giants — John R. Mott and his disciples — among whom it was taken for granted that if you were going to live the Christian life at all, you would give at least one hour daily, before the first meal of the day, to seeking God through his Word and to listening to his voice.

BISHOP STEPHEN NEILL

———o———

If you do not feel as close to God as you once did, make no mistake about which one of you has moved.

———o———

In religion, as in every other profession, practicing is the great thing. Lawyers practice law, doctors practice medicine, and ministers must practice what they preach. So, too, Christians must practice their religion.

JACOBUS

———o———

Serving Christ is not overwork but overflow.

CURTIS B. AKENSON

———o———

Keep your lamp burning, and let God place it where He will.

———o———

An old story always worth a chuckle is the story of the little girl who stood before her mother one day, the picture of guilt and dejection.

"Mother," she began, "you know the priceless vase that has been handed down in our family from one generation to another? Well, this generation just dropped it!"

But the story ceases to be funny when one realizes that in many families the Christian religion is suffering the fate of that priceless vase.

As a Christian, you owe it to yourself and God to be an evangelist for Christ. Invite people to come to church. Be a witness. Express your faith. Evangelism is the calling of your faith.

Evangelism Committee

———o———

God doesn't need lawyers, He needs witnesses.

J. STEWART HOLDEN

———o———

A Christian worker is a physician of souls.

———o———

The Mind Of Christ In Me

May the mind of Christ our Saviour,
    Live in me from day to day,
By His love and power controlling
    All I do and say.

May the Word of God dwell richly
    In my heart from hour to hour,
So that all may see I triumph
    Only through His power.

May the peace of God my Father
    Rule my life in everything,
That I may be calm to comfort
    Sick and sorrowing.

May the love of Jesus fill me,
    As the waters fill the sea,
Him exalting, self abasing,
    This is victory.

May I run the race before me,
    Strong and brave to face the foe,
Looking only unto Jesus
    As I onward go.

May His beauty rest upon me
    As I seek the lost to win,
And may they forget the channel,
    Seeing only Him.

KATE B. WILKINSON

Christianity

According to Wilberforce, the great English preacher, Christianity can be condensed into four words — admit, submit, commit, transmit.

———o———

Christianity has not been tried and found wanting; it has been found difficult and *not* tried.

GILBERT KEITH CHESTERTON

———o———

Christianity is not a human speculation about God, it is a divine revelation to man.

———o———

Christianity demands the homage of the intellect, that the truth be believed; it also requires the homage of the heart, that truth be felt; and of the life, that truth be obeyed.

CLIFF COLE

———o———

Christianity is like the seafaring life — a smooth sea never made a good sailor.

———o———

The primary declaration of Christianity is not "This do!" but "This happened!"

EVELYN UNDERHILL

———o———

What reality is there in your Christianity if you look at men struggling in darkness and you are content to congratulate yourselves that you are in the light?

FREDERICK WILLIAM ROBERTSON

———o———

The greatest proof of Christianity for others, is not how far a man can logically analyze his reasons for believing, but how far in practice he will stake his life on his belief.

T. S. ELIOT

———o———

Is your Christianity ancient history or current events?

SAMUEL M. SHOEMAKER

———o———

Christianity begins where conventionality leaves off; it turns the other cheek, goes the second mile, does more than the expected, and learns what it is to sacrifice.

———o———

The world is equally shocked at hearing Christianity criticized and seeing it practiced.

D. ELTON TRUEBLOOD

———o———

There are no crown-wearers in heaven who were not cross-bearers here below.

CHARLES HADDON SPURGEON

———o———

When Christianity assumes an aggressive attitude, the first result is a great exhibition of Satanic power.

GEORGE BOWEN,
American missionary to India

———o———

A Christianity which does not prove its worth in practice degenerates into dry scholasticism and idle talk.

ABRAHAM KUYPER

———o———

Columbus discovered America. Yes, but what did he find out about its rivers, lakes, and plains? Just so with one who "discovers" Christianity. Wait till you explore!

———o———

Christianity is either relevant all the time or useless anytime. It is not just a phase of life; it is life itself.

RICHARD C. HALVERSON

———o———

He who shall introduce into public affairs the principles of primitive Christianity will change the face of the world.

BENJAMIN FRANKLIN

———o———

My understanding of Christianity is God in search of lost men, not men in search of a lost God.

RONALD R. HATCH
in a letter to *Time Magazine*

———o———

It is not Christianity that is failing, but Christians who fail to do their task.

JAMES BOLARIN

Some people use Christianity like a bus; they ride on it only when it is going their way.

———o———

Too many of us have been inoculated with small doses of Christianity — which keep us from catching the real thing.

LESLIE D. WEATHERHEAD

———o———

The world does not doubt Christianity as much as it does Christians.

Christmas

Christmas Meditation

I wonder — if Christ were here today
In person, as we are, face to face —
Could I place in His hand this offering,
And say, "It is all I have to bring
To spread the work of redeeming grace"?
Watching our gifts of thankfulness,
Could I make this offering honestly,
With His loving eyes fixed full on me,
And feel it was something He could bless?
I wonder! *For Christ is here* today
And no heart motive is hid from Him.
Can it be that He finds me hesitate
To sacrifice for a cause so great?
It was worth a Cross to Him!

Selected

———o———

A little boy in a Christmas program had but one sentence to say, "Behold, I bring you good tidings." After the rehearsal he asked his mother what tidings meant, and she told him it meant "news." When the program was put on, he was stage-struck and forgot his line. Finally the idea came back to him and he cried out, "Hey, I got news for you!"

———o———

God's Gift

He did not use a silvery box,
  Or paper green and red;
God laid His Christmas gift to men
  Within a manger bed.

No silken cord was used to bind
  The gift sent from above.

'Twas wrapped in swaddling clothes and bound
  In cords of tender love.

There was no evergreen to which
  His precious gift was tied:
Upon a bare tree on a hill
  His gift was hung . . . and died.

'Twas taken down from off the tree
  And laid beneath the sod,
But death itself could not destroy
  The precious gift of God.

With mighty hand He lifted it
  From out the stony grave;
Forevermore to every man
  A living gift He gave.

RUTH PRENTICE
in *The Log of the Good Ship Grace*

———o———

Christmas in the Heart

It's Christmastime throughout the land
And trees are white with silver snow,
Come, let us take each other's hand
And wander back to long ago.
The wind is cold, the air is clean,
The church bells chime for all to hear.
What loveliness stands in between
Our hearts and God, this time of year!

What happy faces do we see,
Their cares forgotten every one,
This is the way it ought to be
From dawn until the set of sun.
These blessed days of joy and peace,
Bedecked with wonder, set apart,
Through all our years will never cease,
If we keep Christmas . . . in our heart!

GRACE E. EASLEY

———o———

To see his star is good, but to see his face is better.

DWIGHT L. MOODY

———o———

Return of Christmas

The happy Christmas comes once more,
The heavenly Guest is at the door;
The blessed words the shepherds thrill,
The joyous tidings: Peace, good-will!

To David's city let us fly,
Where angels sing beneath the sky;
Through plain and village pressing near,

And news from God which shepherds
hear.

Oh, let us go with quiet mind,
The gentle Babe with shepherds find,
To gaze on Him who gladdens them,
The loveliest Flower of Jesse's stem!

The lowly Saviour meekly lies,
Laid off the splendour of the skies;
No crown bedecks His forehead fair;
No pearl or gem or silk is there.

No human glory, might, and gold,
The lovely infant's form enfold;
The manger and the swaddlings poor
Are His whom angels' songs adore.

Oh, wake our hearts, in gladness sing!
And keep our Christmas with our King,
Till living song, from loving souls,
Like sound of mighty waters rolls.

O Holy Child! Thy manger streams,
Till earth and heaven glow with its
beams,
Till midnight noon's broad light has
won,
And Jacob's Star outshines the sun.

Thou, patriarchs' joy, Thou, prophets'
song,
Thou, heavenly Day-spring, looked for
long,
Thou, Son of man, Incarnate Word,
Great David's Son, great David's Lord!

Come, Jesus, glorious, heavenly Guest,
Keep Thine own Christmas in our
breast!
Then David's harp strings, hushed so
long,
Shall swell our jubilee of song.
                    CHARLES P. KRAUTH
            (Translated from the Danish)

————o————

This old Christmas greeting from a
letter written between 1387-1455 by
Giovanni da Fiesole (Fra Angelico):

I salute you. I am your friend, and
my love for you goes deep. There is
nothing I can give you which you have
not already; but there is much, very
much, which though I cannot give it,
you can take. No heaven can come to
us unless our hearts find rest in today.
Take heaven. No peace lies in the
future which is not hidden in this
precious little instant. Take peace.
The gloom of the world is but a shadow. Behind it, yet within our reach, is
joy. There is radiance and courage in
the darkness could we but see it; and
to see, we have only to look. Life is so
generous a giver, but we, 'judging its
gifts by their coverings, cast them away
as ugly or heavy or hard. Remove the
covering, and you will find beneath it a
living splendor, woven of love, and
wisdom, and power. Welcome it, greet
it, and you touch the angel's hand that
brings it.

Everything we call a trial, a sorrow,
a duty, believe me, that angel's hand
is there, the gift is there, and the wonder of an overshadowing Presence. Our
joys, too, be not content with them as
joys. They, too, conceal diviner gifts.
Life is so full of meaning and purpose,
so full of beauty beneath its covering,
that you will find earth but cloaks your
heaven. Courage, then, to claim it, that
is all! But courage you have, and the
knowledge that we are pilgrims wend-
ing through unknown country our way
home.

And so, at this Christmas time, I
greet you, not quite as the world sends
greeting, but with profound esteem
now and forever.

The day breaks and the shadows
flee away.

————o————

A little child . . .
A shining star,
A stable rude . . .
The door ajar.
Yet in that place . . .
So crude, forlorn,
The Hope of all . . .
The world was born.
                    AUTHOR UNKNOWN

————o————

A Square, Honest Look

The people were being heavily taxed,
and faced every prospect of a sharp
increase to cover expanding military
expenses.

The threat of world domination by
a cruel, ungodly, power-intoxicated

band of men was ever just below the threshold of consciousness.

Moral deterioration had corrupted the upper levels of society and was moving rapidly into the broad base of the populace.

Peace propaganda was heard everywhere in the midst of preparations for war.

The latest rulers were covering the landscape with their statues and images, invoking a subtle form of state-worship.

Intense nationalistic feeling was clashing openly with new and sinister forms of imperialism.

Conformity was the spirit of the age.

Government handouts were being used with increasing lavishness to keep the population from rising up and throwing out the leaders.

Interest rates were spiraling upward in the midst of an inflated economy.

External religious observance was considered a political asset.

An abnormal emphasis was being placed upon sports and athletic competitions.

Social life centered around the banquet and the pool.

Racial tension was at the breaking point.

In such a time and amid such a people, a child was born to a migrant couple who had just signed up for a fresh round of taxation, and who were soon to become political exiles.

The child was called, among other things, the Prince of Peace.

When he had grown up and had entered upon his ministry, he said, "Peace I leave with you, my peace I give unto you . . . Let not your heart be troubled, neither let it be afraid."

SHERWOOD E. WIRT in *Decision Magazine*

———o———

Too often the Christmas bells with the merriest jingle are on the cash register.

———o———

"When Christmas is over," said a merchant to a minister, "it's over, and it's our job to rid this store completely of Christmas in a day."

"Well," said the minister, "I've a bigger job — to keep Christmas in the hearts of my people for a lifetime."

———o———

A little slum lad, whose parents were dead, was left in charge of a drunken woman, who beat and half-starved him.

The greatest delight in his life was to gaze at the beautiful Christmas toys in the shop windows. He knew, however, that these toys were not for him, for there was ever the glass between.

One day the little fellow was run over and taken to a hospital. About a week having passed, to his surprise he saw other children playing with toys they had received for Christmas.

Soon he himself sat up in bed when, wonder of wonders, on the bed were a number of toys for him.

Hardly able to believe his eyes, he stretched out his hand, and said, "There's no glass between!"

It is only sin that can come between us and Jesus, God's loving gift to the world. But sin can be removed through Christ's atoning blood, so that nothing may be between.

Defender

———o———

Lost Christmas

Why wait till Christmas time again is here?
Why spend those precious hours in hectic ways
Doing the things that you could do all year
And let the noise of whirl of festival days
Drown out the angels' song? Why not take time
To lift the eyes to candles in the sky;
To walk some silent night, while carols chime
And hear the hush of wings brush softly by?
Take time to meditate: to catch the spell
Of childish trust, that simple faith you knew
When love was everywhere, and all was well . . .
The gift you lost may now come back to you.

Seek not for Christmas in the busy mart
But cradled somewhere in a trusting heart.

RACHEL VAN CREME

———o———

Christmas-Time

I am the spirit of Christmas-time, when all should gladness be.
I am the light that you see shining upon each Christmas tree.
I am the thought that brings each gift from ones we hold so dear.
I am the good that permeates the world with Christmas cheer.
I am the joy that brightens homes and guides our thoughts above.
All heaven and earth rejoice in me, for I am known as Love.

LEBARON SHARP

———o———

The miracle of Christmas — that a baby can be so decisive.

———o———

There is love at Christmas because Christmas was born of love. Let us, each one, keep alive this spirit of love and glorify God.

JOSEPHA EMMS

———o———

The Christmas List

Give a gift of laughter,
Give a gift of song,
Give a gift of sympathy
To last a whole life long.
Give a cheerful message,
Give a helping hand,
Tell your sorry neighbor
That you understand!
Give a newsy letter
To a far-off friend;
Give a garden flower
With the book you lend.
Wash the supper dishes,
Help to dust the room;
Give a smile to leaven
Someone's hour of gloom!
Give a gift of sharing,
Give a gift of hope;
Light faith's gleaming candle
For the ones who grope
Slowly through the shadows.

Sweeten dreary days
For the lost and lonely.
Give yourself, ALWAYS!

MARGARET E. SANGSTER

———o———

Carol and Tommy were helping put up Christmas decorations. The conversation went like this:

"I like Christmas time — especially Christmas Day," said Tommy thoughtfully. "There's so much to think about. I wish I had been born on Christmas Day, like Jesus was."

Carol's answer was emphatic: "Jesus wasn't born on Christmas Day! He was born on a regular day. But it became Christmas because he was born that day. Before then it wasn't Christmas at all. Now it's Christmas everywhere! Don't you see? He makes it Christmas!"

"But it isn't Christmas everywhere," Tommy disagreed. "Some places don't have Christmas. Can you imagine a place without Christmas?"

"It can be Christmas even if places don't have it," Carol reasoned. "People can have Christmas. When Jesus lives in your heart he makes it Christmas!"

———o———

After Christmas

She needed pots and a new floor broom
And window shades for the children's room;
Her sheets were down to a threadbare three
And her table cloths were a sight to see.
She wanted scarfs and a towel rack
And a good, plain, useful dressing sack,
Some kitchen spoons and a box for bread,
A pair of scissors and sewing thread.
She hoped some practical friend would stop
And figure out that she'd like a mop,
Or a bathroom rug or a lacquered tray
Or a few plain plates for every day.
She hoped and hoped and she wished a lot,
But these, of course, were the things she got:
A cut glass vase and a bonbonniere,

A china thing for receiving hair,
Some oyster forks, a manicure set,
A chafing dish and a cellaret.
A boudoir cap and a drawn-work mat,
And a sterling this and a sterling that;
A gilt-edge book on a lofty theme,
And fancy bags till she longed to scream;
Some curious tongs and a powder puff,
And a bunch of other useless stuff.
And though she inwardly raged, she wrote
To all her friends the self-same note.
And said to all of her generous host —
"Just how did you guess what I needed most?"

ELLA BENTLEY ARTHUR

Church
(Attendance, Membership, etc.)

The holiest moment of the church service is the moment when God's people — strengthened by preaching and sacrament — go out of the church door into the world to be the Church. We don't go to church; we are the Church.

CANON ERNEST SOUTHCOTT

———o———

The church which neglects the children will have children who neglect the church.

———o———

What shall it profit a church if it go round the world to make converts and lose its own sons and daughters?

———o———

A church is a hospital for sinners, not a museum for saints.

ABIGAIL VAN BUREN, McNaught Syndicate

———o———

A Little Poem

The members sleep a little late,
They go to Church a little late,
Then they'll chew their gum a little,
Joke a little, doodle a little.
Brethren in class argue a little,
Commune a little, give a little,
After dismissal they gossip a little,
Go home and forget what little they heard,
And act like they cared but little,
For the greatest, holiest and most
Precious institution on earth —
The Church of the Lord Jesus Christ.
I may have exaggerated a little,
But very little, and I think in some cases have omitted a little.
Brethren, will you think on this a little?

SOURCE UNKNOWN

———o———

The Church's preoccupation must be Christ. Jesus did not say, "I will build your Church; or you will build my Church." He said, "I will build my Church."

ARTHUR F. FOGARTIE in Presbyterian Journal

———o———

Three ministers who served churches near railroad tracks were exchanging troubles.

"Our first Sunday morning hymn is always interrupted by the C & O when it rumbles past the window," the first complained.

"That's nothing," replied the second minister. "Right in the middle of our prayer the L & N drowns me out."

"Brothers," lamented the third, "I wish all I had was your troubles. Everytime the deacons in my church take up collections, I look down the aisle and there comes the Nickel Plate!"

BERNICE SNELL in Together

———o———

Two things ruin a church: loose living and tight giving.

NAT OLSON

———o———

The church's business is not to catch the spirit of the age but to correct it.

———o———

When our daughter was four, she went to church for the first time with her grandma. On her return her father asked her what the minister's sermon was about.

"I don't know, Daddy. He didn't say."

MRS. RANDALL NEAL in Together

The purpose of going to church is not to show that we are better than others but to bring out the best in ourselves.

———o———

The Thief

"Yes, sir, I'm saved and going to heaven," a man told the minister.

Surprised, the minister replied, "Why that's fine. Have you ever united with a church?"

"No. The dying thief didn't and he went to heaven."

"Have you ever partaken of the Lord's Supper?"

"No. The dying thief didn't and Christ accepted him."

"Have you ever given to missions?"

"No. But the dying thief didn't either."

"Well, my friend," the minister replied, "the difference I see between you and the dying thief — is that you are a *living* one!"

C. H. KILMER

———o———

When I see the same fellows ushering year after year in a church I wonder if folks don't think it's short on man power. Perhaps they don't know that one of nature's good masterpieces is a good usher.

———o———

The church is not a gallery for the exhibition of eminent Christians, but a school for the education of imperfect ones, a nursery for the care of weak ones, a hospital for the healing of those who need special care.

HENRY WARD BEECHER

———o———

When you take opportunity to criticize the church and tell how you stay away from its services because of imperfect members, did you ever think how lonely you'd be in a perfect church?

———o———

Two reasons why churches do not do something:
1. They've never tried it before.
2. They've tried it and "it won't work."

It Isn't The Church, It's You!

If you want to have the kind of a Church
Like the kind of the Church you like,
You needn't slip your clothes in a grip
And start on a long, long hike.
You'll only find what you left behind,
For there's nothing really new.
It's a knock at yourself when you knock at your Church;
It isn't the Church — it's you!

When everything seems to be going wrong,
And trouble seems everywhere brewing;
When prayer meeting, young people's meeting, and all,
Seem simmering slowly stewing,
Just take a look at yourself and say,
"What's the use of being blue?"
Are you doing your "bit" to make things "hit"?
It isn't the Church — it's you!

It's really strange sometimes, don't you know,
That things go as well as they do,
When we think of the little — the very small mite —
We add to the work of the few.
We sit, and stand round, and complain of what's done,
And do very little but fuss!
Are we bearing our share of the burdens to bear?
It isn't the Church — it's us!

AUTHOR UNKNOWN

———o———

Skyscraper Church

As noon approaches every day,
Chimes from the church across the way
Rise over the city's busy din
And climb to where the clouds begin.
Here in my office in the sky,
Old hymns plead their way in and vie
With my insistent clicking keys
That type their brisk monotonies.
"Dear Sirs: We have received your bill,
And when the merchandise is stored,"
"Faith of our fathers living still,
In spite of dungeon, fire and sword."
"We are indeed surprised to know
That you will never guarantee,"

"Oh, love that will not let me go,
I rest my weary soul in thee."
They make a very strange duet,
The typewriter and the chimes, and yet
I wonder why it should seem odd
To mix up offices and God!
                                AUTHOR UNKNOWN

———o———

The church must either send or end.

———o———

On Church bulletin board:

"You aren't too bad to come in.
You aren't too good to stay out."

———o———

Many people find the church cold
because they insist on sitting in "Z"
row. Get up front where it's warm!

———o———

One of the things that is wrong with
the church is that it dwells too much on
what's wrong with it, and overlooks its
own greatness and destiny.

———o———

This Is My Church

This is my church. It is composed
of people like me. We make it what
it is. I want it to be a church that is
a light on the path of pilgrims, leading
them to Goodness, Truth and Beauty.
It will be, if I am. It will be friendly,
if I am. Its pews will be filled, if I
help to fill them. It will do a great
work, if I work. It will bring other
people into its worship and fellowship,
if I bring them. It will be a church of
loyalty and love, of fearlessness and
faith; if I who make it what it is, am
filled with these. Therefore, I dedicate
myself to the task of being what I
want my church to be.
                    Brooklyn Central Church Bulletin

———o———

I Found All This

A room of quiet, a temple of peace,
The home of faith where doubting
    cease,
A house of comfort where hope is giv-
en,
A source of strength to make earth
    heaven,
A shrine of worship, a place to pray —
I found all this in my church today.
                                AUTHOR UNKNOWN

———o———

One thing that may still be said
about "a struggling church." As long
as it is struggling, it isn't dead.

———o———

The best way to heat a church is to
have the stove in the pulpit.

———o———

Churches do take many offerings and
collections, and so there are many of
us who figure that religion is a costly
thing; but irreligion costs many times
as much. Think it over.

———o———

It's very strange that heat on Sunday
Seems so much hotter than on Monday,
And weekday pains, that we ignore,
On Sundays seem to hurt much more,
Till we decide to stay in bed
When we should go to church instead.

———o———

In church recently a boy ran a toy
engine up and down the seat, much to
the annoyance of an elderly gent seated
in the pew behind.
    At long last the man protested: "Shh!
Shh!" he said.
    The small boy beamed. "Oh," he
exclaimed, "do you play trains, too?"
                                CHARLES KENNEDY

———o———

The church that is married to the
spirit of the age will find itself a widow
in the next generation.
                                JOSEPH SIZOO

———o———

The best days of the church have
always been its singing days.
                        THEODORE LEDYARD CUYLER

———o———

Prayerless pews make powerless pul-
pits.

———o———

Satan does not do his most subtle
work in the saloon, but in the sanctuary.
                                RALPH H. STOLL

Now I set me down to sleep
    The prayer is long; the subject's
    deep.
If he should stop before I wake
    Please give me a pinch, for goodness'
    sake.

————o————

The church is so subnormal that if it ever got back to the New Testament normal it would seem to people to be abnormal.

VANCE HAVNER

————o————

My Church

I want my church to be a place
Where I can meet God face to face
And meditate upon His grace.

I want each worship hour so sweet
That I can think each time we meet
A Presence comes and takes His seat.

I want her doors to stand so wide
No hungry soul who waits outside
Will think that he has been denied.

I want my church to be much more
Than stone and mortar, pew and door
Or carpet laid upon a floor.

But, oh, I know that it can be
No more than that is found in me,
So teach me, Lord, to show forth Thee.

JESSIE MERLE FRANKLIN

————o————

Churches

Churches!
Thank God for the sight of them,
The beauty, the dreams and the right
    of them,
In country and city, on mountain and
    moor,
Churches with welcome at the door.

Churches that silently testify,
With spires and crosses reared to the
    sky,
That makes us think every time we
    look,
Of God and right and the Holy Book.

Churches!
Thank God for the heart of them,
The people who live as a part of them,
Praying and learning the things to do,

Giving and labouring, proving them
    true,
Mastering lethargy, selfishness, fear,
Dreaming of Heaven, building it here.

Churches!
Thank God for the scope of them,
For the aims and the deeds and the
    hope of them.

CHAUNCEY R. PIETY

————o————

Urgently in need of sleeping cars, a Canadian railroad inserted the following advertisement in one of the trade journals:
"300 Sleepers Wanted. At Once."
A short time later they received a letter from a minister of a church in Iowa offering his entire congregation.

MELVIN E. LUKENBACH in Coronet

————o————

The old problem of getting congregations to occupy the front pews has been solved by the Trenton, Michigan, Community Presbyterian Church. The first three rows — and only the first three rows — are temptingly equipped with foam-rubber cushions.

————o————

A church exists for the double purpose of gathering in and sending out.

————o————

The reason that rain or shine keeps you away from the church is the reason why the church is necessary.

————o————

Are You Going?

It was
Sunday morning
At the breakfast
Table,
And my host asked
Mrs. Host —
Meaning his wife —
If she was
Going to church.

And I thought
That was funny —
If that's the
Right word.

Strange is better
Maybe —
Or tragic —
Or unfortunate.

I couldn't see why
It should be a
Matter for debate;
Because she was
In good health,
And they were
Members of the
Church.

AUTHOR UNKNOWN

———o———

When you think of yourself and your relation to your church it might be a good motto to "be square all week and be 'round on Sunday."

CLIFF COLE

———o———

Across The Pastor's Desk

Sometime ago, a newspaper carried a story about Mrs. Lila Craig, 81, who had not missed in her church attendance in 1,040 Sundays — a perfect record for twenty years. With tongue in cheek, the writer asked, "What's wrong with Mrs. Craig?"

1. Doesn't Mrs. Craig ever have company on Sunday?

2. Doesn't she ever go anywhere on Saturday night, so that she gets up tired on Sunday morning?

3. Doesn't she ever have headaches, colds, nervous spells, tired feelings, poor breakfasts, sudden trips out of the city, business trips, Sunday picnics, family reunions?

4. Doesn't she ever sleep late on Sunday morning?

5. Doesn't she have any friends who invite her to go on a weekend trip?

6. Doesn't she ever read the Sunday paper?

7. Doesn't it ever rain or snow in her town on Sunday?

8. Doesn't she ever become angry at the minister or her teacher?

9. Doesn't she ever get her feelings hurt by someone at church?

10. Doesn't she have a radio or TV set so that she can stay home and hear some good services?

Church attendance is a privilege which each of us has as a Christian. It is a witness to what we believe. It is fortification for our lives. It is the opportunity to meet God in the beauty of His sanctuary.

See you in church!

Chimes of Hope

———o———

You Arx Important!

Whxn you arx txmptxd to takx a Sunday off, and you think that thx absxncx of onx pxrson won't makx too much diffxrxncx at church, you placx your ministxr in thx samx position as a fxllow trying to typx with onx kxy missing. Hx can makx substitutions just as wx havx donx, but thx rxsult is nxvxr thx samx as whxn hx's with all thx mxmbxrs of thx congrxgation!

———o———

A pastor in Daytona Beach, Florida had a good idea. In a recent bulletin he ran a check list; across the top were the words, "I cannot attend church services because: . . ." And then . . . "Please check." Following were some reasons that a person could check: "Too busy. Must go to the movies. Pleasure trip. Company. Have to go fishing. Disinterestedness. Radio and TV programs. Need to rest." And then there was this instruction across the bottom: "Please tear off and mail to God."

ROBERT E. GOODRICH, JR.

———o———

Moribus Sabbaticus

Sunday sickness, or *moribus sabbaticus,* is a sickness peculiar to church members, and it recurs every seventh day. There will be no suggestion of the disease until Sunday morning, and without the least difficulty it can develop very quickly.

The symptoms vary, but the disease never interferes with the appetite. It never lasts more than twenty-four hours, and often much less. It is never necessary to call a physician, yet the disease is very contagious. No symptoms are felt on Saturday night, but the attack develops suddenly on Sunday morning. The patient awakens as usual, feeling well, and eats a hearty breakfast. About nine o'clock the first attack comes on and lasts usually until noon. And in the afternoon, the patient is much improved and is able to ride and read the Sunday papers.

The aftermath is that on Monday morning the patient who is subject to Sunday sickness, is out bright and early, meeting friends at the drugstore corner and attending to business with the usual interest and briskness.

This strange disease has proved very much of an epidemic. In nearly every home there will be one or more cases every Sunday.

Christian Life

————o————

The minister was inquiring of one of his flock why he had not attended church recently. "Well, you see, sir," said the man, "I've been troubled with a bunion on my foot."

"Strange," said the minister, "that a bunion should impede the pilgrim's progress."

Watchman Examiner

————o————

The new preacher looked coldly at Deacon Smith and said he had heard that the deacon went to a ball game instead of to church last Sunday. "That's a lie!" the shocked deacon cried, "And I've got the fish to prove it."

————o————

What kind of church
   Would my church be,
If everyone in it
   Were just like me?

————o————

An Ordinary Member

Just an ordinary member of the church,
   I heard him say.
But you'd always find him present,
   even on a rainy day.
He had a hearty handclasp for the
   stranger in the aisle,
And a friend who was in trouble found
   sunshine in his smile.
When the sermon helped him, he told
   the preacher so

And when he needed comfort, he let
   the pastor know.
He always paid up promptly, and tried
   to do his share
In all the ordinary tasks for which some
   have no care.
His talents were not many but his love
   for God was true;
His prayers were not in public, but he
   prayed for me and you.
An ordinary member? I think that I
   would say
He was extraordinary in a humble sort
   of way.

LILLIAN M. WEEKS
in *First Methodist Messenger*, Pasadena, Calif.

————o————

A statistician has figured that 5% of all church members do not exist; 10% of them cannot be found; 25% never go to church; 50% never contribute a cent to the Lord's work; 75% never attend a midweek prayer service; 90% do not have family worship in their homes, and more than 95% have never tried to win a soul to Christ!

Easygoing religions make the going easy for the devil.

Circumstances

Man is not the creature of circumstances. Circumstances are the creatures of men.

BENJAMIN DISRAELI, *Vivian Grey*

————o————

People are always blaming their circumstances for what they are. I don't believe in circumstances. The people who get on in the world are the people who get up and look for the circumstances they want, and, if they can't find them, make them.

GEORGE BERNARD SHAW,
Mrs. Warren's Profession

————o————

There are no circumstances, no matter how unfortunate, that clever people do not extract some advantage from; and none, no matter how fortunate, that the unwise cannot turn to their own disadvantage.

FRANÇOIS, DUC DE LA ROCHEFOUCAULD

It is our relation to circumstances that determine their influence over us. The same wind that carries one vessel into port may blow another off shore.

———o———

Circumstances are like featherbeds. So long as you're on top of your circumstances, you're fine. But if you allow those circumstances to get on top of you, they'll suffocate you with the pressure of discouragement and hopelessness.

———o———

It is not the circumstances of our lives that give them character, but our relationships to God under any circumstances.

———o———

The ideal man bears the accidents of life with dignity and grace, making the best of the circumstances.

ARISTOTLE

———o———

Superiority to circumstances is one of the most prominent characteristics of great men.

HORACE MANN

———o———

Circumstances may prevent you from building a fortune, but they have no power to prevent you from building character.

Civilization

Perhaps the supreme product of civilization is people who can endure it.

FRANKLIN P. JONES

———o———

Let us not condemn civilization. It has brought us marvels . . . Civilization is good to have; it is dangerous to be lost in.

RABBI ABRAHAM HESCHEL

———o———

It would have helped a lot if the pioneers had located cities closer to airports.

Advertiser, Salisbury, Maryland

Civilization is just a slow process of being kind.

CHARLES L. LUCAS

———o———

When a civilization reaches the phase of worshipping comfort, it is unfailingly conquered by one of tougher ambitions.

WILLIAM S. SCHLAMM

Clean

Church Cleaning

We cleaned our little church today —
Wiped all the dust and dirt away.
We straightened papers, washed the floors;
Wiped off the light and painted doors.

We brushed the dirt stains from the books
And whisked the cobwebs from the nooks.
We polished windows so we'd see
The newly greening shrub and tree.

The menfolks, too, raked up the yard —
They laughed and said it wasn't hard,
And, oh, it felt so very good
To have the place look as it should.

We said, "How wonderful 'twould be
"If we cleaned out what we can't see —
"Such things as grudges, hates, and lies,
"And musty thoughts much worse than flies."

Selected, from *Christian Witness*

———o———

Clean living makes the undertaker wait longer for his money.

———o———

Just as Jesus found it necessary to sweep the money-changers from the Temple porch, so we ourselves need a lot of housecleaning.

DALE EVANS

———o———

Lord, that my words may be as clean
As any sunshine-whitened stone
Within a meadow, vernal-fair;
My thoughts as clean as mountain air
Along a sky-reflecting lake
Where morning-joyful birds awake;

My heart as clean as when beside
An ocean with a shining tide
I stood with Thee and saw the Grace
Upon Thy holy, selfless face.

GRACE V. WATKINS

———o———

Between the dark and the daylight,
When the night is beginning to lower,
Little paws, black from day's occupations,
Make what is known as the "Children's Scour!"

———o———

Cleanliness is, indeed, next to godliness.

JOHN WESLEY

Clothing

Tommy: "Is it true that pigskins make the best shoes?"
Johnny: "I don't know, but banana skins make the best slippers."

———o———

Keeping your clothes well pressed will keep you from looking hard pressed.

COLEMAN COX

———o———

You are never fully dressed until you wear a smile.

———o———

The fashion wears out more apparel than the man.

WILLIAM SHAKESPEARE,
Much Ado About Nothing

———o———

My Sunday Cloak

My Sunday cloak's a lovely thing,
Its pattern woven by a King.
It wraps me close in special grace,
Which knows no strangeness anyplace.
"I'm all you need," it seems to say,
"Why don't you wear me everyday?"

But it doesn't match my Monday shoes.

My feet have many things to do,
Important things that I pursue.

The gods entice; I must adore,
To win their blessing just once more.
Just one more time to know their touch,
Just one more time — that's not too much.

(My Sunday cloak's a lovely thing,
Its pattern woven by a King.)

But it doesn't match my Tuesday mask.

This face pretends it cannot see;
It honors none — not even me.
It makes believe no choices burn,
And so evades its soul's concern.
It's wearing thin? Oh, yes, I know.
But still I cling — I need it so.

(My Sunday cloak's a lovely thing,
Its pattern woven by a King.)

But it doesn't match my Wednesday gloves.

But gloves somehow don't hide my hands
Outstretched to kill with their demands.
They point with hate and faith deny
The love which came — and stayed to die.
But wash them clean from nail to wrist?
I can't; I can't unclench my fist.

(My Sunday cloak's a lovely thing,
Its pattern woven by a King.)

But it doesn't match my Thursday beads.

And stone by stone my necklace glows
To feed the lusts on which it grows.
God's offered plans ignored, denied;
I have my own. They must be tried.
But if they fail, then hear my plea:
"Why me, Oh God? Why Me? Why Me?"

(My Sunday cloak's a lovely thing,
Its pattern woven by a King.)

But it doesn't match my Friday purse.

And to this purse I have to hold,
For this is where I store my gold.
Here the thefts and lies unfurled;
These my treasure — this my world.
For this is how I pay my way!
And give it up? I can't today.

(My Sunday cloak's a lovely thing,
Its pattern woven by a King.)

But it doesn't match my Saturday
mood.

This mood screams back in grim de-
spair,
"It isn't right! It isn't fair!
"Why always theirs and never mine?
"Is this God's plan? A plan divine?"

But still He comes to help me pray.
— To hold my cloak — To lead the way.

My Sunday cloak's a lovely thing,
Its pattern woven by a King.
It wraps me close in special grace,
Which knows no strangeness anyplace.
"I'm all you need," it seems to say,
"Why don't you wear me everyday?"
                                BLANCHE SMITH

Comfort

Oh, the comfort, the inexpressible
comfort, of feeling safe with a person
having neither to weigh thoughts nor
measure words, but pouring them all
right out, just as they are, chaff and
grain together, certain that a faithful
hand will take and sift them, keeping
what is worth keeping, and with the
breath of kindness blow the rest away.
            DINAH MARIA MULOCH CRAIK

God often comforts us, not by changing the circumstances of our lives, but
by changing our attitude towards them.
                        S. H. B. MASTERMAN

The Psalm Of Comfort

The Lord is my Counselor, I shall not
feel insecure.
He leads me into quiet moments of
meditation;
I hear Him bid me be still.
He restores my soul.
He leads me in paths of service that
I may glorify His name.
Even though the darkness of selfishness,
greed and hate would destroy me, I
am not afraid.
The promise of His word keeps me firm.
In the presence of my sin and failure
He proves His love.
His forgiveness washes away all guilt,
my joy knows no bounds.

Surely as I serve Him with love and
humility
He shall abide with me and I shall
know His peace.
                        MARGARETTE A. WOOD

Consolation

When I sink down in gloom or fear,
Hope blighted or delayed,
Thy whisper, Lord, my heart shall
cheer,
" 'Tis I, be not afraid!"

Or, startled at some sudden blow,
If fretful thoughts I feel,
"Fear not, it is but I!" shall flow,
As balm my wound to heal.
                        JOHN H. NEWMAN

Committee

If you want to get a job done, give
it to an individual; if you want to have
it studied, give it to a committee.

Committee work is like an easy chair
— easy to get into but hard to get out
of.

Birth Of Committees

We sat in committee all morning,
discussing the "cons and the pros,"
At noon we adjourned by creating
. . . more committees to re-dig our
rows.
                        LESLIE CONRAD, JR.
                        in Church Management

It's a mighty good thing that the
Ten Commandments were handed
down direct instead of being obliged
to pass through the hands of a few
committees.
                        CLIFF COLE

A committee of one gets things done.
            JOE RYAN, Ben Roth Syndicate

A committee consists of those who
are unwilling to do the unnecessary.

If machines get too powerful we can organize them into committees, and that will do them in.

————o————

Standing committees should sit down often because they tire easily and others especially!

Common Sense

I read, I study, I examine, I listen, I reflect, and out of all this I try to form an idea into which I put as much common sense as I can.

LAFAYETTE

————o————

The only way to play it cool is to wait until you're through being hot under the collar.

————o————

Common sense is instinct. Enough of it is genius.

GEORGE BERNARD SHAW

————o————

O God, give the world common sense, beginning with me.

————o————

Common sense in an uncommon degree is what the world calls wisdom.

SAMUEL TAYLOR COLERIDGE

————o————

A handful of common sense is worth a bushel of learning.

Spanish Proverb

————o————

The finest education is useless without common sense.

E. F. GIRARD

————o————

Lord, if I dig a pit for others
Let me fall into it;
But if I dig it for myself,
Give me sense enough to walk around
it.

SHERWOOD E. WIRT

————o————

Those who keep their feet on the ground aren't likely to lose standing.

Good sense is a thing all need, few have, and none think they want.

BENJAMIN FRANKLIN

Communication

Communication is depositing a part of yourself in another person.

————o————

Strides in communication now permit us to talk with people around the globe, but cannot bridge the ever-widening gaps within our own families.

GLORIA FRANCE

Communion

Communion

In memory of the Saviour's love,
  We keep the sacred feast,
Where every humble, contrite heart
  Is made a welcome guest.
By faith we take the Bread of Life
  With which our souls are fed,
The Cup in token of His blood
  That was for sinners shed.
In faith and memory thus we sing
  The wonders of His love,
And thus anticipate by faith
  The heavenly feast above.

The Evangel

————o————

If the individual can commune with God, then he must matter to God; and if he matters to God, he must share God's eternity.

JOHN BAILLIE

————o————

Silent Communion

O teach me, Lord, that I may teach
The precious things Thou dost impart:
And wing my words that they may reach
The hidden depths of many a heart.
Amen.

FRANCES RIDLEY HAVERGAL

————o————

The measure of the worth of our public activity for God is the private communion we have with Him.

OSWALD CHAMBERS

Oh, to reach up to the heights that He
   planned,
Though they be rough.
Finding His smile and the touch of His
   hand
Always enough.

Communism

To Fight Communism . . .

Alert yourself — learn the true nature
   and tactics of communism.
Make civic programs for social improvement your business.
Exercise your right to vote; elect repre-
   sentatives of integrity.
Respect human dignity — communism
   and individual rights cannot coexist.
Inform yourself . . . know your country
   — its history, traditions and heritage.
Combat public apathy toward communism — indifference can be fatal
   when national survival is at stake.
Attack bigotry and prejudice wherever
   they appear; justice for all is the
   bulwark of democracy.

                    J. EDGAR HOOVER

A communist is like a crocodile.
When it opens its mouth you cannot
tell whether it is trying to smile or
preparing to eat you up.

              SIR WINSTON CHURCHILL

Communism possesses a language
which every people can understand.
Its elements are hunger, envy, and
death.

                 HEINRICH HEINE

In a communist country they name
a street after you one day and chase
you down it the next.

                The Irish Digest

What is a communist? One who has
yearnings for equal division of unequal
earnings. Idler or bungler, he is willing to fork out his penny and pocket
your shilling.

             EBENEZER ELLIOTT

It is clear that we can never cope
with Communism simply by fearing it
and hating it. We must recapture our
own national sense of purpose, our devotion to a great cause, and a vital
faith.

                 BILLY GRAHAM

Every human ideology comes to an
end sometime and Communism, too,
will be a thing of the past, maybe much
sooner than anyone presently thinks.
There already are traces of crumbling
and falling down.

          BISHOP OTTO DIBELIUS

Compensation

Most people don't care how much
they pay for something, as long as it's
not all at once.

Those who reason that "the world
owes me a living" are likely to discover
that the pay days are somewhat ir-
regular.

My Wages

I bargained with Life for a penny and
   Life would pay no more,
However I begged at evening, as I
   counted my scanty score.
For Life is just an employer, he gives
   you what you ask;
But once you have set the wages, you
   must perform the task.
I worked for a menial's hire, only to
   learn, dismayed,
That any wage I had asked of Life,
   Life would have gladly paid.

             AUTHOR UNKNOWN

Competition

A group of clergymen were discussing whether or not they ought to invite
Dwight L. Moody to their city. The
success of the famed evangelist was
brought to the attention of the men.

One unimpressed minister commented, "Does Mr. Moody have a monopoly
on the Holy Ghost?"

Another man quietly replied, "No, but the Holy Ghost seems to have a monopoly on Mr. Moody."

Sunday

———o———

Don't be afraid of opposition. Remember a kite rises against, not with, the wind.

HAMILTON W. MABIE

———o———

Competition comes in place of monopoly; and intelligence and industry ask only for fair play and an open field.

DANIEL WEBSTER

Complain

A noted preacher had a special black book labeled "Complaints of Members Against One Another." When one of his congregation told him about the faults of another, he would say, "Here is my complaint book. I will write down what you say, and you can sign it. Then when I have time I will take up the matter officially concerning this brother." The sight of the open book and the ready pen had its effect. "Oh, no, I couldn't sign anything like that!" they would say. In 40 years this preacher never got anyone to write a line in it.

Voice of Truth

———o———

A repining life is a lingering death.

BENJAMIN WHICHOUTE

———o———

A Christian lady was complaining to a friend about the hardness of life and the circumstances that buffeted her and in anger said: "Oh, I would to God that I had never been made!" "My dear child," replied the friend, "you are not yet made; you are only being made, and you are quarreling with God's processes."

———o———

Constant complaint is the poorest sort of play for all the comforts we enjoy.

BENJAMIN FRANKLIN

Everyone sympathizes with the chronic grouch when he has to be by himself!

———o———

It is easier to complain than it is to get out and hustle.

Compliment

Everybody knows how to express a complaint, but few can utter a graceful compliment.

———o———

Success in dealing with other people is like making rhubarb pie — use all the sugar you can, and then double it.

Banking

———o———

J. A. Persson of Sweden, missionary to Africa, was going home on furlough, and the Christians at his station were having a farewell dinner. An African native paid the missionary the highest compliment he could think of: "Mr. Persson may have a white skin, but his heart is as black as any of us."

Presbyterian Survey

———o———

Everybody likes a praise-giver. Nobody likes a praise-grabber.

———o———

A man's body is so sensitive that when you pat him on the back, his head swells.

———o———

Praise loudly, blame softly.

Compromise

A compromise is the art of dividing a cake in such a way that everyone believes that he has got the biggest piece.

LUDWIG ERHARD, German Minister of Economics in *The Observer*, London

———o———

Compromise is always wrong when it means a sacrifice principle.

———o———

Many things are worse than defeat and compromise with evil is one of them.

Remember the uncertain soldier in our Civil War who, figuring to play it safe, dressed himself in a blue coat and gray pants and tip-toed out into the field of battle. He got shot from both directions.

Paul Harvey News

———o———

The concessions of the weak are the concessions of fear.

EDMUND BURKE

Computer

The only thing a computer can do when a request is made is to call on its memory bank, which is intake. Eventually it may suffer from hardening of the categories.

———o———

Computers will not really have replaced people until and if somebody figures out a way to discipline them for their mistakes.

Conceit

Conceit is what makes a little squirt think that he is a fountain of knowledge.

———o———

A conceited man is like a man up in a balloon: everybody looks small to him and he looks small to everybody.

———o———

I always like to hear a man talk about himself, because then I never hear anything but good.

WILL ROGERS

———o———

Conceit is a closer companion of ignorance than of learning.

———o———

Conceit may puff a man up, but never prop him up.

JOHN RUSKIN

———o———

If you want to know how important you are in the world, stick your finger in a pan of water and see the hole that is left.

The head never begins to swell until the mind stops growing.

———o———

Conceit is a form of disease that makes everybody sick except the one who has it.

———o———

Conceit causes more conversation than wit.

———o———

The arrogant and self-centered fellow is to be pitied: he has no true friends; for in prosperity he knows nobody, and in adversity nobody knows him.

———o———

He that falls in love with himself will have no rivals.

BENJAMIN FRANKLIN

Concern

Could I climb to the highest place in Athens, I would lift up my voice and proclaim: Fellow citizens, why do ye turn and scrape every stone to gather wealth, and take so little care of your children, to whom one day you must relinquish it all?

SOCRATES

———o———

Walter, who was not quite five, knew much about the Lord Jesus and had accepted him as Saviour. The forgiveness of his sin made him happy.

He surprised us with the question, "Did the Lord Jesus know how many people there were in the world and how many more there would be when He died for them?"

Is the fact that One died for all the sins of all people still able to move us? Does that once-and-for-all offering of Jesus still have anything to say in this day and age?

HEDWIG GUT, Berlin, Germany
in *The Gospel Call*

———o———

When To Be Alarmed

If you find yourself . . .
    coveting any pleasure
        more than your prayer times,

enjoying any book
  more than your Bible,
reading the newspapers for relaxation
  more than the Bible or some
  spiritual book,
reverencing any house
  more than the House of God,
satisfied with any table
  more than the Lord's Table,
loving any person
  more than our Lord Jesus Christ,
seeking the fellowship of men
  more than that of the Holy Spirit,
or delighted with any prospect
  more than that of the return of
  Jesus,
  . . . *then take alarm.*

AUTHOR UNKNOWN

Confidence

Confidence is the feeling you have
before you know better.

———o———

Why should there not be a patient
confidence in the ultimate justice of the
people? Is there any better or equal
hope in the world?

ABRAHAM LINCOLN

———o———

A little girl was taking a long journey, and in the course of the day her
train crossed a number of rivers. The
water seen in advance always awakened doubts and fears in the child. She
did not understand how it could
safely be crossed. As they drew near
the river, however, a bridge appeared
and furnished the way over. Several
times the same thing happened, and
finally the child leaned back with a
long breath of relief and confidence:
"Somebody has put bridges for us all
the way." So God does likewise for
His children all through life.

Selected

———o———

The best way to acquire self-confidence is to do exactly what you are
afraid to do.

———o———

Our confidence in Christ does not
make us lazy, negligent or careless, but

on the contrary it awakens us, urges
us on, and makes us active in living
righteous lives and doing good. There
is no self-confidence to compare with
this.

ULRICH ZWINGLI

———o———

A well-adjusted person is one who
makes the same mistake twice without
getting nervous!

JANE HEARD in *The Progressive Farmer*

———o———

Confidence is a thing not to be produced by compulsion. Men cannot be
forced into trust.

DANIEL WEBSTER

———o———

Confidence is that feeling by which
the mind embarks on great and honorable courses with a sure hope and trust
in itself.

MARCUS TULLIUS CICERO

———o———

Skill and confidence are an unconquered enemy.

Confusion

Why do those who "run in circles"
never realize that they always end up
right where they started?

———o———

Give a man some facts and he will
draw his own confusions.

———o———

When you are confused it's when
you don't know enough about a thing
to be worried.

WILL ROGERS

Conquer

A conqueror is one who wins by
fighting; a "more than conqueror" is
one who wins without fighting.

———o———

Me

Today I had a battle,
  The fight was hard and long;
My opponent was so stubborn,
  And I knew him to be wrong.

We didn't need a referee,
   Because, when we were through,
The decision was unquestioned,
   Nor did we start anew.
I never did like fighting,
   And yet I fail to see
How I could help but cheer a bit
   When I had conquered ME.
                    HAZEL V. WOLFE
         in *The Log of the Good Ship Grace*

————o————

They conquer who believe they can.
                         JOHN DRYDEN

————o————

Make me a captive, Lord,
   And then I shall be free.
Force me to render up my sword,
   And I shall conqueror be.
                    GEORGE MATHESON

————o————

If thou wouldst conquer thy weakness thou must not gratify it.
                         WILLIAM PENN

————o————

I count him braver who overcomes his desires than him who conquers his enemies; for the hardest victory is the victory over self.
                            ARISTOTLE

————o————

Who has a harder fight than he who is striving to overcome himself?
                    THOMAS À KEMPIS

————o————

Conquest pursues where courage leads the way.
         SIR SAMUEL GARTH, *The Dispensary*

————o————

Don't try to overcome the inevitable — just don't let the inevitable overcome you.

Conscience

Conscience and reputation are closely related — a man who has a good conscience seldom gets a bad reputation.

————o————

A good conscience is a continual Christmas.
         BENJAMIN FRANKLIN, *Poor Richard*

A twinge of conscience is a glimpse of God.
                        PETER USTINOV

————o————

Conscience is that small voice that makes us feel small when we do something small.
                       EVA JO STEPHEN

————o————

Guilty consciences always make people cowards.
                             PILPAY

————o————

Man's conscience is the oracle of God.
              LORD BYRON, *The Island*

————o————

The Signal Lights

"It was well you stopped when the red
      light flashed,"
She said, as we drove along,
"For an officer stood at the corner
      there,
   In charge of the traffic throng."
And I smiled and said to my daughter
      fair,
   As we waited on the spot,
"I always stop when the red light
      shows,
   Be an officer there or not."
Then she sat in thought as we drove
      along
   And suddenly this she said,
"There ought to be lights for us all
      through life —
   The amber and green and red.
What help 'twould be if a red light
      flashed
   Where danger and shame were near,
And we all might wait till the green
      light came
   To show that the road was clear."
"My dear," said I, "we have tried to
      light
   Life's road for your feet to fare,
And pray you'll stop when the red
      light glows,
   Though none of us may be there.
We have tried to teach you the signs
      of wrong
   And the way to a life serene,
So stop when your conscience post
      shows red —
   And go when it flashes green."
                      EDGAR A. GUEST

Conscience gets a lot of credit that should really belong to cold feet.

———o———

Conscience warns us as a friend before it punishes us as a judge.

STANISLAS I (King of Poland)

———o———

"Conscience," said an Indian, "is a three-cornered thing in my heart that stands still when I am good, but when I am bad, it turns around and the corners hurt a lot. If I keep on doing wrong, the corners wear off and it does not hurt any more."

Construction Digest

———o———

Conscience is thoroughly well-bred, and soon leaves off talking to those who do not wish to hear it.

SAMUEL BUTLER

———o———

The most painful wound in the world is a stab of conscience.

JOHN ELLIS LARGE

———o———

Asked to describe her conscience, one young girl said: "It's a gray ghost inside you with a friendly face but it stops smiling when your nerves begin to write a note to it when you want to do something bad and when the ghost sees this bad note he gets very angry and yells 'Stop!'"

The Secret World of Kids

———o———

Conscience is a weak, inner voice that sometimes doesn't speak your language.

———o———

Conscience is the chamber of justice.

———o———

Conscience is never dilatory in her warnings.

Consecration

A life totally consecrated to God sees all of its tasks as God-appointed.

———o———

I go out to preach with two proposi-tions in mind. First, every person ought to give his life to Christ. Second, whether or not anyone else gives Him his life, I will give Him mine.

JONATHAN EDWARDS

———o———

Consecration

Lord, my greatest is so little,
And my most is yet so small,
When I measure it with Jesus
There is nothing left at all,
And I hesitate to answer
When I hear Thee call.

Can the Lord, who owns the cattle
On a thousand fertile hills,
He who speaks in voice commanding
And the angry water stills —
Can the Lord, who died for sinners
On the cross of Calvary,
Use me even in my weakness?
Yes, for He demands of me
Perfect strength, and then He gives it
In His all-sufficiency.

Take my greatest, Lord — 'tis nothing —
And my strongest, though 'tis less.
Thou canst use the little, Father,
And the humble offering bless;
And I'll serve Thee, Lord, forever
And Thy blessed name confess.

AUTHOR UNKNOWN

———o———

"Kept By The Power Of God"
(I Peter 1:5)

My Life Kept for Jesus. Colossians 3:3, 4
My Time Kept for Jesus. Psalm 31:15
My Hands Kept for Jesus. Psalm 24: 3, 4
My Feet Kept for Jesus. I Samuel 2:9
My Voice Kept for Jesus. Psalm 40:3
My Lips Kept for Jesus. Psalm 51:15
My Intellect Kept for Jesus. Isaiah 26: 3
My Will Kept for Jesus. Hebrews 13: 20, 21
My Heart Kept for Jesus. Luke 24:32
My Love Kept for Jesus. I John 4:19, 21

REV. J. BECHTEL (*Based on a hymn by* FRANCES RIDLEY HAVERGAL, 1874, "Take My Life and Let it Be.")

To be crucified means, first, the man on the cross is facing only one direction; second, he is not going back; and third, he has no further plans of his own.

A. W. TOZER

———o———

Consecration is not giving to God, but taking hands off what belongs to God.

———o———

You cannot give to the world any more than you give to God.

———o———

Our business is to do the will of God. He will take care of the business.

Consequence

Our deeds still travel with us from afar, And what we have been makes us what we are.

GEORGE ELIOT (MARY ANN EVANS)

———o———

No action, whether foul or fair, Is ever done, but it leaves somewhere A record, written by fingers ghostly, As a blessing or a curse.

HENRY WADSWORTH LONGFELLOW, *The Golden Legend*

Consistent

A foolish consistency is the hobgoblin of little minds.

RALPH WALDO EMERSON

———o———

We need to learn to set our course by the stars and not by the lights of every passing ship.

OMAR BRADLEY

———o———

Those who honestly mean to be true contradict themselves more rarely than those who try to be consistent.

OLIVER WENDELL HOLMES

———o———

Always endeavor to be really what you would wish to appear.

GRANVILLE SHARP

———o———

The true man professes only what he practices.

Content, Contentment

It is right to be content with what we have, never with what we are.

SIR JAMES MACKINTOSH

———o———

As Noah's dove found no footing but in the ark, so a Christian finds no contentment but in Christ.

MASON

———o———

O what a happy soul am I; although
    I cannot see,
I am resolved that in this world
Contented I will be;
How many blessings I enjoy
That other people don't!
To weep and sigh because I'm blind,
I cannot, and I won't!

FANNY JANE CROSBY

———o———

Suppose all the joys, the cares, and the opportunities afforded you in life could be gathered into a bag which you could carry on your shoulders. And suppose each person in the world brought his burden to one common heap, there to be given the privilege of depositing his bag and selecting any other bag of his choice. Do you know what would happen? Invariably, each one would be content once again to pick up the bag he had deposited on the heap and go his way.

Based on PLUTARCH, *Consolation to Apollonius*

———o———

Contentment comes when we remember that what God chooses is far better than what we choose.

———o———

Sweet are the thoughts that savour of content;
The quiet mind is richer than a crown.
. . .
A mind content both crown and kingdom is.

ROBERT GREENE, *Farewell to Folly*

———o———

Content's a kingdom.

THOMAS HEYWOOD

He that wants money, means, and content is without three good friends.
WILLIAM SHAKESPEARE, *As You Like It*

———o———

Contentment is natural wealth.
SOCRATES

Control

When it comes to the control of our lives, we are either "body" men or "spirit" men.
ERIC LINDHOLM

———o———

Controls

You cannot control the length of your life, but you can control its width and depth.

You cannot control the contour of your countenance, but you can control its expression.

You cannot control the other fellow's opportunities, but you can grasp your own.

You cannot control the weather, but you can control the moral atmosphere which surrounds you.

You cannot control the distance that your head shall be above the ground, but you can control the height of the contents of your head.

You cannot control the other fellow's faults, but you can see to it that you yourself do not develop or harbor provoking propensities.

Why worry about things you cannot control? Why not get busy controlling the things that depend on you.
Highway of Happiness

Conversation

Conversation is the laboratory and workshop of the student.
RALPH WALDO EMERSON

———o———

Good talk is like good scenery — continuous, yet constantly varying, and full of the charm of novelty and surprise.
RANDOLPH S. BOURNE

———o———

The reason why so few people are agreeable in conversation, is, that each is thinking more of what he is intending to say, than of what others are saying; and we never listen when we are planning to speak.
FRANÇOIS, DUC DE LA ROCHEFOUCAULD

———o———

It may be difficult to practice, but it seems to us that one of the main rules of conversation is never to speak when you ought to be listening. Also it's a fine builder of personal appreciation.

———o———

For a really fetching conversation, three persons are required: two to talk and one to be the topic.
Dixie County Advocate,
Cross City, Florida

———o———

It's surprising how many conversations develop into a monologue.

———o———

A clever young lady was asked to attend a public function. She was assigned a place between a noted bishop and an equally famous rabbi. It was her chance to break into high company and she meant to use it.

"I feel as if I were a leaf between the Old and New Testaments," she said brilliantly, during a lull in the conversation.

"That page, Madam," replied the rabbi, "is usually a blank."

———o———

It's all right to hold a conversation, but you should let go of it now and then.

———o———

The value of the average conversation could be enormously improved by the constant use of four simple words: "I do not know."
ANDRÉ MAUROIS

———o———

A single conversation across the table with a wise man is worth a month's study of books.
Chinese Proverb

———o———

Conversation is an art in which a man has all mankind for competitors.
RALPH WALDO EMERSON

The best guide to conversation is to ask questions.

———o———

Silence is one of the great arts of conversation.

MARCUS TULLIUS CICERO

Conversion

Conversion is not a repairing of the old building; but it takes all down and erects a new structure. It is not the sewing on a patch of holiness; but with the true convert, holiness is woven into all his powers, principles and practice.

JOSEPH ALLEINE,
An Alarm to the Unconverted

———o———

If good books did good, the world would have been converted long ago.

———o———

A man may be convicted yet never converted, but no man is converted unless he has first been convicted.

D. THURLOW YAXLEY

Conviction

If you don't stand for something, you'll fall for anything.

———o———

He who floats with the current, who does not guide himself according to higher principles, who has no ideal, no convictions — such a man is a mere article of the world's furniture — a thing moved, instead of a living and moving being — an echo, not a voice. The man who has no inner life is the slave of his surroundings, as the barometer is the obedient servant of the air at rest and the weathercock the humble servant of the air in motion.

———o———

I can only say that I have acted upon my best convictions, without selfishness or malice, and that by the help of God I shall continue to do so.

ABRAHAM LINCOLN

Real convictions disturb. They also attract.

———o———

In one of the great crises of Martin Luther's life, when he was standing firmly and alone for a conviction that he refused to surrender, he was confronted furiously by a powerful opponent. Did he realize, asked that opponent, what he was doing and what power he was defying? Did he expect any force worth mentioning to take up arms and come to his help? "No," said Luther quietly, "I do not expect that."
"Then where will you be?" thundered the dignitary who had come to challenge him. "Where will you be?"
And to that Luther answered in words that seem to go to the very heart of things, "I shall be where I have always been — in the hands of Almighty God."

———o———

The men who succeed best in public life are those who take the risk of standing by their own convictions.

JAMES A. GARFIELD

Cooperate

Horse Sense

A horse can't pull while kicking
This fact we merely mention,
And he can't kick while pulling,
Which is our chief contention.

Let's imitate the good horse
And lead a life that's fitting;
Just pull an honest load, and
Then there'll be no time for kicking.

———o———

Begin this morning by saying to thyself, I shall meet with the busybody, the ungrateful, arrogant, deceitful, envious, unsocial. All these things happen to them by reason of their ignorance of what is good and evil. But I who have seen the nature of the good, that it is beautiful, and of the bad and that it is ugly, and the nature of him who does wrong, that it is akin to me, not only of the same blood but that it participates in the same intelligence and the same portion of the divinity, I can neither be injured by any of them, nor can I be angry with my kinsman nor hate him. For we are made for cooperation, like feet, like hands. To act against one another, then, is contrary to nature, and it is acting against one another to be vexed and to turn away. The best way of avenging thyself is not to become like the wrong-doer. Men exist for the sake of one another. Teach them, then, or bear with them.

MARCUS AURELIUS

———o———

Getting along in this world depends a lot on getting along well with others.

———o———

A man said to his body, "Today I will go with you three times to eat, but you will come with me three times to pray."

AUTHOR UNKNOWN

———o———

A little boy asked his father for assistance in repairing his broken wagon. When the job was done, the boy looked up and said, "Daddy, when I try to do things by myself, they go wrong. But when you and I work together, they turn out just fine."

———o———

Light is the task when many share the toil.

HOMER

———o———

Cooperation is spelled with two letters — WE.

G. M. VERITY

Cost

It will cost me to be loyal to Christ — but it will also pay.

———o———

What Then?

You've counted the cost of high living, my friend,
The heat, light, water and food.

You've counted the rent, car insurance and gas, all of them,
But have you counted the cost if your soul should be lost? What then?

You've counted the days till your pay check comes,
You've counted the dollars withheld and why,
You've counted the dollars that you can bring home,
And how much those dollars will buy.
But have you counted the cost if your soul should be lost? What then?

You've counted the distance you travel to work,
And the distance you come back again.
You've counted the bills you cannot shirk,
How you can pay them, and when.
But have you counted the cost if your soul should be lost? What then?

You've counted the cost of a new home perhaps,
And the beauties that make home so bright,
Of the children playing around your door —
All of which is proper and right —
But have you thought, my brother, that sometime you'll die, and when?
Have you counted the cost if your soul should be lost? What then?

EDNA UBER
in *The Log of the Good Ship Grace*

Country

To live in the country one must have the soul of a poet, the mind of a philosopher, the simple tastes of a hermit — and a good station wagon.

———o———

The country for a wounded heart.
English Proverb

Courage

The Difference

Sure, it takes a lot of courage
To put things in God's hands . . .
To give ourselves completely,
Our lives, our hopes, our plans;

To follow where He leads us
  And make His will our own . . .
But all it takes is foolishness
  To go the way alone!
BETSEY KLINE

———o———

Courage is, on all hands, considered as an essential of high character.
JAMES ANTHONY FROUDE

———o———

Remember you are your own doctor when it comes to curing cold feet.

———o———

Courage is fear that has said its prayers.

———o———

Courage is no more necessary on the battlefield than in the hourly choice between right and wrong!

———o———

Courage consists not in hazarding without fear, but being resolutely minded in a just cause.
PLUTARCH

———o———

Courage is a great thing. One may lose his money which is much, he may lose a friend and that is worse, but if he loses his courage he almost loses all.

———o———

If the glory of God is to break out in your service, you must be ready to go out into the night.
M. BASILEA SCHLINK

———o———

Courage is the virtue that makes other virtues possible.
SIR WINSTON CHURCHILL

———o———

Oftimes the test of courage becomes rather to live than to die.
VITTORIO ALFIERI, Oreste

———o———

Two small boys entered a dentist's office and one addressed the dentist as follows: "Say, Doc, will you pull a tooth right this minute? Don't want any gas or nothin'. Just give her one yank."

"Surely," replied the dentist. "My little man, that's what I call being brave and courageous. Now just show me the tooth you want pulled."

"Come, Wilfred, show Doc your tooth."

Courtesy

Courtesy, after all, is only kindliness, politeness and civility.

———o———

Courtesy is the eye which overlooks your friend's broken gateway — but sees the rose which blossoms in his garden.
LYMAN ABBOTT

———o———

Courtesy, good cheer, friendliness — the ability to serve without ostentation, the willingness to give freely of that spirit of welcome that warms the heart — this makes friends.

———o———

Once upon a time a man gave up his seat on a bus to a woman. She fainted. On recovering, she thanked him. Then he fainted.

———o———

How sweet and gracious, even in common speech,
  Is that fine sense which men call Courtesy!
Wholesome as air and genial as the light,
  Welcome in every clime as breath of flowers,
It transmutes aliens into trusting friends,
  And gives its owner passport round the globe.
JAMES THOMAS FIELDS, Courtesy

———o———

We must be as courteous to a man as we are to a picture, which we are willing to give the advantage of a good light.
RALPH WALDO EMERSON,
Conduct of Life, Behaviour

———o———

Courtesy comes from the heart. It is the unmistakable sign of good breeding.

Courtesy is made up of petty sacrifices.

———o———

That false courtesy, that smirking smile which comes from the lips only — is like a cheap gold plating, the baser metal soon shows through.

———o———

Some people should be sentenced to solitary refinement.

———o———

Courtesy is a science of the highest importance which ought to be on the curriculum of every Christian.

———o———

The small courtesies sweeten life; the greater ennoble it.

CHRISTIAN NESTELL BOVEE

Coward

There comes a time when silence is not golden — just plain yellow!

———o———

Necessity makes even the coward brave.

Old Proverb

———o———

Coward: one who in a perilous emergency thinks with his legs.

AMBROSE BIERCE

———o———

To sin by silence when they should protest makes cowards out of men.

ABRAHAM LINCOLN

Create, Creation

God creates out of nothing. Wonderful, you say. Yes, to be sure, but He does what is still more wonderful: He makes saints out of sinners.

SÖREN KIERKEGAARD

———o———

God never mends. He creates anew.

DWIGHT L. MOODY

———o———

Posterity will some day laugh at the foolishness of modern materialistic philosophy. The more I study nature, the more I am amazed at the Creator.

LOUIS PASTEUR

The probability of life originating from accident is comparable to the probability of the unabridged dictionary resulting from an explosion in a printing shop.

EDWIN CONKLIN

———o———

A little Ohio lad attending church school for the first time was asked by his teacher, "Who made you?"
"Made me?"
"Yes, who made you?"
"Why, God made me 'bout so long," holding his hands a few inches apart, "but I growed all the rest."

ORIGINAL SOURCE UNKNOWN

———o———

Nothing was made in vain, but the fly came near it.

MARK TWAIN

———o———

God created the world out of nothing. As long as you are not yet nothing, God cannot make something out of you.

MARTIN LUTHER

Credit

Many people would have skinny wallets if they removed the credit cards.

———o———

No man's credit is as good as his money.

EDGAR WATSON HOWE

———o———

You can accomplish almost anything if you don't care who gets the credit for it.

Creeds

I envy those men and women who know how to keep their creeds intact and unchanged throughout the entire journey of life. Their path is peace and their hope is sure.

SIR ARTHUR KEITH

Credo

Not what, but WHOM, I do believe,
That, in my darkest hour of need,
Hath comfort that no mortal creed

To mortal man may give;
Not what, but WHOM!
For Christ is more than all the
creeds,
And His full life of gentle deeds
Shall all the creeds outlive.
Not what I do believe, but WHOM!
WHO walks beside me in the gloom?
WHO shares the burden wearisome?
WHO all the dim way doth illume,
And bids me look beyond the tomb
The larger life to live?
Not what I do believe,
But WHOM!
Not what,
But WHOM!

JOHN OXENHAM

———o———

Here is my creed:
I believe in one God, creator of the
Universe.
That He governs it by His provi-
dence.
That He ought to be worshipped.
That the most acceptable service we
can render Him is doing good to
His other children.
That the soul of man is immortal,
and will be treated with justice in
another life respecting its conduct
in this life.

BENJAMIN FRANKLIN

———o———

The creed of today becomes the
deed of tomorrow.

E. STANLEY JONES

Crime

Permit a child to always get what
he wants when he wants it – and you
have a criminal in the making.

J. EDGAR HOOVER

———o———

The crime of the Christian church is
that we have withheld the Gospel from
the masses of people.

A. B. SIMPSON

———o———

Seven National Crimes

Seven so-called "national crimes,"
which are in reality unwholesome
mental attitudes are as follows:

1. I don't think.
2. I don't know.
3. I don't care.
4. I am too busy.
5. I leave well enough alone.
6. I have no time to read and find
out.
7. I am not interested.

The Record

———o———

Whoever profits by the crime is
guilty of it.

French Proverb

———o———

He who spares the guilty threatens
the innocent.

Legal Maxim

———o———

Every unpunished murder takes
away something from the security of
every man's life.

DANIEL WEBSTER

———o———

Murder may pass unpunished for a
time,
But tardy justice will o'ertake the
crime.

JOHN DRYDEN

Criticize

The world has so many critics because it is so much easier to criticize
than to appreciate.

LUC DE CLAPIERS VAUVENARG

———o———

He who throws mud loses ground

Presbyterian News

———o———

He who shrinks from criticism cannot safely be showered with praise.

———o———

You have to be little to belittle.

———o———

Nothing is easier than fault-finding;
no talent, no self-denial, no brains, no
character is required to set up in the
grumbling business.

———o———

At the close of a meeting a cynic
approached Mr. Moody and said:

"Mr. Moody, during your address this evening I counted eighteen mistakes in your English."

Looking at his critic, Mr. Moody answered:

"Young man, I am using for the glory of God all the grammar that I know. Are you doing the same?"

———o———

Let me give so much time to the improvement of myself that I shall have no time to criticize others.

DEAN CRESHAM

———o———

It is easy to shoot a skylark, but it is not so easy to produce its song.

LIONEL B. FLETCHER

———o———

He has right to criticize who has a heart to help.

ABRAHAM LINCOLN

———o———

Don't fear criticism. Ford forgot to put a reverse gear in his first automobile.

———o———

Some folks escape criticism by doing nothing.

RALPH BREWER

———o———

. . . how much easier it is to be critical than to be correct.

BENJAMIN DISRAELI

———o———

Most of the time, people criticize in order to forget their own weaknesses.

RALPH BREWER

———o———

Everything you reprove in another, you must carefully avoid in yourself.

MARCUS TULLIUS CICERO

———o———

Criticism, like charity, should begin at home.

———o———

A critic is a person who is unable to do a thing the way he thinks it ought to be done.

———o———

I looked upon my brother with the microscope of criticism, and said, "How coarse my brother is!" I looked at him with the telescope of scorn, and said, "How small my brother is!" I looked into the mirror of truth, and I said, "How like me my brother is!"

Cross

We all have crosses to bear, but let us not forget that it depends on the spirit in which we bear the cross as to whether it becomes an agony or a glory.

CLIFF COLE

———o———

The Cross Of Calvary

The Cross of Calvary
Was verily the key
By which our Brother Christ
Unlocked the door
Of immortality
To you and me;
And, passing through Himself before,
He set it wide
Forevermore,
That we, by His grace justified
And by His great love fortified,
Might enter in all fearlessly,
And dwell forever by His side.

JOHN OXENHAM

———o———

The cross is rough, and it is deadly, but it is effective. It does not keep its victim hanging there forever. There comes a moment when its work is finished. . . . After that is resurrection glory and power, and the pain is forgotten for joy that the veil is taken away and we have entered in actual experience the Presence of the living God.

A. W. TOZER, The Pursuit of God

———o———

The Cross is a symbol of God's heartbreak over a world that is gone astray.

SAM JONES

———o———

Jesus hath many lovers of His kingdom but few bearers of the cross. . . . All are disposed to rejoice with Him, but few to suffer for His sake.

THOMAS À KEMPIS, The Imitation of Christ

Crowds

It was the great Methodist evangelist, John Wesley, who told his young preachers: "Don't worry about how to get crowds. Just get on fire and the people will come to see you burn."

———o———

The more the merrier.

JOHN HEYWOOD,
Proverbs (a collection, 1546)

———o———

The reason the way of the transgressor is hard is that it is so crowded.

FRANK MCKINNEY HUBBARD

Culture

By culture many people mean stuffing modern houses full of antique furniture.

PABLO PICASSO

———o———

Culture is not Christianity but Christianity is culture. Christian culture is the apex of all culture.

HUGH C. BENNER

———o———

Culture . . . is a study of perfection.

MATTHEW ARNOLD, *Culture and Anarchy*

———o———

Culture is the fruit of acquainting ourselves with the best that has been known and said in the world.

MATTHEW ARNOLD

———o———

The soul of culture is the culture of the soul.

ALICE REID

———o———

A man should be just cultured enough to be able to look with suspicion upon culture.

SAMUEL BUTLER

Culture is the habit of being pleased with the best and knowing why.

HENRY VAN DYKE

Curiosity

Curiosity is, in great and generous minds, the first passion and the last.

SAMUEL JOHNSON

———o———

Ask me no questions, and I'll tell you no fibs.

OLIVER GOLDSMITH,
She Stoops to Conquer

———o———

The public have an insatiable curiosity to know everything — except what is worth knowing.

OSCAR WILDE

———o———

The farmer was milking a cow who was eating some hay when a child visitor asked, "If you feed your cow milk, will it give some hay?"

Cynic

A cynic is but a sentimentalist on guard.

———o———

It takes a clever man to turn cynic, and a wise man to be clever enough not to.

FANNIE HURST

———o———

A cynic is a man who, when he smells flowers, looks around for a coffin.

H. L. MENCKEN

———o———

What is a cynic? A man who knows the price of everything, and the value of nothing.

OSCAR WILDE, *Lady Windermere's Fan*

D

Daughter

A pretty good way to arrange additional closet space is to marry off a daughter.

Leader, Earlville, Illinois

———o———

Daughter am I in my mother's house;
But mistress in my own.

RUDYARD KIPLING, *Our Lady of the Snows*

———o———

Oh, my son's my son till he gets him a wife,
But my daughter's my daughter all her life.

DINAH MARIA MULOCK CRAIK,
Young and Old

———o———

Raise your daughter to know the Lord and she will have a built-in chaperon.

Day

Days are like suitcases: all nearly the same size, but some people can pack a lot more into them.

———o———

One Day At A Time

One day at a time, with its failures and fears,
With its hurts and mistakes, with its weakness and tears,
With its portion of pain and its burden of care;
One day at a time we must meet and must bear.

One day at a time to be patient and strong,
To be calm under trial and sweet under wrong,
Then its toiling shall pass, and its sorrow shall cease;
It shall darken and die, and the night shall bring peace.

One day at a time — but the day is so long,
And the heart is not brave and the soul is not strong.
O Thou pitiful Christ, be Thou near all the way;
Give courage and patience and strength for the day.

Swift cometh His answer, so clear and so sweet;
"Yea, I will be with thee, thy troubles to meet;
I will not forget thee, nor fail thee, nor grieve;
I will not forsake thee; I never will leave."

Not yesterday's load we are called on to bear,
Nor the morrow's uncertain and shadowy care;
Why should we look forward or back with dismay?
Our needs, as our mercies, are but for the day.

One day at a time, and the day is His day;
He hath numbered its hours, though they haste or delay.
His grace is sufficient; we walk not alone;
As the day, so the strength that He giveth His own.

ANNIE JOHNSON FLINT

———o———

Think that day lost whose descending sun
Views from thy hand no noble action done.

JACOB BOBART

———o———

Count the day lost in which you have not tried to do something for others.

HAROLD C. HOWARD

———o———

Morning

Open the window! Let in the sun!
Let in the morning! Day has begun!
Here at the height of it,
Warm to the sight of it,

Move in the light of it,
Wakening one!
Come from your dreaming in darkness
  and shade
Into a radiance never to fade!
Here at the start of it,
Close to the heart of it,
Know yourself part of it —
All He has made!

IRENE STANLEY

Death

I think of death as a glad awakening from this troubled sleep which we call life; as an emancipation from a world which, beautiful though it be, is still a land of captivity.

LYMAN ABBOTT

———o———

Death has nothing terrible which life has not made so. A faithful Christian life in this world is the best preparation for the next.

TRYON EDWARDS

———o———

Death to an enemy does not determine who was in the right!

———o———

He that lives to live forever, never fears dying.

WILLIAM PENN

———o———

The fear of death is cancelled by faith in Christ.

———o———

Warning!

If you are not prepared to die:

Do *not* ride in or get in the way of automobiles, as they are the cause of 20 percent of all accidents.

Do *not* stay at home, as 17 percent of all accidents happen inside the home. If you must be at home, stay outside; only 8.5 percent of all accidents occur around the outside of the house.

Do *not* walk on the street if you can avoid it, as 14 percent of all accidents occur to pedestrians.

Do *not* travel by air, rail, or water, because 6 percent of all accidents are the result of traveling.

Do *not* indulge in sports or recreation under any circumstances, for 20 percent of all accidents result from this.

Do *not* do anything or go anywhere, for a multitude of miscellaneous accidents may waylay you.

BUT . . . you can "believe on the Lord Jesus Christ, and thou shalt be saved" (Acts 16:31). Then you *will* be prepared to die anytime, anywhere.

T. M. OLSON in *The Shantyman*

———o———

When the small-town minister turned out on Sunday morning, he saw in the church driveway a dead mule, victim of a Saturday night driver. The preacher hastened to the phone and called the mayor.

"Why tell me?" asked his Honor. "I thought you preachers buried the dead."

"We do," said the preacher, "but first we always like to notify next of kin."

LUELLA DAHLSTROM

———o———

One of the world's great tragedies is that so many people die for nothing.

———o———

A man's conception of *death* will determine his philosophy of *life*.

———o———

The Christian Hope

BLESSED ARE THE DEAD WHICH DIE IN THE LORD.

"With Christ — which is far better" (Philippians 1:23).

Fallen asleep in Jesus!
How precious is that word!
Enjoying now for evermore
The presence of the Lord.
This is not death! 'tis only sleep;
The Lord doth now thy loved one keep.

The earthen vessel's broken,
The Treasure now has flown,
The Lord hath taken back again
What is by right His own.
But when He takes what most we store
It is that He may give thee more.

Thou wouldst have gladly kept her
A little longer here,
To soothe, and nurse, and cherish,
And make her wants thy care.
But He, who doeth what is best,
Hath called her to Himself to rest.

As members of one body
In sympathy we weep —
And yet rejoice — because we know
In Jesus she doth sleep.
For all her pain and suffering's o'er;
And joy her portion evermore.

'Tis not "Goodbye," beloved,
'Tis only just "Farewell."
A little while — a "moment,"
We too with Christ shall dwell:
And so we dry the falling tear,
Because we know the Lord is near.

O, may the God of Comfort
His richest grace impart!
Himself fill up the aching void,
Bind up thy broken heart;
And give thee now to look above,
And rest in His unchanging love.

AUTHOR UNKNOWN

———o———

Low-sunk life imagines itself weary of life; but it is death, not life, it is weary of.

GEORGE MACDONALD

———o———

Dying is the last thing I ever intend to do.

———o———

I dreamed Death came the other night,
And Heaven's gate swung wide,
With kindly grace an Angel came,
And ushered me inside.
And there to my astonishment,
Stood folks I'd known on Earth.
Some I'd judged and called "unfit,"
And some of "little worth."
Indignant words rose to my lips,
But never were set free,
For every face showed stunned surprise,
Not one expected me!

AUTHOR UNKNOWN

———o———

'Tis not the dying for a faith that's so hard . . . 'tis the living up to it that's difficult.

WILLIAM MAKEPEACE THACKERAY,
Henry Esmond

———o———

A few hours before entering the "Homeland" Dwight L. Moody caught a glimpse of the glory awaiting him. Awakening from a sleep, he said, "Earth recedes, Heaven opens before me. If this is death, it is sweet! There is no valley here. God is calling me, and I must go!" His son, who was standing by his bedside, said, "No, no, father, you are dreaming."

"No!" said Mr. Moody, "I am not dreaming: I have been within the gates: I have seen the children's faces." A short time elapsed and then, following what seemed to the family to be the death struggle, he spoke again: "This is my triumph; this is my coronation day! It is glorious!"

———o———

One can survive everything nowadays except death.

OSCAR WILDE

———o———

Dear God

(Poem found on the body of an unknown American soldier)

"Dear God, I've never spoken to you,
But now I desperately want to know you, too.
You see, God, they told me you didn't exist,
And, like a fool, I believed all this.
Last night from a shell-hole I saw your sky;
I figured right then they'd told me a lie.
Had I taken time to see things you had made
I'd have known they weren't calling a spade a spade.
I wonder, God, if you'd take my hand;
Somehow I feel that you will understand.
Strange I had to come to this hellish place
Before I had time to see your face.
Well, I guess there isn't much more to say,

But I'm sure glad, Lord, you opened
  the way.
I guess zero hour will soon be here.
But I'm not afraid since I know you
  are near.
The signal! Well, God, I guess I'll
  have to go.
I love you, Lord — this I want you to
  know.
Look now, this will be a horrible fight!
Who knows, I may come to your house
  tonight.
Though I wasn't friends with you be-
  fore,
I wonder, Christ, if You'd wait at Your
  door?
Look, I'm crying — me shedding tears.
How I wish I'd known You these many
  years!
Well, I have to go now, God. Good-
  bye.
Strange, since I met You I'm not
  scared to die."
              The Log of the Good Ship Grace

———o———

John Wesley when dying said:
"Brethren, farewell. The greatest thing
is that God still lives."

———o———

Last words of Francis Willard: "How
beautiful to be with God!"

Deceive

It is easier to deceive yourself than
to deceive anyone else.

———o———

Oh, what a tangled web we weave,
When first we practise to deceive!
              SIR WALTER SCOTT, *Marmion*

———o———

However much we may deceive others and ourselves, we never deceive
God.

———o———

Fool me once, shame on you;
Fool me twice, shame on me.
              Chinese Proverb

———o———

When we put up a bluff we are
sure to tumble over it.

A story is told of old Thomas K.
Beecher, who could not bear deceit in
any form. Finding that a clock in his
church was habitually too fast or too
slow he hung a placard on the wall
above it, reading in large letters:
"DON'T BLAME MY HANDS — THE TROU-
BLE LIES DEEPER." That is where the
trouble lies with us when our hands
do wrong, or our feet, or our lips, or
even our thoughts." The trouble lies
so deep that only God's miracle power
can deal with it. Sin indeed goes deep,
but Christ goes deeper.
              The Elim Evangel

Decision
(See also Choice)

Whenever you face a decision you
have three chances: Do what you
please; do what others do; or do what
is right.
              A. BANNINGISM

———o———

Seed

Seed that is planted in the mind
  Bears fruitage after its own kind;
The choice of which shall die or grow
  Rests with the one who wields the
    hoe.
              MYRA BROOKS WELCH

———o———

When we let somebody else decide
what our reaction shall be, we are no
longer free persons, whether we decide
to agree or disagree.
              SYDNEY J. HARRIS

———o———

A layman visited a great city church
during a business trip. After the service, he congratulated the minister on
his service and sermon. "But," said
the manufacturer, "if you were my
salesman, I'd discharge you. You got
my attention by your appearance, voice
and manner; your prayer, reading and
logical discourse aroused my interest;
you warmed my heart with a desire
for what you preached; and then —
and then you stopped without asking
me to do something about it. In business the important thing is to get them
to sign on the dotted line."
              JAMES DUFF

When an old Indian Chief first heard of the Savior, he said, "The Jesus road is good, but I've followed the old Indian road all my life, and I will follow it to the end."

A year later he was on the border of death. Seeking a pathway through the darkness, he said to the missionary, "Can I turn to Jesus now? My road stops here. It has no path through the valley."

———o———

I saw a tiny little boy in a candy store. He wandered from case to case with the utmost gravity, studying each assortment with deep seriousness.

His mother, tired of waiting, called to him, "Hurry up, son, spend your money. We must be going."

To this he replied, "But Mama, I've only one penny to spend, and I've got to spend it carefully."

———o———

Once to every man and nation comes
   the moment to decide,
In the strife of Truth with Falsehood,
   for the good or evil side.
JAMES RUSSELL LOWELL, *The Present Crisis*

Dedication

God wants your heart every hour in the day, and every day in the week, and every week in the year.
ULDINE UTLEY

———o———

A Mother's Dedication

Dear Lord, I bring to Thee my son
Whose tender years have scarce begun;
In this wee frame I know full well
A living soul has come to dwell
Who needs Thee now at childhood's
   gate
Ere he shall grow to man's estate.
I covenant through hours apart
To pray for him with fervent heart,
To teach Thy Word with winsome
   voice
By day and night until his choice
Be but Thy blood for sin's deep stain,
And my small son is born again;
Then onward shall I pray the more

And teach Thy precepts o'er and o'er
That he may grow, each boyhood hour
By Thine indwelling risen power.
Lord, some small boys with none to
   care
Will never hear a mother's prayer;
Prepare my son with love aflame
To reach them with Thy saving name;
And make him, Lord, a polished tool,
A learner in Thy highest school.
A mother's part seems, oh, so frail!
But Thy strong arm can never fail;
To teach, to pray, to stand are mine;
The miracles must all be Thine.
Expectantly, I yield to Thee
The little boy Thou gavest me.
LOUISE B. EAVEY

———o———

If I had 300 men who feared nothing but God, hated nothing but sin, and were determined to know nothing among men but Jesus Christ, and Him crucified, I would set the world on fire.
JOHN WESLEY

———o———

Many of us would love to have sin taken away. Who loves to have a hasty temper? Who loves to have a proud disposition? Who loves to have a worldly heart? No one. You ask Christ to take it away, and He does not do it. Why does He not do it? It is because you wanted Him to take away the ugly fruits while the poisonous roots remained in you. You did not ask that henceforth you might give up self entirely to the power of His Spirit. Do you suppose that a painter would want to work out a beautiful picture on a canvas which did not belong to him? No. Yet people want Jesus Christ to take away this temper or that other sin while as yet they have not yielded themselves utterly to His command.
ANDREW MURRAY

———o———

The Instrument

As ocean waves that sing upon the
   sand,
Or as a bow held in a master's hand
That sweeps that taut and waiting
   strings, —
So shall my spirit, tuned to heavenly
   things,

Give forth, as they, its tenderest melodies
When God's own hand sweeps o'er the silent keys.
My life an instrument through which is poured
Ecstatically, the music of the Lord!
                    BERNIECE AYERS HALL

———o———

O that I could dedicate my all to God! This is all the return I can make Him.
                    DAVID BRAINERD

———o———

No candle on the altar of a church will ever substitute for a flame in the heart of the preacher in the pulpit.
                    ROY L. SMITH

Deeds

Give me the ready hand rather than the ready tongue.
                    GIUSEPPE GARIBALDI

———o———

The smallest *deed* is better than the greatest *intention*.

———o———

Little deeds of kindness, little words of love,
Help to make earth happy, like the heaven above.
Little deeds of mercy sown by careful hands,
Grow to bless the nations far in heathen lands.
                    JULIA A. FLETCHER CARNEY,
                    Little Things

———o———

Our deeds are like stones cast into the pool of time; though they themselves may disappear, their ripples extend to eternity.
                    Our Daily Bread

———o———

Small deeds done are better than great deeds planned.
                    PETER MARSHALL

———o———

If our faith were greater, our deeds would be larger.

If any little word of ours has made one heart the lighter,
If any little deeds of ours has made one life the brighter;
Lord, take that little word or deed, or any bit of singing,
And drop it in some lonely vale, and set the echoes ringing.
                    AUTHOR UNKNOWN

———o———

Deeds are the X-rays which enable others to discern our inner life. What we are within is revealed through what we are without.

———o———

I count this thing to be grandly true,
That a noble deed is a step toward God,
Lifting the soul from the common sod
To a purer air and a broader view.
                    JOSIAH GILBERT HOLLAND, *Gradatim*

Defeat

When we start talking of defeat, too often the devil has the victory already.
                    JESS KAUFFMAN

———o———

Some defeats are only installments to victory.
                    JACOB A. RIIS

———o———

There are some defeats more triumphant than victories.
                    MICHEL EYQUEM DE MONTAIGNE,
                    Of Cannibals

———o———

Man learns little from victory, but much more from defeat.
                    Japanese Proverb

———o———

Helen Keller became deaf, dumb, and blind shortly after birth . . . her entire life has served as evidence that no one ever is defeated until defeat has been accepted as a reality.

———o———

Robert E. Lee was one of American's greatest men. He was a great general, but his real greatness was shown in defeat. He accepted it without fear, hate, or rancor.

WILLIAM ROSS

———o———

Defeat never comes to any man until he admits it.

———o———

No defeat is final unless you choose to make it so.

Definitions

Alarm Clock: A mechanism used to scare the daylights into you.

———o———

During an oral test the teacher asked one of the students to give a sentence using the word *ambushed.* Answer: "Well, I sat through two TV horror pictures last night and today I sure ambushed!"

———o———

Antique: A piece of furniture that is paid for.

———o———

Auction Sale: Where you get something for nodding.

———o———

Bachelor: A man who believes in life, liberty, and the happiness of pursuit.

———o———

Blarney is simply baloney coated with an Irish smile!

———o———

Modern *Bridegroom*: A fellow who expects some finance firm to carry practically everything over the threshold except the bride.

———o———

Broadmindedness is highmindedness flattened out by experience.

Clipper, Lexington, Nebraska

———o———

Bureaucracy is a giant mechanism operated by pygmies.

HONORÉ DE BALZAC

Career Girl: A girl who'd rather bring home the bacon than fry it.

———o———

Collection: A church function in which many take no more than a passing interest.

HOWIE LASSETER

———o———

Desperation: A man in want of bread is ready for anything.

French Proverb

———o———

Discussion: A method of confronting others in their errors.

AMBROSE BIERCE

———o———

Do-gooder: A person trying to live beyond his spiritual income.

H. A WILLIAMS

———o———

Equator: Menagerie lion running around the earth and ending in Africa with all the wild animals.

———o———

Faith: Reason grown courageous. What Christ asks is that we shall try it out.

WILFRED GRENFELL

———o———

Friend: One who knows everything about us, and yet knows nothing except that which is good.

FRANK JOHNSON

———o———

Generation: The period between the time when a town tears down an historic landmark and the time when it has a fund-raising drive to build an authentic reproduction of it.

———o———

Gentleman: A man who can disagree without being disagreeable.

———o———

Good Breeding: That quality that enables a person to wait in well-mannered silence while the loud mouth gets the service.

———o———

Honeymoon: The period between "I do" and "You'd better."

Kleptomaniac: A rich thief.
AMBROSE BIERCE

———o———

Lyric: Something written to be sung by a liar.

———o———

Manuscript: Something submitted in haste and returned at leisure.
OLIVER HERFORD

———o———

Mealtime: When youngsters sit down to continue eating.
The Office Economist

———o———

Minister: One who will burst inside unless a message from God gets said.
FRANK JOHNSON

———o———

Mockery: Mockery is the child of ignorance; we jest at what we know nothing of.
HONDRÉ DE BALZAC

———o———

Neurotic: A person in a clash by himself.

———o———

Four-year-old's definition of *nursery school*: A place where they try to teach children who hit, not to hit; and children who don't hit, to hit back.
M. S. N. in Parents' Magazine

———o———

Optimist: A fellow who never reads the headlines on today's newspapers.

———o———

Pedestrian: A husband who didn't think the family needed two cars.

———o———

Poise: The ability to continue talking about something else while the other fellow picks up the check.

———o———

Positive: Being mistaken at the top of one's voice.
AMBROSE BIERCE

Radical: A fellow who can out-talk you on any subject.

———o———

A wife's definition of *retirement*: Twice as much husband on half as much income.

———o———

Self-Made Man: One who absolves God of a great responsibility.
FRANK JOHNSON

———o———

Seminary: A place where they bury the dead.

———o———

Sermon: Something that takes a lifetime of experience and twenty hours to prepare, but must be spoken in twenty minutes.
FRANK JOHNSON

———o———

Social Grace: The ability to yawn and not open your mouth.

———o———

Spring: God thinking in gold, laughing in blue, and speaking in green.
FRANK JOHNSON

———o———

One old brother said, "*Status quo* is Latin for the mess we're in."

———o———

Thinking: The talking of the soul with itself.

Delinquent

Rules for Raising Delinquent Children

1. Begin with infancy to give the child everything he wants. In this he will grow up to believe the world owes him a living!

2. When he picks up bad words, laugh at him. This will make him think he's cute. It will also encourage him to pick up "cuter" phrases!

3. Never give him any spiritual training. Wait until he is 21 and then let him decide himself!

4. Avoid use of the word "wrong." It might develop a guilt complex!

5. Pick up everything he leaves lying around — books, shoes, clothes. Do

everything for him so that he will be experienced in throwing all responsibility on others!

6. Let him read any printed matter he can get his hands on. Be careful that the silverware and drinking glasses are sterilized, but let his mind feed on garbage!

7. Quarrel frequently in the presence of your children. In this way they will not be too shocked when the home is broken up later!

8. Give the child all the spending money he wants. Never let him earn his own. Why should he have things as tough as you did!

9. Satisfy his every craving for food, drink and comfort. See that every sensual desire is gratified. Denial may lead him to harmful frustration!

10. Take his part against neighbors, teachers and policemen. They are all prejudiced against your child!

11. When he gets into real trouble, apologize for yourself saying, "I never could do anything for him."

12. Prepare for a life of grief. You will be likely to have it!

Houston, Texas, Police Department

Democracy

Democracy is a method of getting ahead without leaving any of us behind.

T. V. SMITH

A democracy, — that is a government of all the people, by all the people, for all the people; of course, a government of the principles of eternal justice, the unchanging law of God; for shortness sake I will call it the idea of Freedom.

THEODORE PARKER, *The American Idea*

While democracy must have its organization and controls, its vital breath is individual liberty.

CHARLES EVANS HUGHES

The strength of democracy is judged by the quality of its services rendered by its citizens.

PLATO

Desire

An inquirer once asked a student what three things he most wanted, and he said, "Give me books, health and quiet." He asked a miser and he cried, "Money, money, money." He asked a pauper, and he said faintly, "Bread, bread, bread." The drunkard called loudly for strong drink. He turned to the multitude around him, and he heard in a confused cry, "Wealth, fame, pleasure!" Then he asked a poor man who had long been an earnest Christian. He replied that all his wants and wishes were met in Christ. He spoke seriously and explained: "I greatly desire three things: first, that I may be found IN Christ (Philippians 3:9); secondly, that I may be LIKE Christ (Philippians 3:10-11); and thirdly, that I may be WITH Christ (Philippians 1:23).

DWIGHT L. MOODY

Any unmortified desire which a man allows will effectually drive and keep Christ out of the heart.

CHARLES WESLEY

Some of us don't know what we want, but feel sure we don't have it.

Lord, grant that I may always desire more than I can accomplish.

MICHELANGELO

It is not our changing circumstances, but our unregulated desires that rob us of peace.

ALEXANDER MACLAREN

There is not one whom we employ who does not, like ourselves, desire recognition, praise, gentleness, forbearance, patience.

HENRY WARD BEECHER

A young fellow was looking at his pastor's new car.

"My, it's beautiful," he said excitedly. "I'm so glad you could get it."

"Well," his pastor replied, "I'm glad you like it. But, to tell you the truth, I didn't buy it. On my salary, I just couldn't afford it. My brother Bob bought it and gave it to me free of charge."

The pastor expected the usual reaction, the whiney, "My, I wish I had a brother like that."

But instead, the young boy looked up at the pastor thoughtfully and said, "My, I wish I *could be* a brother like that!"

———o———

The man who really wants to do something finds a way; the other kind finds an excuse.

———o———

If you want to be miserable, think about yourself. If you want to be perplexed, think about others. If you want to be filled with joy, meditate on the Lord Jesus Christ.

———o———

The stomach is the only part of man which can be fully satisfied. The yearning of man's brain for new knowledge and experience and for more pleasant and comfortable surroundings never can be completely met. It is an appetite which cannot be appeased.

THOMAS A. EDISON,
quoted in *This Week Magazine*

Destiny

One's destiny is determined, not by what he possesses, but by what possesses him.

———o———

Where one goes hereafter depends largely upon what he goes after here!

———o———

Destiny waits in the hand of God, not in the hands of statesmen.

T. S. ELIOT

———o———

Details will decide destiny.

———o———

The tissue of Life to be
We weave with colors all our own,
And in the field of destiny,
We reap as we have sown.

JOHN GREENLEAF WHITTIER, *Raphael*

Determination

If you have spunk enough, you can make quite a successful career of doing what others should but would rather not.

Times-Leader, West Point, Mississippi

———o———

Let us not be content to wait and see what will happen, but give us the determination to make the right thing happen.

PETER MARSHALL

———o———

A determined soul will do more with a rusty monkey-wrench than a loafer will accomplish with all the tools in a machine shop.

RUPERT HUGHES

———o———

When man is determined to have his own way, he will refuse to examine any evidence that may prove him wrong.

———o———

When life kicks you, let it kick you forward.

E. STANLEY JONES

———o———

A man without determination is but an untempered sword.

Chinese Proverb

———o———

To him that is determined it remains only to act.

Italian Proverb

———o———

What people say you cannot do, you try and find that you can.

HENRY DAVID THOREAU

Devil, Satan

Although the devil be the father of lies, he seems, like other great inventors, to have lost much of his reputation by the continual improvements that have been made upon him.

JONATHAN SWIFT

There are five or six devils working against you and me, affecting our usefulness, our happiness, and our health. They are worry, hate, hurry, fear, disappointment and pride.

———o———

The devil is the top hidden persuader — the master of subliminal motivation.

JESS C. MOODY

———o———

Asked one time how he overcame the Devil, Martin Luther replied: "Well, when he comes knocking upon the door of my heart, and asks, 'Who lives here?' the dear Lord Jesus goes to the door and says, 'Martin Luther used to live here but he has moved out. Now I live here.' The Devil, seeing the nail-prints in His hands, and the pierced side, takes flight immediately."

———o———

The one concern of the devil is to keep Christians from praying.

SAMUEL CHADWICK

———o———

The devil is worthy of some honor; he minds his business and is wide awake in this sleepy, drowsy age.

———o———

The devil is diligent at his plough.

BISHOP HUGH LATIMER,
Sermon on Ploughers

———o———

The cry of theologians that "God is dead" proves very much that the Devil is alive!

The Gospel Call

———o———

Undertake some worthwhile labor that the devil may always find you occupied.

———o———

If the devil catches a man idle, he will set him to work.

———o———

Billy Sunday used to say, "Yes, I know Satan — I've done business with him."

Some people don't seem to realize that whenever they turn their back on God, they face the devil.

Selected

———o———

Satan has many wiles. His favorite is "Wait awhile."

Devotion, Devotional Life

Rules For Daily Life

Begin the day with God,
  Kneel down to Him in prayer;
Lift up thy heart to His abode;
  And seek His love to share.

Open the Book of God
  And read a portion there,
That it may hallow all thy thoughts
  And sweeten all thy care.

Go through the day with God,
  Whate'er thy work may be;
Where e'er thou art — at home, abroad
  He is still near to thee.

Conclude the day with God:
  Thy sins to Him confess,
Trust in His cleansing blood,
  And plead His righteousness.

Lie down at night with God
  Who gives His servants sleep;
And when thou treadest the vale of
    death,
  He will thee guard and keep.

AUTHOR UNKNOWN

———o———

One Day To Live

Had I but this one day to live,
One day to love, one day to give,
One day to work and watch and raise
My voice to God in joyful praise,
One day to succour those in need,
Pour healing balm on hearts that bleed,
Or wipe the tears from sorrow's face,
And hearten those in sad disgrace —
I'd spend, O God, much time with
    THEE
That Thou might'st plan my day for
  me.
Most earnestly I'd seek to know
The way that Thou would'st have me
  go,

For Thou alone canst see the heart —
Thou knowest man's most inward parts.

A.M.M.

———o———

A moment in the morning, take your
Bible in hand,
And catch a gleam of glory from the
peaceful promised land;
It will linger still before you, when
you seek the busy mart,
And like flowers of hope will blossom
into beauty in your heart;
The precious words like jewels, will
glisten all the day
With a rare effulgent glory that will
brighten all the way.

———o———

Thou hast made us O Lord for Thyself and our heart shall find no rest till it rest in Thee.

SAINT AUGUSTINE, Confessions

———o———

Hurried "devotions" become nothing but religious "commotions."

Diet

One thing you can always be sure of — there are more people going on diets tomorrow than are going on diets today.

———o———

Eat all you can cart
Today without sorrow;
You always can start
Your diet tomorrow.

———o———

To find out what a poor loser you are, just start dieting.

———o———

Diets are for persons who are thick and tired of it.

Tit-Bits

———o———

A young mother thought it was time to break her little boy of thumb-sucking, and she decided to do it by psychology. "Now, tell me, Johnny, does your thumb taste good?"

"No," the boy admitted.

"Is it good to chew on?"

The boy shook his head.

"Then what is good about sucking your thumb?"

"Well," the boy said after some thought, "it's non-fattening."

FRANCES BENSON in Family Weekly

———o———

Who ends the day with wholesome food, begins the next in a happy mood.

Ancient Saying

———o———

Some persons diet on any kind of food they can get.

Difference

Honest differences of views and honest debate are not disunity. They are the vital process of policy-making among free men.

HERBERT HOOVER

———o———

There's only a slight difference between keeping your chin up and sticking your neck out, but it's worth knowing.

Grit

———o———

Each of us lives a life that never has been, or ever will be, exactly like that of any other human being.

KEYES

———o———

When men come face to face, their differences often vanish.

Difficulties

There Are Difficulties
And There Are "Difficulties"

A Marine who hadn't got mail for weeks was finally handed a letter while lying in a foxhole on Saipan with bullets whizzing overhead. It was a bill for $3.52, and the note read, "If this bill is not paid in five days, you will find yourself in serious trouble."

———o———

One of the grandest things to live for is to make life less difficult for other people.

CLIFF COLE

Write it over all your difficulties, pen it across all your disappointments, inscribe it on all your fears, post it over all your troubles — GOD IS ABLE.

———o———

Settle one difficulty and you keep a hundred others away.

Chinese Proverb

———o———

Difficulties are opportunities.

Proverb

———o———

Many men owe the grandeur of their lives to their tremendous difficulties.

CHARLES HADDON SPURGEON

———o———

Difficulties increase the nearer we approach our goal.

JOHANN WOLFGANG VON GOETHE

———o———

Some men make difficulties; some difficulties make men.

———o———

It takes the storm to prove the real shelter.

———o———

Out of difficulties grow miracles.

JEAN DE LA BRUYÈRE

———o———

When you are face to face with a difficulty, you are up against a discovery.

———o———

A hard fall means a high bounce — if you're made of the right material.

Diligence

It is better for a pot to boil over than never to boil at all.

———o———

Too many people itch for what they want but won't scratch for it.

Few things are impossible to diligence.

SAMUEL JOHNSON

———o———

Patience and diligence, like faith, remove mountains.

WILLIAM PENN

———o———

Diligence is the mother of good fortune.

MIGUEL DE CERVANTES, *Don Quixote*

———o———

Diligent working makes an expert workman.

Danish Proverb

Diplomacy

Diplomacy is the art of saying, "nice doggy" until you have time to pick up a rock.

———o———

Diplomacy is the art of letting someone else have your way.

———o———

Men, like bullets, go farthest when they are smoothest.

JEAN PAUL RICHTER

Direction

Society has erected the gallows at the end of the lane instead of guide posts and direction boards at the beginning.

EDWARD GEORGE BULWER-LYTTON

———o———

The greater thing in this world is not so much where we stand, as in what direction we are going.

OLIVER WENDELL HOLMES

———o———

Whenever things seem to go dead wrong, it wouldn't be a bad idea to stop and see if you're not facing in the wrong direction.

———o———

God judges a man not by the point he has reached, but by the way he is facing; not by distance, but by direction.

Too often we run across some fellow who seems to think he is ahead of the times, when infact the times are not going in his direction at all.

———o———

When God does the directing our life is useful and full of promise, whatever it is doing and discipline has its perfecting work.

H. E. COBB

———o———

If you don't know where you are going, then you are lost before you start.

Disagree

A church furnishings committee was meeting in the basement because there were no lights in the church auditorium. One committee member made a motion that the church purchase chandeliers. An older man on the committee objected for three reasons.

"First," he said, "no one can play it. Second, we can't afford it, and third, we need lights!"

———o———

Some hair-splitters don't stop with hairs, they go right on through the head.

JOE BLINCO

———o———

It is regrettable that, among the Rights of Man, the right of contradicting oneself has been forgotten.

CHARLES BAUDELAIRE

Discipline

Discipline of Sunday school pupils is making disciples of them.

———o———

Command discipline, do not demand it.

———o———

Raising Billie

Papa said, "Now Billie, don't!"
But Billie said, "I will," and did;
And Papa went to get the rod,
But Mama said, "Don't beat the kid."

So Papa laid aside the rod
While Billie smiled at "poor old Dad,"
And Mama stroked "dear Billie's" head
And called him her poor little lad.

The years have passed and Bill is gone —
Buried in a sinner's grave —
While Mom and Dad still linger on,
So sad they let him misbehave.

The lesson's clear for all to see:
If you would raise a son for God,
Father and Mother must agree
When Billie needs it, use the rod!

R. H. BURROWS

———o———

Sometimes you can straighten out a youngster by bending him over.

Herald, Troy, Alabama

———o———

A lot of child welfare can be done with razor strap.

WILLIAM WARD AYER

———o———

Nothing impresses the young go-to-schooler
Like a teacher who uses the Golden Ruler.

SUSAN LLOYD in *Coronet*

———o———

Discipline effects destiny.

———o———

If a child annoys you, quiet him by brushing his hair. If this doesn't work, use the other side of the brush on the other end of the child.

Shawano, Wisconsin County Journal

———o———

About the only thing that gets an old-fashioned licking around most homes nowadays is a postage stamp.

———o———

The quickest way to be convinced that spanking is unnecessary is to become a grandparent.

———o———

Parents who are afraid to put their foot down usually have children who step on their toes.

What is discipline? As any small boy knows, it's something unpleasant Daddy had when he was little.

———o———

If parents don't mind that their kids don't mind, the kids don't.

———o———

Master easy, servant slack.
Chinese Proverb

———o———

There was more pathos than humor in what a disgruntled five-year-old boy said to his preacher father when the latter tried to take over the discipline in one of his rare visits home at meal time. "Aw, Dad," said the boy, "why don't you go to a meeting?"
Southern California Presbyterian

———o———

More board meetings in the wood-shed would mean fewer cases in the juvenile courts.

———o———

On juvenile delinquency we would say with the poet, "Oh, for the smack of a vanished hand on the place where the spank ought to be."

———o———

A young businessman returned home tired from a hard day at the office to find his two children rushing madly about the house. He gave them both a scolding and sent them to bed as soon as possible. The next morning he found this note pinned to his bedroom door:
"Be good to your children and they will be good to you. Yours truly, God."

Discontent

Discontent is the price we pay for not being thankful for what we have.

———o———

Discontent may become either spur or spite.
DAGOBERT D. RUNES

———o———

Pliny informs us that Zeuxis once painted such a realistic picture of a boy holding a dish full of grapes that the birds were deceived and flew to the grapes to peck at them. Zeuxis, notwithstanding, was dissatisfied with the picture. "For," said he, "had I painted the boy as well as he ought to have been painted, the birds would have been afraid to touch them." Thus does the Christian dwell more on his shortcomings than on his attainments.
F. F. TRENCH

Discouragement

Let discouragement harden your determination, never your heart.

———o———

Discouragement is a handle that fits many tools.

———o———

Perhaps nothing more effectually cripples achievement than does discouragement.

Discover

When I want to discover something, I begin by reading up everything that has been done along the line in the past. I see what has been accomplished at great labor and expense in the past. I gather the data of many thousands of experiments as a starting point, and then I make several thousand more.
THOMAS A. EDISON

———o———

All human discoveries seem to be made only for the purpose of confirming more and more strongly the truths contained in the Holy Scriptures.
SIR JOHN HERSCHEL

———o———

When we find Christ, we find *everything;* when Christ finds us, He finds *nothing.*

———o———

The greatest discovery I made in life was that God was probably right when I thought Him to be wrong.
REUBEN A. TORREY

Disposition

It isn't your position but your disposition that makes you happy or unhappy.

———o———

The most destructive acid in the world is found in a sour disposition.

———o———

Your emotions shape your disposition. You can give way to hate, resentment, worry, fear, jealousy, and grumbling; or you may let love, faith, hope, goodwill, and kindness predominate.

———o———

Most people are just like cats in that if you rub them the right way, they will purr, but if you rub them the wrong way, they will bite and scratch.
WILLIAM ROSS

———o———

The wearer of smiles and the bearer of a kindly disposition needs no introduction, but is welcome anywhere.
O. S. MARDEN

Do, Doing
(See also Acts, etc.)

One never knows what he can do until he tries.

———o———

The world is blessed mostly by men who do things, not by those who merely talk about doing.

———o———

There never was a person who did anything worth doing who did not receive more than he gave.
HENRY WARD BEECHER

———o———

The more we do, the more we can do.
WILLIAM HAZLITT

———o———

No one ever climbed a hill by looking at it.

———o———

As I grow older, I pay less attention to what men say. I just watch what they do.
ANDREW CARNEGIE

———o———

Even though you are on the right track, you will be run over if you sit still.

———o———

Whatever is worth doing at all is worth doing well.
LORD CHESTERFIELD

———o———

Content yourself with doing, leave the talking to others.
BALTASAR GRACIÀN

———o———

Our chief want in life is somebody who shall make us do what we can.
RALPH WALDO EMERSON, Conduct of Life,
Considerations by the Way

———o———

The great pleasure in life is doing what people say you cannot do.
WALTER BAGEHOT

———o———

The shortest answer is doing.
GEORGE HERBERT

Doctor

A man took his wife to the doctor, who put a thermometer in her mouth and told her to keep her mouth shut for three minutes. When departing, the husband called the doctor aside and said, "What will you take for that thing, Doc?"

———o———

The best doctors in the world are Doctor Diet, Doctor Quiet, and Doctor Merryman.
JONATHAN SWIFT, *Polite Conversation*

———o———

No man is a good physician who has never been sick.
Arabian Proverb

———o———

I dressed his wounds, but God healed him.
AMBROISE PARÉ (father of modern surgery)

Inside information is what a doctor gets.

Doors

Doors

Doors are opened many ways,
  By a key, or beam of light,
By gentle touch, or sudden jar,
  Or by the wind at night.

Doors are opened many ways
  Which we may understand;
But most important are the doors
  God opens with His hand.
MILDRED ALLEN JEFFERY

———o———

All doors open to the man with a smile.

Doubt

There lives more faith in honest doubt,
Believe me, than in half the creeds.
ALFRED, LORD TENNYSON, *In Memoriam*

———o———

Philosophy goes no further than probabilities, and in every assertion keeps a doubt in reserve.
JAMES ANTHONY FROUDE

———o———

Skepticism is slow suicide.
RALPH WALDO EMERSON

———o———

If we begin with certainties, we shall end in doubt; but if we begin with doubts, and are patient in them, we shall end in certainties.
FRANCIS BACON

Dream

The Dreamer

They said: "He is only a dreamer of
  dreams,"
And passed him by with a smile;
But, out of his dreams he fashioned a
  song
That made life more worth while.

And who shall say he was less a part
Of the universal plan,

If, instead of building a mighty bridge,
He molded the life of a man?
ANNA M. PRIESTLY

———o———

Dreams are but interludes which fancy makes.
WILLIAM SHAKESPEARE

———o———

We cannot dream ourselves into what we could be.

———o———

Dreams are of great worth if they are carried into practice.

———o———

Dreaming has its values, but never should it become a substitute for work that needs to be done.

Drive, Driver

When motorists ignored "No parking" signs put on the private lot of a minister of one church, he put up a placard reading "Thou Shalt Not Park." It worked.

———o———

He who weaves his car in and out of traffic may be crocheting a shroud.

———o———

Instead of devoting so much time to developing more horsepower for their cars, maybe the auto manufacturers should try to find a way to put more horse sense into drivers.

———o———

Garage attendant to woman driver of badly battered car: "Sorry, lady, we just wash cars — we don't iron them."
CAVALLI in *True*

———o———

Traffic sign near school: Use your eyes and save the pupils.
Exchange

———o———

Man, teaching wife to drive: "Go on green, stop on red, take it easy when I turn white."

Sign on a cemetery along a well-traveled street: "Drive carefully. We can wait."

———o———

Always try to drive so that your license will expire before you do.

———o———

If more drivers would give some ground, there would be fewer of them in it.

———o———

Second-grader boasting about mother's progress in learning to drive: "She's getting real good at paralyze parking.
This Week Magazine

———o———

It's better to have one foot on the brake than six feet under the ground.

———o———

A traffic-choked bridge in London is called "the car-strangled spanner."
Evening Standard, London

———o———

Prayer For Motorists

O ever-present Lord, I pray,
Be with me at the wheel today.
Fill every corner of my mind,
So roaming thoughts no lodging find.
And take control of my two eyes,
That I may be alert and wise,
And take my feet, and take my hands,
That they react to quick demands.
Give me thy guidance, Friend Divine,
For other folks as well as mine.
Then, when we come to journey's end,
My prayer to heaven will ascend
In utter thankfulness to Thee,
Who kept the wheel all day with me.
REV. F. OSWALD BARNETT (Australia)

Duty

Life's Common Duties

Dream not of noble service elsewhere wrought,
The simple duty that awaits thy hand

Is God's voice uttering a divine command;
Life's common duties build what saints have thought.

In wonder-workings, or some bush aflame,
Men look for God and fancy Him concealed;
But in earth's common things He stands revealed,
While grass and flowers and stars spell out His name.
MINOT J. SAVAGE,
In Common Things

———o———

Do the Duty which lies nearest thee; which thou knowest to be a Duty! Thy second Duty will already have become clearer.
THOMAS CARLYLE, *Sartor Resartus*

———o———

The reward of one duty is the power to fulfil another.
GEORGE ELIOT (MARY ANN EVANS)

———o———

Your first duty is to do your duty first.

———o———

You should never wish to do less than your duty.
ROBERT E. LEE

———o———

The best way to get rid of your duties is to discharge them.

———o———

Duty and today are ours; results and the future belong to God.

———o———

When in Rome, do as the Romans ought to do.

———o———

A duty dodged is like a debt unpaid; it is only deferred, and we must come back and settle the account at last.
JOSEPH FORT NEWTON

E

Early

The early morning hours have gold in their mouth.

Dutch Proverb

———o———

Starting an hour earlier in the morning may make you an achiever instead of an almost.

DONALD LAIRD

———o———

Our five-year-old Jeanie took to rising at 5:30 each morning and puttering around just long enough to wake the rest of us before climbing back into bed. Her reason was always the same — she had to see if there was a surprise. Finally we told her firmly that she must stop and that there wouldn't be any surprises until Christmas, which was months away.

"I wasn't talking about living-room surprises," she said through her tears. "I was talking about like yesterday morning it was raining, and this morning real summer's here, and tomorrow morning I'll probably find some pink in the rosebuds."

Jeanie still gets up each morning at 5:30.

MRS. ROY F. CARTER in *Reader's Digest*

———o———

One school morning as I tried for the second or third time to awaken my six-year-old son, he half-opened his eyes, looked at me in disgust, and remarked, "Whoever invented morning sure made it too early."

MRS. JACQUELINE AHLSTRAND in *Teach*

———o———

He that would thrive must rise at five;
He that has thriven may lie till seven.

Ease, Easy

What is easy is seldom excellent.

SAMUEL JOHNSON

———o———

A life of ease is a difficult pursuit.

WILLIAM COWPER

It is easier to go down a hill than up, but the view is best from the top.

ARNOLD BENNETT

Easter

Easter Dawning

There's a whisper in the garden in the
  morning very early,
And the flowers nod serenely in the
  silver of the moon;
And the warbling of the songbirds in
  the olives gnarled and hoary
Tell the story — tell the story
That our Lord is rising soon.

There's a stirring in the branches in
  the morning in the moonlight,
Glad musicians fill the whole earth
  with a burst of wondrous song;
And the sun's rays gild with splendor
  and unearthly light His prison,
And the sky cries: "He is risen!"
While hosannas sweep along.

Sing, my heart, for He is risen, Christ
  is risen, Christ is risen!
Let the mountains shout for gladness,
  let the hills break forth and sing.
Let the seas make known His message,
  let the stars tell out the story,
Let the world proclaim His glory.
He is Lord and He is King!

LOUIS MERTINS

———o———

The message of Easter cannot be written in the past tense. It is a message for today and the days to come. It is God's message which must re-echo through your lives.

FRANK D. GETTY

———o———

Easter Prayer

Lord, make my heart a garden,
  As real a place of prayer
As was night-hushed Gethsemane
  When Jesus suffered there.

Make it a place of flowers,
  Whose fragrant cups distill
The dews of living water
  Ensweetened in Thy will.

Plant there the trees of kindness,
  Where all who look above
May find the shadows softened
  By sunshine of Thy love.

Fill it with Easter gladness
  As fresh and new as spring.
Keep it the clean, pure dwelling
  Of Christ, the risen King.
                          ESTHER BALDWIN YORK

———o———

If Easter Be Not True

If Easter be not true,
Then faith must mount on broken
    wing;
Then hope no more immortal spring;
Then love must lose her mighty urge;
Life prove a phantom, death a dirge —
  If Easter be not true.

If Easter be not true —
But it is true, and Christ is risen!
And mortal spirit from its prison
Of sin and death with Him may rise!
Worthwhile the struggle, sure the
    prize,
  Since Easter, aye, is true!
                          HENRY H. BARSTOW

———o———

Let us place more emphasis on the
Easter heart than on the Easter hat.

———o———

Easter

What whispers to the bulb, " 'Tis
    spring"?
Behold this shriveled, wrinkled thing —
It stirs and grows, bursts into bloom;
Its fragrance perfumes all the room.

Who tells the silent prisoner,
The little worm in tight cocoon,
"Wake up and work, and burst your
    bonds;
"You will be winged and flying soon"?

Who tells the acorn in the ground
To keep on reaching toward the sky?
How could it dream that it would be
A spreading oak tree, wide and high?

Who speaks within my sickroom, where
I live, a prisoner of pain,

And tells me, though this body die,
This very flesh shall live again?

Because He rose, I too shall rise,
Shall rise and walk and dance and
    sing;
And there shall be no grief, no pain,
Nor any tears, remembering!
                    MARTHA SNELL NICHOLSON

———o———

Easter is an awakening
Of every living thing.
A time when soul and spirits rise,
As heaven receives its King.
                      OLIVE DUNKELBERGER

Eat

"Now," said the mother, "you just
eat your spinach. It will put color in
your cheeks."
  "Yes," the little boy said, "but who
wants green cheeks?"

———o———

It's not the minutes you spend at
the table that make you fat, it's the
seconds.

———o———

"Most accidents happen in the kitchen," said a husband reading from
his newspaper. "And we men," he
added grimly, "have to eat them."

———o———

Let Christ stay throughout the meal.
Don't dismiss Him with the blessing.

———o———

Poor Mary

Mary had a little lamb,
A lobster and some prunes;
A glass of rum, a piece of pie
And then some macaroons.
It made the cafe waiters grin
To see her order so,
And when they carried Mary out
Her face was white as snow.
                      Uncle Mat's Magazine

Dad kept passing the pie to the others, finally his little son remarked, "They're all the same size, Dad, it's no use."

Selected

Part of the secret of success in life is to eat what you like and let the food fight it out inside.

The discovery of a new dish does more for the happiness of a man than the discovery of a star.

ANTHELME BRILLAT-SAVARIN

Tell me what you eat, and I will tell you what you are.

ANTHELME BRILLAT-SAVARIN,
Physiology of Gout

A dinner lubricates business.

WILLIAM SCOTT, LORD STOWELL,
quoted in Boswell's *Life of Dr. Johnson*

After a good dinner one can forgive anybody, even one's own relatives.

OSCAR WILDE

Eating little and speaking little can never do harm.

Economy

Economy: A way of spending money without getting any fun out of it.

Economy is half the battle of life; it is not so hard to earn money as to spend it well.

CHARLES HADDON SPURGEON

I favor the policy of economy, not because I wish to save money, but because I wish to save people.

CALVIN COOLIDGE

Economy, the poor man's mint.

MARTIN FARQUHAR TUPPER

There can be no economy where there is no efficiency.

BENJAMIN DISRAELI

Without economy none can be rich, and with it few will be poor.

SAMUEL JOHNSON

Whatever you have, spend less.

SAMUEL JOHNSON

Economy, industry, honesty and kindness form a quartet of virtue that will never be improved upon.

JAMES OLIVER

Limit your wants to your wealth.

Even a penny is too much to pay for something which is not needed.

Just about the time you think you can make ends meet, someone moves the ends!

Education

When a young man was applying for a job the manager said, "I'll give you a job. Sweep out the store."

Amazed, the young applicant said, "But I'm a college graduate."

The manager quietly replied, "Well, that's all right, I'll show you how."

Not all educated men are college graduates, nor are all college graduates educated men. An educated man is one who is useful to humanity, his profession or trade, and to himself.

Financial Management

It is a common fault never to be satisfied with our fortune, nor dissatisfied with our understanding.

FRANÇOIS, DUC DE LA ROCHEFOUCAULD

It is sometimes difficult to talk to a university man because he is so educated.

Education is what you have left over when you subtract what you've forgotten from what you learned.

The best education in the world is that got by struggling to get a living.
WENDELL PHILLIPS

———o———

In an honor system no one learns. The professors have the honor and the kids have the system.

———o———

Some kind of education is always going on. Education is not optional with the church.
HERMAN J. SWEET

———o———

It is not education that costs. It is ignorance that is expensive.
HEROLD C. HUNT

———o———

As often as not, adult education is left up to teen-agers.
FREDERIC G. HOULE

———o———

A pastor from a Latin American country was visiting various churches in the United States to observe operational procedures. While attending a meeting of the budget committee he observed in one report that the church had spent $800. for kitchen supplies and $100. for Teacher Training supplies.

Following the meeting the host pastor asked if there was anything in particular that had impressed him.

Without hesitation the visitor replied, "You spend more eating than you do feeding!"

———o———

When Woodrow Wilson was president of Princeton University, an anxious mother was questioning him closely about what Princeton could do for her son. Wilson replied: "Madam, we guarantee satisfaction or you will get your son back."

———o———

The entire object of true education is to make people not merely do the right things, but enjoy them — not merely industrious, but to love industry — not merely learned, but to love knowledge — not merely pure, but love purity — not merely just, but to hunger and thirst after justice.
JOHN RUSKIN

———o———

The great end of education is to discipline rather than to furnish the mind; to train it to the use of its own powers, rather than fill it with the accumulation of others.
TRYON EDWARDS

———o———

The object of education is to prepare the young to educate themselves throughout their lives.
ROBERT MAYNARD HUTCHENS

———o———

Those who have not distinguished themselves at school need not on that account be discouraged. The greatest minds do not necessarily ripen the quickest.
JOHN LUBBOCK

———o———

An educated man is one who has finally discovered that there are some questions to which nobody has the answers.
Boston Globe

———o———

Education without God is like a ship without a compass.

———o———

The primary purpose of education is not to teach you to earn your bread, but to make every mouthful sweeter.
JAMES ANGELL

———o———

Girl graduate: "Four years of college — and whom has it got me?"

———o———

Said one speaker, in referring to a long string of honorary degrees, "They're like the curl in the tail of a pig — following the main part of the animal, highly ornamental, but in no way improving the quality of the ham."

———o———

The real function of education, as we all well know, is not so much to teach us how to make a living as how to live while we are earning a living.

Too many of us have the cart before the horse.

———o———

Professor: "What three words are used most among college students?"
Freshman: "I don't know."
Professor: "Correct!"
Voiceways

———o———

We can only stimulate a person to education — we cannot stuff it into him.

———o———

Being educated means to prefer the best not only to the worst but to the second-best.

WILLIAM LYON PHELPS

———o———

Education would be much more effective if its purpose was to ensure that by the time they leave school every boy and girl should know how much they do *not* know, and be imbued with a lifelong desire to know it.

SIR WILLIAM HALEY

———o———

I thoroughly believe in a university education; but I believe a knowledge of the Bible without a college course is more valuable than a college course without the Bible.

WILLIAM LYON PHELPS

———o———

For adult education nothing beats children.

Banking

———o———

A man is not educated who does not know the basic truths of the Bible.

———o———

Education is something you get when your father sends you to college. But it isn't complete until you send your son there.

Washington Journal,
quoted in *Chicago Tribune*

———o———

Any man is educated who knows where to get knowledge when he needs it, and how to organize that knowledge into definite plans of action.

NAPOLEON HILL

Education is the ability to listen to almost anything without losing your temper.

ROBERT FROST

———o———

On one occasion Aristotle was asked how much educated men were superior to those uneducated: "As much," said he, "as the living are to the dead."

DIOGENES LAERTIUS, *Aristotle*

———o———

No one is ever finished with an education and the mark of an educated man is the constant struggle for more and more knowledge.

W. BERAN WOLFE

———o———

Men, while teaching, learn.

SENECA

———o———

The world is full of educated derelicts.

CALVIN COOLIDGE

———o———

On Graduating

Well, this is the last
    Of your high school days
Dear grownup lad
    With the winning ways.
I do not know
    What the future holds;
But day by day
    As time unfolds
May you find the hope
    The joy, the love
That comes from serving
    Your God above.
May you find the strength
    And the courage, too,
To do each task
    He plans for you;
Your work is not finished —
    It's just begun;
The world needs a "doer,"
    May you be the one.

PHYLLIS C. MICHAEL

———o———

Martin Luther gave the best reason for further education when he wrote: "The prosperity of a country depends, not on the abundance of its revenues, nor on the strength of its fortifications, nor on the beauty of its public buildings, but it consists in the number of its men of enlightenment and character."

Efficient

Efficiency expert: A man who waits to make up a foursome before going through a revolving door.

Irish Digest

————o————

Efficiency produces more with less effort.

ADMIRAL HUSBAND EDWARD KIMMEL

————o————

The efficient man is the man who thinks for himself and is capable of thinking hard and long.

CHARLES WILLIAM ELIOT

————o————

Efficiency is the ability to do a job well, plus the desire to do it better.

PAUL H. GILBERT

Effort

To achieve success, not by heritage but by individual effort, is the greatest joy of life.

J. P MORGAN

————o————

There is no ceiling on effort!

HARVEY FRUEHAUF

————o————

Prize fruit remains at the top of the tree because it is safer there from lazy pickers.

————o————

The best angle to use in approaching a problem is probably the try angle.

————o————

The Man Who Is Doing His Best

No matter how little he's getting,
  No matter how little he's got,
If he wears a grin, and is trying to win,
  He is doing a mighty lot!
No matter how humble his job is
  If he's striving to reach the crest,
The world has a prize for the fellow
  who tries —
The man who is doing his best!
Today he may be at the bottom
  Of the ladder to wealth or fame;
On the lowest rung, where he's brave-
  ly clung,
  In spite of the knocks — dead game!
And slowly he's gaining a foothold,
  His eyes on the uppermost roun';
It's a hard old climb, but he knows in
  time
  He will "land" — and be looking
  down!
The fellow who never surrenders,
  And is taking things as they come;
Who never says "quit," and exhibits
  grit,
  When the whole world is looking
  glum;
The fellow who stays to the finish,
  That nothing can hinder or stop,
And who works like sin, is the man
  who'll win —
  And some day he'll land on top!

AUTHOR UNKNOWN

————o————

Adam Clarke, a well-known theologian and commentator, was an early riser.
A young preacher wanted the eminent minister to tell him how he managed it. "Do you pray about it?" he asked.
"No," was the reply. "I just get up."

The Standard

————o————

The persistent exercise of a little extra effort is one of the most powerful forces contributing to success.

Grit

————o————

When my five-year-old son came to the table with his hands very dirty, I told him he must go wash and not come back until they were clean.
After a good deal of time had passed, I called, "Billy, how are your hands — are they clean yet?"
"Not clean," he replied. "But I got them to match!"

CAROLINE BECKER in *Grit*

————o————

Two frogs fell into a can of milk,
  Or so I've heard it told;

The sides of the can were shiny and
   steep,
The milk was deep and cold.

"Oh, what's the use?" croaked Number
   One,
"'Tis fate; no help's around.
"Goodbye, my friend! Goodbye, sad
   world!"
And weeping still, he drowned.

But Number Two, of sterner stuff,
   Dog-paddled in surprise,
The while he wiped his milky face
And dried his milky eyes.

"I'll swim awhile, at least," he said —
   Or so I've heard he said.
"It really wouldn't help the world
"If one more frog were dead."

An hour or two he kicked and swam,
   Not once he stopped to mutter,
But kicked and kicked and swam and
   kicked —
Then hopped out, via butter!
       T. C. HAMLET in *The Target*

———o———

There's no need to put your best
foot forward if you drag the other one.

———o———

The men who try to do something
and fail are better than those who try
to do nothing and succeed.

———o———

If effort is organized, accomplishment follows.

Egotist, Egotism

Egotism is the opiate that the devil
administers to dull the pains of medi-
ocrity.

———o———

An egotist is a conceited dolt who
thinks he knows as much as you do.
       HAL CRANE

———o———

An egotist is not a man who thinks
too much of himself; he is a man who
thinks too little of other people.
       JOSEPH FORT NEWTON

To be pleased with oneself is the
surest way of offending everybody
else.
       EDWARD GEORGE BULWER-LYTTON

———o———

Egotist: One who likes mirrors, but
can't understand what others see in
them.
       HAROLD COFFIN in *Coronet*

———o———

Egotism: An internally generated
anesthetic which enables a conceited
person to live painlessly with himself.

———o———

Egotist: A person of low taste, more
interested in himself than in me.
       AMBROSE BIERCE

———o———

Through A Mirror

I have a little ego that is very fond of
   me,
Though what can be the use of him
   I often cannot see.
He follows close beside me wherever
   I may go;
Whenever I'd be good, he always tells
   me, "No!"
He is my sensitive feelings that are
   always getting hurt;
He is my self-conceit that needs rub-
   bing in the dirt;
He's all the little cranky ways to which
   I am so wont.
Lord, help me to get rid of him, this
   pesky little runt!
       IRENE T. COLE in *Clear Horizons*

Eloquence

He from whose lips divine per-
suasion flows.
       HOMER, *Iliad*

———o———

He is an eloquent man who can treat
humble subjects with delicacy, lofty
things impressively, and moderate
things temperately.
       MARCUS TULLIUS CICERO

———o———

When Demosthenes was asked what
was the first part of oratory, he an-

swered, "Action"; and which was the second, he replied, "Action"; and which was the third, he still answered, "Action."

PLUTARCH, *Lives of the Ten Orators*

———o———

Nothing is more eloquent than ready money.

French Proverb

———o———

Eloquence is the power to translate a truth into language perfectly intelligible to the person to whom you speak.

Employment

Never be unemployed and never be triflingly employed.

JOHN WESLEY

———o———

For he lives twice who can at once employ
The present well, and ev'n the past enjoy.

ALEXANDER POPE, *Imitation of Martial*

———o———

When men are employed, they are best contented.

BENJAMIN FRANKLIN, *Autobiography*

———o———

Employment gives health, sobriety, and morals.

DANIEL WEBSTER

———o———

Notice of employer on bulletin board to employees: "Bread is the staff of life, but that is no reason for the life of our staff to be one continual loaf!"

———o———

To All Employees

Due to increased competition and a keen desire to remain in business, we find it necessary to institute a new policy. Effective immediately, we are asking that somewhere between starting time and quitting time, and without infringing too much on the time usually devoted to lunch period, coffee breaks, rest periods, story telling, ticket selling, golfing, vacation planning, and the rehashing of yesterday's TV programs, that each employee endeavor

to find some time that can be set aside and known as the "work break."

To some this may seem a radical innovation, but we honestly believe the idea has great possibilities. It can conceivably be an aid to steady employment and it might also be a means of insuring regular pay checks. While the adoption of the "work break" plan is not compulsory, it is hoped that each employee will find enough time to give the plan a fair trial. It is also hoped that those employees not in favor of adopting the "work break" idea will have fully completed their vacation plans.

Weaver Publishing Company

Encouragement

Encouragement is oxygen to the soul.

GEORGE M. ADAMS

———o———

Saying amen to a preacher is like saying siccum to a dog.

———o———

Correction does much, but encouragement does more. . . . Encouragement after censure is as the sun after a shower.

JOHANN WOLFGANG VON GOETHE

———o———

Secretary to downhearted boss whose desk is piled high with papers: "Allowing for holiday excitement, office parties, postseason letdown and normal absenteeism, we should have December's work cleaned up by January 25th."

HERBRAM in *The Christian Science Monitor*

———o———

A helping word to one in trouble is often like a switch on a railroad track — but one inch between a wreck and smooth rolling prosperity.

HENRY WARD BEECHER

Enemies

An enemy is a danger, but the danger is not what he can do to you. It is what he makes you do. If he fills you with envy, malice, hatred and all uncharitableness, he has done you real harm. But you can prevent that. Pray for him. If you say you cannot trust him, then watch and pray. But you cannot hate a man you pray for.

E. S. WATERHOUSE

———o———

Our foes are feeble in comparison with our Source of Strength.

SANFORD D. RICKER

———o———

He makes no friend who never made a foe.

ALFRED, LORD TENNYSON,
Lancelot and Elaine

———o———

The man who has no enemies has no following.

DON PLATT

———o———

What is a man's chief enemy? Each man is his own.

ANACHARSIS

———o———

Wise men learn much from enemies.

ARISTOPHANES, *Birds*

———o———

It is possible to learn from an enemy things we cannot learn from a friend.

———o———

If you tend to your work, and let your enemy alone, someone will come along some day, and do him up for you.

EDGAR WATSON HOWE

———o———

If you must have enemies — be careful in choosing them.

Energy

To be energetic, act energetic.

CLEMENT STONE

———o———

The world belongs to the energetic.

RALPH WALDO EMERSON

———o———

When men are young, they want experience and when they have gained experience, they want energy.

BENJAMIN DISRAELI

Enjoyment

You were made for enjoyment, and the world was filled with things you will enjoy.

JOHN RUSKIN

———o———

Some people are making such thorough preparation for rainy days that they aren't enjoying today's sunshine.

WILLIAM FEATHER

———o———

Enjoy the little you have while the fool is hunting for more.

Spanish Proverb

———o———

He who is convinced that there remains naught for him to do but to enjoy himself is little more than an erect animal.

RABBI J. LEONARD LEVY

Enthusiasm

Fires cannot be made with dead embers, nor can enthusiasm be stirred by spiritless men.

BALDWIN

———o———

Every man is enthusiastic at times. One man has enthusiasm for thirty minutes, another for thirty days, but it is the man who has it for thirty years who makes a success in life.

EDWARD B. BUTLER

———o———

We need fire without wild fire.

———o———

Every production of genius must be the production of enthusiasm.

BENJAMIN DISRAELI

———o———

The man who is capable of generating enthusiasm can't be whipped.

EDWARD GEORGE BULWER-LYTTON

———o———

A man can succeed at almost anything for which he has unlimited enthusiasm.

CHARLES SCHWAB

None are so old as those who have outlived their enthusiasm.

HENRY DAVID THOREAU

———o———

Merit begets confidence, confidence begets enthusiasm, enthusiasm conquers the world.

WALTER COTTINGHAM

———o———

The world belongs to the enthusiast who keeps cool.

WILLIAM MCFEE,
Casuals of the Sea. Book I

———o———

Enthusiasm is the genius of sincerity, and truth accomplishes no victories without it.

EDWARD GEORGE BULWER-LYTTON

———o———

Be a live wire, then people won't step on you.

Environment

We should seek the atmosphere and the surroundings which call forth the best that is in us.

COUNCILLOR

———o———

There's many a life of sweet content Whose virtue is environment.

WALTER LEARNED

Envy

Too many Christians envy the sinners their pleasure and the saints their joy, because they don't have either one.

MARTIN LUTHER

———o———

Expect not praise without envy until you are dead.

CHARLES CALEB COLTON

———o———

Envy is but the smoke of low estate, Ascending still against the fortunate.

LORD BROOKE

———o———

One cannot be envious and happy at the same time.

HENRY GREBER

Envy is littleness of soul.

WILLIAM HAZLITT

———o———

Envy is an open door to bitterness.

———o———

The envious person is a miserable person.

Epitaph

If tombstones told the truth, everybody would wish to be buried at sea.

JOHN W. RAPER

———o———

The Tired Woman's Epitaph

Here lies a poor woman, who always was tired;
She lived in a house where help was not hired.
Her last words on earth were: "Dear Friends, I am going
"Where washing ain't done, nor sweeping, nor sewing;
"But everything there is exact to my wishes;
"For where they don't eat there's no washing of dishes.
"I'll be where loud anthems will always be ringing,
"But, having no voice, I'll be clear of the singing.
"Don't mourn for me now; don't mourn for me never —
"I'm going to do nothing for ever and ever."

AUTHOR UNKNOWN

———o———

Friend, in your epitaph I'm grieved So very much is said;
One-half will never be believed, The other never read.

———o———

Epitaph of Robert Byrkes:
That I spent, that I had;
That I gave, that I have;
That I left, that I lost.

A.D. 1579

———o———

Epitaph Of Faith

A godly old man asked that on his tombstone be carved the legend "The

Inn of a Traveler on His Way to the New Jerusalem."

He looked on this life as a journey toward the heavenly city where real life would begin. Having set his course toward the full enjoyment of the presence of God, the grave became merely a stopping place on the way.

KATHERINE BEVIS

———o———

Epitaph: A belated advertisement for a line of goods that has permanently been discontinued.

IRVIN SHEWSBURY COBB

———o———

A man once lived the kind of life that inspired his friends to place this epitaph at his grave:
Unawed by opinion,
Unseduced by flattery,
Undismayed by disaster,
He confronted life with courage,
And death with Christian hope.

Errors

Things could be worse. Suppose our errors were tabulated and published every day like those of a ball player.

———o———

Some people throw away a bushel of Truth because it contains a grain of Error; while others swallow a bushel of Error because it contains a grain of Truth.

———o———

Navy Chaplain Lt. Daniel Litt was at 11th Naval District headquarters when a phone call came for another chaplain.

The secretary replied: "We only have one chaplain here just now, and he is Litt."

After what seemed to be an embarrassed silence, the caller hung up.

———o———

A typographical error in a church bulletin was not far off. A roster of the church staff included the name of the "Dustodian."

Minneapolis Tribune

She ended the program with a prelude and fudge by Bach.

Daily Record, Wooster, Ohio

———o———

The least error should humble, but we should never permit even the greatest to discourage us.

WILLIAM JAMES POTTER

———o———

Without error there can be no such thing as truth.

Chinese Saying

———o———

Errors, like straws, upon the surface flow;
He who would search for pearls must dive below.

JOHN DRYDEN, *All For Love*

———o———

Ignorance is a blank sheet on which we may write; but error is a scribbled one on which we must first erase.

CHARLES CALEB COLTON

———o———

Typographical Error

The typographical error is a slippery thing and sly
You can hunt till you are dizzy, but it somehow will get by.
Till the forms are off the presses, it is strange how still it keeps
It shrinks down into a corner and it never stirs or peeps,
That typographical error, too small for human eyes!

Till the ink is on the paper when it grows to mountain size
The boss he stares with horror, then he grabs his hair and groans.
The copy reader drops his head upon his hands and moans —
The remainder of the issues may be clean as clean can be,
But that typographical error is the only thing you see.

AUTHOR UNKNOWN

———o———

The following collection of students' boners are on file in St. Michael's school in Hoban Heights, Pennsylvania:

A *blizzard* is the inside of a fowl.

A *goblet* is a male turkey.

A *spinster* is a bachelor's wife.

A *virgin forest* is a forest in which the hand of man has never set foot.

They only raise *alpaca* grain in Kansas, and they have to irritate it to make it grow.

An *adjective* is a word hanging down from a noun.

The *Prodigal Son* went out a dude and came back a bum.

———o———

It is error only, and not truth, that shrinks from inquiry.

THOMAS PAINE

Eternity

In this world life becomes a new and thrilling thing; in the world to come eternal life with God becomes a certainty.

WILLIAM BARCLAY

———o———

Life with Christ is an endless hope; without Him it is a hopeless end.

———o———

We must live *for* Christ here, if we would live *with* Him hereafter.

———o———

With God Forever

The stars shine over the earth,
The stars shine over the sea;
The stars look up to the mighty God,
The stars look down on me.
The stars have lived for a million years
A million years and a day,
But God and I shall love and live
When the stars have passed away.

AUTHOR UNKNOWN

———o———

Eternity gives nothing back of what one leaves out of his minutes.

———o———

One life — a little gleam of time between two eternities.

PETRARCH

Church announcement board outside Christ Episcopal Church, New Brighton, Pennsylvania: "Christian funeral directors provide many valuable services . . . but they can't 'phone ahead for reservations — you must apply in person for Eternal Life."

Ethics

Evangelical faith without Christian ethics is a travesty on the gospel.

V. RAYMOND EDMAN

———o———

Ethics is the science of human duty.

DAVID SWING

———o———

A man without ethics is a wild beast loosed upon this world.

MANLY HALL

———o———

Ethics and equity and the principles of justice do not change with the calendar.

DAVID LAWRENCE

Etiquette

Ten Commandments For Church Etiquette

I. Thou shalt not come to service late, nor for the Amen refuse to wait.

II. Thy noisy tongue thou shalt restrain when speaks the organ its refrain.

III. And when the hymns are sounded out, thou shalt join in, not look about.

IV. The endmost seat thou shalt leave free, for more to share the pew with thee.

V. Forget thou not the off'ring plate, nor let the usher stand and wait.

VI. Thou shalt not make the pew a place to vainly decorate thy face.

VII. Thou shalt give heed to worship well, and not in thine own business dwell.

VIII. Thou shalt the Sabbath not misuse, nor come to church to take thy snooze.

IX. 'Tis well in church thy friend to meet, but let thy ardor be discreet.

X. Be friendly at the church's door, so shall the stranger love God more.

ARTHUR JAMES LAUGHLIN, JR.

———o———

Etiquette: How you behave every day of your life. Acquiring good manners and skill in the art of gracious living comes in a three-way package: reading, observation, and practice.

Evangelism

Let us go . . .

Because He commands us to go
Because He has made us ambassadors
Because we love Him
Because we do care for the lost

into the highways and hedges

Where a baby is born every two seconds
Where an immigrant crosses our border every two minutes
Where life's highway leads to school, shop, office, store, farm . . .
Where people are groping for reality

and compel them to come in

That the seeker may find the truth
That the weary may find rest.
That the troubled may find peace
That the sinner may find eternal life
That the Christian may find a blessing in service.

A. C. MCKENSIE

———o———

Of all the subjects that have to be discussed and prayed about, there is none which in my judgment is more fascinating and more important than the conversion of children.

F. B. MEYER

———o———

The Redemption Of Youth

Nineteen out of every twenty who ever get saved do so before they reach the age of twenty-five.
After twenty-five, only one in 10,000.

After thirty-five, only one in 50,000.
After forty-five, only one in 200,000.
After fifty-five, only one in 300,000.
After sixty-five, only one in 500,000.
After seventy-five only one in 700,-000.

Dr. Wilbur Chapman tested a meeting where 4,500 were present. The result was:

400 were saved before ten years of age.
600 were saved between twelve and fourteen.
600 were saved between fourteen and sixteen.
1,000 were saved between sixteen and twenty.
Twenty-five were saved after thirty years of age.
1,875 were unsaved.

———o———

Admit God's Word to be His message for you.
Submit to the authority of the book.
Commit Scriptures to memory.
Transmit the message to someone else.

———o———

If you should live to preach the gospel forty years, and be the instrument to saving only one soul, it will be worth all your labors.

———o———

Fireworks evangelism is like a rocket. It goes up in fire and falls like a dead stick.

———o———

Evangelism stands for a certain interpretation of Christianity emphasizing the objective atonement of Christ, the necessity of a new birth, or conversion, and salvation through faith.

W. W. SWEET

———o———

Told of thousands of souls going to Christless graves in foreign lands, men and women are stirred, but they are not stirred by the man dying in the next block into whose home no pastor has ever entered with the Gospel message. Somehow souls far away seem more valuable in the sight of God than souls nearby, or in the next town. There is a confusion of values among us, not derived from the Scriptures.

CHESTER E. TULGA

———o———

Things Not To Do

Don't argue and don't lecture!

Never talk boastfully or sound too familiar.

Don't point your finger in the person's face.

Don't interrupt while someone is speaking; there is danger of offending him and prejudicing him against you and against Christ through you.

Don't run down the person's church.

Don't beg or coax.

Avoid long stories or illustrations.

Don't be in a hurry.

Don't pick green fruit. (Try for an early decision, but don't force one . . . it might be the wrong decision.)

AUTHOR UNKNOWN

———o———

You can hardly have evangelism unless you have Christian scholarship; and the more Christian scholarship you have, so much the more evangelism.

J. GRESHAM MACHEN

———o———

In evangelism we seek the lost; in revival the lost are running to the Lord.

EDWIN ORR

Evil

We could add a fourth monkey to the Chinese where one hears no evil, one sees no evil and one speaks no evil. Our fourth monkey would "think no evil." Seems to us that it is the most important.

———o———

If a man's face is turned toward evil, and he is following his face, you'll find it hard to believe he's on the road to Heaven no matter what he says about it.

Out Or In?

All the water in the world
However hard it tried
Could never sink a ship
Unless it got inside.
All the evil in the world,
The wickedness and sin
Can never sink your soul's fair craft
Unless you let it in.

AUTHOR UNKNOWN

———o———

Evil does not disappear merely by being ignored.

———o———

Evil to him who evil thinks. (*Honi soit qui mal y pense.*)

EDWARD III, King of England
— *Motto of the Order of the Garter*

———o———

For himself doth a man work evil in working evils for another.

HESIOD

———o———

The truest definition of evil is that which represents it as something contrary to nature. Evil is evil because it is unnatural.

FREDERICK WILLIAM ROBERTSON

Exaggerate

An exaggeration is a truth that has lost its temper.

KAHLIL GIBRAN

———o———

You can tell a parrot from a human being because the parrot is content to repeat just what it hears without trying to make a good story out of it.

———o———

The fellow who is always slapping you on the back does this to help you swallow all he tells you!

———o———

When inclined to exaggerate, talk only to yourself.

———o———

We exaggerate misfortune and happiness alike. We are never so wretched or so happy as we say we are.

HONORÉ DE BALZAC

Examination

Examinations are formidable even to the best prepared, for the greatest fool may ask more than the wisest man can answer.

CHARLES CALEB COLTON

———o———

A teacher, annoyed with his clock-watching students, covered the clock with a cardboard which said: "Time will pass. Will you?"

Sunshine Magazine

———o———

In an examination, a high school student defined the humerus as "that part of the body which is commonly called the funny bone."

———o———

In answer to the question, "How can one attain a good posture?" one boy wrote on his class examination paper: "Keep the cows off of it, and let it grow awhile."

Example

(see also Influence)

When he was a small boy his teacher made him stay after school and write fifty times on the board, "I must not talk in class."

Now he was a big boy and a judge and into his court came his former teacher, charged with speeding.

The sentence? She must pay a fine of ten dollars and write one hundred times, "I must not exceed the speed limit."

———o———

A Primary-age child prayed in the worship service, "Dear God, please make me as much like my Jesus as my Sunday School teacher."

———o———

Example is always more efficacious than precept.

SAMUEL JOHNSON, *Rasselas*

———o———

Right example bolsters effectively the fruit of the lips.

Since truth and constancy are vain,
Since neither love, nor sense of pain,
Nor force of reason, can persuade,
Then let example be obey'd.

GEORGE GRANVILLE

———o———

I do not give you to posterity as a pattern to imitate but as an example to deter.

JUNIUS

———o———

Example is the school of mankind, and they will learn at no other.

EDMUND BURKE

———o———

Turning the Fable

When telling your children a story
And you use yourself as a sample,
Perhaps you should do it as warning
And not as a shining example!

LAVONNE MATHISON in *Home Life*

———o———

It's what you are when you pray that influences me.

———o———

Example is not the main thing in influencing others. It is the only thing!

ALBERT SCHWEITZER

———o———

Good example has twice the value of good advice.

———o———

A great man once said: "In early life I had nearly been betrayed into the principles of atheism, but there was one argument in favor of Christianity that I could not refute, and that was the consistent character and example of my own father."

———o———

Shortly after the close of the Civil War, a Negro entered a fashionable church in Richmond, Virginia, one Sunday morning while communion was being served. He walked down the aisle and knelt at the altar. A rustle of shock and anger swept through the congregation. Sensing the situation, a distinguished layman immediately stood up, stepped forward to the altar and knelt beside his colored brother. Captured by his spirit, the congregation followed this magnanimous example. The layman who set the example: Robert E. Lee.

BILLY GRAHAM in *Life*

————o————

Fathers who want their children to end up right must walk upright themselves.

NAT OLSON

————o————

The world wants to see demonstrators of the faith rather than defenders of the faith.

————o————

Nothing is so infectious as example.

CHARLES KINGSLEY

————o————

Not so long ago one of my two boys spoke these sobering words to me. He said, "When the two of us were young, there were times when you and mom would obviously set out to tell me how to live the good life. We could always recognize those moments and we would close our ears and our minds. Your most influential moments were your most inadvertent ones. We were apt to imitate what you really were – not what you said you were or even what you may have believed you were."

JOSEPH N. WELCH in *The Pioneer*

Excellence

Whoever I am or whatever I am doing, some kind of excellence is within my reach.

JOHN W. GARDNER

————o————

There is no excellence uncoupled with difficulties.

OVID

————o————

Excellent things are rare.

PLATO

————o————

Excellence is never granted to man but as the reward of labor.

SIR JOSHUA REYNOLDS

Of course it will only be a matter of time till you reach the top if you can contrive each day to outclass the fellow you were yesterday.

Excess

In the cross of Christ excess in men is met by excess in God; excess of evil is mastered by excess of love.

LOUIS BOURDALOUE

————o————

Excess in anything is a defect.

MONVEL

————o————

Excess kills more than the sword.

————o————

Nothing in excess.

TERENCE

Exclusive

A small Christian sect of an exclusive temperament was holding a convention. Outside the auditorium where they met there was displayed the motto, "Jesus Only."
A strong wind blew away the first three letters and left the sign, "us Only."

HARRY A. IRONSIDE

Excuse

Parents have always found excuses for their children when they failed to make it to school. Some of them have been honest, and some of them have stretched the truth a bit. One of the most widely used, and sometimes abused, excuses has been the breakdown of transportation. To show how this excuse has changed through the years, Frederick J. Moffitt in *Nation's Schools* gives this "History of Transportation."
1860 – Dear Teacher: Please excuse Mary for absence from school yesterday because it was her brother's turn to wear the shoes.
1900 – Dear Professor: John missed school today because the horse succumbed to an attack of glanders on Murder Hill.

1910 — Dear Principal: Jane was absent yesterday because her father broke his arm cranking the Ford.

1950 — Dear Superintendent: Willie overslept, and the school bus wouldn't wait for him.

1960 — Dear Announcer: K a r e n missed her lesson yesterday because the TV tube blew out.

Quote

————o————

We've heard a few times, "No, I didn't get to church but was there in spirit." As a preacher, I've found that it's not easy to preach to disembodied spirits; bodies are really indispensable.

————o————

He that is good at making excuses is seldom good at anything else.

BENJAMIN FRANKLIN

————o————

Church member X: "We really shouldn't be out here fishing on prayer meeting night."

Church member Z: "Oh, well I couldn't be at church tonight anyway. I've got a sick child at home."

Today

————o————

There aren't nearly enough crutches in the world for all the lame excuses.

————o————

"I'm sorry to be late, Mom," said ten-year-old Jimmy as he rushed home from school. "We were making a science display, and I had to stay to finish the universe."

————o————

He who excuses himself accuses himself.

GABRIEL MEURIER

Executive

An executive is a person who is working on the solution of a problem or else is a part of the problem.

————o————

Executive: A man who can make a decision and stick to it — no matter how wrong he is.

An executive is a man who can take as long as he wants to make a snap decision.

————o————

It isn't difficult to determine which executives are big wheels and which are merely spokesmen.

————o————

How to stay in the groove without making it a rut is the problem of every executive.

————o————

A good executive is one who wears the worried look — upon his assistant's face.

MAX SCHUSTER

————o————

The able executive is the man who can train assistants more capable than himself.

ANDREW CARNEGIE

————o————

The ability to influence people is a foremost requirement for every executive.

WILLIAM L. BATT

Exercise

The best exercise for the heart is to reach down and pull other people up.

————o————

Scientists tell us that exercise kills germs. Trouble is in trying to talk them into taking it.

————o————

The only exercise some people get is jumping to conclusions, running down their friends, sidestepping responsibility, and pushing their luck.

Expect

The small-town boy who had gone to fame and fortune decided to visit his birthplace after a twenty-year absence so he could gloat a little over his boyhood friends and surviving relatives.

Half expecting an official greeting and a turnout of the town band, he arrived at high noon to find empty streets, the same sleepy central square, and the old railroad station broiling in the sun.

Getting out of his train, his suitcase in his hand, he wandered over to the white-haired baggage handler and stood waiting for a sign of recognition and welcome.

The old man shuffled forward, squinted in the sun, and smiled. "Hello, Jimmie," he said. "Going away?"

———o———

Life is much like Christmas — you are more likely to get what you expect than what you want.

———o———

It is always first class when we do not expect anything better.

T. J. BACH

———o———

When you expect something for nothing, you deserve to be disappointed. No one is entitled to more than he gives.

THEODORE LANG

Experience

When a youngster sets out to gain experience, he should be cautioned that some experience is a definite loss.

———o———

Experience is what enables you to recognize a mistake when you make it again.

EARL WILSON

———o———

Even if you drop out of the school of experience, it has a wonderful home study program which keeps you constantly in touch.

———o———

I am a part of all that I have met;
Yet all experience is an arch where-
    through
Gleams that untraveled world whose
    margin fades
For ever and for ever when I move.

ALFRED, LORD TENNYSON, *Ulysses*

How Fresh Is Your Experience?

A story is told of an old man who had a wonderful experience twenty-five years ago, so wonderful that he wrote it all down and called it his "Blessed Experience." When people visited him he often would bring it out and read it through to them.

One night when a friend called in he said to his wife, "My dear, just run upstairs and bring down my 'Blessed Experience' from the drawer in the bedroom."

She went upstairs to get it and, on returning, she said, "I am sorry, but the mice have been in the drawer, and have eaten up your 'Blessed Experience'!"

And a good thing, too! If you had a blessing twenty-five years ago, and have not had one since, you had better forget it and get an up-to-date experience.

A. LINDSAY GLEGG in *Gospel Herald*

———o———

On a credit application the applicant signed his name "Bill Smith, BBBFF."

"You have an unusual degree," commented the credit manager. "Where did you get your education?"

"Experience," replied Bill Smith. "Three bankruptcies and two fires!"

———o———

Experience can be costly. But the right kind can be more than a refund in full.

———o———

One reason experience is such a good teacher is that she doesn't allow dropouts.

Changing Times, The Kiplinger Magazine

———o———

We need an experience of Christ in which we think everything about the Christ and not about the experience.

PETER TAYLOR FORSYTH

———o———

Learning teacheth more in one year than experience in twenty.

ROGER ASCHAM, *The Schoolmaster*

He gains wisdom in a happy way, who gains it by another's experience.
                                    PLAUTUS

——o——

Sad experience leaves no room for doubt.
                        ALEXANDER POPE

——o——

Experience is by industry achieved And perfected by the swift course of time.
            WILLIAM SHAKESPEARE,
            Two Gentlemen of Verona

——o——

Experience is what keeps a man who makes the same mistake twice from admitting it the third time around.
            TERRY MCCORMICK in *Quote*

Expert

An expert is a fellow that can hit a bull's eye without shooting the bull.

——o——

An expert is like the bottom part of a double boiler: builds up a lot of steam but doesn't know what's cooking.

——o——

An expert is a person who can take something you already know and make it sound confusing.

——o——

An expert is a man away from home with a set of slides.

——o——

Every skilled person is to be believed with reference to his own art.
                        Legal Maxim

Explanation

When the grass looks greener on the other side of the fence, it may be that they take better care of it over there.
            CECIL SELIG in *Quote*

——o——

One cool morning I was trying to convince my three-year-old son to put on his bathrobe. When I told him he was shivering, he replied: "I am not. I'm just bouncing my teeth."
                    MRS. HARRY WESTON
                    in *The Chicago Tribune*

——o——

The boy explained to his teacher why he hadn't yet returned his report card to her. "You gave me three A's, and the card still is on the rounds of the relatives."
        Times Leader, West Point, Mississippi

——o——

Jay, age three, put his cousin's roller skates on and tried to skate. But he said, "My one foot doesn't wait for the other one."
                        Christian Living

——o——

A four-year-old was overheard by his mother as he talked to his new puppy. "You mustn't chew me," he was saying. "Bones are for chewing. People are for lapping."

——o——

"And what did my little angel do while mother was shopping?" a mother asked her pride and joy.
"I played postman, Mommy," replied the youngster. "I put a letter in every mail box on the street. They were real letters, too. I found a big bundle of them in your drawer tied up in a pink ribbon."
                        V. D. PALAT

Extra

And Then Some . . .

A retired business executive was once asked the secret of his success. He replied that it could be summed up in three words: "and then some."
"I discovered at an early age," he said, "that most of the differences between average people and top people could be explained in three words. The top people did what was expected of them — and then some.
"They were thoughtful of others, they were considerate and kind — and then some.

"They were good friends to their friends — and then some.

"They could be counted on in an emergency — and then some.

"And so it is when we put our trust in God's goodness. He returns our love — and then some."

AUTHOR UNKNOWN

F

Face (Expression)

Take care that the face which looks out from your mirror in the morning is a pleasant one. You may not see it again all day, but others will.

———o———

A long face shortens your list of friends.

———o———

A gesture of a hand, a look upon a face, the silent message sensed in a chance glimpse of another's eyes often speak more eloquently than the finest prose or poetry, the most stirring music, or all the words in the dictionary.

———o———

Some persons think they have to look like a hedgehog to be pious.

BILLY SUNDAY

———o———

One small boy to another, shopping for Halloween masks: "Take your time. Don't fall for the first ugly face ya see!"

HANK KETCHAM, Hall Syndicate

———o———

It Will Show

You don't have to tell how you live every day,
You need not reveal if you work or play;
For a trusty barometer's always in place —
However you live it will show in your face.

The truth or deceit you would hide in your heart,
They will not stay inside when once given a start;
Sinews and blood are like thin veils of lace —

What you wear in your heart you must wear on your face.

If you've battled and won in the great game of life,
If you've striven and conquered through sorrow and strife,
If you've played the game fair but reached only first base,
It shows in your face.

AUTHOR UNKNOWN

———o———

God gave you your face; you make your own countenance.

———o———

A beautiful face is a silent commendation.

FRANCIS BACON

———o———

He had a face like a benediction.

MIGUEL DE CERVANTES, Don Quixote

———o———

A sanctimonious face is no proof of a Spirit-filled heart.

Facts

Jumping at conclusions is not half as good exercise as digging for facts.

———o———

Too many people decide what they want to believe, then go looking around for half-facts to prove they are right.

War Cry

———o———

Every story has three sides — yours, mine and the facts.

———o———

Mark Twain, in his reporting days, was instructed by an editor never to state anything as a fact that he could not verify from personal knowledge. Sent out to cover an important social event soon afterward he turned in the following:

A woman giving the name of Mrs. James Jones, who is reported to be one of the society leaders of the city, is said to have given what purported to be a party yesterday to a number of alleged ladies. The hostess claims to be the wife of a reputed attorney."

———o———

Small boy to friend: "Well, I know all the facts of life, but I don't know if they're true."

CHON DAY in *The Saturday Evening Post*

———o———

God formed us.
    Sin deformed us.
        One Christ can transform us.

———o———

Facts do not cease to exist because they are ignored.

———o———

Facts are stubborn things.

ALAIN RENÉ LE SAGE, *Gil Blas*

———o———

Nothing is so fallacious as facts, except figures.

GEORGE CANNING, quoted by SIDNEY SMITH

Failure

Don't worry when you stumble. Remember, a worm is about the only thing that can't fall down.

———o———

Every unfriendly individual is a failure, so let's all be a success.

———o———

It is better to fail in doing right than to succeed in doing wrong.

———o———

It ain't no disgrace for a man to fall, but to lay there and grunt is.

"JOSH BILLINGS" (HENRY WHEELER SHAW)

———o———

Man takes account of our failures but God of our striving.

The fellow who keeps looking back will soon find himself going that way.

———o———

Straight from the Mighty Bow this truth is driven:
They fail, and they alone, who have not striven.

CLARENCE URMY

———o———

In the lexicon of youth, which fate reserves
For a bright manhood, there is no such word
As "fail."

EDWARD GEORGE BULWER-LYTTON

———o———

More men fail through ignorance of their strength than fail through knowledge of their weakness.

———o———

Not failure, but low aim, is crime.

JAMES RUSSELL LOWELL,
For an Autograph

———o———

A lot of people spend six days sowing wild oats, then go to church on Sunday and pray for a crop failure.

FRED ALLEN

———o———

No man's success should be built on another man's failure.

———o———

Someone asks why so many church members fail. Here's one answer in a parable: When a boy was asked why he fell out of bed, he replied, "I guess it's because I stayed too close to the getting-in place."

Faith

Prayer is the faith that asks; thanksgiving is the faith that takes.

———o———

All I have seen teaches me to trust the Creator for all I have not seen.

RALPH WALDO EMERSON

Faith makes all things possible, and love makes them easy.

———o———

I believe the promises of God enough to venture an eternity on them.

ISAAC WATTS

———o———

Faith marches at the head of the army of progress. It is found beside the most refined life, the freest government, the profoundest philosophy, the noblest poetry, the purest humanity.

THEODORE T. MUNGER

———o———

Skepticism has never founded empires, established principles, or changed the world's heart. The great doers in history have always been men of faith.

EDWIN HUBBELL CHAPIN

———o———

Faith never stands around with its hands in its pockets.

———o———

Faith is more like a verb than a noun . . . Faith *accepts* the Word of God, *affirms* confidence in that Word and *acts* upon it. You never really get going until you act upon what you accept and affirm. Then you are "faithing" your way along.

VANCE HAVNER, *Peace In The Valley*

———o———

Faith gets the most; humility keeps the most; but love works the most.

DWIGHT L. MOODY

———o———

In actual life every great enterprise begins with and takes its first forward step in faith.

AUGUST WILHELM VON SCHLEGEL

———o———

Dwight L. Moody described three kinds of faith in Jesus Christ: struggling faith, which is like a man in deep water; clinging faith, which is like a man hanging to the side of a boat; and resting faith, which finds a man safely within the boat, and able moreover to reach out with a hand to help someone else.

Our faith is tried in order that His faithfulness may be experienced.

———o———

The faith that does not act, is it truly faith?

JEAN BAPTISTE RACINE

———o———

Dr. A. J. Gordon, while traveling on a train, engaged in a spirited conversation with a fellow passenger on the subject of faith. "I differ with you," said the man, "in that any person is admitted to heaven because of a little bit of theological scrip called 'faith.' I believe that when God receives one into heaven He makes a searching inquiry as to his character rather than inspection of his faith."

Presently the conductor came along and examined the tickets. When he had passed, Dr. Gordon said: "Did you ever notice how a conductor always looks at the ticket but takes no pains to inspect the passenger? A railway ticket, if genuine, certifies that the person presenting it has complied with the company's conditions and is entitled to transportation. So faith alone, my friend, entitles one to that saving grace which produces a character well-pleasing to God."

———o———

Faith

Oh for a faith that will be strong
  When angry foes beset,
A faith that will stand fast until
  The victory is met.

Though dark and long the battle rage,
  I pray for faith sincere,
A faith that will stand out, unmoved,
  A strength in time of fear.

A courage born of trust alone,
  I know will see me through;
So Lord, I pray, Thou mayest now,
  My feeble faith renew.

JOHN CALDWELL CRAIG

———o———

Faith makes the uplook good, the outlook bright, the inlook favorable, and the future glorious.

V. RAYMOND EDMAN

Faith

Faith came singing into my room
　And other guests took flight;
Fear and anxiety, grief and gloom
　Sped out into the night.
I wondered that such peace could be.
　But Faith said gently, "Don't you see,
"They really cannot live with me."
                                    AUTHOR UNKNOWN

———o———

Faith is dead to doubt, dumb to discouragement, blind to impossibilities, and knows nothing but success in God.

———o———

Faith is not believing that God can. It is knowing that He *will*.

———o———

While faith makes all things possible, it is love that makes all things easy.
                            EVAN H. HOPKINS,
                    in *The Wesleyan Methodist*

———o———

Faith is the eye by which we look to Jesus. A dim-sighted eye is still an eye; a weeping eye is still an eye.

Faith is the hand with which we lay hold of Jesus. A trembling hand is still a hand. And he is a believer whose heart within him trembles when he touches the hem of the Saviour's garment, that he may be healed.

Faith is the tongue by which we taste how good the Lord is. A feverish tongue is nevertheless a tongue. And then we may believe, when we are without the smallest portion of comfort; for our faith is founded, not upon feelings but upon the promises of God.

Faith is the foot by which we go to Jesus. A lame foot is still a foot. He who comes slowly nevertheless comes.
                            GEORGE MUELLER

———o———

Lord,
in spite of having been with you,
like Peter, James and John,
I find I still can't cope with so much
that seems wrong and frightening in
　the world.

Give me the kind of faith that knows
that even if I can't cope
you can.
                            S. P. G., London

———o———

I prayed for faith and thought it would strike me like lightning. But faith did not come. One day I read, "Now faith comes by hearing, and hearing by the Word of God." I had closed my Bible and prayed for faith. I now began to study my Bible and faith has been growing ever since.
                            DWIGHT L. MOODY

———o———

It is strange we trust each other
And only doubt our Lord.
We take the word of mortals
And yet distrust His Word.
But oh, what light and glory
Would shine o'er all our days,
If we always would remember
God means just what He says.
                            A. B. SIMPSON

———o———

Faith is only worthy of the name when it erupts into action.
                            CATHERINE MARSHALL

———o———

When faith in God goes, man, the thinker, loses his greatest thought.

When faith in God goes, man, the worker, loses his greatest motive.

When faith in God goes, man, the sinner, loses his greatest help.

When faith in God goes, man, the sufferer, loses his securest refuge.

When faith in God goes, man, the lover, loses his fairest vision.

When faith in God goes, man, the mortal, loses his only hope.
                            HARRY EMERSON FOSDICK,
                            The Meaning of Faith

———o———

Faith: you can do very little with it, but you can do nothing without it.
                    SAMUEL BUTLER THE YOUNGER

———o———

I had faith
That God could,
I had hope
That God would;

Then my love
Pleased God
That He should.
FRANCES RHOADS LA CHANCE

———o———

Now that we have seen something of the greatness of faith, let us not forget that Christ is greater than faith in Him. As Maurice says, we spend half our time in thinking of faith, hope and love, instead of believing, hoping and loving.
JAMES HASTINGS

———o———

Lord, Give Me Faith

Lord, give me faith! — to live from day to day,
With tranquil heart to do my simple part,
And, with my hand in Thine, just go Thy way.

Lord, give me faith! — to trust, if not to know;
With quiet mind in all things Thee to find,
And, child-like, go where Thou wouldst have me go.

Lord, give me faith! — to leave it all to Thee,
The future is Thy gift, I would not lift
The veil Thy love has hung 'twixt it and me.
JOHN OXENHAM

———o———

Keystone

At first I only gave God thanks
If I felt well that day,
And everything was tranquil
And going just my way;
But when I learned to thank our Lord
When not one thing went right —
I found His hand was leading me,
His presence my delight,
His keystone *faith*, not sight.
MILDRED ALLEN JEFFERY

———o———

Faith is something like walking over a bridge you know will hold you up.
RAYMOND LINDQUIST

———o———

Faith lets Christ do for us and with us what we could never do alone.

Faithful

I cannot do great things for Him,
Who did so much for me,
But I should like to show my love,
Dear Jesus, unto Thee;
Faithful in very little things,
O Saviour, may I be.

———o———

His Choice Or Ours?

I would like to do something great, but God may appoint something little, and grace in doing that cheerfully may be greater in His sight. Elisha was ploughing, not dreaming, when Elijah brought God's message. Peter and Andrew were fishing, and James and John were mending their nets. "He that is faithful in that which is least is faithful also in much" (Luke 16:10). If we are glorifying God in that which He appoints today, we may be fitted for something more tomorrow. But we are not to live tomorrow today.
Selected

———o———

Fret not because thy place is small.
Thy service need not be,
For thou canst make it all there is
Of joy and ministry.

The dewdrop, as the boundless sea,
In God's great plan has part;
And this is all He asks of thee;
Be faithful where thou art.
Selected

———o———

It is not success that God rewards but faithfulness in doing His will.
Selected

Fame

Fame is a vapor, popularity an accident, riches take wings. Only one thing endures, and that is character.
HORACE GREELEY

———o———

I had rather men should ask why no statue has been erected in my honor, than why one has.
MARCUS PORCIUS CATO,
quoted in PLUTARCH's *Political Precepts*

Fame is no plant that grows on mortal soil.

JOHN MILTON, *Lycidas*

———o———

Seldom comes glory till a man be dead.

ROBERT HERRICK

———o———

Fame is the thirst of youth.

LORD BYRON, *Childe Harold's Pilgrimage*

Family

Someone has said, "The solution of the American family problems is contained in one word — CHRIST."

———o———

"A family man," says Roby Goff, who is one, "is a fellow who has replaced the currency in his wallet with snapshots."

Presbyterian Life

———o———

A family altar would alter many a family.

———o———

What Is Required

There are six essentials of good family life needed by all children.

First — love, affection and security, preferably with their own parents in their own home.

Second — full-time adult supervision and the teaching of self-control.

Third — parents with whom the child learns he can love on the basis of mutual trust.

Fourth — a close sense of family unity, where the members of the family eat together, take vacations together, go to church together.

Fifth — parents who take an interest in the education of their children.

Sixth — parents who set an example of living in accordance with the principles of their religious faith.

JUDGE GEORGE EDWARDS

———o———

Linda, aged nine, went with a neighbor playmate to a revival meeting one night. In telling her experience to the family she said, "The preacher asked everyone who had family *commotions* at their house to raise their hand, so I did."

Christian Home Builder

———o———

It is easy to govern a kingdom, but difficult to rule one's family.

———o———

You Can Always Tell Where a Family Lives

You can always tell where a family lives
By the gay effect that the hallway gives.
There are hooks arranged in a nice, straight row,
And the coats grow shorter and shorter, so
At the very first glance you can surmise
That the people vary in shape and size.
Hats that have streamers mean little girls,
With perky haircuts or ribboned curls.

A wagon and ball and bat reveal
That a boy lives there; and a slim, high heel
Or an overshoe is a certain clew
That a grown-up sister's an inmate, too.
A doll that flopped with a broken neck,
A toy train bunched in a pleasant wreck . . .
The rooms may be still as a sleeping mouse,
But you know there's a family in the house!

HELEN WELSHIMER

———o———

How To Hold A Family Worship

1. Choose a regular time to hold family worship each day — either in the morning or evening.
2. The father will be the leader.
3. Family worship should be a happy gathering, but remember that it must be reverent, too.
4. Let the Bible be the center of family worship. The Bible reading should be clear, careful, and brief.
5. Follow a definite course of Bible reading, either going through one book at a time — e.g. one of the

Gospels — or choosing passages which contain great verses or prayers, or tell of important events and prophecies. Where there are children, it is good to use the Psalms.

6. With young children it is sometimes better to tell a Bible story instead of reading it, or to read from a Bible picture book, which will help to hold their interest.

7. Children should be allowed to ask questions if they wish. They can also recite memory verses.

8. Prayers should be short, and the children encouraged to take part.

9. Invite friends to share in your family worship when they are visiting your home.

10. Remember that the saying of grace before meals is part of family worship too!

SOURCE UNKNOWN

Father

Father's Day

Father's Day, as some might assume, was not conceived in the egotism of a man, but was originated by a woman. To Mrs. John Bruce Dodd belongs the honor.

The day actually came into being about forty-three years ago on a very small scale, when a woman, Mrs. John Dodd, in Spokane, Washington, remembered her father as she sat in church on Mother's Day.

Mrs. Dodd was one girl among six children, the other five were boys. She could recall the day when her mother died.

As little children, they did not understand the finality of death and that night one of the little boys rushed out of the door and started for the cemetery where they had put his mother. Her father ran after him and caught up the little fellow in his arms and brought him back and put his arm about all of them.

"From that moment he became both father and mother to us," she said.

Mrs. Dodd remembered how her father through the years tried to throw about those six children the best influence, how he taught them to live by the Golden Rule, and gave them a faith to live by. He brought the preacher into their home again and again.

Mrs. Dodd went to the ministerial association in Spokane with the idea of honoring her father.

Selected

———o———

Tommy, doing his homework: "Daddy, why is our language called the mother tongue?"

Dad: "Because fathers hardly ever get a chance to use it."

———o———

Nurse: "Congratulations! You are the father of triplets."

Building Contractor: "Whew! I've exceeded my estimate again!"

———o———

Many a son has lost his way among strangers because his father was too busy to get acquainted with him.

WILLIAM L. BROWNELL

———o———

God And Father

My little boy came to me one day,
Placed his tiny hand in mine and said:
"Daddy, what is God like?"
And I said, "God is like love and sunshine,
And all the good things you know."
He smiled into my eyes and said:
"Then, Daddy, God must be just like you!"
I remember how Jesus said
That God is like a father;
And I had to bow my head in shame
That I, a father, was so unlike God!

GEORGE A. TURNER
in *The Log of the Good Ship Grace*

———o———

A little girl was showing her playmate her new home. "This is daddy's den," she explained as they entered one room. "Does your daddy have a den?"

"No," was the answer, "my pop just growls all over the house."

———o———

Small boy's definition of Father's Day: "It's just like Mother's Day, only you don't spend as much on the present."

Toronto Star

———o———

Reflections Of A Father

Say, fellows, I want to tell you I'd be
happy as a clam
If I was just the Daddie that my laddie
thinks I am.
He thinks I'm a wonder and believes
his dear old Dad
Could never think of mixing with mean
things that are bad,
And sometimes I just sit and think how
nice it would be,
If I was just the Daddie that my laddie
thinks he is.

CHELEY

———o———

One father is more than a hundred
schoolmasters.

GEORGE HERBERT, *Jacula Prudentum*

———o———

Definition of an exceptional father:
One who lets the children play with
their Christmas toys more than he does.

———o———

Many a boy at sixteen can't believe
that some day he will be as dumb as
his dad!

———o———

A Father's Ten Commandments

By My Example

I. I shall teach my child respect
for his fellow man.
II. I shall teach him good sports-
manship in work and play.
III. I shall instill in him an appreciation of religion and the family,
the backbone of society.
IV. I shall strive for companionship
and mutual understanding.
V. I shall impart to him a desire
to love and honor his country
and obey its laws.
VI. I shall encourage him to apply
himself to difficult tasks.
VII. I shall teach him the importance
of participation in community
affairs and local government.
VIII. I shall teach him self-reliance

and help him develop an independent spirit.
IX. I shall help him develop a sense
of responsibility in planning for
the future.
X. I shall, above all, prepare him
for the duties and responsibilities of citizenship in a free
society.

Glendale News Press,
Glendale, Calif.

———o———

A Father's Day Prayer

Mender of toys, leader of boys,
Changer of fuses, kisser of bruises,
Bless him, dear Lord.
Mover of couches, soother of ouches
Pounder of nails, teller of tales,
Reward him, O Lord.
Hanger of screens, counselor of teens,
Fixer of bikes, chastiser of tykes,
Help him, O Lord.
Raker of leaves, cleaner of eaves,
Dryer of dishes, fulfiller of wishes . . .
Bless him, O Lord.

JO ANN HEIDBREDER in *The Sign*

———o———

Giddap, Dad

The men who ride in rodeos
Need to be tough, of course —
But they should have a two-year-old
And spend time as a horse!

LAVONNE MATHISON

———o———

Fatherhood

I could have lost him, but pride and
joy
Curbed sharp impatience with my boy.

I shared his joy at triumph's fame
Restored his faith when failure came.

Sometimes with wisdom, often with
hope,
I answered as his mind would grope

In eager questioning. And I would
pray
For guidance for myself, to lead his
way.

I salved his woes, calmed fears and
cries

And saw the father worship in his eyes.

Tired feet trod with his strong ones
To greater heights, to bright new suns!
ROY Z. KEMP

———o———

We think our fathers fools, so wise we
grow;
Our wiser sons, no doubt, will think us
so.
ALEXANDER POPE, *Essay on Criticism*

———o———

A Father's Prayer

Build me a son, O God, who will be
strong enough to know when he is
weak and brave enough to face himself when he is afraid; one who will be
proud and unbending in honest defeat, but humble and gentle in victory.
Build me a son whose wishes will not
replace his actions — a son who will
know Thee, and that to know himself
is the foundation stone of knowledge.
Send him, I pray, not in the path of
ease and comfort but the stress and
spur of difficulties and challenge; here
let him learn to stand up in the storm;
here let him learn compassion for those
who fail.

Build me a son whose heart will be
clear, whose goal will be high; a son
who will master himself before he seeks
to master others; one who will learn to
laugh, yet never forget how to weep;
one who will reach into the future,
yet never forget the past, and after all
these things are his, this I pray, enough
sense of humor that he may always be
serious yet never take himself too seriously. Give him humility so that he
may always remember the simplicity
of true greatness, the open mind of
true wisdom, the meekness of true
strength; then I, his father, will dare
to whisper, "I have not lived in vain."
Quoted by the late
GENERAL DOUGLAS MACARTHUR

Faults

From Day To Day

We all have faults to conquer
You do and I do, too.
We make mistakes quite often
In something that we do.

Not one of us is perfect.
We can only progress,
From day to day attempting
To make our faults grow less.

Then may we aid each other,
Not harshly criticize.
How sweet is understanding
From those who sympathize.

The helping hand, the kindly heart
Are needed everywhere
So let us reach out daily
And show someone we care
LOUISE DARCY

———o———

We can often do more for other men
by correcting our own faults than by
trying to correct theirs.

———o———

We ought to avoid in ourselves the
faults that we blame in others.
MENANDER

———o———

To acknowledge our faults when we
are blamed is modesty; to discover
them to one's friends, in ingenuousness,
is confidence; but to proclaim them to
the world, if one does not take care, is
pride.
CONFUCIUS

———o———

Nothing is easier than faultfinding;
no talent, no self-denial, no brains, no
character are required to set up in the
grumbling business.
The Herald

———o———

What you dislike in another, take
care to correct in yourself.
THOMAS SPAT

———o———

It is a satisfaction for some to ex-
hibit another's faults even if they must
wait six months for a chance.

———o———

But, friend, to me
He is all fault who hath no fault at all.
ALFRED, LORD TENNYSON
Idylls of the King, Lancelot and Elaine

———o———

He has no faults, except that he is
faultless.
PLINY THE YOUNGER

A fault confessed is half redressed.

———o———

To increase your happiness, forget your neighbor's faults.

———o———

I dare no more fret than I dare curse and swear. Nothing is more sure to destroy the joy and peace of a home. Nothing is more sure to finally divide and even separate a home than this habit of fretfulness, grumbling and fault-finding.

JOHN WESLEY

Fear

Near acquaintance doth diminish reverent fear.

SIR PHILIP SIDNEY

———o———

There is much in the world to make us afraid. There is much more in our faith to make us unafraid.

FREDERICK W. CROPP

———o———

The people to fear are not those who disagree with you but those who disagree with you and are too cowardly to let you know.

NAPOLEON BONAPARTE

———o———

He has not learned the lesson of life who does not every day surmount a fear.

RALPH WALDO EMERSON

———o———

Afraid? Of What?

Afraid? Of what?
To feel the spirit's glad release?
To pass from pain to perfect peace?
The strife and strain of life to cease?
Afraid — of that?

Afraid? Of what?
Afraid to see the Savior's face?
To hear His welcome, and to trace
The glory gleam from wounds of grace?
Afraid — of that?

E. H. HAMILTON

No power is strong enough to be lasting if it labors under the weight of fear.

MARCUS TULLIUS CICERO

———o———

We can easily forgive a child who is afraid of the dark; the real tragedy of life is when men are afraid of the light.

PLATO

———o———

Six-year-old Tommy was far from anxious to enter the first grade when school started in a few weeks. Finally he told his parents the reason for his fears. "I don't want to go to first grade because my teeth will begin to fall out like Johnny's did when he started to school!"

———o———

He who fears the Lord can expect help when his case is at the worst.

———o———

No one loves him whom he fears.

ARISTOTLE, *Rhetoric*

———o———

Our fears do make us traitors.

WILLIAM SHAKESPEARE, *Macbeth*

———o———

To be free from all fear, we must have but one fear — the fear of God.

———o———

What we are afraid to do before men we may well be afraid to think before God.

———o———

The function of fear is to warn us of danger, not to make us afraid to face it.

Fellowship

A habit of devout fellowship with God is the spring of all our life, and the strength of it. Such prayer, meditation and converse with God restores and renews the temper of our minds; so that by this contact with the world unseen we receive continual accesses of strength.

HENRY E. MANNING

Fellowship is heaven, and lack of fellowship is hell: fellowship is life, and lack of fellowship is death: and the deeds that ye do on earth, it is for fellowship's sake that ye do them.

WILLIAM MORRIS

———o———

I remember what an African said to a missionary. They had been praying together [in Africa], after the blessing. One was an African Christian, the other a missionary from England. The missionary saw what had happened in the life of this African, that he was changed, and that he came to the missionary and opened his heart — to the amazement of the Englishman. But after a number of times of having a little prayer time in the missionary's house . . ., the missionary turned to the African and said, "Look here. You haven't got as much fellowship with me as you have with your dear African brother [naming a friend]. What's wrong?" The African replied, "Look, we are here like two boxes. Imagine two boxes trying to have fellowship — one having the lock on, and the other wide open. Tell me if that is practical. Can these two boxes have fellowship as long as one is locked?"

Of the two men, one was open.

FESTO KIVENGERE,
in Commission, Conflict, Commitment

———o———

Tell God all that is in your heart, as one unloads one's heart to a dear friend. People who have no secrets from each other never want subjects of conversation; they do not weigh their words, because there is nothing to be kept back. Neither do they seek for something to say; they talk out of the abundance of their hearts, just what they think. Blessed are they who attain to such familiar, unreserved intercourse with God.

FRANÇOIS DE SALIGNAC DE LA MOTHE
FENELON (1651-1715)

Fight

If you aren't wounded then you haven't fought.

The tree that never had to fight
For sun and sky and air and light,
That stood out in the open plain
And always got its share of rain,
Never became a forest king,
But lived and died a scrubby thing.
Where thickest stands the forest growth
We find the patriarchs of both;
And they hold converse with the stars
Whose broken branches show the scars
Of many winds and much of strife.
This is the common law of life.

———o———

One day my youngster brought home a note from his teacher, saying he had been fighting in the schoolyard. "Johnny and I weren't fighting when the teacher came along," my son insisted. "We were just trying to separate each other."

MRS. LILY JACOBSEN in Coronet

———o———

It is easier to fight for one's principles than to live up to them.

ALFRED ADLER

———o———

It is often asked whether the Christian is not to fight in the conflict with personal sin. The answer is that of course he must fight, but it is necessary to remember that it is the "good fight of faith" (I Timothy 6:12), and it is particularly important to realize that the fight is not to obtain, but to maintain. It is a struggle not for a position, but from a position. As has been well said, the Christian is not like a man in the valley struggling to reach the top of the hill, but like a man on the top of the hill fighting to maintain his position there against enemies who are trying to drag him down.

GRIFFITH W. THOMAS

Fire

The same fire that melts the wax hardens the steel.

———o———

Men ablaze are invincible. Hell trembles when men kindle with the flame and fervor of the Holy Spirit. The stronghold of Satan is proof against everything but fire.

SAMUEL CHADWICK

————o————

The supreme need of the Church is the same in the twentieth century as in the first: it is men on fire for Christ.

JAMES S. STEWART

————o————

I will blaze the trail, though my grave may only become a stepping-stone that younger men may follow.

C. T. STUDD

————o————

You cannot kindle a fire in another until it is burning within yourself.

Fish, Fishing

Never fish in troubled waters.

————o————

Seeking diversion by fishing in the streams of Scotland, a literary man went from the city with patent pole and a complete outfit of the most expensive kind. After hours of effort without even a bit, he came across a country boy with only a switch for a pole and a bent pin for a hook — but he had a long string of fish.

"Why is it that I can't catch any?" the man inquired.

"Because you don't keep yourself out of sight," the boy replied.

This is the secret of fishing for men as well as trout. Hold up the Cross of Christ. Send the people away talking about Him, instead of praising you.

————o————

A fishing rod is an instrument with a worm at one end and a fool at the other.

————o————

You will find angling to be like the virtue of humility, which has a calmness of spirit and a world of other blessings attending upon it.

IZAAK WALTON, *The Compleat Angler*

Flag

Flag Day

"I pledge allegiance to my flag" and
    all for which it stands,
  The cradle-home of Freedom, and
    hearts of many lands,
And may I never dim its stars with
    touch of greedy hands!

"One nation indivisible," one banner,
    and one soul,
  For whom through years of blood
    and toil our fathers paid the toll,
And may I come to understand the
    vision of the whole!

"With liberty and justice," for each his
    fighting-chance
  To prove his worth, and win his
    dream in battled circumstance,
And may I never bar the way, nor
    break another's chance!

"I pledge allegiance to my flag," north,
    south, east and west,
  I know not what the years shall bring
    to put me to the test,
But may I guard it with my life, and
    serve it with my best!

MARTHA HASKELL CLARK

————o————

"A song for our banner?" The watch-
  word recall
Which gave the Republic her station;
"United we stand, divided we fall!"
It made and preserves us a nation!

GEORGE POPE MORRIS,
The Flag of Our Union

————o————

The American Flag

When Freedom from her mountain
    height
Unfurled her standard to the air,
She tore the azure robe of night,
  And set the stars of glory there.
She mingled with its gorgeous dyes
  The milky baldric of the skies,
And striped its pure, celestial white,
With streakings of the morning light.

Flag of the free heart's hope and home!
  By angel hands to valor given;
Thy stars have lit the welkin dome,

And all thy hues were born in heaven.

Forever float that standard sheet!
Where breathes the foe but falls before us,
With Freedom's soil beneath our feet,
And Freedom's banner streaming o'er us?

JOSEPH RODMAN DRAKE

Flattery

Flattery is to be used like perfume — smell and enjoy it, but don't swallow it.

———o———

Flattery is soft soap
and soap is 90% lye.

Christian Leader

———o———

Flattery is often a gift-wrapped insult.

———o———

Flattery is the art of telling another person exactly what he thinks of himself.

———o———

Flatterers look like friends, as wolves like dogs.

GEORGE CHAPMAN

———o———

Flattery corrupts both the receiver and the giver; and adulation is not of more service to the people than to kings.

EDMUND BURKE

———o———

He that loves to be flattered is worthy of the flattery.

WILLIAM SHAKESPEARE

———o———

'Tis an old maxim in the schools,
That flattery's the food of fools;
Yet now and then your men of wit
Will condescend to take a bit.

JONATHAN SWIFT, *Cadenus and Vanessa*

Follow

Followers

They followed Him by thousands when He took some fish and bread
And a banquet in the desert by His miracle was spread.

They sang aloud, "Hosanna!" and they shouted, "Praise His name!"
When in an hour of glory to Jerusalem He came.
They followed when He told them of a kingdom and a throne,
But when He went to Calvary, He went there all alone.

It seems that many people still would follow Him today
If He only went to places where everything was gay.
For the kingdom that they're seeking isn't one the world scorns,
And the crown of which they're singing isn't one that's made of thorns.
Oh, they'll follow for the fishes over land and over sea,
And they'll join the church at Zion, but not at Calvary.

It's so easy, friends, to follow when the nets are full of fish,
When the loaves are spread before you and you're eating all you wish,
When no lands, nor lots, nor houses and no friendships are at stake,
When there's no mob to mock you and you have no cross to take.
But you'll need some faith to follow down through Gethsemane,
And you'll need some love to follow up to Calvary!

AUTHOR UNKNOWN

———o———

If you haven't learned to follow, you can't lead.

HENRIETTA C. MEARS

———o———

A telegram was received by a famous girls' school in which the father of the applicant, on observing the question, "Outline the leadership capabilities of your daughter," responded by saying, "My daughter has no leadership capacities. However, she is an intelligent follower."

The president of the college telephoned the father directly and admitted his daughter to the college without qualification, stating that, of the thousands of applicants to the college, this was the first girl who was not a natural-born leader.

GENE L. SCHWILCK in *Indiana Teacher*

When I follow someone I at least want to know where he's going.

CLARA FRANCES SMITH

———o———

Others follow in your footsteps quicker than they follow your advice.

———o———

Anyone can praise Christ, but it takes a man of courage to follow Him.

———o———

The grandchildren of Mr. and Mrs. W. W. Evans, owners of a ranch near Panhandle, Texas, were thrilled by the gift of seventeen sheep — which they played with and fed until one day the sheep wandered off the ranch. Another rancher, finding the strays and thinking they belonged to his son, put them in with his son's 200 sheep. When he realized he had taken the Evans children's sheep, he was quite sorry and willing to give them back. But how could they tell which of the sheep belonged to which owner?

Then Billy, one of the children, had an idea. Taking a bucket of oats, he went out to the flock, and gave his usual feed call. Immediately sixteen of the sheep hurried to him — and the seventeenth followed as soon as he came near enough to hear!

This brings home Christ's description of Himself as the Good Shepherd calling to His sheep: "And the sheep follow Him: for they know His voice" (John 10:4).

Fool, Foolish

A foolish man uses wisdom to explain his foolishness; a wise man uses foolishness to explain his wisdom.

———o———

Much more painful than acting like a fool is suddenly to realize that you were not acting!

———o———

You can always tell a fool, but the chances are he won't know what you're talking about.

Many a man who is counted a fool by financiers has laid up an enviable fortune in Heaven.

———o———

He who asks a question is a fool for five minutes; he who does not ask a question remains a fool forever.

Chinese Proverb

———o———

If there were a law against being foolish, we'd all be in jail.

———o———

Being considered a fool for Christ's sake is not a license to act like one.

C. J. FOSTER

———o———

If things go awry, must we then turn the world over into the hands of the fools?

———o———

The only way to keep from seeing a fool is to remain in your bedroom and break the mirror.

———o———

Dr. P. S. Hensen was engaged to speak for a Chautauqua on the subject of "Fools." He was introduced by Bishop John H. Vincent with the remark, "Ladies and Gentlemen, we are about to have a lecture on 'Fools' by one of the most distinguished . . ." The bishop paused as if finished, then resumed: ". . . men of Chicago." Dr. Hensen, unperturbed began his speech: "I am not so great a fool as Bishop Vincent . . ." The audience gasped during his pause, and then he concluded: ". . . would have you think."

———o———

Wise men learn more from fools than fools from wise men; for wise men avoid the faults of fools, but fools will not imitate the good examples of wise men.

MARCUS PORCIUS CATO,
quoted in PLUTARCH'S *Lives*

Forbearance

If I Knew You And You Knew Me

If I knew you and you knew me,
'Tis seldom we would disagree;

But never having yet clasped hand,
Both often fail to understand
That each intends to do what's right
And treat each other "honor bright,"
How little to complain there'd be
If I knew you and you knew me.

Whene'er I ship you my mistake
Or in your bill some error make,
From irritation you'd be free
If I knew you and you knew me.
Or when the checks don't come on
    time
And customers send nary a line,
I'd wait without anxiety
If I knew you and you knew me.

Or when some goods you "fire back,"
Or make a "kick" on this or that,
I'd take it in good part, you see,
If I knew you and you knew me.
With customers a million strong,
Occasionally things go wrong —
Sometimes my fault, sometimes theirs —
Forbearance would decrease all cares.
Kind friend, how pleasant things would
    be
If I knew you and you knew me!
Herbalist Almanac, 1938

———o———

Cultivate forbearance till your heart
yields a fine crop of it. Pray for a short
memory as to all unkindnesses.
CHARLES HADDON SPURGEON

Foreign

After hearing his teacher talk about
a missionary family which the church
supported serving in a foreign field, the
three-year-old prayed as follows during
the prayer time: "Dear God, help the
Butler family in the corn field."

———o———

A Foreigner

Within the walls of hate and shunning
I am placed.
I am a foreigner.
Outside the walls of love and friend-
ship
I am placed.
I am a foreigner.
Because I am dark,
Because I speak with an unharmoniz-
ing tone,

Because I am a foreigner
I am placed
Within the walls of ridicule,
Outside the walls of understanding.
MARYBETH ANDERSON

Forget

Forget yourself for others, and others
will never forget you.

———o———

When a man forgets himself, he usually does something that everyone else
remembers.

———o———

The Year That Has Gone

Let us forget the things that vexed and
    tried us.
The worrying things that caused our
    soul to fret,
The hopes that cherished long, where
    still denied us,
Let us forget.

Let us forget the little slights that
    pained us,
The greater wrongs that rankle some-
    times yet,
The pride with which some lofty one
    disdained us,
Let us forget.

But blessings manifold past all deserv-
    ing,
Kind words and helpful deeds, a count-
    less throng,
The fault o'ercome, the rectitude un-
    swerving —
Let us remember long.

The sacrifice of love, the generous giv-
    ing,
Where friends were few, the hand-
    clasp warm and strong,
The fragrance of each life of holy liv-
    ing,
Let us remember long.

So pondering well the lesson it has
    taught us,
We tenderly may bid the year "Good-
    bye,"
Holding in memory all the good that
    it has brought us,
Letting the evil die.
AUTHOR UNKNOWN

Your brother's sins write in the sand
Where waters may erase them
But carve his virtues in your heart
And let not time efface them!

JAMES GALLAGHER

————o————

The Forward Look

Lord, make me deaf, and dumb and
   blind
To all, "those things which are behind."
Dead to the voice that memory brings,
Accusing me of many things.
Dumb to the things my tongue could
   speak,
Reminding me when I was weak.
Blind to the things I still might see,
When they come back to trouble me.
Let me press on to Thy high calling,
In Christ, who keepeth me from falling.
Forgetting all that lies behind —
Lord, make me deaf, and dumb and
   blind.
Like Paul, I then shall win the race,
I would have lost but for Thy grace!
Forgetting all that I have done —
'Twas Thee, dear Lord, not I that won!

GEORGE T. KENYON
in Herald of His Coming

Forgive

He who has mastered the grace of
forgiveness is far more triumphant than
he who has managed to see that no
wrong to him is gone unavenged.

LLOYD D. MATTSON

————o————

How can we gain a forgiving heart?
Only by going to the Cross and there
seeing how much our Lord has forgiven us and at what a cost. Then we
shall see that the utmost we are called
upon to forgive, compared with what
we have been forgiven, is a very little
thing.

————o————

Forgiveness of sins does not qualify
a person to live; it only qualifies him
to die.

LLOYD AHLEM

————o————

Dinny Malone, a retired sea captain
of unusual integrity, was reading his
Bible when the minister came to call.
The 80-year-old seaman greeted the
minister with the news that he had
been trying to get God to forgive him
for six years — "and He won't!"

The minister looked at him keenly.
"Have you repented?" Dinny nodded
solemnly. "Have you trusted God?"
"Yes," answered Dinny. "Then you
must have found Him!"

Dinny shook his head. "I never feel
it in my heart — the forgiveness."

The minister took the Bible from
Dinny's hand and together they went
over the invitations of Christ and such
verses as I John 1:9: "If we confess our
sins, he is faithful and just to forgive us
our sins, and to cleanse us from all
unrighteousness."

"Dinny," said the minister, "when
you give your word, do you keep it?"
"Sure I do!" roared Dinny. "Doesn't
a gentleman always?" The minister
leaned toward him. "Dinny, don't you
think God is a gentleman?"

A light that never was on land or sea
shone on Dinny's face. "What a fool
I've been! I see it now. He does forgive me, and now I feel it!"

The Pentecostal Evangel

————o————

Forgiveness does not leave the
hatchet handle sticking out of the
ground.

————o————

The offender never pardons.

GEORGE HERBERT, Jacula Prudentum

————o————

Being all fashioned of the self-same
   dust,
Let us be merciful as well as just.

HENRY WADSWORTH LONGFELLOW

————o————

When you are forgiven, someone
must pay, and the one who forgives is
the one who suffers.

EDWIN ORR

————o————

Yesterday

A typical day, crowded full of things —
   Household chores and a phone that
   rings

The children rushing in at three —
  Shouting with laughter and full of
  glee.

She tried to be helpful — saying, "Here
  I'll pour"
And milk is spilled on the freshly
  waxed floor.
"Shame on you — now see what you've
  done."
  (Was that my voice?) "You naughty
  one!"

"I'm sorry, Mommy" — "Sorry, won't
  do —
You go to your room 'til I call you."
The hours slip by — supper is past,
  The children are bathed and in bed
  at last.

When out of the darkness a question
  from Sue,
"When you're naughty, Mommy,
  who punishes you?"
The house is quiet — my day is through
And so I turn, Dear God, to You —

To You who gives me each new day.
  Another chance to go Thy way.
Another chance — all sins forgiven,
  A gift of love from God in Heaven.

And suddenly the teardrops start,
  For I have failed to do my part,
To teach my children the kind of love,
  Given to us from God above.

I, whose sins are so much more
  Than a glass of milk spilled on the
  floor,
Forget how much I count on Thee ac-
  cepting
"I'm sorry" each day from me.

Forgive me, Father — Forgive me,
  Sue —
And help me remember my whole
  life through
"When you're naughty, Mommy — who
  punishes you?"

                            MARIAN PALMER

Fortune

When Fortune is on our side, popular favor bears her company.

                    PUBLILIUS SYRUS, *Maxim 275*

Not only is fortune herself blind, but
she generally blinds those on whom
she bestows her favors.

                    MARCUS TULLIUS CICERO

———o———

Fortune makes him a fool, whom she
makes her darling.

                            FRANCIS BACON

———o———

Fortune is like glass — the brighter
the glitter, the more easily broken.

                    PUBLILIUS SYRUS, *Maxim 280*

Free, Freedom

Once upon a time there was a kite
who wanted to be free. He was quite
thrilled the day his master took him
out, and he rose high above the earth.
But suddenly he found he could go no
farther. His master had quit letting out
the string.
  "Why does he hold me back like
this?" he fretted. "You think I am high
in the sky now, but if my master would
only let me loose and give me freedom,
I'd show you how high I could go."
  One day while the kite was fretting
thus, the string broke. The kite wavered for a minute, was blown from
side to side, then suddenly turned
topsy-turvy, and came floating down,
down, down, unable to right itself.
Finally it was swept by the strong
wind up against a telegraph wire and
there it hung, all tattered and torn. Its
freedom was its ruin.

                    The Evangelical Christian

———o———

Let us give thanks that we live in a
free country where a man can say what
he thinks if he isn't afraid of his wife,
his neighbors, or his boss, and if he's
sure it won't hurt his business.

                    Changing Times, The Kiplinger Magazine

———o———

False freedom leaves a man free to
do what he likes; true freedom, to do
what he ought.

———o———

Moody tells of a man who said he
would like to come to Jesus, but he was
chained and could not break away. A

Christian said to him, "But, man, why don't you come, chain and all?" He said, "I never thought of that. And I will." He did and Christ broke every fetter.

———o———

One who knows by the assurance of the witnessing Spirit that he is born of God, knows he must be free.

BISHOP WARREN CANDLER

———o———

Christianity promises to make men free; it never promises to make them independent.

WILLIAM R. INGE

———o———

You have freedom *of* choice but not freedom *from* choice.

WENDELL JONES

———o———

. . . freedom of religion; freedom of the press; freedom of person under the protection of the *habeas corpus*. . . . these principles form the bright constellation which has gone before us, and guided our steps through an age of revolution and reformation.

THOMAS JEFFERSON,
First Inaugural Address

———o———

No one can be free who does not work for the freedom of others.

———o———

Sunsets For Sale

Suppose that people had to pay
To see a sunset's crimson play
And the magic stars of the Milky Way.
Suppose it was fifty cents a night
To watch the pale moon's silvery light,
Or watch a gull in graceful flight.

Suppose God charged us for the rain,
Or put a price on a song-bird's strain
Of music — the dawn-mist on the plain.
How much would autumn landscapes cost,
Or a window etched with winter's frost,
And the rainbow's glory so quickly lost?

How much, I wonder, would it be worth
To smell the good, brown, fragrant earth

In spring? The miracle of birth —
How much do you think would people pay
For a baby's laugh at the close of day?
Suppose God charged us for them, I say!

Suppose we paid to look at the hills,
For the rippling mountain rills,
Or the mating song of whippoorwills,
Or curving breakers of the sea,
For grace and beauty and majesty?
And all these things He gives us free!

Ah! what poor return for these
We yield at night on bended knees,
Without thanksgiving we mumble pleas;
Ignoring the moonlight across the floor,
The voice of a friend at the open door,
We beg the Master for more and more!

AUTHOR UNKNOWN

———o———

Without a free press there can be no free society.

FELIX FRANKFURTER

———o———

Land Of The Free

Freedom to worship God.
Our pilgrim fathers came
Bearing aloft this torch,
A high and holy flame.

Freedom to worship God.
With this they lit the world;
Beneath this burning brand
A bright new flag unfurled.

Freedom to worship God.
And now, on speeding wheels,
Their children crowd the earth.
Today, who bows, who kneels?

Freedom to worship God.
This was their battle cry.
And now that we are free —
Have we forgotten why?

HELEN FRAZEE-BOWER

———o———

Three Needs

I know three things must always be,
To keep a nation strong and free;
One, a hearthstone, bright and clear

With busy, happy loved ones near.
One is a ready heart and hand
To love and serve, and keep the land.
One is a worn and beaten way
To where the people go to pray.
So long as these are kept alive,
Nation and people will survive.
God keep them always, everywhere —
The hearth, the flag, the place of
   prayer.

                    BERTHA CLARKE HUGHES

———o———

Here is J. Edgar Hoover's answer to
the question, "Where do you believe
freedom has its beginnings?"

In religion. Christ championed the
sanctity of the individual. There is
respect for human dignity only where
Christ and the Bible are a way of life.
The philosophy of Christ has meant
freedom from despair and tyranny
throughout history.

Friend

The older we grow the more we are
disquieted over the lack of attention
people show to their friends. An old
Scandinavian adage puts it this way:
"Go often to the house of thy friend,
for weeds choke up an unused path."

———o———

A friend of mine dropped by, dear
   God, for just a friendly chat . . .
We sipped a cup of coffee and we
   talked of this and that . . .
Our visit was not planned at all, but
   as he passed my way . . .
My friend just stopped to say "hello"
   and pass the time of day . . .

You know how much I'm grateful, God,
   for kind and thoughtful friends . . .
It's folks like these that bring my life
   its richest dividends . . .
Because they bring a friendly word,
   they share a smile or two . . .
And skies that had a tinge of gray become a brighter blue.

                    GEORGE BILBY WALKER

———o———

It is my joy in life to find
   At every turning of the road

The strong arms of a comrade kind
   To help me onward with my load.
And since I have no gold to give
   And love alone can make amends,
My only prayer is, "While I live,
   God, make me worthy of my friends!"

                    AUTHOR UNKNOWN

———o———

A real friend is one who will continue to talk to you over the back fence
even though he knows he's missing his
favorite television program.

———o———

The ornaments of a house are the
friends who visit it.

———o———

Old Friends

Make new friends, but keep the old;
Those are silver, these are gold.
New-made friendships, like new wine,
Age will mellow and refine.

Friendships that have stood the test —
Time and change — are surely best;
Brow may wrinkle, hair grow gray,
Friendship never knows decay.

For 'mid old friends, tried and true,
Once more we our youth renew.
But old friends, alas! may die,
New friends must their place supply.

Cherish friendship in your breast —
New is good, but old is best;
Make new friends, but keep the old;
Those are silver, these are gold.

                    JOSEPH PARRY

———o———

He who would have friends must
show himself friendly. Love begets
love. Kindness secures kindness. Whatsoever we sow we shall reap.

———o———

Treat your friend as if he might
become an enemy.

                    PUBLILIUS SYRUS, Maxim 402

———o———

Some take their gold in minted mold
   And some in harps hereafter;
But give me mine in friendship fine;
   Keep the change in laughter.

I awake this morning with devout thanksgiving for my friends, the old and the new.

RALPH WALDO EMERSON

————o————

The way to keep a circle of friends is to keep on the square with them.

————o————

We can never replace a friend. When a man is fortunate enough to have several, he finds they are all different. No one has a double in friendship.

JOHANN VON SCHILLER

————o————

A friend is someone you can count on to count on you.

————o————

A friend whom it has taken years to win should not be displeasing to you in a moment. A stone is many years becoming a ruby — take care that you do not destroy its luster in an instant.

————o————

True friendship is loyalty to a friend in trouble.

RALPH BREWER

————o————

Prosperity makes friends and adversity tries them.

PUBLILIUS SYRUS, *Maxim 872*

————o————

To God, thy country, and thy friend be true.

HENRY VAUGHAN,
Rules and Lessons, No. 8

————o————

Chance makes our parents, but choice makes our friends.

JACQUES DELILLE

————o————

I lay it down as a fact that, if all men knew what others say of them, there would not be four friends in the world.

BLAISE PASCAL, *Pensées*

————o————

Unless you bear with the faults of a friend you betray your own.

PUBLILIUS SYRUS

Growing Friendship

Friendship is like a garden of flowers, fine and rare,
It cannot reach perfection except through loving care;
Then, new and lovely blossoms with each new day appear . . .
For Friendship like a garden, grows in beauty year by year.

AUTHOR UNKNOWN

————o————

Friendship is a chain of God
Shaped in God's all perfect mold.
Each link a smile, a laugh, a tear,
A grip of the hand, a word of cheer.
Steadfast as the ages roll,
Binding closer soul to soul.
No matter how far or heavy the load,
Sweet is the journey on friendship's road.

AUTHOR UNKNOWN

Fruitful

Fruitful Christian witness grows from roots of faithful obedience to Christ.

————o————

The fruits of the Spirit are nothing but the virtues of Christ.

FRIEDRICH ERNST SCHLEIERMACHER

————o————

He that plants thorns must never expect to gather roses.

PILPAY

Frustration

A good definition of frustration: Missing your turn in a revolving door.

————o————

Frustration

Traveling with a four-year-old
Explains the word "frustration" . . .
You have to stop . . . he has to go
At every service station.

ALBERTA KNOCH in *Home Life*

————o————

He overcomes the frustration of the times whose plans and purposes belong to God.

Fun

Mix a little folly with your wisdom; a little nonsense is pleasant now and then.

HORACE, *Odes*

———o———

There ain't much fun in medicine, but there's a good deal of medicine in fun.

———o———

When a thing is funny, search it for a hidden truth.

GEORGE BERNARD SHAW

———o———

A little folly is desirable in him that will not be guilty of stupidity.

MICHEL EYQUEM DE MONTAIGNE, *Of Vanity*

———o———

A little nonsense now and then
Is relished by the wisest men.

ANONYMOUS

———o———

Your funny-bone is where you laugh in your sleeve.

———o———

Everything is funny as long as it is happening to somebody else.

WILL ROGERS, *The Illiterate Digest*

Funeral

A new minister, who was called to pastor a church in a small town in Oklahoma, the first few days visited the homes of the members, urging them to attend his first service that coming Sunday.

But when Sunday came, only a handful of people showed up.

The next day, in desperation, the young minister placed a notice in the local newspaper stating that, because such-and-such a church was dead, it was his duty, as a minister, to give it a decent Christian burial.

"The funeral will be held the following Sunday afternoon at the Church" the advertisement said.

Morbidly curious, the entire community turned out for this unusual funeral.

In front of the pulpit, they saw a casket, smothered with flowers. The pastor read the obituary and delivered the eulogy.

He then invited his congregation to step forward and pay their respect to the dearly beloved who had departed.

The long line filed by. Each "mourner" peeped into the coffin, and turned away with a guilty, sheepish look.

In the coffin, tilted at the correct angle, was a large mirror.

Each person saw himself — as the reason for the death of the old church.

Future

The Uncertain Future

We know not what the future holds
In times like these today;
The castles that we start to build
May crumble and decay,
With all earth's vast uncertainty —
Some poverty, some wealth,
For some the best that heart could wish;
For others failing health.

Hold on to God's unchanging hand
No matter where you go;
Relinquish not your trust in Him
Though weakened by the foe.
May God's eternal leadership
Our stronghold ever be.
Oh, strengthen, Lord, our faith and hope
For what we cannot see!

AUTHOR UNKNOWN

———o———

The future is always a fairy land to the young.

———o———

To The Future

The past has its store of joys we remember,
The future is ours undefiled . . .
Let us carry our weight with courage of men,
But proceed with the trust of a child.

KATHLEEN PARTRIDGE

———o———

I do not know what the future holds, but I do know who holds the future. Because of the character and the invincible purpose of God, there can be no doubt of the ultimate triumph of righteousness.

GEORGE W. TRUETT

I know of no way of judging the future but by the past.

PATRICK HENRY, *Speech*, March 23, 1775

G

Gain

A great point is gained when we have learned not to struggle against the circumstances God has appointed for us.

H. L. SIDNEY LEAR

———o———

I gave up all for Christ, and what have I found? I have found everything in Christ.

JOHN CALVIN

———o———

He who seeks for gain must be at some expense.

PLAUTUS

Gambling

Gambling is the child of avarice, the brother of iniquity, and the father of mischief.

GEORGE WASHINGTON

———o———

Gambling is the one sure way of getting nothing for something.

———o———

He who gambles picks his own pockets.

———o———

There are two times in a man's life when he should not speculate: when he can't afford it, and when he can.

———o———

The gambling known as business looks with austere disfavor upon the business known as gambling.

AMBROSE BIERCE

Games

Little Diane was lying on her back on the floor singing a happy song. The next time her mother looked, she was lying on her stomach, shrilling a different tune.

"Playing a game, dear?" Mother asked.

"Yes," Diane replied. "I'm pretending I'm a phonograph record, and I've just turned myself over."

The Instructor

———o———

Dare to err and to dream; a higher meaning often lies in childish play.

JOHANN CHRISTOPH FRIEDRICH VON SCHILLER

———o———

In play there are two pleasures for
  your choosing —
The one is winning, and the other losing.

LORD BYRON

Garden

God almighty first planted a garden; and, indeed, it is the purest of human pleasures. It is the greatest refreshment to the spirits of man; without which buildings and palaces are but gross handiworks. . . .

FRANCIS BACON, *Of Gardens*

———o———

My Garden

A Garden is a lovesome thing, God
  wot!
Rose plot,
Fringed pool,
Ferned grot —
The veriest school
Of Peace; and yet the fool
Contends that God is not —
Not God! in Gardens! when the eve is
  cool?
Nay, but I have a sign:
'Tis very sure God walks in mine.

THOMAS EDWARD BROWN

Practically everybody grows five things in the garden: peas, radishes, beans, tomatoes, and tired.

———o———

Gardening tip: To tell real plants from weeds, pull them out. If they come up again, they're weeds.

———o———

In order to live off a garden, you practically have to live in it.

FRANK MCKINNEY HUBBARD

———o———

Oh, Adam was a gardener, and God who made him sees
That half a proper gardener's work is done upon his knees.

RUDYARD KIPLING,
The Glory of the Garden

———o———

What a man needs in gardening is a cast-iron back, with a hinge in it.

Generous

A farmer had just finished telling his friend how much he loved the Lord and how much he loved to give. His friend asked him, "John, if you had twenty horses, would you give God two of them?"
"Why, of course," replied the farmer; "however, I have no horses."
"But if you had ten cows, would you give God one of them?"
"Certainly," was his prompt answer, "but I have no cows."
"Well, John, if you had ten pigs, would you give one of them to God?"
"Hold on there," cried John. "That isn't fair! You know I've got ten pigs!"

IVY MOODY

———o———

Men are very generous with that which costs them nothing.

———o———

Generosity during life is a very different thing from generosity in the hour of death; one proceeds from genuine liberality and benevolence, the other from pride or fear.

HORACE MANN

Genius

One of the strongest characteristics of genius is the power of lighting its own fire.

JOHN WATSON FOSTER

———o———

A genius is usually a crackpot until he hits the jackpot.

———o———

Genius is one per cent inspiration and ninety-nine per cent perspiration.

THOMAS A. EDISON

———o———

Genius, that power which dazzles mortal eyes,
Is oft but perseverance in disguise.

HENRY WILLARD AUSTIN,
Perseverance Conquers All

———o———

Talent is that which is in a man's power; genius is that in whose power a man is.

JAMES RUSSELL LOWELL
Rousseau and the Sentimentalists

———o———

Patience is a necessary ingredient of genius.

BENJAMIN DISRAELI, *The Young Duke*

———o———

Genius is mainly an affair of energy.

MATTHEW ARNOLD

———o———

It is the privilege of genius that to it life never grows commonplace as to the rest of us.

JAMES RUSSELL LOWELL

———o———

If people knew how hard I have to work to gain my mastery it wouldn't seem wonderful at all.

MICHELANGELO

Gentle, Gentlemen

Give me a gentle heart, that I may do
Naught but the gentle thing my whole life through.
Give me a heart as kind as heart can be,

That I may give before 'tis asked of me.

PERCY THOMAS

———o———

Nothing is so strong as gentleness; nothing so gentle as real strength.

ST. FRANCIS DE SALES

———o———

The gentleness of Christ is the comeliest ornament that a Christian can wear.

WILLIAM D. ARNOT

———o———

Be gentle in old age; peevishness is worse in second childhood than in first.

GEORGE D. PRENTICE

———o———

A gentleman is a man who can disagree without being disagreeable.

———o———

A man can never be a true gentleman in manner until he is a true gentleman at heart.

CHARLES DICKENS

———o———

A man may learn from his Bible to be a more thorough gentleman than if he had been brought up in all the drawing-rooms in London.

CHARLES KINGSLEY

Gifts

Instead of a gem, or even a flower, cast the gift of a lovely thought into the heart of a friend.

GEORGE MACDONALD

———o———

Rings and jewels are not gifts, but apologies for gifts. The only gift is a portion of thyself.

RALPH WALDO EMERSON, *Essays: Gifts*

———o———

The finest gift a man can give to his age and time is the gift of a constructive and creative life.

———o———

By the gates of the treasury still He sits,
And watches the gifts we bring —
And He measures the gold that we give to Him
By the gold to which we cling.
How much to revive a starving world?
How much for our pampered plates?
How much to extend the King's frontiers?
How much for our own estates?

F. C. WELLMAN

———o———

The most valuable gift of a man or woman to this world is not money, nor books, but a noble life.

———o———

It is the will, and not the gift that makes the giver.

GOTTHOLD EPHRAIM LESSING

———o———

Don't let the abundance of God's gifts make you forget the Giver in your satisfaction over the gifts.

Girls

The man is, as a first creation, genuine;
The woman is the clearer, softer, and diviner,
For he was from the inorganic dirt unfolded,
But she came forth from clay which life before has molded.

JOHN DRYDEN

———o———

A Girl Is A Girl

A girl is a girl so frilly and sweet
You'd just like to hug her the moment you meet.

She's little pink ruffles and nylon and lace;
She's an innocent look on a little pink face;

She's dozens of dollies of ev'ry known size —
This cute little angel with stars in her eyes;

She's little toy dishes and parties and teas —
A princess at heart, you can say what you please;

She's all kinds of ribbons and buttons
and bows,
A pleasure to have as any one knows.

She's little play houses and red rocking
chairs
Soft pink eyed bunnies and brown
teddy bears;

She's the pictures she colored and
wants you to see,
This wee little pixie who climbs on
your knee;

She's roses and sunshine, yes, she's all
that —
Wearing pink gloves and a little pink
hat;

In Mother's lace curtain this minia-
ture bride
Is really quite charming it can't be denied.

She's an artist, a teacher, a nurse all in
white,
Yet the mother of four from morning
till night;

She's perfume and powder and all
pretty things
Like bracelets and beads and play
diamond rings;

She's ice cream and candy and pink
birthday cake
She's also the cookies she helped Mother bake;

She's the one perfect nuisance to each
little boy
But she's Daddy's own sweetheart, his
pride and his joy;

She can pout, she can stomp, she can
tease, she can cry,
But still she's his pet, the very apple of
his eye.

She's kittens and everything cuddly
and nice —
Ah, sure 'n she's a bit of God's own
paradise.

PHYLLIS C. MICHAEL,
Poems for Mothers

Give

If you want to give something very
small to the Lord, give yourself.

All that we have comes from God,
and we give it out of His hand.
I Chronicles 29:14b, Dutch Paraphrase

———o———

Give all He asks;
Take all He gives.
S. D. GORDON

———o———

Getters generally don't get happi-
ness; givers get it. You simply give to
others a bit of yourself:
A thoughtful act,
A helpful idea,
A word of appreciation,
A lift over a rough spot,
A sense of understanding,
A timely suggestion.
You take something out of your
mind, garnished in kindness out of your
heart, and put it into the other fellow's
mind and heart.

CHARLES H. BURR

———o———

All that we can hold in our dead
hands is what we have given away.
Sanskrit Proverb

———o———

If you want to be rich, give; if you
want to be poor, grasp; if you want
abundance, scatter; if you want to be
needy, hoard!

———o———

God has given us two hands — one
to receive with and the other to give
with. We are not cisterns made for
hoarding; we are channels made for
sharing. If we fail to fulfill this divine
duty and privilege we have missed
the meaning of Christianity.

BILLY GRAHAM

———o———

What I kept I lost.
What I spent I had.
What I gave I have.
Persian Proverb

———o———

True Giving

We lose what on ourselves we spend:
We have as treasure without end,
Whatever, Lord, to Thee we lend
Who givest all.

Whatever, Lord, we lend to Thee,
  Repaid a thousand-fold will be;
And gladly will we give to Thee,
  Who givest all.

CHRISTOPHER WORDSWORTH,
Giving to God

———o———

For Our Sakes

He did not even own a bed,
He had no place to lay His head;
A cattle stall, His crib at birth;
He had no bank account on earth.
He laid the wealth of Heaven down
For earthly rags, and thorny crown.
He passed the praise of angels by,
And came where men cried
  "Crucify!"
He left a throne for you and me
And bore our sins upon a tree.
So strong His claim, so clear His call,
How dare I give Him less than all?

BARBARA C. RYBERG

———o———

Let Your Dollars Testify

An anxious father, fearful that his son had lost all interest in the church, asked the minister to speak with the boy.

At the first opportunity the minister said to the boy, "I should think you would want to keep your interest in the church if for no other reason than that your father is so interested."

"You don't know my father," the boy replied, adding, "By the way, how much does Dad give to the church each year?"

The minister thought for a moment and said, "I'm not so sure what he gives, but I know he is one of our most generous members. I should say he gives five dollars a Sunday."

The boy figured a bit. "That makes $260 a year. But it costs him $600 a year to belong to the country club, and he gave $5,000 to help elect his friend the mayor. You say I ought to attend church because Dad is so interested. I don't think he is as interested as you think. Go ask him to give $500 a year to the church and then come and talk with me."

ARTHUR V. BOAND

No man is known by what he receives, but by what he gives.

———o———

He gives double who gives unasked.

———o———

The preacher wrote to some parishioners asking financial aid for the church. One man turned him down with a curt note: "So far as I can see, this Christian business is one continuous give, give, give." The pastor meditated on that, then wrote the man again. "Thank you for the best definition of the Christian life I have ever heard."

———o———

God requires our persons before He asks our purses.

———o———

Who gives to me teaches me to give.

Dutch Saying

———o———

The world will never be won to Christ with what people can conveniently spare.

BERNARD EDINGER

———o———

A godly woman unexpectedly received a legacy of $5,000. True to her practice maintained in poverty, she at once put $500 into her tenth box and it was used in Christ's work. She never mentioned the disposal of the tenth, but after her death there was found entered in her diary the day she received the legacy: "Quick, quick, before my heart gets hard."

———o———

Let Me Be A Giver

God, let me be a giver, and not one
  Who only takes and takes unceasingly;
God, let me give so that not just my own,
  But others' lives as well, may richer be.

Let me give out whatever I may hold
  Of what material things life
    May be heaping.

Let me give raiment, shelter, food or
   gold,
  If these are, through Thy bounty,
   In my keeping.

But greater than such fleeting treas-
   ures,
  May I give my faith and hope and
   Cheerfulness,
Belief and dreams and joy and laughter
Gay some lonely soul to bless.

                      MARY DAVIES

———o———

I have held many things in my hands
and lost them all; but whatever I have
placed in God's hands, that I still possess.

                 MARTIN LUTHER

———o———

Giving

It is strange, but very true — giving
   just enriches you.
If you give a kindly deed, if you plant
   a friendship seed,
If you share a laugh or song, if your
   giving rights a wrong,
Then joy you feel and share makes
   more goodness everywhere.
It is strange, but very true — *giving*
   just enriches *you!*

———o———

How Much Ought I To Give?

Give as you would if an angel
Awaited your gift at the door;
Give as you would if tomorrow
Found you where giving was o'er.
Give as you would to the Master
If you met His loving look;
Give as you would of your substance
If His hand your offering took.

             AUTHOR UNKNOWN

———o———

Spender

The fountains flash across his lawn,
His yard is full of flowers.
His house has thirty rooms or more
With half a dozen showers.
He slumbers in a massive bed,
Some king once owned it, it seems.
The table where he eats is long
And silver brightly gleams.
He drives a gleaming mammoth car

That has the latest shape.
He sits before a mighty desk
And reads a ticker tape.
He goes to church when Sunday comes,
He sits up very straight,
And with a pious look he drops
A dollar in the plate!

             LON WOODRUM

———o———

Let Me Give

I do not know how long I'll live,
  But while I live, Lord, let me give,
Some comfort to someone in need,
  By smile or nod, kind word or deed.
And let me do whate'er I can
  To ease things for my fellow man.
I want naught but to do my part
  To lift a tired or weary heart,
To change folks' frowns to smiles again.
  Then I will not have lived in vain.
And I'll not care how long I'll live
  If I can give — and give — and give.

            AUTHOR UNKNOWN

———o———

Most people apportion their giving
according to their earnings. If the process were reversed and the Giver of
All were to apportion our earnings according to our giving, some of us would
be very poor indeed.

             The Christian

———o———

Three Kinds Of Giving

There are three kinds of giving:
Grudge giving, duty giving, and thanks
giving. Grudge giving says, "I hate to";
duty giving says, "I ought to"; thanks
giving says, "I want to."

The first comes from constraint, the
second from a sense of obligation and
the third from a full heart. Nothing
much is conveyed in grudge giving,
since the gift without the giver is
bare. Something more happens in duty
giving, but there is no song in it.
Thanks giving is an open gate into
the rewards.

         ROBERT N. RODENMAYER

———o———

Little Ships

I sent my little ships to sea,
But none returned to comfort me;

Then Jesus came, and I'm content
Because He told me where they went:

"The tracts went where you cannot go;
Supplies sent folk you do not know;
The little ships you sent to sea,
All that you gave — returned to Me."

And I am glad that this is so,
For giving is a debt I owe
To Him who gave His life for me
Upon the cross of Calvary.
                    MILDRED ALLEN JEFFERY

————o————

Giving And Receiving

Is thy cruse of comfort wasting?
    Rise and share it with another,
And through all the years of famine
    It shall save thee and thy brother,
Love divine will fill thy warehouse,
    Or thy handful still renew;
Scanty fare for one will often
    Make a royal feast for two.

For the heart grows rich in giving;
    All its wealth is living grain;
Seeds which mildew in the garner,
    Scattered, fill with gold the plain.
Is thy burden hard and heavy?
    Do thy steps drag wearily?
Help to bear thy brother's burden;
God will bear both it and thee.

Numb and weary on the mountain,
    Wouldst thou sleep amidst the snow?
Chafe that frozen form beside thee,
    And together both shall glow.
Art thou stricken in life's battle?
    Many wounded round thee moan;
Lavish in their wounds thy balsams,
    And that balm shall heal thine own.

Is thy heart a well left empty?
    None but God its void can fill;
Nothing but a ceaseless fountain,
    Can its ceaseless longing still.
Is thy heart a living power?
    Self-entwined its strength sinks low;
It can only live in loving,
    And by serving love will grow.
                    AUTHOR UNKNOWN

————o————

Seven Ways Of Giving

1. The Careless Way — To give something to every cause that is presented without inquiry into its merits.

2. The Impulsive Way — To give from impulse, as much and as often as love and pity and sensibility prompt.

3. The Lazy Way — To make a special offer to earn money for benevolent objects by fairs, festivals, etc.

4. The Self-Denying Way — To save the cost of luxuries and apply them for purposes of religion and charity. This may lead to asceticism and self-complacence.

5. The Systematic Way — To lay aside as an offering to God a definite portion of our gains: one-tenth, one-fifth, one-third or one-half. This is adaptable if this method were generally practiced.

6. The Equal Way — To give to God and the needy just as much as we spend on ourselves, balancing our personal expenditures by our gifts.

7. The Heroic Way — To limit our own expenditures to a certain sum, and give away all the rest of our income. This was John Wesley's way.
                    A. T. PIERSON

————o————

If truth takes possession of a man's heart, it will direct his hand to his pocketbook.

————o————

Numbers 7 is the longest chapter in the Bible, containing nearly 2,000 words — all about giving.

————o————

When the heart is converted the purse will be inverted.

————o————

"What! Giving again?"
    I asked in dismay,
"And must I keep giving
    And giving alway?"
"Oh no," cried the Angel,
    Piercing me through.
"Just give 'til the Father
    Stops giving to you."
                    AUTHOR UNKNOWN

Glory

How swiftly passes the glory of the world!

THOMAS À KEMPIS,
The Imitation of Christ

———o———

Glory is like a circle in the water,
Which never ceaseth to enlarge itself
Till by broad spreading it disperse to nought.

WILLIAM SHAKESPEARE,
King Henry VI, Part I

Goals

Promise yourself:

To be so strong that nothing can disturb your peace of mind;
To talk health, happiness and prosperity;
To make your friends feel that there is something in them;
To look on the sunny side of everything;
To think only of the best;
To be just as enthusiastic about the success of others as you are about your own;
To forget the mistakes of the past and profit by them;
To wear a cheerful countenance and give a smile to everyone you meet;
To be too large for worry, too noble for anger, too strong for fear, and too happy to permit the presence of trouble.

CHRISTIAN D. LARSON

———o———

The ripest peach is highest on the tree.

JAMES WHITCOMB RILEY,
The Ripest Peach

———o———

If called to be a missionary, don't stoop to be a king.

CHARLES HADDON SPURGEON

———o———

The man that I want to be is so much better than the man that I am that I am desperately afraid that the man I am can never be the man I want to be. How is it with you?

Before you can score you must first have a goal.

Greek Proverb

———o———

Obstacles are those frightful things you see when you take your eyes off the goal.

HANNAH MORE

———o———

Not everything that is desirable is attainable, and not everything that is worthwhile knowing is knowable.

JOHANN WOLFGANG VON GOETHE

———o———

People with goals find a meaning in life.

God

The living God is my Partner.

GEORGE MUELLER

———o———

My great concern is not whether God is on our side; my great concern is to be on God's side.

ABRAHAM LINCOLN

———o———

Any step away from the true, living God is a step in the direction of strife.

BILLY GRAHAM

———o———

Evidence

The fool has said in his heart,
"There is no God,"
But the fool has not the mind to know.
Cycles of coppery suns and silvered moons
Declare the wonderment of God,
And all the things of earth
Silently proclaim His handiwork.
He spoke, and there was light;
He breathed, and man became a living soul.
Aeons of time declare the everlastingness of Him.
The fragrance of a flower,
And the mystery of a throbbing heart
Witness to His creative power.
The wise have not the minds to understand,
Yet, they must say in all humility,
"There is a God!"

HELEN MILLER LEHMAN

If

If man could fling a trillion stars
Beyond the sun and moon and Mars,
Far out in vast sidereal space,
And keep them spinning in their place;

If man could make a tiny flower
And make it grow by his own power;
If he the ocean could command
And measure it within his hand;

If man could make a living soul
That should endure while ages roll;
Would I be then by man so awed
That I'd acclaim him e'en as God?

Ah, no! for had he all this might,
He could not guide his life aright;
He could not cleanse his own lost soul,
Nor make a sin-sick sinner whole.

Though man-made spheres may come
    and go,
There's only one true God, I know,
Who holds the worlds within His hand,
And on that Rock secure I'll stand.

MARGARET K. FRASER

———o———

A man should be ashamed to run
his own life the minute he finds out
there is a God.

PAUL RADER

———o———

A little boy being asked, "How many
Gods are there?" replied "One!" "How
do you know that?" "Because," said
the boy, "there is only room for one,
for He fills heaven and earth."

———o———

God always fills in all hearts all the
room which is left Him there.

FREDERICK W. FABER

———o———

God be in my head,
    And in my understanding;
God be in my eyes,
    And in my looking;
God be in my mouth,
    And in my speaking;
God be in my heart,
    And in my thinking;
God be at my end,
    And at my departing.

Old Sarum Primer, 1558

When I think of God, my heart is so
full of joy that the notes leap and
dance as they leave my pen; and since
God has given me a cheerful heart, I
serve Him with a cheerful spirit.

FRANZ JOSEPH HAYDN

———o———

Thou Art God

Thou art the triumph of the race well
    run,
The spring of virtue, rock of purity,
The Giver of all blessings through Thy
    Son,
And spark of hope set fire at Calvary.
In Thee alone I find abiding peace;
Thou art my fruitful valley, rich and
    deep.
Thy Grace and tender mercy shall not
    cease,
For time is Thine to fashion and to
    keep.

And yet I sorrow that these make-
    shift thoughts
Are as toy boats upon a mighty sea,
Or sparrows that would follow eagle
    wings:
Frail evidence of insufficiency.
O might my thunder peal Thy Name
    abroad!
Instead I choke and whisper, "Thou
    art God!"

ESTHER BELLE HEINS

———o———

God In A Box

God in a box? Unlikely thought —
And yet men do declare
It came to pass (Sing, angels, sing!),
And in a manger bare.

God in a box? Say rather, tent —
Not metal, wood or stone,
But like our own: See the Lord
    Christ
Wrapped 'round with flesh and bone.

God in a box? A coffin bleak,
So dark, and cold, and grim?
Yes, even here God stooped to seek
Men who would bury him.

See, then! This box, though doubly
    bound

With sin and death's strong cord,
Still could not hold his majesty —
Behold! The risen Lord!

RUTH HEARD

———o———

I fear God, yet am not afraid of
Him.

SIR THOMAS BROWNE

God's Goodness

God's Extras

God could have made the sun to rise
　Without such splendor in the skies;
He could have made the sun to set
　Without a glory greater yet.

He could have made the corn to grow
　Without that sunny, golden glow;
The fruits without those colors bright,
　So pleasant to the taste and sight.

And caused the apple trees to bloom
　Without the scent that doth perfume
Those dainty blossoms, pink and white,
　That fill our hearts with sheer de-
　　light.

He could have made the ocean roll
　Without such music for the soul —
The mighty anthem, loud and strong —
　And birds without their clear, sweet
　　song.

The charm of kittens' dainty grace,
　The dimples in a baby's face —
All these are "extras" from His hand,
　Whose love we cannot understand.

The God Who fashioned flowers and
　trees,
　Delights to give us things that please,
And all His handiwork so fair
　His glory and His love declare.

Yes, He Who made the earth and skies
　Gave "extras" for our ears and eyes,
And while my heart with rapture sings,
　I thank Him for the "extra things."

MARGARET K. FRASER

———o———

God's ways are not like human ways,
　He wears such strange disguises;
He tries us by His long delays
　And then our faith surprises.

While we in unbelief deplore
　And wonder at His staying,
He stands already at the door
　And interrupts our praying.

J. E. RANKIN

———o———

He Giveth More

He giveth more grace when the bur-
　dens grow greater,
He sendeth more strength when the
　labors increase;
To added affliction He addeth His
　mercy,
To multiplied trials, His multiplied
　peace.

When we have exhausted our store of
　endurance,
When our strength has failed ere the
　day is half done,
When we reach the end of our hoarded
　resources,
Our Father's full giving is only begun.

His love has no limit, His grace has no
　measure,
His power no boundary known unto
　men;
For out of His infinite riches in Jesus
He giveth and giveth and giveth again.

ANNIE JOHNSON FLINT

———o———

God gives our blessings but we have
to take them.

God's Love and Care

No foe can cast me down,
　No fear can make me flee,
No sorrow fill my life with ill;
　Thy love surroundeth me.

Warm as the glowing sun,
　So shines Thy love on me;
It wraps me round with kindly care,
　It draws me unto Thee.

OSCAR CLUTE

———o———

I know not where His islands lift
　Their fronded palms in air;
I only know I cannot drift
　Beyond His love and care.

JOHN GREENLEAF WHITTIER,
The Eternal Goodness

The God of Love

And can he who smiles on all
Hear the wren with sorrows small,
Hear the small bird's grief and care,
Hear the woes that infants bear,

And not sit beside that nest,
Pouring pity in their breast;
And not sit that cradle near,
Weeping tear on infant's tear;

And not sit both night and day
Wiping all our tears away?
Oh, no! never can it be!

Never, never can it be!
He doth give his joy to all;
He becomes an infant small;
He becomes a man of woe.
He doth feel the sorrow too.

Think not thou canst sigh a sigh,
And thy Maker is not by;
Think not thou canst weep a tear,
And thy Maker is not near.

WILLIAM BLAKE,
On Another's Sorrow

———o———

How often we look upon God as our last and feeblest resource! We go to Him because we have no where else to go. And then we learn that the storms of life have driven us, not upon the rocks, but into the desired havens.

GEORGE MACDONALD

———o———

If God did not hold us back every moment, we should be devils incarnate.

DAVID BRAINERD

———o———

You can rest the weight of all your anxieties upon God, for you are always in His care.

Paraphrase of *I Peter 5:7*

God's Power and Greatness

God tempers the wind . . . to the shorn lamb.

LAURENCE STERNE, *A Sentimental Journey*

———o———

God regulates the cold to the shorn lamb.

HENRI ESTIENNE, *Prémices*

God is as great in minuteness as He is in magnitude.

———o———

When Martin Luther's friends wrote despairingly of the negotiations at the Diet of Worms, Luther replied from Coburg that he had been looking up at the night sky, spangled and studded with stars, and had found no pillars to hold them up. And yet they did not fall. God needs no props for His stars and planets. He hangs them on nothing. So, in the working of God's providence, the unseen is prop enough for the seen.

AUGUSTUS HOPKINS STRONG

———o———

And I smiled to think God's greatness
    flowed around our incompleteness, —
Round our restlessness His rest.

ELIZABETH BARRETT BROWNING,
Rhyme of the Duchess May

———o———

As the marsh-hen secretly builds on the
    watery sod,
Behold I will build me a nest on the
    greatness of God:
I will fly in the greatness of God as the
    marsh-hen flies
In the freedom that fills all the space
    'twixt the marsh and the skies:
By so many roots as the marsh-grass
    sends in the sod
I will heartily lay me a-hold on the
    greatness of God.

SIDNEY LANIER, *The Marshes of Glynn*

God's Presence

My Presence Shall Go With Thee

Life's dark shadows turn to sunshine
When the Light of Life appears;
And the rainbow of His promise
Brightly beams above my fears.

He who guides the countless planets
Through the endless realms of space,
Walks beside me, guards and guides
    me
By His never-failing grace.

He whom angels serve and worship
In the Glory Land above,

Deigns to be my blest companion,
In the greatness of His love.

Why then should I grieve my Savior
By my needless fret and care?
He will never, never leave me,
All my burdens He will share.

Heartaches? He knows all about them;
His own heart was pierced for me.
"Man of Sorrows" once they called Him,
He who died to make me free.

Yes, His presence will go with me,
For He always keeps His word,
And my soul shall rest serenely
In the love of Christ, my Lord.

ALBERT SIMPSON REITZ

———o———

God Is Here

(The following words are to be found engraved on the floor of the church where John Wesley preached his first sermon.)

Enter this door
As if the floor
Within were gold
And every wall
Of jewels, all
Of wealth untold;
As if a choir
In robes of fire
Were singing here
Nor shout, nor rush
But hush —
For God is here.

AUTHOR UNKNOWN

———o———

We are always punched in on God's timecard.

RICHARD RIIS

———o———

Tomorrow

God is in every tomorrow,
    Therefore I live for today,
Certain of finding at sunrise
Guidance and strength for the way;
Power for each moment of weakness,
    Hope for each moment of pain,
Comfort for every sorrow,
    Sunshine and joy after rain.

God is in every tomorrow,
    Planning for you and me;

E'en in the dark will I follow —
Trust where my eyes cannot see;
Stilled by His promise of blessing,
Soothed by the touch of His hand,
    Confident in His protection,
Knowing my life path is planned.

God is in every tomorrow,
    Life with its changes may come;
He is behind and before me;
    While in the distance shines Home!
Home — where no thought of tomorrow
    Ever can shadow my brow;
Home — in the presence of Jesus
    Through all eternity — now.

Exchange

———o———

God is the silent partner in all great enterprises.

ABRAHAM LINCOLN

God's Strength and Help

It is at the point where we are just about to faint, that God gives us strength to go on.

———o———

Only when you attempt the impossible do you test the resources of God.

———o———

Cheered by the presence of God, I will do each moment, without anxiety, according to the strength which He shall give me, the work that His providence assigns me.

FRANCOIS DE SALIGNAC DE LA MOTHE FÉNELON

———o———

Never does he who clings to God despair, because he is never without resources.

JACQUES BÉNIGNE BOSSUET

God's Ways

God's ways are behind the scenes, but He moves all the scenes which He is behind.

JOHN NELSON DARBY

———o———

Never make a plan without seeking God's guidance; never achieve a success without giving God the praise.

Though the mills of God grind slowly,
Yet they grind exceeding small;
Though with patience He stands wait-
  ing,
With exactness grinds He all.

HENRY WADSWORTH LONGFELLOW
(Translation of *Retribution* by F. VON LOGAN)

———o———

God writes with a pen that never
blots, speaks with a tongue that never
slips, acts with a hand that never fails.

———o———

Going God's Way

I arise today, equipped and fortified
to meet life's problems, with —
  God's strength to pilot me.
  God's wisdom to guide me.
  God's eye to look before me.
  God's ear to hear me.
  God's Word to speak for me.
  God's hand to guard me.
  God's way of life before me.
  God's shield to protect me.
  God's host to save me.

Selected

God's Will

God's Will

It is God's will that I should cast
  My care on Him each day (I Peter
  5).
He also asks me not to cast
  My confidence away (Hebrews 10).
But, oh, how stupidly I act
  When taken unaware;
I cast away my confidence
  And carry all my care.

T. BAIRD

———o———

Missionary Betty Elliot, whose husband was murdered by the fierce Auca
Indians of Ecuador, tells why she went
back to the Aucas. "I didn't return
because I thought it would be safe, or
even to carry on my husband's work.
The only reason is my belief that going back is the next step in a series of
steps that God wills."

———o———

William E. Gladstone, talking about
the questions of the day, said, "There
is but one question, and that is the will
of God. That settles all other questions."

———o———

If the will of God is our will, and
if He always has His way, then we
always have our way also.

HANNAH WHITALL SMITH

———o———

Those Things Beyond My Control

There are some things in life, O God,
  Beyond my own control.
And when they come,
  I pray that they will never warp my
  soul.

Sometimes my well-laid plans don't
  work,
  And everything goes wrong.
And then it is that
  I'm in need of courage to be strong.

In times that I have spent my strength
  In trying to resist,
The things that I could never change,
  It seems I've always missed.
A living opportunity to help myself
  adjust
  To changeless situations, God,
And walk with You in trust.

GEORGE BILBY WALKER

———o———

O Thou who hast taught us that we
are most truly free when we lose our
wills in Thine, help us to gain that
liberty by continual surrender unto
Thee, that we may walk in the way
which Thou hast prepared for us, and
in doing Thy will may find our life,
through Jesus Christ our Lord.

Gelasian Sacramentary

———o———

Try to make an instantaneous act of
conformity to God's will, at everything
which vexes you.

EDWARD B. PUSEY

———o———

Through His will, loved and done,
lies the path to His love.

ANDREW MURRAY

———o———

A man should be encouraged to do
what the Maker of him has intended

by the making of him, according as the gifts have been bestowed on him for that purpose. His happiness, and that of others around him, [depends upon] such a relation to the Maker's will.

THOMAS CARLYLE

Grace To Do Without

My heart rejoices in God's will,
'Tis ever best — I do not doubt;
He may not give me what I ask,
But gives me grace to do without!

I blindly ask for what I crave,
With haughty heart and will so stout;
He oft denies me what I seek,
But gives me grace to do without!

He makes me love the way He leads,
And every fear is put to rout;
When with my fondest wish denied,
He gives me grace to do without!

O blessed, hallowed will of God,
To it I bow with heart devout;
I will abide in all God's will,
His way is best, I do not doubt;
He may not give me what I ask,
But gives me grace to do without!

Selected

"Everything goes against me," said a man to Luther. "None of my wishes come true. My hopes go wrong. My plans never work out."

"My dear friend, that is your own fault," said Luther.

"My own fault?"

"Yes," said Luther. "Why do you pray every day, *Thy* will be done'? You ought to pray, *My* will be done. But if you pray that God's will should be done and not yours, you should be satisfied if God does as you pray."

Lutheran Witness

When I was crossing the Irish Channel one dark, starless night, I stood on the deck by the captain and asked him, "How do you know Holyhead Harbor on so dark a night as this?"

He said, "You see those three lights? Those three must line up behind each other as one, and when we see them so united we know the exact position of the harbor's mouth."

When we want to know God's will there are three things which always concur: the inward impulse, the Word of God, and the trend of circumstances! God in the heart, impelling you forward; God in His book corroborating whatever He says in the heart; and God in circumstances, which are always indicative of His will. Never start until these three things agree.

F. B. MEYER

God's Will

I wanted to go, He said stay.
I wanted to do, He said pray;
I wanted to work, He said wait,
I wanted to live for His sake!
"Love Me, child," He softly said,
"Oh, yes, Lord," I bowed my head;
"I want your way, I am your son,
Not my will, but Thine be done!"

GRACE OPPERMAN

The hardness of God is kinder than the softness of men, and His compulsion is our liberation.

C. S. LEWIS, *Surprised by Joy*

Jesus taught, first, that a man's business is to do the will of God; second, that God takes upon Himself the care of that man; third, therefore, that a man must never be afraid of anything, and so, fourth, be left free to love God with all his heart, and his neighbor as himself.

GEORGE MACDONALD

A knowledge of the will of God is relative to one's desire to do the will of God. God does not reveal His will to those who are not gladly committed to it. A commission from God is relative to our commitment to God. Commitment is prerequisite to commission. There is no substitute for the bent knee, the surrendered heart, the open Bible, the listening ear and the voice of the Spirit in discovering the will of God.

DON W. HILLIS
in *The Missionary Broadcaster*

Sooner or later you will find that it is harder to shun the will of God than it is to yield yourself to it.

———o———

Passive to His holy will
Trust I in my Master still,
Even though He slay me.
JOHN GREENLEAF WHITTIER,
Barclay of Ury

God's Work

God's work done in God's way will never lack God's supplies.
J. HUDSON TAYLOR

———o———

God works slowly but surely; we spoil His work when we get in a hurry and interfere.

———o———

God requires on our part, nothing that we are unable, with His help, to do.

Godliness

Keep company with the more cheerful sort of the godly; there is no mirth like the mirth of believers.
RICHARD BAXTER

———o———

Unless there is within us that which is above us, we shall soon yield to that which is about us.
PETER TAYLOR FORSYTHE

———o———

Godliness is the knowledge of God in the mind; the grace of God in the soul; the love of God in the heart; the obedience to God in the life.
JAMES DRUMMOND BURNS

Good, Goodness

There is a very simple test by which we can tell good people from bad: if a smile improves a man's face, he is a good man; if a smile disfigures his face, he is a bad man.
WILLIAM LYON PHELPS

———o———

Be not only good; be good for something.
HENRIETTA C. MEARS

Goodness and love mold the form into their own image, and cause the joy and beauty of love to shine forth from every part of the face. When this form of love is seen, it appears ineffably beautiful, and effects with delight the inmost life of the soul.
EMANUEL SWEDENBORG

———o———

The truly good do good for no other reason than doing good.
ROY DALE

———o———

There are two kinds of people: good and bad. The classifying is done by the good.

———o———

Four-year-old Jimmie was saying his prayers one evening. His mother was shocked to hear him say:
"O God, make me a good boy — not real good, but just good enough to keep from getting spanked."
Gospel Banner

———o———

Good, the more
Communicated, more abundant grows.
JOHN MILTON, *Paradise Lost, Book IV*

———o———

If you can see good in everybody, almost everyone will see some good in you.
HENRY F. HENRICHS

———o———

It is not enough to do good; one must do it the right way.
JOHN VISCOUNT MORLEY, *On Compromise*

———o———

People seldom get dizzy from doing good turns.

———o———

"Who's telling the truth?" asked nine-year-old Bill.
"Why?" asked Father.
"Because," the boy explained, "my Sunday School teacher said that if I was good I would go to heaven and you said that if I was good I would go to the circus."

———o———

A Christian should always remember that the value of his good works is not based on their number and excellence, but on the love of God which prompts him to do these things.

SAN JUAN DE LA CRUZ

Gospel

The Gospel is a declaration, not a debate.

JAMES S. STEWART

———o———

We do not need to defend the Gospel, we need only to proclaim it.

———o———

The world has many religions; it has but one Gospel.

GEORGE OWEN

———o———

The Gospel is not a challenge, it is an offer.

JOE BLINCO

———o———

The Gospel is not simply for the sanctuary but for the open road.

RICHARD C. HALVERSON

———o———

The Gospel is not something we go to church to hear; it is something we go from church to tell.

VANCE HAVNER

———o———

The Gospel is God's News — not Man's Views.

JAMES L. FOWLE

———o———

Hear the good news — then tell it!

———o———

A thief broke into a Buffalo, New York, church and got away with some valuable equipment and several dollars from a collection box. The next day the church's outdoor bulletin board carried the words, "If the person who burglarized this church will contact the pastor, he will receive important news."

Interested, reporters called on the pastor. "What's the good news?" they wanted to know.

Replied the pastor, "If we confess our sins, He is faithful and just to forgive us our sins, and to cleanse us from all unrighteousness."

A man may want liberty, and yet be happy; a man may want food, and yet be content; a man may want clothing, and yet be comfortable; but he that wants the Gospel, wants everything that can do him good in this life and the next. Nothing worse can be imagined than to be without hope and without God in this world.

Traveller's Guide

Gossip

Tale-bearers are as bad as the tale-makers.

RICHARD BRINSLEY SHERIDAN,
School for Scandal

———o———

Gossip always travels faster over grapevines that are slightly sour.

———o———

A gossip turns an earful into a mouthful.

———o———

A gossip is a person who will never tell a lie when the truth will do more damage.

———o———

If we had buttons or zippers on our lips, we'd do less gossiping, and hold on to our respect for others.

———o———

Gossip

The longer I live, the more I feel the importance of adhering to the following rules, which I have laid down for myself in relation to such matters:

1. To hear as little as possible what is to the prejudice of others.

2. To believe nothing of the kind until I am absolutely forced to.

3. Always to moderate, so far as I can, the unkindness which is expressed toward others.

4. Always to believe that, if the other side were heard, very different accounts would be given of the matter.

An Old Scotch Writer

———o———

A five-year-old "preacher" lined his friends up on the curb and gravely announced, "This morning we will preach the gossip."

Teach

———o———

Had you ever thought that while we despise the gossiper it is almost as bad to listen eagerly, like most of us do, to his tales? Should we refuse to listen to gossip, it is likely that none would ever be spread.

———o———

Never believe anything bad about anybody unless you feel that it is absolutely necessary — and that God is listening while you tell it.

HENRY VAN DYKE

———o———

Someone has said that a gossip is one who talks too much about others. A bore is one who talks too much about himself. A wise man is one who talks little but says much.

———o———

Thy friend has a friend, and thy friend's friend has a friend, so be discreet.

The Talmud

———o———

Great minds discuss ideas, average minds discuss events, small minds discuss people.

———o———

Gossip is what no one claims to like — but everybody enjoys.

JOSEPH CONRAD

———o———

There is nothing that can't be made worse by telling.

TERENCE

Govern

Men must be governed by God or they will be ruled by tyrants.

WILLIAM PENN

———o———

A man must first govern himself, before he is fit to govern a family; and his family before he is fit to bear the government of the Commonwealth.

SIR WALTER RALEIGH

No man is good enough to govern another man without the other's consent.

ABRAHAM LINCOLN

———o———

Realms are households which the great must guide.

JOHN DRYDEN

———o———

They that govern the most make the least noise.

JOHN SELDEN, *Table Talk; Power*

———o———

It is impossible to govern the world without God.

GEORGE WASHINGTON

———o———

God rules in the realms to which he is admitted.

MARY WELCH

———o———

Never expect to govern others until you have learned to govern yourself.

———o———

The rule that governs my life is this: Anything that dims my vision of Christ, or takes away my taste for Bible study, or cramps my prayer life, or makes Christian work difficult, is wrong for me, and I must, as a Christian, turn away from it. This simple rule may help you find a safe road for your feet along life's road.

J. WILBUR CHAPMAN

Government

History has demonstrated that nations thrive and grow strong as they develop individual citizens. Law and order without loss of individual freedom can be maintained only as the personal ethics of individual citizens call for and support the laws of the state. Good government can exist and persist only as it is rooted in self-government by the millions of individual citizens.

DR. ALFRED HAAKE

———o———

A grade school teacher reports this answer was turned in on a question about government: "The main political parties are the GOP, AFL, CIO, and PTA."

Glendale News Press, Glendale, Calif.

———o———

If we did not believe in the spiritual character of man, we would be foolish indeed to be supporting the concept of free government in the world.

DWIGHT DAVID EISENHOWER

———o———

Whenever the pillars of Christianity shall be overthrown, our present republican forms of government, and all the blessings which flow from them, must fall with them.

JEDIDIAH MORSE

———o———

Government is a trust, and the officers of the government are trustees; and both the trust and the trustees are created for the benefit of the people.

HENRY CLAY, *Speech,* March, 1829

———o———

The lessons of paternalism ought to be unlearned and the better lesson taught that while the people should patriotically support their Government, its functions do not include the support of the people.

GROVER CLEVELAND, *Inaugural Address,* March 4, 1893

———o———

The Bible is for the government of the people, by the people, and of the people.

WYCLIFFE AND HEREFORD (Preface to their translation of the Bible — 1384)

———o———

The people's government, made for the people, made by the people, and answerable to the people.

DANIEL WEBSTER, *Speech,* January 26, 1830

———o———

. . . our aim in founding the Commonwealth was not to make any one class specially happy, but to secure the greatest possible happiness for the community as a whole.

PLATO, *The Republic*

There is no qualification for government but virtue and wisdom.

EDMUND BURKE

Grace

An ounce of quiet-working grace does what tons of effort can never accomplish.

———o———

There is a saving grace for sinners and a serving grace for Christians.

———o———

I was going to say that faith turns on the faucet of Grace, but I'll put it the other way: unbelief turns the faucet off.

WILLIAM R. NEWELL

———o———

The Father never fails to cheer our hearts with sweet surprises of His Grace. He hides them through all our fleeting years, and every day we are finding them: friends old and new, the joys of home, new aspirations, new tasks, new fields of labor, new knowledge, new understandings of the heart of Christ, new experiences with Him. Often they fall into our laps when we are least expecting them.

This is God's antidote for weariness and dullness. We greet each day with expectancy. We grow old gracefully, eagerly waiting to know what is that grandest gift of all — eternal life.

COSTEN J. HARRELL, *Walking With God*

———o———

'Twas grace that taught my heart to fear,
And grace my fears relieved;
How precious did that grace appear
The hour I first believed.

JOHN NEWTON, *Amazing Grace*

———o———

God's Grace is the only Grace,
And all Grace is the Grace of God.

COVENTRY PATMORE

———o———

It takes less grace to criticize than to cooperate.

J. B. CHAPMAN

Sin had no sooner come into the world than God came in Grace seeking the sinner, and so from the first question, "Adam where art thou?" on to the incarnation, God has been speaking to man.

HARRY A. IRONSIDE

———o———

Grace freely justifies me and sets me free from slavery to sin.

ST. BERNARD OF CLAIRVAUX

———o———

If we do less under grace than we do under law, it is a disgrace.

———o———

The word 'Grace' is unquestionably the most significant single word in the Bible.

ILION T. JONES

———o———

God's providence will never place you where His grace cannot keep you.

———o———

One who is saved by grace should live graciously.

———o———

Grace humbles man without degrading him and exalts him without deflating him.

———o———

Grace is everything for nothing to one who deserves nothing but judgment and destruction.

———o———

The dross of my cross gathered a scum of fears in the fire, doubtings, impatience, unbelief, challenging of Providence as sleeping and not regarding my sorrow. But my Goldsmith, Christ, was pleased to take off the scum and burn it in the fire. And blessed be my Refiner, He has made the metal better, and has furnished new supply of Grace, to cause me hold out weight; and I hope that He has not lost one grain-weight by burning His servant.

SAMUEL RUTHERFORD

Grammar

Christian Grammar

A well-known Bishop of the Church of England gave a class he was teaching a lesson in what he called "Christian Grammar."

"We have all learned to say in school:
    'First person — I;
    Second person — Thou;
    Third person — He.'
"But that is wrong in Christian grammar, so wrong that to put it right, one has to turn it upside down. The Christian's grammar is:
    'First person — He;
    Second person — Thou;
    Third person — I.'
"And 'he' means God, the first person in the first place. Then 'thou' means one's fellow-man; and 'I' myself comes last."

———o———

My son had been having trouble with his grammar studies in school. For several weeks we worked at night on the three degrees of adjectives and adverbs. After patiently emphasizing that the comparative degree was stronger and that the superlative was strongest, I dictated a list of words to compare, which included the adjective "high."

On his tablet I was amazed to find: "Positive degree — Hi. Comparative degree — Hello. Superlative degree — How do you do?"

ERNEST BLEVINS in *Your Life*

———o———

Grammar In A Nutshell

Three little words you often see
Are Articles — A, An, and The.

A Noun's the name of anything,
As School, or Garden, Hoop or Swing.

Adjectives tell the kind of Noun,
As Great, Small, Pretty, White or Brown.

Instead of Nouns the Pronouns stand —
Her head, His face, Your arm, My hand.

Verbs tell of something being done —
To Read, Count, Laugh, Sing, Jump or
Run.

How things are done the Adverbs tell,
As Slowly, Quickly, Ill, or Well.

Conjunctions join the words together,
As men And women, wind Or weather.

The Preposition stands before
A Noun, as In or Through a door.

The Interjection shows surprise
As Oh! how pretty! Ah! how wise!

The Whole are called Nine Parts of
Speech,
Which reading, writing, speaking teach.
                          AUTHOR UNKNOWN

———o———

Teacher: "Name three relative pronouns."
Student: "Aunt, uncle, brother."

———o———

Teacher: "What gender is the word
hurricane?"
Boy student: "Neuter gender, singular number."
Girl student: "No it isn't! Don't you
remember Mrs. Roseberry said last
week, 'Who ever heard of a *hima*cane.
It's always a *her*-a-cane!'"
                          RUTH ROSEBERRY

———o———

One day in an English class a boy
was asked, "What parts of speech are
'my' and 'mine'?"
Quickly he replied, "Aggressive pronouns."
                          RUTH ROSEBERRY

———o———

One of our elementary school teachers gave her small charges a lecture on
the merits of brevity and then asked
them to write a sentence or two describing something exciting. One of
them promptly submitted the following: "Help! Help!"
                 PATRICIA LAITIN in *Coronet*

Grandparents

Grandma

My grandma likes to play with God,
They have a kind of game.

She plants the garden full of seeds,
He sends the sun and rain.

She likes to sit and talk with God
And knows He is right there.
She prays about the whole wide world,
Then leaves us in His care.
                 ANN JOHNSON, age 8 in
                      The Lutheran Standard

———o———

One of the most influential hand-
clasps is that of a grandchild around
the finger of a grandparent.
           Gazette, High Bridge, New Jersey

———o———

Any grandmother can tell you what's
new in people. And she has pictures
to go with her wonderful story.
                 Herald, Azusa, California

———o———

My sister, the harassed mother of
five, was asked by a friend, "Well, Nell,
what do you want your next one to
be?"
"A grandchild!" she replied.
        MRS. FRANK WATSON in *Reader's Digest*

———o———

Grandbabies are better than babies.
You can tote them around the church,
collecting compliments, whereas it
would be unseemly if you were merely
the father.
                 OREN ARNOLD in *Home Life*

Gratitude

Thou hast giv'n so much to me;
Give one thing more — a grateful heart.
. . . .
Not thankful when it pleases me
As if Thy blessings had spare days,
But such a heart, whose pulse may be
Thy praise.
           GEORGE HERBERT, *Gratefulness*

———o———

Gratitude is a fruit of great cultivation; you do not find it among gross
people.
        SAMUEL JOHNSON, *Tour to the Hebrides*

———o———

Gratitude takes three forms: a feeling in the heart, an expression in
words, and a giving in return.

We Thank Thee

A little sunshine, a little rain,
A little loss and a little gain,
Courage to walk the unknown road,
Strength to carry the tiring load,
Blossoming flowers and beauteous trees,
Singing birds — for all of these
  We thank Thee, God.

For memories of voices sweet,
Of beauty fresh and eager feet
That will not run again our way,
For all the joys of yesterday,
For vision to undo the bars
Of doubting night and see the stars,
  We thank Thee, God.

ADELAIDE R. KEMP

-----o-----

Gratitude is the sign of noble souls.

AESOP, *Androcles*

Great

The greatest truths are the simplest; and so are the greatest men.

AUGUSTUS WILLIAM HARE

-----o-----

The price of greatness is responsibility.

SIR WINSTON CHURCHILL

-----o-----

Those people who are always improving never become great. Greatness is an eminence, the ascent to which is steep and lofty, and which a man must seize on at once by natural boldness and vigor, and not by patient, wary steps.

WILLIAM HAZLITT

-----o-----

He is great who inspires others to think for themselves.

ELBERT HUBBARD

-----o-----

If a man is not great when it doesn't matter . . . he will not be when it does!

RICHARD C. HALVERSON

-----o-----

The all-important factor in national greatness is national character.

THEODORE ROOSEVELT

Popularity comes from pleasing people, but greatness comes from pleasing God.

-----o-----

No man is greater than his prayer life.

LEONARD RAVENHILL

-----o-----

They're only truly great who are truly good.

GEORGE CHAPMAN, *Revenge for Honour*

-----o-----

The smallest things become great when God requires them of us; they are small only in themselves; they are always great when they are done for God, and when they serve to unite us with Him eternally.

FRANCOIS DE SALIGNAC DE LA MOTHE FÉNELON

-----o-----

Great men never feel great.
Small men never feel small.

Chinese Saying

-----o-----

It is not required of every man and woman to be or do something great. Most of us must content ourselves with taking small parts in the chorus, as far as possible without discord.

HENRY VAN DYKE

-----o-----

Great Things

Great things are only done by men
Who, having failed, will try again:
Who risk their all to venture out,
And having ventured, never doubt:
Whose confidence in self is strong,
And dare defy the doubting throng.

AUTHOR UNKNOWN

-----o-----

A really great man is known by three signs: generosity in the design, humanity in the execution, and moderation in success.

OTTO VON BISMARCK

-----o-----

Great men never complain about the lack of time. Alexander the Great and John Wesley accomplished everything they did in 24-hour days.

FRED SMITH

Signs of True Greatness

The ability to apologize; to forgive and forget;
To avoid arguments; to avoid being self-conscious;
To take snubs and reproof well; to have mastery over the flesh;
To stoop to help others.

———o———

The great man is he who does not lose his child's heart.

———o———

The world's greatness is measured by authority and lordliness, but divine greatness is a meek and gentle influence.

———o———

The world's great men have not commonly been great scholars, nor the great scholars great men.
OLIVER WENDELL HOLMES,
The Autocrat of the Breakfast Table

———o———

Man is not great until he beholds his own littleness.

Grief

Some of your griefs you have cured,
And the sharpest you still have survived;
But what torments of pain you endured
From evils which never arrived!
RALPH WALDO EMERSON,
Borrowing (from the French)

———o———

Ah, surely nothing dies but something mourns.
LORD BYRON, *Don Juan*

———o———

Those who have known grief seldom seem sad.
BENJAMIN DISRAELI

———o———

The flood of grief decreaseth when it can swell no longer.
FRANCIS BACON

There is not a grief which time does not lessen and soften.
MARCUS TULLIUS CICERO

———o———

Nothing speaks our grief so well as to speak nothing.
RICHARD CRASHAW

Grow

God never puts any man in a place too small to grow in.

———o———

Every youth who is ambitious to grow to the full stature of noble manhood must make up his mind at the start that he has got to be bigger than the things that are trying to down him. If he doesn't, he will go down with them.

———o———

When a child was asked why a tree in his yard was crooked, he replied, "I 'sposed somebody must have stepped on it when it was a little fellow."

———o———

There could be no growth if there were not something planted . . . Until the new man is born, or begotten, the soul abideth in death, and therefore cannot grow.
HORACE BUSHNELL

———o———

If you are alive, you will grow; death begins where growth ends.

———o———

Most of us get so scared, so civilized, that we invent a disguise for ourselves, and we walk around looking serious and acting self-important, and we call it Grown Up.
ALLAN SHERMAN

———o———

We always grow in the direction in which we express ourselves.

———o———

An acorn is not an oak tree when it is sprouted. It must go through long summers and fierce winters; it has to endure all that frost and snow and side-striking winds can bring before it is a full grown oak. These are rough teachers; but rugged schoolmasters make rugged pupils. So a man when he is created; he is only begun. His manhood must come with years.

HENRY WARD BEECHER

———o———

Unless you try to do something beyond what you have already mastered, you will never grow.

———o———

Everybody wants to be somebody; nobody wants to grow.

JOHANN WOLFGANG VON GOETHE

Grudge

The high-minded man does not bear grudges, for it is not the mark of a great soul to remember injuries, but to forget them.

ARISTOTLE

———o———

Very often the chip on a person's shoulder is just bark.

———o———

No matter how much you nurse a grudge, it won't get better.

———o———

The heaviest piece of wood in the world is the chip a man carries on his shoulder.

———o———

The most inflammable wood is the chip on a Christian's shoulder.

———o———

Grudges are too heavy a load to bear.

———o———

To nurse a grudge is to keep alive a thing that will destroy you.

———o———

The surest way to knock the chip off a fellow's shoulder is by patting him on the back.

Guide, Guidance

When a door slams behind you, look for the one God is opening.

———o———

Divine Guidance

Forth into the darkness passing
  Nothing can I hear or see,
Save the Hand outstretched to guide me,
  And the Voice that calls to me.
"I will bring the blind by pathways
  That they know not, nor have known;
'Tis a way untried, untrodden,
  But they shall not walk alone."

Lead the way then, where Thou pleasest,
  Only keep me close to Thee,
Craving not to see the distance,
  Well content that Thou dost see.
Have I not my all committed
  To Thy keeping long ago?
Knowing Him Whom I have trusted,
  More I do not need to know!

AUTHOR UNKNOWN

———o———

I helped a little child to see
That God had made a willow tree,
And God became more real to me.
I tried to lead a child through play
To grow more Christlike every day,
And I myself became that way.
I joined a little child in prayer,
And as we bowed in worship there,
I felt anew God's loving care.
Thank You, dear Lord;
How grandly true:
By guiding children, we find You!

———o———

Step By Step

He does not lead me year by year
  Nor even day by day.
But step by step my path unfolds;
  My Lord directs my way.

Tomorrow's plans I do not know,
  I only know this minute:
But He will say, "This is the way,
  By faith now walk ye in it."

And I am glad that it is so;
  Today's enough to bear,
And when tomorrow comes, His grace
  Shall far exceed its care.

What need to worry then or fret;
  The God who gave His Son
Holds all the moments in His hand,
  And gives them one by one.
BARBARA C. RYBERG

———o———

If God has made your program, He
will carry it out.

———o———

A sound head, an honest heart, and
a humble spirit are the three best
guides through time and eternity.

———o———

Men give advice; God gives guidance.
LEONARD RAVENHILL

———o———

My Pilot

I care not if the tempest rage,
  Or if the billows roar,
I care not if the surges roll
  And break upon the shore;
I have a Pilot in my ship
  Whom wind and wave obey,
And when He whispers, "Peace, be
  still!"
The storm must die away.

I care not if the sky be black
  And wild the lightning flash,
I care not if the fierce winds blow,
  And loud the thunders crash;
I have a Pilot in my ship
  Who made the mighty sea,
Who made the thunder and the storm,
  And He abides with me.

I care not if the waves wash high,
  And treacherous waters roll,
O'er hidden bar, and jagged rock,
  Or over perilous shoal;
I have a Pilot in my ship
  Who knows the trackless sea,
And He will guide me safely Home
  To His Eternity!
E. MARGARET CLARKSON

Guilt, Guilty

Loud shouting about the sins in another person's life is often due to the
fact that those same sins are in the life
of the shouter
DAVID HAMMAR

———o———

The burden of guilt is a heavy burden.

———o———

Suspicion always haunts the guilty
mind;
The thief doth fear each bush an officer.
WILLIAM SHAKESPEARE, King Henry VI,
Part III

Habits

Nothing so needs reforming as other
people's habits.
MARK TWAIN, Pudd'nhead Wilson

———o———

Talk about the slave habit! The true
galley slave is the man who, because
he is not the slave of habit, is always
mislaying things and hunting for them.
ROBERT LYND

———o———

Habits are at first cobwebs, then
cables.
Old Proverb

The chains of habit are generally too
small to be felt till they are too strong
to be broken.
SAMUEL JOHNSON

———o———

Habit is a cable. We weave a thread
of it every day until it becomes so
strong we cannot break it.
HORACE MANN

———o———

We first make our habits, and then
our habits make us.

———o———

Habit, if not resisted, soon becomes
necessity.
ST. AUGUSTINE

A bad habit is at first a caller, then a guest, and at last a master.

———o———

Guess Who I Am?

It is mighty hard to shake me,
In my brawny arms I take thee;
I can either make or break thee,
    I am Habit!
Through each day I slowly mold thee;
Soon my tightening chains enfold thee;
Then it is with ease I hold thee;
    This is Habit!
Choose me well when you are starting,
Seldom is there easy parting;
I'm a devil or a darling!
    I am habit!

ROBERT E. SLY, in *Junior Class Paper*

———o———

Our bad habits make us prisoners, and our false pride is the jailor that keeps us there.

———o———

Habits are either bobs or sinkers, cork or lead. They hold you up or hold you down.

———o———

I never knew a man to overcome a bad habit gradually.

JOHN R. MOTT

Hands

His Hands

The hands of Christ
    Seem very frail
For they were broken
    By a nail.

But only they
    Reach heaven at last
Whom these frail, broken
    Hands hold fast.

JOHN RICHARD MORELAND

———o———

My Mother's Hands

My mother's hands! So capable!
    I love them — every wrinkle there.
Though toil has made them rough and
        worn
    These hands to me are wondrous fair.

AUTHOR UNKNOWN

Hands

Hands given to God, surrendered
        hands,
    Muscle and bone, and nerve and rich
        red blood,
Hands made for service and for selfless
        toil;
    I yield them gladly to the Lord I
        love,
For His high tasks as His wise love
        demands;
    But should I tire of work and minis-
        try,
If to life's challenge I disloyal am,
    And stretch not forth my hands in
        helpful deed,
Then, Jesus, in Thy mercy let me see
    Thy hands that toiled and served in
        Galilee,
Thy nail-pierced hands upon the sa-
        cred Tree,
    Lord, show me then the hands that
        bled for me;
So stab my soul that I may follow Thee,
    That life and hands re-dedicated be.

KENRED SMITH

———o———

Blessed are the horny hands of toil.

JAMES RUSSELL LOWELL,
A Glance Behind the Curtain

———o———

Helen Keller, the famous blind personality, says: "The hands of those I meet are dumbly eloquent to me. The touch of some hands is an impertinence. I have met people so empty of joy that when I clasped their frosty fingertips it seemed as if I were shaking hands with a north east storm. Others there are whose hands have sunbeams in them, so that their grasp warms my heart. It may be only the clinging touch of a child's hand, but there is as much potential sunshine in it for me as there is in a living glance for others (who can see)."

Happiness, Happy

The Way To Happiness

I met a man the other day
Whose sunny manner seemed to say
That he had found the happy way.
I asked the secret of his smile;

He gave a thoughtful look the while
And answered somewhat in this style:
"Six things have I that spell content,
Six things that mean a life well-spent,
That make for real accomplishment.
A peaceful mind,
A grateful heart,
A love for all that's true,
A helping hand,
Real tolerance,
And lots of things to do."
I took my way with courage new,
With kindlier feelings, broader view,
Trying to think his answer through.
That man had found the secret key
Of how to live and what to be,
And passed it on to you and me.
Then let us try his simple plan
Of faith in God and love for man,
And imitate him if we can.

S. W. GRAFFIN

———o———

On Finding Happiness

Once there was a little puppy chasing its tail. It kept chasing its tail all day long, day after day. The puppy never seemed to tire of chasing its tail.

But one day a large dog stopped near where the puppy was chasing its tail, and the puppy stopped long enough to have a short conversation with the large dog.

The large dog said to the puppy, "Why are you always chasing your tail?"

"Well," answered the puppy, "when I was a very young puppy I learned that happiness was in my tail. So long as it was up and wagging, I was happy. When it dropped, or fell between my legs, I was not so happy. So I've just decided to always chase my tail, since that is my source of happiness. But the trouble is that I never really catch it!"

The older and more mature dog said to the puppy, "When I was a puppy like you that's exactly the way I thought too. But one day I forgot to chase my tail. And, lo and behold, when I looked around, happiness was following me where I went."

C. EDWIN HOUK

———o———

God cannot give us happiness and peace apart from Himself, because it is not there. There is no such thing.

C. S. LEWIS,
Mere Christianity, What Christians Believe

———o———

Much happiness is overlooked because it doesn't cost anything.

OGDON

———o———

Recipe For A Happy Day

1 cup of friendly words
2 cups of understanding
4 heaping tablespoons of time
A pinch of warm personality
A dash of humor
Mix well and serve in generous portions.

———o———

A Recipe For Happiness

I mixed a little loving with my giving,
   And found it made my life much
      more complete;
I mixed some understanding with my
      living,
   And found it made the bitter waters
      sweet.

I took some oil of gladness in the morning
   And mixed it with the work I had to
      do,
Then suddenly I found my heart was
      warming,
   And I felt at peace with every one I
      knew.

I took some sympathy for those in
      trouble
   And mixed it very gently with a
      smile;
Then I felt the joy within begin to
      bubble,
   And I knew I'd found a mixture
      quite worthwhile.

I took a lot of love and godly pleasure
   And mixed it all together with the
      rest;
I then poured in more faith than I
      could measure,
   And it made a life of joy and happiness.

HOWARD ALEXANDER

Happiness is that certain something you acquire while you're too busy to be miserable.

———o———

The Happy Heart

The happy heart is that which is content with little things,
The heart that loves the simple life, the heart from which there springs
A sense of joy with each fresh day; a prayer of gratitude
For the morning miracle of health and strength renewed.

The heart that builds about itself a shell of quietness,
A heart that keeps its faith amidst disaster and distress;
A heart serene, unmoved by envy, doubt, defeat or fear,
Filled with hope unfailing, rich in charity and fear.

No greater gift could be bestowed than this: the happy heart.
The world becomes a better place when once we've learned the art
Of putting golden edges round the clouds that blow along,
Of turning sorrows into smiles and discord into song.

PATIENCE STRONG

———o———

The secret of happiness is not in doing what one likes, but in liking what one has to do.

GEORGE V, King of England

———o———

There is no personal charm so great as the charm of a cheerful and happy temperament.

HENRY VAN DYKE

———o———

Happiness in one respect is like potato salad: when shared with others, it's a picnic.

RALPH SCOTT

———o———

Nine-tenths of our unhappiness is selfishness, and is an insult cast in the face of God.

G. H. MORRISON

The greatest happiness of life is the conviction that we are loved, loved for ourselves, or rather loved in spite of ourselves.

VICTOR HUGO

———o———

The happiness which brings enduring worth to life is not the superficial happiness that is dependent on circumstances. It is the happiness and contentment that fills the soul even in the midst of the most distressing of circumstances and the most bitter environment.

BILLY GRAHAM

———o———

Now, if happiness were only as contagious as the common cold.

———o———

Whoever wishes to be happier than he is no longer is happy.

BEN THOMAS

———o———

It isn't your position that makes you happy or unhappy; it's your disposition.

———o———

In the happiness of others, I find my own happiness.

PIERRE CORNEILLE

———o———

There is no duty we underrate so much as the duty of being happy.

ROBERT LOUIS STEVENSON,
Virginibus Puerisque,
An Apology for Idlers

———o———

Making an issue of little things is one of the surest ways to spoil happiness.

———o———

Man's happiness consists in present peace, even in the midst of the greatest trials, and in more than hope of a glorious future.

CHARLES G. GORDON

———o———

Most People Think:

Happy are the pushers:
        For they get on in the world.
Happy are the hard-boiled:
        For they never let life hurt them.

Happy are they who complain:
  For they get their own way in
  the end.
Happy are the blasé:
  For they never worry over their
  sins.
Happy are the slave-drivers:
  For they get results.
Happy are the knowledgeable men of
  the world:
  For they know their way
  around.
Happy are the trouble-makers:
  For people have to take notice
  of them.

Jesus Christ Said:

Happy are those who realize their
  spiritual poverty:
  They have already entered the
  kingdom of reality.
Happy are they who bear their share
  of the world's pain:
  In the long run they will know
  more happiness than those
  who avoid it.
Happy are those who accept life and
  their own limitations:
  They will find more in life than
  anybody.
Happy are those who long to be truly
  "good":
  They will fully realize their
  ambition.
Happy are those who are ready to
  make allowances and to forgive:
  They will know the love of
  God.
Happy are those who are real in their
  thoughts and feelings:
  In the end they will see the
  ultimate Reality, God.
Happy are those who help others to
  live together:
  They will be known to be doing God's work.
                              J. B. PHILLIPS,
                         Your God Is Too Small

———o———

Seek not happiness; bestow it, and
it will come to you.

Happiness is nothing more than good
health and a bad memory.
                         ALBERT SCHWEITZER

———o———

The happier the time, the quicker it
passes.
                         PLINY THE YOUNGER

———o———

Be merry if you are wise.
                                   MARTIAL

———o———

A light heart lives long.
                         WILLIAM SHAKESPEARE

———o———

Happiness is not a station you arrive
at; but a manner of traveling.
                         MARGARET LEE RUNBECK

———o———

Possibly the greatest source of human happiness is in personal achievement.
                              HERBERT HOOVER

———o———

You traverse the world in search of
happiness, which is within the reach
of every man. A contented mind confers it on all.
                                   HORACE

———o———

The way to bliss lies not on beds of
  down,
And he that has no cross deserves no
  crown.
                         FRANCIS QUARLES, *Esther*

Hate

Hate is a prolonged form of suicide.
JOHANN CHRISTOPH FRIEDRICH VON SCHILLER

———o———

Unless love embrace the world, hate
will crush it.
———o———

Hate and mistrust are the children
of blindness.
                              WILLIAM WATSON

———o———

We are more inclined to hate one
another for points on which we differ
than to love one another for points on
which we agree.

One of the fine arts — to hate sin without hating sinners.

---o---

I shall allow no man to belittle my soul by making me hate him.

BOOKER T. WASHINGTON

---o---

Hatred is by far the longest pleasure,
Men love in haste, but they detest at leisure.

LORD BYRON

---o---

Contempt is a kind of gangrene, which, if it seizes one' part of a character, corrupts all the rest.

SAMUEL JOHNSON

---o---

Who love too much, hate in the like extreme.

HOMER

Head

To handle yourself, use your head; to handle others, use your heart.

The English Digest

---o---

A man is like a tack, he can go only as far as his head will take him.

---o---

I think there is only one quality worse than hardness of heart and that is softness of head.

THEODORE ROOSEVELT

---o---

One good head is better than a hundred strong hands.

---o---

Nobody can steal what's in your head or in your heart.

HAL STEBBINS

Health

Health Note: One way to keep your "ticker" ticking is not to continually wind it too tight.

---o---

He who has health, has hope; and he who has hope, has everything.

Arabian Proverb

Health is a trust from God.

---o---

To be the picture of health, keep in a good frame of mind.

---o---

Our good health always seems much more valuable after we lose it.

---o---

Health is a gift, but you have to work to keep it.

HUBBARD

---o---

He spent his health to get his wealth, and then with might and main
He turned around and spent his wealth to regain his health again.

---o---

Life is not mere living, but the enjoyment of health.

MARTIAL

---o---

Late to bed, early to rise,
Makes dark circles under your eyes.

---o---

I cannot take care of my soul. God can keep that. But my body is for me to take care of.

GEORGE MUELLER

Hear

He hears but half who hears one side only.

AESCHYLUS

---o---

What you hear never sounds half so important as what you overhear.

---o---

Nature has given to men one tongue, but two ears, that we may hear from others twice as much as we speak.

EPICTETUS

---o---

The hearing ear is always found close to the speaking tongue.

RALPH WALDO EMERSON

---o---

Hear twice before you speak once.

Heart

God will accept a broken heart, but He must have all the pieces.

———o———

The best exercise for the heart is to bend down several times a day to help someone else.

———o———

The human heart generates enough energy in twelve hours to lift sixty-five tons one foot off the ground!

———o———

Whatever is seen, touched, heard, tasted, or smelled is likely to produce reactions in the heart!

———o———

"This is where your heart is," said the teacher, pointing to her chest.

"Mine is where I sit down," a little boy called from the back of the class.

"Whatever gave you that idea?" the startled teacher asked.

"Well," the youngster replied, "every time I do something good, my grandmother pats me there and says, 'Bless your little heart.'"

EDWARD JAMES BERRY

———o———

As God Sees

Man sees the kingly features,
    The confidence and charm,
The large, impressive stature,
    The strength of will and arm;
But God looks through the semblance
    And reads the hidden part,
And chooses for His servants
    The truly great at heart.
Man hears the spacious promise,
    The boast of statesmanship,
And worships him whose praises
    Are heard on every lip;
But God's ears are attentive
    To hear the thought instead,
And catch the secret meaning
    Of everything that's said.
God's ways with men are baffling,
    And oft to our surprise
He passes by the famous,
    The mighty and the wise.

He searches out a shepherd,
    A tollman in the mart,
And fishers by the seaside —
    The truly great at heart.

RALPH T. NORDLUND

———o———

It is not flesh and blood but the heart which makes us fathers and sons.

JOHANN CHRISTOPH FRIEDRICH VON SCHILLER

———o———

Whatever is to reach the heart must come from above.

LUDWIG VON BEETHOVEN

———o———

A Quiet Heart

O Lord, give me a quiet heart—
    So oft my heart is filled with fear;
I need the peace Thou canst impart;
    I need to feel that Thou art near.

Help me to walk by faith each day.
    Though shadows hide the path from view;
Give me a quiet heart, I pray
    To trust Thee as Thou bid'st me do.

I cannot see the journey's end,
    I know not what lies just ahead;
But, oh I have a Heav'nly Friend
    Who knows the path my feet must tread.

So now, my heart, be still and trust,
    Although thou canst not see the way:
For He who formed thee from the dust
    Wilt lead thee on from day to day.

A quiet heart — a quiet heart,
    From which are banished doubts and fears;
O Lord, give me a quiet heart
    That trusts Thee for the coming years.

W. M. NIENHUIS

———o———

The average heart is made to pump 2,000,000,000 times without failure, or more than ten times the performance expected from a cylinder in the engine of the highest-priced car.

———o———

In days of great need the world around there are too many folks worrying about hardening of the arteries who ought to be treated for hardening of the heart.

————o————

No man can tell whether he is rich or poor by turning to his ledger. It is the heart that makes a man rich. He is rich according to what he is, not according to what he has.

HENRY WARD BEECHER

————o————

If there is righteousness in the heart, there will be beauty in character, there will be harmony in the home. If there is harmony in the home, there will be order in the nation. Where there is order in the nation, there will be peace in the world.

Chinese Proverb

Heaven

Weep Not For Me

Would you like to know where I am?
   I am at home in my Father's house,
     in the mansions prepared for me
     there.
   I am where I would be —
   No longer on the stormy sea, but in
     the safe and quiet harbor.
   My working time is done and I am
     resting;
   My sowing time is done and I am
     reaping;
   My joy is as the joy of harvest.

Would you know how it is with me?
   I am made perfect in holiness.
   Grace is swallowed up in glory.
   The top-stone of the building is
     brought forth.

Would you know what I am doing?
   I see God.
   I see Him as He is, not as through
     a glass darkly, but face to face,
   And the sight is transforming, it
     makes me like Him.
   I am in the sweet enjoyment of my
     blessed Redeemer.
   I am here singing hallelujahs inces-
     santly to Him who sits upon the
     throne,
   And rest not day or night from
     praising Him.

Would you know what company I
     keep?
   Blessed company —
   Better than the best on earth.
   Here are holy angels and the spirits
     of just men made perfect.
   I am set down with Abraham, Isaac
     and Jacob in the Kingdom of God,
   With the blessed Paul and Peter,
     James and John and all the saints.
   And here I meet with many of my
     old acquaintances with whom I
     worked,
   And with whom I prayed who came
     hither before me.
   And lastly . . .

Would you know how long this is to
     continue?
   It is a garland that never withers,
   The crown of glory that fades not
     away.
   After millions and millions of ages it
     will be as fresh as it is now,
   And therefore, weep not for me.

Ascribed to MATTHEW HENRY

————o————

From A Loved One In Heaven

I would not have you grieve for me
   today
Nor weep beside my vacant chair.
Could you but know my daily portion
   here
You would not, could not, wish me
   there.

I know now why He said, "Ear hath
   not heard."
I have no words, no alphabet.
Or even if I had I DARE not tell
Because you could not bear it yet.

So, only this — I am the same, though
   changed,
Like Him! A joy more rich and strong
Than I had dreamed that any heart
   could hold,
And all my life is one glad song.

Sometimes when you are talking to
   our Lord
He turns and speaks to me . . . Dear
   heart,
In that rare moment you and I are just
The distance of a word apart!

And so my loved ones, do not grieve
  for me
Around the family board today;
Instead, rejoice, for we are one in Him,
And so I am not far away.
                    MARTHA SNELL NICHOLSON

———o———

Billy was gazing at his one-day-old
brother, who lay squealing and yelling
in his cradle.
  "Has he come from Heaven?" inquired Billy.
  "Yes, dear."
  "No wonder they put him out."

———o———

A devout Scotchman, being asked
if he ever expected to go to Heaven,
gave this reply: "Why, mon, I live
there!" All the way to Heaven is
Heaven begun to the Christian who
walks near enough to God to hear the
secrets He has to impart. There is such
a thing as having an inner Heaven in
the heart. "The Kingdom of God is
within you."
                              B. F. HALLECK

———o———

Heaven is a prepared place for a
prepared people, and they that enter
shall find that they are neither unknown
or unexpected.
                              BISHOP RYAL

———o———

A would-be soapbox orator who had
reached the argumentative stage sat
down next to a clergyman on a bus.
Wishing to get into an argument, he
turned and said, "I'm not going to
heaven because there is no heaven."
  His words, however, got no response.
  "I said I'm not going to heaven because there is no heaven," he said
again, almost shouting as he came to
the end of his sentence.
  "Well, then," replied the clergyman
calmly, "go to hell, but be quiet about
it."

———o———

Teacher: "How many of you children
want to go to heaven?"
  The children all raised their hands
except Johnny.
  Teacher: "But, Johnny, don't you
want to go to heaven?"

Johnny: "I can't, teacher, 'cause
mother told me to come home right
after school."

———o———

A little girl taking an evening walk
with her father looked up at the stars
and exclaimed, "Oh, Daddy, if the
wrong side of heaven is so beautiful
what must the right side be!"

———o———

Think —

Of stepping on shore and finding it
  Heaven;
Of taking hold of a hand and finding
  it God's hand;
Of breathing a new air and finding it
  celestial air;
Of feeling invigorated and finding it
  immortality;
Of passing from storm and tempest to
  an unbroken calm;
Of waking up, and finding it Home!"
                              ANONYMOUS

———o———

In order to be heaven-bound, we
must be heaven-born.

———o———

He who is on the road to heaven will
not be content to go there alone.

———o———

Sequence

After the sea, the harbor;
  After the storm, the calm;
After the road, the arbor;
  After the bleeding, balm;
After the gladness, weeping;
  After the bloom, the clod;
After the labor, sleeping;
  After the sleeping — God!
                    EDGAR DANIEL KRAMER

———o———

One tear, one sigh, one fear, one
loss, one thought of trouble cannot find
lodging there.

———o———

Jesus came to earth from heaven
that we might go to heaven from
earth.

We can't enter heaven before heaven enters us!

————o————

There is a land of pure delight
    Where saints immortal reign;
Infinite day excludes the night,
    And pleasures banish pain.

ISAAC WATTS, *Hymn 66*

————o————

When I can read my title clear
    To mansions in the skies,
I'll bid farewell to every fear,
    And wipe my weeping eyes.

ISAAC WATTS, *Hymn 65*

————o————

Trying to impress on my son that he should take good care of a souvenir from Jerusalem, I said, "This is from the Holy Land, and it is so far away we'll never be able to go there."

Next day when showing his gift to a neighbor girl, he announced, "This is from heaven, and that's one place our family will never go."

MRS. B. J. WILZ in *Together*

————o————

The man who expects to go to heaven should take the trouble to learn what route will get him there!

————o————

If you read history you will find that the Christians who did most for the present world were just those who thought most of the next. The Apostles themselves who set on foot the conversion of the Roman Empire, . . . the English Evangelicals who abolished the Slave Trade, all left their mark on Earth, precisely because their minds were occupied with Heaven. It is since Christians have largely ceased to think of the other world that they have become so ineffective in this. Aim at Heaven and you will get earth "thrown in"; aim at earth and you will get neither.

C. S. LEWIS,
Mere Christianity, Christian Behaviour

————o————

A discussion of heaven with the boys and girls in children's church brought to light a hitherto unexplored advantage when four-year-old Becky said,

"We won't have to take naps when we get there!"

IRENE ROYCE in *Teach*

————o————

The blue of heaven is larger than the clouds.

ELIZABETH BARRETT BROWNING

————o————

If God hath made this world so fair
    Where sin and death abound,
How beautiful beyond compare
    Will paradise be found.

JAMES MONTGOMERY

Hell

Time flies, death urges, knells call, heaven invites, hell threatens.

EDWARD YOUNG

————o————

As sure as night follows day and winter follows summer, so shall wrath follow sin.

————o————

The wisest of men are those who spend most pains in keeping out of hell rather than to exercise themselves with disputes about it.

Help

When God puts a burden upon you He puts His own arm under you.

————o————

Boy Overboard

A surgeon on an ocean-going vessel told how a boy fell overboard, and the crew rescued him. They brought him on board, worked his hands and feet, and tried to revive him, but in vain. When the surgeon arrived on the scene the crew members said, "It's no use; he's dead."

The surgeon replied, "I think you have done all you could," and he was about to turn away, when a sudden impulse told him he ought to examine the boy and make sure there was nothing he could do to revive him.

When he went to where the lad was and looked down into his face, he discovered it was his own son!

The surgeon immediately got busy.

He pulled off his coat, bent over the boy, breathed into his mouth, blew into his nostrils. He turned him over and over. He prayed. For four hours he worked, and at last he saw signs of life in his boy.

"Oh, I will never see another boy drown," said the surgeon, "without taking off my coat and doing all I can to save him — just as if I knew he were my own boy!"

When we see a boy or girl in spiritual danger, are we as sympathetic and as concerned as if it were our own child? Do we really do all we can to help the situation?

The Log of the Good Ship Grace

———o———

The woman who helps her neighbor does herself a good turn.

BRENDAN FRANCIS

———o———

No one is useless in this world who lightens the burden of it to any one else.

CHARLES DICKENS

———o———

Not enough people realize that the helping hand they always are looking for is at the end of their own wrist.

NICK KOZMENIUK

———o———

The truest help we can render to an afflicted man is not to take his burden from him, but to call out his best strength, that he may be able to bear the burden.

PHILLIPS BROOKS

———o———

No man can sincerely try to help another without helping himself.

J. B. WEBSTER

———o———

The hands that tend the sick tend Christ.

ARTHUR F. WINNINGTON INGRAM

———o———

It would be much nicer if everyone tempted to point a finger would instead hold out a hand.

———o———

It is not so much our friends' help

that helps us as the confidence in their help.

EPICURUS

———o———

To look up and not down,
To look forward and not back,
To look out and not in, and
To lend a hand.

EDWARD EVERETT HALE,
Ten Times One Is Ten

———o———

Nothing lightens one's burdens so quickly as helping others carry theirs.

———o———

You can't help someone else uphill without getting closer to the top yourself.

———o———

One lightning bug to another: "Give me a push; my battery's dead."

———o———

The Lord helps those who help others.

———o———

When my third-graders come to an unfamiliar word in oral reading, they usually stop and wait until I pronounce it for them.

One day I was reading a story when one child began whispering. Hoping that silence would remind her of her good manners, I stopped reading but did not look up. Whereupon a boy said sympathetically, "If you'll spell the word for me, Miss Carroll, maybe I can tell you what it is."

DOROTHY M. CARROLL in *NEA Journal*

Heredity

Heredity is when a teen-age boy winds up with his mother's big brown eyes and his father's long yellow convertible.

———o———

Heredity: Something you believe in when your child's report card is all A's.

DR. L. BINDER in *Coronet*

———o———

Every man believes in heredity until his son begins making a fool of himself.

Heredity is what makes the mother and father of teen-agers wonder a little about each other.

———o———

When one has nothing else to blame, he falls back on his heredity.

———o———

It is of no consequence of what parents a man is born, so he be a man of merit.

HORACE

Heroes

God is preparing His heroes and when the opportunity comes, he can fit them into their places in a moment and the world will wonder where they came from.

A. B. SIMPSON

———o———

Heroes are as necessary to a child's growth as vitamins.

———o———

Whosoever excels in what we prize, Appears a hero in our eyes.

JONATHAN SWIFT

———o———

Unbounded courage and compassion joined proclaim him good and great, and make the hero and the man complete.

JOSEPH ADDISON

———o———

Heroes are made every little while, but only one in a million conduct themselves afterwards so that it makes us proud that we honored them at the time.

WILL ROGERS

———o———

As employment interviewer for a large aircraft company, I meet and talk with many kinds of people. I thought nothing could surprise me, but the other day a recently discharged sailor set me back on my heels.

Well-dressed in civvies, he wore on his lapel the Purple Heart, as well as his honorable discharge button. However, it was another large gold star-shaped medal, suspended from a ladder of ten bars, which really took my eye.

My curiosity grew. I was sure he had won the medal through some unprecedented act of valor. The details of his employment being completed, I did something I don't ordinarily do. I asked him how it happened.

"Oh," he replied proudly, yet with the modesty befitting a hero, "I got that *before* I went into the Navy. I won it for going to Sunday School for ten years without missing a Sunday."

ALFRED SEALE in *Coronet*

History

There is properly no history, only biography.

RALPH WALDO EMERSON

———o———

History keeps right on repeating itself, while statesmen act as though they expected it to do something different.

———o———

Some of the biggest improvements in history are made by writers of history.

Record-Herald, Butler, Indiana

———o———

The supreme purpose of history is a better world.

HERBERT HOOVER

———o———

What are all histories but God manifesting himself, shaking down and trampling under foot whatever he hath not planted.

OLIVER CROMWELL

———o———

[History] hath triumphed over time, which besides it nothing but eternity hath triumphed over.

SIR WALTER RALEIGH, *Historie of the World*

———o———

History is only a confused heap of facts.

LORD CHESTERFIELD

He is happiest of whom the world says least, good or bad.

THOMAS JEFFERSON

———o———

There is a saying among men, that a noble deed ought not to be buried in the silent grave.

PINDAR

Holy

A holy God could require of man nothing less than holiness.

———o———

Holiness

1. Not inability to sin, but ability not to sin.
2. Not freedom from temptation, but power to overcome temptation.
3. Not infallible judgment, but earnest and honest endeavor to follow the higher wisdom.
4. Not deliverance from infirmities of the flesh, but triumph over all bodily affliction.
5. Not exemption from conflict, but victory through conflict.
6. Not freedom from liability and falling, but gracious ability to prevent falling.
7. Not the end of progress, but deliverance from standing still.

What real Christians would not desire the beauty and blessedness of such a life?

G. CAMPBELL MORGAN

———o———

More holiness give me,
More striving within;
More patience in suffering,
More sorrow for sin;
More faith in my Savior,
More sense of His care;
More joy in His service,
More purpose in prayer.

P. P. BLISS

———o———

I am certain of nothing but the holiness of the heart's affections and the truth of imagination.

JOHN KEATS,
Letter to Benjamin Bailey

Holiness is righteousness expressed.

Holy Spirit

Without the Holy Spirit, the preacher is as helpless before a sinner needing a Saviour, as Samson before Delilah.

ARTHUR F. FOGARTIE in *Presbyterian Journal*

———o———

If the Church is to rise to its fullest stature in God, if it is to enjoy the abundant life, if it is to meet all foes in the spirit of triumph, it must rely, not upon its numbers or skills, but upon the power of the Holy Spirit.

AUTHUR J. MOORE

———o———

I am in Christ
Christ is in me,
My body his temple,
Sin's captive set free;
My heart His altar,
Divine love the flame,
Cleansing for service
In His matchless Name;
My life and His life
Co-mingled shall be,
With God's very Spirit
Enthroned in me.

FRANCES RHOADS LA CHANCE

———o———

I have learned to place myself before God every day as a vessel to be filled with His Holy Spirit. He has filled me with the blessed assurance that He, as the everlasting God, has guaranteed His own work in me.

ANDREW MURRAY

———o———

A man praying at a conference in England for the outpouring of the Holy Spirit, said: "O Lord, we can't hold much, but we can overflow lots."

S. D. GORDON

———o———

Every time we say, "I believe in the Holy Spirit," we mean that we believe that there is a living God able and willing to enter human personality and change it.

J. B. PHILLIPS

All that has been done by God the Father and by God the Son must be ineffectual to us, unless the Spirit shall reveal those things to our souls.

CHARLES HADDON SPURGEON

———o———

To build temples is easier than to be temples of the Holy Spirit.

———o———

One taught by the Spirit knows the will of God.

Home

Most of our homes are having this painful contemplation: A child is born in the home and for twenty years makes so much noise we think we can hardly stand it, and then he departs leaving the home so silent that we think we'll go mad.

———o———

Children may learn at home those things which enable them to live rich, happy, useful lives or they may become unhappy, maladjusted people, suspicious of the motives of others and unwilling to cooperate with anyone. Most children fall somewhere between these two extremes.

ALICE SOWERS

———o———

Home is the chief school of human virtues.

———o———

A house is built by human hands, but a home is built by human hearts.

———o———

The Christian Home

How God must love a friendly home
Which has a warming smile
To welcome everyone who comes
To bide a little while!

How God must love a happy home
Where song and laughter show
Hearts full of joyous certainty
That life means ways to grow!

How God must love a loyal home
Serenely sound and sure!
When troubles come to those within,
They still can feel secure.

How God must love a Christian Home
Where faith and love attest
That every moment, every hour,
He is the honored Guest!

GAIL BROOKS BURKET

———o———

Friday Night

The house is full of the gayest noise,
It's Friday night, and our two big boys
Are home from college, and the place
   seems glad;
The spaniel's crazy, the cat's gone mad;
The old stairs creak, and the windows
   rattle,
We gird our loins for banter and battle,
For clash of wits and laughter and
   song,
For the week-end's short, and they'll
   soon be gone.
The old house rumbles, and the shingles crack,
As it chuckles for joy, when the boys
   come back!

MARGERY COFFMAN in *Gospel Herald*

———o———

Men make a camp; a swarm of bees a
   comb;
Birds make a nest; a woman makes a
   home.

ARTHUR GUITERMAN

———o———

Nothing makes your home look so attractive as pricing the new ones.

FRANKLIN P. JONES

———o———

Tied Down

I am tied down . . .
By clothes lines
On which I hang
Small blue and yellow rompers.
By strings . . .
Just commonplace white threads
With which I sew on buttons,
Mend wee pockets,
Patch faded threadbare little suits.
Ropes tie me down,
Red jumping ropes
And those that pull
Small animals about.
Young, bleeding grimy thumbs there
are

To kiss and bind with lengths
Of clean white gauze.
And baby arms about my neck . . .
Oh, yes . . . I am tied down . . . thank
  God!

AUTHOR UNKNOWN

---o---

Motto For A Home

Lord, enter Thou my home with me,
Until I enter Thine with Thee.

---o---

A house is built of logs and stone,
  Of tiles and posts and piers;
A home is built of loving deeds
  That stand a thousand years.

VICTOR HUGO

---o---

God bless this home and those who
  love it;
Fair be the skies which bend above it.
May never anger's thoughtless word
Within these sheltering walls be heard.
May all who rest beside this fire
And then depart, glad thoughts in-
  spire;
And make them feel who close the
  door,
Friendship has graced their home once
  more.

God bless this house and those who
  keep it;
In the sweet oils of gladness steep it.
Endow these walls with lasting wealth,
The light of love, the glow of health,
The palm of peace, the charm of mirth,
Good friends to sit around the hearth;
And with each nightfall perfect rest —
Here let them live their happiest.

AUTHOR UNKNOWN

---o---

A visitor in a large Eastern city was
being taken around by a friend.
Among other features of interest he
was shown the beautiful homes of the
fine residential area. "Your homes are
palatial," the visitor remarked. "Yes,"
replied his host, "it is not so difficult
for us to build palatial mansions, but
it is extremely difficult to build prince-
ly men to live in them."

Light

If you want to find the pot of gold
at the end of the rainbow, start digging at home.

---o---

A house is not home unless it contains food and fire for the mind as
well as for the body.

---o---

Homes are the building blocks of
civilization.

ARNOLD J. TOYNBEE

---o---

Blest be that spot, where cheerful
  guests retire
To pause from toil, and trim their
  evening fire;
Blest that abode, where want and pain
  repair,
And every stranger finds a ready chair;
Blest be those feasts with simple
  plenty crowned,
Where all the ruddy family around
Laugh at the jests or pranks that never
  fail,
Or sigh with pity at some mournful
  tale,
Or press the bashful stranger to his
  food,
And learn the luxury of doing good.

OLIVER GOLDSMITH, *The Traveller*

Honesty

A commentary on the times is that
the noun "honesty" now is preceded
by the adjective "old-fashioned."

Modern Times

---o---

Make yourself an honest man, and
then you may be sure there is one
rascal less in the world.

THOMAS CARLYLE

---o---

I hope I shall always possess firm-
ness and virtue enough to maintain
what I consider the most enviable of
all titles, the character of an honest
man.

GEORGE WASHINGTON

---o---

Honesty is the first chapter of the
book of wisdom.

THOMAS JEFFERSON

An honest man's the noblest work of God.

ALEXANDER POPE,
Essay on Man, Epistle IV

———o———

How happy is he born and taught,
That serveth not another's will;
Whose armour is his honest thought
And simple truth his utmost skill!

SIR HENRY WOTTON

———o———

The badge of honesty is simplicity.

———o———

To be honest with others, one must be thoroughly honest with himself.

Honor

No one was ever honored for what he received; honor is the reward for what he gave.

———o———

He who wishes to retain his honor, let him be humble and seek no honors; for in trying to receive honors and recognition, he reveals that he lacks something.

———o———

God has given us something to do in this world. Do we appreciate the honor?

———o———

Honor lies in honest toil.

GROVER CLEVELAND

Hope

Next to the gospel of love, the gospel of hope is perhaps the most blessed story in life. It makes us optimists for tomorrow, and we look for bright skies, good health, congenial work, true friends and a happy future.

AUTHOR UNKNOWN

———o———

Other men see only a hopeless end, but the Christian rejoices in an endless hope.

GILBERT M. BEENKEN

———o———

While there is life there is hope.

MARCUS TULLIUS CICERO

As froth on the face of the deep,
As foam on the crest of the sea,
As dreams at the waking of sleep,
As a gourd of a day and a night
As harvest that no man shall reap,
As vintage that never shall be
Is hope if it cling not aright,
O my God, unto Thee.

CHRISTINA GEORGINA ROSSETTI

———o———

Hope, alone, accomplishes nothing. Thought, effort, determination — these are among the other ingredients of accomplishment. But without hope, there is naught to nourish these other elements in our souls, minds and sinews.

———o———

Whatever happens don't lose your hold on the two main ropes of life: Hope and Faith. If you do, God pity you because then you are adrift without sail or anchor.

WILLIAM L. BROWNELL

———o———

Everything that is done in the world is done by hope.

MARTIN LUTHER

———o———

There is no medicine like hope, no incentive so great, and no tonic so powerful as expectation of something better tomorrow.

O. S. MARDEN

———o———

The time I live in is a time of turmoil, my hope is in God.

FREDERICK THE GREAT, King of Prussia

———o———

Be still, sad heart, and cease repining;
Behind the clouds the sun is shining;
Thy fate is the common fate of all,
Into each life some rain must fall,
Some days must be dark and dreary.

HENRY WADSWORTH LONGFELLOW,
The Rainy Day

———o———

Hope ever urges on, and tells us tomorrow will be better.

TIBULLUS

———o———

Hope, like the gleaming taper's light,
Adorns and cheers our way;

And still, as darker grows the night,
Emits a brighter ray.
OLIVER GOLDSMITH, *The Captivity*

Hospitality

The ultimate in hospitality is to be able to make your guest feel at home when you wish he were.

———o———

Alike he thwarts the hospitable end
Who drives the free or stays the hasty friend;
True friendship's laws are by this rule expressed,
Welcome the coming, speed the parting guest.
HOMER

———o———

Come in the evening, or come in the morning,
Come when you're looked for, or come without warning,
Kisses and welcome you'll find here before you,
And the oftener you come here the more I'll adore you.
THOMAS O. DAVIS, *The Welcome*

Housework

Housework is something you do that nobody notices unless you don't do it.

———o———

A Minneapolis housewife went into her kitchen early one morning on April Fool's Day and found a "Good Morning!" sign hung from the center light fixture. The door of a cabinet had been removed for fixing. At that point she found a sign "Closed For Repair." In the refrigerator crisper was another message "Lettuce Pray." In the freezer was another: "Help! I'm freezing!" In the egg compartment she found "I'll bet you didn't eggspect me in here." In the sink was "What depths some people won't sink to!" The dustpan had a note: "Remember, man, that thou art dust." A bar of soap was decorated with "Once again, Ivory returned." In the kitchenware drawer was "Hey! I've discovered silver!" On the glassware shelf she found:

"Big Tyrone presents: 'The Glass Menagerie.'" Inside a rubber glove was "Why, we would just glove to have you." These were thought up and planted by her sons, ages 12 and 19.
BOB MURPHY

———o———

Christ moves among the pots and pans.
ST. THERESA

Human

Human beings divide the human race horizontally: upper class, middle class, lower class. But Christ divides it vertically: to the right and to the left; and it's Christ's division which will stand.

———o———

He who helps a child helps humanity with an immediateness which no other help given to human creatures in any other stage of their life can possibly give again.
PHILLIPS BROOKS

———o———

Human beings generally respond to loving concern. There is more power in a thimbleful of tears than in a barrel of logic.
C. FRANKLIN ALLEE

———o———

Honor humanity, if for no other reason than that Jesus died and shed His blood for all.

———o———

Human action can be modified to some extent, but human nature cannot be changed.
ABRAHAM LINCOLN

Humility

The late Queen Mary visited a hospital ward one day and paused for a moment at the bed of a little girl. She asked the child where she lived and the child said in Battersea, a poor district in London.
"Where do you live?" the girl asked, unaware of the rank of her visitor.
"Oh, just behind Gorringe's department store," Queen Mary replied.
New York Herald Tribune

Whom God would greatly exalt He first humbles.

———o———

A city boy visiting on a farm for the first time saw a field of ripening wheat. He noticed that some of the yellowing stems stood up tall and straight while others gracefully bent their heads. "Those stalks that stand up so tall and straight must be the best," he remarked to the farm boy who was his companion. "They look as if they were proud of what they were doing."

The country boy laughed. "That's because you don't know much about wheat," he explained. He plucked a head of each and rubbing them in his hands showed that the tall, straight stalks held very little grain, while the bending heads were filled with the promise of a rich harvest. One of the surest evidences of greatness is a humble spirit.

———o———

Do you want to enter what people call "the higher life"? Then go a step lower down.

ANDREW MURRAY

———o———

The Lord fishes on the bottom, and if you want to get his bait and hook, brother, you've got to get right down on the bottom.

SAM JONES

———o———

I believe the first test of a truly great man is his humility.

JOHN RUSKIN

———o———

A humble person can neither be put down nor exalted; he can neither be humiliated nor honored: he remains the same person under all circumstances.

———o———

He that is down need fear no fall,
   He that is low no pride;
He that is humble ever shall
   Have God to be his guide.

JOHN BUNYAN,
Pilgrim's Progress, Part II

———o———

Humility is the acceptance of the place appointed by God, whether it be in the front or in the rear.

God will deny no blessing to a thoroughly humbled spirit.

CHARLES HADDON SPURGEON

———o———

The man who humbly bows before God, is sure to walk upright before men.

———o———

Humbleness is always grace; always dignity.

JAMES RUSSELL LOWELL

———o———

Sense shines with a double luster when it is set in humility. An able and yet humble man is a jewel worth a kingdom.

WILLIAM PENN

———o———

Humility is the solid foundation of all the virtues.

CONFUCIUS

———o———

He who blushes at the discovery of his own hidden virtues is a true gentleman.

———o———

Few people have a lower opinion of themselves than they deserve.

———o———

Humility is a virtue all preach, none practice, and yet everybody is content to hear.

JOHN SELDEN

———o———

The flower of sweetest smell is shy and lowly.

WILLIAM WORDSWORTH

———o———

In becoming a little child, and remaining a little child, there is all the difference between a simpleton and a saint.

Humor

A sense of humor . . . is not so much the ability to appreciate humorous stories as it is . . . the capacity to recognize the absurdity of the positions one gets into from time to time together with skill in retreating from them with dignity.

DANA L. FARNSWORTH in Think

Humor is emotional chaos remembered in tranquillity.

JAMES THURBER

————o————

A pun is the lowest form of humor — when you don't think of it first.

LEVANT

————o————

Lost!

I lost my sense of humor. Oh, wherever did it go?
Didn't know I'd lost it 'til it was needed so.
It wasn't in the kitchen; I couldn't find it there.
It wasn't in the parlor or in the room of prayer.

I couldn't laugh with children. Their pranks had vexed me sore.
I couldn't see the humorous side; I found life such a bore.
I took myself too seriously. My errors left me smarting.
I found the faults of those about excuse for my departing.

I wanted more perfection in everyone, and me,
Expected right to be the way I wanted it to be.
Then I heard God's chiding whisper, and suddenly I knew
I'd lost my sense of humor. Whatever could I do?

I looked and searched most everywhere
To find this needed treasure,
And there is was, obscured from sight,
By SELF grown out of measure.

DORIS REICHERT

————o————

A sense of humor is the lubricant of life's machinery.

————o————

Man is the only creature endowed with the gift of laughter; is he not also the only one that deserves to be laughed at?

FULKE GREVILLE

————o————

Cheer up and smile; it's gravity that holds things down.

Humor is the harmony of the heart.

DOUGLAS JERROLD

————o————

Good humor is a tonic for the mind and body.
It is the best antidote for anxiety and depression.
It is a business asset.
It attracts and keeps friends.
It lightens human burdens.
It is the direct route to serenity and contentment.

GRENVILLE KLEISER

————o————

More to be pitied than the unlearned person who cannot appreciate intellectual conversation is the learned person who cannot enjoy nonsense.

————o————

A humorist is a man who feels bad but who feels good about it.

————o————

There are very few good judges of humor, and they don't agree.

"JOSH BILLINGS" (HENRY WHEELER SHAW)

————o————

Humor makes the educated mind a safer mind.

WALTER LIPPMANN

————o————

A man, fond of practical jokes, late one night sent his friend a telegram out of a clear sky, collect which read: "I am perfectly well."

A week later the joker received a heavy parcel, collect, on which he had to pay considerable charges. On opening it, he found a big block of concrete on which was pasted this message:

"This is the weight your telegram lifted from my mind."

————o————

Mirth cannot move a soul in agony.

WILLIAM SHAKESPEARE

Hurry

Someone has said that modern life can be spelled in three words, "Hurry, worry, bury." One thinks of a senator who was asked, as he rushed breathlessly along, "What do you think of the world crisis?"

He replied, "Don't bother me; I'm in a hurry to make a radio speech. A crisis like this is no time to think!"

The Bible has as much to say about resting as about working. Our Lord would have us come apart and rest awhile, for if we don't we shall come apart!

VANCE HAVNER

I will not hurry through this day.
Lord, I will listen by the way
To humming bees and singing birds,
To murmuring trees and friendly words;
And for the moments in between
Seek glimpses of thy great unseen.

I will not hurry through this day,
I will take time to think and pray;
I will look up into the sky
Where fleecy clouds and swallows fly;
And somewhere in the day, maybe
I will catch whispers, Lord, from Thee.

ROBERT SPAULDING CUSHMAN

No man who is in a hurry is quite civilized.

WILL DURANT

Though I am always in haste, I am never in a hurry.

JOHN WESLEY

Christ was never in a hurry. There was no rushing forward, no anticipating, no fretting over what might be. Each day's duties were done as every day brought them, and the rest was left with God.

MARY SLESSOR

To go slowly and to live a long time are two brothers.

Dutch Proverb

Make haste slowly.

AUGUSTUS CAESAR

Ease and speed in doing a thing do not give the work lasting solidity or exactness of beauty.

PLUTARCH

Hurt

They say the world is round, and yet, it must be square;
So many little hurts we get from corners here and there.
We flatter those we scarcely know, we please the fleeting guest,
And deal full many a thoughtless blow to those we love the best.

WALTER LOG

Sometimes we are helped by being hurt. A skilled physician about to perform a delicate operation upon the ear said reassuringly, "I may hurt you, but I will not injure you." How often the Great Physician speaks to us the same message if we would only listen! Richer life, more abundant health for every child of His — that is His only purpose. Why defeat that purpose?

The Sunday School Times

Husband

Often, you can make him a good husband by making him a good wife.

Times, Holbrook, Massachusetts

Husband: A bachelor who became a yes-man.

The average husband is one who lays down the law to his wife and then accepts all the amendments.

A husband is a man who lost his liberty in the pursuit of happiness.

Good husband: One who feels in his pockets every time he passes a mailbox.

Husband: A curious creature who buys his football tickets in June and his wife's Christmas present on December 24.

Hypocrisy

Hypocrisy Versus Life

Ye call Me Master and obey Me not;
Ye call Me Light and see Me not;
Ye call Me Way and walk not;

Ye call Me Life and desire Me not;
Ye call Me Wise and follow Me not;
Ye call Me Fair and love Me not;
Ye call Me Rich and ask Me not;
Ye call Me Eternal and seek Me not;
Ye call Me Gracious and trust Me
not;
Ye call Me Mighty and honor Me not;
Ye call Me Just and fear Me not;
If I condemn you blame Me not!

————o————

Hypocrisy is the homage that vice pays to virtue.

FRANCOIS DUC DE LA ROCHEFOUCAULD

————o————

Our Father

There is one thing more pitiable, almost worse, than even cold, black, miserable atheism:

To kneel down and say, "Our Father," and then to get up and live an orphaned life.

To stand and say, "I believe in God the Father Almighty," and then to go fretting and fearing.

Saying with a thousand tongues, "I believe in the love of God!" — but it stoppeth short at the stars.

To say, "I believe in the providence of God!" — but it is limited to the saints in Scripture.

To say, "I believe that the Lord reigneth" — only with reference to some far-off time with which we have nothing to do.

That is more insulting to our Heavenly Father, more harmful to the world, more cheating to ourselves, than to have no God at all.

MARK GUY PEARSE

————o————

For neither man nor angel can discern Hypocrisy, the only evil that walks Invisible, except to God alone.

JOHN MILTON, *Paradise Lost, Book III*

————o————

The man who says he is kept away from religion by hypocrites is not influenced by them in any other area of life.

Business is full of them, but if he sees a chance at making money he does not stop for that.

Society is crowded with them, and yet he never thinks of becoming a hermit.

Married life is full of them, but that doesn't make him remain a bachelor.

Hell is full of them, and yet he doesn't do a thing to keep himself from going there.

He wants to have you think that he is trying to avoid the society of hypocrites, and yet he takes not a single step toward Heaven, the one place where no hypocrites go!

Today

Idea, Ideas

A mind, once stretched by a great idea, can never return to its original dimensions.

OLIVER WENDELL HOLMES

————o————

Man is always ready to die for an idea, provided that idea is not quite clear to him.

————o————

I like people who have ideas and talk about them. Deliver me from the sphinxes of the world. A simple "yes" or "no" leaves me feeling flat and depressed. One of the nicest things in life is communicating with fellow creatures. There's just no substitute for good talk. There are three levels of conversation: the lowest is about other people, the second concerns events, and the highest is about ideas.

Journal, Louisville, Mississippi

————o————

Good ideas are subjected to solitary confinement when they get into an empty head.

GENTRY SERENADER

The university is not engaged in making ideas safe for students; it is engaged in making students safe for ideas.

KERR

———o———

We always think a man's ideas are good if they coincide with ours.

———o———

The man with an idea has ever changed the face of the world.

———o———

Nothing is as powerful as an idea whose time has come.

VICTOR HUGO

———o———

Ideas control the world.

JAMES A. GARFIELD

———o———

Man is a dispenser of words and a generator of ideas.

ERNEST REEVES

Ideals

Some people are more concerned about "deals" than ideals.

———o———

To live with a high ideal is a successful life. It is not what one does, but what one tries to do, that makes the soul strong and fit for a noble career.

E. P. TENNEY

———o———

He who dedicates his life to a great ideal, himself becomes great.

GILL R. WILSON

———o———

Ideals are like tuning forks: sound them often to bring your life up to standard pitch.

S. D. GORDON

———o———

Our ideals are our better selves.

AMOS BRONSON ALCOTT

———o———

Ideals are worthless unless we act on them.

———o———

The ideal man is the man who knows how to get what he ought to want.

EDWARD SHEFFIELD BRIGHTMAN

Idle

To be idle and to be poor have always been reproaches, and therefore every man endeavors with his utmost care to hide his poverty from others, and his idleness from himself.

SAMUEL JOHNSON

———o———

Too much idleness, I have observed, fills up a man's time much more completely, and leaves him less his own master, than any sort of employment whatsoever.

EDMUND BURKE

———o———

Idleness is leisure gone to seed.

ELI J. SCHLEIFER

———o———

Absence of occupation is not a rest;
A mind quite vacant is a mind distressed.

WILLIAM COWPER, *Retirement*

———o———

Idleness travels so slowly that poverty soon overtakes it.

———o———

Idleness is the parent of shame and poverty.

———o———

Idleness rusts the mind.

———o———

In works of labor, or of skill,
 I would be busy too,
For Satan finds some mischief still
 For idle hands to do.

ISAAC WATTS

Ignore, Ignorance

The only thing more expensive than education is ignorance.

———o———

Little can give you peace of mind like ignorance.

Independent-Review, Aztec, New Mexico

The person who doesn't know his own mind hasn't missed a thing.

———o———

Sometimes it would be better to be unborn than untaught or wrongly taught, for ignorance is the root of about every kind of misfortune that a person falls heir to.

———o———

Ignorance is a voluntary misfortune.
NICHOLAS LING

———o———

A man's ignorance is as much his private property, and as precious in his own eyes, as his family Bible.
OLIVER WENDELL HOLMES

———o———

What you don't know won't hurt you, but it may make you look pretty stupid.

———o———

Everyone is ignorant, only on different subjects.
WILL ROGERS

———o———

Ignorance of wrongdoing does not make one innocent for having done wrong.

———o———

If thou art wise, thou knowest thine own ignorance; and thou art ignorant if thou knowest not thyself.
MARTIN LUTHER

———o———

He that voluntarily continues to ignorance, is guilty of all the crimes which ignorance produces.
SAMUEL JOHNSON

———o———

Ignorance is not innocence but sin.
ROBERT BROWNING

———o———

The fool is happy that he knows no more.
ALEXANDER POPE,
Essay on Man, Epistle II

Illness

When Ma Is Sick

When Ma is sick, she pegs away,
She's quiet though, not much to say.
She goes right on adoin' things,
An' sometimes laughs, or even sings.
She says she don't feel extry well,
But then it's just a kind of spell.
She'll be all right tomorrow sure,
A good old sleep will be the cure.
An' Pa he sniffs, an' makes no kick,
For women folks is always sick.
And Ma she smiles, let's on she's glad;
When Ma is sick, it ain't so bad.
AUTHOR UNKNOWN

———o———

When Pa Is Sick

When Pa is sick, he's scared to death,
An' Ma and us just holds our breath.
He crawls in bed, and puffs and grunts
An' does all kinds of crazy stunts.
He wants "Doc" at once, an' mighty quick,
For when Pa's ill, he's awful sick.
He gasps an' groans, an' sort o' sighs,
He talks so queer, an' rolls his eyes.
Ma jumps an' runs, an' all of us,
Are plum worn out by all his fuss,
An' peace an' joy is mighty skeerce.
When Pa is sick, it's somethin' fierce.
AUTHOR UNKNOWN

———o———

Don't let us make imaginary ills when we know we have so many real ones to encounter.
OLIVER GOLDSMITH

———o———

For a sick man the world begins at his pillow and ends at the foot of his bed.
HONORÉ DE BALZAC

———o———

A little girl whose father was a minister was very sick. She asked to see her daddy but her mother explained that he was busy preparing his sermon.

A short time later the child asked a second time to see her daddy. She got the same answer.

After asking a third time and getting the same answer she said, "I'm a sick woman and I want to see my minister!"

———o———

Someone asked the church decorator what she did with the flowers after the services. She replied innocently,

"Oh, we take them to the people who are sick after the sermon."

———o———

Diseases enter by the mouth, misfortunes issue from it.

———o———

I'm so full of penicillin that if I sneeze in here I'm sure going to cure somebody.

———o———

The Presbyterian minister had been summoned to the bedside of a Methodist woman who was very ill. As he went up the walk, he met the little daughter and said to her, "I am very glad your mother remembered me in her illness. Is your minister out of town?"

"No," answered the child. "He's at home, but we thought it might be something contagious and we didn't want to expose him to it."

Imagination

Rife Imagination

Let tomorrow take care of tomorrow;
  Leave things of the future to fate;
What's the use to anticipate sorrow?
Life's troubles come never too late.
If to hope overmuch be an error, 'tis
  One that the wise have preferred;
And how often have hearts been in terror
Of evils that never occurred!

Let tomorrow take care of tomorrow;
  Short and dark as our life may appear,
We may make it still darker by sorrow,
  Still shorter by folly and fear!
Half our troubles are half our invention
  And often from blessings conferred
Have we shrunk, in the wild apprehension
Of evils that never occurred.

CHARLES SWAIN

———o———

It is wrong for any adult to impair the imagination of a child.

———o———

Several years ago when I was teaching kindergarten in a school for blind children, five-year-old John (who had sufficient sight to recognize color but not form) was finger-painting with bright red paint. When both of his hands were completely covered with the paint, he cupped them, turned to me and said:

"Look at my hands! They look as if they were . . ."

As he paused in the middle of his thought, I half expected him to say that they looked as if they were covered with blood. Instead he said: ". . . full of red roses!"

His charming imagination made such an impression on me that countless times since then, his lesson has helped me to "think beauty" and then see beauty when something unpleasant, either real or imagined, is more obvious. How much I owe to Johnny.

FLORENCE S. ATKINSON in *Guideposts*

———o———

When I was a beggarly boy,
  And lived in a cellar damp,
I had not a friend nor a toy,
  But I had Aladdin's lamp;

When I could not sleep for cold
  I had fire enough in my brain,
And builded with roofs of gold
  My beautiful castles in Spain.

JAMES RUSSELL LOWELL, *Aladdin*

———o———

Love is the triumph of imagination over intelligence.

H. L. MENCKEN

Imitate

It has been well said, "Everyone is born an original and dies a copy."

Decision Magazine

———o———

Little boy to his sister: "Come on, let's play soldiers. I'll be a general, you be my secretary, and I'll dictate my memoirs."

L'Orient, Beirut, Lebanon

———o———

Small boy in barber's chair: "I want my hair cut like daddy's — with a round hole on top."

The class was having a composition lesson. The teacher instructed: "Do not imitate what other people write. Simply be yourself and write what is in you."

Following this advice, Bobby turned in the following composition:

"We should not imitate others. We should write what is in us. In me there are my stomach, heart, liver, two apples, one piece of pie, a lemon drop, and my lunch."

Impossible

The actual is limited,
The impossible is immense.

ALPHONSE DE LAMARTINE

———o———

You do not test the resources of God until you try the impossible.

F. B. MEYER

———o———

Nothing is impossible to the man who doesn't have to do it himself.

———o———

God does not demand impossibilities.

ST. AUGUSTINE

———o———

God raises the level of the impossible.

CORRIE TEN BOOM

———o———

Nothing is impossible to a faithful and willing heart.

———o———

Nothing is impossible to a valiant heart.

Motto of JEANNE D'ALBERT,
mother of Henry IV

———o———

You cannot have faith and tension at the same time.

GANDHI

———o———

What are Christians put into the world for except to do the impossible in the strength of God?

Ten Cannots

You cannot bring about prosperity by discouraging thrift.

You cannot help small men by tearing down big men.

You cannot strengthen the weak by weakening the strong.

You cannot lift the wage earner by pulling down the wage payer.

You cannot help the poor man by destroying the rich.

You cannot keep out of trouble by spending more than your income.

You cannot further the brotherhood of man by inciting class hatred.

You cannot establish security on borrowed money.

You cannot build character and courage by taking away man's initiative and independence.

You cannot help men permanently by doing for them what they could and should do for themselves.

ABRAHAM LINCOLN

———o———

A little boy was told to sit down in front.

"I can't," he replied. "I'm not made that way."

———o———

To the timid and hesitating everything is impossible because it seems so.

JOHN SCOTT

———o———

He who can see the invisible can do the impossible.

———o———

Few things are impossible to diligence and skill.

SAMUEL JOHNSON, *Rasselas*

———o———

Patient industry overcomes impossibilities.

BALTASAR GRACIÀN

Improve

People seldom improve when they have no other model but themselves to copy after.

OLIVER GOLDSMITH

The human race seems to have gone to a lot of trouble to improve everything but people.

———o———

Everyone can do something to make the world better. He can at least improve himself!

———o———

God has no self-improvement course for the flesh.

———o———

There is one person whom it is my duty to make good, and that is myself.

ROBERT LOUIS STEVENSON

———o———

If you don't keep becoming better, you will stop being good.

———o———

The improvement of the mind improves the heart and corrects the understanding.

AGATHON

———o———

Everything can be improved.

C. W. BARRON

Income

The reason many people don't live within their incomes is that they don't consider that living.

———o———

Our incomes should be like our shoes: if too small, they will gall and pinch us, but if too large they will cause us to stumble and to trip.

CHARLES CALEB COLTON

———o———

It is better to have a permanent income than to be fascinating.

OSCAR WILDE

———o———

If you live within your income you'll be without many things, the most important of which is worry.

WILLIAM WARD AYER

Individual

The modern world began with Christ's discovery of the individual.

JOHN MACMURRAY

———o———

Jesus Christ never met an unimportant person. That is why God sent His Son to die for us. If someone dies for you, you must be important.

DR. M. C. CLEVELAND

———o———

The worker is far more important to our Lord than the work.

MRS. CHARLES E. COWMAN

———o———

Everything of importance in the world was begun by one man or one woman.

CHANNING POLLOCK

———o———

Every great man is unique.

RALPH WALDO EMERSON

———o———

I fear uniformity. You cannot manufacture great men any more than you can manufacture gold.

JOHN RUSKIN

Industry

A. H. Smith, former president of the New York Central Railroad once defined his industry this way: "A railway is 95 percent man and 5 percent iron."

———o———

Poverty cannot overtake industry.

Japanese Proverb

———o———

The tree of industry bears golden fruit.

Japanese Proverb

———o———

God commends us to the ceaseless industry of the ant for noiseless eloquence.

———o———

The great end of all human industry is the attainment of happiness.

DAVID HUME

Andrew Carnegie was once asked which he considered to be the most important factor in industry: labor, capital, or brains? The canny Scot replied with a merry twinkle in his eye, "Which is the most important leg of a three-legged stool?"

Infidel

Replying to an infidel who had mailed him some literature, one Christian gave the following answer:
"My Dear Sir,
If you have anything better than the Sermon on the Mount, the story of the Prodigal Son; or if you have any code of morals superior to the Ten Commandments; if you can supply anything that will throw more light on the future and reveal to me a Father more merciful and kind than the New Testament does, please send it along."
There was no answer.

———o———

An infidel had just completed an eloquent address to a large audience. "And now, does anyone have any questions?" he asked.

An old man who had been a drunkard most of his life, but who had recently become a Christian, shuffled down the aisle and ascended the platform. Taking an orange from his pocket, he began to peel it.

The lecturer asked him to state his question, but the old man just went on — peeling his orange and eating it section by section.

Finally, wiping his hands on his pocket handkerchief, the old man turned to the lecturer and said: "No, here's my question. Can you tell me, was that orange sour or sweet?"

"Idiot!" retorted the lecturer in anger. "How do I know? I never tasted it!" To which the elderly man replied: "And how can you know anything about Christ, if you have never tasted Him?"

Influence
(See also Example)

Influence is the exhalation of character.

WILLIAM MACKERGO TAYLOR

We can foretell what our children will believe — what they will say and do, what they will praise and condemn — just by examining what is being planted in their minds by means of books, periodicals, television and radio.

FRANK C. LAUBACH

———o———

The proper time to influence the character of a child is about a hundred years before he is born.

WILLIAM RALPH INGE

———o———

A Father's Influence

An incident which impressed me deeply then and its impress has never faded happened when I was in the vicinity of ten years old. My father had told me to go to bed. I honestly thought he meant when I had finished a quite legitimate and proper occupation, for I was hobnobbing with a little crony of my age who had come to the house with an older person.

I remained talking with him. My father, later passing through the room and finding that I had not obeyed him, spoke with that directness of which he was capable, called brusqueness by some, and ordered me to bed at once. There was no standing on the order of my going after this.

I retreated, frightened and in tears, for such a tone of voice was a new experience in my life. I hurried to bed, but before I had time to fall asleep, he was at my bedside, kneeling and asking my forgiveness for the harsh way in which he had spoken to me, the tears falling down over his rugged, bearded face.

That was nearly half a century ago, but I would exchange any memory of life before I would surrender that. For all unknowing he was laying for me the consciousness of the Fatherhood of God, and the love of God. No sermon on the prodigal's father, and no words on the love of God have cast quite such a light as his huge figure kneeling in the twilight by my bed, asking the forgiveness of a child.

PAUL DWIGHT MOODY

"Who influenced you most toward Christ?" a friend once asked Henry Ward Beecher. "Was it some college professor, some great preacher, or a faithful Sunday School teacher?"

Beecher replied, "I doubt if the man knew at the time what an influence he was. He used to lie on his cot and read the New Testament, hardly aware that I was in the room. Then he'd talk to himself about what he read. Sometimes he would smile as he read. I never saw the Bible enjoyed like that. It challenged me more than any other thing."

"But you didn't tell me who this great man was."

"Oh, I'm sorry — that man was Charles Smith, a hired man on my father's farm."

———o———

SOME PARENTS SAY: "We will not influence our children in making choices and decisions in matters of religion!"
WHY NOT?
The ads will!
The press will!
The radio will!
The movies will!
The TV will!
Their neighbors will!
Their business will!
Their politicians will!
We can use our influence over flowers, vegetables, cattle.
Shall we ignore our children?

———o———

The length and breadth of our influence upon others depends upon the depth of our concern for others.

———o———

Had not Susannah Wesley been the mother of John Wesley, it is not likely that John Wesley would have been the founder of Methodism.

Susannah Wesley was the mother of John and Charles and seventeen other children. She was beautiful, energetic, devout. She knew Greek, Latin, French and theology.

In counsel to John she said, "Take this rule: Whatever weakens your reason, impairs the tenderness of your conscience, obscures your sense of God, or takes off the relish of spiritual things — in short, whatever increases the strength and authority of your body over your mind, that thing is sin so you, however innocent it may be in itself."

This Christian mother's counsel to her son John needs the attention of every mother and father and child today. If more parents would be Christian in character as Mrs. Wesley was, there would be less sabotaging of the children's lives with parental delinquency.

Gospel Banner

———o———

No man's actions stop with himself.

———o———

May every soul that touches mine,
Be it the slightest contact,
Get therefrom some good . . .
Some little grace . . . one kindly thought,
One aspiration yet unfelt,
One bit of courage from the darkening sky;
One gleam of faith
To brave the thickening ills of life;
One glimpse of brighter skies
Beyond the gathering mists
To make this life worth while.
GEORGE ELIOT (MARY ANN EVANS)

———o———

You cannot antagonize and influence at the same time.
JOHN KNOX

———o———

A *Child Learns*

If a child lives with hostility,
  He learns to fight.
If a child lives with criticism,
  He learns to condemn.
If a child lives with fear,
  He learns to be apprehensive.
If a child lives with jealousy,
  He learns to hate.
If a child lives with self-pity,
  He learns to be sorry for himself.
If a child lives with encouragement,
  He learns self-confidence and integrity.
If a child lives with praise,
  He learns to be appreciative.

If a child lives with acceptance,
He learns to love.
If a child lives with approval,
He learns to like himself.
If a child lives with fairness,
He learns justice.
If a child lives with honesty,
He learns what truth is.
If a child lives with friendliness,
He learns that the world is a nice
place in which to live.
AUTHOR UNKNOWN

Ingratitude

I refuse to think that there is as much ingratitude in the world as is commonly maintained. A great deal of water is flowing underground which never comes up as a spring.
ALBERT SCHWEITZER

———o———

Next to ingratitude, the most painful thing to bear is gratitude.
HENRY WARD BEECHER

———o———

A man is very apt to complain of the ingratitude of those who have risen far above him.
SAMUEL JOHNSON

Instruction

Instruction

Shape them, mold them, but leave them whole,
Children with mind and thought and soul.
Free to progress, inquire and soar
Far from the classroom's dusty core.

Light their genius! Give it wings
To overcome trite, mundane things.
Alert for the future's needs they rise
Children of God! His greatest prize.
BETH M. APPLEGATE in *This Day*

———o———

When you don't succeed after you've tried again, you might read the instructions if they are still around.
Herald, Meeker, Oklahoma

———o———

Instruction enlarges the natural powers of the mind.
HORACE

The wise are instructed by reason; ordinary minds, by experience; the stupid, by necessity; and brutes by instincts.
MARCUS TULLIUS CICERO

Integrity

Men Of Integrity

God give us men in times like these
With hope and courage strong;
Men like Daniel in days of old
Who'll stand against the wrong.

God give us men in times like these
With hearts and purpose true,
Who'll stand for right with all their might
Despite what others do.

God give us men who will not swerve
From all that's fair and just,
With faith in Thee through war or peace,
A steadfast perfect trust.

God give us men with vision keen,
Men of integrity,
Men who will put their hand in Thine,
Lead with humility.
War Cry

———o———

There is no better test for a man's ultimate integrity than his behavior when he is wrong.

———o———

Integrity without knowledge is weak and useless.

Intellect, Intelligence

The intellect may acquire much information about how to live, but it is the province of the will to make good.

———o———

It would be better to abandon our over-rapid development of the intellect and to aim rather at training the heart and the affections.
VICTOR HUGO

———o———

If we encounter a man of rare intellect, we should ask him what books he reads.
RALPH WALDO EMERSON

Intelligence consists in recognizing opportunity.

Chinese Proverb

———o———

Your stock of intelligence is not so much what you can remember as what you can forget.

———o———

There are four aspects to intelligence: thinking, reflection, projection, and application.

THOMAS BLANDI

Intentions

Among the most commonly used paving materials in this country are concrete, macadam and good intentions.

FRANKLIN P. JONES

———o———

Unless good intentions are followed by deeds, they avail nothing.

———o———

Well intentioned persons who have never succeeded in managing their private affairs are ready to take over the destinies of worlds.

MANLY HALL

Interest

Few kindnesses are as warmly welcomed as sincere, objective interest.

NORMAN G. SHIDLE

———o———

It is easy to lose interest in a church in which you have nothing invested.

———o———

A pastor, calling in the luxurious office of one of his members who was a top executive, noticed that all of the man's drawers were labeled. He was not surprised. He knew the man had efficient habits. Left alone in the office for awhile, however, he grew curious. What would a man like this keep in his top drawer? He looked. The top drawer bore just one word: CHURCH.

Every man has his "top drawer" interest. The apostle Paul said: "For me to live is Christ." Jesus Himself taught His believers to "Seek . . . first the kingdom of God and His righteousness." Put Him first and you will rate your church high too. Higher than anything measurable by dollars and cents.

Today

———o———

It is the personal that interests mankind, that fires their imagination, and wins their hearts.

BENJAMIN DISRAELI

Intuition

Intuition is what enables a woman to contradict her husband before he says anything.

———o———

Let your intuitive powers, when developed, help you get the things in life you want.

HAROLD SHERMAN

———o———

All great men are gifted with intuition. They know without reasoning or analysis what they need to know.

Invitation

On church bulletin board: "You aren't too bad to come in. You aren't too good to stay out."

LOWELL NUSSBAUM in *Indianapolis Star*

———o———

The world says: "Come to me and I will fail you."
The flesh says: "Come to me and I will destroy you."
Christ says: "Come to Me and I will give you rest."

ST. BERNARD of Clairvaux

J

Jealousy

It is jealousy's peculiar nature,
To swell small things to great, nay, out
of nought,
To conjure much; and then to lose its
reason
Amid the hideous phantoms it has
formed.

EDWARD YOUNG, The Revenge

———o———

O jealousy thou magnifier of trifles!

JOHANN CHRISTOPH FRIEDRICH VON SCHILLER

———o———

Jealousy lives upon suspicion, and
it turns into fury or it ends as soon as
we pass from suspicion to certainty.

FRANÇOIS DUC DE LA ROCHEFOUCAULD
— Maxim 32

———o———

Jealousy dislikes the world to know
it.

LORD BYRON

———o———

Jealousy is a horse which the devil
likes to ride.

Job

The dreaded job takes more time
than the done job.

———o———

A veteran missionary to China was
approached by an American businessman to accept a position with his cor-
poration.

"You know the language and the culture of China very well," the business
executive said, "and for this knowledge
we will be happy to pay you well.
Let's begin with say — $10,000?"

"No," replied the missionary quickly.

"What about $15,000?" asked the ex-
ecutive.

Once more the missionary kindly
but firmly refused. Finally the offer
reached its ultimate — $25,000. But
still the missionary shook his head neg-
atively.

"Well, just how much would it take
to get you?" the executive asked in
desperation.

"Oh," replied the missionary, "your
first offer was more than enough. The
salary is fine, but your job is too small.
I have more important work to do."

———o———

It's a mistake to stop looking for
work as soon as you've landed a job.

———o———

One of life's hardest jobs is to keep
up the easy payments.

———o———

Doing nothing is the most tiresome
job in the world because you can't
quit and rest.

———o———

There is only one job in which you
can start at the top — and that's digging a hole.

Journey

A journey of a thousand steps begins with one.

Chinese Proverb

———o———

Good company in a journey makes
the way to seem the shorter.

Italian Proverb

———o———

We Go This Way But Once

We go this way but once, O heart of
mine,
So why not make the journey well
worthwhile,
Giving to those who travel on with us
A helping hand, a word of cheer, a
smile?

We go this way but once. Ah! never
more
Can we go back along the selfsame
way,
To get more out of life, undo the
wrongs,

Or speak love's words we knew, but
did not say.

We go this way but once. Then, let
us make
The road we travel blossomy and sweet
With helpful, kindly deeds and tender words,
Smoothing the path of bruised and
stumbling feet.

AUTHOR UNKNOWN

Joy

All who joy would win
Must share it, — happiness was born
a twin.

LORD BYRON, *Don Juan*

———o———

With trumpets and sound of the cornet
Be joyful before Him, the King.
Let the oceans burst forth with great
gladness,
The hills with His happiness ring.

NAOMI A. DALLAS

———o———

Joy is not gush; joy is not jolliness.
Joy is just perfect acquiescence in
God's will because the soul delights
itself in God Himself.

HAMMER WILLIAM WEBB-PEPLOE

———o———

Science cannot restore the joy of
life and help us laugh again. Joy and
laughter are the products of faith.
Men can laugh only when they believe.

GERALD KENNEDY

———o———

Joy is the standard that flies on the
battlements of the heart when the King
is in residence.

R. LEONARD SMALL

———o———

Jesus Christ can put joy into the joy-
less work of the twentieth century.

BERNARD RAMM

———o———

Great joy is only earned by great
exertion.

JOHANN WOLFGANG VON GOETHE

Without kindness there can be no
true joy.

THOMAS CARLYLE

———o———

Grief can take care of itself; but to
get the full value of joy you must have
somebody to divide it with.

MARK TWAIN

———o———

There is sweet joy in feeling that
God knows all and notwithstanding,
loves us still.

J. HUDSON TAYLOR

———o———

If you will but live up to your
privileges, you can rejoice with unspeakable joy.

———o———

The reflections on a day well spent
furnishes us with joys more pleasing
than ten thousand triumphs.

THOMAS À KEMPIS

———o———

Joy comes, grief goes, we know not
how.

JAMES RUSSELL LOWELL

Judge, Judgment

Great Spirit, help me never to judge
another until I have walked in his
moccasins for two weeks.

Sioux Indian Prayer

———o———

There is no fear of judgment for the
man who judges himself according to
the Word of God.

HOWARD G. HENDRICKS

———o———

We aren't judged by what we want
to do and can't, but by what we ought
to do and don't.

———o———

The habit of judging and condemn-
ing others can be a more serious blem-
ish than the things we so glibly point
out as others' faults.

———o———

God will judge us for what we retain.

J HUDSON TAYLOR

Refuse to believe everything you hear, and you will rarely be embarrassed by your bad judgment.

———o———

We judge ourselves by what we feel capable of doing; others judge us by what we have done.

HENRY WADSWORTH LONGFELLOW

———o———

Judge of a tree from its fruit, not from its leaves.

PHAEDRUS

———o———

Be slow to judge but quick to forgive.

———o———

A fox should not be of the jury at a goose's trial.

THOMAS FULLER

———o———

The more one judges, the less one loves.

HONORÉ DE BALZAC

———o———

Be occupied with improving yourself and you will have little time to criticize and judge others.

———o———

Never judge a man's actions until you know his motives.

———o———

Others applaud your good judgment when you agree with them.

———o———

Better err on the side of charity than to misjudge anyone.

Just, Justice

Be just before you're generous.

RICHARD BRINSLEY SHERIDAN

Justice is the great interest of man on earth.

DANIEL WEBSTER

———o———

A man's vanity tells him what is honor, a man's conscience what is justice.

WALTER SAVAGE LANDOR

———o———

Justice discards party, friendship, and kindred, and is therefore, represented as blind.

JOSEPH ADDISON

———o———

Nothing can be honorable where justice is absent.

MARCUS TULLIUS CICERO

———o———

There is no virtue so truly great and godlike as justice.

JOSEPH ADDISON

Juvenile

Paul's exhortation to juveniles is timely: "To be subject to principalities and powers to obey magistrates, to be ready to every good work."

———o———

Perhaps the best antidote to juvenile delinquency is to stop trying to understand it, justify it, rationalize it; get old-fashioned and just punish it.

———o———

Juvenile delinquency is proving that some parents just are not getting at the seat of the problem.

KENNETH J. SHIVELY

K

Kind, Kindness

You have not lived a perfect day, even though you have earned your money, unless you have done something for someone who will never be able to repay you.

You cannot do a kindness too soon, because you never know how soon it will be too late.

Every right implies a responsibility, every opportunity an obligation, every possession a duty.

You'll never get hurt by the things you didn't say.

There are four things that will never come back: the spoken word, the sped arrow, the past life, the neglected opportunity.

From the Scrap Book of JOAN WINCHELL

———o———

If We Only Knew

If we only knew that the smiles we see
Often hide the tears that would fain be
    free,
Would we not more tender and loving
    be,
    If we only knew?

If we only knew that the words we say
Oft may drive the peace from some
    heart away,
Would we speak those words in the
    selfsame way,
    If we only knew?

If we only knew that some weary
    heart
Has been burdened more by our
    thoughtless art,
Would we cause the tears from those
    eyes to start,
    If we only knew?

If we only knew, as we onward go,
Many things that here we can never
    know,
For more patient love we would often
    show,
    If we only knew.

AUTHOR UNKNOWN

Let Me Be A Little Kinder

Let me be a little kinder,
Let me be a little blinder
To the faults of those about me;
Let me praise a little more;
Let me be, when I am weary,
Just a little bit more cheery;
Let me serve a little better
Those that I am striving for.

Let me be a little braver
When temptation bids we waver;
Let me strive a little harder
To be all that I should be;
Let me be a little meeker
With the brother that is weaker;
Let me think more of my neighbor
And a little less of me.

AUTHOR UNKNOWN

———o———

Kindness, if you show it to others, will radiate from you like the warmth of the sun over the hill tops.

———o———

Kindness, and courtesy, are infectious.

———o———

Guard within yourself that treasure, kindness. Know how to give without hesitation, how to lose without regret and how to acquire without meanness. Know how to replace in your heart by the happiness of those you love, the happiness that may be wanting to yourself.

GEORGE SAND

———o———

Seek to cultivate a buoyant, joyous sense of the crowded kindness of God in your daily life.

ALEXANDER MACLAREN

———o———

Shall we make a new rule of life . . . always to try to be a little kinder than is necessary.

SIR JAMES MATTHEW BARRIE,
The Little White Bird

The Day's Result

Is anybody happier because you passed
  his way?
Does anyone remember that you spoke
  to him today?
The day is almost over and its toiling
  time is through;
Is there anyone to utter now a kindly
  word of you?
Did you give a cheerful greeting to
  the friend who came along,
Or a churlish sort of "Howdy"; then
  vanish in the throng?
Were you selfish, pure and simple, as
  you rushed along your way,
Or is someone mighty grateful for a
  deed you did today?
Can you say tonight, in parting with
  the day that's slipping fast,
That you helped a single brother of
  the many that you passed?
Is a single heart rejoicing over what
  you did or said?
Does the man whose hopes were fading now with courage look ahead?
Did you waste the day or lose it, was
  it well or poorly spent?
Did you leave a trail of kindness, or a
  scar of discontent?
As you close your eyes in slumber, do
  you think that God would say,
"You have earned one more tomorrow
  by the work you did today?"

AUTHOR UNKNOWN

————o————

Small kindnesses, small courtesies,
small considerations, habitually practiced in our social intercourse, give a
greater charm to the character than
the display of great talent and accomplishments.

MARY ANN KELTY

————o————

Kindness is a hard thing to give
away. It keeps coming back to the
giver.

RALPH SCOTT

————o————

Kindness is the kingpin of success
in life; it is the prime factor in overcoming friction and making the human
machinery run smoothly.

ANDREW CHAPMAN

I expect to pass through life but
once. If therefore, there be any kindness I can show, or any good thing I
can do to any fellow-being, let me
do it now, and not defer or neglect it,
as I shall not pass this way again.

WILLIAM PENN

————o————

Kindness is a language which the
deaf can hear and the blind can read.

MARK TWAIN

————o————

The best portion of a good man's life,
His little, nameless, unremembered
  acts
Of kindness and of love.

WILLIAM WORDSWORTH, *Tintern Abbey*

————o————

A little word in kindness spoken,
  A motion or a tear,
Has often healed a heart that's broken,
  And made a friend sincere.

AUTHOR UNKNOWN

————o————

If you are not kind, you are the
wrong kind.

Kindergarten

Young Keith Flaniken reported
graphically on his first day at kindergarten:
  "Well," he told his grandmother,
"we sang a while. Then we cried a
while. Then we sang a while."

Glendale News Press

————o————

The world is a great university.
From the cradle to the grave we are
always in God's great kindergarten,
where everything is trying to teach us
its lesson.

O. S. MARDEN

————o————

A kindergarten teacher is a smart
girl who knows how to make little
things count.

————o————

The five most important questions a
kindergarten child asks are:

1. Why?
2. Why?

3. Why?
4. Why?
5. Why?

———o———

A child's explanation of the kindergarten: "A garden full of children."

King, Kingdom

The king reigns but does not govern.

———o———

Kings are like stars — they rise and set,
they have
The worship of the world, but no repose.

PERCY BYSSHE SHELLEY, *Hellas*

———o———

There is no king who has not had a slave among his ancestors, and no slave who has not had a king among his.

HELEN KELLER

———o———

Though invisible, the kingdom of heaven is a reality among men.

———o———

Never does man enter the kingdom of heaven except as God, by the miracle of the new birth, make him a member of that kingdom.

Knowledge

Knowledge is awareness that fire will burn; wisdom is remembrance of the blister.

———o———

The only thing worse than a man who knows it all is a woman who hears it all.

———o———

Knowledge comes, but wisdom lingers.

ALFRED LORD TENNYSON, *Locksley Hall*

———o———

Some people know a lot more when you try to tell them something than when you ask them something.

———o———

Knowledge is of two kinds: we know a subject ourselves, or we know where we can find information upon it.

SAMUEL JOHNSON,
Boswell's *Life of Dr. Johnson*

None so dumb as he who knows all the facts of life and none of the paradoxes.

DON HEROLD

———o———

The Tree of Knowledge

The
Bible contains 3,566,480
letters, 773,693
words, 31,102 verses,
1,189 chapters and
66 books. The longest chapter is the 119th
Psalm, the shortest and
middle chapter the 117th
Psalm. The middle verse is
8th of the 118th Psalm. The
longest name is in the 8th chapter of Isaiah. The word "and" occurs 46,227 times. The word "Jehovah" 6,855 times. The 37th chapter of Isaiah and the 19th chapter of
of the 2nd book of Kings are alike.
The longest verse is the 9th of the 8th
chapter of Esther; the shortest verse is
the 35th of the 11th chapter of John.
The 21st verse of the 7th chapter of
Ezra contains all the letters of the
alphabet except the letter J. The
finest piece of reading is
the 26th chapter of Acts.
The name of God is
not mentioned
in the
book of
Esther. The Bible
contains knowledge,
wisdom, holiness and love.

AUTHOR UNKNOWN

———o———

There is no knowledge which is not valuable.

EDMUND BURKE

———o———

If you have knowledge, let others light their candles by it.

THOMAS FULLER

———o———

Know Or Guess

The word "know" is found 200 times in the Bible. "Guess" is not found at all. Jesus said, "These things have I written unto you that believe on the name of the Son of God; that ye may *know* that ye have eternal life, and that ye may believe on the name of the Son of God" (I John 5:13).

———o———

Perhaps the greatest tragedy of man is that his knowledge increases so much faster than his wisdom.

———o———

He who does not increase his knowledge decreases it.

———o———

You do not need the acquirement of fresh knowledge half so much as to put in practice that which you already possess.

FRANCOIS DE SALIGNAC DE LA MOTHE FÉNELON

———o———

I may know, if I wish to know, all that I need to know.

———o———

Mere knowledge, apart from divine love, puffs one up with pride.

———o———

It is important to know what the Bible says before you try to figure out what it means.

———o———

To know is well; to do is better.

L

Labor

This is the gospel of labor, ring it, ye
　　bells of the kirk!
The Lord of Love came down from
　　above, to live with the men who
　　work;
This is the rose that He planted, here
　　is the thorn-curst soil:
Heaven is blest with perfect rest, but
　　the blessing of Earth is toil.

HENRY VAN DYKE,
The Toiling of Felix. III, Envoy

———o———

Genius begins great works; labor alone finishes them.

JOSEPH JOUBERT

———o———

The end of labor is to gain leisure.

———o———

Life has granted nothing to mankind save through great labor.

HORACE

———o———

Toiling — rejoicing — sorrowing,
　　Onward through life he goes;
Each morning sees some task begin,
　　Each evening sees it close;
Something attempted, something done,
　　Has earned a night's repose.

HENRY WADSWORTH LONGFELLOW,
The Village Blacksmith

Language

Profanity is unreasonable and unmanly; it is an offense against God and man.

———o———

Language may be a vehicle of thought, but in some cases it is just an empty wagon.

———o———

Where God is concerned the only language open to us is prayer.

J. H. OLDHAM

———o———

Perhaps of all the creations of man language is the most astonishing.

LYTTON STRACHEY

———o———

Language Test Answers

A metaphor is a surprised simile.
To indicate an omission, insert a carrot.

LAURA A. NELSON in *NEA Journal*

She had cheeks like rose peddles.

SARA THOMASSON in *NEA Journal*

———o———

Language is the dress of thought.

SAMUEL JOHNSON

———o———

The finest command of language is often shown by saying nothing.

ROGER BABSON

Late

Troubled by latecomers to his church, Rowland Hill delivered this prayer: "O Lord, bless those mightily who are in their places; give grace to those who are on their way; and have mercy on those who are getting ready to come and will never arrive."

EDWIN WYLE in *Religious Digest*

———o———

The reason that some people come late is that we don't give them a reason for coming early.

———o———

He gets through too late who goes too fast.

PUBLILIUS SYRUS, *Maxim 767*

Laugh

When you laugh at your boss' joke, it may not prove you have a sense of humor, but it proves you have sense.

———o———

After a hard day's work in serious discussions, Theodore Cuyler and Charles H. Spurgeon went out into the country together for a holiday. They roamed the fields in high spirits like boys let loose from school, chatting and laughing and free from care. Dr. Cuyler had just told a story at which Pastor Spurgeon laughed uproariously. Then suddenly he turned to Dr. Cuyler and exclaimed:
"Theodore, let's kneel down and thank God for laughter!"
And there, on the green carpet of grass, under the trees, two of the world's greatest men knelt and thanked the dear Lord for the bright and joyous gift of laughter.
There is no antagonism between prayer and laughter. One is conclusive of spiritual health, the other of physical health.

The Sunday School World

———o———

A good laugh is sunshine in a house.

WILLIAM MAKEPEACE THACKERAY

Laugh and the world laughs with you. Cry and you simply get wet!

———o———

The fool will laugh though there be nought to laugh at.

MENANDER, *Monosticha 1081*

———o———

Men show their characters in nothing more clearly than in what they think laughable.

JOHANN WOLFGANG VON GOETHE

———o———

Laughter is the best medicine for a long and happy life. He who laughs — lasts.

WILFRED A. PETERSON

Law, Legal

The young lawyer was presenting his first case and wanted to be impressive. He began, "Long ago, before the world was created . . ." when the judge interrupted with: "We are very busy this morning; would you mind starting after the flood?"

———o———

Where law ends, tyranny begins.

WILLIAM PITT

———o———

Laws should be like clothes. They should be made to fit the people they are meant to serve.

CLARENCE DARROW

———o———

I sometimes wish that people would put a little more emphasis on the observance of the law than they do on its enforcement.

CALVIN COOLIDGE

———o———

The laws of God are for our guidance and perfecting.

———o———

The law — It has honored us; we may honor it.

DANIEL WEBSTER, *Speech at the Charleston Bar Dinner* [May 10, 1847]

———o———

Let a man keep the law — any law

—and his way will be strewn with satisfaction.

RALPH WALDO EMERSON

———o———

When a lawyer dies, he lies still.

———o———

While the legalist is severe with others and charitable with himself, the true saint is severe with himself and understanding and loving with others.

MYRON AUGSBURGER
in *From the Mennonite Pulpit*

———o———

The best use of good laws is to teach men to trample bad laws under their feet. One on God's side is a majority.

WENDELL PHILLIPS

Layman

It's The Laymen

Leave it only to the pastors, and soon
    the church will die;
Leave it to the womenfolk, the young
    will pass it by.
For the church is all that lifts us from
    the coarse and selfish mob,
And the church that is to prosper
    needs the layman on the job.
Now a layman has his business, and a
    layman has his joys,
But he also has the training of all our
    girls and boys;
And I wonder how he'd like it if
    there were no churches here,
And he had to raise his children in a
    godless atmosphere.
It's the church's special function to up-
    hold the finer things,
To teach that way of living from
    which all that's noble springs;
But the pastor can't do it single-hand-
    ed and alone,
For the laymen of the country are the
    church's buildingstones.
When you see a church that's empty,
    though its doors are open wide,
It's not the church that's dying — it's
    the laymen who have died.
It's not just by song or sermon that
    the church's work is done,
It's the laymen of the country who for
    God must carry on.

EDGAR A. GUEST

Lazy

The lazier a man is, the more he plans to do tomorrow.

Norwegian Proverb

———o———

Some men remind us of blisters. They don't show up until the work is done.

———o———

All good things will come to the other fellow if you will only sit down and wait!

———o———

Even if you are on the right track, you will get run over if you just sit there.

———o———

Too many people are ready to carry the stool when there's a piano to be moved.

———o———

He that rises late must trot all day, and shall scarce overtake his business at night, while laziness travels so slowly that poverty soon overtakes him.

BENJAMIN FRANKLIN,
Preface to Poor Richard Improved

Leader

The footsteps a boy follows in are apt to be those his father thought he'd covered up.

FRANKLIN P. JONES

———o———

Leaders must be readers.

DONALD LAIRD

———o———

A tactful leader must overlook as well as look over the work of his associates.

LARRY WARD

———o———

One reason the big apples are always on top of the basket is that there are always a lot of little ones holding them up there.

———o———

There are no bad soldiers, only bad officers!

NAPOLEON BONAPARTE

Reason and judgment are the qualities of a leader.

TACITUS

—o—

An efficient leader may, through his knowledge of his job and the magnetism of his personality, greatly increase the efficiency of others.

—o—

No matter what happens in this world there will always be room at the top and there will always be room for the pioneer.

—o—

He isn't a real boss until he has trained subordinates to shoulder most of his responsibilities.

—o—

Tomorrow's Christian leaders need Christian training today.

—o—

A strong leader knows that if he develops his associates he will be even stronger.

JAMES F. LINCOLN,
President Lincoln Electric Company

—o—

Any leader worth following gives credit easily where credit is due.

FRANKLIN J. LUNDBERG,
Chairman Jewel Tea Company

—o—

No man can lead who does not love the men he leads.

—o—

You can handle people more successfully by enlisting their feelings than by convincing their reason.

PAUL P. PARKER

Learn

We have learned to fly through the air like birds and to swim through the sea like fish. When will we learn to walk the earth like men?

R. W. HUGH JONES

—o—

It is better to learn late than never.

PUBLILIUS SYRUS, *Maxim 864*

A man learns only by two things: one is reading and the other is association with smarter people.

WILL ROGERS

—o—

What we have to learn to do we learn by doing.

ARISTOTLE

—o—

It is impossible for one to learn what he already thinks he knows.

—o—

We must unlearn some things before we can become truly learned.

—o—

To be proud of learning is a mark of great ignorance.

—o—

Better be ignorant of a matter than half know it.

PUBLILIUS SYRUS, *Maxim 865*

—o—

Learning without thought is labor lost; thought without learning is perilous.

CONFUCIUS

—o—

The bookful blockhead, ignorantly read,
With loads of learned lumber in his head,
With his own tongue still edifies his ears,
And always list'ning to himself appears.

ALEXANDER POPE,
Essay on Criticism, Part III

—o—

One pound of learning requires ten pounds of common sense to apply it.

Persian Proverb

—o—

Love of learning is seldom unrequited.

ARNOLD H. GLASOW in *Quote*

—o—

To learn to walk, the child must walk.
To learn to think, the child must think.

To learn to feel, the child must feel.
To learn to live, the child must live.
To make a life, the child must be free to make his own life. His activity is the molding influence which determines the nature of his attitudes and ideals. His own choices determine his destiny.

C. B. EAVEY

The test of a learned man is the ability to express himself so simply that the unlearned say, "He can't be so smart: I can understand him perfectly!"

The Banner

The light of learning does not have to burn brilliantly, but it must burn constantly.

Anyone who stops learning is old whether this happens at twenty or eighty. Anyone who keeps on learning not only remains young but becomes constantly more valuable, regardless of physical capacity.

HENRY FORD

We have learned no portion of Scripture until we have done what it teaches.

MALCOLM E. VAN ANTWERP

The end of learning is to know God, and out of that knowledge to love Him and imitate Him.

JOHN MILTON

If you get out of school today and stop learning tomorrow, you are uneducated the next day.

Learn the blessedness of the unoffended in the face of the unexplainable.

AMY CARMICHAEL

Seeing much, suffering much, and studying much, are the three pillars of learning.

BENJAMIN DISRAELI

Professor to class: If you get this in your head, you'll have it in a nutshell.

After his first day of school little Gary said, "I have to go back tomorrow because I haven't learned how to read or write yet."

Leisure

The advantage of leisure is mainly that we have the power of choosing our work; not certainly that it confers any privilege of idleness.

SIR JOHN LUBBOCK

Leisure time is when your wife can't find you.

Leisure is a beautiful garment, but it will not do for constant wear.

He hath no leisure who useth it not.

GEORGE HERBERT, Jacula Prudentum

Employ thy time well if thou meanest to gain leisure; and since thou art not sure of a minute, throw not away an hour.

BENJAMIN FRANKLIN

Letter

Dear letter, go upon your way,
O'er mountain, plain or sea;
God bless all who speed your flight
To where I wish you'd be.

And bless all those beneath the roof
Where I would bid you rest;
But bless even more the one
To whom this letter is addressed.

AUTHOR UNKNOWN

Liberty

Liberty without obedience is confusion, and obedience without liberty is slavery.

WILLIAM PENN

Liberty is the only thing you cannot

have unless you are willing to give it to others.

WILLIAM ALLEN WHITE

---o---

Experience teaches us to be most on our guard to protect liberty when the government's purposes are beneficent.

LOUIS DEMBITZ BRANDEIS

---o---

The real destroyer of the liberties of any people is he who spreads among them bounties, donations and largess.

PLUTARCH

---o---

There can be no such thing as liberty where there is not rational reflection and choice.

WILLIAM GRAHAM SUMNER

---o---

The God who gave us life gave us liberty at the same time.

THOMAS JEFFERSON

---o---

Our Heritage

Would that each true American, however great or small,
Might journey to that shrine of shrines, old Independence Hall.
And there within those sacred walls where those immortals met,
Renew our pledge to keep the faith, "Lest we forget — lest we forget."
Lest we forget that we must be
The keepers of our liberty.

JAMES WILLARD PARKS

---o---

Draw near and learn the faithful American lesson. Liberty is poorly served by those who are quelled by one failure or any number of failures, or from the casual indifference of the people, or from the sharp show of the tushes of power. Liberty relies on itself, invites no one, promises nothing, sits in calmness and light and knows no discouragement.

WALT WHITMAN

---o---

A day, an hour, of virtuous liberty
Is worth a whole eternity of bondage.

JOSEPH ADDISON

Liberty exists in proportion to wholesome restraining.

DANIEL WEBSTER

---o---

Is life so dear, or peace so sweet, as to be purchased at. the price of chains and slavery? Forbid it, Almighty God! I know not what course others may take, but as for me, give me liberty, or give me death!

PATRICK HENRY

Lie, Lying

White lies are but the ushers to black ones.

---o---

Parents who tell the bus driver that their fourteen-year-old son is too YOUNG to pay fare are the same ones who will tell the Department of Motor Vehicles that he is plenty OLD enough to get a driver's license.

---o---

A lie can be dressed up to look like the truth, but the dress will wear out.

---o---

An untruth a day old is called a lie; a year old it is called a falsehood; a century old it is called a legend. But the nature of a false statement is not altered by age.

CHARLES HADDON SPURGEON

---o---

Some persons profit by lying convincingly; I profit by telling the truth unconvincingly. It is not so difficult as you might suppose, for in this world, where actually nothing is commonplace, people believe only in the commonplace, in that which they are accustomed to see.

ROBERT L. RIPLEY

---o---

Figures don't lie, but liars figure.

---o---

A lie travels around the world while Truth is putting on her boots.

CHARLES HADDON SPURGEON

---o---

A truth that's told with bad intent
Beats all the lies you can invent.

WILLIAM BLAKE, *Auguries of Innocence*

The person who feels it is all right to tell white lies soon goes completely color-blind.

———o———

Once there was a mother who asked her young daughter, "Do you know what happens to little girls who tell lies?" To which the little girl replied, "Of course I do. They grow up and tell their little girls they'll get curly hair if they eat their spinach."

———o———

Exaggeration is a blood relation to falsehood, and nearly as blamable.
                                        HOSEA BALLOU

———o———

Lie not, neither to thyself, nor man, nor God.
                                        GEORGE HERBERT

———o———

If you tell the truth you don't have to remember anything.
                                        MARK TWAIN

———o———

A liar should have a good memory.
            QUINTILIAN, *Institutiones Oratoriae*

———o———

Some lie beneath the churchyard stone,
And some — before the speaker.
                    WINTHROP MACKWORTH PRAED

Life

Life leaps like a geyser for those who drill through the rock of inertia.
                                        ALEXIS CARREL

———o———

The life of every man is a diary in which he means to write one story, and writes another; and his humblest hour is when he compares the volume as it is with what he hoped to make it.
                    SIR JAMES MATTHEW BARRIE

———o———

Since there is but a brief span between birth and death, learn to enjoy the span!

———o———

Up-hill

Does the road wind up-hill all the way?
Yes, to the very end.

Will the day's journey take the whole long day?
From morn to night my friend.

But is there for the night a resting place?
A roof for when the slow dark hours began.

May not the darkness hide it from my face?
You cannot miss that inn.

Shall I meet other wayfarers at night?
Those who have gone before.

Then must I knock, or call when just in sight?
They will not keep you standing at that door.

Shall I find comfort, travel-sore and weak?
Of labour you shall find the sum.

Will there be beds for me and all who seek?
Yea, beds for all who come.
                    CHRISTINA GEORGINA ROSSETT

———o———

Thirteen Progressions Of Life

At Five: "The stork brought us a new baby sister."

At Ten: "My Dad can lick any man twice his size."

At Fifteen: "Girls are just . . . blaaaah!"

At Twenty: "Just give me a chance. I'll show everybody!"

At Thirty: "In a few years, people will wake up and demand their rights."

At Thirty-five: "I'd be rich, if I'd stayed single."

At Forty: "I think I'd better have some more of those vitamin pills."

At Fifty-five: "Thank goodness I have a good bed."

At Sixty: "I was mighty fortunate to pick such a good wife."

At Sixty-five: "Why, I feel as young as I did twenty years ago."

At Seventy: "I don't know what these modern young people are coming to."
                                The King's Business

———o———

Life is fragile,
Handle with prayer.

Life is a mission. Every other definition of life is false, and leads all who accept it astray. Religion, science, philosophy, though still at variance upon many points, all agree in this, that every existence is an aim.

GIUSEPPE MAZZINE, *Life and Writings*

———o———

All of the animals except man know that the principle business of life is to enjoy it.

SAMUEL BUTLER

———o———

Life itself can't give you joy
Unless you really will it.
Life just gives you time of space —
It's up to you to fill it.

AUTHOR UNKNOWN

———o———

Life is like playing a violin solo in public and learning the instrument as one goes on.

SAMUEL BUTLER

———o———

Life is no brief candle to me. It is a sort of splendid torch which I have got hold of for the moment, and I want to make it burn as brightly as possible before handing it on to future generations.

GEORGE BERNARD SHAW

———o———

Someone's Bible

Thy life is someone's Bible, where
  Each day adds one new page;
Where chapters rise from little deeds
  That fill thy youth and age.

The friend who meets thee now and
    then
  Will read a line therein,
And find some cheer to strive anew,
  Or pretext for his sin.

Someday these speeding years —
  Their work of record done —
May show how often reading thee,
  His soul was lost or won.

Should Christ be grieved in him, thy
    Lord
  Thou mayest scarce requite,
If his resolve be framed from what
  Thy daily needs may write.

A godless act may fix his doom;
  Thy thoughtlessness he heeds;
Be careful friend, for where thou art,
  Someone his Bible reads.

E. C. KURTZ

———o———

Life is full of shadows but the sunshine makes them all.

———o———

Not only around our infancy
Doth heaven with all its splendors lie;
Daily, with souls that cringe and plot
We Sinais climb and know it not.

JAMES RUSSELL LOWELL,
Vision of Sir Launfal

———o———

Life's Melody

There is no music in a rest —
  Composers place it there
That we may pause and catch the note
  That follows, with more care;
God sends each life sometimes a "rest,"
  And we lament and grieve
That sickness, disappointing plans
  Give us unsought reprieve.
God writes the music of our lives,
  Our part to beat the time
And sing, and rest, pick up the tune —
  Go on with note sublime.

RUTH SMELTZER in *Sunshine Magazine*

———o———

True Life

Ah, life is lonely without God —
  A desert drear and wild;
One feels an exile far from home
  And like an orphan child.

Though weak and sinful, God is found
  By those who are sincere;
To hearts that hunger for His love
  He tenderly draws near.

To know the Father and the Son
  Is everlasting bliss;
Earth's fading joys cannot compare
  With joy as pure as this!

We leave earth's joys to seek in Him
  The good earth cannot give;
When fellowship with God is found,
  Then we begin to live.

MAX I. REICH

LIFE is built around:
  Love
  Integrity
  Faith
  Enthusiasm

———o———

Life is a hard, unceasing battle between man and his enemies, between woman and her friends.

———o———

Live your own life and you will die your own death.

Latin Proverb

———o———

I like trees because they seem more resigned to the way they have to live than other things do.

WILLA SIBERT CATHER, *O Pioneers!*

———o———

The best education in the world: struggling to get a living.

WENDELL PHILLIPS

———o———

Life is short and we have never too much time for gladdening the heart of those who are travelling the dark way with us.

HENRI-FRÉDÉRIC AMIEL

———o———

When my life
is past, how
glad I shall
Be that the
lamp of my
life has been shining for Thee.
I shall then not regret what I gave,
Of labor, or money for sinners
to save. I shall not mind that
the way has been rough. That my
Savior led me
— that will be
enough. When
I am dying
how glad I
shall be, that
the lamp of
my life has
been shin-
ing for THEE.

CLEAVER, *Missionary to Egypt*

———o———

Life is something that is happening to us while we are busy making other plans.

Life is short to the fortunate, long to the unfortunate.

APOLLONIUS of Tyana

———o———

Man always knows his life will shortly cease,
Yet madly lives as if he knew it not.

RICHARD BAXTER

———o———

I am drawing near to the close of my career; I am fast shuffling off the stage, I have been perhaps the most voluminous author of the day; and it is a comfort to me to think I have tried to unsettle no man's faith, to corrupt no man's principle, and that I have written nothing which on my deathbed I should wish blotted.

SIR WALTER SCOTT

———o———

In an old print shop there hangs a sign which reads: "Life is a grindstone and whether it grinds a man down or polishes him up depends on the stuff he's made of."

———o———

The hour which gives us life begins to take it away.

SENECA

———o———

Dost thou love life? Then do not squander time, for that is the stuff life is made of.

BENJAMIN FRANKLIN, *Almanac*

———o———

The life of man is a journey; a journey that must be travelled, however bad the roads or the accommodations.

OLIVER GOLDSMITH

Light

A group of tourists were visiting Carlsbad Caverns in New Mexico. Among those observing the wonders of the phenomenal underground labyrinth were a girl of twelve and her seven-year-old brother. When they had reached the deepest part of the caverns, as was customary, the guide turned off the lights for a moment's meditation and silence. The little boy became frightened and began to cry. And there in the pitch-black darkness and quietness of the cavern, many an adult received a moral lift from the clear whisper of the girl to her little brother, "Don't cry. Don't be afraid. There's someone here who knows where the lights are, and he can turn them on."

For many people there seems to be too much darkness in the world today. Yet, have you stopped to think of this: God knows where the lights are, and He can turn them on.

———o———

In darkness there is no choice. It is light that enables us to see the differences between things; and it is Christ who gives us light.

MRS. C. T. WHITMELL

———o———

God will never leave you without light enough to take one step; don't stop walking till the light gives out.

———o———

A traveler visiting the lighthouse at Calais said to the keeper, "But what if one of your lights should go out at night?"

"Never! Impossible!" he cried. "Yonder are ships sailing to all parts of the world. If tonight one of my burners were out, in six months I should hear from America and India, saying that on such a night the lights of Calais Lighthouse gave no warning and some vessel had been wrecked."

What a lesson to the people of God! Our lights must shine steadily and always, that other storm-tossed souls may be guided to Christ!

———o———

Lighthouses don't ring bells or fire guns to call attention to their light: they just shine.

———o———

We don't pretend to know anything about the speed of light, except that it gets here too early in the morning.

———o———

Whitewash always shows up blackest in the limelight.

———o———

When He came — there was no light; when He left — there was no darkness.

AUTHOR UNKNOWN

The man with time to burn never gave the world any light.

———o———

God sometimes puts us in the dark to prove to us that He is light.

Limit

Pull Me Out Of My Narrow Field

Lord, I confess unto Thee that I have lived in a narrow world. I have moved in the treadmill of my own thoughts, going around and around in the paralyzing circle of my restricted ideas.

I have kept myself dangerously confined to a small group of friends.

I have loved a few pictures, read a few books, touched the vast orbit of Thy truth and will at a few points.

Thrust me out of this small world into a large and expanding one, O Lord.

Transform me through ideas that come from the deep places of Thy plan and reach far into the distant confines of Thy unachieved will.

Enlarge and enrich my heart through many and varied and contagious friends.

Bring the islands of the sea next door to me through knowledge.

People my home and my heart with the mighty souls of all time through my sympathetic awareness of what they were and did. In His Name.

SOURCE UNKNOWN

———o———

We Limit God

Man's mind is small. We are, each day,
Concerned with things the eye can see,
With things to measure, count, or weigh;
Forgetting that, on bended knee,
The mind of God is ours to claim.
We limit God. We're halt and lame,
Though we might run, in His dear Name.

Unsearchable, God's wisdom, and
Unlimited, His wealth and might;
Yet worlds beneath His mighty Hand

Are seared and withered by the blight
Of unbelief. What loss! What shame!
Poor human clods: we fail to claim
Our riches in His precious Name!

VADYS MOTE VAUGHT

Listen

Nobody ever listened himself out of
a job.

CALVIN COOLIDGE

———o———

Some people are easily entertained
All you have to do is sit down and
listen to them.

———o———

You may wish to jot in the back of
your Bible these "hearing aids" to help
you get more from the pastor's mes-
sage. Listen —
Reverently — Habakkuk 2:20
Expectantly — Psalm 62:5
Prayerfully — I Samuel 3:10
Attentively — Acts 15:12
Understandingly — Nehemiah 8:8
Discerningly — Acts 17:11
Obediently — Matthew 7:24-27

ROY ROBERTSON

———o———

The best way to make a long story
short is to stop listening.

———o———

One way to be popular is to listen
to a lot of things you already know.

———o———

Let a man talk about himself and he
will think you're mighty interesting!

———o———

Train yourself to listen. You'll be
amazed at what you can learn when
your mouth is shut.

———o———

Some people think that God does
not speak to men today, but He does!
The trouble is that men refuse to listen.

———o———

A poor listener seldom hears a good
sermon.

We have two ears and only one
tongue in order that we may hear more
and speak less.

DIOGENES LAERTIUS

Literature

Grace Nies Fletcher in her book
Preacher's Kids says: "At ten I had
devoured Dickens; I had galloped with
Scott's armored knights, shivered
through the Paris sewers with Victor
Hugo. Cutting down a vocabulary to
fit the child's age as we do today always seem to me like cutting off the
baby to fit the crib. We offer our children Pablum instead of the red meat
of real literature."

Lutheran Education

———o———

No man but a blockhead ever wrote
except for money.

SAMUEL JOHNSON,
Boswell's *Life of Dr. Johnson*

———o———

In science, read, by preference, the
newest works; in literature, the oldest. The classic literature is always
modern.

EDWARD GEORGE BULWER- LYTTON,
Hints on Mental Culture

———o———

Literature is a very bad crutch, but
a very good walking-stick.

CHARLES LAMB

———o———

Literature is the thought of thinking
souls.

THOMAS CARLYLE

Little

Think not anything little, wherein we
may fulfill His commandments.

EDWARD B. PUSEY

———o———

Little Things

Lord, let me do the little things
    Which may fall to my lot;
Those little inconspicuous ones
    By others oft forgot.

A staff for age to lean upon,
  Strong hands to help the weak;
A loving heart with open door
  To all who solace seek.

To sit beside some silent bier
  And share their lonely grief;
To hold the palsied hand of care,
  Until there comes relief.

To hold my tongue when hot words
    rise,
  Speak kindly ones instead;
Nor harshly judge my fellow men
  In what they've done or said.

To share another's heavy load
  By word of courage given;
To help a fallen brother rise
  And bring him nearer Heaven.

If, like the Master, I can give
  Myself for those I love,
Rich joy and peace shall come to me,
  Sweet rest in Heaven above.

I know not when the day shall cease,
  But when life's curfew rings,
I want my Lord to find me then
  Still doing little things.

MRS. MORTON SIMS

———o———

Things insignificant to man may be
great in the sight of God.

———o———

He is a narrow-minded person who
despises little things.

———o———

Often the most useful Christians are
those who serve their Master in little
things. He never despises the day of
small things, or else He would not hide
His oaks in tiny acorns, or the wealth
of a wheat field in bags of little seeds.

THEODORE LEDYARD CUYLER

———o———

Little Things

This is a world of little things. The
tallest mountain is only a gigantic mass
of little things. The sky-piercing office
buildings are composed of millions of
little things. Man's activities in every
field of endeavor are made up of trifles, little things that apparently count
for little.

If it had not rained the night before
Waterloo, Napoleon would have won
the battle. Rain was a little thing.

It was a little thing that led to the
discovery of America. Columbus was
about to turn his ships and go back to
Europe when a lookout saw seaweed
floating near the ship.

The lamp swinging in the cathedral
furnished the idea of the pendulum,
and from that idea we have our clocks.

Mankind has grown great and
strong, has subdued the earth, the water, and the air by a succession of little
victories.

We are building our lives of little
things. Habit is made up of countless
unnoticed actions. And from these we
weave our future. The veriest trifles
control our destinies.

Personality

———o———

Little things are great to little men.
OLIVER GOLDSMITH

Live, Living

Facing The Dawn

Sunrise and morning star,
  And one clear call to give;
And may there be no clouding of the
    skies
  When I set forth to live.
But such a glow as, shining, seems
    ablaze,
  Too full for shade or night,
When that which drew from out the
    sun's vast rays
  Bursts forth in light.

Daylight and morning bell,
  And after that to work;
And may there be no soft and subtle
    spell
  To make me shirk.
For though into the maze of toil and
    strife
  My tasks may set my way,
I hope to meet my Master life to life,
  As I shall live this day.

WILLIAM HIRAM FOULKES

Men will wrangle for Christianity, write for it, fight for it, die for it, anything but live for it.

———o———

Write your name in kindness, love, and mercy on the hearts of thousands you come in contact with year by year, and you will never be forgotten.

THOMAS CHALMERS

———o———

Let us live as people who are prepared to die, and die as people who are prepared to live.

JAMES S. STEWART

———o———

We must live our convictions and be willing to be misunderstood. Live in God.

W. B. MUSSELMAN

———o———

Nothing can get between God and me when I live close enough to Him.

———o———

A four-year-old boy was so quiet his mother wondered what he was up to. Looking for him, she found him sitting quietly on the steps.

"What are you doing, Billy?" she asked.

He sighed and answered patiently, "Mother, can't you see I'm only living?"

———o———

Live each day as if it were thy last.

DRUMMOND of Hawthornden

———o———

Let us live in a great spirit, then we shall be ready for a great occasion.

GEORGE HODGES

———o———

To work fearlessly, to follow earnestly after truth, to rest with childlike confidence in God's guidance, to leave one's lot willingly and heartily to Him — this is my sermon to myself. If we could live more within sight of Heaven, we should care less for the turmoil of earth.

JOHN RICHARD GREEN

Take Time To Live

Take time to live;
The world has much to give
Of faith and hope and love:
Of faith, that life is good,
That human brotherhood
Shall no illusion prove;
Of hope, that future years
Shall bring the best in spite
Of those whose darkened sight
Would stir our doubts and fears;
Of love, that makes of life,
With all its griefs, a song;
A friend, of conquered wrong;
A symphony, of strife.
Take time to live,
Nor to vain mammon give
Your fruitful years.
Take time to live;
The world has much to give
Of sweet content; of joy
At duty bravely done;
Of hope, that every sun
Shall bring more fair employ.
Take time to live,
For life has much to give
Despite the cynic's sneer
That all's forever wrong;
There's much that calls for song.
To fate lend not your ear.
Take time to live;
The world has much to give.

THOMAS CURTIS CLARK

———o———

The man who lives by the Golden Rule today never has to apologize for his actions tomorrow.

Grit

———o———

The man who lives for Christ does not conform to his environment. He is drawn into a new one.

———o———

No one can live wrong and pray right. And no one who prays right can live wrong.

DAVID C. HALL

———o———

So live that when they check over your footprints on the sands of time, they won't find only the marks of a heel.

The only real way to "prepare to meet thy God" is to live with thy God so that to meet Him will be nothing strange.

PHILLIPS BROOKS

———o———

A child, hearing the minister shout when he prayed, said to his mother, "Don't you think that if he lived nearer to God he wouldn't have to talk so loud?"

———o———

Not everyone who wants to make a good living wants to earn it.

———o———

A man has to live with himself, and he should see to it that he always has good company.

CHARLES EVANS HUGHES

———o———

O Lord, let us not live to be useless.

JOHN WESLEY

———o———

To live with saints in heaven
    Will be eternal glory;
But to live with them on earth
    Is quite a different story!

———o———

Many who say "Our Father" on Sunday spend the rest of the week acting like orphans.

———o———

New Road Map

Proverbs 3:5-6 may well be labeled "The Road-Map for Christian Living." If we heed these directions not relying on our own insights alone, trusting the Lord with all our hearts, acknowledging the Lord in all we do and say each day, we will be sure to arrive safely at our destination, because the road will be made straight.

This age needs a road map for daily living. In God's Word, we have the master-plan and if we heed the Holy Spirit and obey the words of the wise man, we will have no regrets or fears — for we shall arrive home safely at eventide.

HARRY J. FISHER

I like to see a man proud of the place in which he lives; and so live that the place will be proud of him.

ABRAHAM LINCOLN

———o———

Live like Moses:

His first 40 years he was somebody.
His second 40 years he became nobody.
His third 40 years God became everybody.

———o———

It is not how many years we live, but what we do with them.

It is not what we receive, but what we give unto others.

GENERAL EVANGELINE BOOTH

———o———

Lessons In Living

Learn to laugh. A good laugh is better than medicine.
Learn to attend to your own business. Few men can handle their own well.
Learn to tell a story. A well-told story is like a sunbeam in a sick room.
Learn to say kind things. Nobody ever resents them.
Learn to avoid sarcastic remarks. They give neither the hearer nor the speaker any lasting satisfaction.
Learn to stop grumbling. If you can't see any good in the world, keep the bad to yourself.
Learn to hide aches with a smile. Nobody else is interested anyway.
Learn to keep troubles to yourself. Nobody wants to take them from you.
Above all, learn to smile. It pays!

———o———

Gracious living is when you have the house air-conditioned, and then load the yard with chairs, lounges and an outdoor oven so you can spend all your time in the hot sun.

Detroit News, Detroit, Michigan

———o———

The real art of living is beginning where you are.

———o———

Don't go around saying the world owes you a living. The world owes you nothing. It was here first.

MARK TWAIN

Live your life while you have it.
Life is a splendid gift —
There is nothing small about it.
FLORENCE NIGHTINGALE

———o———

At one time Edward Rijnders gave no indication that he would ever serve the Lord. At the age of 16, he said to his father, pastor of the Dutch Reformed Church in Doorn, "Do you believe what you are saying every Sunday?"

"Why, yes."

"Well, I don't."

"Then I forbid you to go to church. When you say there is no God, you stay at home Sunday morning. Now you have to live in the thought that God does not exist. You can come to the table after grace."

"It was a great experience," Rijnders said. "My father is a wise man. After three months I said to him, 'Father, I'm not able to live without God. It is impossible.'"
MARY SETH in *Presbyterian Life*

———o———

Upside-down Days

Some of my days fall into place
  Like soldiers on parade.
In half a jiffy — maybe less,
  My plans are wisely made.
No matter what I do, things go
  Like clockwork all day long,
And work out just as I desire,
  And things just can't go wrong.
But some days march in upside down,
  And simply won't be good;
So when I find things going wrong
  Instead of as they should,
I use a lot of extra care,
  And faith instead of doubting.
And extra effort now and then,
  And smiles instead of pouting,
And soon, I find, the day turns kind;
  Relenting, it rewards me.
And things I want, the way I want,
  It very soon accords me.
WILFRED T. COOKE in *Pilot*

———o———

Some wish to live within the sound
Of church or chapel bell,

I want to run a rescue shop
Within a yard of hell.
C. T. STUDD

———o———

Those who live with too much tension seldom live to enjoy a pension.

———o———

So live that you will have a good inside to show outside.

———o———

More people are reading the Bible which is bound in human skin than they are the one bound in leather.

Loan

Only Loaned

God didn't say that I might keep
This lovely autumn day,
Nor did He mean that through all time
The world could look this way.
He sent the beauty of the fall —
The changing autumn leaves,
And yet I know within my heart
God only loaned me these.

I marvelled at the reds and golds,
The mountains smiling fair,
And filled my mind with wondrous
  sights
I found most everywhere,
So much in beauty to behold
October's pleasantries,
And yet so soon will change, I know
God only loaned me these.

God only lends life's lovely things
However large or small.
He keeps them ever in His power
Then lends a share to all;
Old Mother Nature's golden days,
The mountains, plains and trees,
The joys and gladness they impart
God only lends us these.
GARNETT ANN SCHULTZ

Lonely

No man is lonely while eating spaghetti — it requires so much attention.
CHRISTOPHER MORLEY

A person isn't lonesome because he is alone but because he is not with some other person.

Breeze, Berlin, New Jersey

———o———

The Solitary Way

There is a mystery in human hearts,
And though we be encircled by a host
Of those who love us well, and are be-
loved,
To every one of us, from time to time,
There comes a sense of utter loneliness;
Our dearest friend is "stranger" to our
joy,
And cannot realize our bitterness.
"There is not one who really under-
stands,
Not one to enter into all I feel;"
Such is the cry of each of us in turn.
We wander in a "solitary way,"
No matter what or where our lot may
be;
Each heart, mysterious even to itself,
Must live its inner life in solitude.

And would you know the reason why
this is?
It is because the Lord desires our love.
In every heart He wishes to be first;
He therefore keeps the secret-key Him-
self,
To open all its chambers, and to bless,
With perfect sympathy and holy peace
Each solitary soul which comes to Him.
So when we feel this loneliness, it is
The voice of Jesus saying, "Come to
me;"
And every time we are "not under-
stood,"
It is a call to us to come again,
For Christ alone can satisfy the long-
ing soul,
And those who walk with Him from
day to day
Can never have a "Solitary Way."

And when beneath some heavy cross
you faint
And say, "I cannot bear this load
alone,"
You say the truth, Christ made it pur-
posely
So heavy that you must return to Him.
The bitter grief that "no one understands"

Conveys a secret message from the
King,
Entreating you to come to Him again;
The Man of Sorrows understands it
well.
In all points tempted He can feel with
you;
You cannot come too often or too near;
The Son of God is infinite in grace,
His presence satisfies the longing soul.
And those who walk with Him from
day to day,
Can never have a "Solitary Way."

AUTHOR UNKNOWN

———o———

A young man once asked F. B. Meyer to help him find a new job, because
he was the only Christian in the entire
establishment, and found it so lonely
to stand by himself. "But," said Meyer,
"is not that one reason to hold your
ground? Surely the loneliness of a light
is the more reason why it should shine.
If there were more than one, it might
with some grace retire, but not if it is
alone."

———o———

He overcomes his lonely days who
walks with Christ, who walks with man.

JOHN HOWARD BLOUGH

———o———

Seldom can a heart be lonely
If it seek a lonelier still —
Self-forgetting, seeking only,
Emptier cups of love to fill.

FRANCES RIDLEY HAVERGAL

———o———

It is proper and beneficial sometimes
to be left to thyself.

THOMAS À KEMPIS

Look

In the Scriptures we are given four
commands to *look*:

1) *Look* into the Scriptures
"Whosoever looketh into the perfect law of liberty and continueth
therein . . . shall be blessed in his
deed" (James 1:25).

2) *Look* unto Jesus
"Looking unto Jesus the author

and finisher of our faith" (Hebrews 12:2).

3) *Look* on the fields

"Lift up your eyes and look on the fields for they are white unto harvest" (John 4:35).

4) *Look* for His coming

"Looking for that blessed hope and the glorious appearing of the great God and our Saviour Jesus Christ" (Titus 2:13).

T. J. BACH

———o———

If we are shut in by life's troubles, we can look to the open heaven above us.

JAMES M. CAMPBELL

———o———

Man is the only being God has created to look up.

———o———

Looking to self makes one miserable.

———o———

Look Up

Some people pass through this wonderful world
And never look up at the sky . . .
It's nothing to them that the lark sings there
While the great white clouds sail by.

It's nothing to them that the millions of stars
Weave a silver web at night . . .
They do not know of the hush that falls
When the dawn gives birth to light.

Oh, pity the people with all your heart,
Who never look up at the sky . . .
So many beautiful sights they miss
As the pageant of God goes by.

AUTHOR UNKNOWN

———o———

If we look around, like Moses,
We will be afraid.
If we look down, like Peter,
We will sink.
If we look on others, like Miriam,
We will be envious.
If we look up to Jesus,
We will be transformed.

AUTHOR UNKNOWN

Lose, Lost

Born To Lose

The expression: "I would give my right arm for it," has often been uttered.

One day it was unexpectedly fulfilled in New York.

A 22-year-old burglar gave his right arm for a television set he tried to steal.

He and two friends broke the window of a store in which the TV set was displayed. As he reached through the broken window to seize the set, a falling section of the plate glass fell on his right arm, almost severing it.

He was rushed to the hospital, where amputation above the elbow was completed.

His left arm was tattooed with the words, "Born to lose."

How mistaken can a person be? He was born to glorify God and to enjoy Him forever. He was not born to lose, but to win; for God is "long-suffering to usward, not willing that any should perish, but that all should come to repentance." (II Peter 3:9).

TOM OLSON in *Now*

———o———

The trouble with being a good sport is that you have to lose to prove it.

Times, Alamo, Tennessee

———o———

No man can lose what he never had.

IZAAK WALTON, *The Compleat Angler*

———o———

Prefer a loss to a dishonest gain. The one brings pain at the moment, the other for all time to come.

———o———

I left the tent where we were holding meetings one night, and among the number who left last was a young man to whom I was especially attracted by his fine looks. I walked down the street with him, and put to him the invariable question, "Are you a Christian?"

He said, "No sir; I am not."

Then I used every Scripture and every argument to get him to promise me to give his heart to God, but could not succeed. When about to separate, I asked him, "Are your father and mother alive?"

"Both alive," said he.

"Is your father a Christian?"

"Don't know; he has been a steward in the church for several years."

"Is your mother a Christian?"

"Don't know; she has been superintendent of the Sabbath school of the same church for some time."

"Do your father and mother ever ask the blessing at the table?"

"No sir."

"Did your father, mother, or sister ever ask you to be a Christian?"

"Mr. Sunday, as long as I can remember, my father or mother or sister never said a word to me about my soul. Do you believe they think I am lost?"

BILLY SUNDAY

———o———

For 'tis a truth well known to most,
That whatsoever thing is lost,
We seek it, ere it come to light,
In every cranny but the right.

WILLIAM COWPER

———o———

The loss of wealth is much; the loss of health is more; but the loss of Christ is such a loss that no man can restore.

E. W. P.

———o———

Sheep get lost, not because of the thicket, but because they wander away too far from the shepherd.

———o———

Sorrowfully, the little lost boy looked up and down the street, then went up to the policeman on the corner. "Sir," he asked hopefully, "did you see a lady go by without me?"

———o———

What Would It Profit?

If all the riches of this world were mine,
And all the lovely gems that brightly shine;
If I possessed a large estate and grand,
And choicest fruitful fields, and timber-land;
What would it profit me, if death should call,
And I should be compelled to leave it all?

If I could somehow win this world's applause,
And rise to lofty heights in some great cause;
If I could have my fondest hopes fulfilled,
And with the prestige won be greatly thrilled:
What would it profit if I reached my goal,
And then should die in sin, and lose my soul?

If I could boast myself of noble birth,
And consort with the greatest ones of earth;
If I could make some friends in every land,
And find in every place an outstretched hand:
How dreadful in the end would be my lot,
If Christ should then declare, "I know you not!"

Love

Love is a feeling of a feeling like a feeling we've never felt before.

———o———

To love oneself is the beginning of a lifelong romance.

OSCAR WILDE, An Ideal Husband

———o———

Love sacrifices all things
To bless the thing it loves.

EDWARD GEORGE BULWER-LYTTON

———o———

Let those love now who never loved before;
Let those who always loved, now love the more.

THOMAS PARNELL,
Translation of the Pervigilium Veneris

———o———

Love is a gift, take it, let it grow.
Love is a sign we should wear, let it show.
Love is an act, do it, let it go.

Love is indeed heaven upon earth; since heaven above would not be heaven without it.

WILLIAM PENN

———o———

If thou didst know the whole Bible by heart, and the sayings of all the philosophers, what would all that profit thee without the love of God, and without His grace? Vanity of vanities; all is vanity except to love God and to serve Him only.

THOMAS À KEMPIS

———o———

Love

There is a love that passeth understanding,
    A love whose greatness cannot measured be;
Like a vast ocean, without shore or landing;
    And that great love, it loveth you and me!

Nor height, nor depth, nor breadth, nor length can show it;
    No words of man can speak its tale to thee;
And yet thy poor weak heart may learn to know it —
    That wondrous love that loveth you and me!

For God so loved, He sent His Well-Beloved,
    His only Son, to die for you and me;
And thus His love to all the world He proved —
    Oh, proof divine; that cannot questioned be;
And Jesus died, and rose, and went to heaven,
    God's gift of love and life to you and me:
Oh, gift unspeakable! to be forgiven,
    And dwell with God and Christ eternally!

WILLIAM R. NEWELL

———o———

We hear a good deal about the power of love. If you really want to put it to the test, see what happens when it is applied to an enemy.

Those who deserve love least, need it most!

———o———

The Second Mile

Stern Duty said, "Go walk a mile
    And help thy brother bear his load."
I walked reluctant, but, meanwhile,
    My heart grew soft with help bestowed.
Then Love said, "Go another mile."
    I went, and Duty spake no more,
But Love arose and with a smile
    Took all the burden that I bore.
'Tis ever thus when Duty calls;
    If we spring quickly to obey,
Love comes, and whatso'er befalls,
    We're glad to help another day.
The second mile we walk with joy;
    Heaven's peace goes with us on the road,
So let us all our powers employ
    To help our brother bear life's load.

STEPHEN MOORE

———o———

If slighted, slight the slight, and love the slighter.

———o———

He loves not Christ at all who does not love Christ above all.

———o———

God and I have this in common — we both love His Son, Jesus Christ.

LANCE ZAVITZ

———o———

The law of love will keep us from doing a great many things which mere impulse would often do, and will make us very careful of every word and action.

A. B. SIMPSON

———o———

Before Christ, a man loves things and uses people. After Christ, he loves people and uses things.

HORACE WOOD

———o———

Love makes everything lovely; hate concentrates itself on the one thing hated.

GEORGE MACDONALD

Be persuaded, timid soul, that He has loved you too much to cease loving you.

FRANCOIS DE SALIGNAC DE LA MOTHE FÉNELON

———o———

One thing that we may have but which we cannot keep for ourselves is divine love. Love unexpressed will soon be love dispossessed.

———o———

Enjoying each other's good is heaven begun.

LUCY C. SMITH

———o———

The greatest happiness of life is the conviction that we are loved, loved for ourselves, or rather loved in spite of ourselves.

VICTOR HUGO, Les Misérables

———o———

On the whole, God's love for us is a much safer subject to think about than our love for Him.

C. S. LEWIS,
Mere Christianity, Christian Behaviour

———o———

What is love? It's when you don't give a thought for all the if's and want-to's in the world.

EUGENE O'NEILL

———o———

Love is the goal. Love is the way we wend.

CHRISTINA GEORGINA ROSSETTI

———o———

Though love is weak and hate is strong,
Yet hate is short, and love is very long.

KENNETH BOULDING

———o———

You want to compete with His affection before you have understood it: that is your mistake. Show a little more deference to our Lord and allow Him to go first. Let Him love you a great deal before you have succeeded in loving Him even a little as you would wish to love Him. That is all that our Lord asks of you.

HENRI DE TOURVILLE

The Need And The Supply

O Love, my hunger is too deep
For bread alone to still;
The void within too vast for aught
Save deathless love to fill.

Where shall I find the nourishment
That satisfied the soul?
Where is the potent remedy
That makes the sin-sick whole?

O Love that died for me, Thou art
My only resting place;
The answer to my deepest need
I read in Jesus' face.

MAX I. REICH

———o———

Rooted In Love

Our strength and soul's integrity
Are deeper gifts of God's own grace:
As wind-bent branches of a tree
Return, in calm, to their own place,
We may be tossed by passing gales
Of sorrow, but our roots below
Hold to the love that never fails,
And in His peace we stand . . . and grow!

JEAN HOGAN DUDLEY

———o———

I look at her, somewhat resigned,
And guess the workings of her mind.
She's restless as a little wren,
And says that she's in love again.

Seems he has nice teeth, dark brown hair,
And wears his clothes with careless air.
Now I'm not jealous, y'understand,
But when he's here, I'm contraband.

I grin, and that she can't condone.
She waits for him to telephone.
It rings — she leaps — to hear him say,
"Gramma, I gotta 'A' today."

PAUL P. WENTZ in Sunshine Magazine

———o———

Are there some Christians that you just don't like? Remember that they are the Lord's possession, and then love them for His sake. To grasp this truth is to walk as the saints should walk.

Love feels no burden, thinks nothing of trouble, attempts what is above its strength, pleads no excuse of impracticability; for it thinks all things lawful for itself if possible.

THOMAS À KEMPIS

———o———

To be loved is better than to be famous.

———o———

Love is not soured by injustice; nor crushed by men's contempt.

A. S. LONDON

———o———

If thou neglectest thy love to thy neighbor, in vain thou professest thy love to God; for by thy love to God, the love to thy neighbor is begotten, and by the love to thy neighbor, thy love to God is nourished.

FRANCIS QUARLES

———o———

How shall we become lovely? By loving Him who is ever lovely.

ST. AUGUSTINE

———o———

There is in the world far more hunger for love and appreciation than there is for bread.

"Love is the fulfilling of the Law." It is the rule for fulfilling all rules, the new commandment for keeping all old commandments, Christ's one secret of the Christian life.

HENRY DRUMMOND

———o———

Love stops at nothing but possession.

THOMAS SOUTHERNE, *Oroonoko*

———o———

For the love of God is broader
Than the measure of man's mind,
And the heart of the Eternal
Is most wonderfully kind.

If our love were but more simple
We should take Him at His word;
And our lives would be all sunshine
In the sweetness of our Lord.

FREDERICK W. FABER,
Souls of Men Why Will Ye Scatter

———o———

Love is a wonder-worker, but it gets along better when it has brains to direct it.

BILLY SUNDAY

———o———

Love is life, and lovelessness is death.

FRANCES PAGET

M

Magic

Johnny came running home from school and announced excitedly, "They've got a magic record player at our school. It runs without anything!"

"A magic record player — it runs without anything?" asked his puzzled mother.

"Yes," explained Johnny, "you don't have to plug it into electricity — you don't even use electricity to make it play. All you have to do is wind it up with a crank!"

———o———

Grandfather Ba Te was a Baptist evangelist, and while he was preaching on the Burma-China border a Chinese chief, wishing to obstruct his work by devious means, sent a spy to a gospel session. Afterward the villagers lingered for a chat, and green tea was served. Grandfather declined, saying he preferred plain boiled water. "I regret that there is none ready," his host said apologetically. "Do you mind a short wait?"

"Oh, a glass of cold water will do — I'll boil it myself," replied Grandfather, who loved a practical joke. Surreptitiously taking a bottle of Eno's Fruit Salts from his bag, he poured a little into the water. Then he held the glass high for all to see the water bubbling, and drained it.

Later he learned that the spy had

hurried back across the border to warn his chief: "Do not try any tricks. Ba Te can boil water without fire. What is more, he can drink it while it is boiling!"

LOUISE PAW (Rangoon, Burma)
in *Reader's Digest*

Man, Mankind

Man is the greatest marvel in the universe. Not because his heart beats forty million times a year, driving the bloodstream a distance of over sixty thousand miles in that time; not because of the wonderful mechanism of eye and ear; not because of his conquest over disease and the lengthening of human life; not because of the unique quality of his mind, but because he may walk and talk with God.
The Nazarene Weekly

———o———

Man is the Only Animal that blushes. Or needs to.
MARK TWAIN, *Following the Equator.* Vol. I

———o———

Man is not truly man until he is God's man.
JOHN A. MACKAY

———o———

Man without God is a beast, and never more beastly than when he is most intelligent about his beastliness.
WHITTAKER CHAMBERS

———o———

For man is man and master of his fate.
ALFRED, LORD TENNYSON,
Idylls of the King

———o———

An old maid heard a rumor that she had found *the* man.
"Modesty and honesty," she said, "compel me to deny it, but thank God for the rumor."

———o———

Man is not the creature of circumstances. Circumstances are the creatures of men.
BENJAMIN DISRAELI, *Vivian Grey.* Book I

No man is more than another unless he does more than another.
MIGUEL DE CERVANTES

———o———

Man! thou pendulum betwixt a smile and a tear.
LORD BYRON

———o———

I mean to make myself a man, and if I succeed in that, I shall succeed in everything else.
JAMES A. GARFIELD

———o———

The man, whom I call deserving the name, is one whose thoughts and exertions are for others rather than himself.
SIR WALTER SCOTT

———o———

The bulk of mankind are schoolboys through life.
THOMAS JEFFERSON

———o———

Of all wonders, man himself is the most wonderful.

———o———

Man is but breath and shadow, nothing more.
SOPHOCLES

———o———

You Are Not Cheap

There is an old story of Muretus, a Christian scholar of the 16th century. One time he became ill while on a trip. The doctors who were called in to treat him did not know him. He looked so much like an ordinary individual that they said, "Let's try an experiment on him, for he looks of no importance." In the next room Muretus heard this remark, and he called to the doctors, "Call not any man cheap for whom Christ died."

It is so easy for us to downgrade individuals. Even Christian churches close their doors to people because their skin is of a different color. We are so prone to measure a man's importance according to the street on which he lives. It never bothers us that refugees continue to live in camps marked by squalor and poverty because, well, they are expendable. And then, too, we so often undervalue our own lives and willingly sell our birthright for a mess of pottage. For the cheapest price we sell our most precious heritage. Christ did not think of you that way. He believed you were worth the giving of His own life on the cross. Indeed, "call not any man cheap for whom Christ died." Not even yourself.

WILLIAM R. BUITENDORP in *Church Herald*

———o———

Someone knew what he was talking about when he said there are three states of man: "Yes, sir!" "No, sir!" and "Ulcer!"

———o———

It's a busy man who lives up to his wife's expectations.

———o———

Man is the head, but woman turns it.

Chinese Proverb

———o———

Every man is a volume, if you know how to read him.

WILLIAM ELLERY CHANNING

———o———

Women can resist a man's love, a man's fame, a man's personal appearance and a man's money, but they cannot resist a man's tongue when he knows how to use it.

WILKIE COLLINS

———o———

No man has an enemy worse than himself.

MARCUS TULLIUS CICERO

———o———

You can take my steel mills, my banks, my money, but leave me my men and I will build it all again.

ANDREW CARNEGIE

———o———

Gold is good in its place but living, brave, patriotic men are better than gold.

ABRAHAM LINCOLN

Rebellious Man

The plan and scheme of earth and
    heaven
By God's hands were devised,
While all the things that man may boast
    Are only improvised.
The sun, the moon and all the stars,
    The tides that ebb and flow,
Year after year return again,
    For God has willed it so.

Year after year come storms and rain
    The seasons come and go,
And in dark, island solitudes
    Some bright-hued blossoms grow.
The morning breaks on forests dark,
    Never traversed by man;
The sun beams on the desert wide
    According to God's plan;

But man, alone, defies the hand
    Of God that placed him here;
The most rebellious of all things
    Created on this sphere.
What, then, is man that he should
    boast?
Who is he to be proud?
Not one flower can he cause to bloom,
    Nor stem the smallest cloud.

CHARLES F. SMITH

———o———

The world needs fewer man-made goods and more God-made men and women.

SARAH ANNE JEPSON

Management

To handle yourself, use your head; to handle others, use your heart.

———o———

Good management is showing average people how to do the work of average people.

JOHN D. ROCKEFELLER, SR.

———o———

The job of management is to get the good out of a man without letting the bad interfere.

———o———

Management is the art of getting things done through people.

LAWRENCE APPLEY

Before we begin to manage the moon, it might be well to set our house in order here on earth.

Manners

Children are born mimics, so it is important that good manners should be the rule in the home. When you meet a youngster who is polite and thoughtful, you can be sure that he comes from a home where consideration for others' rights and feelings is taught and observed.

Tit-Bits

———o———

The test of good manners is to put up pleasantly with bad ones.

WENDELL WILKIE

———o———

Manners are noises you don't make when eating soup.

———o———

Good manners and soft words have brought many a difficult thing to pass.

SIR JOHN VANBRUGH, *Aesop*

———o———

Graciousness of manner is built upon very definite qualities of character, and chief among these is — adaptability, tact and poise.

Marriage

In married life no wife gets what she expected, and no husband expected what he's getting.

The Christian Parent

———o———

Lawyer: "But you can't marry again. If you do, your husband clearly specified in his will that his fortune will go to his brother."
Widow: "I know — it's the brother I'm marrying."

———o———

A woman must be a genius to create a good husband.

HONORÉ DE BALZAC

———o———

Men marry because they are tired, women because they are curious; both are disappointed.

OSCAR WILDE

You girls aspiring to get married — hearken to this voice of experience: a beautiful woman fascinates a man; a brilliant one interests him; a good one inspires him; but a sympathetic one gets him.

———o———

Any man who thinks he's more intelligent than his wife is married to a smart woman.

———o———

A truly happy marriage is one in which a woman gives the best years of her life to the man who has made them the best.

———o———

If there's any one thing a woman doesn't understand about marriage it's a husband.

———o———

"Does your husband live up to the promises he made during his courtship days?"
"Always. In those days he said he wasn't good enough for me."

———o———

Marriage starts with billing and cooing. The billing lasts.

———o———

When a man stops taking out a girl, it doesn't always mean they've broken up. He may have married her.

HERM ALBRIGHT in *Family Weekly*

———o———

A successful marriage requires falling in love many times, always with the same person.

MIGNON MCLAUGHLIN
in *The Atlantic Monthly*

———o———

Man's love is of man's life a thing apart;
'Tis a woman's whole existence.

LORD BYRON, *Don Juan*

———o———

Before marriage he talks and she listens. After marriage she talks and he listens. Later they both talk and the neighbors listen.

Common sense would avoid many divorces and also quite a few marriages.

———o———

The woman next door believes marriage is a give and take proposition. If her husband doesn't give her enough, she takes it out of his pocket.

———o———

The secret of happy marriage is simple: just keep on being as polite to each other as you are to your best friends.

ROBERT QUILLEN

———o———

A honeymoon is the vacation a man takes before starting to work for a new boss.

———o———

The main reason why some married folks don't pull together like a team is that one of them is just a nag.

———o———

Hasty marriage seldom proveth well.

WILLIAM SHAKESPEARE, *King Henry VI*

———o———

The one word above all others that makes marriage successful is "ours."

ROBERT QUILLEN

———o———

All marriages are happy — it's the living together afterwards that's tough.

———o———

Love is blind but marriage opens their eyes.

———o———

A real home is a picture of heaven on earth.

———o———

Success in marriage is more than finding the right person; it is a matter of being the right person.

———o———

Single women say they wouldn't marry the best man in the world. Married women know they didn't.

———o———

Make this agreement with your wife: if she will quit driving from the back seat, you will quit cooking from the dining room table.

Martyr

Blood of the martyrs is the seed of the Church.

TERTULLIAN, *Apologeticus*

———o———

Martyrdom is the only way in which a man can become famous without ability.

GEORGE BERNARD SHAW

———o———

Some ministers would make good martyrs; they are so dry they would burn well.

CHARLES HADDON SPURGEON

———o———

A death for love's no death but martyrdom.

C. CHAPMAN

Mathematics

To work out life's problems, we need to add love, subtract hate, multiply good, and divide between truth and error.

JANET T. COLEMAN

———o———

A schoolteacher was trying to explain subtraction to his young pupils.

"You have ten fingers," he said. "Suppose you had three less fingers, what would you have?"

A sweet little girl gave the quick answer, "I'd have no music lesson."

Sunshine Magazine

———o———

The greatest mathematician is he who daily counts his blessings.

DAVID PHELPS

———o———

A story has been written by Frederick Hall about the lad who played such an important role in the miracle of the loaves and fishes. It tells how the boy reported the exciting incident to his mother when he returned home that evening at sunset. When, with eyes still big with the wonder of it all, he had told how his five barley cakes and two dried lake fish had increased in the Master's hands until the vast crowd had been fed to a sufficiency, he added, "I wonder, Mother, if it would be that way with everything you gave Him?"

The Sunday School Times

Maturity

To be able to rejoice with another who succeeds when you have failed — that is a mark of real maturity!

———o———

Maturity: The capacity to endure uncertainty.

JOHN FINLEY, Harvard Professor

———o———

Maturity is the ability to live in someone else's world.

OREN ARNOLD in *The Kiwanis Magazine*

———o———

Maturity

If you can see a work which you have begun taken from you and given to another without feeling bitterness — that is maturity.

If you can listen to someone criticize you, even unkindly, and receive instruction from it without hard feelings — that is maturity.

If you can see others chosen for a job which you yourself are better qualified to do without feeling hurt — that is maturity.

If you can see a person do an act which is against your Christian standards and react without self-righteousness — that is maturity.

If you can hear a man argue a point of view which is contrary to your own and accept his right to his own opinion without a feeling of smugness — that is maturity.

If you can see someone you know deliberately snub you, and still make allowance for his actions — that is maturity.

If you can suffer nagging pain or ache, still singing and praising God, hiding your feelings for the sake of others — that is maturity.

If you can give yourself to help someone else who needs you, without having the idea that you are "a pretty good fellow" — that is maturity.

If you can crawl out of bed at an early hour to pray when you would rather sleep, because you realize that here lies your power with God — that is maturity.

If you can look upon every man as an object of God's yearning, so that you become burdened for his soul — that is maturity.

ANNE NUNEMAKER in *Moody Monthly*

Maxim

The winds and waves are always on the side of the ablest navigators.

EDWARD GIBBON, *Decline and Fall of the Roman Empire*

———o———

There are two things in the world that are only as big as the one who owns them: A dollar and a minute.

———o———

Do good by stealth, and blush to find it fame.

ALEXANDER POPE, *Satires, Epistles and Odes of Horace*

———o———

He who falls down gets up faster than he who lies down.

———o———

A hammer shatters glass but forges steel.

———o———

There is no right way to do a wrong thing.

———o———

Whitewashing the pump won't make the water pure.

DWIGHT L. MOODY

———o———

For, as I like a young man in whom there is something of the old, so I like an old man in whom there is something of the young; and he who follows this maxim, in body will possibly be an old man, but he will never be an old man in mind.

MARCUS TULLIUS CICERO, *De Senectute*

Pithy sentences are like sharp nails which force truth upon our memory.

DENIS DIDEROT

Memorial Day

The Dash Between The Dates

Memorial Day was over now,
All had left and I was alone.
I began to read the names and dates
Chiseled there on every stone.
The dates which showed whether it
    was Mom or Dad
Or daughter or baby son.
The dates were different but the
    amount the same,
There were two on every one.

It was then I noticed something,
It was but a simple line;
It was the dash between the dates
Placed there, it stood for time.
All at once it dawned on me
How important that little line.
The dates placed there belonged to
    God,
But that line is yours and mine.

It's God who gives this precious life
And God who takes away;
But that line between He gives to us
To do with what we may.
We know God's written the first date
    down
Of each and every one,
And we know those hands will write
    again,
For the last date has to come.

We know He'll write the last date
    down,
And soon, we know, for some.
But upon the line between my dates
I hope He'll write "well done."

LUCILLE BRITT
in *The Log of the Good Ship Grace*

Memory, Memorize

Strong Box

I have a treasured strong box,
    Its contents are pure gold;
Where all these precious moments
    Are mind to have and hold.

Inside I've put my baby's smile,
    The sound of pattering feet;
My little girl's first childish song,
    In babbling accent sweet.

There was a time when guests arrived.
    My walls were scarred and marked;
I washed the handprints all away,
    But framed them in my heart.

Now when my children both have
    grown,
    And I am old and gray,
I'll turn the lock with mem'ry's key,
    And while the hours away.

IRENE C. WALLIS

———o———

The true art of memory is the art of attention.

SAMUEL JOHNSON

———o———

A Bible stored in the mind is worth a dozen stored in the bottom of one's trunk.

———o———

The Chinese Christians, fearful that someday their precious Bibles might be taken away from them, hid the Word away in the most secure place possible, in their hearts. They memorized whole chapters of Scripture. In one district a missionary said that he knew of two hundred people who had memorized the entire New Testament. What strength and peace it must give them in the fiery trials they must endure under a Communist government.

F. S. DONNELSON

———o———

The good old days are the result of memory over misery.

Journal, Moro, Oregon

———o———

The memory is a treasurer to whom we must give funds, if we would draw the assistance we need.

NICHOLAS ROWE

———o———

In a Midwestern state, a newspaper reported that a local man had donated a loudspeaker to his church in memory of his wife.

———o———

Memory is a good thing if we learn to use it and do not let it use us.

EUGENIA PRICE

I remember your name perfectly, but I just can't think of your face.

————o————

No statue was ever erected to the memory of a man or woman who thought it was best to let well enough alone.

————o————

"It's a poor sort of memory that only works backwards."

LEWIS CARROLL,
Alice Through the Looking-Glass

————o————

Memory is the diary that we all carry about with us.

OSCAR WILDE,
The Importance of Being Earnest

————o————

For he lives twice who can at once employ
The present well, and ev'n the past enjoy.

ALEXANDER POPE, *Imitation of Martial*

————o————

I have a room whereinto no one enters
 Save I myself alone:
There sits a blessed memory on a throne,
There my life centers.

CHRISTINA GEORGINA ROSSETTI,
Memory (II)

————o————

A Sunday School teacher had been teaching the Bible verse, "Draw nigh to God, and He will draw nigh to you" (James 4:8). By the time Charles got home he happily repeated his memory verse to Grandmother — his own version: "Draw a line unto me and I will draw a line unto you."

————o————

We commit the Golden Rule to memory and forget to commit it to life.

Mercy

A Tigress Saved By Mercy Gun

An angry tigress was saved from death by a "mercy gun" in Templar Park, near Kuala Lumpur, Malaya.

She was caught in an illegal wild boar trap; and she struggled for hours to free herself.

All conventional attempts to shoot the tigress out of the trap failed in the thick underbrush.

Five barbiturate capsules fired from Malaya's only "mercy gun" by Game Warden G. C. Metcalfe finally put the beast to sleep and into a coma that lasted four days!

It is mercy, but it is not in the shape of a gun, which the Lord uses to release human beings from the traps of sin and unbelief in which they are securely held — and from which their own efforts cannot extricate them.

TOM OLSON in *Now*

————o————

For Those Who Love

Have mercy always on the ones who
 love you.
Deny yourself the sharp impatient
 word.
When they are over-anxious, over-kind,
 Your careless, hasty utterance is
 heard
Through all the lonely hollows of the
 heart
 That loves, and loving, yearns.

Refrain! Refrain
In mercy from self-will, for those who
 love
Are desperately vulnerable to pain.

AUTHOR UNKNOWN

————o————

Teach me to feel another's woe,
 To hide the fault I see;
That mercy I to others show,
 That mercy show to me.

ALEXANDER POPE, *The Universal Prayer*

————o————

Mercy's indeed the attribute of heaven.

THOMAS OTWAY

————o————

Being all fashioned of the self-same dust,
Let us be merciful as well as just.

HENRY WADSWORTH LONGFELLOW,
Tales of a Wayside Inn

Merit

True merit, like a river, the deeper it is, the less noise it makes.

GEORGE SAVILE, LORD HALIFAX

———o———

Speak little and well if you wish to be considered as possessing merit.

French Proverb

———o———

Real merit of any kind, cannot long be concealed; it will be discovered, and nothing can depreciate it but a man exhibiting it himself. It may not always be rewarded as it ought; but it will always be known.

LORD CHESTERFIELD

Methods

Someone told Billy Sunday that they didn't like his methods. He answered, "How do you do it?" "Well, I don't try to preach," was the answer. "Then," said Billy, "I like the way I do it better than the way you don't do it."

———o———

We are looking for better methods; God is looking for better men.

JAMES WHITCOMB BROUGHER

Mind

It is easy to give another a "piece of your mind," but when you are through, you have lost your peace of mind.

———o———

Making up your mind is like making a bed; it usually helps to have someone on the other side.

———o———

Training the mind and overlooking the emotions may give us only monstrous machines long on thinking and short on feeling.

———o———

Most of us carry our own stumbling block around with us. We camouflage it with a hat.

Healthways

Most people take better care of their automobiles than their brains — they seldom put cheap fuel in their cars.

ROSCOE BROWN FISHER

———o———

A great many so-called open minds should be closed for repairs.

———o———

There are times when we need an open mind and a closed mouth, but there is never a time when we need a closed mind and an open mouth.

———o———

When a fellow ain't got much mind it don't take him long to make it up.

WILL ROGERS

———o———

I cannot put any price on that which I now value most — a mind.

———o———

As a field, however fertile, cannot be fruitful without cultivation, neither can a mind without learning.

MARCUS TULLIUS CICERO

———o———

The mind is not a vessel to be stuffed; it is a vessel made to transmute something.

———o———

Do not measure God's mind by your own.

GEORGE MACDONALD

———o———

Content is wealth, the riches of the mind;
And happy he who can such riches find.

JOHN DRYDEN

———o———

"Thou wilt keep him in perfect peace, whose mind is stayed on Thee: because he trusteth in Thee" (Isaiah 26:3).

An 86-year-old woman who has been a Christian for 79 years has tacked up in her room these words:

These things I have tried:

1. Laughing at difficulties, and found them disappearing.
2. Attempting heavy responsibility, and found it growing lighter.

3. Facing a bad situation and found it clearing up.
4. Telling the truth and found it most rewarding.
5. Believing men honest, and found them living up to expectation.
6. Trusting God each day, and found Him surprising me with His bountiful goodness.
7. Keeping my mind stayed on Him, and experiencing perfect peace.

———o———

When your mind goes blank, turn off the sound.

———o———

If you wish to know the mind of a man, listen to his words.

Chinese Proverb

———o———

As land is improved by sowing it with various seeds, so is the mind by exercising it with different studies.

PLINY THE ELDER

———o———

Were I so tall to reach the pole,
Or grasp the ocean with my span,
I must be measured by my soul:
The mind's the standard of the man.

ISAAC WATTS, *Horae Lyricae*

———o———

Measure your mind's height by the shade it casts!

ROBERT BROWNING, *Paracelsus*

———o———

The diseases of the mind are more destructive than those of the body.

MARCUS TULLIUS CICERO

———o———

Great minds have purposes, others have wishes. Little minds are tanned and subdued by misfortune; but great minds rise above them.

WASHINGTON IRVING

———o———

Cultivation of the mind is as necessary as food to the body.

MARCUS TULLIUS CICERO

———o———

Nurture your mind with great thoughts.

BENJAMIN DISRAELI

Minister

Minister's Moment

Here it is . . .
Saturday night.
Wonder what everyone's doing?

Me?
I'm waiting for another
wedding party to arrive.
Sermon's all done . . .
(Been working on it all week)
Bulletin is printed.
(Secretary has worked too).

I'm trying to relax a little . . .
store up my strength . . .
physical and spiritual for tomorrow.
Wonder how many will come to church?

A terrible responsibility . . .
(trying to speak of God)
Sometimes on Saturday night
I want to run.

But I pray . . .
and sweat a little too
(or is perspire nicer?)
thinking about Sunday.

What about you?
Do you ever think about Sunday?

ART MORGAN

———o———

The new Methodist minister was introducing his small son to a welcoming layman. "And this is my son John."
"Well," said the layman, "are you John the Baptist?"
"Oh, no," said the boy. "I'm John the Med'odist."

MRS. DAVID LETWAS in *Together*

———o———

Church member talking about her minister: "Six days of the week he's invisible and on the seventh he's incomprehensible."

News, Charlotte, North Carolina

———o———

The ministry of the Gospel is the poorest of trades and the noblest of callings.

THEODORE LEDYARD CUYLER

The world looks at ministers out of the pulpit to know what they mean in it.

RICHARD CECIL

———o———

A Methodist minister was found to have diabetes and while under treatment acted as hospital chaplain. His popularity in that post led to his retirement from the church, which made him a pastor emeritus. He was then hired by the hospital.

A woman in his former church, misunderstanding his honorary status, spread the word: "Poor Mr. Johnson — first he had diabetes, and now he has emeritus."

VIDA HOWARD in *Together*

———o———

We heard of a church service so solemn that a little girl whispered to her mother, "Does the minister live here or does he come down from Heaven every Sunday?"

———o———

Two ministers, given to arguing about their respective faiths, were in a very heated discussion. "That's all right," said one, calmly. "We'll just agree to disagree. After all, we're both doing the Lord's work — you in your way and I in His."

———o———

I would have every minister of the Gospel address his audience with the zeal of a friend, with the generous energy of a father, and with the exuberant affection of a mother.

FRANÇOIS DE SALIGNAC DE LA FÉNELON

———o———

A minister was called by the tax collector about a $500.00 church donation claimed by a parishioner.

"Did he give that amount?" asked the tax gatherer. The minister hesitated, then replied:

"No — but he will!"

MAXINE BARTLETT in *Together*

Miracles

The man for whom a miracle has been done never recognizes it as a miracle.

Miracles

The age of miracles is past,
    I hear the skeptic say;
How little does he understand
    Christ's miracles today.
His great and marv'lous works go on.
    How do I know, my friend?
He wrought His miracles in me,
    His wonders never end.

Did Jesus make the blind to see?
    My sight He has restored.
He caused the dumb to speak, you say?
    My lips now praise the Lord.
He also made the deaf to hear?
    But my ears too were sealed,
I could not hear His gentle voice
    'Til by His love He healed.

He passed through crowds and was
        not seen?
    Each day He walks with me
Through busy streets and thoroughfares
    And none but I can see.
He healed all manner of disease?
    With them I had my part;
He cured my sin-sick soul, you see,
    And healed my broken heart.

Did Peter walk upon the sea?
    When I'm cast down with care
He takes my hand — my spirit soars —
    And O, I walk on air.
No miracles today, you say?
    How wrong you are, my friend,
For what the Lord has done for me
    All human works transcend.

Yes — these are miracles to me —
    All blessings from above.
But, O, the greatest one of all —
    The wonder of His love.

LENA TRAAS

———o———

To have faith is to create; to have hope is to call down blessing; to have love is to work miracles.

———o———

Jesus was Himself the one convincing and permanent miracle.

IAN MACLAREN

———o———

Miracle Of Miracles!

My face is lined with living,
    My hair is touched with snow.

My hands are gnarled with giving,
My feet are aged and slow.
The years are creeping on me
As night descends on day,
Silently, like the shadows
That steal the light away.
But when each night I kneel in faith
At Jesus' feet to pray,
It's wonderful how young I feel,
How peaceful and how gay!
My timid troubles disappear
Before His throne, and then,
O miracle of miracles!
I am a child again!

JESSIE CANNO ELDRIDGE

Misery

The comfort derived from the misery of others is slight.

MARCUS TULLIUS CICERO

———o———

There is no time so miserable but that a man may be true to himself.

———o———

Misery still delights to trace
Its semblance in another's vase.

WILLIAM COWPER

Missions, Missionary

First Missionaries

Was this the One the world had waited for?
Some thought He was. The woman at the well,
Astonished at the truth He dared to tell
Shared her conviction door to village door.
Was this the One? Mary and Martha swore
Not only by the awe He could compel
Or by the act of death that He could quell,
This was the Lord the people could adore.
But was He Saviour and the Son of God,
This carpenter of Nazareth, a man
So young to be so gently wise? Because

His touch held healing though He used no rod.
Was this Messiah sought since time began?
They changed our world who first believed He was.

DONNA DICKEY GUYER
in *Church Management*

———o———

Every heart with Christ is a missionary and every heart without Christ is a mission field.

DICK HILLIS

———o———

A colporteur missionary told the Christmas story to a group of people in a village in North India. Then he read the story from the Scriptures. "How long ago was this great day when God's Son was born?" one person asked. "About two thousand years ago," replied the missionary. "Then why has the news been so long in reaching us?" asked the villager in surprise. "Who has been hiding the Book all this time?"

CHARLES R. WOODSON

———o———

A missionary fell into the hands of cannibals.
"Going to eat me, I presume?" asked the missionary. The chief grunted.
"Don't do it," he advised, "you won't like me." Thereupon the missionary took out a knife, sliced a piece from the calf of his leg and handed it to him. "Try this and see for yourself."
The chief took one bite and choked.
The missionary worked on the island for fifty years. He had a cork leg.

———o———

You cannot spell gospel without spelling GO.

———o———

The High Cost Of Missions

In 1839, John Williams, dubbed "The Apostle of the South Seas," and a missionary named Harris, sailed to the New Hebrides Islands and were clubbed to death by savages after a period of service for Christ.
Eighteen years later, G. N. Gordon and his wife took up the work on these islands and were killed in 1861.

Mr. Gordon's brother went to the same place and was killed in 1872.

A couple of missionaries named Turner and Nisbet later disembarked on the island of Tanna, stayed seven months, then fled for their lives by night in an open boat.

John G. Paton also heard the call of God to the New Hebrides. When he confided to a friend these plans, he was warned: "You will be eaten by cannibals!"

Paton replied, "Mr. Dickson, you are old . . . soon you will be put into the grave and eaten by worms. But if I can live and die serving the Lord Jesus Christ, it doesn't make any difference to me whether I'm eaten by cannibals or worms."

So Paton shoved off on his dangerous but God-appointed mission.

He learned the language, won for Christ many brute savages and held his first communion service in 1869 with twelve Christian natives partaking.

"I shall never taste a deeper bliss," he said, "until I gaze in the glorified face of Jesus Himself!"

Paton lived to see 16,000 South Sea islanders sing of God's love. And on the plains where savages once killed and ate each other, now stand Christian churches, schools and printing presses.

His life work behind him, John G. Paton is today enjoying his "deeper bliss" — gazing upon the glorified face of Him he served so well.

——o——

If I had a thousand lives to live, Africa should have them all.

BISHOP MACKENZIE

——o——

That land is henceforth my country which most needs the Gospel.

NIKOLAUS LUDWIG VON ZINZENDORF

——o——

A little girl just entering school said that she was from a missionary family.

"What is it like being a missionary?" the teacher asked.

"A barrel," the child replied.

It was a Jew who brought the Gospel to Rome, a Roman who took it to France, a Frenchman who took it to Scandinavia, a Scandinavian who took it to Scotland, a Scotsman who evangelized Ireland, and an Irishman who, in turn, made the missionary conquest of Scotland.

No country ever originally received the Gospel except at the hands of an alien.

Survey Bulletin

——o——

Your love has a broken wing if it cannot fly across the sea.

MALTBIE D. BABCOCK

——o——

You cannot do effective missionary work today without miracles.

ROBERT MCALISTER

——o——

A missionary is a person who never gets used to the thud of Christless feet on the way to eternity.

——o——

God had only one Son — and He was a missionary.

DAVID LIVINGSTONE

——o——

Unprayed for I feel like a diver at the bottom of a river with no connecting airline to the surface, or like a fireman wielding an empty hose on a burning building. With prayer I feel like David facing Goliath.

JAMES GILMOUR, Missionary to Mongolia

——o——

A one-legged school teacher from Scotland came to Hudson Taylor to offer himself for service in China.

"Why do you, with only one leg, think of going as a missionary?" asked Taylor.

"I do not see those with two legs going, so I must," replied George Stott.

He was accepted.

The Christian Beacon

——o——

The Voice Of One Who Wept

Today I heard the voice of one who wept in far-off lands,

Because of sin and misery, and begged
  with outstretched hands
For one small lamp to light his dark.
  Now fain I would have slept,
So stopped my ears, but in my heart
  that sobbing voice still wept.

And then I heard the voice of One who
  counted not the cost,
But left His ivory palaces to seek and
  save the lost.
He said, "The sound of one who weeps
  is coming up to Me.
Dost thou forget that last command
  which I gave unto thee,

"To preach My Word to all the world?"
  . . . O bitter be our shame!
Still hopeless millions walk the earth
  who never heard His name,
And still the world spends lavishly in
  every crowded mart,
And still the voice of Him who wept
  is sobbing in my heart!

MARTHA SNELL NICHOLSON

———o———

Missions is taking the whole gospel
to the whole world by the whole
church.

———o———

I do not know that I shall live to see
a single convert, but I would not leave
my present field of labor to be made
king of the greatest empire on the
globe.

ADONIRAM JUDSON

———o———

Many of us will never reach the
mission field on our feet, but we can
reach them on our knees.

———o———

The only generation that can reach
this generation is our generation.

OSWALD SMITH

———o———

The funds of missionary societies depend not so much on the condition of
men's purses as on the state of their
soul. Unless a man cultivates a habit
of systematic giving when he had not
much to give, he will give little when
he is rich.

SAMUEL CHADWICK

Foreign missions are not an extra;
they are the acid test of whether or
not the Church believes the Gospel.

LESSLIE NEWBIGIN

———o———

In foreign missions, plant a tree;
don't import fruit.

LESTER SUMRALL

———o———

If God wants you on the mission
field, neither your money nor your
prayers will ever prove an acceptable
substitute.

———o———

When James Calvert went out as a
missionary to the cannibals of the Fiji
Islands, the captain of the ship sought
to turn him back. "You will lose your
life and the lives of those with you if
you go among such savages," he cried.
Calvert only replied, "We died before
we came here."

DAVID AUGSBURGER

———o———

Do we still want missionaries? Yes,
but we want missionaries who are God-
intoxicated men.

BISHOP ODUTOLA of Nigeria

———o———

A Missionary's Plea

Please pray for me, my friend — I need
  your prayers
    For there are burdens pressing hard
    and many cares.
Pray, too, that Christ will make of me
    The missionary that I ought to be.

Do pray for me, my friend, at morning
  hour
    That I may not be overcome by
    Satan's power.
That mid the whirl and maze of things
    My soul may drink of hidden springs.

And pray for me, my friend, when
  night comes on alone,
    God's stars look down upon us both,
    apart.
Will you, dear friend, before you sleep,
    Pray Him my soul with yours to
    keep?

Cease not to pray for me — tho' sun-
  dered far,

Come, meet me at the mercy seat
from where you are;
Nor time nor distance can divide
Our hearts that in His love abide.

AUTHOR UNKNOWN

———o———

Sophie had been praying for twelve years to become a foreign missionary. One day she had so prayed and the heavenly Father seemed to say:

"Sophie, stop! Where were you born?" "In Holland, Father." "Where are you now?" "In America, Father." "Well, are you not a foreign missionary already?"

Then the Father said, "Who lives on the floor above you?" "A family of Swedes." "And who above them?" "Why, some French." "And who in the rear?" "Some Italians." "And a block away?" "Some Chinese."

"And you have never said a word to these people about My Son? Do you think I will send you thousands of miles to the foreigner and the heathen when you never care enough about those at your own door to speak to them about their souls?"

———o———

The Spirit of Christ is the spirit of missions, and the nearer we get to Him the more intensely missionary we must become.

HENRY MARTYN

———o———

My son, if God has called you to be a missionary, your Father in Heaven would grieve to see you shrivel down into a king.

CHARLES HADDON SPURGEON

———o———

Where Shall I Work?

"Master, where shall I work today?"
And my love flowed warm and free.
Then He pointed out a tiny plot,
And He said, "Work there for me."
But I answered quickly: "Oh, no, not there,
Not anyone could see,
No matter how well my task is done —
Not that small place for me!"
And His voice, when He spoke, it was so stern,

But He answered me tenderly:
"Disciple, search that heart of thine.
Are you working for them, or for Me?
Nazareth was just a little place,
And so was Galilee."

AUTHOR UNKNOWN

Mistakes

We recently heard about an editor who explained away the mistakes that crept into his publication with the following notice: "If you find any mistakes, please consider that they appear for the benefit of those readers who always look for them. We try to print something for everybody."

———o———

A story is told of the great Biblical scholar, Bengel, as he lay on his deathbed. One of his friends quoted, or rather misquoted, a well-known verse of Scripture, adding the word "in" where it did not belong: "I know in whom I have believed."

"No, no," said the dying believer, "do not allow even a preposition to come between my Savior and me: I know whom I have believed!"

Gospel Witness

———o———

Among the floral displays received by a new store on the occasion of its opening was one that bore a card reading, "Deepest Sympathy."

The manager immediately telephoned the florist.

"But," the disturbed florist replied, "what about the other party who received the card intended for you? It read: 'Congratulations on your new location'."

———o———

Admitting Mistakes

How often when we blunder, and are filled with guilty shame,
Do we invent excuses, and attempt to shift the blame!
But when we make mistakes, I find it's sensible and wise
To honestly admit them, and omit the alibis.

MARY HAMLETT GOODMAN

Nature DOES make mistakes. Sometimes she puts all the bones in the head and none in the back.

———o———

Nothing is opened by mistake as often as the mouth.

———o———

There is nothing final about a mistake, except its being taken as final.

PHYLLIS BOTTOME

———o———

I have made mistakes, but I have never made the mistake of saying that I never made one.

JAMES GORDON BENNETT

———o———

The quickest way to get a lot of undivided attention is to make a mistake.

Modern Life

Old-timers: Those who can remember when people were just people, instead of a bunch of numbers — Social Security, Zip Code, Area Code. . . .

———o———

Little Willie was in a store with his mother when he was given candy by one of the clerks.

"What must you say, Willie?"

"Charge it," he replied.

———o———

The materialistic age in which we live has blinded the eyes of many who fail to see that only what we do for, and through Christ, will live forever.

———o———

In this modern electric era, all a woman has to do to run her home is to keep on plugging.

Modesty

Modesty is the citadel of beauty and virtue.

DEMADES

———o———

Modesty is becoming to the great. What is difficult is to be modest when one is a nobody.

The Journal of Jules Renard

Modesty is a wonderful thing; it doesn't cost a cent and makes you look like a million.

———o———

Modesty: The gentle art of enhancing your charm by pretending not to be aware of it.

OLIVER HERFORD

Money

A dime is a dollar with the taxes taken out.

———o———

Why?

Why should we give money to save the heathen abroad when there are heathen in our own country?

Why should I give money to save those in other parts of the country when there are needy ones in my own town?

Why should I give to the poor of the town when my own church needs the money?

Why should I give to the church when my own family wants it?

Why should I give to my family what I want myself?

Why? Because I am a Christian; not a heathen.

A. P. UPHAM

———o———

One reason men's faces are put on money is that women are satisfied just to get their hands on it.

———o———

In presenting to his congregation the findings of the finance committee and explaining the need for more contributions, the minister sought to praise the laymen who have the best interests of the church at heart.

"You know," he said, "the preacher is the shepherd of his flock, and the finance committee acts as his crook."

MRS. ROBERT MOULTON in *Together*

———o———

He was not an outstanding Christian, as such. But he was very faithful. He seldom missed a service. Quietly he came and went each week, doing willingly whatever he could to help. Yes, there was something strange about him.

Each payday he made a special trip to the church office with his tithe from his modest income. One day the church secretary asked him why he made this special trip. Why not wait until Sunday? His answer: "I have a bad heart, and I don't want God's money in my pocket when I go."

————o————

It is good to check up once in a while, and make sure you have not lost the things that money cannot buy.

GEORGE HORACE LORIMER

————o————

Gold will be slave or master.

HORACE

————o————

A man's treatment of money is the most decisive test of his character, how he makes it and how he spends it.

JAMES MOFFATT

————o————

The poorest of all men is the one who has nothing but money.

————o————

The money you intend to save draws no interest.

————o————

A purse is doubly empty when it is full of borrowed money.

————o————

One day a certain old, rich man of a miserable disposition visited a rabbi, who took the rich man by the hand and led him to a window.

"Look out there," he said.

The rich man looked into the street.

"What do you see?" asked the rabbi.

"I see men, women, and children," answered the rich man.

Again the rabbi took him by the hand and this time led him to a mirror. "Now what do you see?"

"Now I see myself," the rich man replied.

Then the rabbi said, "Behold, in the window there is glass, and in the mirror there is glass. But the glass of the mirror is covered with a little silver, and no sooner is the silver added than you cease to see others, but you see only yourself."

Moody Monthly

The kindergarten teacher was trying to teach her class to count money.

Placing a half dollar on her desk, she asked, "What is that?"

Said a small voice from the back row, "Tails."

————o————

Money is a form of power so intimately related to the possessor that one cannot consistently give money without giving self, nor can one give self without giving money. When a man gives money to a cause, he inevitably gives a part of himself, for his money is definitely a measure of his toil and talent. He supports with his money what he really values. Look at a man's budget, and you can quickly tell what matters most to him.

HENRY B. TRIMBLE

————o————

Earning maketh an industrious man; spending, a well-furnished man; saving, a prepared man; giving, a blessed man.

The Pentecostal Holiness Advocate

————o————

You will never win the world for Christ with your spare cash.

————o————

Money is like dynamite. It will destroy its possessor, according to the way it's handled.

————o————

Inflation is like putting on weight. It's easier to start than stop.

————o————

A budget is something that allows you to live within your means and without almost everything else.

————o————

One of the first things children learn at school is that other children get allowances.

Empire-Courier, Craig, Colorado

————o————

Often all it takes to start down the path to bankruptcy is a small raise in pay.

Having "money to burn" is a good way to start a fire which you can't put out.

————o————

Take care of your dollars and you will show more cents than your friends give you credit for.

————o————

Money never was made a fool of anybody; it only shows 'em up.

FRANK MCKINNEY HUBBARD

————o————

You can't take your money to heaven but you can send it on ahead.

Monument

The best monument is one with two legs going about the world witnessing for the Lord Jesus Christ to others.

DWIGHT L. MOODY

————o————

Those only deserve a monument who do not need one; that is, who have raised themselves a monument in the minds and memories of men.

WILLIAM HAZLITT

————o————

Who builds a church to God, and not to fame,
Will never mark the marble with his name.

ALEXANDER POPE, *Moral Essays, Epistle III*

Mother

Her Day

She cooked the breakfast first of all,
    Washed the cups and plates,
Dressed the children and made sure
    Stockings all were mates.
Combed their heads and made their
    beds,
    Sent them out to play.
Gathered up their motley toys,
    Put some books away.
Dusted chairs and mopped the stairs,
    Ironed an hour or two,
Baked a jar of cookies and a pie,
    Then made a stew.
The telephone rang constantly,
    The doorbell did the same,

A youngster fell and stubbed his toe,
    And then the laundry came.
She picked up blocks and mended
    socks
And then she polished up the stove.
(Gypsy folks were fortunate with
    carefree ways to rove!)
And when her husband came at six
He said: "I envy you!
It must be nice to sit at home
Without a thing to do!"

AUTHOR UNKNOWN

————o————

Mother's Love

Her love is like an island in life's ocean,
    vast and wide,
A peaceful, quiet shelter from the
    wind, and rain, and tide.

'Tis bound on the north by Hope, by
    Patience on the west,
By tender Counsel on the south,
    and on the east by Rest.

Above it like a beacon light shine Faith,
    and Truth, and Prayer;
And through the changing scenes of
    life,
    I find a haven there.

AUTHOR UNKNOWN

————o————

Mother's Hands

What can be said of mother's hands
    can also not be said,
For who can count the vast drudgeries
    performed each day —
And who can surmise if drudgeries
    are really joys, because it is their
    pride . . .
And they also minister kindness.

LINDA CLARKE

————o————

Some mothers love their children selfishly: Their children exist for them.

Other mothers love their children slavishly: They exist for their children.

But some mothers love their children sacrificially: Their children and they exist for God.

JAMES SPRUNT

————o————

Maternal love: a miraculous substance which God multiplies as He divides it.

VICTOR HUGO

A Mother's Prayer

Lord, give me patience when wee
hands
Tug at me with their small demands.
Give me gentle and smiling eyes;
Keep my lips from hasty replies.
Let not weariness, confusion, or noise
Obscure my vision of life's fleeting joys.
So, when in years to come, my house
is still —
No bitter memories its rooms may fill.
Amen.

———o———

Sign on a supermarket bulletin:
"Help a poor unwed mother. Take one
of her kittens!"

———o———

Sign in a London maternity wear
shop: "Two can look as chic as one."

———o———

Some men were discussing the various versions of the Bible. After they
were finished giving the pros and cons
of each Bible, a man who had been
silent spoke up and said, "The best
version of the Bible is the one my
mother lived!"

———o———

One day a certain young mother was
running on endlessly about the shortcomings of her children. Finally she
paused long enough to ask, "What do
you want out of life, anyway?" One
child cautiously replied, "A quiet mother!"

The Christian Mother

———o———

A little boy, who was told by his
mother that it was God who made
people good, responded, "Yes, I know
it is God, but Mothers help a lot."

Christian Guardian

———o———

A godly mother will point her children to God by the force of her example as much as by the power of her
words.

———o———

You may have tangible wealth untold;
Caskets of jewels and coffins of gold,

Richer than I you can never be —
I had a mother who read to me.
STRICKLAND W. GILLILAN,
The Reading Mother

Motivation

Show me. Dare you. Prove it. If
those words won't start you going, nothing will.

———o———

Man considereth the deeds, but God
weigheth the intentions.

———o———

We only truly believe that which
activates us.

DICK HILLIS

———o———

Triumphant father to mother watching teen-age son mow lawn: "I told
him I lost the car keys in the grass."
DICK TURNER,
Newspaper Enterprise Association

Mottoes

A church in Kansas City has as its
slogan:
"Wake up, sing up, preach up, pray
up, but never give up, or let up, or
back up, or shut up until the cause of
Christ in this church and in the world
is built up."

The Roundtable

———o———

A Good Motto

Talk less,
Pray more,
Obey God.
Rush less,
Love more,
Prove God.

———o———

Walk softly; speak tenderly; pray
fervently.

T. J. BACH

———o———

If I falter — push me on.
If I stumble — pick me up.
If I retreat — shoot me.
Motto of the French Foreign Legion

Gentle in manner, strong in performance.

Motto of LORD NEWBOROUGH

Mouth

The mouth is the microphone of the heart.

ELEANOR L. DOAN

———o———

A lot of trouble in this world is caused by combining a narrow mind and wide mouth.

———o———

Mouth: The grocer's friend, the dentist's fortune, the orator's pride, and the fool's trap.

———o———

Nature did not make your ears so that they could be shut but did a perfect job on your mouth.

———o———

No man is so full of wisdom that he has to use his mouth as a safety valve.

Music

After teaching my second-graders "America the Beautiful," I listened while they sang it for me. And one voice rang out above the rest: "Oh, beautiful for space-ship skies . . ."

MARILYN KILBY in NEA Journal

———o———

The teacher played the "Star Spangled Banner" and asked her first-grade class to identify it. "That's easy," shouted a pupil. "It's what they play every Friday on television just before the fights."

———o———

Music, once admitted to the soul, becomes a sort of spirit, and never dies. It wanders perturbedly through the halls and galleries of the memory, and is often heard again, distinct and living, as when it first displaced the wavelets of the air.

EDWARD GEORGE BULWER-LYTTON

Sunday Nights

Some years ago within our small household
A simple formula my parents found
Whereby on Sunday nights, quite safe and sound,
We sang together — young as well as old.

The heat of Summer or king Winter cold
Lost their attractions when a jolly round
Or hymn or carol would indeed resound.
A choicer heritage all this than gold!

My mother, playing on the rare Rosewood
Was lovely in a flowing gown of blue:
And father, with his bass, was just the one
To harmonize the way a master should.

Such treasured nights I would bequeath to you
Who seek a sense of peace when day is done.

DORA FLICK FLOOD in The Churchman

———o———

Music should strike fire from the heart of man, and bring tears from the eyes of women.

LUDWIG VON BEETHOVEN

———o———

Music hath charms to soothe a savage breast,
To soften rocks, or bend a knotted oak.
I've read that things inanimate have moved,
And, as with living souls, have been informed
By magic numbers and persuasive sound.

WILLIAM CONGREVE, The Mourning Bride

———o———

Is there a heart that music cannot melt?
Alas! how is that rugged heart forlorn!

JAMES BEATTIE, The Minstrel

———o———

Music is nothing else but wild sounds civilized into time and tune.

THOMAS FULLER

Music is one of the fairest and most glorious gifts of God.

MARTIN LUTHER

———o———

Six-year-old Larry disagreed with his Sunday School teacher after the singing of the song, "The Light of the World Is Jesus."

"Jesus," Larry said, "is not the light of the world. The Sun and the Moon give the light."

———o———

Maybe the prayer hymn which was misprinted in the songbook wasn't too incongruous when, instead of "Land Me Safe On Canaan's Shore," it read, "Land My Safe On Canaan's Shore."

Mystery

Mystery Of Moods

Why are we whipped by our moods?
Why do we get the blues?
Why do we sigh and cry
Until we feel, "Oh, what's the use?"
Why after all this dejection,
Does our spirit soar like a breeze?
Why are we gay and blithesome and glad,
When a short while before,
We were lonely and sad?
Will somebody tell me . . . please?

BERNICE SMITH

———o———

A mystery is a fact every mind can see, but no one can explain. To reject an obvious fact because you cannot understand or explain it is childish.

———o———

One of the minor mysteries to many an angler is why fish decide to take their vacations at the same time the fisherman does.

N

Name

Many a man's name appears in the papers only three times: When he's too young to read, when he's too dazed to read, and when he's too dead to read.

———o———

Your Name

You got it from your father,
'Twas the best he had to give,
And right gladly bestowed it;
It is yours the while you live.
You may lose the watch he gave you
And another you may claim,
But remember, when you're tempted,
To be careful of his name.
It was fair the day you got it
And a worthy name to wear;
When he took it from his father
There was no dishonor there.

Through the years he proudly wore it,
To his father he was true,
And that name was clean and spotless
When he passed it on to you.

It is yours to wear forever,
Yours, perhaps, some distant morning,
To another boy to give,
And you'll smile as did your father
Smile above that baby there,
If a clean name and a good name
You are giving him to wear.

AUTHOR UNKNOWN

———o———

A census taker asked a woman how many children she had.

"Well," she began, "there's Billy, and Harry, and Martha, and —"

"Never mind the names," he interrupted, impatiently, "just give me the number."

The mother became indignant. "They haven't got numbers; they've all got names."

———o———

I know a life that is lost to God,
Bound down by the things of earth;
But I know a Name, a Name, a Name
That can bring that soul new birth.

AUTHOR UNKNOWN

I cannot love my lord, and not his name.

ALFRED, LORD TENNYSON

Narrow

Narrow-Minded

The preacher is sometimes accused of being narrow-minded because he insists upon the Christian's forsaking all to follow Christ.

But all of life is narrow, and success is to be found only by passing through the narrow gate and down the straight way.

There is no room for broad-mindedness in the chemical laboratory. Water is composed of two parts hydrogen and one part oxygen. The slightest deviation from that formula is forbidden.

There is no room for broad-mindedness in the mathematics classroom. Neither geometry, calculus, nor trigonometry allows any variation from exact accuracy, even for old times' sake. The solution of the problem is either right or it is wrong — no tolerance there.

There is no room for broad-mindedness in the garage. The mechanic there says that the piston rings must fit the cylinder walls within one-thousandth part of an inch. Even between friends there cannot be any variation if the motor is to run smoothly.

How, then, shall we expect that broad-mindedness shall rule in the realm of religion and morals?

The Log of the Good Ship Grace

Nature

Flowers are the poetry of earth, as stars are the poetry of heaven.

AUTHOR UNKNOWN

———o———

In a little church in the far south of Ireland, every window but one is of painted glass. Through that single exception may be seen a breathtaking view: a lake of deepest blue, studded with green islets, and backed by range after range of purple hills. Under the window is the inscription: "The heavens declare the glory of God, and the firmament showeth His handiwork."

ROBERT GIBBINGS

———o———

Invitation

Come and ride with me to the mountain side
Where the road leads up and the world is wide.

Come and bring your dreams that have gone astray,
You will find new ones on my tree-lined way.

Come and tour with me to the canyon's rim
And listen spellbound to nature's hymn.

Come and lift your eyes to the star-hushed night,
And release your soul for the wind's delight.

You will know at last that your heart is free
When you follow this path and ride with me.

AUTHOR UNKNOWN

———o———

He that follows nature is never out of his way. Nature is sometimes subdued, but seldom extinguished.

FRANCIS BACON

———o———

Nature gives to every time and season some beauties of its own; and from morning to night, as from the cradle to the grave, is but a succession of changes so gentle and easy that we can scarcely mark their progress.

CHARLES DICKENS

———o———

God's Gifts In Nature

We plow the fields and scatter
  The good seed on the land,
But it is fed and watered
  By God's almighty hand;
He sends the snow in winter,
The warmth to swell the grain,
The breezes and the sunshine,
  And soft refreshing rain.

He only is the Maker
  Of all things near and far;

He paints the wayside flower,
 He lights the evening star;
The winds and waves obey Him,
 By Him the birds are fed;
Much more to us, His children,
 He gives our daily bread.

We thank Thee, then, O Father,
 For all things bright and good,
The seed-time and the harvest,
 Our life, our health, our food.
Accept the gifts we offer
 For all Thy love imparts,
And, what Thou most desirest,
 Our humble, thankful hearts.

MATTHIAS CLAUDIUS

————o————

His eyes are dim who cannot see
A mountain's purple majesty.
His ears are deaf who cannot hear
Love songs of birds in spring of year.
His feet are numb who never seeks
A mountain breeze to cool his cheeks.
His soul is dead who gets no thrills
From rocks and woods and templed
 hills.
He who no wilderness has trod
Has missed a chance to walk with God.

————o————

Longing For The Mountains

There is a place where I long to be,
A place in the mountains high and
 free;

Away from the routine, procedures and
 strife,
Where one draws nearer to the beauties
 of life.

Where lonely streams plunge to depths
 below,
Churning from summits of sparkling
 snow;

Where the laurel, aspen and lofty pine
Remain untouched as in the beginning
 of time.

Where the eagle in his domain so ma-
 jestically fair,
Reels by the hour in the turbulent air.

Where at twilight is heard the voice
 of the thrush,
Which leaves me oblivious to the modern day rush.

CARMON F. BECKER

Climb the mountains and get their
 good tidings.
Nature's peace will flow into you as
 sunshine flows into trees.
The winds will blow their own fresh-
 ness into you,
And the storms their energy,
While cares will drop off like falling
 leaves.

JOHN MUIR

————o————

A group of scientists in Chicago
were conducting an experiment. They
placed a female moth of a rare species
in a room. Four miles away a male
moth of the same species was released.
Despite the din and smoke of the city,
the distance, and the fact that the
female was in a CLOSED room, in a
few hours the male moth was found
beating its wings against the window
of the room in which the female was
confined! Can you explain such a phe-
nomenon? It's a miracle – a miracle
of nature. God made it so!

The Log of the Good Ship Grace

————o————

There is a serene and settled majesty
to woodland scenery that enters into
the soul and delights and elevates it,
and fills it with noble inclinations.

WASHINGTON IRVING

————o————

If you wish your children to think
deep thoughts, to know the holiest emotions, take them to the woods and hills,
and give them the freedom of the
meadows; the hills purify those who
walk upon them.

RICHARD JEFFERIES

————o————

Walk with me a little mile down shimmering sunlit trails;
Listen with me a little while to nature's
 whispered tales.
If man could only understand the
 words that nature speaks,
He'd have the world at his command
 and find the truth he seeks.

DEL BARTON

————o————

I saw two clouds at morning
 Tinged by the rising sun,

And in the dawn they floated on,
And mingled into one.

JOHN GARDINER CALKINS BRAINARD,
Epithalamium

———o———

The Voice Of Nature

A thousand sounds, and each a joy-
ous sound;
The dragon-flies are humming as they
please,
The humming birds are humming all
around,
The clithra all alive with buzzing bees,
Each playful leaf its separate whisper
found,
As laughing winds went rustling
through the grove;
And I saw thousands of such sights as
these
And heard a thousand sounds of joy
and love.
And yet so dull I was, I did not know
That He was there who all this love
displayed,
Shared all my joy, was glad that I
was glad;
And all because I did not hear the
word
In English accents say, "It is the Lord."

AUTHOR UNKNOWN

———o———

I can enjoy society in a room; but
out-of-doors, nature is company enough
for me.

WILLIAM HAZLITT

Needs, Necessity

I Must Go Shopping

One of these days I must go shopping. I am completely out of SELF-
RESPECT. I want to exchange the
SELF-RIGHTEOUSNESS I picked up
the other day for some HUMILITY,
which they say is less expensive and
wears better.

I want to look at some TOLERANCE
which is being used for wraps this
season; and someone showed me some
pretty samples of PEACE; we are so
low on that and we can never have
too much of it.

By the way, I must try to match
some PATIENCE that my neighbor
wears. It is very becoming to her and
I think would look equally good on me.
I might try that garment of LONG-
SUFFERING that they are displaying.
I never thought I would want to wear
it. And I must not forget to have my
SENSE OF HUMOR mended, and
look for some inexpensive EVERYDAY
GOODNESS.

It is surprising how quickly one's
stock of goods is depleted. Yes, I must
go shopping soon.

PATRICIA MUELLER

———o———

A great necessity is a great opportunity.

HENRY PARRY LIDDON

———o———

The world's most basic needs can be
summed up in four words: bread,
brains, belief, and brotherhood.

J. WALLACE HAMILTON
in *Tarbell's Teacher's Guide*

———o———

Necessity never made a good bargain.

BENJAMIN FRANKLIN

———o———

Many are our wants; few are our
needs.

———o———

Someone Needs You

If you're feeling low and worthless,
There seems nothing you can do,
Just take courage and remember
There is someone needing you.

You were created for a purpose,
For a part in God's great Plan;
Bear ye one another's burdens,
So fulfill Christ's law to man.

Are you Father, Son or Daughter?
You've a work, none else can do.
Are you Husband, Wife or Mother?
There is someone needing you.

If perhaps in bed you're lying,
You can smile or press the hand
Of the one who tells his story.
He will know you understand.

There are many sad and lonely,
And discouraged, not a few,
Who a little cheer are needing,
And there's someone needing you.

Someone needs your faith and courage,
Someone needs your love and prayer,
Someone needs your inspiration,
Thus to help their cross to bear.

Do not think your work is ended,
There is much that you can do,
And as long as you're on earth,
There is someone needing you.

SUSIE B. MARR

Neighbor

Who Is My Neighbor?

Thy neighbor? It is he whom thou
Hast the power to aid and bless —
Whose aching heart or burning brow
Thy soothing hand may press.

Thy neighbor? 'Tis the fainting poor
Whose eye with want is dim —
Whom hunger sends from door to door.
Go thou and succor him.

Thy neighbor? 'Tis that weary man
Whose years are at their brim —
Bent low with sickness, care and pain.
Go thou and comfort him.

Thy neighbor? 'Tis the heart bereft
Of every earthly gem —
Widow and orphan, helpless left,
Go thou and shelter them.

When thou meetest a human form
Less favored than thine own,
Remember, He thy neighbor is —
Give bread instead of stone.

O, pass not, pass not heedless by,
Perhaps thou canst redeem
The breaking heart from misery;
Go — share thy lot with him.

AUTHOR UNKNOWN

———o———

There's an ideal height for a back-
yard fence: just high enough to keep
the dogs out but low enough to shake
hands over.

———o———

Neighbors are good when they are
neighborly.

News, Newspaper

Pupils at a Canadian grade school
were asked why their families chose
the newspaper read in their homes.
One young fellow gave the following
reason: "Mom says she likes our paper
because when folded in two it exactly
fits the bottom of the bird cage."

EDDIE OLYNUK in *Coronet*

———o———

In The News From The Headlines:

"Cemetery Site Is Approved By Body."
Manhattan, Kansas Mercury

"Ike Pledges Federal Aid in Lynching."
Harrisburg, Pennsylvania Patriot

"Beast Bites Bride, Harasses Trip."
Minot, North Dakota Daily News

"Writer Slaughter To Be At Fooley's."
Houston, Texas Post

———o———

A headline on the church page of a
California paper: "Church School
Women Want More Children."

———o———

On an October Sunday, an important eastern newspaper made the following listing in its radio schedule:
"1:00 — Back to God. (If no World
Series game.)"

This Week Magazine

———o———

Let the greatest part of the news
thou hearest be the least part of what
thou believest, lest the greater part of
what thou believest be the least part
of what is true. Where lies are easily
admitted the father of lies will not
easily be excluded.

FRANCIS QUARLES

———o———

The day the Rev. Smith took a turn
for the better after a long and serious
illness, the old church janitor decided
to give townspeople the good news.
They had been calling continuously to
ask about the minister. So on the bulletin board outside the church, the
janitor posted this announcement:
"God is good — Smith is better!"

GLORIA FOSTER in *Together*

New Year

A New Year's Wish

To be of greater service, Lord,
A closer student of Thy Word;
To help to bear a brother's load
And cheer him on the heavenly road;
To tell the lost of Jesus' love,
And how to reach the home above;
To trust in God whate'er befall,
Be ready at the Master's call
For any task that He may give;
And thus through all the year to live
For Him who gave Himself for me
And taught me that my life should be
A life unselfish, not self-willed,
But with the Holy Spirit filled.

Selected

New Year's Thoughts

What is a year? A group of days
That may be used in many ways.
A year may be a priceless boon —
Alas, that it is gone so soon!
And yet we need not feel forlorn,
For now another year is born.
Our days and years are wisely planned.
They lie within the Master's hand.
So, with glad hope and right good cheer,
We welcome this, another year.

RALPH H. DUMONT

A New Year Wish

What shall I wish thee this New Year?
Health, wealth, prosperity, good cheer,
All sunshine — not a cloud or tear?
  Nay! Only this:
That God may lead thee His own way,
That He may choose thy path each day,
That thou mayest feel Him near alway,
  For this is bliss!

AUTHOR UNKNOWN

A Prayer Upon A Threshold

Here on my threshold, eager to start
  Out through a New Year, Lord, I stand,
Waiting a moment, a prayer in my heart:

Go with me, Lord, and hold my hand.

There are such beautiful days ahead,
  Blinding my eyes, Lord, may there be
Springs by the wayside, manna for bread,
  And You, a companion, to walk with me.

Through any dark day, talk with me,
  I am a small child, often afraid;
Lead through the darkness, let me see
  Light ahead that Your lamp has made.

Here on the threshold, ready to start
  Out through a year, untrod, unknown —
Now with a small child's trusting heart
  I go, but I do not go alone.

GRACE NOLL CROWELL

The darkness hides the path ahead,
  The stones we cannot see;
So many struggle on life's road
  Complaining shamefully!
Fumbling, grumbling, stumbling on
  Waiting for the light to dawn!

The light has dawned, for Christ has said:
  "I am this dark world's Light."
Then why continue in the dark?
  Without Him it is night!

So, as another New Year dawns,
  May we walk close to Him;
The dazzling glory of His light
  Will make all else grow dim;
His beaming, gleaming, streaming Light
Will shine, and make the pathway bright!

AUTHOR UNKNOWN

Still upward be thine onward course;
  For this I pray today;
Still upward as the years go by
  And seasons pass away.
Still upward in this coming year,
  Thy path is all untried
Still upward may'st thou journey on,
  Close by Thy Savior's side.

AUTHOR UNKNOWN

I Am The New Year

I am what you dreamed to be — but did not dare.

I am what you hoped to do — but did not will.

I am the distant country of achievement which you saw afar but the path to which you have not found.

I am the fellowships you have been too busy to form.

I am the books which, in spite of plans, you didn't take time to read.

I am the habits of yesterday crystallizing into the character of tomorrow.

I am the decisions of the old year, coming back into your life to empower or to imperil those of the new.

I am the vigor of a new purpose, putting life into your half-formed ambitions.

I am the Eternal Will of God at work within you.

I am the NEW YEAR!

PERCY R. HAYWARD

———o———

Seven Blessings For The New Year

May the Lord's presence this coming year be:

ABOVE YOU — to guard. "Know therefore this day . . . that the Lord He is God in heaven above" (Deuteronomy 4:39).

UNDERNEATH — to support. "The eternal God is thy refuge and underneath are the everlasting arms" (Deuteronomy 33:27).

BEHIND — as a rereward. "The God of Israel will be your rereward" (Isaiah 52:12).

AT YOUR RIGHT HAND — to protect. "Because He is at my right hand I shall not be moved" (Psalm 16:8).

BEFORE — to lead. "I will go before thee and make the crooked places straight" (Isaiah 45:2).

ROUND ABOUT — to shield from storms. "As the mountains are round about Jerusalem so the Lord is round about His people from henceforth even forever" (Psalm 125:2).

WITHIN — as Companion and Comforter. "And I will put my Spirit within you" (Ezekiel 36:27). "I am crucified with Christ nevertheless I live; yet not I, but Christ liveth in me" (Galatians 2:20).

MRS. JONATHAN GOFORTH
in *The Sunday School Times*

———o———

Correct Thou, Lord, for me
What ringeth harsh to Thee,
That heart and life may sing
Thy perfect song
The New Year long.

Night

Good Night

Some things go to sleep in such a funny way;
Little birds stand on one leg and tuck their heads away;
Chickens do the same, standing on their perch;
Little mice lie soft and still as if they were in church;
Kittens curl up close in such a funny ball;
Horses hang their sleepy heads and stand still in the stall;
Sometimes dogs stretch out, or curl up in a heap;
Cows lie down upon their sides when they would go to sleep.
But little babies dear are snugly tucked in beds,
Warm with blankets, all so soft and pillows for their heads.
Birds and beast and babe — I wonder which of all
Dream the dearest dreams that down from dreamland fall.

Child Lore

———o———

Night is the time to weep,
To wet with unseen tears
Those graves of memory where sleep
The joys of other years.

JAMES MONTGOMERY

Noble, Nobility

Be noble! and the nobleness that lies
  In other men, sleeping, but never
    dead,
Will rise in majesty to meet thine
    own.

JAMES RUSSELL LOWELL

———o———

The beginning of true nobility comes
when a man ceases to be interested in
the judgment of men, and becomes interested in the judgment of God.

J. GRESHAM MACHEN

———o———

Better not to be at all than not be
noble.

ALFRED, LORD TENNYSON

Nothing

Since it is God's nature to make
something out of nothing, we must become nothing before He can make
something out of us.

MARTIN LUTHER

———o———

It's dangerous to try and be number
one because it's next to nothing.

———o———

Nothing can be obtained from nothing.

———o———

Nothing is cheap if you don't want
it.

Nothing is simpler than faith, and
nothing more sublime.

———o———

Man is as a circle whose circumfer-
ence has been erased.

Now

Life Is Too Short

To remember slights or insults.
To cherish grudges that rob me of
  happiness.
To waste time in doing things that are
  of no value.
To let past sins or mistakes cloud
  future happiness.
To miss making friends because I am
  too busy making money.
To give my youth to the devil and my
  old age to God.
To dream of tomorrow when I may
  never have one.
To put off making a confession of
  Christ now.

CHARLES M. SHELDON

———o———

The only period of time you can
ever act upon is right now.

PAUL PARKER

———o———

"Now" is the watchword of the wise.

CHARLES HADDON SPURGEON

O

Obedience, Obey

Throughout the Bible . . . when God
asked a man to do something, methods,
means, materials and specific directions were always provided. The man
had one thing to do: obey.

ELISABETH ELLIOT

———o———

Obedience

I said, "Let me walk in the fields."
He said, "No, walk in the town."

I said, "There are no flowers there."
He said, "No flowers, but a crown."

I said, "But the skies are black;
"There is nothing but noise and din."

And He wept as He sent me back.
"There is more," He said; "there is
  sin."

I said, "But the air is thick,
  And fogs are veiling the sun."

He answered: "Yet souls are sick,
  "And souls in the dark undone."

I said, "I shall miss the light
"And friends will miss me, they say."

He answered: "Choose ye tonight
"If I am to miss you, or they."

I pleaded for time to be given.
He said, "Is it hard to decide?"

"It will not seem hard in heaven
"To have followed the steps of your
   Guide."

I cast one look at the fields,
Then set my face to the town;

He said, "My child, do you yield?
Will you leave the flowers for the
   crown?"

Then into His hand went mine,
And into my heart came He;

And I walk in a light divine
The path I had feared to see.
                              GEORGE MACDONALD

——o——

The child who obeys without question is probably too young to talk.
                              JEANNE OPALACH

——o——

Have you learned that being obedient is better than being obstreperous?

——o——

In John 15, the secret of abounding
is abiding, the secret of abiding is obeying, and the secret of obeying is aban-
donment to Christ.
                              WILLIAM MIEROP

——o——

Cheerful obedience is the only kind
worth practicing.

——o——

The man who would lift others must
be uplifted himself, and he who would
command others must learn to obey.
                              CHARLES K. OBER

——o——

Where the need is greatest let us be
found gladly obeying the Master's command.
                              J. HUDSON TAYLOR

——o——

I believe that we get an answer to
our prayers when we are willing to
obey what is implicit in that answer.
I believe that we get a vision of God
when we are willing to accept what
that vision does to us.
                              ELSIE CHAMBERLAIN

——o——

The Breath Of God

May I in will and deed and word
   Obey Thee as a little child;
And keep me in Thy love, my Lord,
   For ever holy, undefiled;
Within me teach, and strive, and pray,
Lest I should choose my own wild way.

My spirit turns to Thee and clings,
   All else forsaking, unto Thee;
Forgetting all created things,
   Remembering only "God in me."
O living Stream; O gracious rain,
None wait for Thee, and wait in vain.
                              GERHARDT TER STEEGEN

——o——

"Mommy," said little Phil, "Tommy
never will learn to swim 'cause his
mommy won't let him go near the
water."
"Yes? He is a good little boy to listen
to his mother."
"Unhuh," agreed Phil, thoughtfully,
"and he'll go straight to Heaven the
first time he falls in."
                              TED DOUGLAS

——o——

A policeman noticed a boy with a
lot of stuff packed on his back riding a
tricycle around and around the block.
Finally he asked him where he was
going.
"I'm running away from home," the
boy said.
The policeman then asked him,
"Why do you keep going around and
around the block?"
The boy answered, "My mother won't
let me cross the street."
                              Teach

——o——

Tom: "Did you know that Lot's wife
turned into a pillar of salt because she
did not obey God?"
Charles: "That's nothing. My mother
turned into a telephone pole because
she didn't obey the traffic signal."

Obedience should be a child's first lesson.

BENJAMIN FRANKLIN

Obstacles

Obstacles are those frightful things you see when you take your eyes off the goal.

———o———

The block of granite which was an obstacle in the path of the weak, becomes a stepping-stone in the path of the strong.

THOMAS CARLYLE

———o———

The barriers of life may be ranked among its greatest benedictions.

FREDERICK B. MEYER

Offering

In a little parish church in Scotland one Sunday, so the story goes, a parishioner was horrified to discover that he had accidentally dropped a sovereign into the usher's basket, instead of the shilling he had intended.

After the service he went up to the head usher and, explaining, tried to get his money back. "Not on your life!" was the head usher's firm reply. "Money paid to the Lord is not returnable."

"Well," said the man, after reflection, "at least I'll get a sovereign's worth o' credit in heaven."

"That you weel not," announced the elder. "You'll get the shilling's worth you meant to drap in. The balance be just velvet for the Lord."

Onward, Canada, quoted in *The Liguorian*

———o———

If it weren't for parking meters and the church collection plates, the government could do away with nickels.

———o———

He dropped a quarter in the plate,
Then meekly raised his eyes;
Glad that his weekly rent was paid
To mansions in the skies.

———o———

There are many signs along the highways saying, "Keep the state green." It's a good idea to keep the offering the same way.

ELEANOR L. DOAN

———o———

When we place our offering in the plate, we are not really giving to God; we are simply taking our hands off of what belongs to Him.

———o———

A lady arriving at a church concert found two men at the door selling tickets.

"Oh," she said, "you're selling tickets! Why, I thought you were going to take up a collection, so I didn't bring any money along."

———o———

Does your religion stand up under the collection plate test?

———o———

A poor blind woman in Paris put twenty-seven francs into a plate at a missionary meeting. "You cannot afford so much," said one. "Yes, sir, I can," she answered.

On being pressed to explain, she said, "I am blind, and I said to my fellow straw-workers, 'How much money do you spend in a year for oil for your lamps when it is too dark to work nights?' They replied, 'Twenty-seven francs.'

"So," said the poor woman, "I found that I have so much in the year because I am blind and do not need a lamp, and I give it to shed light to the dark heathen lands."

Christian Endeavor World

Opinion

If you insist on sticking to your guns in any situation, be sure they are loaded.

———o———

"How well you and your wife get on," a friend remarked to a man whose marriage was very happy. "Don't you ever have differences of opinion?"

"Oh, yes," was the reply, "very often."

"You must get over them quickly."

"Ah, that's the secret," said the husband. "I never tell her about them."

Another person's good opinion of you is something to live up to, not to lean on.

———o———

One of the hardest secrets for a man to keep is his opinion of himself.

———o———

Public opinion in this country is everything.

ABRAHAM LINCOLN

———o———

Some men haven't any opinions but yours until they meet the next fellow.

Opportunity

Next to knowing when to seize an opportunity, the most important thing in life is to know when to forego an advantage.

BENJAMIN DISRAELI

———o———

Believe it or not, opportunity will look for you if you're worth finding.

———o———

No opportunity is ever lost — someone else picks up the ones you miss.

———o———

Why doesn't opportunity kick down the door instead of just knocking? Temptation does.

———o———

When opportunity knocks at the door some people are out in the yard looking for four-leaf clovers.

———o———

It's Up To Me

I get discouraged now and then
When there are clouds of gray,
Until I think about the things
That happened yesterday.
I do not mean the day before,
Or those of months ago.
But all the yesterdays in which
I had the chance to grow.
I think of opportunities
That I allowed to die
And those I took advantage of
Before they passed me by.

And I remember that the past
Presented quite a plight.
But somehow I endured it and
The future seemed all right.
And I remind myself that I
Am capable and free,
And my success and happiness
Are really up to me.

JAMES J. METCALFE

———o———

To see each morning a world made anew, as if it were the morning of the very first day; to treasure and use it, as if it were the final hour of the very last day.

FAY HARTZELL ARNOLD

———o———

Opportunity never comes — it's here.

———o———

God, teach us to take advantage of the opportunities offered us — not the people offering them.

———o———

The door of opportunity is so wide open that it's off its hinges.

ERNIE REB

———o———

Opportunities correspond with almost mathematical accuracy to the ability to use them.

———o———

An opportunist is a person who, finding himself in hot water, decides he needs a bath anyway.

———o———

When opportunity does knock,
By some uncanny quirk
It often goes unrecognized —
It so resembles work!

———o———

There are two kinds of opportunities, according to an old Japanese saying: those we chance upon and those we create. Either kind may represent the opportunity of a lifetime to any one individual but we are far more likely to recognize and take advantage of those we create.

With every rising of the sun
Think of your life as just begun.

AUTHOR UNKNOWN

———o———

A minister in a town is used to having his tiny daughter hustle up from Sunday School to help him shake hands with the congregation on the way out of church. He was a bit taken aback one Sunday, however, to notice that his eldest son had also joined the line and was busily collecting from customers on his paper route whom he had missed the day before on his regular rounds.

Maclean's Magazine

———o———

Opportunities are seldom labeled.

JOHN SHEDD

———o———

Opportunity often reveals great men in small places and small men in great places.

———o———

The hour of opportunity lies near the hours of prayer.

Opposite

Selfishness and service are at opposite poles. It is impossible to be characterized by both at the same time.

CAROL S. GISH

———o———

Our antagonist is our helper.

EDMOND BURKE,
Reflections on the Revolution in France

Optimism, Optimist

An optimist is one who thinks the good old days are yet to come!

———o———

An optimist is wrong as often as a pessimist, but he has a lot more fun.

———o———

The optimist proclaims that we live in the best of all possible worlds; and the pessimist fears this is true.

JAMES BRANCH CABELL, *The Silver Stallion*

———o———

Optimist: Happychondriac.

An optimist is a woman who starts hunting for her shoes when the guest speaker says "in conclusion . . ."

———o———

It would be interesting to know what an optimist and a pessimist see when both look into the same mirror at the same time.

———o———

Write in your heart that every day is the best day in the year.

RALPH WALDO EMERSON

———o———

Optimism is the content of small men in high places.

F. SCOTT FITZGERALD

———o———

An optimist laughs to forget, and a pessimist forgets to laugh.

———o———

The photographer had just taken a picture of an old man on his ninety-eighth birthday. He thanked the old gentleman, saying, "I hope I'll be around to take your picture when you're one hundred."

The old man replied: "Why not? You look healthy to me."

———o———

An optimist is a fisherman who brings along his camera.

———o———

Optimist: A man who can turn his car over to a parking lot attendant without looking back.

———o———

Optimist: A father who will let his son take the new car on a date.
Pessimist: One who won't.
Cynic: One who did.

———o———

An optimist is a bald-headed man who thinks his condition is only temporary.

———o———

No man ever impaired his eyesight by looking on the bright side of things!

The optimist says his glass is half full. The pessimist says his is half empty.

———o———

Optimism is one of the chief members of the faith family.

Organize

An organizer is the person who is the center of confusion.

———o———

Ninety percent of failure is due to lack of organization.

HENRIETTA C. MEARS

———o———

Well-arranged time is a mark of a well-arranged mind.

———o———

After forming a club, girls in my third-grade class gave me a list of their officers: the usual President, Vice-President, Roll Caller, Treasurer. But I was intrigued by the last officer listed — Decider!

ETHEL M. ANDERSON in *Reader's Digest*

Original, Originality

Originality is the act of forgetting where you read it.

———o———

If you want to be original, be yourself. God never made two people exactly alike.

Others

Plea For Others

You cannot pray the Lord's Prayer
  And even once say "I."
You cannot pray the Lord's Prayer
  And even once say "my."
Nor can you say the Lord's Prayer
  And not pray for another.
For when you ask for daily bread
  You must include your brother.
For others are included
  In each and every plea;
From the beginning to the end of it,
  It does not once say "me."

AUTHOR UNKNOWN

If a man be gracious and courteous to strangers, it shows he is a citizen of the world, and that his heart is no island cut off from other lands, but a continent that joins to them. If he be compassionate toward the afflictions of others, it shows that his heart is like the noble [myrrh] tree that is wounded itself when it gives the balm. If he easily pardons and remits offenses, it shows that his mind is planted above injuries. If he be thankful for small benefits, it shows that he weighs men's minds and not their trash. But above all, if he has St. Paul's wish to be *anathema* from Christ for the salvation of his brethren (Romans 9:3), it shows a nature that has a kind of conformity with Christ Himself.

FRANCIS BACON

———o———

To be subject to others is the worst kind of suffering for some people.

———o———

When you are good to others, you are best to yourself.

———o———

He who wishes to secure the good of others has already secured his own.

———o———

O merciful Father, who in compassion for Thy sinful children didst send Thy Son Jesus Christ to be the Savior of the world: Give us grace to serve one another in all lowliness, and to enter into the fellowship of His sufferings, who liveth and reigneth with Thee and the Holy Spirit, one God, world without end. Amen.

Book of Common Worship

———o———

As John Glenn orbited the earth, through those strange transitions from sunrise to sunset, men and instruments in marvelously sensitive attunement were keeping touch with him. Again and again, as messages came through from earth, he said, "I read you loud and clear."

We're given a strange, wonderful power for tuning in — at least to some extent — to one another as persons. Also, yet, how often we steel our thoughts against one another, or turn a cold shoulder to some other! God gives holy heart-ears for responding, for listening, and for turning to others with voluntary warmth, kindness, help. Only because He first loved us can we learn love. "Without us God will not, without Him we cannot!"

REV. A. C. FESSENDEN

P

Paradox

When a boy gets up at four o'clock in the morning to deliver papers, people say he is a go-getter. If the church should ask that same boy to get up at four to do some work for the Lord, they would say: "That's asking too much of a boy."

If a woman spends eight hours away from her home working in a factory or office or her garden, she is called an energetic wife. If, however, she is willing to do the same thing for the Lord, they say: "Religion has gone to her head."

———o———

If one ties himself down to making payments of $30 each week for some time on a item for personal enjoyment, he pays willingly. But if that same person is approached on tithing and asked to put the same amount in the offering plate, people say: "The preacher's crazy."

This is a crazy world indeed, where first things come last, and last things come first.

Evangelical Friend

———o———

A good many people soak up information like a blotter, but they seem to get it backward, also like a blotter.

———o———

One of the paradoxes of life is that the young are always wishing they were just a little older and the old are usually wishing they were a whole lot younger.

———o———

You can reach the top by staying on the level.

He enjoys much who is thankful for a little.

———o———

Paradox

With eight-year-old disdain, he balks
  At polishing his shoes;
Wears cowboy garb, and wants his shirts
  In bold, conflicting hues.
He likes odd caps, and every pair
  Of blue jeans sports a patch.
It's up to me to scrub his neck
  And see that both socks match.
But when it rains and I remind:
  "Now, wear your rubbers, dear,"
He argues back in all good faith —
  "But, Mom, I'll look so queer!"

MILDRED R. BENSMILLER

Pardon

How Far Is East From West?

How far is the East from the West?
It cannot be measured or proved;
But farther than this, so the Bible tells me,
My sins have fore'er been removed.

How high are the heavens above?
An infinite measureless space;
But higher than this is the gift of God's love,
So great is His mercy and grace.

How deep are the depths of the sea?
A fathomless measure, you say;
But farther than this, so my Saviour tells me,
My sins are fore'er cast away.

They're gone and forgotten by God,
And God has removed every doubt;

For covered by blood are my many
transgressions,
My sins are fore'er blotted out.

"Return unto Me," saith the Lord,
For I have redeemed thee by blood,
Thy name is engraved on the palms of
My hands,
And pardoned thou art, by thy God.

To Him we would joyfully sing,
Our praises to Him would ascend;
Our Saviour, our Shepherd, our Priest
and our King,
Our true and unchangeable Friend.

AUTHOR UNKNOWN

———o———

He allowed no interval between assault and forgiveness; so that he was
almost robbed of pain itself by the
speed of pardon.

ST. GREGORY OF NAZIANZUS of his father

Parents

Child To Parent

1. Don't spoil me. I know quite well
   that I ought not to have all I ask
   for. I am only testing you.
2. Don't be afraid to be firm with
   me. I prefer it. It makes me feel
   more secure.
3. Don't let me form bad habits. I
   have to rely on you to detect them
   in the early stages.
4. Don't make me feel smaller than I
   am. It only makes me behave stupidly "big."
5. Don't correct me in front of people
   if you can avoid it. I'll take much
   more notice if you talk quietly with
   me in private.
6. Don't protect me from consequences. I need to learn the painful way sometimes.
7. Don't take too much notice of my
   small ailments. I am quite capable
   of trading on them.
8. Don't nag. If you do, I shall have
   to protect myself by appearing
   deaf.
9. Don't make rash promises. Remember that I feel badly let down
   when promises are broken.
10. Don't forget that I cannot explain

myself as well as I should like.
That is why I am not always very
accurate.
11. Don't tax my honesty too much. I
    am easily frightened into telling
    lies.
12. Don't be inconsistent. That com-
    pletely confuses me and makes me
    lose faith in you.
13. Don't put me off when I ask ques-
    tions. If you do you will find I will
    stop asking and seek my informa-
    tion elsewhere.
14. Don't tell me my fears are silly.
    They are terribly real, and you can
    do much to reassure me if you try
    to understand.
15. Don't neglect me; I do not *want*
    to be a delinquent.

On And Off Duty

———o———

One trouble in raising a boy is that
father always expects son to do exactly as much work as he never did.

———o———

In dealing with their children, many
parents give in because they've given
out.

———o———

Only fair but stern action against
delinquent parents and snarling young
thugs can bring a halt to the present
plague of youthful lawlessness.

J. EDGAR HOOVER

———o———

Spare the rod when Junior is willful
and disobedient — and when he grows
up he'll probably carry one.

———o———

Parents are people who bear children, bore teen-agers and board new-
lyweds.

———o———

Small girl's essay on parents: "The
trouble with parents is they are so old
when we get them, it's hard to change
their habits."

———o———

Some parents solve their toughest
homework problems by sending their
children to a boarding school.

Parents are just baby-sitters for God.

———o———

Too many parents expect strict obedience in other people's children.

———o———

As a gardener is dependent upon God to grow a plant, so a parent is dependent upon God to grow a life.

C. B. EAVEY

Past

We live in the present, we dream of the future, but we learn eternal truths from the past.

MADAME CHIANG KAI-SHEK

———o———

The past is never dead . . . it's not even past.

WILLIAM FAULKNER

———o———

It's never safe to be nostalgic about anything until you're absolutely sure there's no chance of its coming back.

———o———

What calls back the past, like the rich pumpkin pie?

JOHN GREENLEAF WHITTIER, *The Pumpkin*

———o———

He who learns nothing from the past will be punished by the future.

———o———

You can't change the past, but you can ruin the present by worrying over the future.

Patience

Patience will do wonders, but it was not much help to the fellow who planted an orange grove in Maine.

———o———

Patience can accomplish much. It blunts the edge of misfortunes. By its steady exertion, success can be won a little bit at a time. Unfortunately, though, patience sometimes is confused with procrastination.

Be patient enough to live one day at a time as Jesus taught us, letting yesterday go, and leaving tomorrow till it arrives.

JOHN F. NEWTON

———o———

Living would be easier if men showed as much patience at home as they do when they're waiting for a fish to bite.

———o———

Patience on the road may often prevent patients in the hospital.

———o———

Patience is a quality most needed when it is exhausted.

———o———

Whenever our judgments and our feelings lack patience, they also lack wisdom and virtue.

JOSEPH JOUBERT

———o———

Beware the fury of a patient man.

JOHN DRYDEN, *Absalom and Achitophel*

———o———

Nothing is so full of victory as patience.

Chinese Proverb

———o———

Patience is the ability to keep your motor idling when you feel like stripping the gears.

———o———

All men commend patience, although few be willing to practice it.

THOMAS A KEMPIS

———o———

God sometimes permits us to be perplexed so that we may learn patience and better recognize our dependence upon Him.

Patriotism

There are no points of the compass on the chart of true patriotism.

ROBERT CHARLES WINTHROP

———o———

What a pity it is that we can die but once to save our country.

JOSEPH ADDISON

Patriotism is your conviction that this country is superior to all other countries because you were born in it.

GEORGE BERNARD SHAW

———o———

I only regret that I have but one life to lose for my country.

NATHAN HALE

———o———

He who loves not his country, can love nothing.

LORD BYRON

———o———

Far dearer, the grave or the prison,
Illumed by one patriot name,
Than the trophies of all who have risen
On Liberty's ruins to fame.

THOMAS MOORE

———o———

One who is a patriot is as willing to live sacrificially for his country as he is to die for it.

Peace

Peace with God helps mightily in living peaceably with men.

———o———

No man enjoys the serene calm of inner peace unless he has first known the harassing moments of a disquieted soul.

JOHN J. ZIER

———o———

Christ spells peace. When everything else in life fails Jesus draws near to support. He makes real, through His living Presence, that those whose minds are stayed on God shall be kept in perfect peace.

———o———

Drop thy still dews of quietness
Till all our striving cease;
Take from our souls the strain and stress,
And let our ordered lives confess
The beauty of thy Peace.

JOHN GREENLEAF WHITTIER

———o———

I never have found
Peace of mind
By giving folks a
Piece of mine.

LAURENCE C. SMITH

Peace, when "ruling" the heart and "ruling" the mind, opens in both every avenue of joy.

SARAH W. STEPHEN

———o———

Peace is not as much a goal to be achieved as a way to be walked.

———o———

Perfect Peace

I gazed into the storm-swept sky
Gray clouds piled high as eye could see.
A picture of my storm-swept soul
Not clouds, but troubles piled on me.

I   fought — and   struggled — planned and schemed
I'd solve each problem as it came,
And this I did for oh so long,
But trouble piled up just the same.

Now, all my time and strength were spent
As troubles piled up one by one,
But still my proud and stubborn heart
Refused to say — "God's will be done."

I would not fail — but still I did,
And then in utter anguish cried
For God to help me. Then I knew
Why I had failed, though I had tried.

Oh! Willful heart, you had to learn
How empty all our efforts, when
We trust in self, and not in God!
As empty as the world of men.

My storm-swept soul is calm at last.
These words of peace God spoke to me —
"Thou wilt keep him in perfect peace
Whose mind is stayed on Thee."

FLORA SORENSON

———o———

It is lamentable that peace does not come in capsules.

S. I. MCMILLEN

———o———

A little girl wrote an answer to a question in an examination: "Armistice was signed on November 11, 1918, and since then we have had two minutes of peace every year."

Before we can enjoy the peace of God we must know the God of peace.

———o———

We [do not] eschew concord and peace, but to have peace with man we will not be at war with God.

JOHN JEWELL

———o———

Peace is such a precious jewel that I would give anything for it but truth.

MATTHEW HENRY

———o———

Peace Today

Today Christ stilled a storm — not Galilee,
  But in my heart; I heard His "Peace, be still."
There raged a storm and tempest here, in me,
  And fear that I might perish made me ill.

The boat that is my life seemed tempest-tossed,
  And I forgot the Christ who knows our ships.
My heart sank low, I felt that all was lost,
  So that a cry of "Help me!" reached my lips.

I turned to Him and knew that He could save,
  That all my trials yield to His great will;
I felt the calming smoothness of the wave
  On which I rode, as Christ said, "Peace, be still."

HAZEL HARTWELL SIMON

People

There are three kinds of people: those who make things happen, those who watch things happen, and those who have no idea what happens.

Powergrams

———o———

I love mankind; it's people I can't stand.

He liked to like people, therefore people liked him.

MARK TWAIN

———o———

Two Kinds Of People

There are two kinds of people on earth today,
Just two kinds of people, no more, I say,
Not the good and the bad, for 'tis Well understood
The good are half bad and the bad Are half good.

Not the humble and proud, for in Life's busy span
Who puts on vain airs is not counted a man.
No! The two kinds of people on earth I mean,
Are the people who lift, and the People who lean.

Wherever you go, you will find The world's masses
Are ever divided in just these two classes.
And, strangely enough, you will Find, too, I wean,
There is only one lifter to twenty who lean.

This one question I ask. Are you Easing the load
Of overtaxed lifters who toil down the road?
Or are you a leaner who lets others bear
Your portion of worry and labor and care?

ELLA WHEELER WILCOX

———o———

You are not one person but three: the one you think you are, the one other people think you are and the person you really are.

———o———

I thought I heard the voice of God And climbed the highest steeple;
But God declared, "Go down again, I dwell among the people."

To get along with people and be successful in life, forget yourself and learn to love and be interested in other people.

NORMAN VINCENT PEALE

Perfect, Perfection

The nearest to perfection most people ever come is when filling out an employment application.

KEN KRAFT

——o——

Perfection consists not in doing extraordinary things, but in doing ordinary things extraordinarily well. Neglect nothing; the most trivial action may be performed to God.

ANGÉLIQUE ARNAULD

——o——

A man cannot have an idea of perfection in another, which he was never sensible of in himself.

SIR RICHARD STEELE

——o——

He who boasts of being perfect is perfect in folly. I never saw a perfect man.

CHARLES HADDON SPURGEON

——o——

Aim at perfection in everything, though in most things it is unattainable.

LORD CHESTERFIELD

——o——

This is the very perfection of a man, to find out his own imperfection.

ST. AUGUSTINE

Perseverance, Persistence

When you get into a tight place and everything goes against you, till it seems that you could not hold on a minute longer, never give up then, for that is just the place and time that the tide will turn.

HARRIET BEECHER STOWE

——o——

Perseverance is usually considered to be an admirable characteristic. Still it depends upon what it is at which one perseveres.

It's a wise person who knows how to draw the line between persistence and obstinance.

——o——

When a man has equipped himself by thought and study for a bigger job, it usually happens that promotion comes along even before it is expected.

P. G. WINNETT

——o——

Even a turtle gets nowhere until it sticks its neck out.

——o——

Consider the postage stamp: its usefulness consists in the ability to stick to one thing until it gets there.

"JOSH BILLINGS" (HENRY WHEELER SHAW)

——o——

Great works are performed, not by strength but by perseverance.

SAMUEL JOHNSON

——o——

Ninety thousand Norwegians stood for seven hours in biting cold weather to watch the ski jumpers in Oslo, Norway. The wind was so stiff the jumps had to be postponed several hours, but all ninety thousand braced themselves and stood fast. That's perseverance!

——o——

Thomas Edison made about 18,000 experiments before he perfected the arc light. Dr. Jonas Salk worked sixteen hours a day for three years to perfect the polio vaccine. A chemist, Paul Ehrlich worked day and night for years to perfect a chemical called "606" which would destroy the germ that causes syphilis. He had made 605 unsuccessful experiments, but the 606th was a success — thus the name: 606. Perseverance!

——o——

Do the best you can with what you
   possess,
Though it isn't much, yet it could be
   less.
He invites defeat who gives up to
   sighing,
But the battle is won if you keep on
   trying.

ISLA PASCHAL RICHARDSON

Persistent people begin their success where others end in failure.

EDWARD EGGLESTON

———o———

Neither snow, nor rain, nor heat, nor gloom of night stays these couriers from the swift completion of their appointed rounds.

Adaptation from HERODOTUS on the Main Post Office, New York City

———o———

An eight-year-old boy had been pestering his father for a watch. Finally his father said, "I don't want to hear about your wanting a watch again."

At dinner that night the family each gave a scripture verse at the dinner table and the boy repeated Mark 13:37: "And what I say unto you I say unto all, Watch."

———o———

Diamonds are pieces of coal that stuck to their jobs.

Personality

By a myriad observations we know of no effect greater than its corresponding cause — not even atomic chain reaction with its accompanying devastation. . . . On what rational grounds could we assume that an effect such as personality (the supreme distinction of mortal man in the animal world) was produced by a cause which lacked what it somehow managed to produce?

LEITH SAMUEL, *The Impossibility of Agnosticism*

———o———

Christ never *forces* the door of our personality. He gently knocks by circumstances, coincidences and providential leadings.

———o———

Life demands a great deal of sameness of all those who participate in living. But human differences are as precious as human conformity. Personality is the highest attribute of human life, and personality depends in major part on differences. But personality goes deeper than merely an outward show of differences. It is the mysterious spirit which can transform the tedium of sameness into spired differences.

Peabody Journal of Education

———o———

His personality is like a bent safety pin: it doesn't fit any place and is always sticking people in the wrong place.

———o———

The personality of the therapist is the most important human element in the therapeutic process.

THOMAS TYNDALL

———o———

Our possibilities of success are much more limited by our personality traits than by our intellect.

HENRY GREBER

Pessimist

A pessimist: If you give him an inch, he'd measure it.

———o———

A pessimist is one who feels bad when he feels good, for fear he'll feel worse when he feels better.

———o———

A pessimist is someone who likes to listen to the patter of little defeats.

———o———

It Can't Be Done

The man who misses all the fun
Is he who says, "It can't be done."
In solemn pride, he stands aloof
And greets each venture with reproof.
Had he the power, he would efface
The history of the human race.
We'd have no radio, no cars,
No streets lit by electric stars;
No telegraph, no telephone;
We'd linger in the age of stone.
The world would sleep if things were run
By folks who say, "It CAN'T be done."

AUTHOR UNKNOWN

Philosophy

A philosopher sees less on his tiptoes than a Christian on his knees.

A walk to the top of a hill at night to gaze at the stars may reveal more philosophy than the reading of many books.

———o———

Some people take everything philosophically. Like the man who slipped and fell on the ice one day in January. Gazing at the ice, he said: "I'm not angry. July will take care of you."

This Day

———o———

Philosophy is unintelligible answers to unsolvable problems.

HENRY ADAMS

———o———

Philosophy, rightly defined, is simply the love of wisdom.

MARCUS TULLIUS CICERO

———o———

A philosopher is one who desires to discern the truth.

PLATO

Picnic

The ideal place for a picnic is usually a little farther on.

———o———

Beach Picnic

The outing was really
A lulu, a dilly.
The fog was dense
And dank and chilly
But everyone tanned —
To third-degree burns —
And the kiddies fell over
The cliff by turns.

The hampers were bulging,
The menu faultless,
Though salads were sandy
And sandwiches saltless.
Some cutup went swimming
With Mother's new hat on,
And Gladys was nipped
By a crab that she sat on.

And then when the rains came —
They're sudden, you know —
We found all our things
As we started to go

Except Grandma's teeth,
Bill's swimming fins,
The keys to the car
And one of the twins.

ETHEL JACOBSON
in *New York Times Magazine*

Plans

There is no magic in little plans.

HENRIETTA C. MEARS

———o———

Some people who plan to get right with God at the eleventh hour, die at ten-thirty.

———o———

Plans get you into things, but you got to work your way out.

WILL ROGERS

Pleasure

The greatest pleasure I know is to do a good action by stealth, and to have it found out by accident.

CHARLES LAMB, *Table Talk*

———o———

We tire of those pleasures we take, but never of those we give.

———o———

The pleasantest thing in the world is to have pleasant thoughts, and the greatest art of living is to cultivate more pleasant thoughts.

———o———

Pleasure admitted in undue degree
Enslaves the will, nor leaves the judgment free.

WILLIAM COWPER

———o———

Your greatest pleasure is that which rebounds from hearts that you have made glad.

HENRY WARD BEECHER

Polite

Nothing is ever lost by politeness — except your seat on a bus.

———o———

Politeness comes from within, from the heart: but if the forms of politeness are dispensed with, the spirit and the thing itself soon die away.

JOHN HALL

———o———

Politeness to superiors is duty — to equals courtesy — to inferiors nobleness.

BENJAMIN FRANKLIN

———o———

Politeness costs nothing, and gains everything.

LADY MARY WORTLEY MONTAGU, *Letters*

———o———

Daddy and little son were repairing wire.

"Sing, 'Thank You, Lord, For Saving My Soul,'" said the little fellow. Daddy sang it twice.

"Do you think Jesus is saying, 'You're welcome'?"

Christian Living

Politics

An empty stomach is not a good political adviser.

ALBERT EINSTEIN

———o———

A politician is an animal who can sit on a fence and yet keep both ears to the ground.

———o———

Christopher Columbus was the world's greatest politician. He did not know where he was going, he went on borrowed money, and he did not know where he was when he got there.

YMCA Bulletin

———o———

The biggest trouble with political promises is that they go in one year and out the other.

Toastmaster

———o———

This country has gotten to where it is in spite of politics, not by the aid of it.

WILL ROGERS

———o———

He serves his party best who serves the country best.

RUTHERFORD BIRCHARD HAYES

Possess, Possessions

A wise man will desire no more than he may get justly, use soberly, distribute cheerfully, and leave contentedly.

———o———

Think About This . . .

Love that is hoarded moulds at last
Until we know some day
The only thing we ever have
Is what we give away.

And kindness that is never used
But hidden all alone
Will slowly harden till it is
As hard as any stone.

It is the things we always hold
That we will lose someday;
The only things we ever keep
Are what we give away.

LOUIS GINSBERG, *Song*

———o———

How To Possess

If you want to possess something, help create it. If you want to possess a landscape, try to reproduce it. To others it may seem very crude and ugly, but to you it will hold all the beauty of the original and more, for you have put your life into it. If you want to possess a flower, help it grow. If you want a share in the life of another, do something to make that life larger and better. So shall you become a part of the creative energy of God and share with Him as a son and heir a portion of His divine life.

FRANK O. HALL

———o———

He did not have a house where He could go
When it was night, — when other men went down
Small streets where children watched with eager eyes,
Each one assured of shelter in the town,
The Christ sought refuge anywhere at all.
A house, an inn, the roadside, or a stall.

HELEN WELSHEIMER, *The Transient*

It is not the possession of extraordinary gifts that makes extraordinary usefulness, but the dedication of what we have to the service of God.

FREDERICK WILLIAM ROBERTSON

——o——

The greatest possession is self-possession.

——o——

What you possess in the world will be found at the day of your death to belong to someone else, but what you are will be yours forever.

HENRY VAN DYKE

——o——

The more you have, the more you are in debt to God; and you have no reason to be proud of that which makes you a debtor.

——o——

What you have is God's; He has put you in charge of it for a time.

Poverty

Poverty is not dishonorable in itself, but only when it comes from idleness, intemperance, extravagance, and folly.

PLUTARCH

——o——

Poverty is a virtue greatly overrated by those who no longer practice it.

BARNABY C. KEENEY in Saturday Review

——o——

Poverty is usually the side-partner of laziness.

——o——

If you spend all your time collecting money for fear of poverty, you are practicing poverty already.

——o——

Poverty is very good in poems but very bad in the house; very good in maxims and sermons but very bad in practical life.

HENRY WARD BEECHER

——o——

Poverty is a state of being helpless to help the helpless!

I never feel sorry for poor boys. It is the children of wealth who deserve sympathy; too often they are starved for incentive to create success for themselves.

J. C. PENNEY

——o——

The poorest and most pitiable man is the one who has more than he needs but feels that he hasn't enough.

Power

The most efficient water power let
loose through all the ages,
Is found in a married woman's tears,
according to the sages.

——o——

The Lord Jesus said, "Ye shall find rest." Someone may say, "I had not thought of rest and peace: I want power." Please notice that peace and power are two sides of the same thing; peace is the inside, and power is the outgoing side. We are never promised the consciousness of power. We are promised power, but never the consciousness of it. We know the peace: others know the power.

S. D. GORDON

——o——

I can count on God to let power loose in my life when I am ready to let something loose — the hurtful habit, the crippling compromise, the unsurrendered ambition.

PAUL S. REES

——o——

Power with men proceeds from power with God.

——o——

Thinking we have some power of our own prevents our taking all power from Christ.

——o——

He is truly great in power who has power over himself.

CHARLES HADDON SPURGEON

——o——

Power tends to corrupt; absolute power corrupts absolutely.

LORD ACTON,
Letters to Bishop Mandell Creighton

Power is harder to handle than weakness.

———o———

Christ spells power. He is the power that releases us from death's hold. He is the power that keeps us true. He is the power that opens the door unto the Father's home for us. He is the power that guarantees life eternal and rich.

Practice

Practice makes perfect even when we are practicing a bad habit.

———o———

The more you practice what you know, the more you shall know what to practice.

———o———

Everything gets easier with practice — except getting up in the morning.
DAVE EASTMAN,
Los Angeles Times Syndicate

Praise

He who praises everybody praises nobody.
SAMUEL JOHNSON

———o———

What Shall I Render To My God?

What shall I render to my God
For all His gifts to me?
Sing, heaven and earth, rejoice and praise
In glorious majesty.

O let me praise Thee while I live,
And praise Thee when I die,
And praise Thee when I rise again,
And to eternity.

Mysterious depths of endless love
Our admiration raise;
My God, Thy name exalted is
Above our highest praise.
JOHN MASON

———o———

It's better to shout than to doubt,
It's better to rise than to fall,
It's better to let the glory out
Than to have no glory at all.
S. V. M. DOGGEREL

Praising and blessing God is work that is never out of season. Nothing better prepares the mind for receiving the Holy Ghost than holy joy and praise. Fears are silenced, sorrows sweetened, and hopes kept up.
MATTHEW HENRY

———o———

Matthew Henry said that he would not huddle up his praises in a corner. His sins had been open, God's mercy had been open, and he would make open profession and open payment.
JAMES BARR in *Lang Syne*

———o———

We often praise the evening clouds,
And tints so gay and bold,
But seldom think upon our God,
Who tinged these clouds with gold.
SIR WALTER SCOTT, *The Setting Sun*

———o———

A bit of praise goes far in giving confidence.

———o———

As the Greeks said, Many men know how to flatter, few know how to priase.
WENDELL PHILLIPS

———o———

If Christians praised God more, the world would doubt Him less.
CHARLES E. JEFFERSON

Prayer

When we work we work, when we pray, God works.
OSWALD SMITH

———o———

A Child's Prayer

Now I lay me down to sleep,
I pray Thee, Lord, the souls to keep
Of other children, far away
Who have no homes in which to stay,
Nor know where is their daily bread,
Nor where at night to lay their head,
But wander through a broken land
Alone and helpless —
Take their hand!
A German Prayer

The Place Of Power

There is a place where thou canst touch
the eyes
   Of blinded men to instant perfect
   sight,
There is a place where thou canst say
"Arise"
   To dying captives bound in chains
   of might.
There is a place where thou canst
reach the store
   Of hoarded gold and free it for the
   Lord,
There is a place upon some distant
shore
   Where thou canst send the worker
   or the Word.
There is a place where God's resistless
power
   Responsive moves to thine insistent
   plea,
There is a place — a simple trusting
place
   Where God Himself descends and
   fights for thee.
Where is that blessed place? Dost thou
ask where?
   O soul, it is the secret place of
   prayer.

ADELAIDE A. POLLARD

———o———

Five young college students, before
ordination, spent a Sunday in London,
and were anxious to hear some well-
known preachers in churches other than
their own. They found their way on a
hot Sunday to Spurgeon's Tabernacle.
While waiting for the doors to open a
stranger came up to them and said:
"Gentlemen, would you like to see the
heating apparatus of the church?"
They were not particularly anxious to
do so on a broiling day in July, but con-
sented. They were taken down some
steps, and a door was thrown open,
and their guide whispered, "There,
Sirs, is our heating apparatus." They
saw before them 700 souls bowed in
prayer seeking a blessing on the service about to be held in the tabernacle
above. Their unknown guide was
Spurgeon himself. Are we surprised
that Spurgeon's sermons are still circulated?

Living Links

Prayer is not monologue, but dialogue.

ANDREW MURRAY

———o———

Talking to men for God is a great
thing, but talking to God for men is the
first thing.

———o———

Count it a blessing when God delays
the answer to your prayer in order to
enlarge your capacity to receive.

———o———

Many prayers go to the dead-letter
office of heaven for want of sufficient
direction.

———o———

Prayernik

From its launching pad of suff'ring
   Soars my missile through the air,
Past the sun and moon and planets
   Freighted heavily with prayer.

Faith divine is the propellant,
   (Faith, that God cannot deny)
Sending it a 'zillion light years
   To the city in the sky.

There, the Father hears the beeping,
   Knows the signal as His own;
Tunes in lovingly and listens
   As it orbits 'round the throne.

Back it zooms; the answers bearing
   From the One, whom I adore;
Balm and Blessing! . . . Peace and
   Power!
Praise His Name forevermore.

SARAH SMITH REED

———o———

Traveling On My Knees

Last night I took a journey
   To a land across the seas.
I didn't go by boat or plane,
   I traveled on my knees.

I saw so many people there
   In deepest depths of sin.
And Jesus told me I should go —
   That there were souls to win.

But I said, "Jesus, I can't go
   And work with such as these."
He answered quickly, "Yes, you can,
   By traveling on your knees."

He said, "You pray; I'll meet the need.
  You call and I will hear.
Be anxious over all lost souls,
  Of those both far and near."

And so I tried it, knelt in prayer,
  Gave up some hours of ease;
I felt the Lord right by my side
While traveling on my knees.

As I prayed on and saw souls saved,
  And twisted bodies healed,
I saw God's workers' strength renewed
While laboring in the field.

I said, "Yes Lord, I have a job,
  'Tis Thee I'd ever please.
I'll gladly go and heed Thy call
By traveling on my knees."

SANDRA GOODWIN

———o———

The Power House
Is always there,
So push the button,
Labeled "Prayer."

RALPH H. DUMONT

———o———

Pray often, for prayer is a shield for the soul, a sacrifice to God, and a scourge for Satan.

Prayer is as the pitcher that fetcheth water from the brook, therewith to water the herbs. Break the pitcher and it will fetch no water, and for want of water the garden withers.

JOHN BUNYAN

———o———

If you can beat the devil in the matter of regular daily prayer, you can beat him anywhere. If he can beat you there, he can possibly beat you anywhere.

PAUL RADER

———o———

Prayer is the highest use to which speech can be put.

PETER TAYLOR FORSYTH

———o———

Prayer is not overcoming God's reluctance; it is laying hold of His highest willingness.

RICHARD CHENEVIX TRENCH

———o———

Satan trembles when he sees
A contrite nation on its knees.

Lord, we pray not for tranquility; we pray that Thou grant us strength and grace to overcome adversity.

SAVONARDLA

———o———

Gypsy Smith, when converted, immediately desired the conversion of his uncle. Among gypsies it is not proper for children to address their elders on the subject of duty; so the boy just prayed, and waited. One day his uncle noticed a hole in his trousers, and said, "Rodney, how is it that you have worn the knees of your pants so much faster than the rest of them?"

"Uncle, I have worn them out praying for you, that God would have you."

Then the tears came. The uncle put his arm around the boy, drew him to his side, and soon bent his knees to the same Saviour.

Selected

———o———

Each prayer is answered,
That is so;
But for our good
It may be, "No!"

———o———

The spectacle of a nation praying is more awe-inspiring than the explosion of an atomic bomb.

J. EDGAR HOOVER

———o———

When praying, do not give God instructions — report for duty!

AUTHOR UNKNOWN

———o———

If your burdens seem great, remember this: "Daily prayers lessen daily cares."

———o———

If we would have God hear what we say to Him by prayer, we must be ready to hear what He saith to us by His Word.

MATTHEW HENRY

———o———

Prayer is a preparation for danger; it is the armor for battle.

FREDERICK WILLIAM ROBERTSON

Certain thoughts are prayers. There are moments when, whatever be the attitude of the body, the soul is on its knees.

VICTOR HUGO

None can believe how powerful prayer is, and what it is able to effect, but those who have learned it by experience.

MARTIN LUTHER

The equipment for the inner life of prayer is simple. It consists of a quiet place, a quiet hour and a quiet heart.

Selected

Pray hardest when it is hardest to pray.

CHARLES H. BRENT

Lord, make me a channel of Thy peace,
That where there is hatred I may bring love;
That where there is wrong I may bring the spirit of forgiveness;
That where there is discord I may bring harmony;
That where there is error I may bring truth;
That where there is doubt I may bring faith;
That where there is despair I may bring hope;
And where there are shadows I may bring Thy light;
That where there is sadness I may bring joy;
Lord, grant that I may seek rather to comfort than be comforted,
To understand than be understood,
To love than be loved;
For it is by giving that one receives,
It is by self-forgetting that one finds,
It is by forgiving that one is forgiven,
It is by dying that one awakens to eternal life.

ST. FRANCIS OF ASSISI

Prayers of Children

A little boy prayed: "Lord, if you can't make me a better boy, don't worry about it. I'm having a real good time as it is."

A mother, interested in her son's learning some prayers, gave him a tract put out by the church board.

Some nights later she was pleased to hear him recite a prayer at dinner.

"Amen," he concluded. "This prayer is sponsored by the United Board of Churches."

E. RUTH ZIEGLER in *Together*

A little girl was overheard ending the Lord's Prayer thus: "For thine is the kingdom and the flowers that are growing. Amen."

OREN ARNOLD in *Home Life*

Five-year-old Jan likes long prayers, probably to forestall bedtime. She prays, "Jesus, bless Daddy and Mother. Bless everybody in the church. Bless everybody in the whole world."

The other night, however, after a moment's hesitation, she added, ". . . and everybody in outer space."

MRS. J. C. RAINEY in *Teach*

Five-year-old Kathie had a habit of making long drawn-out bedtime prayers. On one occasion her mother, thinking to shorten them, said, "Amen" during a slight pause. Kathie prayed on. Again her mother suggested, "Amen."

Then Kathie said, "God, don't pay any attention to her. She doesn't know when I'm done."

MRS. FREDA B. ELLIOTT in *Teach*

A tiny four-year-old was spending a night away from home. At bedtime, she knelt at her hostess' knee to say her prayers, expecting the usual prompting.

Finding the hostess unable to help her, concluded thus:

"Please, God, 'scuse me. I can't remember my prayers, and I'm staying with a lady who don't know any."

My children had been praying for a baby brother or sister and had been told to expect one. One week-end when we were camping out in the hills, young Herbert called out after bedtime that he had to get up and pray some more.

He got out of bed, knelt down, and said: "God you better not send the baby tonight. There isn't anyone home to take care of him."

MRS. M. NELLIE in *Teach*

---o---

A small boy knelt at his mother's knee and offered his evening prayer. When he had finished, he continued to speak softly while on his knees.

"What did you ask for?" his mother questioned.

"It isn't nice to always ask for things," replied the little fellow. "I just told God that I love Him."

Pentecostal Evangel

Preach, Preacher

Comment about a preacher: "He speaks very well, if he just had something to say!"

---o---

Any preacher who preaches beyond that which he has experienced is incapable of preaching with conviction.

BILLY GRAHAM

---o---

Inadvertent announcement by a pastor: "Next Sunday, I will preach my last sermon in this Lenten series. The choir will sing, 'Now All My Woes Are Over'."

MRS. LAURA JOHNSTON in *Together*

---o---

The pastor announced he was about to preach on "Christian Marriage and Family Life," but his choir got in a warning first by singing, "Turn Back, O Man, Foreswear Thy Foolish Ways."

---o---

A preacher tape-recorded his sermon, then sat down to listen to it and fell fast asleep.

---o---

Daniel Webster, the noted Senator and statesman, was once asked why he generally went to hear a poor country minister preach instead of one of the more brilliant clergymen of Washington.

"Well, you see," he explained, "in Washington they preach to Daniel Webster, the renowned individual, but this country preacher preaches to Daniel Webster, the sinner."

HAROLD HELFER in *Coronet*

---o---

A young man while preaching the Gospel in an open-air meeting heard this sarcastic remark: "Poor fellow, he's cracked." "Yes," he answered quickly, "thank God, that is where the light shone in."

---o---

A minister, but still a man.

ALEXANDER POPE, *Epistle to James Craggs*

---o---

The pastor was hoping to get a discount on the price of his suit. "I'm a poor preacher," he said.

"Yes, I know that," said the salesman, "I've heard you preach."

MARTIN P. SIMON, *Points for Parents*

---o---

My advice to pastors is to give up preaching for the next few months. Take an outline and spend time in prayer over it, and then enter the pulpit and tell the story of Jesus. People have had too much preaching.

J. WILBUR CHAPMAN

---o---

It often requires more courage to preach to one than to a thousand.

ADONIRAM J. GORDON

---o---

In order to preach aright take three looks before every sermon: one at thine own sinfulness; another at the depth of human wretchedness all around thee; and a third at the love of God in Christ Jesus, so that, empty of self and full of compassion toward thy fellowman, thou mayest be enabled to administer God's comfort to souls.

NIKOLAUS LUDWIG VON ZINZENDORF

---o---

"Did I preach too long?" asked Dr. H. C. Morrison, the great Methodist preacher, after one of his earliest sermons. "No, you did not preach too long," his friend answered, much to Morrison's relief; "but you talked too long after you stopped preaching."

———o———

Preachers can talk,
But never teach
Unless they practice
What they preach.
Defender

———o———

The preacher should tell people where to get on, not where to get off.

———o———

One preacher's calling cards had this sentence significantly printed on them: "What on earth are you doing for heaven's sake?"

———o———

None preaches better than the ant, and she says nothing.
BENJAMIN FRANKLIN, *Poor Richard*

———o———

I preached as never sure to preach again,
And as a dying man to dying men.
RICHARD BAXTER,
Love Breathing Thanks and Praise

———o———

To love to preach is one thing — to love those to whom we preach, quite another.
RICHARD CECIL

Prejudice

Opinions founded on prejudices are always sustained with the greatest violence.
SIR FRANCIS JEFFREY, LORD JEFFREY

———o———

Prejudice is the child of ignorance.
WILLIAM HAZLITT

———o———

Most of us have found by experience that it is a good thing to overhaul certain machinery. It would be a good thing for all of us to overhaul our prejudices once in awhile.

It is never too late to give up our prejudices.
HENRY DAVID THOREAU

———o———

Prejudice is a great timesaver; it enables us to form opinions without bothering to get the facts.

———o———

Beware of prejudices. They are like rats, and men's minds are like traps. Prejudices get in easily, but rarely do they get out. We cannot hold anyone in contempt without at the same time attracting contempt toward us. We cannot elevate a man without ourselves being elevated. Likewise, you cannot degrade another without falling into degradation yourself. Prejudice places you in bondage . . . it curtails your opportunities for success and happiness. Why not enjoy the freedom that calm reasoning and an understanding heart will give you! Human nature is so constituted that all see, and judge better, in the affairs of other men, than in our own.
TERENCE

———o———

Be careful that prejudice never closes its eyes to evidence.

Preparation

The great cry of our heart is that God will help us to be ready for whatever He has for us.
BOB PIERCE

———o———

Prepare today for tomorrow and forget about yesterday.
MARTIN VANBEE

———o———

God is preparing his heroes; and when the opportunity comes, he can fit them into their places in a moment, and the world will wonder where they came from.
A. B. SIMPSON

———o———

One who is not prepared today will be less so tomorrow.

I will study and get ready, and perhaps my chance will come.

ABRAHAM LINCOLN

Present

One of the devil's snares is so to occupy us with the past and the future as to weaken us for the present.

———o———

Historians explain the past, and economists the future. Thus only the present is confusing.

MRS. R. E. MILLARD
in *The Log of the Good Ship Grace*

———o———

Children have neither past nor future; they enjoy the present, which very few of us do.

JAMES ABRAM GARFIELD

———o———

Now and Then

NOW as through a glass, but darkly,
 Future hopes by faith we trace;
THEN in realms of radiant glory
 We shall see our Savior's face.

NOW by faith we see Him only,
 Our reflections may be dim;
THEN when He appears to call us,
 We shall really be like Him.

NOW, by scientific finds,
 Men attempt to conquer space;
THEN, our mighty Lord will take us
 Where He has prepared our place.

NOW, by His command, we're spreading
 His great Gospel Truth abroad;
THEN, we'll see in His blest presence
 Those we brought to Christ our
 Lord.

MABEL E. PALMER in *Now*

Pride

A crowd of people at the Franklin Park Zoo in Boston watched a peacock slowly spread its large tail and display its beautiful plumage. The bird held itself erect and strutted regally about the enclosure. Just then an old, drab-colored duck waddled slowly from a nearby pond and passed between the proud peacock and the admiring crowd. The peacock became enraged and drove the duck back into the water. The beautiful bird suddenly became ugly with anger. The plain and awkward duck, having returned to the pond, was no longer unattractive. He swam and dove gracefully in the pond, unaware that many eyes were watching him. The people who had admired the peacock loved the duck. They were reminded of the dangers of pride and that true happiness comes from being ourselves.

———o———

The Ashes Of Pride

Who was that man I saw today,
The one from whom I turned away
To hide the revulsion I felt inside?
That man in the gutter! Had he no
 pride?
A picture of weak-willed moral decay,
Such a sordid sight to spoil my day!

Who was that man? I can tell you to-
 night,
For the answer came like a flickering
 light
That grew until it enveloped me
In the ashes of pride — humility.
The answer came as I read God's
 Word
And it seemed as though His Voice I
 heard —

"Who was that man you saw today?
The one from whom you turned away
Was you, My son, had I let you race
The course of life without My Grace.
If left on your own, you would have
 been
Beside that man your pride condemns.

"Who was that man you saw today?
The one from whom you turned away
Is so loved by Me that I died for him!
Can you still in your foolish pride con-
 demn?
That sordid sight was My child astray,
Did you stop to show him — and your-
 self —
 The Way?"

ART MOSSBERG

One feather in their cap and some persons topple over!

————o————

You can have no greater sign of a confirmed pride than when you think you are humble enough.

WILLIAM LAW

————o————

Most people spend money they don't have to buy things they don't want to impress people they don't like.

WILL ROGERS

————o————

Be not proud of race, face, place, or Grace.

CHARLES HADDON SPURGEON

————o————

A proud man is always looking down on things and people: and, of course, as long as you're looking down, you can't see something that's above you.

C. S. LEWIS,
Mere Christianity, Christian Behaviour

————o————

Pride was the sin of the angels in heaven.

————o————

A proud man is seldom a grateful man, for he never thinks he gets as much as he deserves.

HENRY WARD BEECHER

Problems

It is the first of all problems for a man to find out what kind of work he is to do in this universe.

THOMAS CARLYLE

————o————

If more problems were settled in the house of the Lord, fewer problems would be settled in the house of correction.

HENRIETTA C. MEARS

————o————

People are always trying to solve other people's problems and the world is full of wrong answers.

————o————

You're either helping solve the problem — or you're part of the problem.

BERNARD EDINGER

A sad looking character was shown into the office of a prominent psychiatrist. "I've lost all desire to go on, doctor. Life has become too hectic, too confused."

"Yes," said the doctor, clucking sympathetically. "I understand. We all have our problems. You'll need a year or two of treatments at fifty dollars a week."

There was a pause. "Well, that solves your problem, Doc. Now what about mine?"

————o————

Problems are the price of progress. Don't bring me anything but trouble. Good news weakens me.

CHARLES F. KETTERING

Procrastinate

If you put off until tomorrow what you should do today, someone may invent a machine to do it for you.

————o————

A successful procrastinator puts off his work so long that by the time it's finished, there's no time not to like what he's done.

JIM BULLOCK

————o————

Only two things come to him who waits: whiskers and bills.

————o————

Procrastination is not only the thief of time but it clutters up our lives with an appalling number of half-done things and with slovenly habits.

CLIFF COLE

————o————

He who waits to do a great deal of good at once will never do anything. Life is made up of little things.

————o————

Procrastination is the art of keeping up with yesterday.

DONALD MARQUIS, *Archy and Mehitabel*

————o————

Procrastination is the Thief of time;
Year after year it steals, till all are fled,
And to the mercies of a moment leaves
The vast concerns of an eternal scene.

EDWARD YOUNG, *Night Thoughts*

Procrastination is the thief of time. Collar him!

CHARLES DICKENS

---o---

Someday

Someday — I'm going down the street
And sit and chat with one whose feet
Have had to pause and rest awhile
Before they travel that last mile;
Well — someday.

Someday — A cake or pie I'll bake
And with a cheery smile I'll take
It to a home where there is need;
Just folks, of quite a different creed;
Well — someday.

Someday — a letter I will send
To that distant, lonely friend;
I'll tell her every little thing
That will joy and comfort bring;
Well — someday.

Someday — a quiet place I'll seek
Where I can hear my Father speak,
Where I can listen undisturbed
To His precious guiding Word;
Someday.

Someday — I'll surely take the time
To tell some soul of love divine,
Of salvation full and free,
Meant for them as well as me;
Someday.

Someday — I said it long ago.
The days slip by, and well I know
"Someday" will never come until
Today bends to my Father's will.
Why not today?

ROSELYN C. STEERE

---o---

It's surprising how many times some tasks have to be put off before they completely slip your mind.

---o---

Satan cares not how spiritual your intentions, or how holy your resolutions, if only they are fixed for Tomorrow!

J. C. RYLE

Progress

It's fine to be on the right track. But keep in mind the fact that you'll get run over if you just sit there.

OREN ARNOLD

All growth that is not toward God is growing to decay.

GEORGE MACDONALD

---o---

The best way to get from a lower position to a higher one is to be conspicuously efficient in the lower one.

---o---

What we call progress is the exchange of one nuisance for another nuisance.

HAVELOCK ELLIS

---o---

The time of day I do not tell as some
  do by the clock,
Or by the distant chiming bell set on
  some steepled rock,
But by the progress that I see in what
  I have to do;
It's either 'Done O'Clock' for me, or
  only 'Half-Past Through.'

---o---

Real progress sometimes means retracting our steps. Progress for Abraham meant going back to the place of an altar.

W. LYNN CROWDING

---o---

Progress always involves risks. You can't steal second base and keep your foot on first.

---o---

In our age of rapid advance, you have to run like mad to keep standing still.

---o---

The People Go

From bondage to spiritual faith
From spiritual faith to great courage
From courage to liberty
From liberty to selfishness
From selfishness to complacency
From complacency to apathy
From apathy to dependency
From dependency . . .
    Back into bondage.
    Where are we?

Promise

A promise: one thing you can and should keep after giving.

What many promising young men become is promising older men.

FRANKLIN P. JONES

———o———

The promises of God are just as good as ready money any day.

BILLY BRAY

———o———

God makes a promise.
Faith believes it.
Hope anticipates it.
Patience quietly awaits it.

AUTHOR UNKNOWN

———o———

Promise is most given when the least is said.

GEORGE CHAPMAN, Hero and Leander

———o———

Have you ever noticed how those who are the quickest with promises so often have the slowest memories for keeping them?

———o———

The prospect is as bright as the promises of God.

ADONIRAM JUDSON

———o———

The Promises

My Savior's grace is promised me,
　His tender love and care,
His deep concern in every grief
　Each burden He will share.

My Father's care is promised me,
　His faithful, guiding hand
To lead me on and bear me up
　To Heaven's golden strand.

My Father's wealth is promised me,
　Supplying all my need;
He is a King, and I, His own,
　Am rich, yes, rich indeed.

The Holy Ghost is promised me,
　To in my heart abide,
To hold me steady, pray for me,
　And keep me sanctified.

GEORGE H. TALBERT

Prosperity

Prosperity is only an instrument to be used, not a deity to be worshipped.

CALVIN COOLIDGE

Prosperity hides far more perils than does poverty.

———o———

Continued worldly prosperity is a fiery trial.

CHARLES HADDON SPURGEON

———o———

In prosperity men ask too little of God; in adversity they are likely to ask too much.

———o———

Prosperity has often proved more damaging to human character than adversity.

Proverbs

A proverb is one man's wit, and all men's wisdom.

LORD JOHN RUSSELL

———o———

A stitch on time costs plenty of carrying charges.

———o———

Angels rush in when fools fail to retread.

———o———

A man is judged by the finance companies he keeps.

———o———

A proverb is a short sentence based on long experience.

MIGUEL DE CERVANTES

———o———

Three things cannot be taught: generosity, poetry, and a singing voice.

Irish Proverb

———o———

There's a time to wink as well as to see.

BENJAMIN FRANKLIN

———o———

He gives twice who gives quickly.

Roman Proverb

———o———

Love does to us what life finds in us.

Old English Proverb

Psychiatrist, Psychology

A psychiatrist is a person who can tell you what everyone knows in terms that no one understands, and gets paid for it.

————o————

Woman to small child in store: "Behave! I have no time for psychology today."

————o————

The difference between a psychotic and a neurotic: The psychotic thinks two plus two is five. The neurotic knows two plus two is four, but he hates it!

————o————

A psychiatrist is a man who uses other people's heads to make money.

————o————

Anyone who goes to a psychiatrist must be out of his head.

————o————

A psychiatrist is "a mind-sweeper."

————o————

Modern psychology tells us that it's bad to be an orphan, terrible to be an only child, damaging to be the youngest, crushing to be in the middle, and taxing to be the oldest. There seems no way out except to be born an adult.

SIDNEY J. HARRIS in
Chicago Daily News

Pure, Purity

Visiting in a mining town, a young minister was being escorted through one of the coal mines. In one of the dark, dirty passageways, he spied a beautiful white flower growing out of the black mine earth. "How can there be a flower of such purity and beauty in this dirty mine?" the minister asked the miner. "Throw some of the coal dust on it and see," was the reply. He did and was surprised that as fast as the dirt touched those snowy petals, it slid right off to the ground, leaving the flower just as lovely as before. It was so smooth that the dirt could not cling to the flower.

Our hearts can be the same way. We cannot help it that we have to live in a world that is filled with sin, any more than that the flower could change the place where it was growing. But God can keep us so pure and clean that though we touch sin on every side, it will not cling to us. We can stand in the midst of it just as white and beautiful as that flower.

Hi Call

————o————

It is better to have clean hands and a pure heart than to have clever hands and a smooth tongue.

Purpose

At the age of nine Harry Dixon Loes was advised by his father not to waste time writing songs. But when he died at the age of seventy-two, he left the world with more than 3,000 gospel songs which he composed. Much of his work was published under pen names, as well as his own. Some of his best-known songs include, "Love Found A Way," "Blessed Redeemer" and "All Things in Jesus."

Alliance Witness

————o————

Men fail through lack of purpose rather than through lack of talent.

BILLY SUNDAY

————o————

Some time ago the tallest of HCJB's antenna towers in Quito, Ecuador came crumbling to the ground after lightning hit it, causing expensive damage and loss of air time. Staff members had varying interpretations. Some said, "Satan caused this." Others declared, "God is trying to say something to us."

Perhaps the two viewpoints together expressed the whole truth. Whatever the final definition, we know this: the lightning bolt somehow stood within the circle of God's sovereignty. In His larger purpose the loss became gain.

ABE C. VAN DER PUY

————o————

We mostly spend our lives conjugating three verbs: "to want," "to have" and "to do," forgetting that these verbs have no significance except as they are included in the verb "to be."

EVELYN UNDERHILL

———o———

The world steps aside for the fellow who knows where he is going.

I go at what I have to do as if there were nothing else in the world for me to do.

CHARLES KINGSLEY

———o———

The secret of success is constancy to purpose.

BENJAMIN DISRAELI

Q

Quarrel

Most quarrels are inevitable at the time, incredible afterward.

FORSTER

———o———

But, children, you should never let
Such angry passions rise;
Your little hands were never made
To tear each other's eyes.

ISAAC WATTS, *Divine Songs*

———o———

The quarrel is a very pretty quarrel as it stands; we should only spoil it by trying to explain it.

RICHARD BRINSLEY SHERIDAN,
The Rivals

———o———

A little explained, a little endured,
A little forgiven, the quarrel's cured.

———o———

I hate a quarrel because it interrupts an argument.

GILBERT KEITH CHESTERTON

Questions

Everywhere in life, the true question is not what we gain, but what we do.

THOMAS CARLYLE

———o———

No question is ever settled
Until it is settled right.

ELLA WHEELER WILCOX,
Settle the Question Right

———o———

To a quick question, give a slow answer.

Italian Adage

It is better to debate a question without settling it than to settle a question without debating it.

JOSEPH JOUBERT

———o———

When a child was questioned about the Bible story he had heard in Sunday School, the following was his version of it:
"When Noah's Ark came to rest on the mountain, Noah said to all the animals, 'Go forth and multiply.'
"All of the creatures came out of the ark except the adders. When Noah called them to come, they said, 'We can't, we're adders, we can't multiply.'"

———o———

Teacher: "Which is the most popular cow in America?"
Pupil: "Magnesia. You can buy her milk in any drugstore."

Quiet

In times of quietness our hearts should
    be like trees,
Lifting their branches to the sky to
    draw down strength
Which they will need to face the storms
That will surely come.

TOYOHIKO KAGAWA

———o———

I Needed The Quiet

I needed the quiet so He drew me
    aside,
Into the shadows where we could confide.
Away from the bustle where all the day
    long

I hurried and worried when active and
strong.

I needed the quiet tho' at first I re-
belled

But gently, so gently, my cross He up-
held

And whispered so sweetly of spiritual
things

Tho weakened in body, my spirit took
wings

To heights never dreamed of when active and gay.

He loved me so greatly He drew me
away.

I needed the quiet. No prison my bed,
But a beautiful valley of blessings instead —

A place to grow richer in Jesus to hide.
I needed the quiet so He drew me
aside.

ALICE HANSCHE MORTENSON

——o——

Quiet sleep feels no foul weather.

——o——

Slow Me Down!

Slow me down, Lord!
Ease the pounding of my heart by
the quieting of my mind. Steady my
hurried pace with a vision of the eternal
reach of time. Give me, amidst the
confusion of my day, the calmness of
the everlasting hills. Break the tension of my nerves and muscles with
the soothing music of the singing
streams that live in my memory. Help
me to know the magical restorative
power of sleep.

Teach me the art of taking minute
vacations — of slowing down to look at
a flower, to chat with a friend, to pet a
dog, to read from a good book. Remind
me each day of the fable of the hare
and the tortoise, that I may know that
the race is not always to the swift;
that there is more to life than increasing its speed. Let me look upward into
the branches of the towering trees, and
know that they grow tall because they
grow slowly and well.

Slow me down, Lord, and inspire
me to send my roots deep into the
soil of life's ending values, that I may
grow toward the stars of my greater
destiny. Amen.

AUTHOR UNKNOWN

——o——

Quiet

"In quietness and confidence
shall be your strength" (Isaiah 30:15).

"Quiet." What a strange old word
To use on this day's air!
'Tis many years since it was stressed
By humans anywhere.

Our very entertainment,
And the daily tools we need,
Either prattle, shriek, or roar,
To help our work succeed.

When some youngsters try to study,
Or type themes, or even think,
There must be a radio blaring,
(For mere quiet makes them shrink).

Hot impatience rules our living;
We can't wait for anything.
Things jump into place on order,
Or we rant instead of sing.

Our Bible bids us to be quiet;
— And our God proves values, too.
'Tis BELIEVING, that He asks for;
That's one thing that we can do.

MRS. F. MCQUAT

R

Race

A group of Negroes entered a classy restaurant.

"Sorry, it isn't our policy to serve members of the Negro race," the waitress said.

One of the visitors replied, "That's all right. We don't eat them anyway."

———o———

No race can prosper till it learns that there is as much dignity in tilling a field as in writing a poem.

BOOKER T. WASHINGTON,
Up From Slavery

———o———

If you hate me because I am ignorant I'll educate myself. If you hate me because I am dirty, I'll clean myself. If you hate me because I am pagan, I will become a Christian. But if you hate me because I am black, I can only refer you to God who made me black.

MILAN DAVID

Read

In the "good old days" it was a boy himself, rather than his teacher, who had to explain why he could not read.

CY N. PEACEL

———o———

The reading of good books is one of the most helpful ways in which young people can develop themselves. To read good books casually will not suffice. One must study every sentence and make sure of its full message. Good writers do not intend that we should get their full meaning without effort. They expect us to dig as one is compelled to dig for gold. Gold, you know, is not generally found in large openings, but in tiny veins. The ore must be subjected to a white heat in order to get the pure gold. Remember this when you read.

Young men and women who are seeking to learn all they can, have minds capable of receiving and retaining new impressions. There is nothing that will strengthen the mind, broaden the vision, enrich the soul more than the reading of good books.

J. C. PENNEY
in *Christian Herald*

———o———

Force yourself to reflect on what you read, paragraph by paragraph.

SAMUEL TAYLOR COLERIDGE

———o———

Learn to read slow: all other graces
Will follow in their proper places.

WILLIAM WALKER,
The Art of Reading

———o———

We learn six percent of what we hear but eighty-six percent of all we learn we learn from what we read.

———o———

Four-year-old Billy stood in awe of the great accomplishments of his six-year-old brother Johnny. "Can you really read?" Billy asked one day, admiration obvious in his voice.

"Sure," Johnny replied.

"What does that reading on the stove say?" Billy demanded.

Johnny regarded the brand name printed on the stove. For several seconds he tried to figure out the unfamiliar word. "I don't read stoves," he said at last. "I just read books."

———o———

Tell me what you read and I will tell you what you are.

———o———

Have you ever rightly considered what the mere ability to read means? That it is the key which admits us to the whole world of thought and fancy and imagination? To the company of saint and sage, of the wisest and the wittiest at their wisest and wittiest moment? That it enables us to see with the keenest eyes, hear with the finest ears, and listen to the sweetest voices of all time?

JAMES RUSSELL LOWELL

———o———

Reading maketh a full man, conference a ready man, and writing an exact man.

SIR FRANCIS BACON, *Of Studies*

———o———

To read without reflecting, is like eating without digesting.

EDMUND BURKE

Reason

Some reasons that sound good may not be sound reasons.

———o———

There are many reasons for doing a thing, but one of the most effective is the lack of an alternative; if you gotta do it, you gotta do it.

Transcript, Milton, Massachusetts

———o———

It is useless to attempt to reason a man out of a thing he was never reasoned into.

JONATHAN SWIFT

———o———

Where reason is most needed, usually it is not allowed to enter.

———o———

We don't want a thing because we have found a reason for it; we find a reason for it because we want it.

WILL DURANT

———o———

A four-year-old boy buckled on his new overshoes and went flippety-floppety down the street to visit his grandfather.

"You've got those overshoes on the wrong feet," grumbled Grandpa.

"But they're the only feet I have," said the grandson.

———o———

Reveal'd Religion first inform'd thy sight,

And Reason saw not, till Faith sprung the light.

JOHN DRYDEN, *Religio Laici*

———o———

Passion and prejudice govern the world; only under the name of reason.

JOHN WESLEY

Redemption

Humanitarian programs, though deep and sincere, are not enough. The world may be greatly blessed by them but not redeemed. As worthy as an act may be, simply painting the pump doesn't purify the water.

———o———

Two Hours

Two hours outshine upon the roll of Time
  All other earthly hours as stars aloof;
One tells the moment, throbbing and sublime,
  When He was born beneath the stable roof,
Whose advent hosts of winging angels sang,
While all the sky with alleluias rang.

The other, when with glad unerring wing,
  The Easter Angel at command divine
Unsealed the stone and Love rose triumphing;
  (That tomb, were He unrisen, were mine and thine.)
For the first hour, all earthly hours are named,
But for the other's sake, a lost world is reclaimed.

LOUISE MANNING HODGKINS

———o———

When we say, "Something should be done about Skid Row," God is saying the same thing about us. That is why He sent His Son to help us.

J. VERNON MCGEE

Reflection

The world is a looking glass, and gives back to every man the reflection of his own face. Frown at it, and it will turn and look sourly upon you; laugh at it, and with it, and it is a jolly companion.

WILLIAM MAKEPEACE THACKERAY

———o———

You will find as you look back on your life that the moments that stand out above everything else are the moments when you have done things in a spirit of love.

HENRY DRUMMOND

———o———

A moment's insight is sometimes worth a life's experience.

OLIVER WENDELL HOLMES

———o———

The mirror always tells the truth, but the viewer interprets the reflection to suit himself.

———o———

There is one art which every man should be a master — the art of reflection.

SAMUEL TAYLOR COLERIDGE

Reform, Reformation

O Lord, reform thy world — beginning with me.

A Chinese Christian's Prayer

———o———

There's so much good in the worst of us, and so much bad in the best of us — that it's rather difficult to tell which of us ought to reform the rest of us.

———o———

Ah for a man to arise in me,
That the man I am may cease to be!

ALFRED, LORD TENNYSON

Regret

Might Have Been

The saddest words
Of tongue or pen
May well be
"It might have been,"
Especially silence
Left unbroken
And healing words
We might have spoken.

MAY RICHSTONE, adapted from
JOHN GREENLEAF WHITTIER, Maud Muller

Make the most of your regrets. To regret deeply is to live afresh.

HENRY DAVID THOREAU

Relatives

Small girl's definition of relatives: People who come to dinner who aren't friends.

———o———

He has more kinfolk than a microbe.

IRVIN SHREWSBURY COBB

———o———

Fate makes our relatives, choice makes our friends.

JACQUES DELILLE, La Pitié

Reliable

A small boy explained reliable this way: "A man lied once, then he lied again. He was reliable!"

———o———

Reliability is more important than ability; tackle-ability is really more to be commended than capability.

Religion

If we have an attack of real religion it will be contagious.

———o———

Religion is no more possible without prayer than poetry without language or music without atmosphere.

JAMES MARTINEAU

———o———

If your attitude toward religion were only a private matter you might take it as it comes without concerning yourself about it very seriously. But the trouble is it isn't private, it affects others.

———o———

He that has doctrinal knowledge and speculation only, without holy affection, never is engaged in the business of religion. True religion is a powerful thing . . . a ferment, a vigorous engagedness of the heart.

JONATHAN EDWARDS

We have just enough religion to make us hate, but not enough to make us love another.

JONATHAN SWIFT,
Thoughts on Various Subjects

———o———

To put more heart in your religion, you must have more religion in your heart.

———o———

When your religion gets into the past tense, it becomes pretense.

———o———

A seen religion is not always real, but a real religion is always seen.

———o———

To be furious in religion is to be irreligiously religious.

WILLIAM PENN

———o———

Too many people use religion like a spare tire — only in emergencies.

Banking

———o———

The aim of religion is not to get us into heaven, but to get heaven into us.

ULYSSES G. B. PIERCE

———o———

A near-sighted woman, called a "crank on religion," was once discovered talking religion to a wooden Indian in front of a cigar store. When chided for such "an undignified act," she said, "I would rather be a Christian and talk religion to a wooden Indian, than a wooden Christian who never talks religion to anyone."

———o———

Lord, let not my religion be a thing of
  selfish ecstasy;
But something warm with tender care
  and fellowship which I can share.
Let me not walk the other side of
  trouble's highway long and wide;
Make me a Good Samaritan, and
  neighbor unto every man.

CLARENCE M. BURKHOLDER

———o———

No one is dressed shabbier than he who uses his religion as a cloak.

DAVID YOUNG

Remedy

Our remedies oft in ourselves do lie, Which we ascribe to Heaven.

WILLIAM SHAKESPEARE,
All's Well that Ends Well

———o———

There are some remedies worse than the disease.

PUBLILIUS SYRUS, *Maxim 301*

———o———

Extreme remedies are very appropriate for extreme diseases.

HIPPOCRATES, *Aphorisms*

———o———

He destroys his health by the pains he takes to preserve it.

VIRGIL

Remember

Things to remember: the value of time; the success of perseverance; the pleasure of working; the worth of character; the power of kindness; the influence of example; the obligation of duty; the wisdom of economy, the virtue of patience; the sound of laughter; the joy of originating; the thrill of accomplishing.

CARL YODER

———o———

Recollection is the only paradise from which we cannot be turned out.

JEAN PAUL RICHTER

———o———

To be a noble person it is a holy joy to remember.

ABRAHAM JOSHUA HESCHEL

———o———

Pleasure is the flower that fades; remembrance is the lasting perfume.

MARQUIS STANISLAS JEAN DE BOUFFLERS

———o———

Remembered
(Jeremiah 2:2)

Not forgotten, but remembered!
  Child of God, trust on with cheer!
Thy great Father's help is promised
  Every day throughout the year.

Not forsaken—but most precious
    Thou wilt ever to Him be;
Tenderly He whispers, "Fear not!
    I, the Lord, remember thee!"

Not forgotten, but remembered,
    Is the pledge of Love Divine!
He who loves and understands us,
    Best can plan thy path and mine.
His own Word cannot be broken,
    "As thy days thy strength shall be,"
He, Himself, the word hath spoken—
    "I, the Lord, remember thee!"

Not forgotten, but remembered—
    In His love for thee He planned,
Chosen, sealed, thy name engraven
    On His pierced and peerless hand.
When He calls thee, "Come up higher,"
    Thou shalt then His wonders see—
Wonders of His mighty promise—
    "I, the Lord, remember thee!"

                              L. C. HASLER

———o———

An old southerner, being questioned by a census taker, was having trouble remembering the birthdates of all his grandchildren. He asked his wife when one of the girls was born.

"Well," answered the wife, "I know she was born in 'tater time, but I'm blessed if I can remember if it was diggin' or plantin' time!"

Repentance

Real repentance thinks God's thoughts about sin and hates it; takes God's side against self and dies to it; turns to God Himself and serves Him.

———o———

For making a man repent his sins, there's nothing quite so convincing as catching him.

———o———

If we put off repentance another day, we have a day more to repent of and a day less to repent in.

                                    MASON

———o———

Real repentance is sorrow for the deed, not for being caught.

Repentance is sorrow for sin converted into action, into change in manner of life.

Reputation

No man will ever bring out of the Presidency the reputation which carries him into it.

                        THOMAS JEFFERSON

———o———

When I devoted to God my ease, my time, my future, my life, I did not except my reputation.

                            JOHN WESLEY

———o———

Another way to get a reputation for enlightenment and wisdom is to say the things all men know, but which most of them have forgotten.

———o———

Lasting reputations are of slow growth; the man who wakes up famous some morning is very apt to go to bed some night and sleep it off.

    "JOSH BILLINGS" (HENRY WHEELER SHAW)

———o———

What people say behind your back is your standing in the community.

                        EDGAR WATSON HOWE,
                        Country Town Sayings

———o———

Reputation is for time; character is for eternity.

                            JOHN B. GOFF

———o———

A good reputation is more valuable than money.

                    PUBLILIUS SYRUS, Maxim 108

———o———

Your reputation is the outcome of what you do; your character is determined by what you think.

———o———

A reputation for good judgment, fair dealing, truth, and rectitude, is itself a fortune.

                        HENRY WARD BEECHER

Credible Fable

Two brothers, convicted of stealing sheep, were branded on the forehead with the letters "S.T." meaning "Sheep Thief." One of the brothers was unable to bear the stigma, and tried to bury himself in a foreign land; but men asked him about the strange letters, so he kept on wandering restlessly, and at length, full of bitterness, died and was buried far from home.

The other brother said to himself, "I can't run away from the fact that I stole sheep. I will stay here and win back the respect of my neighbors and myself."

As years passed he built a reputation for integrity. Decades later, a stranger one day saw the old man with the letters on his forehead. He asked a native what they signified. "It happened a great while ago," said the villager. "I've forgotten the particulars, but I think the letters are an abbreviation of 'Saint'."

Rescue

A child was in a house in which a fire was raging away up in the fourth story. The child came to the window, and as the flames were shooting up higher and higher, she cried out for help. A fireman started up the ladder. The wind swept the flames near him, and it was getting so hot that he wavered. Thousands looked on, and their hearts quaked at the thought of the child having to perish. Someone in the crowd cried: "Give him a cheer!" Cheer after cheer went up, and as the man heard, he gathered fresh courage. Up he went into the midst of the smoke and the fire, and brought down the child in safety.

If you cannot go and rescue the perishing yourself, you can at least pray for those who do, and cheer them on. If you do, the Lord will bless the effort. Do not grumble and criticize; it takes neither heart nor brains to do that.

Daily Gems in Moody Monthly

He that turneth from the road to rescue another,
Turneth toward his goal:
He shall arrive by the foot-path of mercy,
God will be his Guide.

HENRY VAN DYKE,
The Tribe of the Helpers

Resolve, Resolutions

If it be my lot to crawl, I will crawl contentedly; if to fly, I will fly with alacrity; but, as long as I can avoid it, I will never be unhappy.

SYDNEY SMITH

———o———

Resolved, never to reprove another except I experience at the same time a peculiar contrition of heart.

HENRY MARTYN, in his diary

———o———

Beware of having too many resolutions and too little action.

———o———

I have never heard anything about the resolutions of the apostles, but a good deal about the *Acts* of the apostles.

HORACE MANN

———o———

January 2 is when most people find that it's easier to break a resolution than a habit.

Farm Journal

———o———

One reason we so often fail in our New Year's resolutions is that they are so often negative.

B. V. SEALS

———o———

The Backslider's Resolutions

January
"I hereby resolve to start to church this year. But I'll wait till February. Gotta get over the holidays. They take a lot out of a fellow, you know."

February
"Weather is terrible. I'll start when it warms up a bit. My blood is so thin this time of the year."

March
"Lots of sickness just now. Got to keep away from those bugs. A per-

son can't afford to take a chance."

April

"Easter . . . big crowds. You can't get a decent seat. Anyhow they won't miss me. It would look strange if I showed up only at Easter."

May

"I've been holed up all winter and now that the weather is getting pretty . . . It's time for reunions, too."

June

"I'll wait until the baby is older . . . how on earth do some folks bring their babies at two weeks of age and then never miss a Sunday?"

July

"Boy! Is the heat terrific! We've got that cabin that we still owe for . . . and that boat for Sunday pleasure."

August

"Preacher's on vacation. He'll never know if I miss this once. Never liked guest preachers anyhow . . . but when the preacher gets back . . ."

September

"School's started. Vacation threw me behind with my work. Gotta make one last visit to grandma's before the snow flies."

October

"Leaves are beautiful . . . I can worship God outdoors anyhow . . . and the kids will be cooped up all winter."

November

"My heart is bursting with gratitude and thanksgiving – the Christmas season will be a wonderful time to start back."

December

"What a madhouse . . . right after this is over my family and I will start back to church . . . the first Sunday in January. This next year I will resolve . . ."

ARNOLD PRATER in
The Miami Christian

———o———

Always bear in mind that your own resolution to succeed is more important than any other one thing.

Resources

One day an undergraduate came in to see me, blue in spirit because of the blue slip of those days which stated his indebtedness due that day in the college business office. So as to pray more intelligently with him I felt led to inquire as to his bill ($28.75, as I recall), and his resources ($.79).

Before we prayed I suggested he write an equation on the back of that bill. He wrote as I dictated:

$.79: $28.75 = 5$ loaves $+ 2$ small fishes: 5000 men $+$ women & children

"Which side of that equation is unbalanced?" I asked, but by that time his eyes had filled with tears. Together we prayed in faith to the Faithful One Who fed the multitude.

The next day unexpected money came in and the bill was paid.

And before you pray, take time to write down your resources and responsibilities and likewise learn anew our Lord's love and faithfulness.

V. RAYMOND EDMAN

———o———

Few men during their life-time come anywhere near exhausting the resources dwelling within them. There are deep wells of strength that are never used.

ADMIRAL RICHARD E. BYRD

Responsibility

Many are chosen, but they don't always accept.

———o———

The man who likes to shoulder his responsibilities never has room for a chip.

O. A. BATTISTA

———o———

Responsibility without accountability brings no result.

———o———

It is easy to dodge our responsibilities, but we cannot dodge the consequences of dodging our responsibilities.

SIR JOSIAH STAMP,
in The English Digest

———o———

Responsibilities move toward him who will shoulder them, and power flows to him who acts with energy.

I will go down, but remember that you must hold the ropes.

WILLIAM CAREY

———o———

Responsibility's like a string, we can only see the middle of. Both ends are out of sight.

WILLIAM McFEE

———o———

You cannot escape the responsibility of tomorrow by evading it today.

ABRAHAM LINCOLN

Resurrection

The Gospels do not explain the resurrection; the resurrection explains the Gospels.

JOHN S. WHALE

———o———

Christianity begins where religion ends, with the resurrection.

———o———

Song Of Resurrection

"Because Christ lives, I too shall live!"
O glorious truth divine!
To think that resurrection life was His
And shall be mine!

"Because Christ lives, I too shall live!"
I'll leave this lump of clay
And lift my wings to higher heights
On resurrection day!

"Because Christ lives, I too shall live!"
With Him I'll ever be
Rejoicing that He broke death's chains
And set my spirit free!

NAT OLSON

———o———

Simple markers are set upon the graves in the churchyard at Oberhofen, Switzerland. One who was too poor to purchase an engraved brass marker printed on a board the name and dates of birth and death of a departed loved one and placed it on the grave. Over this marker was put a little protective roof. In time a caterpillar fastened itself on the underside of the roof. There it passed through the death-like state of a chrysalis, and ultimately emerged as a beautiful butterfly, leaving its former corpse-like abode behind.

What a beautiful picture of the resurrection when Christ as His Second Coming "shall change our vile body, that it may be fashioned like unto His glorious body" (Philippians 3:21).

———o———

Belief in the resurrection is not an appendage to the Christian faith; it *is* the Christian faith.

JOHN S. WHALE

Retribution, Revenge

It was three o'clock in the morning when the telephone suddenly began to ring. Sleepily, Jones struggled out of bed and made his way across the room to answer it. "This is your neighbor," announced the angry voice on the other end. "Your dog has been barking all night, and I can't get to sleep. If you don't do something about it, I'm calling the police!"

The following night at three in the morning Jones phoned his neighbor. The sleepy man fumbled about for his slippers, then stumbled to the phone.

"Listen, buster," Jones said, "I don't own a dog!"

———o———

Some people do odd things to get even!

———o———

Revenge proves its own executioner.

FORD

———o———

It costs more to revenge injuries than to bear them.

THOMAS WILSON

———o———

Revenge converts a little right into a great wrong.

Reverence, Reverently

Enter A Church Reverently

Enter a church reverently;
Leave it reverently, too,
Go alone, that the quiet
May strengthen you.

Each one alone — so it was meant —
Though a thousand are there;

Each heart emptied and waiting,
Each heart at prayer.

Then through the still sanctuary
Falls a communal peace,
God to each heart has spoken,
Each heart has peace.

CAROL M. RITCHIE

———o———

Oliver Wendell Holmes was once
asked why he troubled to attend a
small church where the preacher was
a most ordinary man with no originality as a thinker. Dr. Holmes gave
this fine reply:
"I go because I have a little plant
called 'Reverence,' and I must needs
water it once a week or it would die."

Revival

Revival is a renewing and a reformation of the church for action.

MAX WARREN

———o———

"How can we have revival?" someone asked the great evangelist, Gypsy
Smith.
The wise, old preacher replied, "Take
a piece of chalk, and draw a circle on
the floor. Then step inside the circle
and pray: 'Lord, send a revival inside
this circle.'"

———o———

A native of India, writing to a friend
about a great revival they were having,
said, "We're having a rebible." Not a
bad idea. The church needs to be "re-
bibled."

———o———

An old-fashioned minister asked the
Lord to revive his church.
"You're asking the revival to start in
the wrong place," the Lord told him.
"Get the revival fires burning in your
members' homes, and then your church
will have a new glow."

———o———

In the hydraulics of evangelism, nar-
rowness builds up pressure; that is to
say, revivalism is still bringing in the
sheaves.

GEORGE E. SWEAZEY

Reward

To receive a reward is a good thing;
to deserve it is much better.

———o———

If we always have faith, hope and love,
Our reward is sure in heaven above.

———o———

The day is always his who worked in
it with serenity and great aims.

RALPH WALDO EMERSON

———o———

The Day Of Rewards

I'm looking forward to a day, the day
    of eternal rewards
When Christians shall be given crowns
    from the hands of Christ, our Lord;
Oh, what a glorious sight to see the re-
    deemed ones all march past
With wonderful, heavenly dividends,
    the riches that will last.

I can see the pastors, those godly men
    who have guided and fed the flock,
I can see them there, with their crowns
    so fair, humbly and steadily walk
On the streets of gold, while their mem-
    bers behold the reward for faithful-
    ness;
And the missionaries, too, who've
    stayed pure and true, with their
    trophies of fruitfulness.

Yes, I'm looking forward to that day,
    the day of eternal rewards;
And I'm working, and praying, and giv-
    ing, that I might receive from Christ,
    the Lord
Some trophy, some crown, some divi-
    dend to show I've not lived in vain;
Right now, I'm rather pressed for time
    for soon He'll come again!

NAT OLSON

———o———

A man's better reward is what he
becomes, not what he gets.

———o———

An award can pick up a good deal
of prestige by being refused by the
right person.

Herald-Journal, Clarinda, Iowa

"I think you're going to get an award at the end of the year," a first-grade teacher commented to a pupil for her perfect attendance.

A student excitedly spoke up from the back of the room: "I've got one of those on my hand – I think I got it playing with a frog."

Rich, Riches

It is better to live rich, than to die rich.

SAMUEL JOHNSON,
Boswell's *Life of Dr. Johnson, Vol. II*

———o———

A rich man is one who isn't afraid to ask the clerk to show him something cheaper.

———o———

We grow rich by depositing the Word of God in our hearts.

WILBUR SMITH

———o———

The futility of riches is stated very plainly in two places: the Bible and the income-tax form.

The Gilcrafter

———o———

A man is rich according to what he IS, not according to what he HAS.

———o———

Riches

How rich you may be, or how poor,
There is a way to tell for sure.
The method is a simple one,
And it is very quickly done.
How much or little is your part,
Your wealth is carried in your heart.
Your money, houses, bonds, and lands,
Slip easily from clutching hands.
The hours of happiness you share
With hands that cling and hearts that
  care,
The knowledge that you have a friend
Upon whose faith you can depend,
Love for your work, a sense of worth,
The joy and beauty of the earth,
Courage and confidence to meet
Whatever comes without defeat,
The worth you give on any day,
Nothing can take these things away.
Of riches this, friend, is your part,
All you can carry in your heart.

AUTHOR UNKNOWN

A tax collector one day came to a poor minister in order to assess the value of his property and to determine the amount of his taxes.

"I am a rich man," said the minister.

The official quickly sharpened his pencil and asked intently, "Well, what do you own?"

The pastor replied, "I am the possessor of a Saviour who earned for me everlasting life and who has prepared a place for me in the Eternal City."

"What else?"

"I have a brave, pious wife, and in the Bible it says, 'Who can find a virtuous woman? for her price is far above rubies.' "

"What else?"

"Healthy and obedient children."

"What else?"

"A merry heart which enables me to pass through life joyfully."

"What else?"

"That is all," replied the minister.

The official closed his book, arose, took his hat, and said, "You are indeed a rich man, Sir, but your property is not subject to taxation."

The King's Business

———o———

In this world, it is not what we take up, but what we give up, that makes us rich.

HENRY WARD BEECHER

———o———

We need not have riches in order to make life rich.

Right, Righteous

Better, though difficult, the right way to go,
Than wrong, 'tho easy, where the end is woe.

JOHN BUNYAN,
Pilgrim's Progress, Part I

———o———

Be sure you are right, then go ahead.
Motto of David Crockett in War of 1812

———o———

Sir, I would rather be right than be President.

HENRY CLAY, *Speech* (1850)

Rival

The best way to kill off a rival is to make him a friend.

———o———

He that falls in love with himself will have no rivals.

BENJAMIN FRANKLIN

Rule

No rule is so general, which admits not some exception.

ROBERT BURTON,
Anatomy of Melancholy

———o———

Don't blame the rule if you don't measure up.

———o———

Why is it that it's so much easier to make rules than to follow them?

———o———

We need to commit the Golden Rule to life as well as to memory.

S

Sacrifice

People talk of the sacrifice I have made in spending so much of my life in Africa. Can that be called a sacrifice which is simply paid back as a small part of a great debt owed to our God, which we can never repay? Is that a sacrifice which brings its own best reward in healthful activity, the consciousness of doing good, peace of mind, and the bright hope of a glorious destiny hereafter. I never made a sacrifice.

DAVID LIVINGSTONE

———o———

Once For All

Once into the holy place,
Spotless, free from sin,
With His blood the sacrifice,
Jesus entered in.
Once a year the high priest came
Others' blood to bring,
But Christ suffered once for all,
Himself sin's offering.
All the blood of bulls and goats
Never could suffice:
Christ must offer once for all
Perfect sacrifice.
Hanging there upon the cross,
For lost men He pleaded;
"It is finished!" was His cry,
Nothing more was needed.
No more daily sacrifice:
Salvation's work complete,

Our High Priest at God's right hand
Forever took His seat.
Can I add to such a work
By my weak endeavor?
No! I rest secure in His
Sacrifice forever.

BARBARA C. RYBERG

———o———

In a lonely valley in Switzerland a small band of patriots once marched against an invading force of ten times their strength. They found themselves one day at the head of a narrow pass, confronted by a solid wall of spears. They made assault after assault, but the bristling line remained unbroken. Time after time they were driven back decimated with hopeless slaughter. The forlorn hope rallied for the last time. As they charged, their leader suddenly advanced before them with outstretched arms, and every spear for three or four yards of the line was buried in his body. He fell dead. But he prepared a place for his followers. Through the open breach, over his dead body, they rushed to victory and won the freedom of their country. So the Lord Jesus went before His people, the Captain of our salvation, sheathing the weapons of death and judgment to Himself, and preparing a place for us with His dead body.

HENRY DRUMMOND

Sacrifice is only that which is given after the heart has given all that it can spare. To sacrifice for Christ's sake brings joy unbounded and peace unmoved by the fleeting things of this life.

Saints

Every saint in heaven is as a flower in the garden of God, and every soul there is as a note in some concert of delightful music. All together blend in rapturous strains in praising God and the Lamb forever.

JONATHAN EDWARDS

———o———

A little child on a summer morning stood in a great cathedral. The sunlight streamed through the beautiful stained glass windows and the figures in them of the servants of God were bright with brilliant color. A little later the question was asked, "What is a saint?" The child replied, "A saint is a person who lets the light shine through."

———o———

Saints are persons who make it easier for others to believe in God.

NATHAN SÖDERBLOM

Sales

A woman who was taking her first plane ride was seated next to a minister. During some turbulence, the lady became fearful and turned to the minister, asking him if he couldn't do something.

"Lady," he replied, "I'm in sales, not management!"

———o———

A Bargain Sale

I'm offering for sale today
 A lot of things I'll need no more;
Come, please, and take them all away,
 I've piled them up outside my door.
I'll make the prices low enough,
 And trust you, if it's trust you need;
Here I have listed all my stuff,
 Make your selection as you read:

A lot of prejudices which
 Have ceased to be of use to me;
A stock of envy of the rich,
 Some slightly shopworn jealousy;
A large supply of gloom that I
 Must not permit to clog my shelves;
I offer bargains — who will buy?
 Name prices that will suit yourselves.

A lot of wishes I've outgrown,
 A stock of silly old beliefs;
Some pride I once was proud to own,
 A bulky line of dreads and griefs;
An old assortment of ill will,
 A job lot of bad faith and doubt,
Harsh words that have their poison
  still;
 Choose as you please — I'm closing
  out.

I need more room for kindliness,
 For hope and courage and good
  cheer,
Take all the hatred I possess,
 The superstitions and the fear;
A large supply of frailties I
 Shall have no use for from today;
I offer bargains; who will buy?
 The rubbish must be cleared away!

S. E. KISER in
The Log of the Good Ship Grace

———o———

Salesmanship consists of transferring a conviction by a seller to a buyer.

PAUL G. HOFFMAN

Salvation

There is not a child born into the world but that would go straight to Christ except that someone hinders him.

G. CAMPBELL MORGAN

———o———

As soon as a child is capable of being damned, it is capable of being saved.

CHARLES HADDON SPURGEON

———o———

Win the man, you win the family;
 Win the family, you win the home;
Win the home and you win the community;
 Win the community and you win the nation.

A Parent's Prayer

To us, we pray, Lord give the joy
Of leading our own girl and boy
To that most bless'd and holy place
Where they will meet Thee face to
    face,
Confess their sins, see Christ's oblation,
Then in faith receive salvation.

We who have brought them, by Thy
    help
Into this world of sin and pain
Would be the ones to lead their steps
Within th' eternal King's domain.

So guard our words and guide our
    ways,
That in their very early days
Our little ones may grace receive
To see Christ dying — and believe.

While they are still beneath our wing
Accomplish, Lord, this holy thing.
This joy, more sweet than any other,
Belongs to Christian father and
    mother.

AUTHOR UNKNOWN

E'er a child has reached to seven,
Teach him all the way to heaven,
Better still the work will thrive
If he learn before he's five.

Why should men pay such a high
price for damnation when salvation is
free?

The Man Next Door

Jesus died to bring salvation,
    For the rich and for the poor;
Men of every tribe and nation —
    He includes the man next door.

Millions are in heathen darkness
    And with pleading hearts implore
For the gospel of salvation:
    What about the man next door?

We are stewards of our possessions
    And we bring from out our store
Means to spread abroad this gospel —
    Don't forget the man next door.

"Go into all the world," said Jesus,
    Tell them of my mighty power.
Bring your sheaves from every nation,
    Bring with you the man next door.

When we stand before our Saviour
    On that glad eternal shore,
Heaven's glory will be brighter
    If we've brought the man next door.

SELECTED

God is the originating cause of salva-
tion.
Jesus is the meritorious cause.
The Bible is the instrumental cause.
Faith is the conditional cause.
The Spirit is the efficient cause.
In other words:
God thought it.
Jesus bought it.
The Word taught it.
The mind caught it.
The soul sought it.
Faith brought it.
The Spirit wrought it.
The devil fought it.
But I've got it.

American Holiness Journal.

The elect are the "whosoever wills,"
the non-elect are the "whosoever
won'ts."

DWIGHT L. MOODY

An evangelist visited a man in a
pottery district who, in his younger
days, had been an infidel. The visitor
gazed upon two magnificent vases contained in a glass case. "What lovely
vases!" he remarked. "I suppose they
are very valuable?"
"Yes," was the reply.
"How much would you sell them
for?"
With a shake of the head, the man
turned to his questioner. "All the money in the world wouldn't tempt me to
part with either of them," he answered.
"Years ago I was a drunkard, a
gambler — one who sold his soul to the
devil. One day I was persuaded to
attend a revival meeting. I did so, and
on going home I passed a rubbish heap.
I saw there a piece of clay. Evidently

someone had thrown it away as being useless. I picked it up, took it home, kneaded it and molded it. Then I went to the wheel, and out of that worthless piece of clay I made those two vases. I thought to myself that if I could do such a thing as that, then God could do so with me. And thereafter I placed myself into His hands, and He has made me a new man."

———o———

The late Bishop Taylor Smith, the beloved evangelical of the Anglican faith, never lost an opportunity of introducing the subject of salvation to the ordinary people whom he met. On one occasion he sat in a barber's chair to have a shave, and ventured very courteously to mention the matter of salvation.

"I do my best," snapped the barber, "and that's enough for me."

The Bishop was silent until the shave was over, and when the next customer was seated the Bishop asked, "May I shave this man?"

"No, I'm afraid not," replied the barber, with a grin.

"But I would do my best," answered the Bishop.

"So you might, but your best would not be good enough for this gentleman."

"No," replied the Bishop quietly. "And neither is your best good enough for God."

———o———

We are saved by a Person, and only by a Person, and only by one Person.
WILLIAM F. MCDOWELL

———o———

He that will not be saved needs no preacher.

Satisfaction

A Good Day

To waken in the morning serene and quiet with the thought of His love and His strength — joyous in the thought of those whom He has given us to love and serve — humble in our weakness, and free from the shadow of self.

To care for our bodies as His temples and for our homes as His dwelling-place; striving to maintain in them that order, that beauty, and that law which He has ordained in His world.

To meet those who serve us with appreciation and sympathy, and those whom we serve with forethought and consideration.

To do the small duties with a sense that all faithful service ranks equally with God.

To pass over the rough places with joy, and through the dark places with peace.

To practice always His presence.

To see the beauty He has made.

To be where we are needed, and to make time for those who need us.

To pass on our way unhurried, without care, realizing that His is the Kingdom, the Power and the Glory.
SELECTED

———o———

Show me a thoroughly satisfied man — I will show you a failure.
THOMAS ALVA EDISON

———o———

If you are satisfied just to get by, step aside for the man who isn't.

Saving

The toughest part of putting something away for a rainy day is finding a clear day to do it.
Wall Street Journal

———o———

A man who both spends and saves has both enjoyments.
SAMUEL JOHNSON

———o———

When a man begins to think seriously of saving for a rainy day, it's probably a rainy day.
FRANKLIN P. JONES

———o———

At twenty a man thinks he can save the world;
At thirty he is happy if he can save part of his salary.

School

I feel so tired of school work, God, and
  every night it seems
That when I put away my books, I see
  them in my dreams.
Regardless of the many things that I
  would rather do,
I first must finish homework, God, and
  that is never through!
In spite of my complaining, though, I
  really can't deny
That I am very fortunate, because I
  know that I
Am learning things that I am sure will
  help me day by day
To meet whatever needs, O God, I
  have along the way.

GEORGE BILBY WALKER

———o———

Little Jerry's mother was crying when
he started for his first day at school.
"Aw, Mom, don't take it so hard," he
consoled her. "Just as soon as I learn
to write and read comics, I'll quit."

The Christian Science Monitor

———o———

School Days

The call to school it comes! It comes!
A muffler on the gypsy drums!
And birds and beasts and children sigh
While Summer murmurs soft, "Good-
  bye."
And gruff old Autumn paints his name
On leaves in shades of gold and flame.

Back to the classrooms and the books;
Back from vacation's cherished nooks;
Back with a sigh of deep regret;
Back to the cry of "Teacher's pet!"
Back to the place where pencils fly,
And love notes, too, upon the sly.

The call to school, it comes! It comes!
Recalling youth to maps and sums,
Athletic meets and frantic cheers,
But sad it falls on adult ears . . .
For hearts of grown-ups long in vain
To be a kid at school again!

NICK KENNY

———o———

Monday was the first day of school
for the little boy, and he enjoyed it
tremendously. Each day that followed,
he seemed to like it more. Then Friday came, and he returned home despondent. "Mom," he complained, "I've
been laid off for two days."

ANNA HERBERT in *Family Weekly*

Science

Everything science has taught me —
and continues to teach me — strengthens my belief in the continuity of our
spiritual existence after death.

WERNHER VON BRAUN

———o———

Science is but a mere heap of facts,
not a gold chain of truths, if we refuse
to link it to the throne of God.

FRANCES P. COBBE

———o———

There is something in man which
your science cannot satisfy.

THOMAS CARLYLE to Professor Tyndall

———o———

Science is a first-rate piece of furniture for a man's upper chamber, if
he has common sense on the ground
floor.

OLIVER WENDELL HOLMES

———o———

In this scientific age, the only impossible things are people.

———o———

Scientists are debating whether or not
splitting the atom was a wise crack.

———o———

Human science is an uncertain guess.

MATTHEW PRIOR

Scripture

It is very difficult for an individual
who knows the Scripture ever to get
away from it. It haunts him like an
old song. It follows him like the memory of his mother. It remains with him
like the word of a reverenced teacher.
It forms a part of the warp and woof
of his life.

WOODROW WILSON

Twenty-Third Psalm
(Vest-Pocket Edition)

Beneath me:	green pastures;
Beside me:	still waters;
With me:	my Shepherd;
Before me:	a table;
Around me:	my enemies,
After me:	goodness and mercy;
Beyond me:	the house of the Lord.

———o———

Two texts preachers ought to use for sermons more often than they do are: "Thou God seest me," and "The eyes of the Lord are in every place beholding the evil and the good."

———o———

A minister stood to read the Scripture at an evening camp meeting. As he opened his mouth and drew a deep breath, he sucked in a moth. Gulping but undaunted he said, "I was a stranger and ye took me in . . ."

Seasons

The seasons slip by and, before you know it, it's time for the bulbs you didn't get planted last fall not to come up.

Changing Times, The Kiplinger Magazine

———o———

To be interested in the changing seasons is a happier state of mind than to be hopelessly in love with spring.

GEORGE SANTAYANA

———o———

A few years ago in one of our first-grade classes, the teacher wanted to teach her students about the seasons of the year. One bright little lad waved his hand anxiously and said, "Teacher, I know what the four seasons are. They are squirrel season, quail season, duck season, and deer season."

MILDRED DANIELS in *Grade Teacher*

Secret

It's not so hard for a woman to keep a secret as it is for her to keep it a secret that she's keeping a secret.

SYDNEY J. HARRIS in *Coronet*

A secret is something you tell only one person at a time.

———o———

Some people have two ideas about a secret: it's either not worth keeping or it's too good to keep.

———o———

Let everyone carry his belongings in his own suitcase and his secrets in his own heart.

———o———

If you don't believe a ten-year-old boy can keep a secret, ask him where he left the family hammer.

Independent-Review, Aztec, New Mexico

———o———

One of the hardest secrets for a man to keep is his opinion of himself.

———o———

Secret sins seldom stay secret.

Security

Jesus Christ is no security against storms, but He is perfect security in storms.

———o———

God Holds The Key

God holds the key of all unknown
And I am glad;
If other hands should hold the key,
Or if He trusted it to me,
I might be sad.

The very dimness of my sight
Makes me secure;
For, groping my misty way,
I feel His hand: I hear Him say,
"My help is sure."

I cannot read His future plans;
But this I know:
I have the smiling of His face,
And all the refuge of His grace,
While here below.

J. PARKER

Self

God Pity Him!

God pity him who lives for self —
That one who does not share

The griefs and joys of other men,
That one who does not care.

God pity him who does not give
To others when in need;
God pity him who works and plans
For only selfish greed.

God pity him when sorrow comes
And no kind friend is there,
No one to grasp his trembling hand
And whisper low, "I care!"

God pity him when death shall come
And few stand by his bier;
So little missed by those he left,
They scarcely shed a tear!

God pity him who lives for self,
When the Master he shall see,
And Jesus says, "As you've done to
   them,
You've done it unto Me."

MRS. EDNA B. HUGHES in
The Log of the Good Ship Grace

———o———

Sin has four characteristics:
   Self-sufficiency instead of faith;
   Self-will instead of submission;
   Self-seeking instead of benevolence;
   Self-righteousness instead of humil-
   ity.

———o———

If you wish to know yourself, observe
how others act; if you wish to understand others, look into your own heart.
JOHANN CHRISTOPH FRIEDRICH VON SCHILLER

———o———

God hath entrusted me with myself.
EPICTETUS

———o———

We go on fancying that each man is
thinking of us, but he is not; he is like
us — he is thinking of himself.
CHARLES READE

———o———

It is the weight of self that overpowers;
Take up another's load, it carries ours.

———o———

Self-denial is an excellent guard of
virtue.
THOMAS TOWNSON

In the earlier years of my life I
studied the peculiarities of others.
Lately I am studying my own.
EDGAR WATSON HOWE

———o———

Nothing dies harder than the desire
to think well of oneself.
T. S. ELIOT,
Shakespeare and the Stoicism of Seneca

———o———

You can't be cheerful until you forget yourself. And you can't forget yourself until you remember others.

———o———

Selfishness aims for happiness but
always cheats itself out of it.

———o———

Lord, make me big enough to live
outside myself.
J. SHERMAN WALLACE

———o———

There's only one corner of the universe you can be certain of improving,
and that's your own self.
ALDOUS LEONARD HUXLEY

Serenity

To walk when others are running;
To whisper when others are shouting;
To sleep when others are restless;
To smile when others are angry;
To work when others are idle;
To pause when others are hurrying;
To pray when others are doubting;
To think when others are in confusion;
To face turmoil, yet feel composure;
To know inner calm in spite of every-
   thing —
This is the test of serenity.
DORIS LAGRASSE in *Sunshine Magazine*

Sermons

A sermon can help people in different ways. Some rise from it greatly
strengthened; others wake from it re-
freshed.

———o———

Parishioners' comments to their pastor upon leaving the church at the
close of services:

"Your sermons have been more meaningful ever since my husband lost his mind."

"Each of your sermons is better than the next one."

"I listened to every word you said and didn't understand any of them, but you have a nice face."

————o————

Child watching her father prepare his Sunday sermon: "Daddy, does God tell you what to say?"
Father: "He surely does. Why do you ask?"
Child: "Then, why do you scratch some of it out?"

Westminster Tidings

————o————

It warms the heart of a preacher to tell him how much you enjoyed his sermon, but if you want to pay him a real compliment tell him you will bring a friend to hear his next sermon.

————o————

You'd be surprised to know how many sermons are like blank cartridges, fired into the air just to hear a noise.

————o————

A sermon that gets only as far as the ear is like a dinner eaten in a dream.

CHARLES HADDON SPURGEON

————o————

An old Scottish woman said to her pastor, "That was a grand sermon you preached last Sabbath at the Kirk!"
Seeking to test her sincerity, he asked, "And what was the text?"
"Ah, meenister! I dinna ken the text or the words. But I came home and took the false bottom out o' my peck measure!"

Serve, Service

The story is told of a certain church in Europe which was bombed in World War II. In the explosion, a statue of Christ was mutilated by having the hands blown off. The statue has not been restored. It stands there today with the hands missing. But underneath has been put this well-known sentence: "Christ hath no hands but yours."

————o————

He has always chosen earthen vessels to be ambassadors of His grace. He proclaims His great Gospel through provincial dialects and He fills uncultured mouths with mighty arguments.

————o————

No man, no matter what may be his background can rise to the stature of spiritual manhood who has not found it nobler to serve somebody else than to serve himself.

————o————

It pays to serve the Lord; but don't serve the Lord because it pays — for if you serve the Lord because it pays, it then may not pay.

ROBERT G. LETOURNEAU

————o————

Have you been trying to serve God by halves or some other fraction? God asks total commitment.

————o————

O God, help us to be masters of ourselves that we may be servants of others.

SIR ALEC PATERSON

————o————

A New York City minister was pleased to have a churchgoer come to him to ask some questions about joining his church. After a long talk with the man the minister said, "One of the things that you will want to think about is the department of the church in which you would prefer to serve."

"Oh, I am not interested in anything like that," the man said. "I just want to join the church."

The minister was patient. "It is our custom to have all members divided into different service groups. Some work in the Sunday School, others in the music department, on the finance committee, the missionary emphasis group; many serve as church visitors. There are others who . . ."

"I didn't know that this was that kind of a church," the man interrupted. "I believe I will visit other churches before making a decision about joining."

The minister smiled kindly. "This church, you know, is known as 'The Church of the Saviour.' Maybe you are looking for 'The Church of the Heavenly Rest.'"

Adapted from *The Expositor*

———o———

Find out what God would have thee
    do,
Perform that service well;
For what is great and what is small,
'Tis only He can tell!

———o———

Some folks are bad spellers; they spell service "serve-us."

———o———

If you wish to be a leader you will be frustrated, for very few people wish to be led. If you aim to be a servant you will never be frustrated.

FRANK F. WARREN

Share

We cannot share what we do not possess.

———o———

We share our mutual woes,
Our mutual burdens bear,
And often for each other flows
The sympathizing tear.

JOHN FAWCETT,
Blest Be the Tie That Binds

———o———

About the only two things a child will share willingly are communicable diseases and his mother's age.

Wall Street Journal

———o———

Oh, many a shaft at random sent
Finds mark the archer little meant!
And many a word, at random spoken,
May soothe or wound a heart that's
    broken.

SIR WALTER SCOTT, *The Lord of the Isles*

There is a destiny that makes us brothers;
None goes his way alone.
All that we send into the lives of others
Comes back into our own.

EDWIN MARKHAM

Shut-Ins

God's Shut-Ins

A special glory seems to crown
The shut-in saint of God
A radiance of joy and peace
Bespeaks the way they've trod.

A patience and a yieldedness
To God's own precious will —
A steadfast faith and trust in Him
A purpose to fulfill.

Just like sweet flowers hidden there
Away from stress and strain,
They bloom in Christian loveliness
Midst loneliness and pain.

Shut out from Christian fellowship
They've loved and held most dear;
But now, shut in with Him alone
Who casts out every fear.

Within their quiet little room
Grow flowers of sweet content,
With fragrance of God's wondrous
    grace
And glory — heaven sent.

AUTHOR UNKNOWN

Signs

Sign on a new lawn in Alexandria, Virginia: "Please Don't Ruin The Gay Young Blades."

———o———

A New York bookstore, going out of business, had this sign in its window: "Words failed us."

———o———

No matter how clearly printed, "Keep Off The Grass" signs always seem to be illegible to two kinds of creatures: birds and some people.

———o———

Sign in the window of a vacant store: "We undersold everyone."

When a sign, "Stop for Pedestrians," was erected in a town square a near-sighted Baptist lady asked, "Why do we have to stop for Presbyterians?"

Silence

Well-timed silence hath more eloquence than speech.
MARTIN FARQUHAR TUPPER,
Proverbial Philosophy of Discretion

——o——

Silence is the unbearable repartee.
GILBERT KEITH CHESTERTON

——o——

Few men have ever repented of silence.
PATRICK HENRY

——o——

Silence

In silence comes all loveliness,
The dawn is ever still,
No noise accompanies the dew
That glistens on the hill.

The sunrise slips up quietly,
The moon is never heard,
And love that animates the eye
Surpasses any word.

So prayer is best in solitude,
It seems so very odd
That long ago, I did not know
In silence I'd find God.
JANE SAYRE

——o——

It does not mean that man has lost an argument when he is silent. He may be silent because he has won.

——o——

How can you expect God to speak to you in that gentle and inward voice which melts the soul, when you are making so much noise with your rapid reflections? Be silent, and God will speak again.
FRANÇOIS DE SALIGNAC DE LA MOTHE FÉNELON

——o——

Silence is the element in which great things fashion themselves.
THOMAS CARLYLE

Who is first silent in a quarrel springs from a good family.

——o——

The fact that silence is golden may explain why there's so little of it.

——o——

Silence is one of the hardest arguments to refute.
"JOSH BILLINGS" (HENRY WHEELER SHAW)

——o——

A man is known by the silence he keeps.
OLIVER HERFORD

——o——

Be silent or say something better than silence.

——o——

Silence is a better clue to intelligence than senseless chatter.

——o——

Think all you speak; but speak not all you think.
DELAUNE

——o——

Speech is great, but silence is greater.
THOMAS CARLYLE

Simplicity

Simplicity is an essential characteristic of greatness.

——o——

"The three greatest pieces in literature," observes an editor, "are the Lord's Prayer, the Twenty-Third Psalm and Lincoln's Gettysburg Address.

"Our Father which art in heaven, hallowed be Thy name . . . The Lord is my shepherd; I shall not want . . . Fourscore and seven years ago . . .

"Not a three-syllable word in them; hardly any two-syllable words. All the greatest things in human life are one-syllable things — love, joy, hope, home, wife, child, trust, faith, God. ALL great things are simple."

——o——

The simplicity which is in Christ is rarely found among us. In its stead are programs, methods, organizations, and a world of nervous activities which occupy time and attention, but can never satisfy the longing of the heart.

A. W. TOZER

———o———

A simple life is its own reward.

GEORGE SANTAYANA

———o———

God is not found in multiplicity, but in simplicity of thoughts and words.

MARGARET MARY HALLAHAN

Sin, Sinners

You can't put your sins behind you until you face them.

———o———

A small boy, fighting the town bully, was winning the battle. But while sitting astride the bully, he kept calling for help at the top of his voice. A passer-by asked him why he needed help. "I need help," answered the boy, because I can feel him starting to get up." So it is in our battle with sin. We constantly need God's help to win.

———o———

The Bible does not command sinners to go to church but it does tell the church to go out and seek the sinners.

———o———

One reason sin flourishes is that it is treated like a cream puff instead of a rattlesnake.

BILLY SUNDAY

———o———

Whenever a man is ready to uncover his sins, God is always ready to cover them with His blood.

———o———

A painstaking scientist discovered that the younger leaves of the compass plant, which grows in Texas, point north and south. By referring to them, one can find his direction even at night.

The younger leaves of the plant tilt edgewise to the ground and always point north and south. The older leaves, however, become weighted with dew and dust and point in all directions.

How tragic it is when a Christian becomes soiled and sullied by sin and worldliness and loses his power to effectively witness for Christ and point to "the Lamb of God, which taketh away the sin of the world" (John 1: 29).

WALTER B. KNIGHT

———o———

Remembered Sin

I made a lash of my remembered sins;
  I wove it firm and strong, with cruel tip,
And though my quivering flesh shrank from the scourge,
  With steady arm I plied the ruthless whip.

For surely I who had betrayed my Lord,
  Must needs endure this sting of memory.
But though my stripes grew sore, there came no peace,
  And so I looked again to Calvary.

His tender eyes beneath the crown of thorns
  Met mine, His sweet voice said, "My child, although
Those oft-remembered sins of thine have been
  Like crimson, scarlet, they are now like snow.

"My blood, shed here, has washed them all away,
  And there remaineth not the least dark spot,
Nor any memory of them, and so
  Should you remember sins which God forgot?"

I stood there trembling, bathed in light, though scarce
  My tired heart dared to hope. His voice went on,
"Look at thy feet, My child." I looked, and lo,
  The whip of my remembered sins was gone!

MARTHA SNELL NICHOLSON

———o———

Sin has many tools, but a lie is the handle which fits them all.

OLIVER WENDELL HOLMES,
The Autocrat of the Breakfast Table

The Law was broken in the people's hearts before it was broken by Moses' hand.

———o———

The ultimate proof of the sinner is that he does not recognize his own sin.

MARTIN LUTHER

———o———

A baker living in a small village bought his butter from a neighboring farmer. One day he became suspicious that the butter was not of the same weight as at first. For several days he weighed the butter, and concluded that the rolls of butter which the farmer brought were gradually diminishing in weight.

This angered the baker so that he had the farmer arrested. "I presume you have weights," said the judge. "No, sir," replied the farmer.

"How then do you manage to weigh the butter that you sell?"

"That's easily explained," said the farmer. "When the baker began buying his butter from me, I thought I'd get my bread from him, and it's his one-pound loaf I've been using as a weight for the butter I sell. If the weight of the butter is wrong, he has himself to blame."

Sin is like that. If it becomes the rule of our lives, it turns upon us to betray us when we least expect it. The deceiver becomes the deceived.

Sincerity

Does Your Life Ring True?

You may testify in public
That you love the Lord,
You may sing aloud His praises
And proclaim His Word;
You may tell of sins forgiven
Just as others do;
But the question comes, my brother,
Does your life ring true?

How about your daily conduct
As you come and go?
Are you careless in your dealings?
Does your grocer know
He can trust you for the payment
When your bill comes due?
True religion bears this testing:
Does your life ring true?

Are you kind to those who hate you,
Helping when you can?
Are you patient and forgiving
Towards your fellow-man?
Are you doing unto others
As you'd have them do
Were they in your stead, my brother,
Does your life ring true?

People see as well as hear you:
More than words are deeds;
When your life and lips speak discord,
Who respects your creeds?
'Tis the faithful, daily witness
Of the blood-washed, who
Give to God the glory due Him,
For their lives ring true.

AUTHOR UNKNOWN

———o———

The first virtue of all really great men is that they are sincere. They eradicate hypocrisy from their hearts. They bravely unveil their weaknesses, their doubts, their defects. They are courageous. They boldly ride a-tilt against prejudices. No civil, moral, nor immoral power overawes them. They love their fellowmen profoundly. They are generous. They allow their hearts to expand. They have compassion for all forms of suffering. Pity is the very foundation-stone of genius.

ANATOLE FRANCE

Sing

He started to sing
As he tackled the thing
That couldn't be done,
And he did it.

EDGAR A. GUEST

———o———

During a song service the congregation was singing "Glad Day." On the second stanza the song leader suggested that the women sing the first phrase, "I may go home today," and the men sing the response, "Glad day, glad day."

———o———

Little boy: "Didn't God love Adam?"
Teacher: "Yes, of course. Why?"
Boy: "Well, we sing 'Jesus Loves Eve'n Me.'"

Teach

A Primary boy was enthusiastically singing "From fig tree unto fig tree" as he went from the departmental worship service to his Sunday School class. The dismayed superintendent, recognizing the tune, realized that he had not been careful in teaching these words to the song: "From victory unto victory."

———o———

"Who put the stars in the sky?" asked the Sunday School teacher in reviewing the previous week's lesson.

"I know," said Jimmy. "It was America!"

"How do you know it was America?" the teacher asked with interest.

"Well, for one thing, we sang about it in church," Jimmy explained. "You know, that song that goes, 'It took America to put the stars in place!'"

———o———

"What song would you like to sing today?" asked the Bible Club leader.

"The Andy song," quickly answered a little girl.

"But we don't know that song," the teacher said.

"Yes we do," answered the little girl. "We sing, 'Andy walks with me, Andy talks with me . . .'"

Skepticism

Skepticism can easily become the most fraudulant of all dogmatisms.

———o———

A laborer was asked by a skeptic, "Sam, how do you know you are saved?"

The laborer who was carrying a heavy sack of potatoes on his back took several steps, then suddenly dropped the bag. "How do I know I have dropped the bag?" he asked the skeptic. "I haven't looked around to see if it's gone from my back!"

"No," replied the skeptic. "But you can tell by the lessening of the weight."

"Yes," conceded the laborer. "And that is how I know I am saved. I lost the weight of sin and guilt I carried.

Instead I have found peace and satisfaction in the Lord Jesus Christ."

———o———

Most of the skepticism about the Bible arises from utter ignorance of it.

Sleep

Insomnia is what a person has when he lies awake all night for an hour.

———o———

Sweet are the slumbers of the virtuous man.

JOSEPH ADDISON, *Cato*

———o———

Sleep is the best cure for waking troubles.

MIGUEL DE CERVANTES

Smile

It takes seventy-two muscles to frown and only fourteen to smile. So, smile!

———o———

Keep smiling. It makes everybody wonder what you've been up to.

———o———

Smiles are the reflections of kindness, which the deaf can hear and the dumb can understand.

———o———

A smile is a wrinkle that shouldn't be removed.

Coast Federal Magazine

———o———

Smile And Smile

I gave a smile to one I met,
  She passed it to another;
He started running home to give
  It to his baby brother.

The baby smiled at its own dad,
  He passed it to his neighbor;
Next it slipped into a pit
  Where men were hard at labor.

So, on and on, from heart to heart,
  That smile kept ever spreading;
A light of life and cheerfulness
  It kept on ever shedding.

And when at night, as I sat down,
All tired and warm from duty,
That smile came winging back to me —
I marveled at its beauty!

GLADYS MELROSE GEARHART
in *Log of the Good Ship Grace*

———o———

A Smile

Let others cheer the winning man,
There's one I hold worthwhile;
'Tis he who does the best he can.
Then loses with a smile.

Beaten he is, but not to stay
Down with the rank and file;
That man will win some other day
Who loses with a smile.

AUTHOR UNKNOWN

———o———

Smiles give birth to smiles; "sour pusses" beget sour kittens.

———o———

A smile can add a great deal to one's face value.

———o———

A smile is a curve that can set lots of things straight.

Houston Bulletin

———o———

The world is like a mirror,
Reflecting what you do.
And if your face is smiling,
It smiles right back to you.

AUTHOR UNKNOWN

———o———

If a customer doesn't have a smile, give him one of yours.

Sorrow

Christ, who in the hour of sorrow
Bore the curse alone;
I, who through the lonely desert
Trod where He had gone.
He and I, in that bright glory
One deep joy shall share;
Mine, to be forever with Him,
His, that I am there.

PAUL GERHARDT

No sorrow touches man until it has been filtered through the heart of God.

JOE BLINCO

———o———

Sorrow leaves us good; it teaches us to know our friends.

HONORÉ DE BALZAC

———o———

Most of our sorrows spring from forgetfulness of God.

———o———

The remedy for sadness is prayer.

WILLIAM BERNARD ULLATHORNE

———o———

Only the soul that knows the mighty grief can know the mighty rapture. Sorrows come to stretch out spaces in the heart for joy.

EDWIN MARKHAM

Soul, Soul Winning

I Felt God Touch My Soul

I felt God touch my soul today —
What holy, tranquil rest!
What blessed hope through faith in Him
Came surging through my breast!
My mind was clear, my heart made pure,
Touched by His sacred flame,
Plus every joy I could possess,
Through faith in Jesus' name.

One touch from God, our Friend divine,
Gives strength each trying hour,
And lends us courage, grace and love
To foil the tempter's power.
Touch me again, dear Lord, I pray —
I need Thee, oh, so much!
Please keep me zealous for Thy cause,
Encouraged by Thy touch.

F. W. DAVIS

———o———

Your soul is eternal; feed it well.

DOUGLAS STIMERS

———o———

If your soul is hungry, don't quibble about the things you don't understand. Partake of the Bread of Life; then you'll live.

Sign on church bulletin board: "Be the soul support of your children."

———o———

Whenever the soul comes to itself and attains something of its natural soundness, it speaks of God.

TERTULLIAN

———o———

My soul is like a mirror in which the glory of God is reflected, but sin, however insignificant, covers the mirror with smoke.

ST. THERESA

———o———

As the flower turns to the sun, or the dog to his master, so the soul turns to God.

WILLIAM TEMPLE

———o———

When we reach for the souls of men, we touch Satan at his most sensitive spot.

CHARLES W. ANDERSON

———o———

Soul winners are not soul winners because of what they know, but because of Whom they know, and how well they know Him, and how much they long for others to know Him.

DAWSON TROTMAN

———o———

The soul in its highest sense is a vast capacity for God.

HENRY DRUMMOND

———o———

One can hardly think too little of oneself. One can hardly think too much of one's soul.

GILBERT KEITH CHESTERTON

———o———

Before any congregation can hope to excel in soul winning, the officers and members must first be at peace with each other.

ANDREW W. BLACKWOOD

———o———

The last thing the devil wants you to do is to win a soul definitely to Christ. If you don't believe it, try it.

The devil will let you go to prayer meeting, he will let you talk religious subjects and do "many mighty deeds," if only you will stop short of persuading men to accept Christ as Lord and openly confess Him before men.

CHARLES ALEXANDER

———o———

Said Dr. G. Campbell Morgan, "There was a time in my evangelistic work when I feared to talk to people of high position and culture in the inquiry room. Then one night I knelt beside an old man whom sin had all but wrecked. I spoke to him of the cleansing blood of Christ, and of the possibility of his becoming a new creature in Christ. Presently, someone asked, 'Please speak to the other man kneeling beside you.' I turned and recognized the mayor of the city, who six weeks before had sentenced the oldster to a month's hard labor. Both men were equally lost. Both accepted Christ. The mayor joyfully shook hands with the old man and said, 'Well, we didn't meet here the last time!'"

The old man recognized the mayor and said, "No, and we will never meet again as we did the last time! I'm a new man in Christ, and we are brothers!"

"That scene," said Dr. Morgan, "lingers with me yet. It removed my fear to speak to anyone about Christ."

WALTER B. KNIGHT

———o———

Evangelist Billy Sunday had returned to a city for a second series of meetings. One evening when the invitation was given for sinners to come forward, a man staggered up the aisle and stood before Sunday. "Do you remember me?" he asked.

"I don't believe I do," the evangelist answered.

"You should," the man said. "You saved me when you were here before."

"Yes," said Billy, "I imagine I did. You look like the kind of job I'd do. I know the Lord wouldn't do a job like that."

LULA M. OLDS in Reader's Digest

Space, Space Age

The true end in life is not to explore outer space for man's self-aggrandizement, but to prepare this inner space for God's glory.

———o———

The little boy's father was reading him nursery rhymes and doing quite well until he came to the account of the cow jumping over the moon. The boy thought a moment before asking: "That's interesting. Now tell me how the cow developed that much thrust."

F. G. KERNAN in *Family Weekly*

———o———

On bulletin board in front of the High Street Christian Church in Lexington, Kentucky: "Traveling to outer space? Instructions inside!"

———o———

A sign of our astronautical times occurred in the Kindergarten Department during prayer time for the pastor who was leaving on a world tour.

"Did you know Mr. Houk was going *around the world?*" asked the superintendent impressively.

To which one five-year-old replied, "How many times?"

Chimes, Glendale Presbyterian Church

———o———

The second graders' project on space travel hit a snag. One boy complained, "The girls want to put up curtains in our space ship."

Michigan Educational Journal

———o———

From Outer Space

He came — our God from outer space,
Became a man — to join our race;
But left His throne and glory there,
Our woes to take — our sins to bear.

In manger there — a little one,
'Twas known by few — this was God's Son;
The angels sang to shepherds lone,
The rest of men took ways their own.

This One from outer space was poor,
No pillow his — nor home secure;
On dusty paths with lesser speed,
As Roman guard each rode his steed.

The multitude He gladly fed —
Those lost in sin He homeward led;
The blind received their sight again,
And suff'ring ones — relief from pain.

He was not known — e'en by His kin,
His synagogue — He did not win;
His nation then received Him not,
And Pilate too joined in the plot.

At last the storm broke o'er His head,
No rest until they saw Him dead;
With seal and guard the tomb they close —
'Twas but three days — AND HE AROSE.

To outer space He now returned,
This One — the world had killed and spurned;
His promise is — "I'll come again" —
He's told us how but not the when.

If He's your Lord and Saviour — Friend
Your life on earth will safely end;
And you to outer space will go,
Your Glory Lord by face to know.

JOHN W. DUNLOP

Speak, Speakers, Speeches

Our speaker needs no introduction, just an early conclusion.

———o———

What You Say

What you say in a hurry
May cause you much worry;
So weight your words well —
What you'd say.

Ill-chosen expressions,
Oft give wrong impressions.
So think first, then speak;
It will pay.

W. LANGHORST

———o———

One critic of a speaker said, "He did not put enough fire in his speech."

A second critic replied, "He did not put enough of his speech in the fire!"

The best recipe for an after-dinner speech is to add a good portion of shortening.

———o———

Never rise to speak till you have something to say; and when you have said it, cease.

JOHN WITHERSPOON

———o———

The tire is as great as the length of the spoke.

———o———

World's best after-dinner speech: "Waiter, give me both checks."

———o———

Backward, turn backward, O Time, in thy flight,
I've just thought of a "come-back" I needed last night.

Sunshine Magazine

———o———

Briefly Speaking

We gave him thirty minutes,
He finished up in ten.
Oh, there's a prince of speakers
And a servant unto men.
His diction wasn't much as such,
He hemmed and hawed a bit,
And still he spoke a lot of sense
And after that — he quit.
At first we sat plumb paralyzed,
Then cheered and cheered again;
We gave him thirty minutes
And he finished up in ten!

From A Trade Magazine

———o———

Blessed is the man who, having nothing to say, abstains from giving in words evidence of the fact.

GEORGE ELIOT (MARY ANN EVANS),
Impressions of Theophrastus Such

———o———

"Our guest speaker needs no introduction — we don't have time for his speech!"

DALE MCFEATTERS

———o———

Generally speaking, preachers are.

Blessed are they that speak short for they shall be invited again.

———o———

Hint To Speakers:

Be brief,
Be bright,
Be gone.

———o———

There are two kinds of cleverness, and both are priceless. One consists of thinking of a bright remark in time to say it. The other consists of thinking of it in time not to say it.

The English Digest

———o———

What some public speakers lack in depth, they give you in length.

———o———

After the Sunday School Conference speaker had finished, the chairman said, "Now without wasting any more time we will go to our workshops."

———o———

A speaker's reply to a flowery introduction: "I appreciate those sweet words. They are like perfume: you can smell it but you can't swallow it."

———o———

The effective public speaker is one who forgets himself, looks at his audience, loves them, blesses them, gets the feel of their needs, and then seeks to fill those needs.

ERIC BUTTERWORTH in *Good Business*

———o———

Introduction of the last speaker at a banquet: "And he that is last, must be brief."

———o———

Some speakers who don't know what to do with their hands should try clamping them over their mouths.

G. NORMAN COLLIE
in *Saturday Evening Post*

———o———

Applause at the beginning of an address is faith, during the address is hope, at the end is charity.

He is considered the most graceful speaker who can say nothing in most words.

SAMUEL BUTLER

———o———

Lecturer: One with his hand in your pocket, his tongue in your ear, and his faith in your patience.

AMBROSE BIERCE

———o———

Why doesn't the fellow who says, "I'm no speech-maker," let it go at that instead of giving a demonstration.

FRANK MCKINNEY HUBBARD

———o———

"How long shall I speak?" asked the banquet speaker.

"As long as you wish," replied the master of ceremonies, "but the rest of us will leave about 8:30!"

———o———

A good many people can make a speech, but saying something is more difficult.

HERBERT V. PROCHNOW

———o———

Let us say what we feel, and feel what we say; let speech harmonize with life.

SENECA

———o———

Before we can speak God's message, we must learn to listen. The opened ear comes before the opened mouth.

A. B. SIMPSON

———o———

Guard Thy Lips

Words are things of little cost
Quickly spoken, quickly lost,
We forget them, but they stand
Witnesses at God's right hand
And their testimony bear
For us or against us there,
Oh how often ours have been
Idle words, and words of sin!
Words of anger, scorn and pride,
Or desire our faults to hide
Envious tales, or strife unkind
Leaving bitter thoughts behind.
Grant us, Lord, from day to day
Strength to watch and grace to pray;
May our lips from sin set free

Love to speak and sing of Thee
Till in Heaven we learn to raise
Hymns of everlasting praise.

AUTHOR UNKNOWN

———o———

Speech

Talk happiness. The world is sad enough
Without your woe. No path is wholly rough.
Look for the places that are smooth and clear,
And speak of them to rest the weary ear
Of earth, so hurt by one continuous strain
Of mortal discontent and grief and pain.

Talk faith. The world is better off without
Your uttered ignorance and morbid doubt.
If you have faith in God, or man, or self,
Say so; if not, push back upon the shelf
Of silence all your thoughts till faith shall come.
No one will grieve because your lips are dumb.

Talk health. The dreary, never-ending tale
Of mortal maladies is more than stale;
You cannot charm or interest or please
By harping on that minor chord, disease,
Say you are well, or all is well with you,
And God shall hear your words, and make them true.

ELLA WHEELER WILCOX

———o———

If you your lips would keep from slips,
Five things observe with care:
To whom you speak; of whom you speak;
And how, and when, and where.
If you your ears would save from jeers,
These things keep meekly hid:
Myself and I, and mine and my,
And how I do and did.

WILLIAM EDWARD NORRIS,
Nursery Rhyme, quoted in Thirlby Hall

God's great gift of speech abused
Makes thy memory confused.

ALFRED, LORD TENNYSON

Spirit, Spiritual

A solemn and religious regard to
spiritual and eternal things is an indispensable element of all true greatness.

DANIEL WEBSTER

———o———

You can't win over the devil with
physical force, with human influence,
with scientific skill, with money, with
arguments or threats or promises. It
takes spiritual armor and weapons provided by God and Him alone.

———o———

Spiritual Bath

So you "already know" the Bible
stories, and don't read the Good Book?
A teenager answers: "Nobody has to
bathe every day, but you'll smell if
you don't. Reading the Bible a bit
everyday is like taking a spiritual bath."

———o———

The spiritually successful person did
the things that you intended to do.

———o———

Spiritual gifts are given, not for competition but for cooperation.

GERALD W. COX

Spring

Spring unlocks the flowers to paint
the laughing soil.

REGINALD HEBER

———o———

Stately spring!
Whose robe-folds are valleys,
Whose breast-bouquet is gardens,
And whose blush is vernal evening.

JEAN PAUL RICHTER

———o———

It is always springtime in the heart
that loves God.

JEAN-MARIE VIANNEY

———o———

Spring

Now Spring has passed my way again
And left me with a trace of loveliness
within her charm of tenderness and
grace;
Calling forth the songs of birds, the
flowers, and budding trees
And, with her warm and tender kiss,
awakened memories.
To me she has been just as sweet as
when, at ten,
I roamed the daisy fields of yore, and
picked flowers in the glen.
I say that Spring has passed my way
And still it plays a part of all the lovely
things of life I keep within my heart.

J. EVANS ANDERSON

———o———

Close to my heart I fold each lovely
thing
The sweet day yields; and not discon-
solate
With calm impatience of the woods, I
wait
For leaf and blossom, when God gives
us Spring.

JOHN GREENLEAF WHITTIER

———o———

Spring bursts today, for Christ is
risen and all the earth's at play.

CHRISTINA GEORGINA ROSSETTI

———o———

Boy In Spring

He rolls his marbles, flies his kite,
And shares each day the fresh delight
Awakening across the land.
He has a baseball in his hand
When he goes out to join his friends.
So many happy hours he spends
Fishing beside a little stream
Where sunlight casts a shimmering
gleam.
Oh, there is so much to enjoy
When beckoning Spring meets eager
boy!

LOUISE DARCY

Stand

When pulling together means pulling
away from God, a Christian must be
willing to stand alone.

MAJOR MARGARET TROUTT

I'm standing, Lord.
There is a mist that blinds my sight.
Steep jagged rocks, front, left, and
right,
Lower, dim, gigantic, in the night.
Where is the way?

I'm standing, Lord.
Since Thou hast spoken, Lord, I see
Thou hast beset — these rocks are Thee!
And since Thy love encloses me,
I stand and sing.

BETTY STAM

Stand Close To All

Stand close to all, but lean on none,
And if the crowd desert you,
Stand just as fearlessly alone,
As if a throng begirt you;
And learn what long the wise have
known
Self-flight alone can hurt you.

WILLIAM S. SHURTLEFF

Stewardship

Stewardship: Keeping your hands off
that which belongs to God.

Stewardship

Steward I — and not possessor
Of the wealth entrusted me.
What, were God Himself the holder,
Would His disposition be?
This I ask myself each morning,
Every noon and night,
As I view His gentle goodness
With an ever new delight.

Steward only — never owner —
Of the time that He has lent.
How, were He my life's custodian,
Would my years on earth be spent?
Thus I ask myself each hour,
As I plod my pilgrim way,
Steeped in gratefulest amazement
At His mercy day by day.

Steward only — not possessor —
Of that part of Him that's I.
Clearer grows this truth and dearer,
As the years go slipping by.

May I softly go, and humbly,
Head and heart in reverence bent,
That I may not fear to show Him
How my stewardship was spent.

STRICKLAND W. GILLILAN

In stewardship no man can perform
the duty of another. No proxy is allowed or possible. Stewardship involves personal responsibility.

C. A. COOK

The story is told of a good farmer
who loved the Lord and believed in
stewardship. He was very generous indeed, and was asked by his friends why
he gave so much and yet remained so
prosperous? "We cannot understand
you," his friends said. "Why, you seem
to give more than the rest of us, and
yet you always seem to have greater
prosperity."

"Oh," said the farmer, "that is very
easy to explain. You see, I keep shoveling into God's bin and God keeps
shoveling more and more into mine,
and God has the bigger shovel."

HERBERT LOCKYER

What Is A Pledge?

A pledge is more than money or a
figure on a check.
It is the gift of a part of one's self to
Christ for His work.
It is a contribution to Christian edu-
cation.
It is an investment in a better com-
munity.
It is a gift of gratitude to God.
It is a vote for a Christian world.
It is an outreaching hand to other
nations in a ministry of health and
healing through missions.
It is a gesture of goodwill.
It is a service to those in sorrow.
It is an aid to our youth.
It is an expression of faith in the fu-
ture.
It is an effort to extend one's Chris-
tian influence.
A pledge is a holy thing, dedicated
to God for the service of all men.

Christmas Evans was hard pressed to make ends meet. This early nineteenth century pastor, beloved widely as the "Bunyan of Wales," preached to huge congregations which responded marvelously to his fervent eloquence. But his paydays were usually disappointing. Evans was often perplexed. He could not reconcile his hearers' insatiable appetite for sermons with their utter indifference to his material needs.

After an especially stirring message Christmas Evans was accosted by a leading woman of the congregation. "Well, Christmas Evans," she greeted, "I understand that we are again in arrears on your salary. I do hope you will be paid at the resurrection. You surely gave us a wonderful sermon today."

Evans eyed the woman closely. Her own prosperity was quite evident. "No doubt I will be rewarded at the resurrection," Evans answered, "but what am I to live on until that time? And what about my horse — what will she do? For her there will be no resurrection. But she does need to eat now!"

The pastor paused and the fashionable parishioner started to stammer an embarrassed apology. But Christmas Evans interrupted. "Moreover, what about people like you — what reward will you get at the resurrection for your unfaithfulness in stewardship? You get on so well in this world, are you not concerned lest it be hard with you at the resurrection?"

Adapted from *Gospel Herald*, printed in *The Sunday School World*

———o———

A man may decide to accept or reject Jesus Christ. But once he has accepted Christ, it is not for him to decide whether or not he will be a steward, for he becomes one when he becomes a Christian. He may be a poor steward, or a good steward, nevertheless, he is a steward. He has been entrusted with the gospel of Jesus Christ, and has been given the gift of eternal life, and it is his high calling to share this gift with others. The one requirement that is placed on a steward is that he be found faithful (I Corin-

thians 4:2). The ministry of Christian giving is fulfilled to the extent that a man is faithful in the stewardship of the gospel and of all that is his to share.

LUTHER POWELL in *Money and the Church*

———o———

In San Antonio, Texas, some church workers were soliciting contributions for the year. A woman said, "My husband lost his job, and we are on unemployment compensation for $28 per week. And so we are going to revise our contribution."

The workers expressed sympathy, and offered assistance to the family.

The woman said, "I said we would revise our contribution to the church. We will pay $2.80 per week."

A check of the church's congregation revealed that if the entire membership had been on unemployment compensation and given ten percent, the total contribution would have doubled.

Stranger

A stranger is a friend I have not yet met.

———o———

Not A Stranger

I shall not behold a stranger when I look upon the face
Of my own beloved Saviour, who redeemed me by His grace;
He will be the same dear Jesus that I've known for many years,
Who has comforted in sorrow, cheered my heart and wiped my tears.

I shall not behold a stranger when some day I'll open wide
These mine eyes and in the glory find myself quite satisfied.
Then I'll be with Him forever, sins and fears and longings past,
In the house of many mansions I will be at home at last.

AUTHOR UNKNOWN

Strength

Dwight L. Moody tells the story of an Atlantic passenger who lay in his bunk in a storm, deathly seasick. A cry of "Man overboard!" was heard. "May God help the poor fellow," prayed the man, "there is nothing I can do." Then he thought, "At least I can put my lantern in the porthold," which he did. The man was rescued, and recounting the story the next day, said, "I was going down in the darkness for the last time when someone put a light in a porthole. It shone on my hand, and a sailor in the life boat grabbed it and pulled me in."

Weakness is no excuse for our not putting forth all the little strength we have, and who can tell how God will use it?

———o———

Our strength is shown in the things we stand for. Our weaknesses are shown in the things we fall for.

HUGH A. COWAN

———o———

"Look, Daddy, I pulled up this great big cornstalk all by myself."

"My, but you're strong, Dickie," said Daddy.

"I guess I am!" said Dickie. "The whole world had hold of the other end of it."

———o———

Little Johnny (his eyes filled with tears, to mother peeling onions): "Those onions are strong, Mom; I can smell them with my eyes!"

———o———

Prayer For Strength

This is my prayer to Thee, my Lord — Strike, strike at the root of penury in my heart.
Give me the strength lightly to bear my joys and sorrows.
Give me the strength to make my love fruitful in service.
Give me the strength never to disown the poor or bend my knees before insolent might.
Give me the strength to raise my mind above daily trifles.
And give me the strength to surrender my strength to Thy will with love.

RABINDRANATH TAGORE

Do not pray for an easy task. Pray to be stronger!

Strikes

Strikes

Strikes are quite proper, but mind you strike right:
Strike at your vices at once with your might.
Strike off the fetters of fashion and pride,
Strike at the follies which swarm at your side.
Strike at the customs which lead men to drink,
Strike for the freedom to think and let think.
Strike for your friend and be thoughtful and kind,
Strike for the truth and speak out your own mind.
Strike in the strength which comes from above,
Strike for the cause of peace and of love.
Strike not with the fist, and give no man a blow.
Strike in the spirit which blesses the foe.
Strike in that fashion, strike home and strike straight,
Strike now, my good friends, there's no reason to wait.

CHARLES HADDON SPURGEON

Study

There are more men ennobled by study than by nature.

MARCUS TULLIUS CICERO

———o———

There is no study that is not capable of delighting us after a little application to it.

ALEXANDER POPE

———o———

In cheerfulness is the success of our studies.

PLINY

———o———

Let the great book of the world be your principal study.

LORD CHESTERFIELD

Success

Success is the fine art of making mistakes when nobody is looking.

———o———

The measure of success is not whether you have a tough problem to deal with, but whether it's the same problem you had last year.

JOHN FOSTER DULLES

———o———

Success formula: Think up a product that costs a dime to make, sells for a dollar and is habit-forming.

———o———

Success comes in cans. Failure comes in can'ts.

FRED SEELEY

———o———

Only in dictionaries does success come before work.

———o———

If you wish to succeed in life, make perseverance your bosom friend, experience your wise counselor, caution your elder brother, and hope your guardian genius.

JOSEPH ADDISON

———o———

To succeed in the world, you must assert yourself;
To succeed in God's sight, you must deny yourself.

———o———

I would rather fail in a cause that will someday succeed than to succeed in a cause that will someday fail.

WOODROW WILSON

———o———

To laugh often and much; to win the respect of intelligent people and the affection of children; to earn the appreciation of honest critics and endure the betrayal of false friends; to appreciate beauty, to find the best in others; to leave the world a bit better, whether by a healthy child, a garden patch, or a redeemed social condition; to know even one life has breathed easier because you lived. This is to have succeeded.

RALPH WALDO EMERSON

Success is the ability to get along with some people — and ahead of others.

———o———

Some people got to the top just by being stuck in the back of the elevator.

———o———

There is so much I have learned, I sometimes wonder whether I have been a success at all.

ABRAHAM LINCOLN

———o———

Success measured merely by money is too cheap.

———o———

If success made the heart swell the way the head does, this would be a great deal better world.

———o———

To succeed, work your tongue little, your hands much, and your brains most.

———o———

Our successes we ascribe to ourselves; our failures to destiny.

———o———

The man who wakes up and finds himself successful in God's work has not been asleep.

———o———

If at first you don't succeed, you are running about average.

The Lion

———o———

Self-trust is the first secret of success.

RALPH WALDO EMERSON

———o———

If at first you don't succeed, don't succumb.

ARNOLD H. GLASGOW

———o———

If you think you cannot succeed you are probably right!

———o———

If success turns your head, you're facing in the wrong direction.

———o———

You're on the road to success when

you realize that failure is merely a detour.

WILLIAM G. MILNES, JR.

———o———

Success is to be measured not so much by the position that one has reached in life as by the obstacles which he has overcome while trying to succeed.

BOOKER T. WASHINGTON

———o———

Success is never final and failure never fatal. It's courage that counts.

GEORGE F. TILTON

Suffering

No pain, no palm; no thorns, no throne; no gall, no glory; no cross, no crown.

WILLIAM PENN

———o———

My mind is absorbed with the sufferings of man. Since I was twenty-four there never [has been] any vagueness in my plans or ideas as to what God's work was for me.

FLORENCE NIGHTINGALE

———o———

It is suffering and then glory. Not to have the suffering means not to have the glory.

ROBERT C. MCQUILKIN

———o———

We that are sick
Must suffer pain,
Yes, that may be —
But this our comfort,
That it leaves us free
To look up quietly
At Calvary.

HIROMI

———o———

We learn from the things we suffer.

AESOP

———o———

Suffering for Christ is not when we are buffeted for our faults, or when we are busybodies in other men's matters, but when we are straight for God, not men-pleasers. Have convictions for God and obey them.

Pain is no evil unless it conquers us.

GEORGE ELIOT (MARY ANN EVANS)

Summer

Summer is the topsy-turvy season when the goldfish have to be boarded out while the family goes on a fishing trip.

The English Digest

———o———

Summertime is the time when it's too hot to do the things it was too cold to do during the winter.

———o———

If I Could

If I could take my brush and paint
  heaven's azure blue,
Or could I etch the hush of early morning dew;

If I could set the fleecy white of every
  drifting cloud,
Or capture glowing, golden tones with
  autumn hues endowed;

But I can only watch the tender hand
  of God
Pull back each summer's curtain from
  off this changing sod!

Upon earth's mighty easel God paints
  His pictures rare,
And grants His humble creatures a
  sanctuary there.

JANET MILLER

———o———

Summer Gold

The hills are decked with gold nuggets
As summer puts on her display.
Bright dandelions break through the
  earth
And seem to appear in a day.

Roadsides glisten with yellow
Like a million suns in the grass,
And children can have all the gold
By gathering when they pass.

A few short weeks and the gold is gone
And silver has taken its place
As little seeds wing their way in the
  air . . .
Parachutes of delicate lace.

NORMA REESER

Sunday

Sunday Morning

If I could turn life's pages back and
    from its golden store
Could take some precious moments
    and make them mine once more,
I would not ask for wealth or fame,
    not far-flung fields to roam,
But just for Sunday morning on the old
    farm home.

Those were the days of toil and hard-
    ship, care that could not be denied,
But the Sabbath brought a respite —
    worldly tasks were laid aside.
House all shining, quiet, peaceful,
    mother's face so dear, so blest,
Father's voice in prayer uplifted, "Lord,
    we thank Thee for Thy rest."

Clean white cloth upon the table, silver
    gleaming, china gay,
With a place laid for the preacher,
    should he honor us today;
On the spare bed little garments, dainty
    ruffles snowy white,
All that mother love could compass to
    make Sunday a delight.

No stained windows, no grand organ
    made that little church so fair;
Plain the people were and humble, but
    'twas love that brought them there.
And the awe and holy quiet, emblem
    of the heavenly grace,
God was near and very precious as we
    met Him in His place.

                              MABEL TACKABURY

———o———

I feel as if God had, by giving the
Sabbath, given fifty-two springs in every year.

                  SAMUEL TAYLOR COLERIDGE

———o———

Sunday used to be the day of rest
but in recent years it seems that far
too many of us have to spend the
other six days resting up from Sunday.

———o———

Dismissed, But Promoted

Stephen Girard, the late Philadelphia
millionaire, one Saturday bade his
clerks come the next day and unload
a vessel which had just arrived. One
young man stepped up to the desk
and said, as he turned pale, "Mr.
Girard, I cannot work tomorrow."

"Well, sir, if you cannot do as I wish,
we can separate."

"I know that, sir," said the young
man. "I also know that I have a
widowed mother to care for, but I cannot work on Sunday."

"Very well, sir," said the proprietor,
"go to the cashier's desk and he will
settle with you."

For three weeks the young man
tramped the streets of Philadelphia
looking for work. One day a bank
president asked Mr. Girard to name a
suitable person for cashier of a new
bank about to be started. After reflection Mr. Girard named this young
man.

"But I thought you discharged him?"

"I did," was the answer, "because he
would not work on Sunday; and the
man who will lose his situation from
principle is the man to whom you can
entrust your money."

                              Fellowship News

———o———

In answer to a query about working
on Sunday, Billy Graham said, "It
should not detract from a man's reverence to do what is required. Even Jesus spoke about the ox in the ditch on
the Sabbath. But if your ox gets in
the ditch every Sabbath, you should
either get rid of the ox or fill up the
ditch."

Chicago Tribune-New York News Snydicate

Sunday School

Everybody who believes that Sunday School ought to be, ought to be in
Sunday School.

Everybody who comes to Sunday
School ought to stay for church. Everybody who comes to church ought
to come in time for Sunday School.

There's a place for both. There's a
place for both in both, and if both are
not in both there's something wrong
with both.

                              CLATE RISLEY

A young minister had been asked quite unexpectedly to address a Sunday School class. To give himself time to collect his thoughts, he said to the class, "Well, children, what shall I speak about?"

One little girl, who had herself memorized several declamations, called out: "What do you know?"

————o————

The Sunday School is perpetuated by its own products.

HENRIETTA C. MEARS

————o————

It Is

If the gospel of Jesus Christ is the hope of the world —
And it is.

If the church is the divinely appointed agency for the dissemination of the gospel —
And it is.

If the church school is the recruiting station and training camp of the church —
And it is.

Then the church school is the hope of the world.

JAMES DE FOREST MURCH,
Christian Education And The Local Church

————o————

Labor Not In Vain

My dishes went unwashed today,
  I didn't make the bed,
I took God's hand and followed
  To Bible School instead.

O yes, we went adventuring,
  My young people and I,
Explaining in the Bible,
  The truths none can deny.

That my house was neglected,
  That I didn't sweep the stair,
In twenty years no one on earth
  Will know, or even care.

But that I've helped a girl or boy,
  In Christian witness grow,
In twenty years, the whole wide world
  May look, and see, and know.

AUTHOR UNKNOWN

Did You Know That . . .

1. One out of every three unsaved people enrolled in Sunday School is won to Christ, but one out of 250 unsaved people not enrolled in the Sunday School is won to Christ.

2. Church members who are enrolled in Sunday School give twenty times as much per capita as members not in Sunday School.

3. Every church member is equally responsible for winning the lost, attending Sunday School, and supporting the church in prayer, participation and giving.

First Baptist Reminder

————o————

Someone asks how we can get rid of the trend toward increased moral delinquencies. The sustained, wholesome moral atmosphere imparted through habitual attendance upon Sunday School and church will do it.

————o————

A young friend, who attended Sunday School for the first time, was asked how she liked it. "What did your teacher tell you?" her mother inquired. The little girl replied, "To be quiet."

HELEN GAINES in *Together*

————o————

One of the great Sunday School leaders of our time has quoted some figures to prove that an older person seldom accepts Christianity who hasn't been taught at his mother's knee or in the Sunday School.

————o————

If pupils are not here in Sunday School, they won't hear.

————o————

What I See

His trousers were torn, rolled up at
  the knees,
A hole in his shirt, which he caught on
  a tree.
But I see a soul for whom Jesus died,
Clothed in righteousness, pressed to
  His side.

I see not the labour and hours of prayer,
Spent for that freckled face boy over there.
But I see a Saviour with arms opened wide,
Waiting in heaven to take him inside.

I see not the freckles, but a man fully grown,
A heart filled with God's Word, that I've carefully sown,
A life speaking forth, for the Saviour each day,
O Lord, for this boy, I earnestly pray.

I see not his energy in mischief bent,
But put to the task where the Lord meant it spent.
Oh Lord, make this little mischievous boy,
A power for Thee, to Thy heart a great joy.

WILLIAM E. KIRSCHKE
in *The Sunday School News*

———o———

Our Sunday School lessons need to be up-to-date and down-to-earth.

CLATE RISLEY

———o———

A little four-year-old suddenly lost interest in Sunday School. When her mother asked her why she no longer wanted to go, the child replied, "I just don't want to go anymore since Moses died."

———o———

A little girl in Sunday School was drawing something on her paper. The pastor happened by and asked her what it was. She said it was a picture of God. Gently he explained that nobody really knows what God looks like. Said she, "They will when I finish this picture."

Sunday School Superintendent

Every Sunday School superintendent should have two schools in mind: the one he has and the one he wants to have.

———o———

A successful Sunday School superintendent is one who is maladjusted to the status quo.

Sunday School Journal

Surrender

We learn from Saul's failure that the surrendered life is the only secure and truly successful life.

HENRIETTA C. MEARS

———o———

Surrendering one's will to the divine will may seem to be a negative procedure, but it gives positive dividends.

S. I. MCMILLEN

———o———

One who will not surrender cannot be permanently overcome.

Suspicion

Suspicion is about the only thing that can feed on itself and grow larger all the while.

———o———

There is nothing makes a man suspect much, more than to know little, and therefore men should remedy suspicion by procuring to know more, and not keep their suspicions in smother.

FRANCIS BACON

———o———

If you have no confidence in man, you are to be suspected.

Sympathy

A woman working in a greeting card shop asked a teenager who had been looking through the selection of cards, if she needed help. The girl answered, "Yes, do you have a sympathy card for a girl whose telephone is out of order?"

Chicago Tribune

———o———

Being myself no stranger to suffering, I have learned to relieve the suffering of others.

VIRGIL

It is reported that a sympathy note to a parson injured on a ski slope read in part: "It is my understanding that while Methodists fall from grace, Presbyterians fall from awkwardness."

We have lived and loved together
Through many changing years;
We have shared each other's gladness,
And wept each other's tears.

CHARLES JEFFERYS

T

Tact

Tact is the art of saying nothing when there is nothing to say.

——o——

Tact is the art of making other people think they know more than you do.

——o——

Tact is the ability to shut your mouth before someone else wants to.

Talent

The Talent

God gave me a talent;
And I threw it away;
Into the winds of yesterday.
I had no time to work for God;
  Nor follow the paths my dear Saviour had trod.
So He gave it again to this unworthy soul;
  Taking me humbly into His fold.
He said, "My child, what will you do with
  This talent I have twice given you?"
I cried, "Oh Lord, forgive me I pray,
  I'll take the talent and use it today.
I'll teach others that they might see
  The wonderful life that's found in Thee."

DEANE CHARLTON

——o——

The Hidden Talent

My vessel is almost empty,
My lamp is burning low;
The day is fast approaching
When I must surely go

To stand before the Saviour
A strict account to give

Of how I've used my talent
While in this world I lived.

Shall I hear His words of welcome
As He bids me enter in?
Or His words of condemnation
Because I lived in sin?

Then I pray Thee, Lord, have mercy
And I shall ever faithful be
To use the precious talent
That Thou hast given me,

So when my work is finished
And the victory has been won
May I stand before Thee unashamed
And hear Thee say, "Well done,

"Thou hast improved thy talent
And faithful thou hast been;
So good and faithful servant
Come thou and enter in."

What have you done with your talent?
Are you using it today?
Or is it in a napkin
Wrapped and hidden away?

GLENNA CORDELL

——o——

Talent is built in solitude; character in the stream of the world.

JOHANN WOLFGANG VON GOETHE

——o——

Buried seeds may grow but buried talents never.

ROGER BABSON

——o——

Use what talents you possess: the woods would be very silent if no birds sang there except those that sang best.

HENRY VAN DYKE

——o——

Your unused talents give you no advantage over one who has no talents at all.

Talk

Tommy: "Mommy, canIgooutsideand playwithmyballandbat?"

Mommy: "Tommy, slow down! You talk so fast no one can understand you!"

Tommy: "You just don't LISTEN fast enough!"

———o———

A henpecked weatherman claims: "My wife speaks 150 words a minute with gusts up to 180."

———o———

You cannot learn and talk at the same time.

———o———

Monopoly Note

To hold conversations
Is normal, I know,
But there are some people
Who hate to let go!

F. G. KERNAN

———o———

Those who have nothing to say generally take the longest to say it.

———o———

"I am afraid, doctor," said a woman to her physician, "that my husband has some terrible mental affliction. Sometimes I talk to him for hours and then discover that he literally hasn't heard a word I said."

"That isn't an affliction," was the reply; "that's a divine gift."

———o———

He who talks without thinking runs more risks than he who thinks without talking.

———o———

Two women were just ready to board a big airliner. One of them turned to the pilot and commented: "Now, please don't go faster than sound. We want to talk."

———o———

To those who talk and talk and talk,
This adage doth appeal:
The steam that toots the whistle
Will never turn a wheel.

JOSEPH LINWOOD

A Bore talks mostly in the first person, a Gossip in the third and a Brilliant Conversationalist in the second.

———o———

If God intended that we should talk more than we listen, He would have given us two mouths and one ear.

———o———

Children live in a world of sound. Perhaps because there is so much of it, many children learn to ignore talk.

DAVID AND ELIZABETH RUSSEL
in *Listening Aids Through the Grades*

———o———

If All That We Say

If all that we say in a single day,
With never a word left out,
Were printed each night in clear black
  and white,
'Twould prove queer reading, no
  doubt.
And then just suppose, ere our eyes
  we could close
We must read the whole record
  through;
Then wouldn't we sigh and wouldn't
  we try.
A great deal less talking to do?
And I more than half think
That many a kink
Would be smoother in life's tangled
  thread,
If half that we say in a single day were
  left forever unsaid.

AUTHOR UNKNOWN

———o———

Man can read some people like a book, but cannot shut them up so easily.

———o———

The average woman talks twenty-five percent faster than her husband — listens.

———o———

Take a lesson from the whale: The only time he gets harpooned is when he comes up to spout.

The Liguorian

———o———

I don't care how much a man talks, if he only says it in a few words.

"JOSH BILLINGS" (HENRY WHEELER SHAW)

He that thinketh by the inch
And talketh by the yard
Deserveth to be kicked by the foot.

———o———

Wise men talk because they have something to say; fools, because they have to say something.

PLATO

———o———

No longer talk at all about the kind of man a good man ought to be — but be such.

———o———

Our deeds and our conversation usually resemble each other like twins. If we like what we are doing, we are inclined to talk about it; and if we like very much to talk about something, we shall probably become involved with it.

DELBERT R. GISH

———o———

The little boy was taking his baby sister for a walk when a neighbor stopped them. "What an adorable child," she gushed. "Does she talk yet?"

"No," the boy replied. "She has her teeth, but her words haven't come in yet."

FRANK BENNING

———o———

Those who have but little business to attend to, are great talkers. The less men think, the more they talk.

CHARLES DE SECONDAT MONTESQUIEU

———o———

Talking to men about God is a great thing, but talking to God for men is greater still.

———o———

Talk little and do much, without caring to be seen.

FRANÇOIS DE SALIGNAC DE LA MOTHE FÉNELON

———o———

One way to keep people from jumping down your throat is to keep your mouth shut.

———o———

Trying to get a word in edgewise with some people is like trying to thread a sewing machine with the motor running.

A famous publisher declares, "If you are an articulate person, you utter some thirty thousand words each day." If put in print, this would mean enough books to fill an entire college library. How many pages of these volumes you are constantly writing will be denounced by God as "worthless speech"?

We read in Matthew 12:36, 37: "Every idle word that men shall speak, they shall give account thereof in the day of judgment. For by thy words thou shalt be justified, and by thy words thou shalt be condemned." Words are so dangerous. We utter them so frequently without thought or consideration, little realizing that every word we speak either curses or blesses.

J. ALLEN BLAIR

———o———

There's only one rule for being a good talker: learn to listen.

CHRISTOPHER MORLEY

———o———

Blessed are they who have nothing to say, and who can be persuaded to say it.

JAMES RUSSELL LOWELL

Task

If you find yourself face to face with an impossible task, regard it as a compliment God has paid you. He knows you are the person who can do that task.

———o———

The task of life is not to be engaged in perpetual rebellion, but to find and serve our true Master.

E. L. ALLEN

———o———

No unwelcome tasks become any the less unwelcome by putting them off till tomorrow.

ALEXANDER MACLAREN

———o———

You are not required to complete the task; neither are you permitted to lay it down.

The Talmud

Taxes

Taxpayers: Those who don't have to pass a civil service examination to work for the government.

———o———

It seems a little silly now, but this country was founded as a protest against taxation.

———o———

Go ahead and be thrilled when you sign the check for your income tax. What you write may not be history, but it provides the stuff that makes the making of history possible.

Advocate, Manawa, Wisconsin

———o———

One of my eighth-graders listed these as local, state, and federal taxes: Gas tax, income tax, and thumb tax.

ETHEL KAISER in *NEA Journal*

———o———

There are said to be 112 hidden taxes in a pair of shoes. No wonder a lot of shoes pinch.

Grit

———o———

In this world nothing is certain but death and taxes.

BENJAMIN FRANKLIN, *Letter to M. Leroy*

Teacher, Teaching

It is easier to teach the book of Matthew to a boy than it is to teach a boy the book of Matthew.

ESTHER ELLINGHUSEN

———o———

The teacher was having her trials and finally wrote the mother: "Your son is the brightest boy in my class, but he is also the most mischievous. What shall I do?"

The reply came duly: "Do as you please. I am having my own troubles with his father."

———o———

Problem For Parents

Most any family secret
This lady soon gets word of,
And most domestic squabbles
She certain has heard of!

But is she just a gossip
Who has no moral scruples? . . .
No, she's the first-grade teacher
With confiding little pupils!

MARGARET SCHUMACHER

———o———

To teach something you don't know is like coming back from somewhere you haven't been.

———o———

If, instructing a child, you are vexed with it for want of adroitness, try, if you have never tried before, to write with your left hand, and then remember that a child is all left hand.

JOHN FREDERICK BOYES

———o———

The only way we can teach the Word of God is to live the Word of God.

HENRIETTA C. MEARS

———o———

There are two classes of teachers: those who say it can't be done, and those who are doing it.

———o———

In a way, the great teacher does not teach anything quantitatively measurable. He performs certain actions, says certain things that create another teacher. This other teacher is the one hidden inside the student. When the master teacher is finished, the newborn professor inside the youngster takes over, and with any luck the process of education continues till death.

CLIFTON FADIMAN in *Holiday*

———o———

To The Beginning Teacher

One bleak fact will confront you
And, briefly, shred plans to rubble.
For each student sparked with genius,
There'll be ten with ignition trouble.

BETH BLUE in *NEA Journal*

———o———

What Is A Teacher?

To a child thrust into a strange world, a teacher is the best thing that can happen.

A teacher is courage with Kleenex

in her pocket, Sympathy struggling with a snowsuit, and Patience with papers to grade.

Teachers spend twelve hours a day searching for truth and the other twelve searching for error.

A teacher does not really mind sniffles, squirmings, stomach-aches, and spills. Neither does she disintegrate before tears, fights, futility, excuses, parents who spout, little boys who shout and little girls who pout.

———o———

Most of all, a teacher is somebody who likes somebody else's children — and has strength left to go to the PTA meeting.

AUTHOR UNKNOWN

———o———

Re: *Teacher Merit Rating*

In days gone by
When friends I met
Asked, "How are you?"
I would reply,
"I'm fine, thank you!"
(I meant it, too!)
But I've been Rated,
And Berated,
Investigated,
Evaluated,
Annotated,
And Tabulated.
Now when I'm asked,
"How are you?"
I may reply,
"You're fine, thank you,
But how am I?"
(I wonder, too!)

JUSTA TEECHER in *Montana Education*

———o———

One teacher plus a piece of chalk equals two teachers.

———o———

A Teacher Speaks

Thank you, dear Lord, for giving me
Life's greatest opportunity;
Though I'm not worthy, Lord, to teach,
I pray that thro' me Thou shalt reach
The heart of each small girl and boy
Ere Satan comes to rob, destroy.

I pray that my whole aim might be
To lead each child to Calvary;
To make Thy Word live in his heart,
And warn him never to depart;
I know when I have done my best
That Thou art there to do the rest.

Forever conscious may I be
Of such responsibility;
Help me fore'er to keep in mind
That I must show them how to find
The One Who waits so patiently,
And says to them, "Come unto Me."

When from my class I am away,
Still keep me true, dear Lord, I pray;
If anywhere by chance I pass
A member of my little class,
May he see Christ the Crucified
And Him in me exemplified.

MATILDA CLOER

———o———

You sit still while I instill.

A. V. WASHBURN

———o———

First grade teacher: "Dickie, what am I going to do with you? The closing bell has rung already and your picture isn't colored, and you don't know your memory verse. I don't suppose you learned a thing today. Now why is that, Dickie?"

Dickie: "Well, you made me sit down and be still and listen, and you *teached* me and *teached* me and *teached* me 'till I couldn't learn anything!"

Teach Magazine

———o———

The main idea in Sunday School teaching is to drive home the point, not the class.

Sunday School Promoter

———o———

The mayor met the principal of the toughest school in town. The principal was obviously downcast and the mayor asked him why.

"School's been open only a short time," the educator explained, "and already we've had thirty-nine dropouts."

"It's that bad?" the mayor said. "After all, you're in the roughest section of town.

"That's the trouble," replied the principal, "thirty-eight of the thirty-nine dropouts were teachers."

How to tell students what to look for without telling them what to see is the dilemma of teaching.

LASCELLES ABERCROMBIE

———o———

Begin early to teach children, for they begin early to sin. What is learned young is learned for life. What we hear at the first, we remember to the last. A child's first lesson should be obedience, and after that you may teach it what you please. Yet the young mind must not be laced too tight, or you may hurt its growth and hinder its strength. A child's back must be made to bend, but not be broken. He must be ruled, but not with a rod of iron. His spirit must be conquered, but not crushed.

Ere your boy has reached to seven,
Teach him well the way to heaven;
Better still the work will thrive
If he learns before he's five.

CHARLES HADDON SPURGEON

———o———

A child promoted to a new class said to a dearly beloved teacher: "I wish you knew enough to teach me next year."

———o———

A Plea For Junior

Teacher, teacher, shed a tear,
Junior comes to school this year.
He has never known restraint,
He, in short, is not a saint!

You will sprout some new gray hair
Teaching Junior to be fair,
Since his Mama let him do
Just what Junior wanted to.

Now he is a problem child,
Selfish, stubborn, cruel, wild.
Gentle teacher, need I say,
Mama should be spanked today?

AUTHUR UNKNOWN
printed in *Christian Parents*

———o———

The Teacher

Leader, educator, counselor of youth
who will tomorrow lead the nation
and the world.

Object of the hero worship of those
who need and seek a mentor and
friend.
Giver of courage to him who would
falter;
Strength to him who would despair;
Faith to him who is afraid;
Understanding to him who is confused;
Confidence to him who feels inadequate;
Inspiration to him whose toil seems
pointless;
Guidance to him whose path is unclear;
Friendship to him who feels alone;
Direction through discipline to him
whose feet would stray from the
path of duty.
Slow to anger, quick to forgive, eager
to heal.
Teacher — in whose ranks are found
the best that history of mankind
offers;
Mohammed, Socrates, Moses, Jesus of
Nazareth —
Teacher — hold your head proudly,
though heart and soul and mind
be humble,
Humble in the humility that prepares
the way for wisdom:
For you are the symbol of the quest
for knowledge that recognizes no
goal —
The mountain with no top, the path
without an end.
You are the seeker after the ever elusive truth,
And the leader of others who will pick
up and continue the quest,
The unending quest that leads man
out of the darkness of ignorance,
And into the light that God has prepared
For His supreme creation, mankind.

NORMA LUCE JUNE in *The Instructor*

Teen-Agers

Teen-Ager . . .

She uses my nail polish, wears my hose;
Swipes my make-up to powder her
nose;

Borrows my lipstick, the sweater I
  knitted
(A trifle too large, but she said it just
  fitted!);
She reads all my magazines, samples
  my books,
Commandeers my compact to check
  on her looks;
Talks me out of that hat that I'd only
  worn twice.
She takes all that I give all — except
  my advice!

                              JEAN CONDER SOULE

To a teen-ager, walking distance is
that between the telephone and the
garage.
                              IVERN BOYETT

The father of a rapidly growing teen-
ager was asked by a friend how the
boy was.
  "Okay," grumbled the parent, "but
he's getting too smart to out-argue and
too big to spank. I can hardly wait for
him to fall in love so's some little girl
will take him down a notch or two!"
                              F. G. KERNAN

There's no getting around it. The
chief difference between teen-agers
and middle-agers is simply thirty
pounds and thirty years.

The trouble with teen-agers and
transistors is that they're both portable.
  Changing Times, The Kiplinger Magazine

Too Young

He drops in on our daughter daily
To spend the evening munching gaily.

And while I do not hit the ceiling,
Lately I have started feeling

As our bills for food grow greater
That maybe our refrigerator

Is too young to be already
Going steady!

                              THOMAS USK

Adolescence is when children start
bringing up their parents.

You can always tell a teen-age boy,
and odds are he'll argue.

A teen-age fad is something the
grown-ups find out about three months
after it is out of date.

A teen-ager said he'd rather be dead
than be different.

The best way to tie down a teen-
ager is with a telephone cord.
                              ROBERT S. WILLETT

The basic trouble with teen-agers is
that they are forever acting like a
bunch of adolescents.

One way to keep your teen-age
daughter out of hot water is to put
dirty dishes in it.

When the teacher discovered that
one of her ninth-graders was well stuck
up with bubble gum, she reproved him
and sent him out to remedy the situation. As he left the class, came a voice
from the rear: "Have gum. Will travel."

Telephone

The man who said one half of the
world does not know how the other
half lives never was on a rural phone
line!

"Well," the father congratulated his
teen-age daughter, "you usually talk on
the phone two hours. This time only
forty-five minutes. What happened?"
  "Wrong number," replied the girl.

One day a man telephoned his
butcher but mis-dialed and, without
knowing it, reached his pastor.
  "Do you have any brains today?" the
caller asked.
  "No," the pastor replied, "but I do
have some heart."

Temper

Evangelist Billy Sunday once said, "You say that you have a bad temper but it's over in a minute. So's a shotgun, but it blows everything to pieces."

BILLY GRAHAM

———o———

We must interpret a bad temper as the sign of an inferiority complex.

ALFRED ADLER

———o———

While there may be some things that don't improve the longer you keep them, there are others that do. One is your temper.

———o———

Hitting the ceiling is the wrong way to get up in the world.

War Cry

———o———

Bad temper is murder in the heart, whether it be hot anger or the cold acid of sarcasm.

J. EDWIN ORR

Temper

When I have lost my temper
    I have lost my reason too.
I'm never proud of anything
    Which angrily I do.

When I have talked in anger,
    And my cheeks were flaming red,
I have always uttered something
    Which I wish I had not said.

In anger I have never
    Done a kindly deed or wise,
But many things for which I felt
    I should apologize.

In looking back across my life,
    And all I've lost or made,
I can't recall a single time
    When fury ever paid.

So I struggle to be patient,
    For I've reached a wiser age;
I do not want to do a thing
    Or speak a word in rage.

I have learned by sad experience
    That when my temper flies
I never do a worthy deed,
    A decent deed or wise.

AUTHOR UNKNOWN

Bad temper is its own scourge. Few things are more bitter than to feel bitter. A man's venom poisons himself more than his victim.

CHARLES BUXTON

Temperance

The teacher was presenting a lesson on temperance, telling his Junior boys that it was harmful to smoke. As a review he asked the question, "Where do boys go who learn to smoke?"
One boy replied, "Up the alley."

———o———

One misses, by abstaining, no enjoyment at parties he must attend as a part of his official duties; rather, his faculties are completely at his command if his alertness is not numbed, if his decisions — social, domestic, governmental — are uninfluenced by that which brings tragedy, heartaches, headache, embarrassment, illness, and loss of touch with reality.

SENATOR MARK HATFIELD

———o———

Temperance means the abstinence from all that is evil, and the moderate use of all that is good.

NED H. HOLMGREN

Temptation

When you flee temptation, be sure you don't leave a forwarding address.

———o———

To avoid unnecessary temptations is half of the battle in overcoming evil.

———o———

Temptations need not be hindrances. As we put them beneath our feet, they lift us to higher ground.

LOIS F. BLANCHARD

———o———

Temptation is the stuff of which Christians are made. If the devil never tempts you, you can't develop your resistance to sin.

BILLY SUNDAY

———o———

When you meet temptation, turn to the right!

Many men have too much will power. It's won't power they lack.

JOHN A. SHEDD

---o---

Most of us keep one eye on the temptation we pray not to be led into.

MARY H. WALDRIP in *Advertiser and News*

---o---

I have found in all my experience that in every temptation the victory depends on resisting the first attack. To stop and reason for a moment is dangerous. Is the object or gratification forbidden? That is enough if we truly love the Lord our God. But when we deliberate, we throw ourselves into the arms of Satan.

Neither ought consequences to be considered. God will see to them; better suffer anything than His frown. Oh, may I ever walk by this rule, and live to please my God alone!

WILLIAM CARVOSSO

---o---

Three great temptations which face us all:

The temptation to recline;
The temptation to shine;
The temptation to whine.

DAVID CHRISTIE

Ten Commandments

A high school senior was trying out for a summer job on the small town newspaper. "Would you be any good at rewrite?" the editor asked him.

"Sure," said the teen-ager brashly.

"Okay. Let's see you rewrite this and make it short and to the point." With that, the editor handed the boy a copy of the Ten Commandments.

The boy looked at them, scratched his head, and then in a burst of inspiration scribbled something across the top of the paper, which he then handed back.

The editor took one look and said, "You're hired, boy!"

The teen-ager had written the word "Don't!"

---o---

The Ten Commandments still cover all human relations and all spiritual relations.

RALPH BREWER

---o---

When the editor of a small newspaper was short of material to fill his columns one week, he asked his typesetter to fill in with the Ten Commandments.

After that week's issue had been circulated, the editor received a letter from one reader saying, "Cancel my subscription. You are getting too personal."

Testimony

Dim eyes cannot read fine print. Let your testimony for Christ be written in large letters that the world may see.

WILLIAM WARD AYER

---o---

An ounce of testimony is worth a ton of propaganda.

---o---

Listening to a group of people talking one day about the fine testimony meetings which were held in their church, a lawyer quietly remarked, "To a lawyer there is a vast difference between testimony and evidence."

---o---

A woman testifying at a prayer meeting: "I ain't what I ought to be; and I ain't what I'm going to be; but anyway, I ain't what I was."

Northern Lights

---o---

It is one thing to testify in a church service surrounded by people who agree and appreciate the testimony; but it is an entirely different matter to testify to the person outside of Christ who is ignorant of the Gospel or in opposition to its truth.

LORA LEE PARROTT

Testing

Faithful Is He Who Has Promised

Are you passing through a testing?
Is your pillow wet with tears?

Do you wonder what the reason,
  Why it seems God never hears?
Why it is you have no answer
  To your oft-repeated plea?
Why the heaven still is leaden
  As you wait on bended knee?

Do you wonder as you suffer,
  Whether God does understand?
And if so, why He ignores you,
  Fails to hold you in His hand?
Do black doubts creep in, assail you,
  Fears without, and fears within
Till your brave heart almost falters
  And gives way to deadly sin?

All God's testings have a purpose —
  Some day you will see the light.
All He asks is that you trust Him,
  Walk by faith and not by sight.
Do not fear when doubts beset you,
  Just remember — He is near.
He will never, never leave you.
  He will always, always hear.

When the darkened veil is lifted,
  Then, dear heart, you'll understand
Why it is you had to suffer,
  Why you could not feel His hand
Giving strength when it was needed,
  Giving power and peace within.
Giving joy through tears and trial,
  Giving victory over sin.

JOHN E. ZOLLER

———o———

The test of love is not feeling, but
obedience.

WILLIAM BERNARD ULLATHORNE

———o———

Seventh-graders' answers on a quiz:
  Three types of clouds are cumulus,
nimbus, and stimulus.
  Ku Klux Klan was a relative of
Kublai Khan.

JANE WOODWORTH in NEA Journal

Thankfulness, Thanksgiving
(See also Gratitude)

He enjoys much who is thankful for
a little.

WILLIAM SECKER

———o———

Thanksgiving is possible only for
those who take time to remember.

No one can give thanks who has a
short memory.

———o———

Our despondent moods are, for the
most part, moods of ingratitude.

———o———

I Give Thee Humble Thanks

For all the gifts that Thou dost send,
For every kind and loyal friend,
For prompt supply of all my need,
For all that's good in word or deed,
For gift of health along life's way,
For strength to work from day to day,
  I give Thee humble thanks.

For ready hands to help and cheer,
For listening ears Thy voice to hear,
For yielded tongue Thy love to talk,
For willing feet Thy paths to walk,
For open eyes Thy Word to read,
For loving heart Thy will to heed,
  I give Thee humble thanks.

For Christ who came from Heaven
  above,
For the Cross and His redeeming love,
For His mighty power to seek and
  save,
For His glorious triumph o'er the
  grave,
For the lovely mansions in the sky,
For His blessed coming by-and-by,
  I give Thee humble thanks.

CLIFFORD LEWIS

———o———

During a harvest festival in India, an
old widow arrived at her church with
an extraordinarily large offering of rice
— far more than the poor woman could
be expected to afford.

The itinerant pastor of the church
did not know the widow well. But he
did know that she was very poor and
so he asked her if she were making the
offering in gratitude for some unusual
blessing.

"Yes," replied the woman. "My son
was sick and I promised a large gift to
God if he got well."

"And your son has recovered?" asked the pastor.

The widow paused. "No," she said. "He died last week. But I know that he is in God's care; for that I am especially thankful."

———o———

If one should give me a dish of sand, and tell me there were particles of iron in it, I might look for them with my eyes and search for them with my clumsy fingers, and be unable to detect them; but let me take a magnet and sweep through it, and how would it draw to itself the almost invisible particles by the mere power of attraction.

The unthankful heart, like my finger in the sand, discovers no mercies; but let the thankful heart sweep through the day, and as the magnet finds the iron, so it will find, in every hour, some heavenly blessings, only the iron in God's sand is gold!

HENRY WARD BEECHER

———o———

Thanksgiving Day

The snow is flying and trees are bare;
The birds have left us . . . Thanksgiving is here!
There's laughter outside and stomping of feet,
The children, all nine, have come home to eat.

With the ice thick and glassy on the pond down the lane,
There is skating and merriment since Thanksgiving came.
There's even a sled ride for the fearless and daring
While the women are busy the meal preparing.

The turkey's full of stuffing and is baked a golden brown,
The tantalizing odor brings the hungry children round.
There's a hush and a silence as the blessing is said . . .
In deepest reverence each bows his head
And offers a prayer of gratitude and praise

For bountiful blessings these Thanksgiving days.

MRS. PAUL E. KING

———o———

A thankful heart is not only the greatest virtue, but the parent of all other virtues.

MARCUS TULLIUS CICERO,
Oratio Pro Caeno Plancio, XXXIII

———o———

I Thank God

For the glorious sunshine;
For the gentle showers;
For the fields and mountains;
For the birds and flowers;
For my home and parents;
For Thy care of me;
All my heart, dear Father,
Now I give to Thee.
Amen.
Little Folks

———o———

Matthew Henry, the famous Bible scholar, was once accosted by thieves and robbed of his purse. He wrote these words in his diary:

"Let me be thankful first because I was never robbed before; second, although they took my purse, they did not take my life; third, because, although they took my all, it was not much; and fourth, because it was I who was robbed, not I who robbed."

———o———

He scurried down the gnarled old tree
While two sharp eyes peered out at me,
A bushy tail wagged to-and-fro,
I found a hazelnut to throw.

And on his two hind legs he rose
To catch it; then, in comic pose
He entertained with cunning pranks
Squirrel talk denoting "Many thanks!"

LORRAINE GOOD

Theology

It's about time we gave up all this theological grand opera and went back to practicing the scales.

VANCE HAVNER

Brethren, if you are not theologians, you in your pastorates are just nothing at all.

CHARLES HADDON SPURGEON

———o———

We are not interested in armchair theology but rather that every pastor should be a theologian.

BRUCE D. NICHOLAS, *Yeotmal*

———o———

Your theology may be as clear as ice, but unless you put it into practice it will leave you just as cold.

Think, Thought

Great thought is no longer the privilege of the few. It is given to all men but for the price of concentration and dedication.

———o———

Be careful of your thoughts. They may break into words at any time.

———o———

Think It Through

Are you worried or depressed?
  Think it through.
Feel unequal to the test?
  Think it through.
Concentrate your heart and mind,
Get right down to facts and grind,
A solution you can find —
  Think it through.

Are you out of luck and work?
  Think it through.
Face your problem, do not shirk,
  Think it through.
Seek and find your proper place,
Persevere with smiling face,
Be a hero in the race —
  Think it through.

Do you feel like giving up?
  Think it through.
Is your share a bitter cup?
  Think it through.
God gives you the power to do,
He will make it clear to you,
You must do something too —
  Think it through.

GRENVILLE KLEISER

God's Thoughts And Mine

(Isaiah 55:8; Philippians 4:8)

The Hammer thoughts
  That pound and shatter peace;
The Rodent thoughts
  That gnaw and will not cease;

The Briar thoughts
  That pull and prick and scratch;
The Rover thoughts
  That I can never catch;

The Serpent thoughts
  That leave their lairs at night;
The Shadow thoughts
  That dim the new day's light;

These are my thoughts.
  Oh, take them, Lord, I pray,
Out of my heart
  And cast them far away;

And in their stead
  Give me those thoughts of Thine
So crystal-clear,
  So holy, high and fine,

That I shall grow,
  By their pure grace enticed,
Worthy to think
  The lovely thoughts of Christ.

AUTHOR UNKNOWN

———o———

The Scriptures remind us that "As a man thinketh in his heart, so is he." This Biblical admonition tells us that we cannot think in terms of failure, and then succeed . . . in terms of weakness, and then be strong . . . in terms of fear, and then be courageous . . . in terms of doubt, and then have faith.

W. G. VOLLMER

———o———

The mind is a garden
Where thought flowers grow,
The thoughts that we think
Are seeds that we sow.

AUTHOR UNKNOWN

———o———

Make not your thoughts your prison.

———o———

We often make our duties harder by thinking them hard.

FREDERICK TEMPLE

A man's life is what his thoughts make it.

MARCUS AURELIUS

———o———

A man is what he thinks about all day long.

RALPH WALDO EMERSON

———o———

You become what you allow yourself to think — even when you don't think so.

———o———

Some people are like automatic elevators; they can remember but they don't think.

Southern California Presbyterian

———o———

Take time to deliberate; but when the time for action arrives, stop thinking and go in.

ANDREW JACKSON

———o———

A group of children first visited a planetarium, then looked at tiny flowers. Afterward they drew on paper some of the things they had seen. One boy put a dot in the corner of the drawing. "This is me," he wrote, then added thoughtfully, "but I am bigger than the stars because I can think."

Quote

———o———

Think Right

Think smiles, and smiles shall be;
Think doubt, and hope will flee;
Think love, and love will grow;
Think hate, and hate you'll know.
Think good, and good is here;
Think vice — its jaws appear!
Think joy, and joy ne'er ends;
Think gloom, and dusk descends.
Think faith, and strength's at hand;
Think ill — it stalks the land.
Think peace, sublime and sweet,
And you that peace will meet;
Think fear, with brooding mind,
And failure's close behind.
Think this: "I'm going to win."
Think not on what has been,
Think victory; think "I can!"
Then you're a winning man!

DAVID V. BUSH

He is the rich man, and enjoys the fruit of his riches, who summer and winter forever can find delight in his own thoughts.

HENRY DAVID THOREAU

———o———

An eight-year-old's definition of thinking: When you keep your mouth shut and your head keeps on talking to itself.

———o———

We probably wouldn't care so much what people think of us if we only knew how seldom they do!

———o———

People who have no time, don't think. The more you think, the more time you have.

HENRY FORD

———o———

Thought begets the will to create.

THOMAS J. WATSON

———o———

The ancestor of every action is a thought.

RALPH WALDO EMERSON

———o———

He who has slight thoughts of sin never had great thoughts of God.

JOHN OWEN

———o———

The greatest thought that can occupy a man's mind is his accountability to God.

DANIEL WEBSTER

———o———

The thoughts you think will irradiate you as though you are a transparent vase.

MAURICE MAETERLINCK

Time

If you have work to do — do it now.
If you have a witness to give — give it now.
If you have a soul to win — win him now.
If you have an obligation to discharge — discharge it now.
If you have a debt to pay — pay it now.

If you have a wrong to right — right it now.

If you have a confession to make — make it now.

If you have a preparation to make — make it now.

If you have children to train — train them now.

AUTHOR UNKNOWN

———o———

Time is passing and you are passing out of time.

ROY L. LAURIN

———o———

Take care of the minutes, for the hours will take care of themselves.

ALEXANDER POPE

———o———

Little drops of water, little grains of sand,
Make the mighty ocean and the pleasant land.
Thus the little minutes, humble though they be,
Make the mighty ages of eternity.

JULIA A. FLETCHER CARNEY

———o———

You will never "find" time for anything. If you want time, you must make it.

CHARLES BUXTON

———o———

Lose an hour in the morning and you will be looking for it the rest of the day.

LORD CHESTERFIELD

———o———

Every year it takes less time to fly across the ocean and longer to drive to the office.

RAYMOND DUNCAN
in The Saturday Evening Post

———o———

Years — nothing goes swifter than the years.

OVID

———o———

The years teach much which the days never know.

RALPH WALDO EMERSON

———o———

Kenneth Smith had seven minutes to spare between trips as motorman-conductor on a trolley line in Baltimore. The half-acre loop where his run ended was covered with a dense underbrush and a thicket. He decided to put his seven minutes to work. At the end of each trip he worked at cleaning out the brush and weeds. Eventually he turned the loop that had been an eyesore into a garden.

JAMES KELLER, One Moment, Please

———o———

Time Is

Too Slow for those who Wait,
Too Swift for those who Fear,
Too Long for those who Grieve,
Too Short for those who Rejoice;
But for those who love,
Time is not.

HENRY VAN DYKE, For Katrina's Sun-Dial

———o———

If you want to become a man of the hour, learn first to make every minute count.

———o———

One of the illusions of life is to think that the present hour is not the critical and decisive hour. Write it on your heart that every day is the best day of the year.

RALPH WALDO EMERSON

———o———

Great men never complain about the lack of time. Alexander the Great and John Wesley accomplished everything they did in 24-hour days.

FRED SMITH

———o———

The real secret of how to use time is to pack it as you would your luggage, filling up the small spaces with small things.

HENRY HADDOW

———o———

You wake up in the morning, and lo! your purse is magically filled with twenty-four hours of the magic tissue of the universe of your life. No one can take it from you. It is uneatable. No one receives either more or less than you receive. Waste your infinitely precious commodity as much as you will, and the supply will never be withheld from you. Moreover, you cannot draw on the future. Impossible to get into debt. You can only waste the passing moment. You cannot waste tomorrow; it is kept for you.

ARNOLD BENNETT

———o———

If you spend most of the time dreaming of tomorrow and regretting yesterday, you won't find a great deal of time left for doing anything today.

———o———

No Time For Him?

What! No time for Him today?
For Him who traveled all the way
From that solemn Upper Room
To the Garden's stony tomb?

See Him in Gethsemane,
Where great drops of agony
From His brow fall, one by one,
As He prays, "Thy will be done."

Follow Him to Pilate's hall —
Thence to Calvary's bitter gall.
See Him suffer hell's own pangs
While upon the Cross He hangs.

Hear His words — do they decry
Those who led Him there to die?
He prays for those who hate Him most
As He renders up the ghost.

Well I know He willingly
Lived and died — and all for me.
How then can I ever say,
"I've no time for Him today!"

LOUISE E. SCHILLINGER

———o———

Don't fret over what you'd do with your time if you could live it over again . . . get busy with what you have left.

MARTIN VANBEE

———o———

So valuable is time that God gives only a moment of it at once, and He gives that moment but once in all eternity.

———o———

People who cannot find time for recreation are obliged sooner or later to find time for illness.

JOHN WANAMAKER

Mother (explaining the keeping of time): "Here are the hours, these are the minutes, and these are the seconds."

Little daughter: "Where are the jiffies?"

ROSANN MOELLER in *My Chum*

———o———

An inch of gold will not buy an inch of time.

———o———

A person does the things he really wants to do, but complains about not having time to do the things he pretends he wants to do.

———o———

Well-arranged time is a sure mark of a well-arranged mind.

———o———

Timing is the chief ingredient in judgment.

WILLIAM FEATHER

———o———

Ease Up A Bit

I say, my lad, what's your hurry?
  You can't catch up with time.
No matter how fast you travel,
  You'll always be behind.
So, ease up on the gas a bit,
  Enjoy the trees and sod;
You can't catch up with time, my lad,
  It's in the hand of God.

GARRETT NUVEN

———o———

Take Time

Take time to hear their prayers at
    night,
And cuddle them a bit.
Tell them a story now and then,
And steal a little time to sit
And listen to their childish talk,
Or take them for a walk.

We little know it now — but soon
They will be gone (the years are
    swift).
For life just marches on and on;
And heaven holds no sweeter gift
Than shouting boys with tousled hair,
Who leave their joys just anywhere.

Take time to laugh and sing and play,
To really cherish and enjoy
A little girl with flaxen curls
And the small wonder of a boy.
They ask so little when they're small,
Just love and tenderness — that's all.
AUTHOR UNKNOWN

Tithing

The Tither's Surprises

The Christian who begins to tithe
will have at least six surprises. He will
be surprised:
1. At the amount of money he has
   for the Lord's work.
2. At the deepening of his spiritual
   life in paying the tithe.
3. At the ease in meeting his own
   obligations with the nine-tenths.
4. At the ease of going from one-
   tenth to a larger giving.
5. At the prudent disposal afforded
   to a faithful and wise steward over
   the nine-tenths that remain.
6. At himself in not adopting the
   plan sooner!

———o———

The Tithe

Ah, when I look up at the cross
Where God's great steward suffered
    loss
Of life and shed His blood for me,
A trifling thing it seems to be
To pay a tithe, dear Lord, to Thee,
Of time or talent, wealth or store —
Full well I know I owe Thee more!
But that is just the reason why
I lift my heart to God on high
And pledge, my love, my all in all.
This holy token at Thy cross
I know as gold, must seem but dross,
But in my heart, Lord, Thou dost see
How it has pledged my all to Thee,
That I a steward true may be.
AUTHOR UNKNOWN

———o———

Thy Tithe

My pay-check barely reaching 'round,
In fact, it's sometimes short;
Takes all that I can rake and scrape
To keep up this old fort.

I've doctor bills for aches and ills
And car insurance due.
This traffic ticket must be paid;
The plumber says he'll sue.

I have to get new license tags,
There's income tax to pay,
And then you say give ten percent —
Just show me how, I pray.

Well, here is what the Bible says,
And it is proven true,
"You're putting money in a bag
That has holes thru and thru."

You're paying great "devourers,"
Whom God says He'll rebuke,
Just hold Him to His promise
In six, thirty-eight of Luke.

Right when the hour is darkest
Is time to start this test,
For God can then best show us
Nine-tenths will reach, when blest.
CLESSON K. SCOLES

Today

All the flowers of all the tomorrows
are in the seeds of today.
Chinese Proverb

———o———

Perhaps Today!

Perhaps today shall sound the mystic
    summons,
The shout, the voice, the trump, not
    by all heard;
And, from their scattered silent resting
    places,
The dead in Christ will rise to meet
    the Lord;
While we, the ransomed, living in a
    moment
Shall be caught up — according to His
    Word.

Perhaps today, from every clime and
    nation,
Shall souls redeemed ascend to meet
    the Lord;
To suffering ones — great, glad eman-
    cipation;
To those who toil for Him, a sure re-
    ward;
We look not down a track of unknown
    years;

It may be that today our Lord appears.

Perhaps today, with problems fresh out-breaking,
With growing evils rampant o'er the earth,
When sore distress, nigh every land is shaking, —
Perhaps today the Saviour may come forth.
Earth's leaders fail; the forces are too great;
But — lift your heads, the Lord is at the gate!

AUTHOR UNKNOWN

———o———

One to-day is worth two to-morrows.

FRANCIS QUARLES

———o———

Today And Time

Today is here. I will start with a smile and resolve to be agreeable. I will not criticize. I refuse to waste my valuable time.

Today in one thing I know I am equal with all others — time. All of us draw the same salary in seconds, minutes, and hours.

Today I will not waste my time because the minutes I wasted yesterday are as lost as a vanished thought.

Today I refuse to spend time worrying about what might happen — it usually doesn't. I am going to spend time making things happen.

Today I am determined to study to improve myself, for tomorrow I may be wanted, and I must not be found lacking.

Today I am determined to do the things that I should do. I firmly determine to stop doing the things I should not do.

Today I begin by doing and not wasting my time. In one week I will be miles beyond the person I am today.

Today I will not imagine what I would do if things were different. They are not different. I will make success with what material I have.

Today I will stop saying, "If I had time —" I know I never will "find time" for anything. If I want time, I must make it.

Today I will act toward other people as though this might be my last day on earth. I will not wait for tomorrow. Tomorrow never comes.

GERALD B. KLEIN

———o———

Our todays and yesterdays are the blocks with which we build.

HENRY WADSWORTH LONGFELLOW

———o———

You are younger today than you ever will be; make use of it for the sake of tomorrow.

———o———

Today well-lived, makes every yesterday a dream of happiness and every tomorrow a vision of hope.

OLIVER WENDELL HOLMES

———o———

Begin Today

Dream not too much of what you'll do tomorrow,
How well you'll work perhaps another year;
Tomorrow's chance you do not need to borrow —
Today is here.

Boast not too much of mountains you will master,
The while you linger in the vale below;
To dream is well, but plodding brings us faster
To where we go.

Talk not too much about some new endeavor
You mean to make a little later on;
Who idles now will idle on forever
Till life is done.

Swear not some day to break some habit's fetter,
When this old year is dead and passed away;
If you have need of living wiser, better,
Begin today!

AUTHOR UNKNOWN

Two Care-Free Days

There are two days of the week about which I never worry.

One of these days is *yesterday*. Yesterday, with all its cares and frets, with all its pains and aches, its mistakes and blunders, has passed forever beyond the reach of my recall. I cannot undo any act that I wrought; I cannot unsay a word that I said on yesterday. All that it holds of my life — of wrongs, regret and sorrow is in the hands of the Mighty Love that can bring honey out of the rock, turn weeping into laughter and give beauty for ashes.

And the other day that I do not worry about is *tomorrow*. Tomorrow, with all its possible adversities, its burdens, its perils, its large promise and poor performance, its failures and mistakes . . . is as far beyond the reach of *my* mastery as its dead sister — yesterday. It is a day of God's. It will be mine.

There is left for myself, then, but one day of the week — today. And any man can fight the battles of today. Any woman can carry the burdens of just one day. Any one of us can resist the temptation of the few moments we call today. It is when we willfully add the burden of those two awful eternities — yesterday and tomorrow — to the burdens and cares of today, that we break down.

Only the mighty God Himself can sustain such burdens. And so, in His infinite wisdom, He has carefully measured out to us our "each day's portion" — and gives the promise "As thy day, so shall thy strength be."

W. J. JEFFERS in *New Horizons*

Tolerance

Tolerance is the only real test of civilization.

SIR ARTHUR HELPS

———o———

I believe with all my heart that civilization has produced nothing finer than a man or woman who thinks and practices true tolerance.

FRANK KNOX

Tolerance is the eternal virtue through which good conquers evil and truth vanquishes untruth.

J. EDGAR HOOVER

———o———

Be quick to always spread a little cloak
Of tolerance on faults of other folk.
Remember that if ALL the truth were known,
A circus tent won't cover up your own!

———o———

The most lovable quality that any human being can possess is tolerance. Tolerance is the vision that enables one to see things from any other's viewpoint. It is the generosity that concedes to others the right to their own opinion and their own peculiarities. It is the bigness that enables us to let people be happy in their own way instead of our way.

AUTHOR UNKNOWN

———o———

Tolerance is the ability to let other people be happy in their own way!

EARLEY

Tomorrow

Satan cares not how spiritual your intentions, or how holy your resolutions, if only they are fixed for tomorrow.

J. C. RYLE

———o———

If you want a life of power in your tomorrows you will need to have been obedient to God in your yesterdays.

GARL E. BRAND

———o———

Jimmy, age four, asked his mother, "Is this tomorrow?"

For ten minutes or so she explained the difference between yesterday, today, tomorrow, and he listened intently.

Then he said, "All I asked was 'is this tomorrow!'"

———o———

The only preparation for tomorrow is the right use of today.

Tomorrows

Don't worry 'bout the yesterdays which
   have already gone,
But plan about tomorrows which are
   just beyond the dawn.

Events that happen'd yesterday we
   never can correct,
While those to come tomorrow, we
   can possibly select.

There are so many things to plan for
   days which lie ahead,
That time is wasted when we think of
   yesterdays instead.

Unpleasant memories which clog the
   peacefulness of mind,
Can, with tomorrow's projects, be completely cast behind.

No matter what has taken place upon
   the day before,
It soon will be discarded if the morrow
   we explore.

FRED TOOTHAKER

Tomorrow Will Not Do

The story is told of a man who
dreamed one night that he was carried to a conference of evil spirits.
They were discussing the best means
of destroying men. One rose and said,
"I will go to earth and tell them the
Bible is a fable, and not God's Word."
Said another, "Persuade them that
Christ was only a man." Still another
said, "Let me go; I will tell them there
is no God, no Saviour, no heaven, no
hell." "No, that will not do," they said.
"We could never make men believe
that."
   Finally one old devil, wise as a serpent but not as harmless as a dove,
rose and said: "Let me go; I will tell
them that there is a God, there is a
Saviour, there is a heaven and a hell,
too. But I will tell them there is no
hurry; tomorrow will do; tomorrow will
be even as today!" And he was the
devil they sent!
   The story is fiction, but its message
is a fact. The devil is among us today,
now; but the wise are not deceived by
his lies. "What will you do with Jesus
who is called the Christ?" The man
who thinks that tomorrow will do even
as today is of all men the most deceived.

J. H. MARION, JR.

Faith in tomorrow makes today beautiful.

REX MOBLEY

Tongue

The tongue being in a wet place is
prone to slip!

A loose tongue often gets its owner
into tight places.

Even though the tongue weighs
practically nothing, it's surprising how
few people are able to hold it.

If you can hold your tongue you can
hold your temper.

Some can't help having false teeth,
but everyone can have a true tongue.

The examination was complete. The
surgeon assured the young man that
the only hope of saving his life was
the removal of his tongue. The young
man was already in surgery when he
learned the full story. Tenderly the
surgeon told him that even though the
operation should be successful, he
would never again be able to speak.
He was asked if there was anything
he wished to say before the operation
began.
   The young man on the operating
table was a Christian. When he realized he would never again be able to
testify in song and word for His Lord,
a shadow crossed his face. But soon
the shadow passed and sitting up he
lifted his voice and sang, "There Is A
Fountain Filled With Blood."
   How he sang! His heart was in the
song. Then he came to the last stanza:
"Then in a nobler, sweeter song
I'll sing Thy power to save,

When this poor, lisping, stammering
  tongue
Lies silent in the grave."

The operation was performed, but
the patient never regained consciousness. His last song on earth was pro-
phetic of his first song in heaven.

On Guard

You have a little prisoner;
  He's nimble, and he's clever;
He's sure to get away from you
  Unless you watch him ever.

And when he once gets out, he makes
  More trouble in an hour
Than you can stop in many a day,
  Working with all your power.

He gets your playmates by the ears;
  He says what isn't so,
And uses many ugly words
  Not good for you to know.

Quick, fasten tight the ivory gates,
  And chain him while he's young!
For this most dangerous prisoner
  Is just — your little tongue.
                P. L. in *The Young Soldier*

Prayer For My Tongue

Lord, grant this one request, I pray:
Guide Thou my tongue! The words I
  say
Can never be called back again;
Should they cause anger, sorrow, pain,
Then in an ever wid'ning sphere
They spread their havoc far and near.
So guide my tongue in ev'ry word,
That it may bless where it is heard.
                EUGENE LINCOLN

Better to slip with the foot than with
the tongue.
                English Proverb

The tongue of slander slays three:
the speaker, the spoken to, and the
spoken of.

The human tongue is a deadly weapon, whether it be sharp or blunt.

The old-fashioned doctor used to
diagnose the condition of his patient by
his tongue. The same method might
still be used to determine a person's
moral and spiritual health.

Travel

Two matronly ladies to travel agent:
"We'd like to get completely away from
civilization, near some nice shopping
district."
                FRANKLIN FOLGER, *Newspaper Features*

To travel is to possess the world.
                BURTON HOLMES

If you really look like your passport
photo, chances are you're really not
well enough to travel.
                General Features Corporation

Too often travel, instead of broaden-
ing the mind, merely lengthens the conversation.
                DREW

If you have some hard bumps, you
are probably traveling out of the rut.

Treasure

Opened Treasures

They opened their treasures, the wise
  men of old,
And prostrate they fell on the ground,
Exultant in spirit, they worshiped the
  Lord,
For Jesus, the Savior, they'd found!

The Treasure of Heaven in Bethlehem
  lay,
Incarnate was God from above;
No wonder their treasures they opened
  to Him —
Their feeble expressions of love!

We may not have treasures of glory or
  gold,
Or perfumes to pour at His feet;
Though if we but knew of the worth
  of the Christ,
We would give Him our homage complete.

Our treasured desires we'd open anew,
Our secrets, our dreams and our all —
We would offer as incense our praises
to Him,
Adoring before Him we'd fall!

This Savior from Heaven is worthy
indeed;
And treasures of earth become dim!
But joys everlasting in Jesus are found;
Oh, open your treasures to Him!

MARIE L. OLSON in Now

---o---

Treasures

One by one He took them from me,
  All the things I valued most,
Until I was empty-handed;
  Every glittering toy was lost,

And I walked earth's highways, griev-
  ing,
In my rags and poverty,
Till I heard His voice inviting,
  "Lift your empty hands to Me!"

So I held my hands toward Heaven,
  And He filled them with a store
Of His own transcendent riches,
  Till they could contain no more.

And at last I comprehended
  With my stupid mind and dull,
That God could not pour His riches
  Into hands already full!

MARTHA SNELL NICHOLSON

---o---

Borrowed Treasures

I thank you, God —
For all you've given me.
Your sun,
Your beach,
Your ocean's roar;
Your trees upon the cool
Green shore.
I thank You for the rose
Within my garden;
That is Yours.
The starlit skies,
The twinkle in my infant's
Eyes —
The world.

EVALENA FISHER

Trial

If your cup of trial is sometimes
bitter, put in more of the sugar of
faith. If you feel chilled by the disappointments of your plans or the unkindness of others, get into the sunshine of Christ's love. If income runs
down, invest more in God's precious
promises. A good, stout, healthy faith
will sweeten your affections, and sweet-
en your toils, and sweeten your home,
and sweeten the darkest hours that
may lie between this and heaven. Ad-
herence will bring assurance.

THEODORE LEDYARD CUYLER

---o---

God does not take away trials or
carry us over them, but strengthens us
through them.

EDWARD B. PUSEY

---o---

Nothing will show more accurately
what we are, than the way we meet
trials and difficulties.

---o---

Trials and temptations do not weak-
en us, but they do show us where we
are weak, that we may become strong.

---o---

Every trial that we pass through is
capable of being the seed of a noble
character. Every temptation that we
meet in the path of duty is another
chance of filling our souls with the
power of Heaven.

FREDERICK TEMPLE

---o---

Dr. Paul Carlson in his last tape-
recorded message before his death at
Stanleyville, Congo, said: "Pray that
through the trials we face here we
may be an effective witness for Christ,
and that we may see growth in the
church."

---o---

A blacksmith, about eight years after
he had given his heart to God, was
approached by an intelligent unbeliever
with the question: "Why is it you have
so much trouble? I have been watching you. Since you joined the Church

and began to 'walk square,' and seem to love everybody, you have had twice as many trials and accidents as you had before. I thought that when a man gave himself to God his troubles were over. Isn't that what the parsons tell us?"

With a thoughtful, but glowing face, the blacksmith replied:

"Do you see this piece of iron? It is for the springs of a carriage. I have been 'tempering' it for some time. To do this I heat it red-hot, and then plunge it into a tub of ice-cold water. This I do many times. If I find it taking 'temper,' I heat and hammer it unmercifully. In getting the right piece of iron I found several that were too brittle. So I threw them in the scrap-pile. Those scraps are worth about a cent a pound; this carriage spring is very valuable."

He paused, and his listener nodded. The blacksmith continued:

"God saves us for something more than to have a good time — that's the way I see it. We have the good time all right, for God's smile means heaven. But he wants us for service just as I want this piece of iron. And he has put the 'temper' of Christ in us by testing us with trial. Ever since I saw this I have been saying to him, "Test me in any way you choose, Lord; only don't throw me in the scrap-pile."

————o————

To Be Called A Brick

A brick is made of clay;
    So is man.
A brick is square and plumb and true;
    So a man ought to be.
A brick is useless until it has been
    through the fire;
    So is man.
A brick is not so showy as marble, but
    it is more useful;
    Man is not made for show, but for
    service.
A brick fulfills its purpose only by be-
    coming a part of something greater
    than itself;
    The same is true of a man.
When a man fulfills this description,
    he has a right to be called a brick.
                  AUTHOR UNKNOWN

Trouble

The easiest way to get into trouble is to be right at the wrong time.

————o————

The fellow who's really in trouble is one who's in bad company when he's alone.

————o————

The man was complaining glumly to a friend that family trouble had him down. His friend suggested that perhaps he was taking it too seriously — that there were two sides to every question.

"That's right," agreed the morose one, "but in my house the two sides are always my wife's and her mother's."

————o————

It's much easier to borrow trouble than it is to give it away.

————o————

During the First World War, a disastrous fire broke out in the Greek city of Salonica. The historic church of St. Demetrius suffered considerably from the fire. The scorching heat destroyed the plaster covering of the west wall, and exposed a seventh century painting of St. Demetrius fighting a ravaging fire in Salonica in his own day. One of the things that the flames through which we pass do for us is to break through the surface of the years and reveal the souls of the saints and heroes of old who fought similar fires in their own day.

————o————

The person who looks for trouble should have his eyes examined.

————o————

Some people bear three kinds of trouble:
    All they ever had,
    All they have now,
    All they expect to have.
            EDWARD EVERETT HALE

————o————

A good way to forget your troubles is to help others out of theirs.

A lot of trouble in this world is caused by combining a narrow mind with a wide mouth.

———o———

I have never met a man who has given me as much trouble as myself.

DWIGHT L. MOODY

———o———

When a neighbor once asked a mother of twelve if she had a lot of trouble with so many children, she replied: "Never trouble. Bother at times, maybe. Bother is in the hands. Trouble is in the heart."

———o———

You don't need help to get into trouble, but usually you have it.

Journal-Enquirer, Grayson, Kentucky

———o———

You don't need references to borrow trouble.

———o———

If you must talk about your troubles, don't bore your friends with them — tell them to your enemies, who will be delighted to hear about them.

OLIN MILLER
in *Chicago Sun-Times Syndicate*

———o———

Borrow trouble for yourself, if that's your nature, but don't lend it to your neighbors.

RUDYARD KIPLING

———o———

All the troubles of life come upon us because we refuse to sit quietly for a while each day in our rooms.

BLAISE PASCAL

———o———

I am an old man and have known a great many troubles, but most of them have never happened.

MARK TWAIN

———o———

When you help out a man in trouble, you can be sure of one thing: he won't forget you — next time he's in trouble.

Illinois General News

———o———

Let us give up our work, our thoughts, our plans, our selves, our lives, our loved ones, over all into His hands. When you have given all unto God, there will be nothing left for you to be troubled about.

J. HUDSON TAYLOR

———o———

Troubles

I've got a heap of troubles
  And I've got to work them out.
But I look around and see
  There's trouble all about.
And when I see my troubles,
  I just look up and grin
And count all the trouble
  That I'm not in.

True, Truth

It is not hard to find the truth; what is hard is not to run away from it once you have found it.

ETIENNE GILSON in *Ladies' Home Journal*

———o———

Truth is the hardest missile one can be pelted with.

GEORGE ELIOT (MARY ANN EVANS)
———o———

In any emergency in life there is nothing so strong and safe as the simple truth.

CHARLES DICKENS
———o———

I do not ask that He must prove
His Word is true to me;
And that before I can believe
He first must let me see.
It is enough for me to know
'Tis true because He says 'tis so.
On His unchanging Word I'll stand,
And trust till I can understand.

AUTHOR UNKNOWN

———o———

Truth does not hurt unless it ought to.

———o———

God requires us to give credit to the truths which He reveals, not because we can prove them, but because He reveals them.

DANIEL WEBSTER
———o———

Truth is tough. It will not break,

like a bubble, at a touch; nay, you may kick it about all day, like a football, and it will be round and full at evening.

———o———

It does not require a long lesson to present a great truth.

———o———

Truth is the secret of eloquence and of virtue, the basis of moral authority; it is the highest summit of art and life.

HENRI-FRÉDÉRIC AMIEL, *Journal*

———o———

The New Testament does not say, "You shall know the rules, and by them you shall be bound," but "You shall know the truth, and the truth shall make you free."

JOHN BAILLIE

———o———

The reason some people arrive at the truth a good deal more quickly than others is not because of their intuition or superior brain power. They simply ask more questions.

———o———

Our world is so exceedingly rich in delusions that a truth is priceless.

CARL GUSTAV JUNG

———o———

There is nothing so powerful as truth, — and often nothing so strange.

DANIEL WEBSTER,
Argument on the Murder of Captain White

———o———

Truth is the most valuable thing we have. Let us economize it.

MARK TWAIN
Following the Equator, Vol. I

———o———

We search the world for truth. We cull
The good, the true, the beautiful,
From graven stone and written scroll,
From all old flower-fields of the soul;
And, weary seekers of the best,
We come back laden from the quest,
To find that all the sages said
Is in the Book our mothers read.

JOHN GREENLEAF WHITTIER, *Miriam*

———o———

If you tell the truth, you have in-

finite power supporting you; but if not, you have infinite power against you.

CHARLES GEORGE GORDON

———o———

Truth sits upon the lips of dying men.

MATTHEW ARNOLD, *Sohrab and Rustum*

———o———

No pleasure is comparable to the standing upon the vantage-ground of truth.

FRANCIS BACON, *Of Truth*

———o———

This above all: to thine own self be true,
And it must follow, as the night the day,
Thou canst not then be false to any man.

WILLIAM SHAKESPEARE, *Hamlet*

———o———

Being True

Think truly and thy thought
Shall the world's famine feed;
Speak truly and thy word
Shall be a fruitful seed;
Live truly and thy life
Shall be a great and noble creed.

HORATIUS BONAR

Trust

Trust in God is an antidote for fear of men.

———o———

Trust is the chief conqueror of difficulties.

———o———

They greatly dare who greatly trust. If our faith were greater, our deeds would be larger.

———o———

God has never been able to use any man in a large way who could not be trusted in an emergency.

———o———

You can trust the man who died for you.

MRS. CHARLES E. COWMAN

We were crowded in the cabin;
  Not a soul would dare to sleep;
It was midnight on the waters
  And the storm was in the deep.

'Tis a fearful thing in winter
  To be shattered by the blast,
And hear the rattling trumpet
  Thunder, "Cut away the mast!"

So we shuddered there in silence,
  For the stoutest held his breath
While the hungry sea was roaring
  And the breakers threatened death.

And as thus we sat in darkness,
  Each one busy in his prayers,
"We are lost!" the captain shouted
  As he staggered down the stairs.

But his little daughter whispered,
  As she took his icy hand,
"Isn't God upon the ocean
  Just the same as on the land?"

Then we kissed the little maiden
  And we spoke in better cheer;
And we anchored safe in harbor
  When the morn was shining clear.
                        JAMES T. FIELDS
                from a *McGuffey Fourth Reader*

———o———

Sure, it takes a lot of courage
  To put things in God's hands,
To give ourselves completely,
  Our lives, our hopes, our plans;
To follow where He leads us
  And make His will our own,
But all it takes is foolishness
  To go the way alone.
                        BETSEY KLINE

———o———

I have no answer for myself or thee,
Save that I learned beside my mother's
    knee:
"All is of God that is, and is to be;
And God is good." Let this suffice us
    still,
Resting in childlike trust upon His will
Who moves to His great ends un-
    thwarted by the ill.
                        WILLIAM COWPER

———o———

When I try I fail; when I trust, He
succeeds.

When you cannot trust God you
cannot trust anything; and when you
cannot trust anything you get the condition of the world as it is today.
                        BASIL KING

———o———

Trusting

You ask how you learn to trust Him?
Dear child, you must just let go!

Let go of your frantic worry,
And the fears which plague you so;

Let go of each black tomorrow
Which you try to live today;

Let go of your fevered planning,
He knoweth all your way.

Fear not lest your slipping fingers
Let go of your Saviour too, —

Trusting is only knowing
He'll not let go of you!
                MARTHA SNELL NICHOLSON

———o———

Trust him little who praises all, him
less who censures all, and him least
who is indifferent about all.
                        JOHANN LARATER

———o———

What does a child do whose mother
or father allows something to be done
which it cannot understand? There is
only one way of peace. The loving
child trusts.
                        AMY CARMICHAEL

———o———

It is an equal failing to trust everybody, and to trust nobody.

Try

Try, Try Again

'Tis a lesson you should heed,
  Try, try again;
If at first you don't succeed,
  Try, try again;
Then your courage should appear,
For, if you will persevere,
You will conquer, never fear;
  Try, try again.

Once or twice though you should fail,
  Try, try again;

If you would at last prevail,
  Try, try again;
If we strive, 'tis no disgrace
Though we do not win the race;
What should you do in the case?
  Try, try again.

If you find your task is hard,
  Try, try again;
Time will bring you your reward,
  Try, try again;
All that other folks can do,
Why, with patience, should not you?
Only keep this rule in view:
  Try, try, again.

                                    T. H. PALMER

————o————

Triumph is just UMPH added to
TRY!

                                    Sunshine Magazine

————o————

You Haven't Tried Yet!

I was busy in my basement worshop
when four-year-old Mike came and
stood at my elbow. "Daddy, will you
fix my scooter?" he asked.

Guiltily, I looked down at the completely wrecked scooter which he held
in his hand. I had backed over it with
the car earlier that day. I couldn't
possibly fix it; it was too badly dam-
aged. Irritated, I said, "Mike, I told
you before that I can't fix your scooter.
I'm sorry."

A troubled expression came over
Mike's face. "But Daddy, you haven't
tried yet!"

How could a father resist such an
appeal? I set to work and, to my
surprise, I discovered that I could fix
the scooter.

Later, I wondered how often we
excuse ourselves from attempting a difficult assignment or taking a new step
in faith by saying, "I can't," when the
truth is we haven't tried yet.

                                    HERBERT GIBSON

U

Unbelief

Unbelief is giving God the lie.

                                    CHARLES HADDON SPURGEON

————o————

Unbelief is something of which the
devils are not guilty.

————o————

God does not think so lightly of our
doubt and unbelief as we do.

Understand, Understanding

The Fifth Commandment

An old schoolmaster said one day to
a clergyman, who came to examine his
school, "I believe the children know the
catchism word for word."

"But do they understand it? That is
the question," said the clergyman.

The schoolmaster bowed respectful-
ly, and the examination began. A little
boy had repeated the fifth commandment, "Honor thy father and thy
mother," and he was asked to explain
it. Instead of trying to do so, the little
boy, with his face covered with blushes, said, almost in a whisper, "Yesterday I showed some strange man over
the mountain, and the sharp stones cut
my feet. The man saw they were
bleeding, and gave me some money
to buy shoes. I gave it to my mother,
for she had no shoes either, and I
thought I could go barefooted better
than she could."

                                    Selected

————o————

Teacher: "Johnny, are your folks
diplomats?"

Johnny: "No, they are Lutherans."

————o————

Man to young boy: "Does your dog
have a pedigree?"

Boy: "No, we cut that off."

The story is told of a young theological student who one day came to the great preacher, Charles H. Spurgeon, telling him that the Bible contained some verses which he could not understand about which he was very much worried. To this Spurgeon replied, "Young man, allow me to give you this word of advice: You must expect to let God know some things which you do not understand."

The Sunday School Times

———o———

It is man's mission to learn to understand.

VANNEVAR BUSH

———o———

O God, help us not to despise or oppose what we do not understand.

WILLIAM PENN

———o———

Seeing may be believing, but it isn't necessarily understanding.

Tribune-News, Cartersville, Georgia

———o———

God — let me be aware.
Stab my soul fiercely with others' pain,
Let me walk seeing horror and stain.
Let my hands, groping, find other hands.
Give me the heart that divines, understands.

MIRIAM TEICHNER

———o———

Whoever would fully and feelingly understand the words of Christ, must endeavor to conform his life wholly to the life of Christ.

THOMAS À KEMPIS

———o———

By comparison with God's perfect understanding, we are like a man inside a barrel looking through a bunghole.

R. R. BROWN

Unhappy, Unhappiness

The worst kind of unhappiness, as well as the greatest amount of it, comes from our conduct to each other.

FREDERICK WILLIAM FABER

Whoever does not regard what he has as most ample wealth, is unhappy, though he be master of the world.

EPICURUS

———o———

A perverse temper, and a discontented, fretful disposition, wherever they prevail, render any state of life unhappy.

MARCUS TULLIUS CICERO

Unknown

The world knows nothing of its greatest men.

SIR HENRY TAYLOR

———o———

Everything unknown is taken to be magnificent.

TACITUS

———o———

Unknown, unmissed.

Urgent

Later Than You Think

A young boy awakened at midnight. He listened to the old grandfather's clock strike out the melody of midnight — one, two, three, four . . . and on to twelve. But something went wrong with the old clock and it kept on striking . . . thirteen . . . fourteen . . . fifteen . . . sixteen. The boy became alarmed and ran into his father's bedroom.

He startled his father with these words, "Daddy, I just heard the old clock strike sixteen! It must be later than it's ever been before!"

There's no time to waste. No time for frivolity, or worldly pursuits. It's time to seek the Lord. It's later than it's ever been before!

The Log of the Good Ship Grace

———o———

We have all eternity to tell of victories won for Christ but we have only a few hours before sunset in which to win them.

JONATHAN GOFORTH

Use, Useful, Useless

Square yourself for use. A stone that may fit in the wall is not left in the way.

Persian Proverb

———o———

Let's quit trying to use God and ask God to use us.

———o———

The really useful worker is so busy being useful that he hasn't time to consider how useful he is.

———o———

Use what you have, that you may have more to use.

CHARLES HADDON SPURGEON

Use is the best estimate of value.

———o———

Use pastime so as to save time.

———o———

A Christian girl who was saved from shipwreck by getting into a lifeboat said, "I was not afraid to die, for Christ is my Savior. But I was ashamed to die, for my life had been so useless."

———o———

We lose what we don't use.

ALFRED ARMAND MONTAPERT

———o———

No one is useless in this world who lightens the burden of another.

CHARLES DICKENS

V

Vacation

A vacation should be just long enough for the boss to miss you, and not long enough for him to discover how well he can get along without you.

———o———

There is no vacation from godliness.

———o———

If all the year were playing holidays, To sport would be as tedious as to work.

WILLIAM SHAKESPEARE, *King Henry IV*

———o———

"You didn't take a vacation this year, did you?"
"No, I thought I needed a rest."

———o———

No man needs a vacation so much as the person who just had one.

ELBERT HUBBARD

———o———

Every now and then go away, have a little relaxation, for when you come back to your work your judgment will be surer, since to remain constantly at work will cause you to lose power of judgment. Go some distance away, because then the work appears smaller, and more of it can be taken in at a glance, and lack of harmony and proportion is more readily seen.

LEONARDO DA VINCI

———o———

Isn't it wonderful how school vacation runs out at about the same time as your patience?

———o———

If a person looks tired and careworn, don't suggest a vacation. He has probably just had one.

Valentine

First Time

The wee man held in one chubby hand
A valentine message so true,
A small red heart and written inside
Those three magic words, "I love you."

This moment both shall long remember,

For nothing is ever so fine
As when a lad gives his first sweet-
heart
Her very first gay valentine.

VIRGINIA K. OLIVER

———o———

Oh! if it be to choose and call thee
mine,
Love, thou art everyday my Valentine.

THOMAS HOOD

———o———

Valentine To A School Teacher:

The bees do the work
And the bees get the honey;
But we do the work
And you get the money!

Value, Values

Sound Values

Marshall Field once indicated the following twelve reminders that can be helpful in obtaining a sound sense of values:
The value of time.
The success of perseverance.
The pleasure of working.
The dignity of simplicity.
The worth of character.
The power of kindness.
The influence of example.
The obligation of duty.
The wisdom of economy.
The virtue of patience.
The improvement of talent.
The joy of originating.

MARSHALL FIELD

———o———

What we obtain too cheaply, we esteem too lightly. It is dearness, that gives everything its value.

THOMAS PAINE

———o———

A sense of values is the most important single element in human personality.

———o———

No inferior form of energy can be simply converted into a superior form unless at the same time a source of higher value lends it support.

CARL GUSTAV JUNG

Treasures

I was standing in Tiffany's great store in New York, and I heard the salesman say to a lady who had asked him about some pearls, "Madam, this pearl is worth $17,000."

As I looked around that beautiful store, I imagined them bringing all their stock up to my house, and saying, "We want you to take care of this tonight." What do you think I would do? I would go as quickly as I could to the telephone and call up the Chief of Police and say, "I have all Tiffany's stock in my house, and it is too great a responsibility. Will you send some of your most trusted officers to help me?"

But I have a little boy in my home, and for him I am responsible. I have had him for nine years, and some of you may have just such another little boy. I turn to this old Book and I read this word: "What shall it profit a man if he gain the whole world and lose his own soul?" It is as if he had all the diamonds and rubies and pearls in the world, and held them in one hand, and just put a little boy in the other, and the boy would be worth more than all the jewels. If you would tremble because you had $17,000 worth of jewels in the house one night, how shall you go up to your Father and your son be not with you?

J. WILBUR CHAPMAN

———o———

The chemical analysis of the human body is:

Sulphur	Enough to rid a dog of fleas.
Lime	Enough to whitewash a chicken coop.
Fat	Enough for six bars of soap.
Iron	Enough for a 6-penny nail.
Phosphorus	Enough for twenty boxes of matches.
Sugar	Enough for ten cups of coffee.
Potassium	Enough to explode a toy cannon.

Total value, ninety-eight cents!
Scientists of Northwestern University

have re-estimated the value of the basic elements in the human body, formerly placed at ninety-eight cents, and consider them now worth $31.04.

———o———

The parent who gives his child seventy-five cents for a movie and a dime for Sunday School is teaching him a set of values that could carry through a lifetime.

———o———

We can only be valued as we make ourselves valuable.

RALPH WALDO EMERSON

Victory

It was Paul who had malaria and poor eyesight, who was whipped, imprisoned, stoned and shipwrecked who said, "God has turned my life into a pageant of triumph."

A. BONNINGRAM

———o———

The first and best victory is to conquer self; to be conquered by self is, of all things, the most shameful and vile.

PLATO

———o———

God will give us the victory if we will go to the fight.

———o———

There is no victory without the stench and heat of battle; there is no shining without burning. But when we finish our spiritual campaign in the battlefield of earth, we will stand before our Lord Jesus Christ and be pleasing to Him.

LIEUTENANT ROBERT C. HOLLAND, JR.

———o———

Christ spells victory. Even though we have trials and tribulations, we experience defeats and frustrations, we can be of good cheer because we know that the One in whom we have placed our confidence has overcome the world.

———o———

Before the winds that blow do cease,
 Teach me to dwell within Thy calm;
Before the pain has passed in peace,

Give me, my God, to sing a psalm,
Let me not lose the chance to prove
 The fulness of enabling love.
O Love of God, do this for me:
 Maintain a constant victory.

AMY CARMICHAEL

———o———

On the day of victory, no fatigue is felt.

Arab Proverb

———o———

The first step on the way to victory is to recognize the enemy.

CORRIE TEN BOOM

———o———

The way to get the most out of a victory is to follow it up with another which makes it look small.

HENRY S. HASKINS

———o———

Victory

Keep on trying, forego sighing,
God will help us do our best.
It's by working, not by shirking,
We find comfort, joy and rest.
It's by loving, not by hating,
That we build the life sublime;
It's our blessing, not our cursing,
That brings victory, every time.

BERNICE SMITH

———o———

To be effective one must be unaffected. Outward defeat often spells inward victory.

———o———

A life of victory hinges upon three things: an act, a purpose, and a habit: an initial act, a fixed purpose, a daily habit.

The initial act is that of personal surrender to the Lord Jesus as Master.

The fixed purpose is that of doing what will please Him, and only that, at every turn, in every matter, regardless of consequences.

The daily habit is that of spending a quiet time daily in prayer alone with the Lord over His Word. After the initial act of surrender, the secret of a strong, winsome Christian life is in spending time daily alone with God over His Word in prayer.

S. D. GORDON

Victory is a thing of the will.

MARSHAL FERDINAND FOCH

Victories that are easy are cheap. Those only are worth having which come as the result of hard fighting.

HENRY WARD BEECHER

If there be no enemy, no fight;
If no fight, no victory;
If no victory, no crown.

SAVONAROLA

Virtue, Virtuous

Sincerity and truth are the basis of every virtue.

CONFUCIUS

When men grow virtuous in their old age, they only make a sacrifice to God of the devil's leavings.

ALEXANDER POPE,
Thoughts on Various Subjects

The [Christian] Puritan held, incredible as it may seem, that morals are more important than athletics, business or art; that the good life must be founded on virtue.

RALPH BARTON PERRY

Virtue has many preachers, but few martyrs.

CLAUDE ADRIEN HELVETIUS

A large part of virtue consists in good habits.

WILLIAM PALEY

Virtue can see the duty regardless of how great the darkness be.

Riches adorn the dwelling; virtue adorns the person.

Chinese Proverb

Virtue herself is her own fairest reward.

SILIUS ITALICUS, *Punica*

Rarely do we like the virtues we do not have.

Virtue is a jewel of great price.

Virtue consists in doing our duty in the various relations we sustain to ourselves, to our fellowmen, and to God, as it is made known by reason, revelation, and Providence.

ARCHIBALD ALEXANDER

The greatest offense against virtue is to speak ill of it.

WILLIAM HAZLITT

We value great men by their virtue and not their success.

CORNELIUS NEPOS

Vision

Poor eyes limit your sight; poor vision limits your deeds.

FRANKLIN FIELD

Vision is the art of seeing things invisible.

JONATHAN SWIFT,
Thoughts on Various Subjects

Vision is of God. A vision comes in advance of any task well done.

KATHERINE LOGAN

The vision of God is the transfiguration of the world; communion with God is the inspiration of the life.

BROOKE FOSS WESTCOTT

Visit, Visitation

Visit neighbors, kith, and kin,
But don't always be about.
Often too much dropping in
Causes falling out.

JANE MERCHANT

One day I rang a door bell,
In a casual sort of way.
'Twas not a formal visit,
And there wasn't much to say.
I don't remember what I said —
It matters not, I guess —
I found a heart in hunger,
A soul in deep distress . . .
It meant so little to me
To knock at a stranger's door,
But it meant heaven to him
And God's peace forever more.

AUTHOR UNKNOWN

———o———

Visits always give pleasure — if not the coming, then the going.

Portuguese Proverb

Vocation
Vocation

By the way I do my job —
keep a ledger,
till the soil,
prepare a meal,
advise a client,
love my child,
serve a customer —
I witness to my faith, and win on
behalf of the church a good reputation
before the world.

FRED C. HOLDER

———o———

Teen-ager to vocational counselor: "How do I know what I want to be when I get out of school? Maybe they haven't even invented my job yet."

The Improvement Era

W

Wait

All things come to him who waits — provided he knows what he is waiting for.

WOODROW WILSON

———o———

Satan has many wiles. His favorite is "Wait a while."

———o———

I Must Wait

I know I am impatient, Lord,
I want to run ahead;
Speak to my heart and make me
Willing to be led.
Your clock is always right, Lord
It never does run late;
Your schedule can't be hurried
So teach me, Lord, to wait.

Your time is never my time —
Oh, make this plain to me
And give me patience so to wait
And Thy fulfillment see.
I see through a glass darkly
And in this earthly state
I only know impatience,
So teach me, Lord, to wait.

I pray for Thy anointing,
I need Thy holy touch;
Oh, send me a full measure —
I need it, oh, so much.
Please keep me calm and trusting
In this world of strife and hate;
And 'mid the hurrying, worrying throng
Oh, teach me, Lord, to wait.

RETA BELLE LYLE

———o———

Waiting for a phone call frets him,
Waiting on his wife upsets him.
Almost any kind of waiting
Starts his temper activating.
He's the guy who finds delight
Waiting for the fish to bite!

S. OMAR BARKER in *Capper's Weekly*

———o———

They Wait Too Long

Some people wait too long in life
To use their clever brains.
And then they find it is too late
To make impressive gains.
They will not take the time to get
The knowledge they require
To reach the glorious success
To which their hearts aspire.

For they would rather have their fun
And play around today,
Than try to reach a certain goal
That seems so far away.
The value of their dreams in life
Is something that they measure
In terms of idle wanderings
And moments made for pleasure.

And strange as it may seem, they have
The nerve to weep and wail
And wonder why with all their brains
Their feeble efforts fail.

JAMES J. METCALFE

Wait Upon The Lord

Wait thou, my soul, upon the Lord —
   He is thy strength and life:
Lift up thy heart — mount up and fly
   Above the stress and strife;
For there thy strength shall be re-
      newed
   In that celestial sphere;
Then through the valley thou canst
      walk
   By faith and not by fear.

Wait thou, my soul, upon the Lord,
   And with the wings of faith,
Rise up to mountain tops of truth
   Where each reviving breath
Shall fill thy soul with songs of joy;
   And on the sacred height,
Renew thy strength to walk the plain,
   Amid the gloom of night.

Thou art too weak to walk the paths
   Where days seem dark and long?
Then wait on Him, thy gracious Lord,
   Until the victor's song
Thou, too, hast heard amid the heights
   And cherished as thine own —
Until on mountain tops of faith
   The triumph has been won.

Wait then upon the Lord; yea, wait
   Till earthly doubts grow dim;
Yea, mount above the clouds of care
   And fellowship with Him.
There He will train thee for the task
   Where common duties call,
And in the strength renewed by Him
   Thou shalt not faint or fall.

AUTHOR UNKNOWN

The man who waits for things to
turn up, usually finds that his toes do
it first.

———o———

While you wait for great things, the
door to the little ones may close.

American Friend

———o———

Patient waiting is often the highest
way of doing God's will.

———o———

All good abides with him who wait-
eth wisely.

HENRY DAVID THOREAU

Walk

It is better to walk straight, even
though alone, than to stagger in the
"best" of circles.

———o———

I'm a slow walker, but I never walk
back.

ABRAHAM LINCOLN

———o———

Men think of a fifty-mile hike as
training in physical fitness. Women
call it shopping.

———o———

The one who walks with God always gets to his destination.

———o———

One who walks with God always
knows in what direction he is going.

———o———

I like long walks, especially when
they are taken by people who annoy
me.

FRED ALLEN

Want

A Man Must Want

It's wanting keeps us young and fit;
It's wanting something just ahead
And striving hard to come to it,
That brightens every road we tread.

The man is old before his time
Who is supremely satisfied,

And does not want some hill to climb
Or something life has still denied.

A man must want from day to day,
Must want to reach a distant goal
Or claim some treasure far away,
For want's the builder of the soul.

He who has ceased to want has
  dropped
The working tools of life, and stands
Much like an old-time clock has
  stopped,
While time is moldering his hands.

Want is the spur that drives us on
And oft its praises should be sung,
For man is old when want is gone —
It's what we want that keeps us young.
                          AUTHOR UNKNOWN

---o---

It's impossible to have everything
you want because if this were so you'd
always be missing the fun of wanting
something.

---o---

Some people think they are poor
just because they do not have everything they want.
                             ROY L. SMITH

---o---

God is waiting to be wanted.
                             A. W. TOZER

War

The tragedy of war is that it uses
man's best to do man's worst.
                      HARRY EMERSON FOSDICK

---o---

I bet you that history don't record
any two nations ever having a war
with each other unless they had a conference first.
                             WILL ROGERS

---o---

The only way to make war impossible
is to stop getting ready for war.
                             FRANK CRANE

---o---

War is death's feast.

---o---

War! that mad game the world so
loves to play.
                      JONATHAN SWIFT,
                   Ode to Sir William Temple

Waste

Waste of Muscle, waste of Brain,
Waste of Patience, waste of Pain,
Waste of Manhood, waste of Health,
Waste of Beauty, waste of Wealth,
Waste of Blood, waste of Tears,
Waste of Youth's most precious years,
Waste of Ways the Saints have trod,
Waste of Glory, waste of God — War!
                      G. A. STUDDERT-KENNEDY

---o---

There never was a good war, or a
bad peace.
                      BENJAMIN FRANKLIN

---o---

War is the business of barbarians.
                      NAPOLEON BONAPARTE

---o---

Take my word for it, if you had seen
but one day of war, you would pray to
Almighty God, that you might never
see such a thing again.
                  THE DUKE OF WELLINGTON

Watch

In the children's meeting we sang
with the smallest children:
  "Be careful, little eyes, what you see.
  Be careful, little ears, what you hear.
  Be careful, little mouth, what you
say . . .
  For the Father up above
  Is looking down on you in love,
  So be careful . . ."
Little almost four-year-old Hans
broke out in tears. "No!" he shouted,
"I don't want to have a father who
watches over me so carefully."
Had he not uttered from his heart
that which we sometimes feel? We
want a loving God who helps us out
of all our difficulties, but not One who
sees the wrong things we do.
                      HEDWIG GUT, in Gospel Call

---o---

A man becomes wise by watching
what happens to him when he isn't!

---o---

Teacher: "Jimmy, what are you doing?"

Jimmy: "Nothing! With you and Mom and God and Santa Claus watching all the time, what can I do?"

———o———

Watching man as our ideal does not make us spiritual.

———o———

No one ever falls into sin as the result of being too watchful.

Water

A crew shipwrecked in the Atlantic had been drifting for days in a small lifeboat, suffering from extreme thirst. When all hope had been abandoned, smoke was discerned on the horizon and a vessel bore down upon them. With all their strength they mustered a pitiful shout, "Water! Water!"
From the bridge came what seemed to be a mocking answer, "Dip your bucket over the side!" Without knowing it, they had drifted into the area where the mighty Amazon River bears its fresh waters out to sea. Unaware, they were floating in an ocean of plenty. "Ho, every one that thirsteth, come . . ." says God's Word.

———o———

Water: A liquid that freezes slippery side up.

Way

You Know The Way

Shortly after 1918, when the Soviets came to power in western Russia, a young baroness of German parentage was thrown into prison and condemned to death. While waiting for execution, Marion Von Klodt, a devout Christian, wrote a hymn, which was immediately taken up by other prisoners and swept through camps across Russia. Today it is sung in many languages in churches across the communist world. Marion Von Klodt sang the hymn as she went before the firing squad.

You know the way,
Though I myself do not,

This thought gives me
A peace beyond compare.
What shall I fear
What terrors fill with anguish,
By night and day,
Although my soul does languish?

You know the way;
You also know the time.
Your plan for me
Has long since been prepared.
I praise you, Lord,
With all my deepest feeling
For all your care,
Your love to me revealing.

You know all things:
From whence the wind doth blow.
The storm of life
You can alone subdue.
I am at peace,
Content, though still not knowing,
For you have planned
The way I am now going.
MARION VON KLODT

Weakness

Although men are accused of not knowing their own weakness, yet perhaps as few know their own strength. It is in men as in soils, where sometimes there is a vein of gold which the owner knows not of.
JONATHAN SWIFT

———o———

The acknowledgement of our weakness is the first step toward repairing our loss.
THOMAS À KEMPIS

———o———

You cannot run away from a weakness; you must some time fight it out or perish; and if that be so, why not now, and where you stand?
ROBERT LOUIS STEVENSON,
The Amateur Emigrant

Wealth

You can use the wealth of this world in the service of the Master. To gain is not wrong. It is only wrong when grasping becomes the main object of life.
CHARLES HADDON SPURGEON

Wealth makes worship.

Old Proverb

———o———

If we command our wealth, we shall be rich and free. If our wealth commands us, we are poor indeed.

EDMUND BURKE

———o———

A thousand times God called his name,
A thousand times God touched his hand;
He turned aside for wealth and fame;
And built his house upon the sand.

FRANKLIN PIERCE RENO

———o———

Wealth consists not in having great possessions, but in having few wants.

EPICURUS

Weddings

The kindest and the happiest pair
　Will find occasion to forbear,
And something every day they live
　To pity, and perhaps forgive.

WILLIAM COWPER

———o———

Dad gets the worst of it, no doubt,
With daughter's wedding frills:
At first the wedding BELLS ring out
Then come the wedding BILLS.

———o———

A golden wedding is when the couple has gone fifty-fifty!

———o———

There's nothin' like a weddin'
　To make a feller learn;
At first he thinks she's his'n,
But later finds he's her'n.

AUTHOR UNKNOWN

Weight

The difference between a career girl and a housewife is twenty pounds.

———o———

It's not the minutes you take at the table that make you overweight — it's the seconds.

———o———

A little girl was describing a set of scales: "It's something you stand on and then get really mad."

———o———

Paunch Lines

Hey diddle, diddle,
I'm watching my middle,
I'm hoping to whittle it soon;
But eating's such fun
I may not get it done,
Till my dish runs away with my spoon!

Printed from *The Owl* in the *Hi-Desert Star*

———o———

One Weigh

I lost five pounds;
No one said a word.
I gained back three —
And that's all I've heard!

LUCY LOLLI RANKIN in *Family Weekly*

———o———

A larger-than-average woman stepped on the scales, not knowing they were out of order. The indicator stopped at seventy-five pounds.

A little boy standing by watched her intently. "Whaddaya know," he marveled. "She's hollow!"

Wicked

There is a method in man's wickedness, —
It grows up by degrees.

FRANCIS BEAUMONT and JOHN FLETCHER,
A King and No King

———o———

No man ever became extremely wicked all at once.

JUVENAL, *Satires*

———o———

For never, never, wicked man was wise.

ALEXANDER POPE, *Odyssey of Homer*

Wife

Nothing lovelier can be found
In woman, than to study household good,
And in good works her husband to promote.

JOHN MILTON

Thy wife is a constellation of virtues; she's the moon, and thou art the man in the moon.

WILLIAM CONGREVE, *Love for Love*

———o———

How much the wife is dearer than the bride.

GEORGE, LORD LYTTELTON

———o———

Ten Commandments For Wives

I. Honor thy own womanhood, that thy days may be long in the house which thy husband provideth for thee.

II. Expect not thy husband to give thee as many luxuries as thy father hath given thee after many years of hard labor and economies.

III. Forget not the virtue of good humor, for verily all that a man hath will he give for a woman's smile.

IV. Thou shalt not nag.

V. Thou shalt coddle thy husband, for verily every man loveth to be fussed over.

VI. Remember that the frank approval of thy husband is worth more to thee than the sidelong glances of many strangers.

VII. Forget not the grace of cleanliness and good dressing.

VIII. Permit no one to assure thee that thou art having a hard time of it; neither thy mother, nor thy sister, nor thy maiden aunt, nor any of thy kinfolk, for the judge will not hold her guiltless who letteth another disparage her husband.

IX. Keep thy home with all diligence, for out of it cometh the joys of thine old age.

X. Commit thy ways unto the Lord thy God and thy children shall rise up and call thee blessed.

———o———

A successful wife knows how much to believe of what she hears about her husband.

Pioneer-Times, Houlton, Maine

———o———

All other good by fortune's hand are given,
A wife is the peculiar gift of heaven.

ALEXANDER POPE

What is there in the vale of life
Half so delightful as a wife,
When friendship, love, and peace combine
To stamp the marriage-bond divine?

WILLIAM COWPER

———o———

His house she enters, there to be a light,
Shining within, when all without is night;
A guardian angel o'er his life presiding,
Doubling his pleasures, and his cares dividing!

SAMUEL ROGERS, *Human Life*

———o———

The world well tried — the sweetest thing in life
Is the unclouded welcome of a wife.

NATHANIEL PARKER WILLIS, *The Lady Jane*

———o———

While the true wife clings and leans, she also helps and inspires.

O. G. WILSON

———o———

An ideal wife is any woman who has an ideal husband.

BOOTH TARKINGTON

———o———

The ideal wife is one who knows when her husband wants to be forced to do something against his will.

SYDNEY J. HARRIS

———o———

A constantly nagging wife had a momentary change of heart and bought her husband two neckties for his birthday. Finding them on his dresser, the surprised husband put one on and went down to the dining room for breakfast.

"Humph!" the wife snorted. "So you don't like the other one?"

Watchman-Examiner

———o———

A perfect wife does not expect a perfect husband.

Courier, Houma, Louisiana

———o———

A wife is one who remodels your funny stories as you tell them.

Will, Willing

He that complies against his will
Is of the same opinion still.
Which he may adhere to, yet disown
For reasons to himself best known.
SAMUEL BUTLER, *Hudibras*

———o———

He is a fool who thinks by force or
skill
To turn the current of a woman's will.
SIR SAMUEL TUKE, *Adventures of Five Hours*

———o———

Where is the man who has the power
and skill
To stem the torrent of a woman's will?
For if she will, she will, you may depend on't;
And if she won't, she won't; so there's
an end on't.
*Inscribed on a pillar on the mount in
the Dane John Field*, Canterbury

———o———

Our wills are ours, we know not how,
Our wills are ours, to make them
thine.
ALFRED, LORD TENNYSON,
In Memoriam

———o———

Where there's a will there's a lawsuit.

———o———

Most parents know from experience
that where there's a will, there's a
won't.
FRANCIS O. WALSH

———o———

If a mother could mix the willingness
of a two-year-old with the brawn of a
sixteen-year-old, she'd have a real
helper.
Journal-Transcript, Franklin, New Hampshire

———o———

All lay hold on the willing horse.

———o———

The secret of an unsettled life lies
too often in an unsurrendered will.

———o———

People do not lack strength; they
lack will.
VICTOR HUGO

Don't make the mistake of taking
your will for God's will.

Winter

I love thee, all unlovely as thou seem'st,
And dreaded as thou art.
WILLIAM COWPER, *The Task*

———o———

God gave us our memories so that
we might have roses in December.
SIR JAMES MATTHEW BARRIE

———o———

Winter lingered so long in the lap of
Spring that it occasioned a great deal
of talk.
EDGAR WILSON NYE

———o———

I crowned thee king of intimate de-
lights,
Fireside enjoyments, home-born happi-
ness,
And all the comforts that the lowly
roof
Of undisturb'd Retirement, and the
hours
Of long uninterrupted evening, know.
WILLIAM COWPER, *The Task*

———o———

Winter Viewpoints

Restful time when the earth slumbers
'neath the snow,
Hiding all her treasures while frosty
north winds blow.

A time when woodland creatures have
need of bounty store,
And yet God watches over them while
winter's at their door.

Enchanted time for children, as crystal
flakes of white
Descend to make a wonderland and
fill hearts with delight.

A fireside time for grown-ups when
home is best of all,
And golden memories of the past are
pleasant to recall.
LAVERNE P. LARSON

The Lovely Days Of Winter

The lovely days of winter come,
The wind is like a muffled drum.
  I did not miss this pastel sky
  When summer roses bloomed near-
    by;
I did not know that on this hill
There was such beauty, chaste and
    still;
  That mirrored ice in frozen stream
  Could catch and hold a vagrant
    dream;
That tall bare trees so hard and brown
Could sing though leaves had fluttered
    down —
  But now with new-found joy I see
  All that summer hid from me.

AUTHOR UNKNOWN

Wise, Wisdom

The only person less popular than a wise guy is a wise guy who's right.

——o——

What this country needs is a special encyclopedia with blank pages for those who know everything.

——o——

The wise man appreciates the good points of the worst things that happen to him.

——o——

It is what we find out after we know it all, that counts.

——o——

There is nothing so like a wise man as a fool who holds his tongue.

ST. FRANCIS DE SALES

——o——

Nine tenths of wisdom consists of being wise in time.

THEODORE ROOSEVELT

——o——

I recall the advice given to me when as a young, green editor I joined the staff of a New York book publishing house. I asked the publisher in just what line he thought I should specialize. His reply was interesting.

"The successful editor may know a little about many things or much about a few things, but one thing is absolutely necessary: He must know how to use the wisdom and experience of others."

WILLIAM H. LEACH in Church Management

——o——

The lesson of wisdom is, be not dismayed by soul-trouble. Count it no strange thing, but a part of ordinary Christian experience. Should the power of depression be more than ordinary, think not that all is over with your usefulness. Cast not away your confidence, for it hath great recompense of reward. Even if the enemy's foot be on your neck, expect to rise and overthrow him. Cast the burden of the present, along with the sin of the past and the fear of the future, upon the Lord. Live by the day — aye, by the hour.

CHARLES HADDON SPURGEON

——o——

The wise man doesn't expect to find life worth living; he makes it that way.

——o——

Wisdom doesn't always mean knowing what to do. It can be just as important to know what not to do.

——o——

Wise people believe only half of what they hear — wiser ones know which half to believe.

——o——

Many might attain to wisdom, if they were not assured that they already possessed it.

SENECA

——o——

The wisdom of today is the fruit of the education of all past centuries. We are heirs to the accomplishments of forgotten ages. The knowledge we possess is as a tree which draws its life from the debris of forests that have crumpled into dust.

HENRY WARD BEECHER

——o——

He is a wise man who does not grieve for the things which he has not, but rejoices for those which he has.

EPICTETUS

The clouds may drop down titles and
  estates;
Wealth may seek us; but wisdom must
  be sought;
Sought before all; (but how unlike all
  else
We seek on earth!) 'tis never sought
  in vain.
                    EDWARD YOUNG, *Night Thoughts*

——o——

Knowledge is proud that he has learned
  so much;
Wisdom is humble that he knows no
  more.
                    WILLIAM COWPER, *The Task*

——o——

It is more easy to be wise for others
than for ourselves.
          FRANÇOIS, DUC DE LA ROCHEFOUCAULD

——o——

Burt, Jr., was one of the Three Wise
Men in the Sunday School pageant,
and so was his father, one Christmas
long ago. "Well, Dad," he said, "wisdom must run in the family."

——o——

Wisdom

When I have ceased to break my wings
Against the faultiness of things,
And learned that compromises wait
Behind each hardly opened gate,
When I can look Life in the eyes,
Grown calm and very coldly wise,
Life will have given me the Truth,
And taken in exchange — my youth.
                    SARA TEASDALE, *Wisdom*

——o——

Wisdom is knowing when to speak
your mind and when to mind your
speech.

——o——

He is wise who has endured all the
pains of mankind — and still smiles in
serenity.

——o——

Wisdom is ofttimes nearer when we
  stoop
Than when we soar.
                    WILLIAM WORDSWORTH

The wise man must be wise before,
not after the event.
                    EPICHARMUS

——o——

"Tommy," said his Uncle John, "do
you have a girl?"
"I should say not," shouted the ten-
year-old and ran off to his baseball
game.
  The little girl next door smiled
wisely at Uncle John and said, "They're
always the last ones to know."
                    FRANK HOLLAND

——o——

Be wiser than other people if you
can; but do not tell them so.
          LORD CHESTERFIELD, *Letter to His Son*

Wish

My Daily Wish

My daily wish is that we may
See good in those who pass our way:
Find in each a worthy trait
That we shall gladly cultivate;
See in each one passing by
The better things that beautify —
A softly spoken word of cheer,
A kindly face, a smile sincere.

I pray each day that we may view
The things that warm one's heart
  anew:
The kindly deeds that can't be
  bought —
That only from the good are wrought,
A burden lightened here and there,
A brother lifted from despair,
The aged ones freed from distress;
The lame, the sick brought happiness.

Grant that before each sun has set
We'll witness deeds we can't forget:
A soothing hand to one in pain,
A sacrifice for love — not gain;
A word to ease the troubled mind
Of one whom fate has dealt unkind.
So, friend, my wish is that we may
See good in all who pass our way.
                    PHIL PERKINS

——o——

For every person who wishes dreams
came true, there are at least ten who
thank heaven that they don't.

Many of us spend half our time wishing for things we could have if we didn't spend half our time wishing.

Talelights

Witness

Who builds a church within his heart
And takes it with him everywhere
Is holier far than he whose church
Is but a one-day house of prayer.

MORRIS ABEL BEER,
The Church in the Heart

———o———

Witnessing is first by being and then by doing.

———o———

They witness best for Christ who say least about themselves.

———o———

Billy Sunday's choir leader, Homer Rodeheaver, told the following touching story about a boy who sang in his choir:

Joey was not quite bright. He would never leave the tabernacle at night till he could shake my hand. He would stand right next to me until the last man had gone in order to say good-bye. It was embarrassing at times. One evening a man came forward to speak to me. He said, "I want to thank you for being so kind to Joey. He isn't quite bright and has never had anything he enjoyed so much as coming here and singing in the choir. He has worked hard during the day in order to be ready in time to come here at night. He has coaxed us to come too, and it is through him that my wife and our five children have been led to the Lord. His grandfather, seventy-five years old and an infidel all his life, and his grandmother have come tonight, and now the whole family is converted."

———o———

Witnessing is not just something a Christian says, but what a Christian is!

Of course words are important — but they are no substitute for Christ-like demeanor. Pious language cannot camouflage profane practice.

Indeed, words constitute an indictment against the man whose actions contradict what he professes.

The world will listen if the life manifests Christian character . . . the world will scoff at the emptiness of words, however pious, if the witness of the life is wanting.

Conditioned to demonstration, modern man awaits the confirmation of the claims by the consistent conduct of the claimant.

Let every serious-minded Christian who would be an effective witness for Christ live as though he had to earn the right to be heard.

RICHARD C. HALVERSON

———o———

Witnessing is the unfulfilled part of man's devotion.

MARK LEE

———o———

Resolution

Could I but dip a brush of flame
Into a pot of gold,
Across the sky I'd write His name
In letters brilliant, bold.
Had I a voice of thunder,
Or the lightning's brilliant flash,
Could I make use of ocean's roar —
The angry waves that dash,
Of these and more I would avail
To make His wonders known,
To cause all mankind to cry "Hail!"
And worship at His throne.
But since I can't make use of these,
I'll faithful witness give
To draw men's hearts,
My God to please —
By how I daily live!

CHARSTEN CHRISTENSEN

———o———

Every called soul is to be a herald and a witness; and we are to aim at nothing less than this, to make every nation, and every creature in every nation, acquainted with the Gospel tidings.

A. T. PIERSON

———o———

Christ did not tell His disciples to sit still and let sinners come to them.

Woman, Women

What a strange thing is man! And
    what a stranger
Is woman! What a whirlwind is her
    head,
And what a whirlpool full of depth
    and danger
Is all the rest about her! Whether
    wed,
Or widow, maid or mother, she can
    change her
Mind like the wind; whatever she has
    said
Or done, is light to what she'll say or
    do; —
The oldest thing on record, and yet
    new!

LORD BYRON

———o———

Woman, they say, was only made of
    man;
Methinks 'tis strange they should be so
    unlike!
It may be all the best was cut away,
To make the woman, and the naught
    was left
Behind with him.

FRANCIS BEAUMONT and JOHN FLETCHER

———o———

If the heart of a man is depress'd
    with cares,
The mist is dispell'd when a woman
    appears.

JOHN GAY, *The Beggar's Opera*

———o———

Earth's noblest thing, a Woman perfected.

JAMES RUSSELL LOWELL, *Irene*

———o———

O woman! lovely woman! Nature
    made thee
To temper man; we had been brutes
    without you;
Angels are painted fair, to look like
    you;
There is in you all that we believe
    of heaven,
Amazing brightness, purity, and truth,
Eternal joy, and everlasting love.

THOMAS OTWAY, *Venice Preserved*

With women the heart argues, not
the mind.

MATTHEW ARNOLD

———o———

An explorer says an Eskimo woman
is old at forty. An American woman
is not so old at forty. In fact, she's
not even forty!

———o———

Not all women give most of their
waking thoughts to the problem of
pleasing men. Some are married.

———o———

As soon as you cannot keep anything from a woman, you love her.

PAUL GERALDY

———o———

A woman will wear a swim suit
when she doesn't swim, a tennis outfit when she doesn't play tennis, and
ski pants when she doesn't ski. But
when she puts on a wedding dress —
she means business.

———o———

Women can never be as successful
as men; they have no wives to advise
them.

———o———

No wonder women live longer than
men — see how long they're girls.

———o———

Women are very loyal. When they
reach an age they like, they stick to it.

———o———

Women are unpredictable. You never know how they're going to manage
to get their own way.

BEATRICE MANN in *Buck Bits*

———o———

A woman needs no eulogy, she
speaks for herself.

———o———

Woman was last at the cross and
first at the grave of Christ.

———o———

Anyone can recognize a nagging
woman except when that woman is
looking in a mirror.

A woman's whole life is a history of the affections.

WASHINGTON IRVING,
Rip Van Winkle. The Broken Heart

———o———

The difference between a beautiful woman and a charming woman: A beautiful woman is a woman you notice, while a charming woman is one who notices you.

Sunshine Magazine

———o———

The only way to understand a woman is to love her — and then it isn't necessary to understand her.

SYDNEY J. HARRIS

———o———

It does not take a very bright woman to dazzle some men.

Wonder

We Wonder

We all have wondered, more or less,
  Why this or that must be.
Why some of us find happiness
  That others fail to see.
Why some of us are lifted high
  And lead throughout life's role,
While others even though they try
  Can never reach their goal.

Why some can meet the tempter's wrath
  And find the strength to stay
Upon the straight and narrow path
  And never lose their way;
While others walking by their side
  Will try to beat life's game,
And wander off where paths are wide
  That lead to sin and shame.

And oftentimes when death draws near,
  With sickle grim and cold,
To reap the life of someone dear,
  The young as well as old;
We'll hear the question asked by some,
  If all of this is just;
If life is worth the struggle from
  The embryo to the dust.

We ponder over many things,
  But here we'll never know

The reason for the happenings
  That mystify us so;
But when earth's scenes recede and we
  Respond to Heaven's call,
We'll see things then as God doth see
  And understand them all.

DONALD LAVERN WALKER

———o———

Wonder is the feeling of a philosopher, and philosophy begins in wonder.

PLATO

Words

The oldest, shortest words — "yes" and "no" — are those which require the most thought.

PYTHAGORAS

———o———

Good words are worth much, and cost little.

GEORGE HERBERT, *Jacula Prudentum*

———o———

Many a blunt word has a sharp edge.

———o———

I'm careful of the words I say
To keep them soft and sweet.
I never know from day to day,
Which ones I'll have to eat.

———o———

The knowledge of words is the gate of scholarship.

JOHN WILSON

———o———

If you insist upon having the last word, make it your first.

———o———

Our words have wings, but fly not where we would.

GEORGE ELIOT (MARY ANN EVANS)

———o———

High praise and honour to the bard is due
Whose dexterous setting makes an old word new.

HORACE

———o———

A word to the wise is enough.

PLAUTUS

Some by old words to fame have made
  pretence,
Ancients in phrase, mere moderns in
  their sense;
Such labored nothings, in so strange a
  style,
Amaze the unlearned, and make the
  learned smile.
ALEXANDER POPE,
Essay on Criticism, Part II

———o———

A blow with a word strikes deeper
than a blow with a sword.
ROBERT BURTON, Anatomy of Melancholy

———o———

Harsh words, though pertinent, un-
  couth appear;
None please the fancy who offend the
  ear.
SIR SAMUEL GARTH, The Dispensary

———o———

O, many a shaft at random sent
Finds mark the archer little meant!
And many a word, at random spoken,
May soothe or wound a heart that's
  broken!
SIR WALTER SCOTT,
The Lord of the Isles. Canto V

———o———

He draweth out the thread of his
verbosity finer than the staple of his
argument.
WILLIAM SHAKESPEARE,
Love's Labour's Lost

Most Important Words

Five most important words: I am
  proud of you.
Four most important words: What is
  your opinion?
Three most important words: If you
  please.
Two most important words: Thank you.
The least important: I.
This Day

———o———

Boy: "Father, may I have an encyclopedia?"
Father: "No, I bought you a bicy-
cle, use it."

One good thing you can give and
still keep is your word.

———o———

How much can you say in a three-
minute phone call? A lot. Slow talkers
can get in about 450 words, while
people who talk fast can whiz through
about 750 words.

Many important ideas can be expressed in three minutes. Consider:

Lincoln needed only 267 words for
the Gettysburg Address.

Shakespeare used just 363 for Hamlet's famous soliloquy, "To Be Or Not
To Be."

The Lord's Prayer has 56 words.

The Ten Commandments, which set
a whole moral code for mankind, 297.

In contrast, the words used in a Federal order dealing with the price of
cabbage totaled 26,911.

———o———

About Words

Never be afraid of big words.
Most big words name little things,
Like microscopical, and mosquito, and
  pediculosis.
Most small words name big things,
Like sky, and land and air and sun,
And man and wife and love and life
  and God.

Try to use small words.
It is hard to do, but they say what
  you mean.
If you don't know what you mean, use
  big words.
They will confuse little people.
AUTHOR UNKNOWN

———o———

Don't stop to pick up the kind words
you drop.

———o———

A timely word may lessen stress, but
a loving word may heal and bless.

———o———

Words

A careless word may kindle strife;
A cruel word may wreck a life.

A bitter word may hate instill;
A brutal word may smite or kill.

A gracious word may smooth the way;
A joyous word may light the day.

A timely word may lessen stress;
A loving word may heal and bless.

MILDRED HOUSTON

———o———

The difference between the right word and the almost right word is the difference between lightning and the lightning bug.

MARK TWAIN

———o———

Words that sound wise to certain people sound ridiculous to others; for some people value only the speaker, others what is said.

Work

A noble life is not a blaze
  Of sudden glory won,
But just an adding up of days
  In which good work is done.

AUTHOR UNKNOWN

———o———

If you owned the company, would you want someone to do the job you're doing the way you're doing it?

BREE SMITH

———o———

Work hard — the job you save may be your own.

———o———

Get your spindle and your distaff ready, and God will send you the flax.

English Proverb

———o———

Be glad for work that's difficult,
  For tasks that challenge you;
Workers find a thousand joys
  The idle never do.

———o———

Put work into your life and life into your work.

———o———

I began by working with my own hands for my daily bread.

HERBERT HOOVER

A Working Prescription

Seldom do physicians of the various medical schools agree in the diagnosis and treatment of diseases, but the following prescription is one that is unanimously recommended and accepted:

If health is threatened — work.

If disappointments come — work.

If you are rich — continue to work.

If faith falters and reason begins to fail — work.

If dreams are shattered and hope seems dead — work.

If sorrow overwhelms you and loved ones are untrue — work.

If you are burdened with seemingly unfair responsibilities — work.

If you are happy — keep right on working. For where there is idleness there is room for doubt and fear.

No matter what ails you — work. Work as if your life were in peril, for it is!

War Cry

———o———

All work and no play makes Jack a big tax bill.

———o———

Too often we attempt to work for God to the limit of our incompetency, rather than to the limit of God's omnipotency.

J. HUDSON TAYLOR

———o———

I learned to work mornings, when I could skim the cream off the day and use the rest for cheese-making.

JOHANN WOLFGANG VON GOETHE

———o———

If He has work for me to do I cannot die.

HENRY MARTYN

———o———

It is better to burn the candle at both ends, and in the middle, too, than to put it away in the closet and let the mice eat it.

HENRY VAN DYKE

———o———

If you must choose between getting a job done and getting credit for it, get it done.

No man is born into the world whose work
Is not born with him; there is always work,
And tools to work withal, for those who will;
And blessed are the horny hands of toil!

JAMES RUSSELL LOWELL,
A Glance Behind the Curtain

———o———

The tendency to work is born in us, but laziness is acquired.

———o———

Absence of occupation is not rest,
A mind quite vacant is a mind distress'd.

WILLIAM COWPER, *Retirement*

———o———

Every community has at least one poor soul who will do all the work if given a few chairmanships.

———o———

An employee entered the manager's office to ask for a raise: "I've been here nearly ten years doing three men's work for one man's pay," he said.
"I'm sorry we can't give you a raise," said the manager, "but if you'll tell me who the other two men are I'll fire them."

———o———

Personnel manager of applicant: "What we're after is a man of vision, a man with drive, determination, fire; a man who never quits; a man who can inspire others; a man who can pull the company's bowling team out of last place!"

———o———

An employment office was checking on an applicant's list of references: "How long did this man work for you?" a former employer was asked.
"About four hours," was the quick reply.
"Why, he told us he'd been there a long time," said the astonished caller.
"Oh, yes," answered the ex-employer, "he's been here two years."

Wall Street Journal

Most people like hard work. Particularly when they are paying for it.

FRANKLIN P. JONES
in *The Saturday Evening Post*

———o———

Lord, temper with tranquillity
My manifold activity,
That I may do my work for Thee
In very great simplicity.

AUTHOR UNKNOWN

———o———

Thank God every morning when you get up that you have something to do that day which must be done, whether you like it or not. Being forced to work, and forced to do your best, will breed in you temperance and self-control, diligence and strength of will, cheerfulness and content, and a hundred virtues which the idle never know.

CHARLES KINGSLEY,
Town and Country Sermons

———o———

Everyone admires a worker. Even a mosquito gets a pat on the back when he starts working.

———o———

Very often we are half out of our predicament the moment we get up and start working.

———o———

I've Often Found

I've often found that working with my hands
Has eased my heart when I have been distressed;
Despair has yielded to a straight, white hem,
A sock to mend, a crumpled gown I've pressed.

And once or twice when hope was strangely lost
The hurt was lessened when I baked a pie,
And I felt gayer when I washed the towels
In crisp, bright suds and hung them out to dry.

There is a rhythm of relief, dear God,
In quiet toil, and so I ask of you
Then when life brings me disappointment, grief,
My hands may find some humble task to do.

HELEN WELSHIMER

———o———

A Psalm Of Life

Let us, then, be up and doing,
With a heart for any fate;
Still achieving, still pursuing,
Learn to labour and to wait.

HENRY WADSWORTH LONGFELLOW

———o———

If the power to do hard work is not a talent, it is the best possible substitute for it.

JAMES ABRAM GARFIELD

———o———

Your work should be a challenge, not a chore; a blessing, not a bore.

HAL STEBBINS

———o———

Waste not your Hour, nor in the vain pursuit
Of This and That endeavour and dispute.

EDWARD FITZGERALD,
Rubáiyát of Omar Khayyám

———o———

Things are never so much appreciated as when, like a chicken, we must do a certain amount of scratching for what we get.

EPICTETUS

———o———

Folks who never do any more than they get paid for, never get paid for any more than they do.

———o———

I never did anything worth doing by accident, nor did any of my inventions come by accident.

THOMAS ALVA EDISON

———o———

If you have built castles in the air, your work need not be lost. Now put the foundations under them.

HENRY DAVID THOREAU

The best preparation for tomorrow's work is to do your work as well as you can today.

ELBERT HUBBARD

———o———

When Henry Ward Beecher expressed his admiration for a horse he was hiring, the liveryman responded enthusiastically. "He'll work any place you put him and will do all that any horse can do."
Beecher regarded the horse with greater appreciation than before and said wistfully, "I wish he were a member of my church! How we need workers like him!"

LEO POLMAN in *Christian Life*

———o———

Nothing makes a man work like being "debt propelled."

———o———

Let me but find it in my heart to say,
This is my work; my blessing, not my doom;
Of all who live, I am the one by whom
This work can best be done in the right way.

HENRY VAN DYKE, *The Three Best Things*

———o———

The Christian cannot have his God without being willing to work in His service. Even Adam was not allowed to be idle in the Garden, but was given something by God to do (Genesis 2: 15).

MARTIN LUTHER

———o———

No rule of success will work if you don't.

———o———

If you want work well done, select a busy man — the other kind has no time.

———o———

The man who does not do more work than he's paid for isn't worth what he gets.

ABRAHAM LINCOLN

World

Attachment to Christ is the only secret of detachment from the world.

Carol Willis, eight, was writing hard, and her lawyer-father sat down to look over her shoulder. "I'm writing a report on the world," she said. Mr. Willis wondered if that wasn't a pretty big order. "It's okay," she said. "Three of us in my class are working on it."

NEIL MORGAN in *San Diego Tribune*

———o———

Ever see a world so fine
As this world of yours and mine?
Sun and moist from end to middle,
Just as sweet as song and fiddle;
Dust and dew, and rest and dream,
Country roads and rippling stream,
Town and city, mill and street —
Ever see a world so sweet?

Baltimore Sun

———o———

A Strip Of Blue

I do not own an inch of land,
  But all I see is mine —
The orchards and the mowing fields,
  The lawns and gardens fine.
The winds my tax collectors are,
  They bring me tithes divine —
Wild scents and subtle essences,
  A tribute rare and free;
And, more magnificent than all,
  My window keeps for me
A glimpse of blue immensity,
  A little strip of sea.

Here I sit as a little child
  The threshold of God's door
Is that clear band of chrysoprase;
  Now the vast temple floor,
The blinding glory of the dome
  I bow my head before.
Thy universe, O God, is home,
  In height or depth to me;
Yet here upon Thy footstool green
  Content I am to be.
Glad when is opened unto my need
  Some sea-like glimpse of Thee.

LUCY LARCOM

———o———

The Bible shows how the world progresses. It begins with a garden, but ends with a holy city.

PHILLIPS BROOKS

———o———

The world is too much with us. Late and soon,

Getting and spending, we lay waste our powers.

WILLIAM WORDSWORTH, *Sonnet*

———o———

The devil will promise you the whole world, but he doesn't own a grain of sand.

———o———

The Christian is not ruined by living in the world, but by the world living in him.

———o———

The world today needs reality, not formality.

LESTER SUMRALL

———o———

Take the world as it is, not as it should be.

German Proverb

Worry

An unusual woman was being interviewed by a reporter. Although a widow for years, she had reared six children of her own and twelve adopted children. In spite of her busy and useful life, she was noted for her poise and charm.

The reporter asked how she had managed.

"You see, I'm in a partnership."

"What kind of partnership?"

She replied, "One day, a long time ago, I said, 'Lord, I'll do the work, and you do the worrying,' and I haven't had a worry since."

War Cry

———o———

Did you know that when you are worrying, you are literally choking yourself to death? The very word "worry" comes from an old Anglo-Saxon word which means "to choke!"

———o———

Worry and faith are incompatible. If your faith is strong, you need not worry. If it is weak, worrying won't help it.

S. T. LUDWIG

———o———

Daily Dozen For Worriers

1. Believe in yourself — you are marvelously endowed.

2. Believe in your job — all honest work is sacred.

3. Believe in this day — every minute contains an opportunity to do good.

4. Believe in your family — create harmony by trust and cooperation.

5. Believe in your neighbor — the more friends you can make the happier you will be.

6. Believe in uprightness — you cannot go wrong doing right.

7. Believe in your decisions — consult God first, then go ahead.

8. Belive in your health — stop taking your pulse . . .

9. Believe in your church — you encourage others to attend by attending yourself.

10. Believe in the now — yesterday is past recall; tomorrow may never come.

11. Believe in God's promises — "I am with you always." He meant it!

12. Believe in God's mercy — if God forgives you, you can forgive yourself. Try again tomorrow.

ALASTAIR MACODRUM in *Christian Herald*

———o———

When Peter Marshall was chaplain of the U.S. Senate he once shocked that dignified body in his opening prayer by saying:

"Help us to do our very best this day and be content with today's troubles, so that we shall not borrow the troubles of tomorrow. Save us from the sin of worrying, lest stomach ulcers be the badge of our lack of faith. Amen."

———o———

It is not the work, but the worry
    That drives all sleep away,
As we toss and turn and wonder
    About the cares of the day.
Do we think of the hands' hard labor
    Or the steps of the tired feet?
Ah, no! But we plan and wonder
    How to make both ends meet.

———o———

Green Pastures

Last night I started counting sheep
    When I had gone to bed,
For I had worries large and small
    Which drove sleep from my head.
The sheep had many little lambs
    And these I counted too,
Thus through the flock I went until
    The Shepherd came in view.
And then I thought, "Why spend the time
    In simply counting sheep
When I can walk with Him and pray
    For folk who cannot sleep?"
I walked with Him awhile, and then
    He smiled, and said to me —
"Look back, where are your worries now?"
    But not one could I see!

MILDRED ALLEN JEFFERY

———o———

Worry empties a day of its strength, not of its trouble.

———o———

When you feel down at the mouth, think of Jonah. He came out all right.

———o———

Worry has nowhere to go, and it gets nowhere.

———o———

Our fatigue is often caused not by work, but by worry, frustration and resentment.

DALE CARNEGIE

———o———

Worry Or Pray?

Worry? Why worry? What can worry do?
It never keeps a trouble from overtaking you.
It gives you indigestion, and wakeful hours at night,
And fills with gloom the days, however fair and bright.

It puts a frown upon the face, and sharpness in the tone,
We're unfit to live with others, and unfit to live alone.
Worry? Why worry? What can worry do?
It never keeps a trouble from overtaking you.

Pray? Why pray? What can praying do?

Praying really changes things, arranges
life anew.
It's good for your digestion, gives
peaceful sleep at night,
And fills the grayest, gloomiest day
with rays of glowing light.

It puts a smile upon your face, the
love note in your tone,
Makes you fit to live with others, and
fit to live alone.
Pray? Why pray? What can praying
do?
It brings God down from Heaven, to
live and work with you.

AUTHOR UNKNOWN

———o———

When you are worried, read:
The Upholding Verses Isaiah 41:10, 13
The Optimism Verse   Romans 8:28
The Waiting Verse   Psalm 27:14

Worship

To worship the Holy Trinity is an
art taught by the Holy Spirit. He uses
various schools: the school of suffering,
the school of experience, the school of
knowledge. He uses people to teach
this art, and one of them is you.

M. L. K. in *Lutheran Education*

———o———

When a fellow claims that he can
worship as well out in the open country, in a mountain resort or at the
beach as he can at church, it seems
that he probably feels no particular
urge to worship at all.

———o———

Worship is more than words, and
communion is deeper than conversation.

NORMAN R. OKE

———o———

True worship doesn't depend on
preacher or place, but on the attitude
of the heart.

———o———

What Is Worship?

It is the exposure of what man is
to what he ought to become.

It is the knife of conscience re-
moving that which offends.
It is the medicine of the Great
Physician for tired bodies and weary
souls.
It is the door into the abundant
life.
It is the hand of a small child seeking the hand of his Father.
It is permitting our bodies to rest
while our souls catch up.
It is the book of memories and aspirations.
It is our little soul seeking the bigness of God.

———o———

What greater calamity can fall upon
a nation than the loss of worship.

THOMAS CARLYLE

———o———

One who knows God, worships God.

———o———

We become like that which we worship — God, self, or anything else.

———o———

As you worship, so you serve.

THOMAS LATHERN JOHNS

———o———

"What do you think about when you
see church doors open to everyone
who wants to worship God there?" a
teacher asked her Sunday School class
in an integrated Washington, D.C.,
church. A Negro junior replied, "It
is like walking into the heart of God."

———o———

True worship is not lip service but
life service.

———o———

Worship refreshes the soul as sleep
refreshes the body.

Worth

To realize the worth of the anchor,
we need to feel the storm.

———o———

So much is a man worth as he es-
teems himself.

FRANCOIS RABELAIS, *Works. Book II*

If one could buy some people at their real worth and sell them for what they think they are worth, he would soon become rich.

————o————

What you are determines your worth.

————o————

The unexamined life is not worth living.

PLATO

————o————

Any worth found in man is the worth of One who was more than man.

Wound

What wound did ever heal but by degrees?

WILLIAM SHAKESPEARE

————o————

Love On, O Heart, Love On!

If wounded by some critic's word,
  Or hurt by tongues that utter lies;
If false reports on you are heard
  By those who watch with faithless
    eyes,
Don't seek revenge and rise to strike
And think your foes will soon be
    gone,
Or hope that God your pluck will like,
  But love, O heart, love on, love on!

Love on in spite of wounding darts,
  In spite of what the critics say;
Love men through grace that God im-
    parts
When at the feet of Christ you pray.
The way of love will bring you out,
  Though dark the night before the
    dawn;
Then keep in faith and shun the doubt,
  And love, O heart, love on, love on!

WALTER E. ISENHOUR

Write

In The Dark

I keep a little memo pad
Beside my bed, to write
The multitude of thoughts and things
Which come to me at night;
Ideas rare are written there,

Reminders — how I need them —
The only trouble is, of course,
Comes morning, I can't read them.

STEPHEN SCHLITZER

————o————

The fellow who can recognize the handwriting on the wall probably has a child who writes legibly.

————o————

A good writer is one who knows that little words never hurt a really big idea.

————o————

A journalism student, while visiting a newspaper plant, came to the editorial room and asked the City Editor: "If you please, sir, could you give me a few pointers on how to run a newspaper?"

"Sorry, son, but you've come to the wrong person," replied the Editor. "Just ask any one of our subscribers."

————o————

"Professor, what is this you wrote at the end of my paper?"

"I only suggested that you write plainer next time."

————o————

The budding author sent a poem to an editor and wrote: "Please let me know at once if you can use it for I have other irons in the fire."

The editor wrote back: "Remove irons and insert poem."

————o————

Editors call themselves "we" so the person who doesn't like an article will think there are too many for him to lick.

————o————

Anybody can make history; only a great man can write it.

OSCAR WILDE

————o————

"Do you think any of your writings will live on after you are gone?"

"Oh, that doesn't worry me at all. What I am anxious about is that my writings keep me living on before I go."

When I started out to write and mispelled a few words, people said I was just plain ignerant. But when I got all the words wrong, they declared I was a humorist and said I was quaint.
WILL ROGERS

———o———

How easy is pen-and-paper piety! I will not say it costs nothing; but it is far cheaper to work one's head than one's heart to goodness. I can write a hundred meditations sooner than subdue the least sin in my soul.
THOMAS FULLER

———o———

He who wields the pen shapes the future.
LUTHER WESLEY SMITH

———o———

The one thing that most men can do better than anyone else is read their own handwriting.

———o———

A Junior High English class, assigned a composition on "My Family" got this classic essay turned in:
"My father is an insurance man and my mother is a tired housewife."

———o———

The only real problem the writer has found since the discovery of papyrus is to write.
HAL G. EVARTS in The Writer

———o———

For men use, if they have an evil turn, to write it in marble: and whoso doth us a good turn we write it in dust.
THOMAS MORE,
Richard III and his Miserable End

———o———

Of writing many books there is no end.
ELIZABETH BARRETT BROWNING

———o———

By a long habit of writing one acquires a greatness of thinking and a mastery of manner which holiday writers, with ten times the genius, may vainly attempt to equal.
OLIVER GOLDSMITH

———o———

Never write what you dare not sign.

I'll make thee glorious by my pen, And famous by my sword.
JAMES GRAHAM MONTROSE,
My Dear and Only Love

———o———

Beneath the rule of men entirely great, The pen is mightier than the sword.
EDWARD GEORGE BULWER-LYTTON, Richelieu

Wrong

It may make a difference to all eternity whether we do right or wrong today.
JAMES F. CLARKE

———o———

One wrong action can cause a lifelong regret.

———o———

There's nothing shameful about being wrong. Nobody can be right all the time.

———o———

It is better to suffer wrong than to do it, and happier to be sometimes cheated than not to trust.
SAMUEL JOHNSON

———o———

Many three-word phrases in our language are powerful or significant or informative; but the one that probably gives the greatest over-all peace of mind is "I was wrong."
Advocate, Allen, Oklahoma

———o———

It is easy to tell when you're on the wrong road. You hardly ever see any detour signs.

———o———

It is a wicked thing to be neutral between right and wrong.
THEODORE ROOSEVELT

———o———

A wrong-doer is often a man that has left something undone, not always he that has done something.
MARCUS AURELIUS, Meditations. VIII

———o———

If things go wrong don't go with them.
ROGER BABSON

Y

Yesterday

Don't let yesterday use up too much of today.

WILL ROGERS

———o———

Live in the sunshine of today and not in the shadows of yesterday.

———o———

Striking from the Calendar
Unborn Tomorrow and dead Yesterday.
EDWARD FITZGERALD,
The Rubáiyát of Omar Khayyám

Yield

We make ourselves the servants of that one to whom we yield.

———o———

It is no virtue to be so unyielding that you cannot consider any position other than your own.

———o———

The willow which bends to the tempest often escapes better than the oak which resists it.

SIR WALTER SCOTT

Yoke

Yokes are good for youthful shoulders.

———o———

Christ has a yoke for our necks as well as a crown for our heads.

———o———

Christ's yoke is lined with love.

———o———

He who said, "My yoke is easy," did not live an easy life.

You, Yourself

You will not be loved yourself if you love none but yourself.

———o———

Be yourself. Ape no greatness. Be willing to pass for what you are. A good farthing is better than a bad sovereign. Affect no oddness; but dare to be right, though you have to be singular.

SAMUEL COLEY

———o———

Be yourself. It is an impossibility to be otherwise, though thousands attempt it.

A. PURNELL BAILEY

———o———

Believe in yourself, and what others think won't matter.

RALPH WALDO EMERSON

———o———

You

"Your task — to build a better world,"
God said.
I answered, "How?
This world is such a large, vast place,
So complicated now!
And I so small and useless am —
There's nothing I can do!"
But God, in all His wisdom, said,
"Just build a better you!"

DOROTHY R. JONES

Young, Youth

If you want to keep young, work with young people. If you want to grow old, try to keep up with them.

———o———

In America, the young are always ready to give those who are older than themselves the full benefit of their inexperience.

OSCAR WILDE

———o———

"Hello, George! You have changed; what's making you look so old?"
"Trying to keep young," was the reply.
"Trying to keep young?" queried the other.
"Yes — nine of them," was the gloomy response.

There's probably nothing wrong with the younger generation that the older generation didn't outgrow.

———o———

Blessed are the young, for they shall inherit the national debt.

HERBERT HOOVER

———o———

Young people are our most priceless national asset.

J. EDGAR HOOVER

———o———

A boy's voice changes when he reaches fourteen; a girl's when she reaches a telephone.

———o———

Young people are alike these days in many disrespects.

———o———

Young people, like soft wax, soon take an impression.

———o———

Youth is not a time of life — it is a state of mind. You are as young as your faith, as old as your doubt; as young as your self-confidence, as old as your fear; as young as your hope, as old as your despair.

J. C. BRASWELL

———o———

Don't say that modern youth is wild,
Just exercise forbearance;
The faults within each problem child
May come from problem parents.

———o———

The problem of youth is not youth — it is the spirit of the age.

———o———

We need to train youth for action but educate them for speech and thought.

———o———

In youth we run into difficulties, in old age difficulties run into us.

"JOSH BILLINGS" (HENRY WHEELER SHAW)

———o———

Happy will he be in old age who learns to trust God in the days of his youth.

Never forget or prove false the dreams of your youth.

———o———

Youth

You see youth as a joyous thing
About which love and laughter cling;
You see youth as a joyous elf
Who sings sweet songs to please himself.
You see his laughing, sparkling eyes
To take earth's wonders with surprise,
You think him free from cares and woes,
And naught of fears you think he knows,
You see him tall, naively bold,
You glimpse these things, for you are old.

———o———

A group of high school girls was practicing the anthem for the Sunday morning service. They lacked breath when they came to the long "A-a-a-men." The leader, a highly trained musician, said: "Now, girls, if you don't hold that 'A' so long you will have more time for the 'men'."

———o———

Youth needs more to learn how to think than what to think.

———o———

The follies of youth become the vices of mankind and the disgrace of old age.

———o———

Wise is the youth who does not employ his first years so as to make his last miserable.

———o———

Don't laugh at a youth for his affectations; he is only trying on one face after another to find his own.

L. P. SMITH

———o———

One young person showing the family album to a friend: "I threw away all my comic books when I found this!"

Z

Zeal, Zealous

Zeal is like fire; it needs both feeding and watching.

———o———

Zeal without knowledge is like haste to a man in the dark.

Zeal that is spiritual is also charitable.

———o———

Zeal without knowledge is fire without light.

JOHN RAY

———o———

INDEX

(Capital letters indicate the main listing of a heading which is a separate subject in the Sourcebook.)

397